THE BLACK WORKER

Vol. II

The Era of the National Labor Union

The Black Worker

A Documentary History from Colonial
Times to the Present

Volume II

The Black Worker During the Era of the National Labor Union

Edited by
Philip S. Foner and Ronald L. Lewis

Temple University Press, Philadelphia

Temple University Press, Philadelphia 19122
© by Temple University. All rights reserved
Published 1978
Printed in the United States of America

Library of Congress Cataloging in Publication Data
Main entry under title:

The Black worker.

    Includes index.
    CONTENTS: v.1. The Black worker to 1869.--v.2. The
era of the national labor union.
    1. Afro-Americans--Employment--History--Sources.
2. Afro-Americans--Economic conditions--Sources.
3. United States--Race relations--Sources. I. Foner,
Philip Sheldon, 1910-   II. Lewis, Ronald L.,
1940-
E185.8.B553   331.6'3'96073   78-2875
ISBN 0-87722-136-7 (v. 1)
ISBN 0-87722-137-5 (v. 2)

PREFACE

This is the second volume in *The Black Worker: A Documentary History From Colonial Times to the Present,* the first compilation of original materials to encompass the entire history of Afro-American labor.

The Black Worker During the Era of the National Labor Union begins with the call for a convention of black leaders from around the nation to meet in Washington, D. C., in December 1869, for the purpose of organizing a counterpart to the white-dominated National Labor Union. The association which emerged from this meeting, the Colored National Labor Union, represented the first confederation of black trade unions. Even though it did not last more than a few years, the CNLU conventions are of considerable historical significance because the assembled black leaders voiced the local concerns of their communities. Therefore, these conventions provide an excellent sounding board for the hopes and fears of black America. Moreover, along with the local and state labor meetings, which also are reproduced in this volume, the proceedings of the CNLU, available here for the first time, reveal the nature and scope of activism among black workers during the 1870s, a decade of complex cross-currents in the labor movement, and a period of economic and political turmoil in the nation at large.

Volume II explores the intricate race relations between black and white workers, who sometimes cooperated, but all too frequently found themselves in conflict. Local black militancy was, nevertheless, vibrant during the 1870s, a conclusion substantiated by the numerous strikes conducted by black workers demanding better pay and conditions, especially in the South. The white response to this militancy was usually one of hostility. Thus, the Ku Klux Klan and other secret societies attempted to control black workers by violent means and to reduce them to the quasi-slave status of a permanent under-class, subordinated socially and exploited economically.

Under these deteriorating conditions, some blacks sought reform panaceas such as "greenbackism," the monetary reform movement which flourished briefly following the Panic of 1874. Other black workers came to support a reordering of society through socialism, while still others dreamed of withdrawing from the struggle for economic survival by resettling in Africa. Volume II concludes with the dramatic Kansas Exodus of 1879, an attempt by black southerners to gain some degree of autonomy and control over their destiny in the isolation of the open plains of the American West.

Like the other volumes in this series, the documents presented are accompanied by introductions and notes, and original spellings have been retained except in cases where they obscure the intended meaning.

The editors wish to express special thanks to those who have been generous in their assistance toward completion of this book. Miss Lila Prieb did an outstanding job of typing the manuscript from very demanding copy, and Ms. Gail Brittingham once again proved herself invaluable to this project. Two more competent typists are not likely to be found. We would also like to express our appreciation to the Black American Studies Program at the University of Delaware for its continued moral and material support. Preparation of the manuscript for this volume was facilitated by a grant-in-aid from the College of Arts and Science, University of Delaware, and we gratefully acknowledge our indebtedness.

Philip S. Foner
Lincoln University,
  Pennsylvania

Ronald L. Lewis
University of Delaware

TABLE OF CONTENTS

PART I

THE CALL AND THE RESPONSE

PART II

FORMATION OF THE COLORED NATIONAL LABOR UNION AND
THE BUREAU OF LABOR

PART III

THE SECOND AND THIRD CONVENTIONS OF THE COLORED NATIONAL LABOR UNION

PART IV

STATE AND LOCAL BLACK LABOR MEETINGS

PART VI

THE KU KLUX KLAN AND BLACK LABOR

PART VII

BLACK SOCIALISM AND GREENBACKISM

PART VIII

BLACK AND WHITE LABOR RELATIONS, 1870-1878

PART IX

THE BLACK EXODUS

I

BLACK WORKERS FORM A NATIONAL ORGANIZATION

THE CALL AND THE RESPONSE

Volume I of this series concluded with the determination of black labor leaders to call a convention in 1869 to organize their own labor union be- cause they found the National Labor Union, a white organization, to be in- sensitive to the special needs of black workers. Even though the NLU was the first American union to admit black representatives to its conventions, the NLU nevertheless found silence the better part of valor on the sensitive issue of member unions barring black workers from membership. The NLU also supported independent political action through the Labor Reform Party, and demanded that blacks abandon the Republican Party to join with the Reformers. Blacks, however, were ardent supporters of the party which had sponsored Radical Reconstruction.

On July 20, 1869, the State Labor Convention of the Colored Men of Mary- land resolved that a national black labor convention should meet in December 1, 1869, in Washington, D.C., to discuss issues central to the particular concerns of blacks (Doc. 1). Throughout the nation, local and state meetings convened to select delegates and to formulate a position on the various is- sues to be discussed at the upcoming convention. The largest and most im- portant of these gatherings was held in Macon, Georgia, in October 1869.

The proceedings of the Macon convention were printed in the conservative Macon Telegraph *(Doc. 2). In a series of editorials, however, the* Telegraph *objected to several of the ideas which blacks articulated at the meeting. The demand for higher wages would only force planters to let land be fallow (Doc. 3). The editors reminded planters that it was not in their interest to defraud blacks of their wages, for through "good management" alone could planters "preserve a dominant influence over the negro." Indeed, it was their "business as white men" to do so (Doc. 4). The Telegraph also dis- agreed with the Convention's outrage over violence against blacks which went unpunished, accepting the jaded assessment of local peace officers that these actions were strictly in "self defense" (Doc. 5). The Telegraph's final judgment on the convention, however, was surprised that while it did "no great amount of harm" the meeting did nothing of importance either (Doc. 6-9).*

The racially liberal National Anti-Slavery Standard *applauded the Macon convention as "the beginning of a new industrial era" in the South "based on free labor" (Doc. 10). In a similar vein, the (Augusta) Georgia Republican a Radical newspaper, viewed the convention as a gathering of "the most in- telligent colored laboring men in Georgia," and expressed relief that "at last the colored laboring men in Georgia are united" (Doc. 11).*

In the wake of the Macon convention, numerous local black workingmens' associations were organized in the South, especially in Georiga. For exam- ple, black workers of Cass County organized themselves into a local union and sought assistance from white Radical sympathizers (Doc. 14-15). Although local meetings were held from Virginia to Texas, the second largest meeting held in the South was at Columbia, South Carolina, in November 1869. Organ- ized by the state's leading black figures, the meeting was attended by 300 black and white participants (Doc. 21-22).

In the North, local black communities formed workers' organizations as well. Of special interest was the meeting in Newport, Rhode Island, which failed to define a policy toward black women. The women complained that they too suffered the degradation and demoralization of prejudice in their employ- ment. As a result, the local executive committee nominated and approved a woman delegate to attend the convention along with the men (Doc. 17).

Most of the state and local conventions underscored their determination to keep politics out of the convention, and to confine their discussions to issues alone. They reaffirmed their conviction that the interests of labor and capital were identical, a view generally accepted by labor organizations of the day. The National Labor Union itself viewed the forthcoming conven- tion of black workers from their usual ambivalent posture, but advised the delegates to let "common sense" rule and to "frown down" any attempt to transform the assembly into a Republican auxiliary (Doc. 30).

CALL FOR THE COLORED NATIONAL LABOR UNION CONVENTION

1. NATIONAL LABOR CONVENTION OF THE COLORED MEN
OF THE UNITED STATES

Fellow Citizens: --At a State Labor Convention of the Colored Men of
Maryland, held July 20th, 1869, it was unanimously resolved that a National
Labor Convention be called to meet in the Union League Hall, City of Wash-
ington, D.C., on the 1st Monday in December, 1869, at 12 M., to consider:

1st. The Present Status of Colored Labor in the United States and its
Relationship to American Industry.

2d. To adopt such rules and devise such means as will systematically
and effectually organize all the departments of said labor, and make it the
more productive in its new Political relationship to Capital, and consolidate the Colored Workingmen of the several States to act in co-operation
with our White Fellow-Workingmen in every State and Territory in the Union,
who are opposed to Distinction in the Apprenticeship Laws on account of
Color, and to so act co-operatively until the necessity for separate organization shall be deemed unnecessary.

3d. To consider the question of the importation of Contract Coolie Labor, and to petition Congress for the adoption of such Laws as will Prevent
its being a system of Slavery.

4th. And to adopt such other means as will best advance the interest
of the Colored Mechanics and Workingmen of the whole country.

Fellow-Citizens: You cannot place too great an estimate upon the important objects this Convention is called to consider, viz: your Industrial
Interests. In the greater portion of the United States, Colored Men are excluded from the workshops on account of their *color*.

The laboring man in a large portion of the Southern States, by a systematic understanding prevailing there, is unjustly deprived of the price of
his labor, and in localities far removed from the Courts of Justice is
forced to endure wrongs and oppression worse than Slavery.

By falsely representing the laborers of the South, certain *interested*
writers and journals are striving to bring Contract Chinese or Coolie Labor
into popular favor there, thus forcing American laborers to work at Coolie
wages or starve.

The Address of the National Executive Committee, created by the National Convention of Colored Americans, convened in Washington on the 13th of
January, 1869, makes a forcible appeal upon this subject. They have and are
making noble efforts to overcome these great wrongs, which we feel can only
be effectually remedied by the meeting in National Council of the Mechanics
and Laborers of this country. We do, as they have, appeal to the white
tradesmen and artizans of this country to conquer their prejudices so far as
to enable Colored Men to have a fair field for the display of competitive
industry; and with this end in view to do away with all pledges and obligations that forbid the taking of Colored Boys as Apprentices to trades, or
the employment of Colored Journeymen therein.

Delegates will be admitted without regard to race or color. State or
City Conventions will be entitled to send one Delegate for each department
of Trade or Labor represented in said Convention. Each Mechanical or Labor
Organization in every State and Territory is entitled to be represented by
one Delegate. It is hoped that all who feel an interest in the welfare and
elevation of our race will take an active part in making this Convention a
grand success.

By order of the Executive Committee.--William W. Hare, John W. Locks,
Wm. L. James, John H. Tabbs, H. C. Hawkins, Geo. Myers, Robert H. Butler, G.
W. Perkins, Wm. Wilks, Geo. Grason, Wesley Howard, Daniel Davis, Jos. Thomas.
J. C. FORTIE, *Secretary*.
ISAAC MYERS, *President*.[1]

Co-operative Executive Committee:--James Ruby, Texas; P. H. Clark, Ohio; John M. Langston, Ohio; William Spradley, Ky.; Rev. James Lynch, Miss.; William H. Hall, Cal.; Mark A. Bell, Oregon; Dr. W. H. C. Steveson, Nevada; Hon. H. D. Norton, Va.; William Brown, Mass.; Col. A. H. Galloway, N.C.; R. H. Cain, S.C.; Rev. H. H. Garnet, Pa.; Isaiah Wears, Pa.; William Rich, N.Y.; Lt. Gov. Oscar Dunn, La.; Jonathan Gibbs, Esq., Fla.; Rev. Jas. Simms, Ga.; Rev. B. T. Tanner, Pa.; Frederick Douglass, Esq., N.Y.; F. G. Barbadoes, Mass.; W. U. Saunders, Md.; Bishop D. A. Payne, Ohio; Bishop A. W. Wayman, Md.; Geo. T. Downing, Esq., R.I.; J. M. Williams, N.J.; Richard De Baptist, Ill.; Moses Dixon, Mobile; W. H. Gibson, Ky.; Alexander Clark, Iowa; Chas. H. Peters, Washington, D.C.; Cornelius Clark, Washington, D.C.

Conventions and Associations will report the names of Delegates to ISAAC MYERS, Box 522 Post-office, Baltimore, Md.

The Christian Recorder, September 18, 1869.

THE RESPONSE

2. LABOR MEETING IN MACON, GEORGIA

First Day--Morning Session.
The delegates to the above Convention assembled yesterday morning in the City Hall, at 10 o'clock. At half past ten, Mr. Jeff. Long, of Macon, being called to the chair, proceeded to call the Convention to order, and read his call for a Convention as published in some of the papers of the State for some time past.

On motion of Rev. H. M. Turner, Mr. Jeff. Long was unanimously chosen temporary President of the Convention, and on motion the deliberation of the body were opened with prayer by Rev. T. G. Campbell, of McIntosh county, who made a very earnest and eloquent appeal to the Throne of Grace that the proceedings of the Convention might be conducted in harmony and love, and its action be of lasting benefit to the colored people of Georgia and redound to the glory of God. [2]

On motion, James H. Deveaux, of Jones county, was chosen Secretary pro. tem., and Wm. H. Artex, of Liberty, Assistant Secretary.

On motion, the President was then requested to ask all persons who were not present as delegates to retire from the room until a permanent organization could be effected, and the spectators all immediately retired.

On motion a committee of three were appointed to examine the credentials of delegates, and in a short while the committee reported present 232 daily authorized delegates, representing about 80 counties of the State.

On motion, a committee of nine was appointed on permanent organization, and were allowed 10 minutes to report. During the absence of the committee, the Convention was addressed by Mr. Penfield, of Richmond county, upon the duty of delegates and the importance of united and harmonious action on the labor question. He was followed in a few brief and pointed remarks by Mr. Smith, of Muscogee, but before he concluded, the committee on permanent organization returned, and through their Chairman, Rev. H. M. Turner, made the following report, which was unanimously adopted:

Hon. JEFFERSON F. LONG. of Bibb, President.

VICE PRESIDENTS.

Hon. T. G. Campbell, of McIntosh--First Vice President.
Hon. Phillip Joiner, of Dougherty--Second Vice President.
Hon. Abraham Smith, of Muscogee--Third Vice President.

Hon. George H. Clower, of Monroe--Fourth Vice President.
Hon. Moses Gardner, of Richmond--Fifth Vice President.
Hon. James A. Jackson, of Clarke--Sixth Vice President.
Hon. William Cokine, of Cobb--Seventh Vice President.

FOUR VICE PRESIDENTS FOR THE STATE AT LARGE.

A. H. Gaston, of Bibb.

On motion, the President appointed a Committee of five on each of the following subjects: Manufacturers, Blacksmiths, Carpenters, Finance, General Labor, Masonry and Brick Work, Education, Professions, Outrages on Laboring men, and Commercial Interests.

On motion, the President then appointed a committee of ten to recommend the organization of labor associations throughout the State of Georgia.

On motion, it was resolved that the hours of session of the Convention be from nine A.M. to one, and from three to five P.M.

On motion the Convention then adjourned at three P.M.

AFTERNOON SESSION.

The Convention was called to order at 3½ o'clock and was opened with prayer by Rev. T. G. Stewart of Bibb county.

On motion of Rev. H. M. Turner, the Convention proceeded to select committees to report business for the action of the Convention. Carried.

The following parties were then appointed on Farming: P. B. Bolden, Richard Reese, S. Artney, C. J. Blackburn, G. H. Clower.

On mechanical Interests: Washington Harris, blacksmith; Isaac Reynolds, blacksmith; G. H. Washington, bricklayer; Chas. Gardner; Robert Fairfax, carpenter; Richard Bassett, carpenter; James C. Blackburn, wheelwright; Lewis Barron, wheel-wright; Isaac Keebber, shoemaker; Alfred Smith, shoemaker; Richard Smith, screwbuilder.

Committee on Finance: H. H. Gaston, J. P. Hutchins, Mr. Whitehead, Henry Porter, Thomas Crayton, Rev. Wm. Benefield.

Committee on Education: Henry Singleton, Floyd Snelson, S. A. Cobb, W. A. Golding, of Liberty; W. J. White to act as Chairman of the committee.

Committee on Professions: Dr. Badger, H. M. Turner, T. G. Campbell.

Committee on Outrages upon Labor: Charles Griffin, Robert Alexander, J. M. Singleton, Paul Armstrong, J. B. Frazer, George Austin, Joshua Sims, Wm. Armstrong, Henry Taylor, W. Bosswell.

Committee on Commercial Interest: A. Smith, Pat Christian, Peter Houston, Wm. H. Artson, J. B. Deveaux, T. G. Steward.

Committee on Associations through the State: C. B. Edwards, T. G. Campbell, Wm. Barefield, Chris Wilson, Phillip Joiner, George Wallace, J. A. Jackson, Peter Houston, J. P. Hutchins, William A. Goulding.

Committee on Savings Bank: Moses Gardner, T. G. Steward, Peter Houston, George Wallace, Dr. Badger.

On motion of W. A. Golding, a committee of two citizens was appointed to act as Sergeants-at-arms and that they receive two dollars per day for the services.

On motion of M. Gardner, a collection was then taken up to defray the expenses of this Convention and as the name of each delegate was called he approached the Secretary's desk and contributed whatever amount he was able toward the object.

On motion the Convention then adjourned till this morning at 9 o'clock.

SECOND DAY--MORNING SESSION.

The Convention was called to order at 6 o'clock. Prayer by Rev. N. B. Beacham, of Sumter county.

The roll was called, and a number of delegates who had not arrived yesterday were enrolled.

The minutes of the preceding day were read, corrected and approved.

Rev. Louis Rose, a native African missionary, was invited to a seat on the floor of the Convention.

Dr. Badger, of Fulton county, moved that a committee of three be appointed to memorialize the Legislature in regard to the outrages that are committed upon colored people. Laid on the table for the present.

The committee on Framing submitted their report, which, after some debate, was recommitted, with an addition of five members.

On motion of Wm. J. White, of Richmond county, this afternoon will be set apart to give the committee on Outrages an opportunity to hear the reports of the delegates from the different counties.

The report of the committee on Savings Banks, as follows, was received and adorned:

Your Committee on the Freedman's Savings and Trust Company, having had the subject under consideration, beg leave to submit the following report:[3]

1st. Having unbounded confidence in the solvency of the Company ourselves, we desire to impress on our people generally the same impression, and to that end give publicity to the following facts:

It has on deposit now, $1,327,010.66.

This amount the bank owes to its depositors and constitutes its entire abilities.

To pay this indebtedness, the Company has on hand:

```
United States Bonds.........................................$997,759
Cash in hand................................................ 231,801 31
Premium on bonds, real estate, etc.......................... 157,110 57
                                                          $1,386,670 88
```

We do not suppose any one of this Convention will attempt to deny that Government bonds constitute the highest class of securities in this country, and the facts of their being exempt from taxation makes them a profitable investment as well. This bank by its charter can invest only in Government securities, and therefore has the advantages of offering both safety and reasonable profits to the patrons.

Having examined its charter and by laws and being highly satisfied with them, we most earnestly commend it to our people generally throughout the State.

> MOSES A. GARDNER,
> GEO. WALLACE,
> T. G. STEWART,   COMMITTEE
> ROBERT BADGER,
> PETER HOUSTON.

The report of the committee on Mechanical Interests being defective, was recommitted.

J. D. Enos, of Lowndes county, was requested to act as Secretary, in place of J. B. Deveaux, who was unexpectedly called away from the city.

The President called the attention of the Convention to an article in the Journal and Messenger, of this city, which he caused to be read. The purport of the article was to ridicule the Convention and those connected with it. The President stated that the paper was owned by J. W. Burke and Co., who sell annually, thousands of dollars worth of Sunday School and other books, papers, etc., to the colored people of Georgia.

He advised them in the future to withdraw their patronage from all parties who use such expressions toward colored people, declaring the time had come for our people to assert their manhood.

The above was received with immense applause.

On motion, the Convention adjourned to 3 o'clock P.M.

AFTERNOON SESSION.

The Convention was called by the President at 3½ o'clock P.M.

Prayer by Wm. Lewis, of Macon county.

The President made a few remarks in relation to delegates leaving.

After some scattering debates the Convention proceeded, in accordance with a resolution passed this forenoon, to hear reports from the different counties. A large number of reports were received.

The Committee on Education made the following report, which was received an unanimously adopted:

The mind of man is that part which, more than any other, indicates the near relation that he sustains towards God, the great source of all knowledge. The past history of man has developed the fact that the mind is capable of a

very high degree of cultivation. Indeed, the limit to which the human mind
is confined has never, and, perhaps, never can be ascertained by man himself.
Our Creator, in his own wise providence, has ordained that while man is primarily dependent on him for everything, even the breath he inhales, still
there is much that he may do for himself which will, in a very large degree
enhance his happiness or misery while he lives upon the earth. There is no
duty required of man that yields such an abundant harvest of true happiness
as the cultivation of the mind. This cultivating the mind is called education. No educated people can be enslaved; no educated people can be robbed
of their labor; no educated people can be kept in a helpless condition, but
will rise with a united voice and assert their manhood.

Your Committee beg leave to say that in their opinion many, if not all
of the disadvantages under which the colored people of Georgia are to-day
laboring, grows out of their great destitution in this respect. We know that
many of them are doing everything in their power to acquire an education
themselves, and to educate their children, still with the light before us we
think much more might be done, and will, we believe, be done if our people
can be made to understand the vast importance of this subject to themselves
and their pasterity.

We have the honor, therefore to recommend to the members of this Convention and the people of Georgia that in the future more attention be given
to this subject, and that in every neighborhood the heads of families and
others interested in the education and elevation of the colored race, unite
themselves together for the purpose of establishing schools for themselves
and children. The well known maxim, "United we stand, divided we fall,"
holds good with us in the work of education. We must work together so that
the strong may help the weak and all prosper together. We recommend that
such arrangement be made by this Convention as they may deem necessary to
assist the people in securing teachers, and that a committee be appointed to
memorialize the General Assembly of this State, at its next session to at
once pass the necessary laws to carry into effect that part of the Constitution of Georgia which provides that there shall be a public school law.
We would further recommend to our people to employ no one to teach their
children unless they be of good moral character, believing as we do that it
would greatly retard their elevation morally to do so.

WM. J. WHITE, Chairman.
HENRY SINGLETON,
FLOYD SNELSON,
S. A. COBB,
W. A. GOLDEN.

The report of the Committee on Workingmen's Association was received
and laid on the table for the present.

Col. J. R. Lewis, Superintendent of Education of Georgia, requested the
delegates from the different counties to furnish the names of teachers,
schools, etc., in their counties.

The Convention then adjourned to 7½ o'clock P.M.

Macon (Ga.) Telegraph, October 22, 1869.

3. THE NEGRO LABOR UNION

According to the American Union (Swayze's paper,) the movement, father-
ed by Jeff Long, to get up a Labor Union among the negroes and pledge them
to demand thirty dollars a month for field hands and fifteen dollars a month
for women, is the work of J. E. Bryant, and Long is the catspaw in the business. If these worthies should succeed in bringing up the negroes to that
line, they will make a case of them; for it is needless to say they will all
necessarily forfeit wages.[4]

Nor it is possible to fix upon a safe minimum of wages for field hands,
simply because that some of them would be dear for their food, while others,

who are intelligent, able, faithful and honest would be comparatively cheap
at twenty dollars a month and rations. Piece work cannot be applied to the
plantation, and therefore the common dead level of the trades unions which
is wholly unjust in respect to them, would be impossible in plantation labor.
    Unquestionably the price of labor will rise this winter, but the demand
of any such minimum by the negroes as thirty dollars a month will destroy
the wages system altogether. Hands must then lie idle and relapse into vagrancy, or be content to labor on shares and take risks with the landowner.

Macon (Ga.) Telegraph, October 8, 1869.

4. THE COLORED LABOR CONVENTION, II

    Every reflecting Georgian must, of course, feel great interest in the
welfare, contentment and prosperity of the colored people of this State.
They are an important portion of our population. Their labor produces perhaps only a little short of two-thirds the total amount of our crop values,
and is rated at one-third the total value of this product. We should estimate it to be worth to itself annually not far from fifteen millions of dollars, and will not undertake to pronounce upon its actual value to the
whole industrial interest of the State. It produces about two hundred thousand bales of our cotton crop, and perhaps more, and we should say at least
twelve millions of bushels of corn; and, therefore, in solving the question
of the value of this labor to Georgia we must consider the possibility of
substituting it by some other, supposing it were suddenly to be withdrawn
from the field.
    In this view of the matter we have no doubt that a good deal of inter-
est will be felt among the whites in knowing the views, feelings, plans and
purposes of this Colored Labor Convention, now in session in Macon; and we,
therefore, invited the Convention to report their proceedings, *in their own
way,* in the TELEGRAPH. Accordingly, we observe that the official record
contains a characteristic flourish of titles, and is set forth in much pomp;
but this is immaterial. The Convention itself, just so far as it indicates
the existence of dissatisfaction among this laboring class, and a determination coupled with the ability to exact increased wages, is an interesting
fact to every planter.
    This movement, it seems, is not confined to Georgia. The "Charleston
Daily Republican," calls a similar one to meet at Columbia in that State,
and proposes to change the Union League into Labor Unions, and put into
force upon the plantations and in every household, all the iron handed despotism of the white labor unions, which, in point of fact destroys *bargain*
in the employment of labor, and makes the employer the victim of compulsion
not only in the wages to be paid, but in pretty much all the details of laboring. It is enough to say that the introduction of the Union labor system
on the farm and in the households, if it were possible, would be attended
with so great convenience and oppression that most people would prefer to
dispense with the labor. It is enough to be bossed in the shop--it would be
intolerable to be mastered at home.[5]
    But we trust, with good management upon the part of the whites, the
mischief done may be limited. It is our business as white men--owners of
the soil and employers--to obtain and preserve a dominant influence over the
negro, by showing him that we are not only his *best* friends, but actually
and truly the *only* friends he has got on earth who can be of any service to
him. Neither his Northern allies or their representatives on our soil, nor
his own race in the South are in any condition to be serviceable to him.
They cannot furnish him with regular supplies of food, clothing and money,
while the Southern whites can do it and find their own advantage in doing it.
    Almost the first point, then, with the good Southern planter who looks
for a permanent and prosperous business, is to secure the entire confidence
and attachment of his colored laborers. This cannot be done even by *fair
dealing* if it is not a kind of dealing in which the negro is able to see for

himself that he is justly and liberally dealt by. A planter may keep an
honest account current, in which everything during the year has been honestly debited and credited, but ten to one the negro will go off from settlement discontented and suspicious.

The practice of some planters of dealing in supplies for their hands of
shoes, clothing, tobacco, etc., is at best a dangerous one and likely to
cost more than it came to. If convenience requires it, then deal in cash.
Sell the wages into the hands of the negro carefully at the end of every
month, and then let him buy if he chooses. It is peculiarly true of the negro that "short reckonings make long friends;" and if you are to have a long
reckoning, compare your notes with his memory every few weeks--so that he
can know exactly how the account is running. Be sure of this: that if by
trafficking with your hands you have managed it so that they will have nothing left at Christmas, you have done a bad business for yourself, however
honest may be the account. You will find it hard to keep him another year.
The great secret of successful planting now is, a force of reliable, faithful and contented laborers. Therefore speculate upon anybody else rather
than your field hands.[6]

Now, we are grateful to believe that the Georgia planters have shown,
as a general thing, great justice and liberality to their field laborers and
yet cases of this trafficking in tobacco, shoes, flour, whisky and calico do
come to our knowledge, and we are sure whenever we hear of it, that the man
in saving a dollar at the cost of twenty. The Charleston Republican, gives
a doleful account of sharp dealing with the negroes of South Carolina--true
or false we know not--but all sharpness with the negroes is a monstrous
dullness on the main question of making money in planting.

The confidence of laborers in the justice of employers must constitute
the main defence against all these schemes at combination by which Jeff Long
or any other Jeff will sit in his barber's shop and prescribe wages for the
county or call a convention for the purpose. Planters and employers must be
willing to pay liberal wages and make all their dealings transparent to the
mind of the laborer. If this or any similar fuss should have the effect of
raising the standard of wages unreasonably, then we must hire on shares, and
we must do with fewer house servants--but we must keep faith with the negro
and increase our influence over him day by day, in the only legitimate way
of a liberal, considerate and just dealing.

Macon (Ga.) Telegraph, October 22, 1869.

5. THE NEGRO CONVENTION ON GEORGIA OUTRAGES

We have again had the misfortune to disturb the sensitive nerves of our
friend of the Savannah News by having published the outrage reports of the
Colored Convention without contemporaneous editorial comments. The News had
had some experience in printing daily journals, and it should perhaps have
occurred to him that very extended reports of meetings prolonged into the
night, and which do not get into the printers' hands till after gas-light,
and are not in type till after midnight, or seen by the editor until the next
day, cannot well be accompanied with contemporaneous editorial comment. But,
while a little surprised at the failure of the News to comprehend the difficulties of a performance which he exacts at our hands, we see he comes up
manfully to supply our short comings and omissions, and comments with much
bitterness if not justice.

The truth is, we view this Convention and their handiwork from a different standpoint from that which the News seems to take. We looked for it
to be a very mischievous and violent body. All its predecessors in Macon
had been of that character. But just in proportion as its influences might
be had, just in that proportion it was important to the whites to know all
about them. The negroes do *not* depend on the press for the dissemination of
intelligence among themselves; but with the whites the press is the sole
dependence.

Consequently, we determined to have the proceedings of the Convention fully reported, and, if possible, by parties in the interest of the Convention. This we succeeded in doing, and the great interest manifested by the people and press of Georgia in reading these accounts, vindicates the propriety of the proceeding. Indeed, there can be nothing more important to us in a material or political point of view, than knowing just what is going on among our colored population, so that we may be prepared to counteract falsehood, and evil pernicious influences, as soon and as far as possible.

With these views of what was to be the probable character of the Convention, we were agreeably surprised to find it not half so bad as we anticipated, and naturally felt a good deal more like praising it for unexpected moderation, than inveighing with any particular bitterness against such errors as it might have committed. The temper it displayed was generally conciliatory and the whites of Georgia should never suffer themselves to be outdone by the negroes. On the contrary, we should take the lead in contributions to harmony between the races, each in its appropriate sphere. We should display great allowance, toleration and forbearance, and encourage with the fullest reciprocity every manifestation of a friendly temper by the colored race. They are a valuable part of our population. Their interests are substantially ours, and never should we suffer the political power with which they have been armed to be used for the common injury if we can prevent it by fair and honorable means. That is so plainly the policy dictated by a common sense view of the situation that few men will call it in question.

When, therefore, we found that the delegates, from most of the countries in the State, in their mixed reports of good and ill, had reported a number of "murders" amounting in gross to only twenty-three, we thought, on the whole, they had done pretty well considering. Last year the Radicals, black and white, native and foreign, made out among them, if our memory serves us, some two or three hundred murders of blacks in Georgia. This, then, was a large improvement. We had no doubt that during the year more than twenty-three blacks, and probably more than twenty-three whites, had been killed, and that in the case of the blacks every instance of killing would be set down as murder. In Bibb county, for illustration, the delegates reported one negro killed, whereas, there have been two or three. The statement, therefore, was not surprising. There have been, as we suppose, more than twenty-three homicides of negroes in Georgia during the past year--but the mass of them were cases of killing in self-defence, or killing when the victim was in the act of robbery or resisting apprehension, or killing in the course of a broil. The number of *murders* of blacks by whites, if any, was exceedingly small, and not one of them, as we believe, had any origin in political causes.

There is not a newspaper in Georgia which has been more sedulous than the TELEGRAPH in its efforts to counteract and refute the slanders upon our political and social condition disseminated by the Radicals for political effect; and if the whole press will be as anxious to maintain the peace and fair fame of Georgia as we, and to avoid all the approaches to violence, by discouraging personal and political acrimony, there will be even less foundation for "reports of outrages."

Macon (Ga.) Telegraph, October 29, 1869.

6. THE COLORED LABOR CONVENTION, III

It is needless for us to say to the readers of the TELEGRAPH, that we did not look for any *good* from the Colored Labor Convention, which has lately held its session in Macon at the call of certain master spirits of the race who are surely not examples in the way of labor. The least that we hoped was that it should do no great amount of *harm*, by unsettling the minds of our plantation laborers and stirring them up to the attempt to establish arbitrary wages of labor and refusing to work unless these rates were conceded.

But in this particular, as well as some others, the convention disappointed us by its good sense, moderation and good temper. It has been the first large gathering of the colored population in Macon, in which some attempt has not been manifested to stir up bad feeling between the races. There was nothing of the sort here; but, on the contrary, the feeling seemed to be kindly.

We are glad to see and to acknowledge this fact. We are glad to be able to compliment the body by saying that, in the main, it has shown sense and prudence and a good spirit, and we know we utter the heartfelt wishes of all the conscientious thoughtful and responsible citizens of Georgia, when we express the earnest hope that the future of Georgia may be marked by a growing kindness and sympathy between the two races. That our intercourse may be characterized, on both sides, by justice, liberality, good will and a sincere and hearty interest in each other's welfare. That both races may prosper in the ways of well-doing--increase in virtue, intelligence, wealth and comfort, and together build up old Georgia on a solid basis of civil and social order and prosperity.

On the part of the great body of the whites, we are sure that we can say with truth, this is the unanimous desire. The colored people will find their strong defence against injustice in the scarcity of labor and the universal longing to increase the cotton product. This will bring them satisfactory wages and prompt and fair dealing. In a country like ours, where the character of every employer, in relation to liberal and honorable dealing, can be easily ascertained, it seems to us no laborer need suffer. He can always find a just and honorable employer, if he himself is disposed to do right.

We feel great confidence in an improving good understanding between the whites and blacks of Georgia. It is so clearly for the interest of the planter to secure the good opinion of the laborers, and for the laborers to settle down quietly and permanently upon the plantation and surround themselves with the conveniences and comforts they desire, that we feel morally certain this will be the steady tendency in the future.

We do not propose to review the somewhat extended proceedings which have been published. The outrage report we might except to; but unfortunately there has been perhaps more than twenty-three blacks and perhaps more then twenty-three whites killed in Georgia the past year. All good men deplore violence and bloodshed; but the bulk of it is not murder; and we believe the life of a peaceable black is as safe in Georgia as that of a white; and we think justice is impartially administered to both races. Some of the county reports say the contrary--but allowance must be made for prejudice. We don't believe there are a hundred white men in Georgia who would not join hands with the blacks in a hearty desire and determination that their rights shall be maintained with even-handed justice.

Macon (Ga.) Telegraph, October 29, 1869.

7.   THE COLORED LABOR CONVENTION, IV

The Griffin Star, of Tuesday, says:

The Macon Convention, while it did not do as much harm as we anticipated--for it did not discuss politics--yet it failed in our opinion to do much that will redound to the benefit of the colored race, and it did some very unwise things. For instance, it recommended the colored people to withdraw their female labor from the field as soon as possible. This thing is one of the worst results of emancipation. Thousands of stout, healthy negro women, have already quit the fields and become a burden instead of a help to their husbands and fathers. They seem to think that because white women don't generally work out doors, it must be degrading to the blacks. This is a mistake.

Another committee "report" upon the great importance of having negro preachers, negro lawyers, negro doctors, philosophers, and editors. This is another mistake. The professions are already crowded. What is needed in this line is--not *more* professional men but *better* ones, while the attempt to crowd the colored race into these professions will only result in discord and strife.

Some of their reports however, betoken some good sense and discretion. *We must also economize labor*. Already the South is making rapid strides in this direction, and yet has made scarcely a beginning. Improved agricultural implements must be found everywhere. The cooking stove, washing machine, sewing machine, etc., must be found in every dwelling. The old kitchens must be torn down and neat little cook rooms attached to the house so that madame, when compelled to, can go to her cooking establishment without getting either head or foot wet. Then every home should have its wood house always full of dry wood, cut and ready for use, and close to the kitchen; also, a washroom and store room and several convenient closets. Even the poor man can have these conveniences after an humble style, at slight expense, while the rich can make them as gorgeous as they please.

We look forward to the accomplishment of all these things with a degree of joy almost inexpressible. It is our politics and almost our religion, and it is of more importance than the fifteenth amendment, or any other demagogue hue and cry.

Macon (Ga.) Telegraph, October 29, 1869.

8. THE COLORED LABOR CONVENTION, V

Which assembled in Macon last week, took an "inventory" of the State and here is what they say of the condition of things in

WASHINGTON COUNTY.--Getting along very well; good wages this year. Two schools. Average ten dollars per month. No murders. Seventy scholars in schools. Daily wages fifty cents. Prejudice gradually dying out.

Very much obliged to them for so much, but it seems they cannot quite go "the whole hog" "Prejudice gradually dying out." What do they mean by that? Is it that prejudice on the part of the blacks against the whites is dying out, or vice versa? Would like to understand the matter fully, but presume that the committee meant to say that the *prejudice* business was all on the part of the white people, and that they are *giving in* at last gradually. Well, let the truth be told though the heavens fall. There never would have been any trouble, "Prejudice" or anything of the kind between whites and blacks in this county, further than the distinction between the two races.--for which heaven, not earth, is responsible--had there been no strolling vagabonds visiting here and sending out their pernicious documents to poison and *prejudice* the minds of the *colored* against the whites.

We are truly gratified to know, however, that our county stands first in the approval of even these fault finders who have constituted themselves the judges in these matters. No charge is laid against Washington at all, while the majority are severely censured. Many of the grave charges alleged against counties of high standing, we are fully persuaded, are without foundation; but we leave the accused to speak for themselves.

As expressed in the Convention, the colored people desire to have their children educated. This is praiseworthy in them, and they should be encouraged in it. Some of them want to become lawyers and doctors right away, and seem to think that their youths and maidens are ready at once to "enter college" and be graduated without further delay. They will learn after time, that primary schools are much more in keeping with their wants than higher institute of learning.

The "Labor Association" has done about all it will do, except to get them into trouble.

The Convention, at the instance of "Hon. George Wallace, passed a resolution extending "the right of fellowship to John Chinaman or any other man," no matter from what "clime, country or previous condition," and bidding him a hearty welcome.[7]

Macon (Ga.) Telegraph, October 29, 1869.

9. THE COLORED CONVENTION, VI

So far as we have heard, Jeff Long's colored Convention has passed off without producing an earthquake, and Jeff is as well as can be expected. Some people were afraid the colored people would demand wages which they could not afford to give, and thus paralyze the planting interests of Georgia for the following year. We rejoice to learn that these fears were unfounded. On the whole, the colored Convention passed off very much like the Leville Convention, without doing much harm or good.

Our colored friends are naturally imitative in their disposition, and Jeff Long, no doubt hearing that the white folks were about having a big convention, immediately determined that the colored folks must have a convention too. And when the convention met, the same difficulty pervaded the colored convention which seemed to affect the Louisville convention. No one seemed to know why they had come together or what to do now they had got there. So after mature deliberation, they passed resolutions, made speeches, and adjourned. We believe that most of those who attended the colored convention were convinced that Jeff Long called the convention merely for the sake of making a big man of himself and don't believe that they were paid for their trouble. From valuable points in Georgia we learn that the most perfect good feeling exists between the two races. Both parties have found out that it is their interest to be on good terms, and to mutually help and assist each other, and this feeling will soon become universal if not prevented by political incendiaries and carpet-baggers from the North. One thing we believe has been too much neglected by both races: It is the interest of both white and colored to make permanent arrangements for a number of years wherever it has be done. This will enable the colored people to improve their houses, and surround themselves with many comforts which they can never do whilst the custom of changing their home every year continues.

Macon (Ga.) Telegraph, October 29, 1869.

10. ORGANIZATION AMONG THE COLORED PEOPLE

We referred last week to the need of organization and cooperation among the colored people. Politically, where they are allowed to vote, they find their places, for the most part, with one of the two general, established party divisions--the Republican. The national guarantee of their right to vote in any or all of the States and Territories of the Union, we trust, will soon be an accomplished fact by the completion of the ratification of the Fifteenth Amendment. Then organization, especially for the promotion of their industrial and educational interests, will be particularly serviceable. This need is already anticipated, and especially in Georgia, the action taken in view of the forthcoming National Convention to be held next month in Washington is timely and important. It is, we infer, the beginning in earnest of a new industrial era at the South, with the healthful free labor stimulus for the basis. The Washington correspondent of the *Tribune*, of November 2d, gives the following synopsis of the proceedings of the recent State Convention held in Georgia, which indicates the present importance, and foreshadows the future good results of the movement:[8]

"The Georgia State Colored Convention, which met at Macon last week, adjourned on Saturday. It numbered 236 delegates, representing 56 counties, resulted in the formation of an organization to be called the 'State Mechanics' and Laborers' Association,' and provided for local workingmen's Unions. They also recommended the formation of auxiliary Workingwomen's Associations. In the resolutions adopted they declared that capital could only be safe when the laborer is protected, and labor is paid its just reward; they also declared that capital could have no advantage over united labor, and that there was no antagonism between the two when justice was done; they recommended the organization of Cooperative Supply Clubs and associations for the purchase of lands, urged the withdrawal of women from field labor whenever possible, and recommended the formation of clubs among those employed on plantations for material defense. An excellent report on education was presented, and the establishment of a paper to support the movement was determined upon, of which the Hon. H. M. Turner is to be editor. A series of strong resolutions favoring emigration, declaring that there is no antagonism between them and any foreign labor, and offering a welcome to the Chinese here, passed unanimously. *Reports were made from the several counties represented, showing that in four-fifths of them a frightful state of disorder prevails. Thirty murders, five of them women, were reported as having occurred during the last six months. Most of the assassins were known, and are yet at large. In only two instances have arrests been made. Only one man has been convicted, and he was only sentenced to ten years' imprisonment.* In thirty-six counties schools were reported, the highest number in any one being eleven, with 1,500 scholars. In thirteen counties there were but two schools, and in ten others but one each. The day wages reported ranged from twenty-five to seventy-five cents, and monthly wages from $5 to $10. Yearly wages averaged $50. In nearly every county great complaint is made of employers failing to fulfill their contracts, and that the laborers have been cheated out of their share of the crops. Only five counties were reported wherein the blacks obtain justice from the civil courts. As this is the first Convention of the kind which has been held in the South, its proceedings are of more than ordinary interest. Before the adjournment, delegates were appointed to the National Convention to be held here in December. Similar conventions will soon be held in nearly all the Southern States."

In this city the colored working people are also awakening. They have already held several meetings which have resulted in bringing together representatives of the different trades and branches of business, with a view of more thorough organization and general cooperation. A very large and enthusiastic meeting was held in Zion's Church (Rev. Mr. Butler's) a few evenings since. It was of a representative character and included clergymen, physicians, bricklayers, engineers, coachmen, carpenters, longshoremen, printers, calciminers, painters, laundresses, dress-makers, moulders, (tobacco) twisters, refiners, etc., etc. It is proposed to have each branch of business represented in the National Convention. Women are eligible as delegates as well as men. Other meetings are to be held for the selection of delegates, and to complete local organizations. The following were among the resolutions adopted: [9]

Resolved, That this organization be called the New York City Labor Council. That it shall be the duty of each member of it to exercise vigilance and perseverance in securing employment and business to each member, in whatever department of labor he or she may be engaged, and to advocate the cause of the equal right to labor with all other classes of our fellow-citizens.

Resolved, That delegates be appointed to represent the views of the colored citizens of New York at the National Labor Convention to be held in the City of Washington in the month of December next.

Resolved, That such delegates be and are hereby requested to urge upon that convention the necessity of recommending to the colored men and women of this country the vast importance of immediately acquiring the possession of lands and homesteads of their own, and for accomplishing that end to make every necessary personal sacrifice, to exercise the greatest diligence in business, and practice rigid economy in their social and domestic arrangements.

Resolved, That our delegates be further requested to ask the convention to recommend the encouragement of mechanical branches amongst the people--

first, by the establishment of workshops by those who have trades, and the thorough instruction of apprentices in every department of skilled labor now known amongst us; second, by the employment of colored artizans; and third, by a more general patronage of colored mechanics and workshops than has hitherto prevailed.

Resolved, That the exclusion of colored persons in this city from the right to labor in almost every department of industry is a strong evidence of the power which the spirit of slavery and caste still holds over the minds of our white fellow citizens, and is alike disgraceful to them as American citizens and deeply injurious to us, who have fought during the several wars for the independence or the dignity of the country, and have sacrificed or perilled our lives with them for the maintenance of the government and the unity of the States.

Resolved, That the thanks of this meeting are due and are hereby tender-ed to Lewis H. Douglass, Esq., for the manly position which he occupies in defence of the right to work at the trade taught him in his father's office, by maintaining his place at the government printing bureau, showing that he is a well cut type of a standard font.[10]

Resolved, That we regard the labor of the country as the common property of the people; that no portion of the people should be excluded therefrom by the mere accident of the division of the globe in which they or their fore-fathers were born, or stature of color; that every man or woman should re-ceive employment according to the ability each may possess to perform the labor required, without any other test.

National Anti-Slavery Standard, November 6, 1869.

11.   "AT LAST THE COLORED LABORING MEN OF GEORGIA ARE UNITED"

The Labor Convention

From the (Augusta) Georgia Republican.

We publish this week the proceedings of the Macon Labor Convention. Our readers, whether employers or employed, cannot fail to be interested in read-ing these proceedings, for the Convention represented the opinions of the most intelligent colored laboring men in Georgia, who represent nearly all of the colored laboring men of the State. The importance of such a movement must be apparent to every intelligent man.

The Convention was composed of abler men than have attended any previous Convention of colored men that has assembled in this State. Several of the ablest colored men who have attended former Conventions were there, a few were absent, but their places were filled by new men of equal ability, while the rank and file was composed of abler colored men than have heretofore at-tended conventions in this State. Nearly all were well dressed. In that respect there was great improvement over former Conventions, thus proving that the condition of the colored people is improving. Col. Avery of the Atlanta *Constitution,* who "stepped into" the Convention, says:

"We found a goodly attendance of all colors. The proceedings were very well conducted. The order was excellent, the members kept their seats, the presiding officer seemed to know parliamentry law very well, and was impartial. The truth is, we have seen deliberative bodies of white men conducted worse.

"Jeff Long, a straw-colored, sharp looking, well dressed negro, seemed the ruling spirit."

It was a *working* Convention, rather than a *talking* Convention, and in that respect was a great improvement over former Conventions. The leaders seemed to realize the importance of the work that they had undertaken, and like sensible men they *worked* more than they talked. It was *in fact,* a Con-vention of colored men. Everything was done by colored men. It is true that there was one white delegate present, by the name of Fitzpatrick, but he was an uneducated man of little ability, and he evidently exerted little influence in the Convention. We believe that he was not appointed on any committee, so that colored men are entitled to the credit of managing the Convention, and writing the reports, resolutions, etc. This whole movement originated with colored men, and has been conducted by them; thus proving their ability to manage their own affairs.

The principal reason given by the enemies of this labor movement for opposing it was that the leaders intended to regulate the price of labor in the State, and that by attempting to do so they would do much harm. We have never believed that it was the intention of Mr. Long and his friends to attempt to control prices, but rather to improve the condition of laboring men and let prices be regulated by the demand for laborers and the supply. We were correct, as the proceedings of the Convention prove. An attempt was made by some delegates to fix a price for the labor of plantation hands, but it was opposed by Mr. Long, Mr. Turner and other influential leaders, who were almost unanimously sustained by the Convention.

The great object which the leaders had in view, as developed by the proceedings, was to improve the condition of colored laboring men--in a word, to make them better citizens. How can any good citizen of Georgia oppose such a movement? Are colored men ignorant? It is proposed to educate them and make them intelligent. Are any vicious? It is proposed to make them good citizens, if possible, and thus promote the interests of Georgia. Such a movement must receive the sympathy, if not the active cooperation of every good citizen.

The report of the committee on education is an able document, and presents concisely, but clearly, the condition of the colored people, and the necessity of their being educated. It is the work of a colored man--Wm. J. White, of this city, who was a slave until the close of the war, but he is a man who understands the condition of his people, and has the ability and disposition to labor for their moral and intellectual elevation. He is the President of the Young Men's Christian Association, of this city.

We call the attention of our readers especially to the report of the committee on outrages. What a record for a civilized country. These men make known to the people of Georgia their condition, and pray for justice. Will not the good men and women of this State listen? Will they not assist these poor people? Shall not the men who commit these crimes be brought to punishment? The worst of all, is that these criminals are not punished except in a few counties.

The most important work done by the Convention was the organization of the Mechanics' and Laborers' Association. If the Convention had adjourned without effecting a permanent organization, it would have greatly disappointed its friends. Associations are to be organized in every county in the State. Thus the most ignorant can be reached and assisted.

Delegates were elected to the National Laboring Men's Convention, which meets in Washington, D. C., in December.

At last the colored laboring men in Georgia are united. Why do not the colored men of other Southern States unite? The battle for political equality has been fought, and the victory won. The great question is now: protection for life and property; food and clothing for wife and children; education for all.

National Anti-Slavery Standard, November 27, 1869.

12.   FRUITS OF THE LABOR CONVENTION

Jeff Long's negro labor convention is beginning to develop its pernicious fruits in those sections of the State that were brought under the influence. Several negroes struck for higher wages in Albany a few days ago, and the employers said, "strike away," and forthwith supplied their places, leaving them to take the chances under Jeff Long's teaching. We find other cases related to the Eatonton Press as follows:

From what we have seen here and can learn from other sections, we are inclined to think Jeff Long's labor movement is going to cause some of his followers to suffer during the coming winter. They are valuing their labor so high employers can't see the profit to be derived from giving them employment, hence they will be forced to idleness and live on short rations, or concede to the terms offered by those who may need their services. It is nonsense, and worse to think of giving the prices some of the negroes are asking, because their labor is not *worth* it. . . .

A man must stand upon the solid rock of justice, truth, and fair and generous dealing before he can indulge one rational hope of prosperity. When he stands there he feels like a man--he knows he is right--he is doing justice, and expects and demands justice in return. His laborers know the same and their own inward consciousness of justice and right are the voiceless advocates of the employer.

But let them detect him in the smallest disposition to take advantage of them and they will return it with interest, and with a comparatively clear conscience. It becomes mere retaliation. It takes the shape of equity.

When a planter, by sharp dealing or by inducing his hands to do what his good sense tells him is not for their real interest, succeeds in reducing very materially, at small cost, the balance of wages against himself at Christmas, he should not be so simple as to persuade himself he has really made that much money. In all probability he has lost, in various ways, ten times the amount of his apparent savings.

And he has made a *bad* loss for himself if, with all, he has lost the *confidence* of his laborers. *That* will lose him their labor, and a bad reputation for kindness, justice, liberality and promptitude is now as indispensable basis for prosperous farming in the South. . . .

The great point is to *content the hands*. A dissatisfied force is a worthless and unprofitable force if you can get it for $5 a month. Let our planters aim, first of all, at relations of entire confidence and friendliness with their hands. Let every one of these negroes feel that he has a "Boss" who not only would not cheat him, if he could, but one who takes a warm and friendly interest in his welfare, and is solicitous for his comfort and prosperity.

Macon (Ga.) Telegraph, November 12, 1869.

13. "NO MOVEMENT IS MORE IMPORTANT"

Colored Labor Convention

The colored people of the South are taking steps to protect their labor interests. Our Augusta, Ga., correspondent has sent us the published proceedings of a large Colored Labor Convention recently held at Macon. The reports of the delegates from the different counties showed that there still exists a deep, bitter feeling against the colored people in the interior of the State. At some places there have been murders without any arrests; at others contracts with colored laborers have been ignored, and the laborer left unrewarded. These instances however, are exceptions; for in the majority of cases the reports are more favorable.

The State Labor Conventions now being held, are preparatory to the great National Labor Convention of colored men to be held in Union League hall at Washington, D.C., on the first Monday in December.

No movement is more important than this. If the objects of this convention be fully carried out, as it is very easy for the colored laborers of this country to do so, they will afford a necessary protection to the labor interests of the colored people that nothing else will.

National Anti-Slavery Standard, December 4, 1869.

14.   LETTER TO GEORGIA NEWSPAPERMAN, J. E. BRYANT.

Cassville, Georgia
November 23, 1869

Mr. Editor deare Sir
     I have glad to recve your thanks. I shall due all in my power to get as
menny Subscribers as i can and Send to you. I hope you Would helpt me by
Sending Some of thouse papers that has the Besniess of the Convintion that
Was in Macon, ga. So i can give them to my peoples.
     They all as anchis to See What Was done and nex Saturday We Expect to
have alarge gathring to come and joine the laboring a Sociathion. So Some of
them papers Will due agrat good and i may get manney to Subscribers and any
thing you Think Would helpt us i Would be glad to have fore my peoples is very
[migrant] and poor at this time.
     i hope you Will Exquse my lines. am yours truley dear Sir
                                             Fraind
                                             Charles R. Edwards

J. E. Bryant Papers, Duke University.
Courtesy of Joseph Reidy, Freedmen's Bureau Project.

15.   MEETING OF THE COLORED MECHANICS AND LABORING MAN'S ASSOCIATION
OF CASS COUNTY, GEORGIA

Cassville, Georgia
December 29, 1869

Mr. Editor
     Please allow me to inform the Public of Our Meeting We have hade in
Cassville, Cass County, G.A. on the 27 Dec 1864 Was Meet at the time apointed
the Meting Was open by Reading the 78 Chapter of Shlams and Singing O god our
help in ages pass. Our help fore years to come by the Rev Charles R. Edwards
and pray by Rev John Megee after witch Rev Charles R. Edwards stated the call
of the Meting one Month ago for to unit the laboring Men in the county into
associations after Witch Rev John Megee Was call and Elected Chairman and the
Rev C. R. Edwards Secetray and Was move and Sent to a Joint committee to choose
candidates to be Elected fore the offeces after witch they Repoted C. R. Edwards and J. Megee & Preston low for Vice P. for Secetray M. F. Churn &
William Saxon fore treasurer John Frost Sectray William Saxson and after With
Meting ajoined untell nex day the 2 day Meeting open at 10 ocl pray by Rev
C. R. Edwards Roll Call and Menets Was read Receved and adopted. [The] com-
mitee apointed on finance Was corlected $79.40 cents and all that Wheres to
come ded not come on the account of bad Rainey Whather committee Was pointed
to get all the amount of crop that Was Made by colored Mens--The Meeting
ajoined to the nex day. . . . On the 29 dec 1869 the Meting Was Call to order
by the charman J. Megee pray Made by the same. Was move by C. R. Edwards
Secetray to take up the onfinshed besness. . . . Send you aletel monney to
have these print. I dont know how much it Will take. You must let me know
and it Was move by the president the Rev Charles R. Edwards that We Meet on
amonth and pay 100 amonth tell We can manag. Some good amount to due Some
good With. We Wants to paye land as Soon as We can to give homes to our poor
peoples for many as be dout homes and land to Worke and Cheated out What many
Workes fore. I have Some promise to take your paper. I Will due all i can to
have this paper among my people. Due What you can for ous. We have the amount
Joined up to date 87 Members and We think We Will have Soon many more.

I am yours truley dear sir
President of the Mechanics and laboring Mens Association of
Cass Co. Ga.
                         Rev Charles R. Edwards
J. E. Bryant Papers, Duke University. Courtesy of Joseph Reidy.

16. BLACKS SELECT DELEGATES IN RHODE ISLAND

National Labor Convention

The Union Congregational Church at Newport, R. I., was well filled on Monday evening by laboring men and their friends to consider the industrial questions of the day. The Providence *Journal* says that the meeting was called to order by Rev. M. Van Horne, and was opened with prayer by Rev. J. P. Shreeves. The following gentlemen were chosen officers for the evening:

Rev. J. P. Shreeves, President; J. W. Palmer and T. G. Williams, Vice Presidents, and John Dosher, Secretary.

Rev. M. Van Horne, George T. Downing, L. D. Davis, Wm. Little and others were called out, and in response addressed the meeting.[11]

Messrs. George T. Downing, Mahlon Van Horne and M. S. Haynes were appointed a Committee on Resolutions, who reported the following, which were unanimously adopted:

Resolved, That we do heartily recognize the call issued for a National Labor Convention to assemble in the city of Washington, D. C., on the first Monday in December.

Resolved, That the colored men of the nation, being to a great extent mechanics and laborers, we regard it our immediate interest, as well as our duty, to do all in our power to add to the dignity and elevation of labor; and as a union of the laboring men of the nation, without regard to race or color, linked by an intelligent, liberal and patriotic spirit, will greatly tend thereto, we should and will strive to effect the same, and shall hope for the sympathy and co-operation of capitalists, with whom labor should be in harmony and accord.

Resolved, That we refer with special satisfaction to the National Labor Convention, which was composed of white men, which assembled in the city of Philadelphia on the 16th of last August, because it adopted a platform in keeping with the above enunciation, as to the importance, duty and interest of union and accord between the laborers of the nation, without regard to race or color.

Resolved, That we are glad to know that the contemplated Convention to assemble in Washington is to convene under these favorable auspices, with a policy in keeping, as its guiding sentiment, that its doors are open to the Irishman, the German, the Englishman, the Frenchman, to all, without regard to race or color.

Resolved, That we will send a delegate to such a Convention, and ask the co-operation to that end of mechanics and the laboring men generally of the State.

Resolved, That a committee of three be appointed to invite such co-operation.

Resolved, That G. T. Downing, M. Van Horne and T. G. Williams be that committee.

Resolved, That Messrs. Shreeves, Van Horne, Palmer, Mary Nichols, Adeline Jones and Miss Bowen be a committee with power to raise funds in aid of this movement.

After some further discussion of the matter at issue the meeting adjourned.

The Christian Recorder, October 9, 1869.

17. FROM THE NEWPORT DAILY NEWS

At the meeting held in the Union Church Monday evening the following appeal was read. It will fully explain itself:

MR. PRESIDENT AND GENTLEMEN: Having attended the meeting called to meet in the Union Congregational church for purpose of taking into consideration the condition of the colored people of Newport in their mechanical and

industrial relations, I was much disappointed in that in all your deliberations, speeches and resolutions, which were excellent so far as the men are
concerned, the poor woman's interests were not mentioned, or referred to.
Now right here are the wives, the mothers, the daughters and the sisters, all
suffering under the same *law*, and in many respects, they are made to feel
more keenly than yourselves the degrading, soul-withering, and demoralizing
influence of prejudice.

Now in your praiseworthy attempt to secure equality in your business
pursuits *are we* to be *left out?* we who have suffered all the evils of which
you so justly complain? Are our daughters to be denied the privilege of
honestly earning a livelihood, by being excluded from the milliner, dressmaker, tailor, or dry good store, in fact every calling, that an intelligent,
respectable, industrious female may strive to obtain, and this merely because
her skin is dusky? These privileges are all denied colored females of Newport. However well they may be fitted for other positions, they are compelled to accept the meanest drudgeries or starve, or leave their childhood
homes, and break away from every cherished association of parent, of birth-
place, of kindred, of friend, and become an exile, aye worse than an exile,
for prejudice grinds its victim in the dust and has no mercy, and simply because our white fellow townsmen and women will not see through our dark
skins the image of their and our God; nevertheless it is stamped there as
clear as the meridian sun. I say in charity they cannot see. I will throw
this as a mantle of charity over their injustice, even while smarting under
its stinging effects.

Are they not aware that we have committed no crime in being blacks, and
hence we ought not to be punished; we had nothing to do with our complexion.
The Almighty alone is responsible for that, he who has declared himself to
be no respecter of persons. The being to whom we all look and say with equal
authority *"Our Father."* Therefore the colored women of Newport would ask
your meeting and the Convention that is to assemble next Monday to remember
us in your deliberations so that when you mount the chariot of equality, in
industrial and mechanical pursuits, we may at least be permitted to cling to
the wheels of your chariot.   A COLORED WOMAN OF NEWPORT.

Mr. D. Nathans and Messrs. M. S. Haynes, G. T. Downing and Wm. Little,
were appointed a committee to nominate a lady to represent the city of Newport in the coming State Convention. The Committee nominated Miss Jennie D.
Harris who was unanimously chosen as a delegate and who will attend the
meeting as such.

National Anti-Slavery Standard, November 30, 1869.

18. THE VIRGINIA CONVENTION

A large and enthusiastic meeting of the colored mechanics, laborers and
farmers of Frederick county, Virginia, was held in the city of Winchester on
Friday evening last, Rev. Robert Armsted was called to the chair, and Mr.
Reuben Bundy was elected Secretary. Randolph Martin, Esq., offered the following resolution which was unanimously adopted.

Resolved, That we unequivocally endorse the call for a National Labor
Convention of the colored men of the nation to meet in the city of Washington
on the first Monday in December, 1869.

Resolved, That in our judgment, the condition of the colored laboring
men of the whole country, demands that we should meet in National Council, to
adopt such measures as will effectually organize the colored labor of the
whole country.

Resolved, That we heartily endorse the action of the Philadelphia Convention in admitting colored delegates, and also their liberal platform, in
making no distinction in the employment of labor, on account of race or col-
or.

Resolved, That we endorse the address of Mr. Isaac Myers, delivered before said Convention, and recommend its careful perusal by the colored

laboring men of the country.

Resolved, That Professor Randolph Martin represent the city of Winchester, and that William A. Evans represent the county at large, in the National Labor Convention that meets in the city of Washington on the first Monday in December next.

A subscription of one hundred dollars was raised to defray the expenses of the delegates.

Mr. Martin has called meetings in other counties. The greatest enthusiasm prevails in Western Virginia.

The colored Coopers of Baltimore have formed an Association, and gone to work in shops with white men, at same rate of wages. The good work moves on. Colored men organize!

The Christian Recorder, October 9, 1869.

19. MARYLAND BLACKS SELECT DELEGATES

The Colored National Labor Convention--The Board of Directors of the Chesapeake Marine Railway Company, at their regular monthly meeting, November 1st, 1869, took the following action in reference to the National Convention of Workingmen:[12]

Resolved, That the call for a National Convention of Colored Workingmen, to meet in Washington, December 6th, 1869, receives our unqualified endorsement, and it is looked forward to as being the beginning of the thorough organization and elevation of colored labor throughout the United States.

Resolved, That the relationship of capital to labor in the Southern States has been so changed by the results of the late civil war that the immunities of every workingman should be equal.

Resolved, That we appeal to the National Convention, when assembled in December next, so to legislate upon the question of labor as will ultimately result in the complete organization and consolidation of all branches of labor without regard to color into one common brotherhood.

The above resolutions were unanimously adopted, and Mr. George Meyers, the Secretary of the company, was elected a delegate to represent the company in the coming Convention. He will represent a constituency of over four hundred, with a capital stock of $40,000, and an enterprise without an equal among colored men in the United States.

National Labor Convention--At the Convention of the Colored Mechanics and Laboring Men of the city of Baltimore, held at the Douglas Institute last evening, the following delegates were elected to represent the different branches of workingmen in the National Labor Convention that meets in the city of Washington on the first Monday in December next: Isaac Myers, State at large; A. Ward Handy, city at large; Daniel Davis, W. W. Hare, Robert B. Sorrell, Daniel Finley, Wm. Gant, Wm. Griffin, Joseph Thomas, Wesley Howard, J. H. C. Pinder, Goerge Dennis, J. H. Tabbs, Augustus Roberts, Henry Jones, James Hammond. Mr. John H. Butler, of Baltimore, has been elected by the Butler Industrial Association of St. Mary's county. Addresses were delivered by Messrs. W. U. Saunders, Isaac Myers, John H. Butler, R. B. Sorrell, and others.[13]

The Christian Recorder, November 20, 1869.

20.   THE LABOR CONVENTION OF COLORED MEN

From the Charleston (S.C.) *Missionary Record*

EVERY day intensifies the interest in this great gathering, which will take place in Washington, D.C., the first Monday in Dec. From every section of the country great interest is felt in this movement. The colored men in Georgia and other States are moving. We call upon the mechanics, and trades-men of every kind in this State to interest themselves in the great living idea of the age now taking deep root in the nation, labor which is the foun-dation stone of every fabric of national prosperity, and civilization, is now being laid deeper and more solid than ever before. The honest yeomanry, the mechanic, artisan, the farmer and the operatives are being recognized as an integral part of the nation, the proper estimate; is being placed on their productions as never before. In the South, we have all the materials, which make these characters, and give prosperity to the country. Let South Caro-lina be fully represented in this Convention, let a delegate be sent from every county, if need be, in this State; chose your most intelligent men of every calling; call county conventions, discuss the various questions of in-terest to the whole people, let no subject be undiscussed which relates to the prosperity of the laboring classes.

Every dispatch brings us news of efforts of the struggling millions of the Old World to obtain a proper recognition, by capital, and wealth, which owe their existence to the industry of the laboring classes. There are, doubtless, twenty thousand mechanics and tradesmen in this State, who ought to be represented there; then there are thousands of inexperienced farmers, who ought to be represented; what is needed in this country is a general diffusion of knowledge among the masses. Let us hope that this convention is the begin-ning of better days for the working men of this country. We hail this as the precursor of a brighter era for our race.

National Anti-Slavery Standard, October 30, 1869.

21.   THE SOUTH CAROLINA CONVENTION

The relations between laborers and employers have formed a prominent top-ic of discussion during the past year, as being closely allied with the in-dustrial reconstruction of the State. A large proportion of the laborers, being freedmen employed upon farms and plantations, have had occasion to com-plain of the unjust conditions imposed upon them by planters in contracts for labor, and of the insufficiency of the wages, and the uncertainty of their prompt collection. Another alleged cause of complaint has been the obstacles encountered by thrifty laborers in their efforts to purchase land in parcels commensurate with their limited means.

In consequence of these grievances, a State Labor Convention, composed chiefly of colored delegates, was held in the latter part of November at Co-lumbia, the object of which was to obtain from the General Assembly then in session the legislation necessary to protect the laborer from the alleged ra-pacity and dishonesty of his employer. In a memorial presented to the Legis-lature, the position and the wants of the agricultural laboring-class of the State were defined, and a redress of their grievances asked in the following terms:

We pray that your honorable body will provide by statute:

1. That the claim of the agricultural laborer for wages due shall oper-ate as a preferred lien upon the land that he works, and that the planter or owner of said land shall not sell or alienate the same, until such claim is satisfied.

2. That the Governor shall appoint a discreet and proper person in each county who shall be designated as "commissioner of contracts." Such persons

shall be charged with the duty of examining and attesting all contracts between the planter and laborer, and shall act as advisory counsel of the laborer upon all questions that may arise under his contract. He shall make a
quarterly report to the Bureau of Agricultural Statistics, setting forth the
number of laborers in his county, how employed, and the rate of wages paid,
and the names of planters and laborers who may have violated their contracts,
all of which shall be laid before the General Assembly, at the commencement
of each session thereof, and shall be published for general information.

3.   That the suits of all classes of laborers and employes for wages due
them shall have precedence on the calendars of the courts, over all other
civil suits, and shall be heard at the first term of the court after the
declaration of the plaintiff in the same shall have been filed.

4.   That the Governor shall be authorized to appoint, in each county, an
officer whose duty it shall be to make up the list of jurors, and superintend
the drawing of the same, in order that the laboring-classes may have a fair
representation on the juries, a privilege which is practically denied them in
the rural districts, under the operation of the present system.

5.   That, when lands are sold under execution, the sheriff shall divide
them, as nearly as practicable, into tracts not exceeding fifty acres each,
in order that the small capitalists may be enabled to purchase.

We believe that this measure will greatly facilitate the acquisition of
land by the landless, and that it can be rendered legally practicable by providing that the decree of sale, in each case, shall declare that only so
much of the debtor's land, or the subdivisions thereof, shall be sold as may
be necessary to satisfy the judgment.

6.   That all due-bills given by planters to laborers shall specify in
terms the special consideration for which the same shall have been given, and
shall be transferable, at the option of the holder, and shall operate as a
lien upon the crop and land whenever such due-bill is given, in lieu of payment for agricultural labor.

7.   That nine hours shall be a lawful day's work for all mechanics and
laborers engaged in manufactures or in any business requiring skilled labor.

8.   Abolish all taxes on sales of cotton and rice, by either State or
municipal authorities.

Your memorialists are satisfied that the enactment of the laws herein
prayed for will be of vast benefit to the agricultural laborers, and will
greatly tend to advance the industrial reconstruction of the entire South.

This action on the part of the laboring-class was not without its effect; for a bill was promptly introduced into the House, with fair prospects
of becoming a law, embodying the main points of the memorial.

Appletons' Annual Cyclopedia, 1869, pp. 635-36.

22.   THE LABOR CONVENTION

300 Delegates Present

                                        Columbia, S. C., Nov. 25.

Janney's Hall was crowded with an intelligent and earnest audience.
The Convention was called to order at four o'clock.
Prayer was made by the Rev. Mr. Perrin.
B. F. Jackson, chairman of the committee which called the Convention,
succinctly stated the reason for calling the Convention. He said that the
time seemed ripe for consultation and concerted action for the elevation and
prosperity of the laboring masses. In obedience to this felt want, the call
was made. That it was a deeply felt want is shown by the response of so
many delegates from all parts of the State. We have met together, not as
politicians or partisans, but as working men, to deliberate, not how to in-
jure or invade the rights of capital, but how the laboring men,
of wealth of the State, those on whom the whole people must depend for their

prosperity, may be secured in their rights and advanced in their social and material interests.

R. B. Elliot was elected temporary chairman. [14]

A printed circular was distributed, containing the following questions to members:

1. What monthly wages is paid in your county and what [do] planters pay?

2. What share of the crop is given where laborers find their own provisions; what share where planters find provisions? What share should be given? Is it better for the laborer to find his own provisions or for the planter to furnish?

3. How do the planters in your county treat the laborers? Do they pay wages as they agree? Do they divide the crops fairly. If not, in what way do they defraud the laborers? What can and ought to be done to prevent these wrongs? Do the magistrates protect the laborers in their rights?

4. What do the planters in your county say about this Convention? Will they agree to a fair system, if proposed by this Convention? What do the laborers say of it? What do they expect us to do? Would the people come to an officer appointed for the purpose of drawing contracts as they should be? Would they adopt a general printed form of contract, if recommended by this Convention and the Legislature?

A committee of five was appointed on credentials.

Pending the report, various speakers were called.

Rev. Mr. Stamford declared that all races and classes should live together, and act kindly and justly toward each other. That this is the desire and purpose of the laborers. He humorously illustrated the situation of the laborer and his aspirations for rising in life.

Hon. F. J. Moses, Jr., was called for. He said we have been steadily denounced as always tearing down, and never building up; but we come to-day to give the lie to this idea--to show that the interests of labor and capital are identical. To close up the chasm between capitalists and laborers we must care for the interests of both. You, laborers, have waited for years for planters and capitalists to do justice. You have waited in vain. You now ask only justice long delayed. You ask not vengeance nor reparation for past wrongs--only for right dealing in the future. Do not allow political ideas to interfere with duty at this time. Some men may think to turn this to a political convention for personal ends. If you see such men, put them aside, and give the control of the Convention into other hands. Let your action be so temperate and judicious that it shall be for the good of all your friends and all the people. [15]

Hon. J. J. Wright, of Beaufort, said we must make this Convention to subserve good purpose, to secure an advance of wages. We cannot divide and distribute land to all, but many men in Beaufort are now ready to sell land. The Agricultural Fair was political. This Convention is for no class or party. If men will pay good wages laborers will do honest and good work. Mr. Wright made several good points and was often cheered. [16]

The Committee on Credentials reported nearly 300 delegates, representing nearly every county of the State. From several counties the people thought best not to incur the expense, and requested their Representatives in the Legislature to attend the Convention.

A committee of one from each county was appointed a permanent organization.

Hon. F. L. Cardoza was invited to speak, and said that the adjustment of the interests of capital and the claims of labor is a question of profound importance and great difficulty. Happy will be that people which can settle and harmonize upon it. Aristocracy is broken down in South Carolina, but it is as much as ever determined to get labor without giving proper return. It is the time to rise and demand just recompense. No class will give justice to another till compelled to do so. The laborers must be united and determined. [17]

Negroes are called lazy. It is libel. Who produced two and a half millions of bales of cotton in the South this year? Give to the laborer such wages that he can live comfortably and lay by something for his old age, and he will work vigorously and faithfully.

A. J. Ransier was called for. He urged that the Convention be kept free from politics. Labor is now honorable. But laborers are ill-paid. To secure increased wages there must be organization and united action. We meet to ask what is good for all classes in society. Wherever the best wages are paid there will be found the most education, thrift, virtue, and the greatest general prosperity. An improvement in the condition of the laboring classes is sure to benefit all classes.[18]

The Committee on Permanent Organization reported officers, nearly all of whom were prominent Republicans. These gentlemen, none of them, craved these positions, but the delegates from the various labor Unions were not acquainted with each other, not as a rule known to the committee, and it was natural to select men well known. When the report was presented there was manifest dissatisfaction, not with any particular gentleman nominated, but because the Labor Unions were not reprsented among the officers. The gentlemen nominated at once agreed to withdraw, as their names came up, and substituted names of men now actually engaged in farming or in some mechanical occupation. A motion to elect separately was made with this view, but a motion to recommit was interposed, and opened discussion.

Mr. Elliot made an address of great power, stating the motives which had actuated him and those with him, and declined to serve as permanent president. Other gentlemen nominated declined to serve.

Short addresses, personalities, motions, and points of order, too numerous for record, followed, amid confusion and clamor.

The report was finally disposed of, an assistant secretary only being elected.

Hon. J. L. Neagle made a judicious and excellent address, closing by nominating R. B. Elliot as permanent president, assuring him that he would gratify all if he would accept. He was elected by a vote so hearty and flattering that he accepted. Hon. J. J. Wright, who had presided with marked ability during the stormy scene of the last hour, surrendered the chair to him, and thus permanent organization was effected.

R. C. De Large, Esq., nominated T. F. Clark, Esq., as Vice President. T. J. Mackey, in seconding the nomination, stated that under the [leadership] of Mr. Clark the longshoremen of Charleston had organized themselves and secured a large advance of wages. The longshoremen are the pioneers in this great labor movement, and well deserve the honor of making their President the first Vice-President of the Convention. Mr. Clark was elected by loud acclamation, and greeted with applause as he took his seat on the platform.[19]

The Convention then adjourned, with good feeling restored.

THURSDAY, Nov. 26.

The Convention met at half-past nine. A committee of one from each county was appointed to prepare and report business to the Convention.

A communication was received from the white laborers of Edgefield county, signed by twenty-eight persons, expressing sympathy with the objects of the Convention and the hope that it would devise such measures as would benefit all classes of laborers. A communication of similar import, from Hon. Simeon Corley, was read, and received with evident approval.

Hon. H. E. Hayne moved that one person be selected from each county to present the views and wants of the working men of the State, and, further, to limit the speeches to ten minutes. This he supported in an admirable speech, and it was carried. It was afterward modified so as to admit one from each delegation and trade.

The business committee reported, by its chairman, B. F. Jackson, for discussion and action of the Convention, a resolution for the appointment of a commissioner in each county to supervise contracts--one on the questions whether the planter should furnish provisions to the hands working on shares of the crop, and one fixing the rate of wages which ought to be paid per month, the rate being left blank, the blank to be filled by the Convention.

After a great waste of time in discussing whether to adjourn while the Legislature was in session, the proposition was voted down, and the Convention proceeded to consider the report.

Counties were called, and to Abberville, H. J. Lomax, Esq., responded. He said that farm laborers received about $6 per month. He thought that the planters ought to pay $12. Laborers on shares received one-third, of the crop. They should receive one-half, the planter furnishing material and mules, and feeding the mules, the men "finding" themselves.

Mr. Ball, of Barnwell, was opposed totally to the system now in practice. He thought that mechanics in winter should get $2.00 per day for eight hours work, and in summer $2.50 for ten hours work. With no less could they pay taxes, rents, board, or doctors' bills. Farm laborers working on shares received one-third, and furnished all things. If they will give one-half the men will agree honestly to work, and honestly to pay rents, doctors' bills, taxes, and all dues. He thought that farm laborers ought to receive $20 a month.

Speaking for Beaufort, Hon. Mr. Whipper said that wages were generally from $10 to $12 a month. The men could live if they could get the pay. Certainty of getting pay according to agreement is the great object. All that we can do here is to form a general plan, and leave laborers in each county to combine and carry it out. Labor cannot go into company with capital. Laborers should agree upon a stipulated sum, and combine to enforce pay.[20]

Mr. Gillings, of Charleston county, said wages are $5 per month and one peck of corn a week for men, women $2 to $3 and one peck of corn a week. Laborers on shares on the Cooper river get one-third of the crop. Our people cannot buy decent clothing, nor buy medicine, nor send children to school. The planter says, when the crop is gathered, "Now, I get two-thirds--you get one-third. You owe me so much, and so much, and this comes out of your third." And then the man has left but two or three dollars. The magistrates do not do justice. The white men swindle and swindle, and the magistrates say the white man is right every time. We cannot get justice.

For the Longshoremen's Protective Union, Mr. Taylor spoke. He earnestly advised the laborers everywhere to form Unions and insist on an advance of wages. The longshoremen ask chartered rights and laws to protect labor Unions.

A delegate from Chester said, except laborers get some relief it seems impossible to live. We ask only enough to live--only what is just and right. Employers say it took a third to keep hands when they held slaves and paid no wages. This is all they give now.

The employer, on a good crop makes from $100 to $140 on each man. The men almost starve. We want some plan and some law to give us fair wages. We ought to get one-half the crop.

We want a just rule for a man to keep his contract. We want a person to help us make such a contract. We are cheated in every way. What can we do? We pray for help. We thought the law would help us long ago. But we have waited and waited in vain. Will our Legislature try to help us?

At the close of this address, the Convention adjourned to meet at half-past four o'clock.

(Special Dispatch to The Daily Republican)

SECOND DAY.

Evening Session.

COLUMBIA, November 26--1 P.M.--Reports from counties continued.

J. H. Rainey, T. J. Mackey, W. B. Nash, and B. G. Yocum, appointed to draft memorial to the General Assembly.[21]

Scores of resolutions presented and referred to committees on business and memorial.

THIRD DAY.

The following gentlemen were appointed delegates to the National Labor Convention:

First Congressional District,
Second Congressional District, J. H. Rainey.
Third Congressional District, Simeon Corley.
Fourth Congressional District, L. Wimbush.
At large--T. J. Mackey, W. B. Nash.

The committee on memorial then made their report.

The following are the committee of nine appointed to prepare an address to the people: B. F. Jackson, Lawrence Cain, J. W. Hogan, Porter Smith, W. W. Tucker, J. H. Rainey, T. J. Mackey, W. B. Nash, and B. G. Yocum.

The Convention adjourned at 1 o'clock.

Charleston Daily Republican, November 26, 1869.

23. A PENNSYLVANIA MEETING

The Labor Question

Shippensburg, Cumberland Co., Pa.,
Nov. 3d, 1869.

Pursuant to notice our citizens met on Wednesday evening, Nov. 3d, 1869, in the A.M.E. Zion church, to consider the question of colored labor, and to elect a delegate to the National Labor Convention. The church was nearly filled. The meeting was called to order by Mr. David Baker. On motion Mr. Richard Baker, Sr., was elected President, and Mr. Elias M. Stanton, Secretary. After singing, and prayer by the Rev. J. D. Brooks, the Secretary read the call, and other documents, concerning the meeting.

The President made some appropriate remarks, and was followed by other gentlemen. They were listened to with interest.

Mr. Elias M. Stanton submitted the following preamble and resolutions, prefaced with a few appropriate remarks.

Whereas, The present status of Colored Labor in the United States, and its affinity to American industry, has had but little or no attention paid thereto by the dominant race of this country, consequently many of us have been compelled, to suffer wrongs, and oppression equal to slavery; and

Whereas, There are certain journalists, individuals and cliques, striving to bring contract Chinese or Coolie labor into popular favor in many parts of the country, thus forcing American laborers to work for Coolie wages or starve, and crowding us out on all sides, and reducing the workingmen of this country to a State worse than slavery; and

Whereas, We are crowded out and shoved aside under all circumstances, and a greater portion of the colored laborers of this place, and in fact, throughout the whole country, are deprived of the proper wages, mechanics excluded from the public work-shops and buildings; journeymen and apprentices denied admittance; tradesmen denied the right of trade; artizans deprived of their right to work with other men and receive the same salary; in fact, all sorts of laborers, yea, even professionals are denied their God-given rights, and debarred from places of competitive industry; therefore

Resolved, That we do hereby cordially indorse the call for a National Labor Convention of the colored men of the United States of America, which convenes in Washington City, D. C., on the first Monday in December, 1869.

Resolved, That we heartily appreciate the forcible appeal that was made upon this subject by the Executive Committee of the National Convention of Colored Americans, which convened in Washington City, on the 13th of December, 1868.

Mr. Henry Gallaway was elected delegate. On motion meeting adjourned.

The Christian Recorder, November 20, 1869.

24.   ANOTHER PENNSYLVANIA MEETING

Labor Movement

Avery College, Allegheny City, Pa., Nov. 8, 1869.

ISAAC MYERS, ESQ: MY DEAR BROTHER: According to your appeal which was sent to me, I secured the co-operation of our leading and influential men in the call of a public meeting.

The meeting, assembled in the lecture room of the college, and Mr. B. F. Pulpress was appointed chairman, and the Rev. Mr. Asbury secretary, October 26th. The meeting adjourned to the 2nd inst. to Brown chapel, when the following delegates were duly elected, representing the following departments of labor:

B. F. Pulpress, Commerce; Robt. Waye, Carpenter; Nelson Williams, Moulder; Noah Marry, Shoemaker; Armstead Morrison, Stone-mason; David Morrison, Plasterer; John Jackson, Blacksmith; Thos. Roach, Calker; Washington Hobbs, Laborer; Jas. Barnes, Bricklayer; B. K. Sampson, Education; A. Cole, the Ministry; H. H. Garnet, Avery College.

May God give the good cause great success and bestow faith and strength.

Yours truly,   H. H.[22]

The Christian Recorder, November 27, 1869.

25.   LABOR REFORM UNION - NEW YORK

Last evening a meeting was held in Bethel church, Sullivan street, under the auspices of the Colored Men and Women's Labor Reform Union. A host of attractive orators was announced to speak, but the only one who put in an appearance was the well known colored Senator A. A. Bradley, of Georgia. There was a large attendance of both sexes. [23]

Rev. Mr. JONES opened the proceedings with prayer, in the course of which he sued for human liberty, in order that the social and moral condition of man might be improved.

Mr. TROUP was the first speaker. He called attention to the proceedings of the Labor Congress at Philadelphia, and alluded to the great sincerity of that body in allowing colored people to participate in the good results of its deliberation. He was aware of the prejudice existing against colored people, but that prejudice must be lived down. The time was come when labor must rise above capital. There had been a difference of opinion in this country about the introduction of colored men into the white men's unions--there had been a difference of opinion among the colored men themselves--but there could be no difference of opinion between white men and colored workingmen that they should go hand and hand in the great struggle for their liberty. He was there to encourage the organizations of colored workingmen in this city. If there were any white workingmen who objected to that he would say they were blind to their own interests. They could not see that it was their interest to organize with the colored men and work harmoniously together. In regard to the coming convention at Washington, he was informed by the President of the National Labor Congress of the United States that he would be present at that convention in order to give his aid and countenance to the movement. The speaker said he would do his utmost to forward the interests of the colored workingmen's organization. (Applause).[24]

Senator BRADLEY then came forward and was warmly received. He said the subjects under consideration were religious labor and political reform. The religious point of the subject had been so ably treated previously that he deemed it superfluous and entirely unnecessary to refer to it. With regard to the other portion of the discourse he would say that in the first periods of the world's history necessity compelled that generals should govern, because men, grouped together in herds, commenced fighting each other and their leaders, chiefs and generals, were obliged to manage them. Among others William the Conqueror, of England, in his time owned everything. People were sold and their masters took care of them. It was then that capital triumphed over labor. It was pretty much the same now in Russia. But at a later period, when people became more enlightened in England, they commenced to own themselves and own land, but they would remember that that was not brought about until the Magna Charta was extorted from King John. Then commenced the history of freedom and independence of the workingmen. The Magna Charta was the foundation of American independence. The speaker then proceeded to dilate at considerable length upon the wars of the country, showing the prominent part colored people had taken in them. It was a colored man who gave the first blow in the great revolution. A colored man named Christopher Attick and two white men were shot down in Boston, the alarm bells were rung and the mighty struggle was commenced. He alluded to the compliments paid the colored troops and finally referred to the action of the negro forces in the late war. The speaker was quite profuse in his eulogies of his brethren, and the announcement of their heroic deeds elicited frequent and loud tokens of approbation. He characterized the rebellion as a great struggle of capital against labor. The speaker reviewed the history of the country since the war, introducing many incidents to show that the acts of reconstruction had not been put into force in the fair and impartial manner intended. At times Senator Bradley was quite humorous; particularly so when narrating his experiences in the Georgia Legislature. Nor did he spare the Massachusetts Legislature in the course of his lengthy address. No less than four hundred and sixty-three special acts had been passed during the last session, a large number being for railroads, while the poor mechanic, the poor St. Crispin, could not get a single act passed. He was particularly severe regarding the street improvements of Boston, and drew comparisons between the municipal legislation of that city and New York, both of which came in for a good round of abuse. And while the Senator wandered away considerably from the subject for which the meeting had assembled he did not fail to draw attention to the important fact that he himself could not live on air--a fact, by the way, all present seemed ready to admit. During the collection the quick ears of the Senator were suddenly startled by the chink of coin, when with much dignity he intimated that paper currency was the order of the evening. The announcement might scarcely have been thoroughly appreciated had it not been that the wily legislator addressed himself to the softer sex and strenuously insisted they had a right to vote; whereupon the stamps fell like rain. The Senator earnestly advocated this point, and read voluminous documents and statutes to substantiate his argument. As the hour was somewhat advanced when Senator Bradley closed his oration, the consideration of the labor question was adjourned and the meeting was brought to a close.[25]

New York Herald, November 17, 1869.

26. BLACK WORKERS CONVENE IN TEXAS

Galveston, Texas, Nov. 5th.

COLORED LABOR CONVENTION.--The Convention met on Friday afternoon at Anderson Hall, and was called to order by Richard Nelson. On motion of John De Bruhl, G. T. Ruby was elected President. On motion of Richard Nelson, John De Bruhl was elected Secretary. Circulars were read from Mr. Isaac Myers, the Chairman of the State Labor Convention at Baltimore. After which a resolution offered by Richard Nelson was adopted, and the Convention took a recess until 9 P.M. The Convention met at the appointed hour, with G. T. Ruby in the chair. The labor question was discussed, and delegates were balloted for and the following persons elected: Rev. Johnson Reed, John De Bruhl and Richard Nelson, and Gen. W. T. Clark was afterwards added to the list. After which the Convention adjourned to meet on Tuesday evening at the A.M.E. church on Broadway.

COLORED LABOR CONVENTION.--The adjourned meeting of this body was held at the A.M.E. church on Broadway last evening.

On motion of Mr. De Bruhl, Mr. Nelson was called to the chair to act as President, until that officer came. Mr. Nelson then called the meeting to order. A resolution offered by Richard Nelson was read and adopted, heartily endorsing the action of the State Labor Convention at Baltimore, and heartily inviting the workingmen of the State to co-operate with the Convention in this movement.

The President proper then took the chair as President of the meeting. On motion of Rev. Mr. Reed the action of the Convention held at Mechanics' Hall, on Friday last, was approved. Mr. Powell then moved that Mr. Reed be appointed one of the delegates to the National Labor Convention, to be held in Washington city in December. Mr. Reed asked that the motion to allow the President to express his views be withdrawn, which was done. After hearing the statement of the President, the motion was renewed and Mr. Reed elected.

Mr. Debbles then stated that Harris county had commissioned him to state to the Convention that that county was willing to send one delegate; and thought it was imposing on Galveston county to ask her to send all the delegates. He thought one delegate was enough to send from Galveston, San Antonio, Austin, Houston and Waco.

Mr. Douglas stated that he thought such was the instruction of the committee.

Major Plumly made a few remarks, which were heartily received.

The thanks of the Convention were tendered Mr. Richard Nelson for his efforts in starting and organizing the first Labor Convention ever held in Galveston.

On motion of Major Plumly a committee of five were appointed to collect funds for the purpose of defraying the expenses of delegates. The following committee was appointed: Maj. Plumly, Miss Maria Corody, Mrs. McIlvane, Miss Cuney, John De Bruhl, Henry Ballinger.

After a short discussion Mr. Reed moved that the Convention adjourn, which was carried.

State Labor Convention of Colored Men.--Third day.

On motion of Hon. H. M. Turner, a committee of seven were appointed to nominate delegates to the National Labor Convention which meets in the city of Washington, D.C., December, 1869. The call of said Convention was then read for the information of members.

Afternoon Session.

The report of the committee for delegates to attend the National Convention at Washington, D.C., was announced by the Hon. H. M. Turner.

On motion, the report was received and adopted.

The Committee on Nominations beg leave to offer the following report:-- 1. Hon. Jas. Porter, of Chatham; 2. Hon. Philip Joiner, of Albany; 3. Hon. Abraham Smith, of Columbus; 4. Hon. J. F. Long, of Macon; 5. Hon. W. J. White, of Augusta; 6. Hon. James A. Jackson, of Athens; 7. Hon. Wm. Cookene, of Marietta.

The Christian Recorder, November 20, 1869 .

27.   COLORED LABOR CONVENTION--GALVESTON

At a Convention of the colored working men of Galveston, which met at the A.M.E. Church, on Tuesday, the 2nd day of October, 1869, the Hon. G. Y. Ruby being President, the following resolutions were read and approved.

WHEREAS, An invitation is extended by the Working Men of Baltimore for a National Labor Convention to be held at the city of Washington, in December, 1869, to consider the prospects and ameliorate the condition of the working men of America, and,

WHEREAS, It is eminently proper that we, who have just emerged from a cruel bondage should co-operate with our more favored brethren of other

States in this great work. Therefore be it

Resolved, That we hereby appoint the Rev. Johnson Reed, and Mr. Henry Powell to be and represent us as our State Delegates in said Labor Convention; and

Resolved, Further, that we hereby nominate and appoint the following named ladies and gentlemen as a committee to collect funds for the purpose of defraying the expenses of our said delegates, viz:

Major B. Rush Plumly, Miss Maria Dewdy, Mrs. McIlvaine, Miss Cuney, John De Bruhl and Henry Ballinger.

G. Y. RUBY, Pres.
JOHN DE BRUHL, Sec.

The Christian Recorder, November 27, 1869.

28. ORGANIZATION--THE COLORED PEOPLE

Not quite a year ago the first truly National Convention, representing the colored people of this country, was held at Washington. The important question then pending before Congress was the proposition for a Fifteenth Amendment of the Constitution, guaranteeing equal political rights, irrespective of color. It was a chief purpose of that Convention to insure the adoption by Congress of that important fundamental measure. During the year it has been sent forth to the States for ratification, and has received the sanction of so large a proportion of the required number, that with the understood bias of the States yet to act, its success is now scarcely a matter of doubt. When it shall be proclaimed as a part of the fundamental law of the land, the colored people will have achieved legal equality with the whites as American citizens. It will be an important vantage ground gained. But it will be found that the ballot is but a tool, a weapon, and that upon its use will depend the measure of its real value. It will be in no sense a substitute for work in gaining bread, in acquiring knowledge. It will afford added means of protection, and of securing better conditions for earnest, compensated labor.

Hitherto, except in churches, and those largely under the indirect control of the whites of kindred denominations, the colored people have gained little strength from organization. Of course there could be no political organizations of importance because until recently they have, as a class, had no political existence. Even yet it is but partial. Of industrial organizations they have had few or none, because prior to the war the major portion of colored laborers, men and women, were held as property, subject to the will of others. Personal, political freedom, at least so far as the letter of the law is concerned, we trust is well nigh assured. We are very glad therefore to see among the colored people of the South, and throughout the country, movements already in progress for organization to promote especially their industrial and educational interests. This is as it should be, and promises well for the future. Labor, and other organizations among the whites, independent of party politics, have done much to advance the interests and to secure better conditions for the working classes. Their real value, however, has as yet been but slightly appreciated and realized among either the whites or the colored people. The existence of slavery in the country was, only in a less aggravated form, a curse to the white laborers as well as the blacks.

We have already published the Call of a large and influential committee for a "National Labor Convention of the colored men of the United States," to meet at Washington on the first Monday in December next. It is proposed that the Convention shall consider:

1st. The Present Status of Colored Labor in the United States and its Relationship to American Industry.

2d. Adopt such rules and devise such means as will systematically and effectually organize all the departments of said labor, and make it the more productive in its new Political relationship to Capital, and consolidate the

Colored Workingmen of the several States to act in cooperation with their White Fellow-Workingmen in every State and Territory in the Union, who are opposed to distinction in the Apprenticeship Laws on account of Color, and to do act cooperatively until the necessity for separate organization shall be deemed unnecessary.

3d. Consider the question of the importation of Contract Coolie Labor and its effects upon American Labor, and to petition Congress for the adoption, of such Laws as will prevent its being a system of Slavery.

4th. And adopt such other means as will best advance the interest of the colored Mechanics and Workingmen of the whole country.

Delegates will be admitted without regard to race or color. Women, we presume, will be admitted to the Convention upon the same terms as men. It will be seen, in another column, that a woman delegate has already been appointed from Newport, R. I., and it is expected, we understand, that others will be, from this city. Colored men, as was shown by the National Convention in Washington last winter, are quite as liberal as the whites in this respect. We are very glad to learn from several of our Southern exchanges that the forthcoming Convention at Washington awakens much interest among the colored people of the South, and that there is good prospect of a large and intelligent representation from that quarter. Organization is probably in a more advanced stage at present in Georgia than elsewhere in the South. The colored people of this and other cities in the North are, we learn, to be well represented. The Convention is likely to mark the beginning of a new and important era for laborers of all classes under the regime of freedom. There is yet a vast deal of unreasonable prejudice against color to conquer among white workingmen. The Printers in their persistent efforts to oust Mr. Douglass from the Government printing office, and the Bricklayers, and others, in their opposition to colored apprentices and mechanics have given abundant and shameful proof of this. But there are other, and more manly white men, mechanics and others, who are superior to such petty prejudice and selfishness, and who are disposed to extend a fraternal recognition to colored workers. With such there can, and doubtless will be, advantageous cooperation.[26]

At the South cooperation among the colored people themselves, and with friendly whites, is a necessity of the situation. Arrayed against them in bitter enmity are the rebel land monopolists. They were formerly slave owners, and are still, in the absence of confiscation, improperly the wealthy, and therefore controlling class. Cooperative associations must be formed among the colored people and friendly whites to gain homesteads and carry on business, farming and manufacturing, independently of the old ruling white class. Landless voters must see to it that their ballots are turned to good account by sending to the Southern Legislatures such representatives as will make the inimical land proprietors give largely, if grudgingly, by taxation for the support of free public education, for State charities and internal improvements. Though not directly a political movement, as it is undoubtedly best that at present it should not be, we hail the beginning of thorough organization among colored laborers, as being auspicious not only for their material welfare but as having for the near future an important political significance.

National Anti-Slavery Standard, October 30, 1869.

29.   THE COLORED LABOR CONVENTION

A Word of Advice

On the 6th of December, 1869, the First National Labor Convention of the colored laboring men of the United States, under the auspices of the National Labor Union, will be held in the city of Washington, D. C. We earnestly trust that its deliberations will be controlled by prudence, candor, and common sense, and that it will frown down any attempt to transform it

into a politico-partizan assemblage. The colored people, have too much at
stake at the present juncture to allow any of the political charlatans, who
are so profuse with their sympathy and advice, and who are ever ready to
ride upon any hobby upon which a little capital may be made, to guide their
councils. They must *act and think for themselves*--independent of party dic-
tation--if they desire or expect the support of their white fellow toilers.
The action of the National Labor Union is in earnest that its professions of
sympathy, are no lip service; that its members are prepared to take them by
the hand, and aid, by every means within their power, the dissemination
among them of those principles, which have proved so advantageous to the
white mechanics of the North. Let them, therefore, eschew all schemes of a
chimerical character, all action calculated to arouse a sectional feeling,
all advice tending to excite the prejudices of race or color; and act on the
principle that their true friends alone can be found in the ranks of labor
and their safest counsellors in those whose interests are identified with
their own; and the results will redound to their lasting welfare, and justify the wisdom which governed their action.

Workingman's Advocate, November 6, 1869.

30. AN APPEAL TO THE LABOR CONVENTION

From every indication the Labor Convention which is to meet in Washington city, the first Monday in December, promises to be numerously attended.
While, indeed, the labor question should be canvassed by all the people,
while every city and considerable town should be represented, yet there is
danger of having the Convention too large. Too many of the people cannot be
interested, but too many of them, by one half, may repair to Washington.
Work is needed, and must be done; but overflowing conventions are never cele-
brated for their *work*. We tremble lest this one, surpassing in practical
importance any ever held by us, will be so crowded, that, by the time each
one of the delegates makes a speech--*and they must do that, you know,* all
will be ready and willing to go home; for we whisper something, and not to
be witty, either, that board is tremendously high at Washington. We trust
the people have sent to represent them, not a crowd, drilled only in talk,--
the most pestiferous class in creation, but a company of prudent, hard working men, men who will speak advisedly with their lips.
       Towering high above every other interest is that of labor. The politi-
cian, the would-be statesman, and we are already troubled with not a few of
them, may cry out, Give us our political rights, but the men who live by the
sweat of their brow, know that their chief want is to have labor properly adjusted. The bawling of politicians never put us in the army, whereby we
struck off our own chains, neither will their bawling ratify the XVth Amendment. Mankind generally only act from necessity. It was the necessity of
the North that put us into the army; the same necessity will ratify the XVth
Amendment. If it be not necessary it will not be done for more than a generation, all the talk of our would-be political leaders to the contrary.
       In the meantime the people want their labor properly adjusted. Let the
convention, which is to meet so soon, inaugurate such measures as will secure
to us our position in the South, and restore it to us in the North. Let organizations and unions be established. Let care be taken to foster all manner of mechanism; as we must therein principally operate in the future. The
Negro has too much of the American in him to be a laborer. He must eventually become a mechanic. The ranks of labor are to be filled by emigrants, of
all races; the ranks of mechanism by Americans, white and black. We appeal
especially to the members who will come from the South; the majority of whom
will doubtless be mechanics. Foster your trades, take no step backward, prepare the minds of the people, to rise to the lofty ranks of the American
mechanic.

The Christian Recorder, November 27, 1869.

FORMATION OF THE COLORED NATIONAL LABOR UNION
AND THE BUREAU OF LABOR

FORMATION OF THE COLORED NATIONAL LABOR UNION
AND THE BUREAU OF LABOR

Delegates to the Colored National Labor Union Convention gathered in an atmosphere of self-conscious drama and heightened expectations. Called to order by Isaac Myers on December 6, 1869, 214 delegates from eighteen states assembled in Union League Hall in Washington, D.C. The proceedings of the founding convention of the first national black union were published in pamphlet form and are reproduced as Doc. 1.

Thus, by 1869, black leaders, North and South, had reached the conclusion that equal employment opportunities and better pay could be achieved only through independent organization. What began in July as a local black workers' union in Baltimore soon expanded into the Colored National Labor Convention in December. That so swift and massive a response by black workingmen could be elicited in such a short period of time underscores the magnitude of the perceived need for an organization to further their special concerns. For the first time Afro-Americans representing a wide variety of trades, occupations, and professions discussed the conditions of Negro labor in the United States and made recommendations for improvements. The Colored National Labor Union was organized as a confederation of autonomous local and state unions. Unlike the NLU, however, the black union would include all workers--industrial, agricultural, skilled craftsmen, and common laborers--men and women alike, not just skilled mechanics. The constitution of the CNLU outlining the structure and purposes of the permanent organization is reproduced as Doc. 2.

The delegates lost little time addressing themselves to the problems of black workers. A permanent National Bureau of Labor with offices in Washington, D.C., was established to furnish information and employment opportunities in various parts of the nation, to lobby for legislation insuring equality of employment opportunity, and to negotiate with "bankers and capitalists" for financial assistance in establishing cooperative business ventures among blacks (Doc. 3). Composed of the chief officers and the nine-man executive committee of the CNLU, the Bureau of Labor was direct in its declaration that the "question of the hour" was how the black worker could "best improve his condition." Blacks were encouraged to organize at the state and local levels, cooperatively pooling their wealth, since "without organization, you stand in danger of being exterminated" (Doc. 4).

The National Labor Union was represented at the CNLU convention by its president, Richard F. Trevellick. The NLU had continued to advocate a uniform platform for the working classes represented in national politics by the Labor Reform Party (Doc. 6-7, 9-10). Apparently, the NLU leadership never understood that they expected blacks to sacrifice their own interests without offering them anything in return. Thus, Trevellick disappointed the black delegates when he called for labor unity on the one hand, while denying the propriety of interfering with local white workers who prevented blacks from working at their trades. Moreover, because it would have caused severe schisms in the black community, the NLU's demand that the CNLU abandon the Republican Party meant certain destruction of the new organization. Trevellick apparently saw no such danger in his position on these two issues, yet for the black worker these were life or death issues.

After several intensively productive days, the CNLU convention adjourned on December 10, 1869. As the delegates disbursed, two representatives of the new organization met with President Ulysses S. Grant at the White House and received his assurance of sympathy and support (Doc. 5).

FORMATION OF THE COLORED NATIONAL LABOR UNION AND THE BUREAU OF LABOR

1. PROCEEDINGS OF THE (COLORED) NATIONAL LABOR UNION CONVENTION

The Convention was called to order by Isaac Myers, Esq., of Maryland, who read the call for the Convention; after which he nominated George T. Downing, of Rhode Island, temporary Chairman, who was unanimously chosen. Mr. Downing, on taking the chair, addressed the Convention:

FELLOW DELEGATES.--Accept my acknowledgment of an appreciation of the honor you have conferred on me, in selecting me to fill the responsible and honorable position of temporary chairman of this important gathering; be assured I shall strive to merit the implied confidence, by being strictly impartial in discharging the duties of the office. I shall know no one personally, but you all as equal delegates.

This convention bears the title "National Labor Convention;" I desire that it shall not falsify its name; that it be a "labor convention;" in a word that it shall labor, that it bring forth something. Much is expected of it; the eyes of every intelligent laborer of the land, without regard to color, are fixed on it; its doings will be eagerly caught up and canvassed by the laborers of Europe, now banding together to the end of causing labor to be respected, and of enjoying its just rewards.

That the colored, as well as the white laborers of the United States, are not satisfied as to the estimate that is placed on their labor, as to their opportunities, as to the remuneration for their labor, the call for this convention, and the very general and highly intelligent response which I gaze on in you, my fellow delegates, attest. No other class of men would be satisfied under the circumstances; why should we be?

The Republican party has been made an effective agent under God in liberating us from unrequited toil, from chattel thraldom--all of my class have been slaves by virtue of proscriptive laws, and still worse, the greater portion have been slaves by positive enactment, been deemed, declared, created and adjudged slaves to all intents and purposes. We owe that party respect and support, in view of its agency in freeing us from that degradation. We think that it should have been more consistent, more positive in its dealings with our and the country's enemies; that it should not have set us free, but that it should have been with us in the wilderness; that should have fed us during our pilgrimage; that it should have given us quails and manna, homes and the letter, the latter, a fitting office of government. We should be secured in the soil, which we have enriched by our toil and blood, to which we have a double entitlement.

When the ratification of the proposed fifteenth amendment to the Constitution shall have been effected, with what has already been accomplished in the same direction, much of the adhesive element which has made the composite Republican party a unit have disappeared; for it to hold together, it must have attractive elements. Let the party have a wise financial policy. Let it be mindful of the fact, that the masses are becoming more and more intelligent; that the laboring man thinks, and is, therefore, restive; the mass are becoming so; they expect and will demand some legislation in their behalf; they realize that by being united, they can be an influence equal to capital. That which is known as the labor movement is growing in strength. I beseech our friends to be mindful of the same, to take such action in the premises as will draw to their party, away from a corrupt dishonorable influence that is striving to ally itself with the labor movement, the honest and intelligent agitators for reform in the matter of labor; they, with the colored laborers and voters, will be a host for the right.

The colored man's struggle until now has been for naked existence, for the right of life and liberty; with the fifteenth amendment, henceforth his struggle will be in pursuit of happiness; in this instance, it is to turn his labor to the most effective account, to be respected therein; this is a great problem; it is racking the brains of the ablest economists; the most we can hope to effect, at this gathering, is a crude organization; the formation of a labor bureau to send out agents, to organize colored labor throughout the land, to effect a union with laborers without regard to color.

Good has come out of Nazareth. Slavery, when it existed, shut out the light to the end of shutting out the right; it had, however, to have some light for its own purposes. It did not permit the educated white mechanic and laborer from the North and abroad to come within its darkened abode; to have done so would have jeopardised its existence; hence, it had to and did teach its subjects, the slaves, mechanical arts; they now have those arts as freemen. In the North, from selfish motives, from prejudice, to serve their then Southern masters, they would not teach or encourage the colored man in mechanism; so that, whatever mechanical acquirements, with some exceptions, exist among colored men in the country, are to be found in the South. They are crying for organization. We desire Union with the white laborer for a common interest; it is the interest of both parties, that such a union should exist, with a fair, open, and unconcealed intent; with no aim to destroy any organization, political or otherwise; with no thought of fostering dishonor, whether in the nation or in individuals; repudiating all attempts to weaken obligations engaged in openly, seriously, with a full knowledge of the same; with an intent to share honorably all obligations "as nominated in the bond." I think that I may say, in behalf of the delegates here assembled, that they stand ready to extend an earnest hand of welcome to every effort, associated or otherwise, that looks to the dignity of labor, to its enjoyment of full remuneration and protection, and which shall manifest a spirit to be in harmony with capital in every instance, when capital shall be properly mindful of its true interest in harmonizing with labor.

Mr. Sampson, of North Carolina, nominated Mr. H. P. Harmon, of Florida, temporary Secretary; adopted.

On motion of Colonel W. U. Saunders, of Nevada, a committee of one from each State, Territory, and the District of Columbia on credentials were appointed.

On motion, Hon. J. H. Harris, of North Carolina, addressed the Convention.

On motion, Mr. Richard Trevellick, President of the National Labor Congress, was invited to address the Convention and to a seat on the platform.[27]

On motion, Mr. John M. Langston, of Ohio, was invited to address the Convention.[28]

The Committee on Credentials reported the names of two hundred and forty delegates, more than half of whom were not present. Report received and adopted.

On motion, a committee of one from each State, Territory, and the District of Columbia was appointed on permanent organization.

Pending the report of the committee, A. M. Powell, Esq., of New York, addressed the Convention.

The Committee on Permanent Organization reported the following, which was adopted:

PRESIDENT--Hon. James H. Harris, North Carolina.

VICE PRESIDENTS.

William F. Butler, New York;	M. Van Horn, Rhode Island;
William U. Saunders, Nevada;	Milton Holland, Ohio;
T. J. Mackey, South Carolina;	William Perkins, Maryland;
Charles H. Peters, D.C.;	James T. Rapier, Alabama;[29]
William T. Hays, North Carolina;	Jeff T. Long, Georgia;
Bishop J. P. Campbell, New Jersey;	Caleb Milburn, Delaware;
Rev. J. P. Evans, Virginia;	J. W. Menard, Louisiana;
Charles McGlynn, Connecticut;	Rev. J. Sella Martin, Massachusetts;
E. S. Francis, Florida;	G. B. Stebbins, Michigan;
O. L. C. Hughes, Pennsylvania;	Abram Smith, Tennessee;

SECRETARIES.

William U. Saunders, Nevada;	Lewis H. Douglas, District of Col.

ASSISTANT SECRETARIES
Hon. H. P. Harmon, Florida;   G. S. Woodson, Pennsylvania.

SERGEANTS-AT-ARMS.
James Hammond, Maryland;   G. M. Mabson, North Carolina.

A committee was appointed to conduct the President to the chair. After a brief speech from the President, the Convention adjourned till 7½ o'clock P.M.

EVENING SESSION.

December 6, 1869.

Convention called to order by the President.

The Committee on Credentials presented the names of W. H. Lewis, of Washington, D.C.; W. U. Derrick, of Virginia, James Copeland, of Virginia; Charles Rolls, of Maryland; Rev. John R. Henry, of Maryland; and S. P. Cummins, of Massachusetts, which were entered on the roll as delegates.

Considerable excitement was created on announcing the name of Mr. McLane, President of the National Plasterer's Union. On obtaining the floor, Mr. Langston made a lengthy speech against his admission to membership, claiming that by his admission the Convention would give a *quasi* endorsement to the views held by the large proscriptive organization which he represented. He claimed that the gentleman alluded to held allegiance to no political party other than the Labor party, and that he intended to use his influence to build up a third party on the ruins of both the Republican and Democratic, that colored men could not in justice to themselves ignore, and, by uniting themselves to the policy of the already existing labor organizations, nullify all the good results of the Republican party; charging the Convention to beware how far they commit themselves, and to adopt a platform so broad that all the laboring men of the world might stand upon it, lending influence to that party only in so far that its members advance the black man side by side with themselves.

Mr. Downing, of Rhode Island, favored the admission of all who presented proper credentials, without regard to the views they had previously expressed in other movements. He proposed to convert those of a different policy to his own, having no fear of the intellect that gentleman might bring to bear against what the world recognized as exact justice to colored men and the interests of the laboring masses.

Mr. Myers, of Maryland, offered a resolution that committees be appointed to take into consideration the following subjects: Business, finance, education, address, platform, constitution and organization, female labor, co-operative labor, homesteads and public lands, railroad travel, national organ, and temperance; each committee to consist of five members.

After a protracted debate and offering of substitutes and amendments, the original resolution was adopted.

His honor the Mayor of the city then came forward and delivered the following address:

GENTLEMEN OF THE CONVENTION: In the name of our good people, and as the chief Executive of this city, I offer you our greetings and the heartfelt welcome to this the metropolis of the nation. I have watched with great interest for a long time past the movements of the workingmen and the friends of labor throughout the country, in perfecting independent organizations for the protection of the rights and the advancement of the interests of labor and the laborer.

These movements I hail as springing naturally from the mighty and beneficent achievements of the great party of freedom and progress in its terrible battle with slavery; and I also hail with unfeigned satisfaction the assembling here in this our National Capital, so long one of the strongholds of the enemy, of a convention of free colored men--of free colored workingmen--in maintenance of the rights and interests of labor.

The old slogans of the oligarch were: "Slavery is the natural and normal condition of the laborer!" "Slavery is right and necessary, whether white or black!" Against these the great party of freedom arrayed its own noble weapons, "Free Speech, Free Labor, and Free Men;" and, planting itself fearlessly and firmly upon these noble principles--the inherent right of all men, of every race, to a perfect equality before the law--an equal right to "life, liberty, and the pursuit of happiness"--it met, fought and conquered the foul demon of slavery, which for so many years had ravaged all parts of our fair land in its conspiracy to debase labor and to degrade the laborer. This wicked spirit was buried forever in a felon's grave by the triumph of the Union armies, composed chiefly of laboring men from the free North.

Gentlemen, the laboring classes have a special history nobler and grander than the oligarch's! To be sure, a distinguished member of the old pro-slavery chivalry some years ago, in the House of Representatives, de-clared that "the existence of laborers and mechanics in organized societies was the result of the partial and progressive emancipation of slavery." Slavery, he contended, was their primordial and only natural condition. But history tells us that, in all ages of the world, the laborer has been the great, the mighty civilizer. Seated, personally free, at the foundation of the earliest societies or civilizations of antiquity, and all the other orders, spurning as degrading all connections with the arts, it was the genius of the laborer, the mechanic, and the cunning of his hand that built up all those magnificent monuments of art which lend a glory and grandeur to the civilization of those early periods.

Long and manfully, too, did the laborer maintain his freedom. But the lust for conquest in the breast of the oligarchy, whose chief occupation was that of war is pursuit of empire, destroyed the industrial classes, and introduced in their stead millions of miserable slaves.

Slavery and the debasement of the industrial classes destroyed in turn every nation of antiquity.

Hence, in modern eras, when the populations of Europe had been debauched by slavery and its accursed influences, they fell an easy prey to the Goth and Vandall--those free and hardy northern nations which established the present States of Europe upon the ruins of Rome. The feudal slavery, the feudal barbarism, which they established, necessarily crushed out what little of industrial art and prosperity remained. The dark ages ensued, and with them every form of misfortune and misery. Had it not been for Christianity and its influences all Europe would have then relapsed into its primeval barbarism.

From this peril Europe, and the world, were rescued by the inherent manhood of the down-trodden laborer. Rising in his misery--

"With strength in his arm and lightning in his eye,"

the laborer, by his prowess and tenacity, soon taught his oligarchical tyrant to dread--

"The might that slumbers in a peasant's arm!"

Nor did he cease his war for freedom, for the rights of his humanity, until he had banished the worst form of bondage from Christendom, and trans-formed, by his genius, the degradation and misery, the barbarism of the dark ages, into the prosperity and comforts, the glory and light of our present civilization.

Gentlemen, this is a brief and rapid survey of this noble history of the laborer. It should be to you a history full of encouragement. Its examples should excite your emulation in your present movements for the vindication of your rights and interests as workingmen; for yours is the cause of human-ity, the cause of civilization; and nothing is more true than that in pro-portion as its people are free, in proportion that its industrial classes are free and happy, just in proportion is the nation free, happy and prosper-ous.

I therefore hail with the liveliest satisfaction your assembling here in the National Capital for the maintenance of the rights and interests of labor. I have always cherished these rights, and have labored to encourage and advance them, believing that in doing so I was fulfilling but my duties as a citizen, as a Christian, and a friend to humanity. It was so in the great battles with slavery.

The oligarch, revolting against the rapid strides of freedom and its beneficent institutions--revolting against a civilization which threatened the destruction of their own debasing tyranny--attempted to hurl back our country into the utter darkness and barbarism, into the poverty, misery, tyranny, and horrible wickedness of feudal times.

Thank God, they failed. Their failure, and the vindication of freedom and the rights of humanity in the triumph of the Union cause, has forever banished the destructive power of the oligarch from our country, and opened up a new era of freedom and manhood, in which all of every race stand before the laws as men and equals.

Hence I rejoice that you, a convention of colored workingmen, should assemble here for the purpose of asserting and securing the rights of your race in the maintenance of the rights of labor. The great and final battle for freedom having been fought and won, it is but proper that as soldiers, citizens, and patriots, you should secure and take the necessary steps to properly preserve the fruits of the victory.

Labor gives energy and activity to the intellect. And I would advise every man--

First. To learn some trade, business, or profession.
Second. To follow the trade, business, or profession through life.
Third. To be regular and prompt in all your affairs.
Fourth. To be honest to yourself and you will be so to others.
Fifth. Do not put off till tomorrow what you can do today.

To the workingmen I would say, in the language of another, "Put on the armor of strength and intelligence, buckle to your side determination and energy, and demand and preserve your rights in the field, in the councils of the nation, and in all things wherein your happiness lies. Be frugal, hospitable, charitable, kind, and generous, and spurn him who would tax your hard toil without giving a fair equivalent. Disdain empty show, parade, and extravagance in everything, for they are incompatible with the dignity of sensible men, and that simplicity of life which conduces the most to health and happiness; and as surely as the sun that rises in the East to illumine your path shall set in the West to close the day the Great Overseer will be ready to pay the laborers their wages, the reward of their toil."

Again I tender you our heartiest greetings. I congratulate you upon the brilliant prospects of your race--upon the opening of our grand, new era and civilization, before which will pass away all the blighting prejudices and tyranny of despotism forever.

A resolution read in the morning session, relative to the action of the Hon. A. M. Clapp in employing colored printers at the Government Printing Office in opposition to the ravings of negro haters, was taken up and passed.

After action on the above resolution the Hon. A. M. Clapp, Congressional Printer, was next discovered to be in the crowded audience who, on motion, was invited to occupy the stand and address the Convention which he did in eloquent terms, noting, the vast changes that politics had produced in the people of the country. Alluding to the time when he commenced active life, men who held the advanced ideas of himself were sometimes socially ostracised, but, having the precepts of the New Testament for his guide, he believed himself to be right, and would continue to do his duty, fearing none but the great God above, who controls the affairs of men. Alluding to the appointment of Mr. Lewis H. Douglass as a compositor in the Government Printing Office, said he (Douglass) asked for employment. He asked him if he was a compositor; receiving an affirmative answer he again asked for his name. On being told it, Mr. Clapp remarked, "I confess there was magic in that name; and I told him to go to work." He said that, having all the respect in the world for the gentlemen as individuals composing the Printers' Union, he has none whatever for their organization, and that Mr. Douglass shall stay in the office as long as he is Congressional Printer. That he requested the Printers' Union to modify their law regulating the number of apprentices that shall be employed to conform to his wishes, which they very graciously did, and that among the number of apprentices he has appointed two colored boys, one of whom is greatly above the average intelligence of boys of his age of any race.

Mr. Clapp was frequently applauded throughout the delivery of his address.

On motion of A. M. Green, of the District of Columbia, the following resolution was adopted:

Resolved, That in the two gentlemen who have addressed us this evening, the Hon. Sayles J. Bowen and the Hon. A. M. Clapp, this Convention recognizes two of its most able and available champions and friends; men who by their aggressions upon the foul prejudice against the black man's right to an equal chance in the race of life entitle them to claim a place in the front rank of the great progressive party of the Republic.

Mr. Allen Coffin, of the District of Columbia, offered the following resolutions:

Resolved, That the accumulated wealth of the nation, being the result of labor already performed, ought to be taxed on a graduated basis, so as to make the burden of taxation to bear heaviest upon those who have reaped the lion's share of American toil.

Resolved, That the national debt ought to be paid in gold, or its equivalent, in accordance with the spirit and intent of the acts of Congress under which it was contracted.

Mr. Coffin made some very suggestive remarks germane to the great question at issue between capital and labor, which were favorably received, applauded, and asked that the resolutions be referred to the Business Committee.

Adjourned until 10 o'clock A.M. Tuesday, December 7, 1869.

SECOND DAY.

The Convention met this morning at 10 o'clock, and opened with prayer by the Rev. M. B. Derrick.

The Committee on Rules made a report, which, after considerable debate, was adopted.

The Committee on Credentials of Delegates from the States made a report, adding several more to the list as reported yesterday; which was adopted.

Mr. Martin moved that distinguished colored and white gentlemen be admitted to seats as honorary members. Adopted.

Mr. William Perkins, of Maryland, from the Committee on Finance, made a report, recommending that a tax of $2 be levied on each delegate to cover expenses.

Mrs. Colby, delegate of the District of Columbia, inquired if the ladies were to be included in the persons taxed.

Rev. Mr. Martin said that there was no distinction to be made on account of race, sex, or color.

Considerable debate took place on the question of taxing female delegates, and as to the amount of tax levied on the members, many taking the ground that two dollars was more than was necessary. This debate was participated in by Prof. A. M. Green, of this District; Isaiah Wear, of Maryland; and B. H. Robinson, of Virginia.

Mr. George T. Downing said he was here at the great expense of his business and he desired the Convention to come to business. Let us show that we can go down into our pockets, if necessary, to cover the expenses of this Convention. We have no right to tax the delegates two dollars without it is necessary. We have got to publish our proceedings and pay for stationery, and let us bear these expenses cheerfully.

It was finally agreed that one dollar be substituted for two dollars as the tax.

At this point a telegram was read from the Secretary of State elect of Mississippi, (Lynch), dated Jackson, as follows:

To the President of the Colored Men's Convention:

Seventy thousand triumphant colored Radicals send greeting. [Applause.]

The Chair stated that the Finance Committee had retired to the basement to receive the fees, and he hoped the delegates would send in their amounts.

Mr. Downing, of New Jersey, offered the following, which was adopted:

That the rule usually termed "point of order" has not its usual controlling force; that the presiding officer has discretionary judgment in the matter.

A recess was here taken of thirty minutes to enable the delegates to settle the tax with the Committee on Finance.

The Convention reassembled at one o'clock.

Secretary Douglass offered a petition of the Engineers' Protective Union of Brooklyn, New York, setting forth the low condition of the colored race, and asking the Convention to encourage equal rights; that they be admitted into work-shops on the same terms as white men. Referred to the Business Committee.

Prof. A. M. Green asked the attention of the Convention to a newspaper article, which he read, in relation to the purposes of this organization, in which a hope was expressed that the colored men would avoid the mistake made by the white men's conventions held at Chicago and New York. In view of these suggestions he offered a resolution "that a committee of five be appointed, in connection with the Secretary, to secure the publication of authentic reports of the Convention in one or more of our city journals, and that said committee are hereby instructed to negotiate with the publishers of these proceedings to retain such matter as can be thrown into circular form for distribution immediately on the rise of the Convention, and that the following gentlemen be designated the committee: J. M. Langston, J. P. W. Leonard, George T. Downing, Cornelius Clark, and F. G. Barbadoes."

The resolution was adopted.

Mr. Jones, of the District of Columbia, offered a resolution that it is expedient that we should use our best endeavors to procure four millions of acres of our public domain for our humble poor for agricultural purposes within the States composing this Union. Referred to same Committee.

Mr. Hayes, of North Carolina, offered the following, which was referred:

Whereas the march of civilization, following our American example, indicates reforms, frequently through revolution, in many parts of the civilized world, particularly in this hemisphere; and whereas the struggling patriots of Cuba have shown by their sacrifice, philanthropy, valor, and conduct of a defense upon the principles of civilized warfare, their capacity to sustain themselves against a monarchical government to the end that "all men everywhere shall be free;" and whereas the future of a million and a half of our brethren and that of their posterity depends upon the success of [30] the patriot arms in Cuba: Therefore be it

Resolved, That the Congress of the United States be assured that it is the sense of this Convention that the *immediate recognition* of the patriot army of Cuba as a belligerent power will meet the approval of the colored people of the country and in the event of war growing out of such recognition this Convention pledges the full strength of colored Americans to sustain the Government.

Mr. Isaac Myers, from the Committee on Platform, reported the following as the platform of the Convention, and it was read; after which the Convention adjourned to $7\frac{1}{2}$ P.M:

Whereas labor has its privileges no less than its duties, one of which is to organize and, if need be, to furnish reasons for its organization: Therefore,

Resolved, That labor was instituted by Almighty God as a means of revealing the rich endowments of inanimate creation to be understood and used by man, and that labor is a duty common to, and the natural heritage of, the human family, each person having a natural right to labor in any field of industry for which he or she is capacitated, the right to be governed and restricted only by the laws of political economy.

Resolved, That capital is an agent or means used by labor for its development and support, and labor is an agent or means used by capital for its development and general enhancement, and that, for the well-being and productiveness of capital and labor, the best harmony and fellowship of action should at all times prevail, that "strikes" may be avoided and the

workingman convinced that justice is done him and that he is receiving an
equivalent for the labor performed.

   Resolved, That there should be a frequent interchange of opinions upon
all questions affecting alike the employer and employed, and that co-operation for the purpose of protection and the better remuneration of labor is
a sure and safe method, invading no specific rights, but is alike beneficial
to the whole community, and tends to lift the working classes to higher
achievements and positions in society, presents the necessity of and increases the desire to give their children a more liberal education, induces
the practice of economy in the distribution of their earnings, and accel-
erates the accumulation of wealth, with all the happiness that must necessarily ensue therefrom.

   Resolved, That intemperance is the natural foe and curse of the
American family, especially the working classes, its terrible effects being
to disease, corrupt, and otherwise disfigure and destroy the constitution,
producing vice, crime, and poverty where peace and plenty would otherwise
exist.

   Resolved, That education is one of the strongest safeguards of republican institutions, the bulwark of American citizenship, and a defense against
the invasion of the rights of man; its liberal distribution to all, without
regard to race, creed, or sex, is necessary for the well being and advancement of society, and that all should enjoy its blessing alike in each of the
States and Territories of the United States; that educated labor is more
productive, is worth, and commands, higher rates of wages, is less dependent
upon capital; therefore it is essentially necessary to the rapid and
permanent development of the agricultural, manufacturing, and mechanical
growth and interests of the nation that there shall be a liberal free school
system enacted by the Legislatures of the several States for the benefit of
all the inhabitants thereof.

   Resolved, That the Government of the United States, republican in form,
is a Government of the people, for the people, and by the people, and that
all men are equal in political rights and entitled to the largest political
and religious liberty compatible with the good order of society, as, also,
the use and enjoyment of the fruits of their labor and talents; and that no
laws should be made by any legislative body to the advantage of one class
and against the interest and advantage of the other, but that all legislation should be for the benefit of all the people of any particular State
and of the United States, to the end that loyalty to and love for the
institutions and the Government of the United States should be a permanent
consideration with all the citizens hereof.

   Resolved, That we feel it to be a duty that we owe to ourselves, to
society, and to our country, to encourage by all the means within our reach
industrial habits among our people, the learning of trades and professions
by our children without regard to sex; to educate and impress them with the
fact that all labor is honorable and a sure road to wealth; that habits of
economy and temperance, combined with industry and education, is the
great safeguard of free republican institutions, the "elevator of the condition of man, the motive power to increase trade and commerce, and to make
the whole people of this land the wealthiest and happiest on the face of the
globe.

   Resolved, That regarding the labor of the country the common property
of all the people, that no portion should be excluded therefrom because of
a geographical division of the globe in which they or their forefathers were
born, or on account of statutes or color, but that every man or woman should
receive employment according to his or her ability to perform the labor
required, without any other test; that the exclusion of colored men and
apprentices from the right to labor in any department of industry or workshops in any of the States and Territories of the United States by what is
known as "Trades' Unions" is an insult to God and injury to us, and disgrace to humanity. While we extend a free and welcome hand to the free
immigration of labor of all nationalities, we emphatically deem imported
contract Coolie labor to be a positive injury to the working people of the
United States; is but the system of slavery in a new form, and we appeal to
the Congress of the United States to rigidly enforce the act of 1862,
prohibiting Coolie importation, and to enact such other laws as will best

protect, and free, American labor against this or any similar form of slavery.

Resolved, That we do not regard capital as the natural enemy of labor; that each is dependent on the other for its existence; that the great conflict daily waged between them is for the want of a better understanding between the representatives of capital and labor, and we therefore recommend the study of political economy in all of our labor organizations as a means to understand the relationships of labor to capital, and as a basis for the adjustment of many of the disputes that arise between employer and employee.

Resolved, That we recommend the establishment of co-operative workshops, land, building, and loan associations among our people as a remedy against their exclusion from other workshops on account of color, as a means of furnishing employment as well as a protection against the aggression of capital, and as the easiest and shortest method of enabling every man to procure a homestead for his family, and to accomplish this end we would particularly impress the greatest importance, of the observance of diligence in business, and the practice of rigid economy in our social and domestic arrangements.

Resolved, That we regard the use of intoxicating liquors as the most damaging and damnable habits practiced by the human family; that we denounce the infamous practice planters have in drenching their employees with this poison drug, (with or without cost,) intended to stupefy their brain and incapacitate them to know the condition of their accounts, the value of their labor, and to rob them of their sense and feelings of humanity; that we appeal to our people to discountenance the use of intoxicating liquors because of its effects to shorten life, and because it is the great cause of so much misery and poverty among the working classes of the country, and we advise the organization of temperance associations as a necessary instrument for the speedy and permanent elevation of our people.

Resolved, That we regard education as one of the greatest blessings that the human family enjoys, and that we earnestly appeal to our fellow-citizens to allow no opportunity, no matter how limited or remote, to pass unimproved; that the thanks of the colored people of this country are due the Congress of the United States for the establishment and maintenance of the Freedmen's Bureau, and to Major General O. O. Howard, Commissioner, Rev. J. W. Alvord and John M. Langston, Esq., General Inspectors, for their co-operative labors in the establishment and good government of hundreds of schools in the Southern States, whereby thousands of men, women and children have been and are now being taught the rudiments of an English education. The thanks of the whole people are due to these philanthropists and friends to the benevolent institutions of this, and other countries, for the means and efforts in money and teachers furnished whereby our race is being elevated to the proper standard of intelligent American citizens, and we appeal to the friends of progress and to our citizens of the several States to continue their efforts; to the various Legislatures until every State can boast of having a free school system that knows no distinction in dissemination of knowledge to its inhabitants on account of race, color, sex, creed or previous conditions; and [31]

Resolved, That we recommend a faithful obedience to the laws of the United States and of the several States in which we may reside; that the Congress and the courts of the United States have ample power to protect its citizens. All grievances, whether personal or public, should be carried to the proper tribunal, and from the lowest to the highest, until justice is granted; that armed resistance against the laws is treason against the United States and ought to be summarily punished. We further appeal to the colored workingmen to form organizations throughout every State and Territory, that they may be able in those districts far removed from courts of justice to communicate with the Bureau of Labor to be established by the National Labor Union and that justice may be meted out to them as though they lived in the large cities where justice is more liberally distributed; that loyalty and love for the Government may be fostered and encouraged, and prosperity and peace may pervade the entire land.

ISAAC MYERS,
HENRY LEE,
HARRY S. HARMON,
REV. JOS. P. EVANS.

The Committee on Business offered a resolution authorizing the Chair to appoint a Committee on Public Meeting, who shall solicit material aid to defray the expenses of this Convention.

The Chair announced the standing committees on the following business of the Convention: On education, address, platform, constitution and organization, female labor, temperance, printing, co-operative labor, public lands, railroads and travel, and banks savings.

J. M. Simms, of Georgia, offered a resolution indorsing the President's message in relation to the State of Georgia and the political condition of that State. Adopted.

Mr. Hays, of North Carolina, introduced a resolution that the colored people sustain the new organ of the colored people to be published in the District of Columbia, to be called the "New Era." Referred to the Business Committee.[32]

The Committee on Addresses was enlarged so as to embrace one from each State and Territory.

The Convention then adjourned at 4 o'clock to meet at 7.30.

EVENING SESSION.

The Convention reassembled in the evening, and after prayer by Bishop Loguen, of New York, Mr. L. H. Douglass offered the following:[33]

Resolved, That a special committee of five, composed of genuine laborers or practical mechanics, or artisans, be appointed by the Chair to draft a plan for the organization of a national union of laboring men to the end of securing a recognition of colored laborers and mechanics in the various workshops of the land; that the said national union submit a plan to the colored people of the country for organizing subordinate unions for the furtherance of the object in view.

Mr. McLean, of Boston, was invited to address the Convention, and made an interesting address.

Senator Wilson, of Massachusetts, was next introduced. He said the Convention had assembled for a great cause, the elevation and improvement of a race who had long been trodden down--the toiling millions. It was important to act with charity to each other, but he thought the people of the country were making rapid progress in intellectual and mechanical improvement. Ten years ago the condition of the colored race was precarious, and none could speak a word for their rights without peril of life; and now the colored race is as free as any other in the land. Ten years ago the colored man was not permitted to go into the Capitol, nor enter the Capitol grounds; now he was as free as any one, and he hoped in a short time to welcome them as Senators. He did not believe in railway dynasties or any other dynasties, and if he had his way he would make a law making free railways. He wanted the public domain administered so as to be of benefit to the poor man, white and black.[34]

At the conclusion of Mr. Wilson's remarks he was greeted by long-continued applause.

Mr. I. C. Wears, of Philadelphia, then addressed the Convention. He doubted very much if a white man is a natural man, or a black man is a natural man. The middle was the normal color of the human race. Both the white and black man are truants from the natural and original color of the human species. The color was only incident to the climate, and the physical development to the condition man is placed in. We demand our right to vote, not because of our color, but because we are men. If a man comes here from China, what right have we to refuse him the right to vote? This right is a protection. He had no objection to making money out of men's muscle. We were all striving to do what we can for ourselves. Every man will gravitate to the condition he is fitted to perform.

Mr. J. T. Rapier, of Georgia, next addressed the Convention, and said if it could do something to relieve these of the South of their burden it will have accomplished a great deal. There never was a class made such progress as the colored laborers in the South. They have to pay high rents to their old masters for the use of their broad acres. If they can obtain the wild lands of Kansas or other new States, they can live and thrive there without

paying tribute. As to the eight-hour law, it will amount to nothing in the
South. As to women's rights, he hoped it would be continued north of the
Ohio River.

Mrs. Mary Carey, of Canada, made a few remarks, and the Convention
adjourned.

THIRD DAY.

The Convention reassembled at 10 o'clock today, and opened with prayer
by Bishop Campbell, of New Jersey.

A committee of three was appointed to revise the roll of delegates.

The Committee on Finance, through its chairman, B. M. Adgers, reported
that $143 had been collected, and the expenses of the Convention had been
$271, leaving a deficit of $128.

Mr. G. S. Woodson, of Pennsylvania, offered a resolution requesting the
Governors of the States where there are Republican Legislatures not as yet
having adopted the Fifteenth Amendment, to call their respective Legislatures
together for the ratification of said amendment. Referred.

Mr. Warren, of Virginia, offered a resolution that we include the use of
tobacco as among the great wastes of our resources, and recommend to all
workingmen to practice economy in this as well as in the use of liquor.
Referred.

The resolution offered by L. H. Douglass at last evening's session,
relative to the appointment of a special committee to draft a plan for the
organization of a national union of laboring men, to the end of securing
recognition of colored laborers and mechanics in the various workshops of
the land, and to submit a plan to the colored people of the country for
organizing subordinate unions for the furtherance of the object in view, was
taken up and discussed at length, and adopted.

Mr. Bowen, of the District of Columbia offered a resolution tendering
thanks to President Grant, the Cabinet officers, and General O. O. Howard
for their kind consideration of the colored race, in giving employment to
them when found competent to fill places of trust. Referred.

Mr. J. J. Wright, of South Carolina, from the Committee on Railroad and
Travel, reported in favor of recommending that a bureau be created to which
this matter, with others relating to the exclusion of colored people from
the cars, be referred, and that a fund be created to prosecute any such case
of exclusion, under the Civil Rights bill, and to test the virtue of that
bill. Referred.

Mr. Myers, of Pennsylvania, offered a resolution that the President and
Vice President of this Convention be a delegation to wait on the President of
the United States and tender the congratulations of this Convention on behalf
of the colored laborers of the United States. Adopted.

The Committee on Printing reported that arrangements had been made to
secure a correct report of the proceedings of the Convention in pamphlet
form.

Mr. W. J. Wilson, of the District of Columbia, from the Committee on
Savings Banks, reported the following:

Gentlemen of the Labor Convention:

In all communities where labor is properly organized the interest of the
poor man is held to be of chief importance. It is the man who, in days of
health and prosperity can save but little above a bare living, and who, in
days of sickness and forced idleness, must, with his family, suffer or live
on charity, whom wise laws seek to protect. And this is right, because the
poor are in all places the vast majority. For this great multitude the way
to a better condition should be laid open, and the free school, the open
Bible, the Savings Bank, and every invitation to intelligence, virtue and
economy meet all who travel it.

After a careful examination of the statistics of Savings Banks, we have
found that wherever labor is best paid, and the improvement of the condition
of the laboring classes most carefully considered, there Savings Banks
abound; there depositors are most numerous, and the aggregate of savings the

largest. Thus--

In Massachusetts, at the date of the latest report to the Legislature, there were in the State, 108 Savings Banks; 350,000 depositors, and $80,431,583.

In the little State of Rhode Island, 25 Banks; 59,071 depositors, and $21,413,648.

In the cities of New York and Brooklyn, 41 Banks; 405,591 depositors, and $116,971,953; and in the whole State of New York, in 1868, the aggregate capital in all the Savings Banks reached the enormous aggregate of $151,127,562.

In the State of Rhode Island one person out of every three has a deposit in some Savings Bank.

In Massachusetts and Connecticut, one in every three and one-half.

In the six New England States, one in every 4.89. In New York, one in 7.22.

But the Savings Bank as an *institution*--as a great conservator of the well-being of the poor, as a perpetual invitation in each city, town, and village to youth and health to put safely by something against the day of old age and sickness--is just beginning to find a footing South of the Potomac. Until the close of the late war there was no civilized labor in the South. The *employer* was at the same time the *owner* of the laboring man. What inducement was there for the toiler to put by his money? What money of his own had he to put by?

With the earnest desire to place within reach of the disenthralled race the opportunity and incentive to careful savings and safe keeping of small earnings, at the close of the war, Congress granted a character to a company called *The Freedman's Savings and Trust Company,* with authority to establish, in any one of our States, Savings Banks for the safe-keeping and investment in the stocks, bonds, and Treasury notes of the United States the savings of the people of color. One of the last acts of the lamented President Lincoln was to affix his signature to the charter giving legal existence to this company. This was in March, 1865. Let us now show, in a few words, what has been done by this company in the space of less than five years:

In that comparatively short time, Banks for savings have been established in Augusta, Macon and Savannah, Georgia; in Beaufort and Charleston, South Carolina; in Jacksonville and Tallahassee, Florida; in Mobile and Huntsville, Alabama; in New Orleans, Louisiana; in Vicksburg, Mississippi; in Chattanooga, Memphis, and Nashville, Tennessee; in Louisville, Kentucky; in St. Louis, Missouri; in Martinsburg, Richmond and Norfolk, Virginia; in Raleigh, Wilmington, and Newbern, North Carolina; and in Washington, Baltimore, and New York, with a parent or principal office office in this city.

Beginning with nothing, of course, in the midst of a people just escaped from the shackles of slavery, at the end of one year from the date of its charter, to wit, on the 1st day of

March, 1866, deposits were - - - - - - - - - - - - - - - - -	$305,167.24
" 1867 " " - - - - - - - - - - - - - - - - -	1,624,853.33
" 1868 " " - - - - - - - - - - - - - - - - -	3,582,378.36
" 1869 " " - - - - - - - - - - - - - - - - -	7,257,798.63

and today the aggregate of all the deposits is over *ten millions!*

Of course there have been constant and heavy drafts from these aggregations. Depositors, when they have accumulated a few hundred dollars in the Bank, quite naturally desire to buy a piece of land, or to enter upon some mercantile or mechanical pursuit. So they draw out money which, but for the Bank, would probably never have been saved, and invest as they see opportunity. A population of small land owners, traders, and mechanics--the very element of a true Democratic civilization--is appearing on the once lordly domains of the planter. The former chattel, thrown upon his own resources, is called, by the necessities of his position, to look out for tomorrow. So he needs his earnings from time to time. The drafts, for the period above specified, were as follows:

Year ending March 1, 1867, - - - - - - - - - - - - - - - - -	$1,225,928.16
" " 1868 - - - - - - - - - - - - - - - - -	2,944,079.36
" " 1869 - - - - - - - - - - - - - - - -	6,184,368.71

At the last date, the net deposit remaining in the Bank, invested in United States securities or in cash and office property, was $1,073,429.92

On the 31st of October, the date of the latest published report, this deposit had reached $1,340,133.94. It will probably have reached *two millions* within the next year.

These savings, as fast as accumulated, are loaned to the United States, *i.e.,* invested in their bonds and stocks. The company has paid up to November 1st, 1869, regularly to its depositors interest at the rate of 5 per cent, in tri-ennial instalments, which, on being entered on the depositor's book as a new deposit, give him really 1-2/3 per cent, each four months, compounded three times per annum.

In connection with the other work of the Bank, it issues monthly,--for gratuitous distribution, to stimulate its patrons to habits of temperance, thrift, and frugality--a newspaper, which is sought for eagerly.

We may add that we find this Bank to be established on the mutual principle. Each depositor is a stockholder to the amount of his deposits. After paying out of its income, the expenses of the business of the institution, the balance of its profits are distributed to its depositors every four months. The larger amount of its deposits the greater the advantage to the stockholder, *i.e.,* to the depositor.

Every man, woman, or child, who is able to deposit $5 in this Bank is a stockholder to that amount, and receives his or her share of the profits which may accrue from the successful management of its business.

Your committee have to report that the opposition among the white people of the South to the progress of these Banks is disappearing; that the security and safety of the Bank is now thoroughly established; that it has purchased, in the city of Washington, a property directly opposite the United States Treasury, where it will build a convenient Banking-house in the coming year; that the best friends of the colored people are the friends and patrons of this Bank. Major General O. O. Howard calls it the "best educator in the field." Among the names of its trustees are found those of Henry D. Cooke, Esq., of the house of Jay Cooke & Co.; Hon. J. M. Brodhead, of the United States Treasury; Gen. B. W. Brice, Paymaster General U.S. Army; Bishop S. Talbot, of the Methodist Episcopal Church, and others well known throughout the land. [35]

But, though the deposits have reached one-and-a-millions of dollars, your committee think that such amount but poorly represents the savings of the colored people within reach of the influence of this company. There are within easy reach it 25 Bank 300,000 laboring people of color. If each had only $10 in the Bank the aggregate would be *three millions*-- more than double the sum now on deposit in the Bank. Or, if out of the three hundred thousand people referred to above, the same porportion were depositors as are found among the laboring people of Rhode Island, the Bank would have 100,000 depositors and $50,000,000.

In conclusion, your committee would report the following resolutions:

Resolved, That, as an aid to the laboring man, affording a safe and profitable place of investment for his small savings, we commend the National Freedman's Savings Bank.

Resolved, That we are of the opinion that in all the principal cities of the South the colored people should unite in establishing Savings Banks, which we believe to be an incentive to economy, as well as a proper place for keeping its fruits.

WILLIAM J. WILSON,
F. G. BARBADOES,
ABRAM SMITH,
J. M. TURNER,
JAMES HARRIS,
Committee

The Committee on National Organ reported the following, which was adopted:

Whereas the necessity of a national journal, to be published in Washington, in the labor, educational, and political interests of the colored people of the country, is deeply felt by all classes of our people, and such an organ having been in contemplation, for some months by our leading men; and

Whereas the scheme now bids fair to be a success under the editorial charge and management of colored men and the paper, to be known as "The New

Era," to be issued in a few days. Therefore be it

    Resolved, That the "New Era" be, and is indorsed, by this Convention as the organ of the laboring men of the country, recommended to our fellow-citizens as the proper exponent of our sentiments.

SELLA MARTIN,
W. U. SAUNDERS,
ISAIAH WEIR,
G. P. ROURK,
F. G. BARBADOES.

    J. M. Langston, from the Committee on Address, reported the following:

ADDRESS

The Relations of the Colored People to American Industry

    The laboring class of any community, educated and united, constitute its strength. And in so far as the leading men thereof realize and appreciate this consideration, they will be able to raise the masses of those identi-fied with them in condition to rank and influence socially and legally.

    Among the colored men of this country there is no small amount of in-dustrial capacity, native and acquired. All over the South and among the colored people of the North, workmen in gold, silver, brass, iron, wood, brick, mortar and the arts, are found doing skillfully and at usual wages, the most difficult tasks in their several departments of labor. Nor are these workmen generally engaged by white men who, superintending their work, can claim, upon any just ground, that the genius and art displayed belong to the employers. As illustrating this statement, it may be appropriately mentioned that perhaps the most accomplished gunsmith among the Americans is a black man, an ex-slave of North Carolina, who not long since received special notice from the Prince of Wales, to whom he presented a pistol of his own make, and received in return, as a token of consideration from the heir apparent of the English throne, a magnificent medal of rare value. It is perhaps true, too, that the most finished cabinet-maker and blacksmith of our country is of the same class. And it is said to be the fact that the most valuable invention given us by the South, the cotton plough, (the paten-tee of which formerly resided in Mississippi,) was the creature of a slave's genius.

    Here, too, it may be mentioned, with no inconsiderable pride, that one of the finest landscape painters of our country, and one of the finest sculptoresses is of African descent; the former distinguished especially as giving life and utterance from canvas to several of Milton's matchless poeti-cal creations in the "Paradise Lost" and the other as making the spirit of the noble Andrew of Massachusetts to breathe and speak through the life-like lips and features of plaster. Individual instances of colored persons en-gaged in commerce as wholesale and retail dealers in many of the larger cities of the North and South might be mentioned New Orleans, Mobile, Charleston, Savannah, Raleigh, Richmond, Nashville, Austin, Helena, Louis-ville, St. Louis, Leavenworth, Chicago, Detroit, Indianapolis, Cincinnati, New York, Philadelphia, several of the largest cities of New England, and the capital of the United States furnish illustrations in proof of this state-ment. [36]

    But it may be claimed that these are isolated and exceptional cases. Let us, therefore, consider this matter from a broader standpoint. Let us take the case of the freedmen in one of the States as presenting a fair average of their condition in this regard--and we name North Carolina. We offer the words of the general inspector of the schools for freedmen, under the Bureau of Refugees, Freedmen and Abandoned Lands, as especially signi-ficant in the bearing on this point. In one of his reports for 1868, in speaking of the freed people of North Carolina, he says:

    "More than one-third of the entire colored population of North Carolina are mechanics. They are nearly six to one as compared with white mechanics. The census gives less than 20,000 of the latter, while there are more than 60,000 of the former. All the mechanical occupations are represented by

them; blacksmiths, gunsmiths, wheelwrights, millwrights, machinists, carpenters, cabinet makers, plasterers, painters, shipbuilders, stonemasons, and
bricklayers are found among them in large numbers. There are also among
them many pilots and engineers. Nor are they behind any class of workmen in
the skill, taste and ability which are usually exhibited in their several
trades. Of the pilots and engineers running steamboats on the different
rivers of this State, many of the very best are colored men. It is said
that the two most trustworthy pilots in North Carolina are freedmen; one of
whom is running a steamboat on Cape Fear river, and the other across Albe-
marle sound, and on the Chowan and Blackwater rivers. The former is paid
$15 per month more than any other pilot on the river, because of his
superior ability. The engineer on the boat run by this pilot, is also a
freedman, and is said to be one of the best in the State.

"The colored mechanics, when employed, command the usual wages paid
others of like calling, and are now constantly taking work upon their own
responsibility, and doing it to the satisfaction of their employers. One of
the most interesting sights which it was my good fortune to witness while
in the State, was the building of a steamboat on Cape Fear river by a
colored shipbuilder, with his gang of colored workmen."

What is thus said of the freed people of North Carolina is in greater
or less degree true of the same class in the various States of the South;
for in the general degradation of labor, produced and fostered by slavery
as it formerly existed, the slave was made to do all kind of work, mechanical
as well as agricultural, and so became the artisan as well as field-hand of
that region.

The consideration that the freedman is the field-hand, the agricultural
laborer of the South, is one of small significance, since the two great
staples which distinguish Southern industry cannot be grown successfully
without his labor. This is abundantly proved by the fact that attempts which
have been made since the war by Northern capitalists to grow cotton and sugar
on Southern plantations upon plans suggested by their Northern experience,
and contrary to the method of culture adopted by the colored laborers of the
South, have proved abortive and disastrous in well nigh every instance, as
too many men, shipwrecked in means by their efforts at fortune-making in
growing these staples are ready to testify.

It is not to be inferred from this statement that the general ignorance
of the ex-slave is forgotten, nor is any one to presume therefrom that
slavery is to be regarded as having been a school with special claims to
consideration by reason of its peculiar adaptability to impart extraordinary
and valuable instruction in the art of cotton and sugar culture. All that
is intended is, that an experience of two hundred and forty-five years as
the laborer in cotton and sugar-fields, has given the negro, though devoid
of school, church and civilizing and elevating influences, such knowledge of
the soil and its improvement, the nature and treatment of the cotton seed
and plant, the tilling and growth of sugar-cane; the seasons and their usual
and abnormal effects upon crops; the agricultural implements and their proper
regulation for use, as to make him, above all others, for the time being,
the successful cultivator of these products.

It will not be denied by any intelligent person that the rough, un-
lettered farmer of Ohio and Illinois, who has had fifty years experience in
the cultivation of corn and wheat in those States, can furnigh better and
more valuable information in regard to the soil, its productiveness, and the
advantageous tillage of these Western staples, than Greeley or Emerson,
although the former writes on topics of political economy, while the latter
announces and expounds theories of philosophy and morals.

With a voting power under our present and just system of reconstruction
of seven hundred and fifty thousand electors, and an actual laboring force
of three millions out of four millions and a quarter of hardy sons and
daughters of toil, native to the soil, inured to the climate, acquainted with
the habits and customs of the people generally, and knowing by an experience
more valuable, perhaps, than the learning of the books, the methods of agriculture, the different systems of mechanical labor, and the common and less
complicated affairs of commerce, we are an element in the industry of the
country of importance, value, and power.

But for our own good and the welfare of our country in all things

pertaining to her material and moral well-being, we seek a better and broader
opportunity to gain knowledge in the fields of agricultural, mechanical,
commercial, artistic, and professional labor, and this knowledge we would
energise, direct, and make more largely effective through the enlightening
and sanctifying influence of education. Our mottoes are liberty and labor,
enfranchisement and education! The spelling-book and the hoe, the hammer and
the vote, the opportunity to work and to rise, a place in which to stand, and
to be and to do, we ask for ourselves and children as the means in the use
of which, under God, we are to compass these achievements which furnish the
measure, the test, and justification of our claim to impartial treatment and
fair dealing.

     That this end may be reached, we ask, first of all, that trades be
opened to the children and that they be given the benefit of a just and
equitable system of apprenticeship; in the second place, that for every day's
labor given we be paid full and fair remuneration, and that no avenue of
honest industry be closed against us; and thirdly, since we believe that the
intelligence, the elevation, and happiness of all people depends in no small
degree upon the diversity of their industrial pursuits, we ask that we may
work in the printing office, whether private or governmental, in the factory,
the foundry, the workshop, upon the railroad, the canal, the river, the steamboat, in the warehouse, the store, wherever labor is to be done and an able
and faithful workman is wanted we conceive that we may claim a place without
distinction as to our color or former condition, since all that can be demanded by the employer is ability, faithful performances of the contract made,
and the employee reasonable treatment and the compensation promised. Hence,
while we condemn that spirit which in its proscriptive regulations denies us
industrial opportunity and the fruits of honest toil, we rejoice in all those
evidences of prospective good which we and other laboring classes see in the
erection of factories and foundries in Maryland, Virginia, Kentucky, Missouri,
Tennessee, Georgia, and Alabama, promising that our strong and labor-hardened
hands, our intellectual powers, quickened by the influences of education, and
our purposes made doubly earnest by considerate treatment and the prospect of
just compensation, shall all be given to the development of the industrial
resources of our several States in the interest of our employers.

     Recognizing ourselves as native Americans, and knowing ourselves as mem-
bers of the great American body politic, while we ask the recognition and
protection due any and all of like political condition, as in the past, so
in all time to come, with unfettered limb and manly endeavor we shall labor
with our white fellow-countrymen, native and naturalized, in mine, on farm,
in workshop, in foundry, in factory, everywhere, to develope the material and
industrial powers of our land, making wind, water, and earth to aid in the
accomplishment of its mission of liberty and law, honor and justice, Christianity and civilization.

     And while this is our purpose, and feeling, as all other intelligent and
honest citizens must, the value of national honesty and honor, and the responsibility of each citizen and every class of citizens for its sacred
maintenance; while we demand that all contracts made in the interest of the
Government be liberally and fully met, according to their terms, we promise,
to this end, more than a tithe, if need be, of the fruits of our industry, as
our influence and votes, that our national obligations receive no detriment.
As we tolerate no political party which favors repudiation, so will we co-
operate with no movement, industrial or other, which proposes or countenances
it. In all laboring men's movements, as in political organizations, we hold
as binding and inviolable the sentiment that the national honor and the
national faith should be maintained in all its fullness, being as sacred as
the sovereignty which we have pledged as its sure guaranty.

     Notwithstanding all these things, said with regard to our purposes of
loyalty, the elements of our strength, as far as labor of an agricultural,
mechanical, commercial, artistic, and other character is concerned; and notwithstanding, in an important sense, the freemen are the laborers and mechanics
of the South, as matters stand necessarily so, supplying the bone and muscle
of the industry of that section, we are not insensible of our weakness in our
disorganized condition, and our utter inability to compel a full and just
recognition of our claims for larger and more certain compensation for services
rendered, and larger opportunity to follow those diversified pursuits of

industry which in New England and our Northern States generally have done so much to enlighten, elevate, and bless the people.

This brings us to a question of vital moment: Is it practicable to so organize our industrial forces and direct our labor as to compel the wealthy classes, the landholders and planters, to recognize and admit our power and respect our claims accordingly?

The importance and difficulty of answering this question every intelligent person friendly to the laboring masses of the world must appreciate. In our case, however, it is indeed doubly difficult and vexing, by two considerations, which make it proper for us to ask and expect legislative action by Congress in our behalf. In the first place, our people are not only poor, but they are the objects in their comparatively new condition of freedom of a hatred which shows itself in demonstrations of outrage and bloodshed in many parts of the South to such an extent as to require, if our interests, in industrial and other, are to be protected, immediate and positive action in the part of state and federal officials. In the second place, by reason of our too long oppressive and degrading life as slaves we are, as far as our masses are concerned, ignorant of the many benefits resulting from co-operative labor.

This latter difficulty will only be overcome as, through education, we more thoroughly comprehend the value of combined effort on the part of the laborer to secure consideration and wealth. Of the good purpose of the Government to protect us and as far as need be, put within our reach the opportunity and means of education, our treatment since our emancipation affords reasonable assurance.

We have attempted the solution of this question, in the organization of our National Bureau of Industry, with none other than anxious and earnest solicitude for the welcome of our working millions and their posterity.

We would unite all these masses upon a principle of common interest, whose accomplishment is practicable, and by which their highest earthly good may be compassed.

We would, therefore, have the laborer understand that acres, however vast, in plantations, however immense--uncultivated, are profitless, like principles promulgated through party platforms unaccepted by popular endorsement at the polls; and besides, that these uncultivated acres cannot be made profitable without labor, any more than political principles can be made influential and effective through party agency, without the approval of the popular will.

We would teach that labor is the parent of capital, and that well-directed, intelligent and united industry brings national wealth, as it brings individual competence and independence.

While our organization is one which springs out of justice and self-defense, aiming not at conflict with capital, but seeking rather, so to adjust the relations of labor and capital, as to secure the just and fair treatment of each by the other, we found it is reason and moderation. Speaking comprehensively, while the interest and welfare of labor are cared for fully, no unwarranted and unfair exactions are made of capital whether its power be exercised through corporate or individual method. In other words, still the mutual and dependent relations of labor and wealth we would neither ignore nor rudely disturb. The laborer needs and must have the compensation which service brings. Without it he cannot secure either the necessaries of life or the means to support and educate his children, nor upon the other hand, is the wealth of the employer of such intrinsic worth as to be valuable above and beyond its use in making effective the muscle and energy of labor.

"The Irishman would starve if not employed by the railroad company," said a brainless and heartless agent thereof. "But," replied the sagacious and philosophical son of the Green Isle, when thus addressed, "there would have been no railroad had God not made the Irishman to dig and shovel." Whether the Irishman be indispensable to railroad building, the principle here indicated is correct. It is digging and shoveling which make capital valuable; and the wealthy of this and other lands once poor but now affluent, can testify that this saying is not altogether figurative.

Such are the interests of capital and labor, so mutual and intertwined in the great aims to be reached, the enterprises to be carried forward for the highest good of mankind, that to disturb them by inconsiderate and ill-advised action, on the part of the people or Government, is to violate a command written in the necessities of the race, and which may be fitly interpreted in the words of the injunction with regard to wedlock, "What God has joined together let no man put asunder." Thus married in interest we would have this bride and groom go forward multiplying their blessings in the earth, their happy relations in nowise disturbed by contentions or acts which show the one a tyrannical lord, or the other a menial cringing slave.

In our organization we make no discrimination as to nationality, sex, or color. A labor movement based upon such discrimination, and embracing a small part of the great working masses of the country, while repelling others because of its partial and sectional character, will prove to be of very little value. Indeed, such a movement, narrow and divisional, will be suicidal, for it arrays against the classes represented by it all other laboring classes which ought to be rather allied in the closest union, and avoid these dissentions and divisions which in the past have given wealth the advantage over labor.

We would have "the poor man" of the South, born to a heritage of poverty and degradation, like his black compeer in social life, feel that labor in our organization seeks the elevation of all its sons and daughters; pledges its united strength not to advance the interests of a special class; but in its spirit of reasonableness and generous catholicity would promote the welfare and happiness of all who "earn their bread in the sweat of their brow."

With us, too, numbers count, and we know the maxim, "in union there is strength." It has its significance in the affairs of labor no less than in politics. Hence our industrial movement, emancipating itself from every national and partial sentiment, broadens and deepens its foundations so as to rear thereon a superstructure capricious enough to accommodate at the altar of common interest the Irish, the negro and the German laborer; to which, so far from being excluded, the "poor white" native of the South, struggling out of moral and pecuniary death into life "real and earnest" the white mechanic and laborer of the North, so long ill-taught and advised that his true interest is gained by hatred and abuse of the laborer of African descent, as well as the Chinaman, whom designing persons, partially enslaving, would make, in the plantation service of the South, the rival and competitor of the former slave class of the country, having with us one and the same interest, are all invited, earnestly urged, to join us in our movement, and thus aid in the protection and conservation of their and our interests.

In the cultivation of such spirit of generosity on our part, and the magnanimous conduct which it prompts, we hope, by argument and appeal addressed to the white mechanics, laborers and trades unions of our country, to our legislators and countrymen at large, to overcome the prejudices now existing against us so far as to secure a fair opportunity for the display and remuneration of our industrial capabilities.

We launch our organization, then, in the fullest confidence, knowing that, if wisely and judiciously managed, it must bring to all concerned, strength and advantage and especially to the colored American, as it earliest fruits, that power which comes from competence and wealth, education and the ballot, made strong through a union whose fundamental principles are just, impartial and catholic.

The resolution before submitted relative to urging upon the Governors of the States to use their endeavors with their Legislature to pass the 15th amendment, was called up, and a lengthy discussion took place on its adoption. Adjourned until 7 o'clock p.m.

EVENING SESSION

The Convention reassembled at 7 o'clock, and was called to order by Sella Martin, Vice President.

The report of the Committee on Savings Banks was received and adopted.

The report of the Committee on the prospective National Organ, to be styled the "New Era," was read, and, after considerable debate, was laid on the table.

Hon. W. D. Kelley, of Pa., was introduced and addressed the Convention. [37]

He had no specific advice to give the colored men here assembled, but he had a claim on them, that if they be true to themselves they must be true to the Republican party--that party belonged to them, and they belonged to that party. After speaking at length of the progress made by the colored race since the first inauguration of President Lincoln, Mr. Kelley closed by warning them not to be seduced into allegiance with any other party but the dominant one. During his remarks he was frequently applauded.

Hon. W. J. White, of Georgia, was next introduced, and gave an interesting description of the natural advantages of that State. At the conclusion of his remarks a collection was again taken up to defray the expenses of the convention, the amount previously collected having been found insufficient, and about $300 were collected.

Mrs. Carey, of Detroit, Michigan, was then introduced, and addressed the Convention at considerable length, her remarks being chiefly confined to the rights of women and the justice of their recognition by the sterner sex. At the conclusion of her remarks, as Chairman of the Committee on Female Suffrage, she offered the following resolution accompanied with the report;

"*Resolved,* That as unjust discrimination in the departments of labor is made against woman, and as the organization of associations for the protection of said interest among the colored people of the United States is in its incipiency, that profiting by the mistakes heretofore made by our white fellow citizens in omitting women as co-workers in such societies, that colored women be cordially included in the invitation to further and organize co-operative societies."

REPORT

The committee, to whom was referred the subject of Woman's Labor, beg leave to report that in their opinion no subject bearing upon the industrial relations of the colored people to community requires more earnest consideration.

The avocations of women hitherto, and particularly colored women, have been lamentably circumscribed, both as to diversity of employment and breadth of operation, seamstresses, laundresses, teachers, clerks, and domestic servants, constituting almost the entire complement of pursuits. In these departments of labor they work without system or organization, there not being, so far as we have been able to learn, but one association among them to promote labor interests, whether by guarding against monopoly or arresting extortion and oppression.

We are pleased, however, to be able to say that a quiet but manifest desire to widen the boundaries of manual and other pursuits, and to invoke aid in protecting the same and other interests, is apparent in examples of noble women of the more favored class who, in the face of a discouraging public opinion, though gradually awakening, now agitate the elective franchise for women, and of colored women who go forth into hitherto forbidden paths of duty or interest with distinguished success.

Miss Edmonia Lewis among sculptors, Mrs. S. M. Douglass and Miss Cole among physicians, Miss Ketchum among clerks, illustrate an aptitude and ability among colored women which, if cordially recognized and encouraged by colored men in their more matured experience in these directions, would be the beginning of an era of thought and effort among colored women creditable to them as a class, and highly promotive of the general well-being.

With women as with the other sex, organized effort, whether in associations with men or in societies of their own, could not fail to be of benefit, as lifting them up from the plane of indifference, frivolity, and dependence, to the nobler sphere of systematized industries and intellectual effort so essential to the growth and prosperity of an enlightened people.

We would recommend to our women, therefore, a steady inculcation of habits of industry, economy, and frugality, to learn trades, to engage in whatever pursuits women of the most highly favored classes now pursue, and in whatever honorable calling besides their inclination or capacities qualify them for, and which will tend to enlarge their sphere and influence of labor.

In addition to present avocations, we would suggest that profitable and health-inspiring employment might be found at market-gardening, small fruit and berry culture, shop and storekeeping, upholstering, telegraphing, and insurance and other agencies, and to connect themselves with co-operative building societies whenever opportunity offers. No women have had a sadder and more varied experience than thousands who have labored in the fields of the South, and to such we would say, engage in agriculture. Bring to the pursuits of freedom the knowledge of husbandry learned when in bondage, and make it magnify and beautify your present improper condition.

An enlarged benevolence is eminently in keeping with the ever-widening sphere of activities into which woman can now enter, as well as with the highest dictates of humanity and religion. The vicissitudes of war, and the accidents inseparable from the great change many have undergone, have thrown to the surface thousands of cases of destitution which appeal to men and women for assistance and remedy. The formation, therefore, of associations, when practical aid and direction can be tended to the thousands of infirm, aged, and poor, could not fail to impress upon the sterner sex the importance of removing all barriers to the full recognition and success of woman as an important industrial and moral agent in the great field of human activities and responsibilities.

All of which is respectfully submitted,   M. A. S. CARY,
                                            CAROLINE E. G. COLBY,
                                            JOSEPH P. EVANS,
                                            BELVA A. LOCKWOOD,
                                            J. S. GRIFFING. [38]

Adopted.

FOURTH DAY

The Convention was called to order at 10 o'clock this morning, the President, J. H. Harris, in the chair. Prayer was offered by Bishop Loguen, of New York.

Mr. Lewis H. Douglas from the committee on the subject, reported a constitution of "The National Labor Union."

On motion to adopt, considerable discussion took place between Messrs. Green and Bowen, of District of Columbia, and Sorrell, of Maryland. It was finally decided to take it up section by section.

At this time Gen. O. O. Howard made his appearance in the room, and was invited to address the Convention. He said that co-operation was what the colored men of this country needed. The practical thought that he would throw out above all others for their improvement was a co-operative system. Labor was of greater importance than capital. He was gratified to see so many men from the South come here for the consideration of these important subjects, and he hoped the movement would be a success.

His remarks were received with applause. General Howard then retired and the Convention proceeded with its business.

Rev. John A. Warren, of Cleveland, Ohio submitted the following; which was referred:

Whereas every form of dissipation tends to waste the resources of labor, and then renders the power of resistance to the evils of poverty and ignorance our common enemies more difficult: Therefore

Resolved, That we include the use of tobacco among the great wastes of our resources, and recommend to all workingmen to practice economy in this as well as the use of liquors.

The consideration of the report of the Committee on Constitution was then proceeded with.

An amendment was adopted that the annual meeting be on the second Monday in December.

The constitution was then adopted as a whole.

Mr. Lewis H. Douglass, chairman of the Committee on Permanent Organization, reported officers for the ensuing year; which report was laid on the table.

Mr. Wm. H. Lester, of Virginia, offered the following:

Whereas the Legislature of Virginia is now largely under the control of a real majority, a result accomplished largely by intimidation on the part of the rebels towards the loyal voters, and especially the colored electors; and whereas there can be no real liberty for our race in that State, much less any safety for the interests of colored and white labor, unless said Legislature is under the control of loyal men therefore

Resolved, That this Convention earnestly invoke the Congress of the United States to enforce its own laws, by causing the test oath to be administered to the rebel Legislature of Virginia, and award the seats of those who cannot take it to their eligible opponents who received the next highest vote, when, from the circumstances, the electors must have known that they were casting their votes for ineligible candidates.

Resolved, That if Congress enforce the law, loyalty and the rights of loyalty will be preserved in Virginia. If not enforced, loyalty will be lost and the colored people, more than 600,000 in that State will be reduced to a condition as deplorable as when they were fastened in chains of slavery.

Resolved, That these resolutions, properly attested, be forwarded by the Secretary to members of Congress and published in the newspapers of the country.

Adopted.

After our report closed yesterday--

The resolution of Mr. T. J. Hayes, of North Carolina, asking Congress to recognize the independence of Cuba, was passed.

Prof. A. M. Green submitted the following:

Resolved, That a delegation of five, of which the President or one of the Vice Presidents of this Convention shall be the chairman, be appointed to wait on Hon. S. J. Bowen, Mayor of Washington, and tender him the best wishes of this Convention for his able and earnest address of welcome to this body, and for the sympathy and the objects of this Convention expressed in that address.

Mr. Lewis H. Douglass thought that as the Mayor had already been thanked by this Convention this resolution smacked somewhat of toadyism and the resolution was laid on the table.

Mr. Rapier, of Alabama, from the Homestead Committee, submitted a report which looked towards organization of a permanent bureau for the purpose of securing homesteads to colored people. Adopted.

Mr. Aaron M. Powell, editor of the Anti-Slavery Standard, New York, submitted a paper detailing the condition of the laboring people in his State. He contended that what was needed most was the power behind the throne--the elective franchise--and recommend the Convention to appeal to Congress to give the poor laboring classes of the South lands belonging to the Government for their use, as it had failed to enact laws to confiscate the rebel lands for this purpose. We find to-day all their estates again in the possession of these rebels. He held the National Government responsible for this state of affairs. Northern capital will not go South because there was no security there for it. Southern freed labor must be protected by Government.

The resolution offered by Rev. J. A. Warren, of Cleveland, Ohio, "that we include the use of tobacco among the great wastes of our resources, and recommend to all workingmen to practice economy in this as well as in the use of liquors," was adopted.

A committee of one from each State and Territory delegation was selected by the respective delegations for the purpose of reporting officers for the National Labor Union, who subsequently submitted the following list: For President, Isaac Myers, of Maryland; Vice President, George T. Downing, of Rhode Island; Secretaries, William U. Saunders, of Nevada, L. H. Douglass of District of Columbia; Treasurer, Collins Crusor, of Georgetown, D. C.; Executive Committee--Isaiah C. Wears, Pennsylvania; Anthony Bowen, District of Columbia; John H. Butler, Maryland; Mrs. M. A. S. Carey, Michigan; J. Booker Hutchins, North Carolina; Hon. C. H. Hamilton, Florida; Sella Martin, Massachusetts, and George Myers, Maryland.

Considerable debate arose on the announcement of the names read, some expressing themselves dissatisfied.

The report was finally adopted, and the Convention adjourned.

EVENING SESSION

The Convention reassembled at 7 o'clock.

Mr. C. H. Peters, of the District of Columbia, offered the following, which was adopted:

Resolved, That the Hon. S. J. Bowen, Mayor of Washington, has in acknowledging the rights of labor throughout the country indiscriminately, kindly extended municipal welcome to this Convention in a most eloquent address; therefore

Resolved, That a committee, consisting of the President and Vice President of this Convention, be appointed to wait upon the Mayor and acknowledge their appreciation and esteem of him who has so nobly espoused the cause of humanity and equality throughout this country.

Senator Sumner, who was expected to address the Convention, having sent his excuse for not appearing.[39]

Hon. J. H. Rainey, of S.C., was introduced, and said that he represented a constituency that could not boast of so much intelligence as this Convention. He regretted that the course pursued here is not of that character that his constituency had expected; that he would not be able to return home and tell them then of some system which had been devised by this Convention whereby some of their wants would be satisfied. They are desirous of knowing from the acts of this Convention what can be done to give them justice; they wanted land, so that they would not be obliged to build up another southern aristocracy. He hoped this Convention would not break up until some plan was devised whereby they could obtain justice, and some action taken that would compel Congress to take notice of the subject.

Bishop Campbell, of N.J., was introduced, and said he confessed and plead guilty to the fact that he belonged to that class of men called preachers, had been one about thirty years, even when slavery held sway all over the South, and when even in the North it was dangerous to agitate the subject. The colored preachers in those days had to contrive all sorts of way to set the people to thinking on this subject. Occasionally they could slip in a word in their sermons. He was sorry to learn that preachers were unpopular in this Labor Convention. He had been a laborer all his life, and he knew no other society but theirs. All the professions here were ruled out. This was not right; all the men here who had rubbed their backs against a college wall were avoided; he was not one of them, but they could not afford to be separated from the working classes. They should make common cause against a common enemy. Oppression was their enemy. He had just returned from among the old rebels of the South. The poor white families there were even in a worse condition than the black. The power that has crushed the black man had not spared the white. If colored men would work together with more earnestness, Georgia would not now be cutting up the devil. [Applause.] [A voice.--"How about Virginia?"] Bishop Campbell.--"Why, the negroes let the rebels pull the wool over their eyes there." [Laughter.] What if the Republican party should stop where they are; what if our Moses should get into the White House again? Where would our race be? Under our gallant Vicksburg general at the White House, he expected to drive the devil out of them yet, if the colored men will at the same time stand by the party that has done so much for them. He owed the people who had crushed them to the earth no ill will, but he wanted them reconstructed and the devil whipped out of them. A rebel had told him that they were now overcome but not subdued.[40]

Mr. Lowry, of Tennessee, was invited to sing "John Brown's body," which he did, and the entire audience joined in the chorus.[41]

Mr. J. K. Rourk, of North Carolina, was next introduced and addressed the meeting.

Mr. Lowry, of Tennessee, gave an interesting account of the political affairs of that State, saying that what the colored people wanted most was education.

Bishop J. W. Loguen, of New York, was next introduced. He said he could go back to his State rejoicing that he had seen so much intelligence congregated as was here. He was not an eloquent speaker, but an eloquent worker, as thousands of his color could testify who had passed over the underground railroad in the days of slavery. He was a co-worker with old John Brown; had ate, slept, and prayed with him, but was not at Harper's Ferry with him. He gave a very interesting account of his (L.'s) escape from slavery when a youth; of his connection with the underground railroad, with which he had been an active agent, of his knowledge of John Brown years ago, and finally of his return back again to his native State--Tennessee--just after the war was over, and the many incidents of his journey there, of his finding his mistress alive, and the changed condition of things there since he had left.

He kept the attention of the audience for nearly an hour, reciting the remarkable experience of his life, detailing very graphically the manner and language of the colored people of the South in the old times, and the over-bearing and proud style of their masters and mistresses.

Mr. John Watson, of Ohio, also spoke, giving a somewhat similar experience.

Hon. Charles H. Porter, of Virginia, addressed the Convention, and after his remarks the Convention adjourned.

FIFTH DAY

The Convention was called to order this morning by Sella Martin, Vice President.

On motion of Mr. Harris, the name of J. B. Hutchins was stricken from the Executive Committee, and that of Mr. G. M. Mabson inserted in its stead.

Sella Martin offered the following resolutions, which were adopted;

Resolved, That, as a labor Convention, it is our bounden duty, and at the same time a great pleasure, to recognize the statesmanlike sentiments contained in the paragraph of the President's message relative to the re-construction of Georgia Labor, to be successful, needs protection opportunity, and just laws. This success can be achieved only through laws made by those who understand the wants and disabilities of the people for whom they legislate.

Resolved, That the Convention tender to President Grant a high appre-ciation of his fairness of mind, fairness of purpose, and fearlessness of utterance in seeking to secure to us, by appropriate legislation, those legal safeguards to our right to labor and to the fruits of our industry, without which the name of freedom is a mockery.

Mr. F. G. Barbadoes offered the following:

Resolved, That, in the opinion of this Convention, the law making eight hours a legal days work in all labor performed for the Government is wise, just, humane and economical in character, and should be interpreted fairly and equitably.

Resolved, That this Convention is unalterably opposed to any repeal or modification of the said law, but that on the contrary they hope the Executive will compel Government contractors, as well as its own officers, to carry out it provisions fully.

After discussion the resolution was adopted.

Mr. J. H. Harris, of N.C., offered the following; which was adopted.

Resolved, That the executive officers and the Bureau of Labor provided by the Convention of the National Labor Union, now being formed, are hereby authorized to appoint one or more suitable persons to represent this organi-zation in the International Labor Congress called to meet in Paris next September, being the fifth annual reunion of the representatives of the industry of the civilized world.

Professor George B. Vashon offered the following report of the Committee on Education:

Mr. President and Members of the Convention:

Your Committee on Education, duly appreciating the extent of the subject consigned to them, and the important relations which it sustains to the question of labor, regret that want of time has prevented them from giving to it as thorough a consideration as it deserves, and they therefore trust that their earnest desire to discharge properly the duty assigned to them, will plead in their behalf for any short-coming in its performance.

The relations which education sustains to labor are, indeed, second in importance only to those which are sustained to it by the attributes of life and freedom. The laborer must be a living man, free in all his acts, thoughts, and volitions; otherwise his efforts, however wearisome to body and mind, or however productive of pecuniary results, cannot, in the estimation of the true political economist, be regarded as a portion of the country's labor; but must be classified as a part of its capital, and with as much propriety, too, as are the workings of a steam-engine or a cotton-gin. Under this view, it follows that the enamcipation of slaves was in effect a conversion of capital into labor, to such an extent as to increase the latter by nearly one tenth

its entire amount. But if labor, in order to be really labor, must be free,
it can be demonstrated very readily that, in order to be productive of its
highest and most desirable results, it must be educated. Who would pretend
to affirm that the savage of the earlier days of Greece, toilfully bringing
together and piling up log after log in the construction of his rude and
comfortless hut, had in so doing accomplished as much as his far-off des-
cendant, who had

> "Learned
> To hew the shaft and lay the architrave
> And spread the roof above them?"

And who would venture to deny that between the one result and the other--be-
tween the clumsy attempt of barbarism and the skillful achievement of civili-
zation--lay a chasm which could be bridged over only by the letters which
Cadmus had brought from Phoenicia? Without their aid there can be no question
that the Greek of the age of Pericles would have shown himself to have been
little, if any, better off than his ancestor centuries removed. The grand
difference between the two was that the one was uncultured, and the other
educated. It is clear, therefore, that education is the necessary condition
of the most efficient labor; and such being the case, it becomes a matter of
great moment to colored workingmen to inquire as to their present condition
and future prospects in reference to it.

Two and a half centuries are now on the eve of completion since a Dutch
vessel landed upon the shores of Virginia the first cargo of human merchandise
that had ever been brought from the ill-fated continent of Africa into a
British colony. Through the servile agency thus introduced, and extended also
to the adjoining provinces, the eminent agricultural resources of the country
were largely developed; and shortly after the epoch of the Revolution, such
an impulse was given to the culture of cotton by the invention of the cotton
gin as to engender a desire for the perpetuation of slavery. But the curse,
thus destined to work so much evil both to Africa and America, did not prove
to its immediate victims one of entirely unmitigated severity. Throughout
the several colonies the relation of master and slave soon lead to the existence of a class in whose veins the blood of the oppressed was mingled with
that of the oppressor; and, in behalf of this class, the voice of nature did
not in many cases plead in vain. Besides, the constant and daily intercourse
of slaveholding families with that portion of their property known as house-
servants was frequently illustrated by such marked instances of devoted
fidelity upon the part of the latter as appealed successfully for a grateful
recognition from their owners in return. To these fortunate individuals,
either the offspring or the favorites of their masters, the rudiments of education, to a greater or less extent, were often imparted. [42]

Through manumission and the privilege granted to slaves to purchase their
freedom, quite a large free colored population was added in course of time to
American society; and in the principal cities a few schools were tolerated for
the benefit of this class. These schools were generally taught by colored persons who had been lucky enough to acquire a sufficiency of education for that
purpose; and through their instrumentality a knowledge of reading and writing
and the other common branches of learning was quite extensively disseminated.
Throughout the free States of the North such schools met with but little opposition; and, indeed, were frequently encouraged; but the case soon became
far different in the South. With that distrust which always characterizes
tyranny, the instruction of the slaves was first vigilantly guarded against
by the imposition of heavy fines and penalties; and afterwards, when the insurrection of Denmark Vesey in South Carolina, and that of Nat Turner in
Virginia had aroused terror and dismay throughout the entire South, public
opinion had universally demanded and secured the prohibition of the schools
for free colored people also. Nor was this prohibition a mere *brutum fulmen,*
as was made apparent in 1854, when a Mrs. Douglass, a white lady of Southern
birth, was imprisoned in the common jail of Norfolk, Virginia, for having
acted in contravention of it. In spite of legislative severity, however, there
is no doubt that, in a few instances, schools for colored children were still
secretly continued. For among the many secret things brought to light by the
opening of the Southern prison-house, there was one at least not challenging
the public attention by its atrocity, but rather by the evidence which

it afforded of the futility of oppressive enactments in crushing out the
South's nobler aspirations. This was a school of the character mentioned,
in Savannah, Georgia. For upwards of thirty years it had existed there, un-
suspected by the slave power, and successfully eluding the keen-eyed vigilance
of its minions. Its teacher, a colored lady by the name of Deveaux, unde-
terred by any dread of penalties, had throughout the long period of time
silently pursued her devoted and assiduous labors in her native city, and in
the very same room that she still occupies; and now she has the satisfaction
of knowing that numbers, who are indebted to her for their early learning,
are, in these more auspicious days, co-workers with her in the elevation of
their common race.[43]

It was reserved for the South itself to abrogate, not only all this iniquitous legislation, but also the slave system which had prompted it, by its
insane attempt to break up the Federal Union. It was reserved, too, for the
shores of Virginia, which had witnessed the inception of the wrong, to behold,
also, the first step in its operation. In the close neighborhood of the very
spot where the first cargo of slaves had been disembarked stands the little
brown building that served as the first school-house for the freedmen. Secure-
ly it nestled under the guns of Fortress Monroe, with the military power of
the nation pledged for its maintenance. Six months had not yet elapsed after
the clouds of war had gathered, when this earliest sunbeam of a dawning
civilization burst through to relieve their gloom. On the 17th day of September, 1861, this school was opened. The honor of its establishment is due
to the American Missionary Association, which had labored, even before the
war, for the educational advancement of colored people in Kentucky and elsewhere, and whose keen-eyed philanthropy eagerly caught sight of this "opening
of the prison-house to those who were bound." Other schools were soon afterwards opened by this Association at Norfolk, Hampton, and Newport News.

With the advance of the Union fleets and armies, the friends of humanity
kept steady pace. In the month of November, 1861, the Port Royal islands
were captured, and in less than three months after, schools were opened at
Beaufort and Hilton Head, South Carolina. The destitution, upon which these
schools cast the first cheering ray was, indeed forlorn. All of the whites
had fled from these islands, leaving there about eight thousand negroes
steeped in ignorance and want. Their deplorable condition appealed strongly
to the officers of the Government for relief, and did not appeal in vain.
At the instigation of General W. T. Sherman and Commodore Dupont, public
meetings were held at once in Boston, New York and Philadelphia, which resulted in the formation of three Freedmen's Aid Societies, viz: the Boston
Educational Commission, the Freedmen's Relief Association, and the Port
Royal Relief Commission. All of these societies straightway sent out teachers,
whose transportation and boarding were furnished by the Government, and in
the month of June, 1862, eighty-six persons were reported in the field.

The year 1863 was ushered in by the Emancipation Proclamation of President Lincoln, which conferred legal freedom upon all the slaves of the nation
except those of certain specified localities, and actual freedom upon all
such as might come within the lines of the national armies. This consequent
enlargement of the area of philanthropic labor was followed by a corresponding
increase in the number of earnest and efficient laborers. Other societies
similar to those already mentioned, were formed at Chicago and Cincinnati in
1863. Hundreds of ladies, tenderly nurtured and refined by all the accomplish-
ments of modern culture, hastened to this field now whitening for the harvest,
and braving privations and the vicissitudes of war, eagerly enrolled themselves among the teachers of the freedmen. Words would fail to depict the
noble devotion and self-sacrifice of those ladies as they carried on their
philanthropic-labors during the remaining years of the war. With a courage
worthy of comparison with that of their brothers on the tented field, they
remained at their posts, braving all the perils of their unwonted situation.[44]

The year 1865 was marked by the fall of Richmond, and the close of the
rebellion. With the opportunities this extended, schools were opened at
every feasible point. The aid of the Government, too, was secured for their
maintenance. On the 3d of March of that year, the Freedmen's Bureau was
created by act of Congress, and through the kind ordering of an all-wise
Providence, Major General O. O. Howard, that gallant Christian soldier, was,
in the following month of May, assigned to duty as its Commissioner. To the

several benevolent agencies already mentioned, he tendered his earnest co-
operation. He gave them efficient aid, by turning over for school purposes,
disused government buildings, and those seized from disloyal owners; by
affording transportation for teachers, books, and school-furniture, and by
assigning quarters and rations to all engaged in the work of instruction,
at the same time that protection was given them through the department com-
manders. By his direction, too, the "Refugees and Freedmen's Fund" was used
to assist in the maintenance of schools supported in part by the freedmen
themselves; and in each State superintendents of schools were appointed to
see to the faithful execution of his plans and purposes. Thus, under the
beneficent administration of General Howard, the Freedmen's Bureau has been,
in the matter of education, as in many other respects, of efficient service
to the freedmen, and has helped to prepare them for a right exercise of the
franchises with which they are now invested as citizens. To bring about this
result, too, the various religious denominations of the country have all
labored to a greater or less extent with commendable zeal. As a consequence
of the several influences at work, the schools at the South have increased
in number, and have prospered greatly every year since the close of the
rebellion. True, they have had to contend with much prejudice and opposition
on the part of a majority of the white population. But there is reason to
believe, from present indications, that these hostile sentiments are gradually
diminishing, and that many who are bitterly opposed to the political equality
of the negro admit the expediency and justice of providing for his education.
And it is an indisputable proposition, that the colored people of the South
have, by their thirst for knowledge and their surprising aptitude for improvement, shown themselves deserving of the interest manifested in their behalf,
and of the aid which has been so generously furnished to them. All classes
among them, both old and young, male and female, have shown that they feel
this thirst, and have exhibited this aptitude. Indeed, when their present
state of advancement is compared with the condition to which slavery had degraded too many of them, there seems to be no exaggeration in Whitter's lyric
     outpouring:

> "Behold the dumb lips speaking!
> The blind eyes seeing!
> Bones of the prophet's vision
> Warmed into being!"

From the report of the General Superintendent of Schools, under the
Freedmen's Bureau, for the six months ending July 1,1869, it appears that
there were in operation during the period mentioned, 2,912 day and night
schools, with an attendance of 149,244 pupils, of whom 73,896 were males and
75,348 females. These schools comprise every grade--quite a number of them,
perhaps thirty, being high schools, several of them colleges, and two universities. In view of this truly respectable exhibit, and of the fact that all
of this surprising progress has been made within the last eight years, surely
there is ample assurance that the colored labor of the South, constituting,
as it does, at least seven-eighths of the colored labor of the Union, will
be, in coming years, not only free, but also rendered effective and honorable
through the generous influences of education.
     In conclusion, your Committee would respectfully submit the following
resolutions for the consideration of the Convention:
     Resolved, That, under the providence of an all-loving God, the members
of this Convention will always hold in grateful remembrance the several educational associations, and their hundreds of auxiliaries throughout the North
and West, that labored in behalf of the Freedmen, together with that noble
band of teachers, who, at the cost of many sacrifices and perils, bore to that
suffering class the blessings of mental and moral culture.
     Resolved, That the system of schools originated by all the agencies re-
ferred to in this report is, to the members of this Convention, the subject of
such grateful regard as leads them to trust that it will continue to be prosperous in its good work until it attains to that perfected state which will
witness the entire South dotted over with normal schools, complete in all
needful educational facilities, from which normal schools as centers will
radiate other schools of inferior grades, to light up every nook and corner
of the land with the beams of useful knowledge.

All of which is respectfully submitted,
                         GEORGE B. VASHON, *Chairman.*
                         JOHN A. WARREN,
                         J. MILTON TURNER,
                         WILLIAM F. BUTLER,
                         J. P. CAMPBELL.

Mr. T. J. Mackey offered the following Memorial of the laboring men of the United States; which was adopted:

To the Honorable the Senate and House of Representatives of the United States
of America:
The memorial of the laboring men of the United States in Convention assembled respectfully showeth, that the condition of the colored laborers of the southern States appeals most forcibly to Congress to intervene in their behalf, by such just and timely measures as properly fall within the scope of the national authority.

Abundant evidence has been laid before this convention showing that the average rate of wages received by the colored agricultural laborer of the South does not exceed sixty dollars ($60) per annum. Out of this small sum he is required to clothe himself and purchase necessary articles for subsistence, for, as a general thing, the only allowance that he receives from his employer consists of one peck of corn meal per week.

Recent returns at the National Bureau of Statistics show that this unrequited labor furnished to the exports of the country during the fiscal year ending June 30, 1869, the enormous amount of one hundred and sixty-eight millions of dollars ($168,000,000) in gold, in the single article of cotton alone. Reliable testimony exhibits the fact that the net profits to the employer from this cotton product, making due allowance for the market value of the land, and deducting every item that enters into cost of production, and allowing each planter at the rate of two thousand dollars ($2,000) per annum for his personal services in superintending his laborers, amount to about fifty (50) per cent, on the capital invested, while the laborers who produced it have not only been left penniless, but are nearly two millions of dollars($2,000,000) in debt, despite the utmost thrift and economy on their part.

Your memorialists are aware of the so-called axiom of political economy which declares that "the price of labor, like that of any other commodity, is regulated by the law of supply and demand." But this proposition, while in its application to a normal condition of society, where the ordinary laws of trade and production alone control prices, it is *not* true as regards the planters and their colored employees in the southern States, for the landowners there can and *do* absolutely regulate the price of labor by combining against the laborer. These combinations would ordinarily be controlled by prudent considerations of profit and loss, which usually govern the investment of capital, and the fear of counter-organizations on the part of the employees would in some measure restrain the oppressive spirit of the employer. But in this case resistance by organized effort is impossible, for the earnings of the laborer leave him no surplus, and when he ceases to labor he begins to starve.

These combinations are very largely inspired and sustained by political causes, as well as by the certainty of ultimate success in securing from the laborer the largest possible amount of work for the smallest possible amount of pay. The political causes above referred to, as stimulating combinations on the part of the landed proprietors against the colored laborers, spring from the well-attested fact that the one class, with but a few exceptions, exhibits an implacable hostility to our system of free government, while the other sustains it with unwavering devotion and uncompromising loyalty to the principles upon which it rests. Hence the possession of civil rights by the colored laborer, conferred upon him not only as an act of justice but as a rational safeguard, and for his self-protection, invites aggression which he cannot repeal, and his political privileges become to him the source of personal peril. The freedom of the ballot is thus sought to be subdued by the necessity for bread, and, with the loyal colored laborer of the South, duty to his country involves danger to himself. Your memorialists believe that this great

wrong is not without a feasible remedy, and that the true and immediately
practicable remedy lies in making a fair proportion of the laborers themselves
land-owners. This will place colored agricultural labor beyond the absolute
control of artificial or political causes by lessening the amount of labor
for hire, and increasing at the same time the demand for that class of laborers. To this end your memorialists pray that the surveyed public lands in the
southern States may be subdivided into tracts of forty (40) each, and that
any freedman who shall settle on one of such subdivisions, and cultivate the
same for the space of one year, shall receive a patent for the same, the
title to such land to vest in the settler and his heirs, and to be inalienable for the period of ten years from the date of entry.

Your memorialists beg leave to invite the attention of your honorable
body to the following exhibit of the public domain now in the southern
States, as shown by the records of the General Land Office:

		Acres.
Alabama,	. . . .	6,496,421
Arkansas,	. . . .	11,307,278
Florida,	. . . .	17,328,344
Louisiana,	. . . .	6,493,499
Mississippi,	. . . .	4,718,517
Total	. . . .	46,344,059

It will thus be seen that there are in the South, in round numbers,
forty-six millions three hundred and forty-four thousand acres of public land.

Estimating the number of freedmen who would probably avail themselves of
the right of settlement, on the terms proposed, at two hundred thousand (200,
000,) or about one-fourth (1/4) of the able-bodied colored males in the
southern States, the Government could give each colored settler forty (40)
acres, and still have a residue of over thirty-eight millions of acres of
public land in the South, the value of which residue would be greatly enhanced by the contiguity of numerous settlements to it, the opening of roads,
&c.; while the population thus endowed would add proportionately to the
sources of national taxation, and would thereby not only swell the aggregate
products of American industry, but would add greatly to the list of consumers
or purchasers of many of those products which they cannot now enjoy.

Your memorialists are assured and believe that the existing homestead
and preemption laws will, with some modifications and extensions, accomplish
the result herein desired.

And your memorialists further pray that your honorable body will enact a
law authorizing the President to appoint a land commission, to consist of
suitable persons, whose duty it shall be to purchase lands in those southern
States in which there are no public lands, and have the same divided into
tracts of forty (40) acres each, and sold to freedmen at cost price, payment
to be made in instalments, and to be completed in five (5) years; the whole
sum to be thus used in the purchase of homesteads for freedmen not to exceed
two millions ($2,000,000) of dollars.

And your memorialists further pray that the railroad grants of public
land made by the Government to several of the railway corporations in the
southern States, and by them forfeited by reason of their non-compliance with
the conditions annexed to the same, be not revived, but that the lands embraced in such lapsed grants be brought within the operations of the homestead
act, as herein prayed for.

And your memorialists will ever pray, &c.

We hereby certify that the above memorial was unanimously adopted in the
National Labor Convention begun to be holden in the city of Washington, D.C.,
on Monday, the 6th day of December, A. D. 1869.

J. H. HARRIS, North Carolina.
President National Labor Convention.

T. J. MACKEY, South Carolina,
SELLA MARTIN, Massachusetts,
JOHN P. SAMPSON, Ohio
W. T. J. HAYES, North Carolina,
WILLIAM J. WILSON, New Jersey,
M. VAN HORN, Rhode Island,

A. WARD HANDY, Pennsylvania,
J. H. RAINEY, South Carolina,
JAMES T. RAPIER, Alabama,
CHARLES H. PETERS, District of Columbia,
WILLIAM PERKINS, Maryland,
J. W. LOGUEN, New York,
CALEB MILBURN, Delaware,
Vice-Presidents National Labor Convention

Attest:
    Lewis H. Douglass,
        Secretary.

On motion of Mr. Waugh, of Rhode Island, it was
Resolved, That we hereby express our most extreme contempt for, and opposition to, the efforts being made to galvanize into active existence the American Colonization Society, and that we entreat the parties, that if they have a spark of honesty in their natures to be consistent and go to Africa themselves, if they be as earnest and sincere in their professions of love for Africa, as they would have us believe, that it is our intention to remain and labor here on our native soil.[45]

Aaron M. Powell, of New York, offered a resolution requesting Congress to authorize the appointment by the President of a land commissioner for the purpose of purchasing eligible land for homesteads, the title thereof to be held until by instalment, without interest, it shall have been paid for, when the money so employed, not exceed $2,000,000, shall be refunded to the National Treasury. Passed.

Allen Coffin, delegate from the Workingmen's Club of the Government Printing Office, introduced the following resolutions, and moved their reference to the Business Committee:

Whereas, The principles announced by the fathers of the Republic, that "all men are created equal" and possess certain "inalienable rights," and that the true purpose of government is to establish and to perpetuate liberty, justice and equality, therefore

Resolved, That all laws, customs, ceremonies, and organizations, either of church or State, which discriminate prejudicially against color, nationality, condition, or laudable avocation, are in direct violation of the fundamental principles of republicanism, and consequently ought not to exist in the United States.

Resolved, That Labor is entitled to its just reward, by whomsoever performed, and the denial of such pay to women because they are women, for equally efficient work is a grievance which demands redress.

Resolved, That it is the duty of the national government to encourage and sustain the associations which seek the elevation of working men and women, particularly those based upon the principle of co-operative industry, inasmuch as labor is the active agent in developing the vast resources of the country, and the real source of national prosperity.

Resolved, That the employment of children of tender years by corporations, as a means of adding to their greed of profit, is a disgrace to the civilization of the age and sadly detrimental to the physical and mental development of American citizens.

Resolved, That the public lands belong to the people, and government has no right to deprive them of their legal possession by granting monopolies of the same to corporate wealth.

Resolved, That while there exists neither reason nor necessity for antagonism between capital and labor, each being essential to the other, no fact is more patent than that capital, as now employed, is inimical to the interests of labor, and the workingmen's remedy is in co-operative industry, in possessing their own capital and emptying their own labor.

Resolved, That the benefits of the eight-hour law ought to be extended to all classes of laborers throughout the country, whether in the employ of the Government, or corporations, or private enterprises. [46]

Resolved, That impartial suffrage, and the representation of minorities ought to be secured and maintained throughout the Republic.

Resolved, That the President of the United States ought to be elected by a direct vote of the people in order that principles of the Republic may be more fully realized.

Hon. C. M. Hamilton, Delegate from Florida offered the following resolution which was referred to the Business Committee:

Whereas, there exists in the Southern States as one of the consequences
of the institution of slavery--an organized *"Land Monopoly"* which is baleful
alike to domestic, and national prosperity; and whereas extensive combinations have been entered into by the land owners in the South, for the purpose of maintaining said land monopoly, pledging themselves to sell not a
foot of land, an implement of agriculture, or a farm-animal to the freed
people, with the willful, malicious design of keeping the freedmen in as
dependent a condition as possible, individually, socially, and politically;
and whereas so long as this land monopoly prevails, the avenues of prosperity,
and personal independence are closed against the national freedmen--the
laboring millions of the south; therefore,

Resolved, By the National Colored Labor Convention, That every possible
legitimate measure be taken, in conjunction with the laboring masses of the
country, to overthrow this cruel barrier to our progress--the monstrous
"Land monopoly" of the South. [47]

Mr. Hamilton said in support of his resolution, that perhaps it was not
generally known to the country that there existed today in the South--as
one of the direful consequences of the institution of slavery--a land monopoly as wide-spread, and as baneful to the liberty, and pursuit of happiness
of the colored people as was that institution itself; that it had its foundation in the barbarous prejudices of the late slave-oligarchy, and preserved
by organizations all over the South for the purpose of keeping the laborers
dependent upon the land-owners not only for employment but for very existence,
with the object of controlling them *politically* as well as that of the *price
of labor.*Here we had the spectacle of labor not simply struggling with capital,
but capital sitting in *judgment* upon labor and controlling it at will. The
Convention assembled for the purpose of putting labor where, in the nature
of things, it belongs--upon the level with capital, and to bind them in the
bonds of wedlock, their proper relation. Labor is the eternal rock upon
which the stately edifice of capital finds its sure foundation--but it is
labor and capital *combined* that erects the temple. The day of inequality has
gone forever, and the Divine influence of the "Kingdom to Come" is pervading
the earth. Let us heed it.

It behooves the Convention to look to the condition of the colored laboring people of the South, where nine hundred and ninety-nine are struggling
with prejudice, poverty, opposition and danger, which you of the North know
nothing about. You may adopt your Constitution, publish your fine addresses,
define theories and policies, for this grand labor movement, but unless this
mountainous obstacle, this land monopoly, is removed from the way of the
advancement, the prosperity, the liberty of the millions of laborers in the
South, this Convention will have proved a failure. I am asked how this is to
be done. That's the question this Convention must consider. It might be
done by a system of taxation--by the Legislatures of the different States--
whereby a certain quantity of land--a homestead--may be taxed at the usual
rate, and all lands over the quantity of this homestead--say of one hundred
and sixty more acres, to be taxed at such rates as to make it more *profitable*
to sell than to hold surplus land. It could be done in this way, and yet have
taxation uniform.

He did not find fault with these men for possessing vast estates, but
when it was to their interest to dispose of a part of them--when the men,
whose sweat and blood and flesh and labor had purchased these estates, were
anxious, and ready to purchase land lying idle, for prejudice and inhumanity
to say *"no* you shall not have a foot of land at any price," is monstrous.
Coming up on the train through South Carolina and Georgia he overheard men--
rebels, discussing this question of land monopoly, and say that it was the
only way to keep the freed people in their proper place--to keep them poor,
and dependent was the only way possible to get along with the colored people.
Because it is thus wilfully and maliciously maintained, I denounce this land
monopoly, as monstrous as it is inhuman, barbarous.

Sella Martin offered the following, which was referred:

Whereas the American Missionary Association is the principal National
Society working in an educational direction among the colored laborers of the

South, expending, at this time, more than $350,000, and employing more than
500 teachers and missionaries among these people, therefore[48]
    Resolved, That this Convention tenders its hearty thanks to, and ex-
presses its full confidence in, this Association and other kindred societies,
and calls upon the colored working people of the country to support these
benevolent labors by sending their children to school, and by contributing to
their funds.
    Sella Martin offered the following, which was referred:

    Resolved, That this Convention regards with great solicitude the efforts
which are still being made to transfer the public domain to the hands of
private speculators through a continuation of the unfortunate policy of
donating the public lands to the railroads and other corporations, and we
earnestly call upon Congress to guard the sacred rights and interests of the
people in the public lands from further encroachments in this direction, and
we especially and earnestly protest against appropriation of these lands except for the occupation in limited quantities by actual settlers.
    Resolved, That we earnestly invite Congress to consider whether some
measures cannot be adopted to facilitate the settlement of Southern colored
and other laborers upon the unoccupied lands, believing that a more independent, and, therefore more intelligent citizenship would be the outgrowth of
the nation's liberality.

    The following resolution was offered by George T. Downing:

    Resolved, That this convention express its most earnest desire that their
shall be brought about, at the earliest possible time, a union of such National
Labor Union as do or may exist on the basis of not proscribing persons on account of their sex or color.

    Mr. J. A. Warren, of Ohio, offered a resolution recommending the *Chris-
tian Recorder,* of Philadelphia, to the support of the colored people.

    Abram Smith, of Tennessee, offered the following, which was referred:
    Resolved, That this Convention endorse the Tennessee Manual Labor Uni-
versal Industrial School, devoted to the elevation and improvement of youth
in industrial art and mental improvement.

    Mr. Cumback, of Mississippi, made a short address congratulating the
Convention on the great success of the Republican party in his State. They
had marched forward with the Star Spangled Banner over them; and had achieved
a great triumph--over 30,000 Radical majority--and he had swam lakes and
rivers to give this Convention the glad tidings.

    R. M. Adger, of Pennsylvania, offered the following:

    Resolved, That it is the desire of the mechanics and laborers of Phila-
delphia that the Convention devise ways and means by which mechanics and
laborers, regardless of color, be admitted to workshops on equal terms; and
that our children may learn the various branches of trade.
    Resolved, That this Convention recommend to the Executive Committee to
elect a delegate to represent the interests of the labor movement in the
Labor Congress.

    L. H. Douglass, Secretary, read a communication from the National Execu-
tive Committee of colored men, expressing satisfaction with the National
Labor Convention, and offering co-operation with them in the interest of
colored labor.
    Mr. Wm. U. Saunders, of Nevada, offered a resolution that the members
of this Convention cheerfully bear testimony to the untiring zeal of the
National Executive Committee of colored men in the performance of an important
trust, and therefore tender to it their hearty thanks for the general good
which it has already accomplished in various matters touching the welfare of
the colored people of the United States.
    Adopted.

The Committee on National Labor Union reported the following Vice-
Presidents:--Albert Somerville, Tennessee; J. F. Rapier, Alabama; W. H. Lester,
Virginia; Wm. Bonner, Louisiana; W. H. Hall, California; Robert H. Small,
Nevada; J. B. Hutchins, North Carolina; W. T. Cumback, Mississippi; J. F.
Long, Georgia; E. S. Traners, Florida; Charles M. Linn, Connecticut; A. E.
Veazey, Delaware; J. A. Warner, Ohio; P. H. Donegan, D.C., J. T. Waugh,
Rhode Island; J. W. Jones, West Virginia, W. H. Fletcher, Massachusetts;
W. P. Brooks, Wisconsin; R. Adger, Pennsylvania; Wm. Perkins, Maryland; S. C.
Watson, Michigan; W. P. Powell, New York; J. H. Rainey, South Carolina; and
J. Woodlin, New Jersey.
     J. R. W. Leonard, of New York, chairman of Committee on Printing, read
a communication from twenty-five colored printers of New York congratulating
the craft on Mr. Lewis H. Douglass, a member of the craft having received
his rights in the District of Columbia in holding his position in the Government Printing Office.

     Mr. Woodlin, New Jersey, offered the following:

     Resolved, That this Convention recommend to our people to abstain from
the use of tobacco, and dealing in lotteries and policies, and the money be
spent in purchasing homesteads.

     Mr. S. Lowry, of Tennessee, offered the following; which was adopted:

     "That, as this is a Convention industrial, composed largely of colored
people in a national council, for the education and elevation of the masses
of our countrymen in the Southern States--
     Resolved, That delegates, upon returning home, will call State con-
ventions, and organize educational and literary societies in the counties,
as far as possible, to work in conjunction with the Bureau, through State
organizations, and ratify the objectives of this body, and place them in
harmony with the Bureau in its purposes."

     Mr. J. Milton Turner, of Missouri, offered the following; which was
adopted:
     Resolved, That this Convention distinctly disavow all responsibility for
the sentiments expressed here today by Senator J. W. D. Bland *apologizing* for
the negro-hating, unreconstructed rebels of Virginia, in the matter of test
oath for office-holders in the State of Virginia.

     The Finance Committee reported that $289. 84 had been collected in cash;
$155.90 expended; $133.44 on hand; and $105 had been pledged; that in order
to carry on the work of this Bureau, more funds were wanted.
Therefore--
     Resolved, That the Vice Presidents of each of the States be requested to
collect and forward to the Treasurer of the Bureau, five dollars from each
of the counties in the States as soon as possible.

     The report was adopted; and the resolution laid on the table.
     Mr. J. P. Evans offered the following; which was adopted.
     Resolved, That we recommend to the delegates here assembled to procure
of their constituencies, on their return home, statistics, showing the number
of societies of various kinds, embracing wealth and strength of said societies,
and forward the same to the Bureau at Washington for publication.

     Mr. A. Manning, of the District of Columbia, offered a resolution of
thanks to the publishers of the Evening Star, National Republican, and Daily
Chronicle, for the favorable reports of the proceedings of this Convention
published in their columns. Adopted.
     Rev. Anthony Bowen, of this District, offered a resolution, that all
ministers of the Gospel, who were delegates here, on their return home would,
with one universal unity of action, offer up prayer to Almighty God for the
amelioration of the condition of their race, and for His blessing on their
efforts as shown in this Convention. Adopted.
     A resolution of thanks was also passed, to the President of this Conven-

tion, Hon. J. H. Harris, for the ability and impartiality with which he has provided over this assembly.

Hon. H. S. Harmon, of Florida, offered the following; what was adopted.

Resolved, That this National Convention, appreciating the noble and untiring service of Mrs. Josephine Griffing during the period of seven years, in aid of the poor people of our race, which has resulted in securing homes and employment for over six thousand needy men, women, and children, and in securing and disbursing, for the benefit of the helpless and friendless of our people, a large sum of money—twelve thousand dollars of which was raised by private contributions through her personal efforts. We hereby publicly tender to her, on behalf of the freed people of the country, our heartfelt gratitude; and may God bless her, who, being a "friend in need is a friend indeed."

A vote of thanks was tendered Mr. Lewis H. Douglass for his services in the Convention.

Mr. Saunders, of Nevada, made remarks congratulating the Convention on the success of its efforts in behalf of the purposes for which it had met and thanked the originator of it. Mr. Isaac Myers, of Maryland, through whose suggestions and efforts it had been called together.

The Chair, Hon. J. H. Harris, made a parting and very able address to the assembly, which was listened to attentively throughout. He thanked the delegates for the respect shown him during their deliberations, and enjoined upon them to labor for the attainment of the ends for which they have met, and, by standing upon the broad principles of the Republican party—broad as the universe, deep as the sea, and high as heaven—angels would smile upon their efforts, and they would be crowned with success. He sat down amidst shouts of applause.

The Convention then adjourned *sine die.*

Proceedings of the National Labor Convention, December 6-10, 1869.

2.   CONSTITUTION OF THE NATIONAL LABOR UNION

Article I.

Section 1. This organization shall be known as the National Labor Union, and its jurisdiction shall be confined to the United States.

Article II.

Section 1. The National Labor Union shall be composed of such organizations as may now or hereafter exist, having for their object the amelioration and advancement of those who labor for a living.

Section 2. Each organization shall be entitled to one representative, and each State Labor Union to three for the State at Large in the National, Labor Union, provided that representatives derive their election direct from the organizations they claim to represent.

Article III.

Section 1. The officers of the National Labor Union shall be elected annually on the third day of the session, and shall hold their offices until their successors are duly elected. They shall consist of a President, Vice-President, Recording and Assistant Secretary, Treasurer, and an Executive Committee of nine members.

Section. 2. The above named officers shall constitute a Bureau of Labor.

Section 3. There shall be one Vice-President for each State, Territory, and the District of Columbia, to be chosen by the State Labor Unions, where they exist. Where there are no State Labor Unions, by the State Labor Conventions at their next meeting preceding the annual meeting of the National Labor Union. If neither elect a Vice-President, then the National Labor Union shall have power to appoint at their regular annual meeting.

Section 4.   The Bureau of Labor shall be located in the City of Washington D.C.

Article IV.

Section 1.   The President shall preside at all meetings of the National Labor Union and "the Bureau of Labor" and preserve order and enforce the laws. He shall sign all orders for money drawn on the Treasurer by the Secretary, and be the Custodian of the Seal, which shall be affixed to all documents emanating from his office, and perform such other duties as may be required of him by the Bureau of Labor, and the interest of the various organizations in the several states demand.
Section 2.   The Vice-President shall, in the absence or disabilities of the President, perform the duties of his office.

Article V.

Section 1.   The Recording Secretary shall keep a correct account of the proceedings of the National Labor Union and the Bureau of Labor. He shall fill all blanks and write all orders for money on the Treasurer. He shall keep a debit and credit account, and shall report the condition of the finances at each meeting of the Bureau of Labor, and perform such other service as may be required by the National Labor Union and Bureau of Labor. In his absence, the Assistant Secretary shall perform the duties of his office.

Article VII.

Section 1.   The Bureau of Labor shall meet at least once in each month, at such time and places as the interest of the Union may require. They shall fill all vacancies in said Bureau. They shall have power to grant charters to the various organizations in the different states. In connection with the President they shall advise and superintend the organization of Labor Unions, land, loan, building and co-operative associations generally, in the different states. They shall inquire into and inform the various organizations as to when, where and how money can be obtained, in what sums, and at what rate of interest, and what security will be required. They shall give especial attention to protecting the rights of workingmen of the various organizations chartered by the National Labor Union by bringing to justice those who may rob them of their wages, and by bringing about such legislation in the several states as may be necessary for the interest and advancement of the condition of the laboring classes.
Section 2.   They shall regulate the salary of the President, Secretary, and such other officers as may be necessary to accomplish the objects of the National Labor Union.
Section 3.   They shall report annually to the National Labor Union the condition of the various organizations, also the general condition of colored labor in the United States, with recommendations, as they may think necessary.
Section 4.   They shall, in connection with the President, act as agent for the securing of employment, to labor of all kinds, and its transfer from one state to another.
Section 5.   All communications in relation to business pertaining to the Labor Union or Bureau of Labor must be marked on the envelope "Official" and addressed to the President, Post Office Box 191, Washington, D.C.

Article VIII.

Section 1.   Seven members, in any organization, shall be sufficient to apply for a charter, which shall be granted on the payment of five dollars.
Section 2.   It shall be the duty of each organization to prepare an annual statement of the condition of said organization, with such other information as may be to the interest of workingmen, and forward it to the Bureau at least one month before the meeting of the National Labor Union, that the reports may be printed for the use and benefit of the National Labor Union at its annual meetings.

Article IX.

Section 1. Each local organization or representative shall pay a tax
of ten cents annually per member. The tax of an organization shall be paid
on the presentation of the credentials of the delegate; and no delegate shall
be allowed to take part in the deliberations of the Union until the tax is
paid.

Article X.

Section 1. The meeting of the National Labor Union shall be held on the
second Monday of December in each year; and shall commence its session at
12M.
Section 2. Special meetings of the National Labor Union may be called
by the President, upon the request of the Bureau of Labor.

Article XI.

ORDER OF BUSINESS:
1. Report of Committee on Credentials.
2. Roll of Members.
3. Reading of Minutes.
4. Report of Bureau of Labor.
5. Report of Standing and Special Committees.
6. Report of Local Organizations.
7. Unfinished Business.
8. New Business.
9. Adjournment.

Article XII.

Section 1. This Constitution shall only be altered or amended at the
regular annual meetings of the National Labor Union by a two-thirds vote of
all members present.

ISAAC MYERS, *President,*
GEO. T. DOWNING, *Vice-President,*
LEWIS H. DOUGLASS, *Secretary,*
CALVIN CRUSOR, *Treasurer.*

EXECUTIVE COMMITTEE

Sella Martin	Hon. C. H. Hamilton	John H. Butler
Isaiah C. Weirs	G. M. Mabson	George Myers
Anthony Bowen	D. M. Simons	F. G. Barbadoes

The New Era, April 21, 1870.

3. ADDRESS OF NATIONAL LABOR UNION TO THE
COLORED PEOPLE OF THE U.S.

OFFICE OF THE NATIONAL BUREAU OF LABOR,[49]
WASHINGTON, D.C.

To the Workingmen of the United States:
FELLOW-CITIZENS: Your representatives from the States of Maryland, Virginia, West Virginia, North Carolina, South Carolina, Georgia, Alabama, Louisiana, Florida, Texas, Tennessee, Kentucky, Missouri, Ohio, Michigan, Pennsylvania, Delaware, New Jersey, New York, Rhode Island, Massachusetts, California,
and Nevada, met in Convention in the City of Washington for the purpose of
considering your industrial condition, and to propose such means as will
speedily relieve and elevate our people. In the course of their deliberations,
which lasted from the 6th to the 10th inst. inclusive, the very important fact
developed itself, that although we constituted a very large portion of the

skilled and unskilled laborers of the country, yet we are almost wholly
without organization in any of the States, and for want of organization our
labor is very poorly remunerated. To change this condition of things, which,
if continued, must shortly prove ruinous to the colored laboring interest of
the United States, your representatives have thought best to establish a
National Labor Union and a Bureau of Labor, the Bureau to be located in the
city of Washington. This Bureau is intended to be the guardian of your interests, both national and local. It will be charged with the special duties
of local organizations: To encourage and superintend the organization of all
the departments of industry:

To furnish information to the various branches or organizations in the
several States where there may be a surplus of labor, as to where that surplus may find employment in other States:

To bring about such legislation, either national or local, as will secure our equality before the law, and enforce the payment of contracts for
labor:

To negotiate with bankers and capitalists to furnish money in aid of the
establishment of co-operative associations. We, therefore, call your attention to the necessity of immediate organization in every State in the Union.
We regret that our white fellow-citizens in many of the States have organized
"Trade Unions," to the exclusion of colored members--that they will not permit
colored men to work in their workshops. This is one of the consequences of
slavery, for which we are not responsible. And yet, we must have work, and
our children must learn trades. This obstruction, or opposition on the part
of a large number of the white mechanics must be met and overcome, not in
angry dispute, or open hostilities, but by organization.

We, therefore, advise the calling of a State Labor Convention in all the
States, Territories, and District of Columbia, and that a State Labor Union
be organized, whose membership shall consist of delegates from the various
labor and industrial organizations in the State.

That in any city or county where there are seven or more mechanics, artisans, or laborers of any particular branch, we advise their immediate organization in separate associations; because, having your labor organized, you
can advertise it for sale in some of the daily papers; and, although the
white mechanics may refuse you work with them, contractors, or those who buy
or employ labor, will be governed more by self-interest than by the power of
Trades Unions, and will negotiate with you as readily as with any other association of mechanics and laborers. Thousands of colored mechanics could obtain immediate employment in cities, where they are hardly known, if they
would adopt the above course.

Every effort should be made to make your labor more remunerative, and
less dependent upon the capitalist; and indeed in most of the States, it is a
necessity at this time, for employment, that you organize co-operative mechanical associations. Let each one lay by a small sum weekly for the purchase of
the necessary tools, then take his labor as capital, and go out and build
houses, forge iron, make bricks, run factories, work plantations, &c. This
has been done, is being done by our white fellow citizens in this country and
in Europe, and can be done by you. All that is wanting, is the will. To aid
you in this work is the duty of the "Bureau."

To acquire a homestead should be the ambition of each man in the land.
To the industrious workman, we say it is your privilege to buy a home at the
same rate at which you pay rent; this can be done by organizing building
associations. We shall aim to furnish you with the most improved plan of
organization.

You will please furnish this Bureau with all information, that will
assist us in finding out our real 'condition,' and that will aid us in the
promotion of the moral, social, intellectual, and industrial welfare of our
people.

N. B. Only those associations, that receive Charters as prescribed by
the Constitution can receive the attention and supervision of the Bureau.

All communications must be addressed Post Office Box 191, Washington,
D.C.

ISAAC MYERS, President,
G. T. DOWNING, Vice President.

W. U. SAUNDERS
L. H. DOUGLASS, Secretaries.

The New Era, February 17, 1870.

4. PROSPECTUS OF THE NATIONAL LABOR UNION AND BUREAU OF LABOR OF THE UNITED STATES OF AMERICA

FELLOW CITIZENS AND WORKINGMEN OF THE UNITED STATES:
   The question of the hour is: How can the workingman best improve his condition? This question is not only being agitated in the United States, but throughout the civilized world. The universal law of our existence is: "In the sweat of thy face thou shalt eat thy bread." We desire to impress you with this fact, that it is a Divine Law, that we must labor, and that the comforts of life can only be attained by honest, patient toil.
   It should be the aim of every man to become a capitalist; that is, every man should try and receive *an exchange* for his labor, which by proper economy and investment, will, in the future, place him in the position of those on whom he is now dependent for a living. At least it should be your aspiration to become the owner of your own homestead, and place that homestead beyond the reach of want and poverty. As workingmen we can only possess these bless ings by being industrious with our brains and hands, temperate in our habits, and economical with our means.
   It is the duty of our National Labor Union, and more particularly the Bureau of Labor created by your delegates assembled from nearly every State in the Union, to advise with you upon the best and most speedy means to better your condition in the United States.
   We look with painful emotions upon the present condition of colored labor in the several States. Disorganized, poorly paid, assaulted, and, in many cases, totally indifferent to its own welfare. After a careful survey and consideration of this vital question, in which we have consulted the wisdom and experience of the most profound economists and labor reformers of our times--
   We advise you, first, to immediately organize, because labor can only protect itself when organized; that is, by being organized thoroughly, you have the command of capital. You receive better pay for your labor. You learn where and how to invest your labor to better advantage. You learn the value of the capital invested with your labor--how to respect that capital, and make that capital respect your labor. You learn how and where to create employment, to give yourselves work when you are debarred by opposite combinations. You learn the wants of your fellow workmen and how to provide for them.
   In a word, without organization, you stand in danger of being extermi- nated. You cannot expect to be profitably employed, and the trades will soon die out in the race. With organization you will find employment, you will force opposite combinations to recognize your claims to work without restric- tion because of our color, and open the way for your children to learn trades and move forward in the enjoyment of all the rights of American citizenship. How shall you organize? We answer, call a general meeting of the workingmen in every city and town, and after discussing the importance of organization, appoint a committee of one from each branch of trade or labor represented, to prepare a plan for organization. When they have reported a plan, then appoint your committee on constitution and permanent organization. When they report, proceed immediately to form yourselves into an association, send a copy of your constitution and list of officers to the Bureau of Labor, and get your charter. We would advise, where there is a sufficient number of any parti- cular branch, that they organize separate associations. As each man desires to follow that business for which he has been educated. As a constitution for the government of a carpenters' association will not suit the government of a laborers' association, it is important that you organize a branch separately. Five men of any one branch organized, can accomplish much in the interest of

that particular branch, than being associated with five hundred men of several branches. Mixed organizations have always proven disastrous in the labor movement, except in delegated bodies. The above organizations referred to, are simple organizations for the protection of labor and wages.

We would call your attention to, and advise, second, that you form yourselves into co-operative Trades Unions. While these are the most beneficial associations of modern times, they require much judgment, and intellectual ability to make them a success. They seem to be a necessity at this time in order to furnish employment to colored men in many States in the Union. We could not furnish a general plan of organization. Each particular association must be governed by special rules. We can only advise you how to organize, when you inform the Bureau what you propose to organize. We can but say the general principle is to each man to take a given amount of stock, and pay that in weekly or monthly installments until they have enough to commence business with, so that, by a combination of their money and labor, they will form a capital and business that will give them an independent living. In organizations of this kind no restriction should be placed upon parties investing, because of their other relations. Let each man who will, take an interest with you.

3. We should advise you to organize building and land associations. They can easily be established in connection with your "Trades and Labor Unions," that will have a tendency to strengthen and perpetuate them. Experience has preached that all men can, by the agency of a well regulated building association, build a house for what he would pay rent for one. We shall be pleased to advise you about the most improved plans of organization.

4. In order to effect a more thorough organization of the colored workingmen of the United States, and advise and enlighten them upon all questions affecting an interest, and battle with the prejudices manifested because of our peculiar position, the Bureau has decided to issue a weekly paper, to be known as the organ of the Colored Workingmen of the United States. It shall be our object to keep informed as to the condition of the trades in each State, rates of wages, demand for labor, value of real estate, forms of organization, and to meet all questions, national and local, affecting the interest of the workingmen.

The necessity for such a paper is admitted by all who are the least acquainted with our present disorganized condition, and as it is barely possible to discount our labor and social interest from our political, we shall at all times, when necessity demands, take a decided stand in advising you upon all questions will be to your interest as a race, and to the good of our common country.

As we shall have one or more agents, who shall travel in and through all States to assist you in organizing all the departments of labor, we hope that each man will make himself an agent to take the paper, and see that his neighbor has one also, until it may be found in every house in the country.

We shall make it, if possible, the cheapest weekly paper in the country, secure the best writers that can be found. Our course is onward! Let every one put his shoulders to the wheel, and victory and success will perch upon our banners. All communications must be marked "official", and addressed to the President, Box 191, Washington, D.C.

P.S.--Your Attention is particularly invited to the Constitution of the National Labor Union, published in the proceedings of the Convention.

ISAAC MYERS, *President,*
GEORGE T. DOWNING, *Vice President,*
W. U. SAUNDERS, *Secretary,*
LEWIS H. DOUGLASS, *Asst. Secretary,*
COLIN CRUSOR, *Treasurer.*

EXECUTIVE COMMITTEE:

SELLA MARTIN,   JOHN H. BUTLER,
ISAIAH C. WEIRS,   GEORGE MYERS,

G. M. MABSON.

The New Era, April 21, 1870.

5. VISIT OF A DELEGATION OF THE COLORED NATIONAL LABOR CONVENTION TO
THE PRESIDENT ON SATURDAY.

Pursuant to a resolution of the National Labor Convention, a delegation
composed of the president and vice president of that body, called on President
Grant.

Mr. Parris, of North Carolina, as president of the Convention, was the
spokesman on the occasion and delivered a brief and forcible address. He
recurred to the past history of his race, and their elevation from chattle-
hood to manhood, and said that issues which it had been supposed were decided
in the field were still being discussed in the forum; that the colored race
would stand by the President in the future, as he and the great party that he
so faithfully represented had stood by them in the past. He stated that he
was especially instructed by the Convention to thank the President for the
view taken by him in his recent message in regard to the reconstruction of
Georgia and said the rights of the loyal laboring classes of that State were
deeply involved in the question, as the local authorities of Georgia are
hostile to every man who is true to the Government of the United States, and
the colored laborer there is today absolutely without protection for his
rights.

The president replied as follows:

"I am very glad to meet a delegation from the working men of the country.
I heartily sympathize with the movements now generally in progress to secure
their rights. If they move in the right direction and organize properly, they
are strong enough to enforce all their just demands. So far as in my power I
will endeavor to secure ample protection for them, and for all classes. The
time has passed when the persons and property of citizens can be endangered
by their loyalty to the Government."

After a brief conversation with the President the delegation retired
highly gratified with their interview.

The Christian Recorder, January 1, 1870.

COMMENTS ON THE NATIONAL COLORED LABOR CONVENTION

6. THE COLORED CONVENTION

We desire to call the attention of our colored friends to the importance
of being properly represented at the ensuing convention, to be held in the
city of Washington, D.C., on Monday, December 6th, and succeeding days. We
assure them in the kindest spirit that it is to their interest to steer clear
of all political partisan humbugs, to allow their reason, their sober common
sense to control them, and refuse to accept any advice, which places them in
antagonism, in any measure, direct or indirect to the National Labor Union.
Such a movement will assuredly prove fatal to their future aspirations, and
we are led to fear that some such action is contemplated, in looking over the
proceedings held in several sections of the country. We are perfectly aware
that the best interests of the producing classes demand that the issues and
isms of the past should be ignored; that the broad eternal principle--that
the interests of *labor* are one and inseparable the world over--no matter
whether the laborer be the skilled, intelligent white mechanic of the New
England States, or the colored emancipated toiler of the South; but this grand
truth can be more surely sown by exhibiting a confidence in the declaration
of friends than by accepting the bogus support of the enemies of the white
mechanic. Of course it will take time to eradicate the prejudices of the
past; to overcome the feelings which it may be, the teachings of a life-time

has inculcated, yet it is well to remember that revolutions never go backwards, and now that the National Labor Union has evinced its honesty and
sincerity of purpose by admitting colored delegates on terms of perfect
equality, it would certainly be the height of folly to raise a barrier which
their enlightened action has removed. Our advice, therefore, is to shove the
reverend humbugs and honorables to the wall; let your *bona fide* labor representatives mould the action of the convention; reaffirm the platform of the
National Labor Union; ignore the blatant demagoguism of these who expect to
ride into public favor on your shoulders; go to work in earnest and organize
in every State of the Union; send your duly accredited delegates to the
Cincinnati Congress, where they will be cordially welcomed, and both you and
your children's children will reap the advantages of taking such a course.
      It is highly probable that our esteemed friend, Mr. R. Trevillick, Pres-
ident of the National Labor Union, whose viewers we have embodied in the
above suggestions, will be in attendance. If not, we trust, he will make it
a point to point out the danger of pursuing a different line of policy.
      We have just learned that it is the intention of Mr. Trevellick to
attend the Convention.

Workingman's Advocate, December 11, 1869.

7.   OBSERVATIONS OF SAMUEL P. CUMMINGS,[50]
A WHITE LABOR UNIONIST

      The Convention of colored men at Washington last week was in some respects
the most remarkable one we ever attended. We had always had full faith in the
capacity of the negro for self-improvement, but were not prepared to see,
fresh from slavery, a body of two hundred men, so thoroughly conversant with
public affairs, so independent in spirit, and so anxious apparently to improve
their social condition, as the men who represented the South, in that convention. Our experience with them has exalted them in our estimation immensely,
and we feel as though the future of the colored race on this continent was
secure. The convention was called to order by Mr. Myers, of Baltimore, and
Geo. T. Downing of Rhode Island, was chosen temporary chairman; and, upon
assuming his position, Mr. D. made one of the best speeches on the labor
question we ever heard. It was a gem in its way, and had his counsels been
heard too, some unpleasant things might have been avoided; but there were a
few, who evidently had some secret purpose to serve, who tried to make the
convention the means of carrying it out. Prominent among these was Mr. J. M.
Langston, the famous colored lawyer of Ohio, who evidently aspires to the
leadership of his race, and who, we hear, has been promised a high position
under the government, if he can control the colored vote of the South, in the
interest of the Republican Party. Mr. Langston certainly possesses ability,
but very little discretion, at least his course indicated it, for on the
first evening of the convention, he took occasion to insult the white delegates from Massachusetts, and warned the delegates to beware of us, intimating
very strongly that we were the emissaries of the Democratic Party, which was
certainly new to us, who have until this year acted with the Republican Party.
      As will be seen by the newspaper reports they formed a National Labor
Union upon a basis similar to that adopted at Philadelphia last August, and
may be said to be fairly in the field as an organized body of laborers. Whether their course in forming an independent National Union was wise or not, time
alone can tell; but we are convinced that for the present at least, they could
not do better. It is useless to attempt to cover up the fact that there is
still a wide gulf between the two races in this country, and for a time at
least they must each in their own way work out a solution of this labor problem. At no very distant day they will become united, and work in harmony
together; and we who have never felt the iron as they have, must be slow to
condemn them because they do not see as we do on this labor movement. For
ourselves, we should have felt better satisfied had they decided to join the
great national movement now in progress, but fresh as they are from slavery,

looking as they naturally do on the Republican Party as their deliverers from
bondage, it is not strange that they hesitate about joining any other movement.
Although they did not distinctly recognize any party in their platform, yet
the sentiment was clearly Republican if their speeches were any indication.
Still, strange as it may seem, parties were ignored in their platform, and
this course was taken mainly through the influence and votes of the southern
delegates.

Isaac Myers, a member of the present Labor Union was chosen their permanent President for the ensuing year, with a good list of other officers, and
in their hands the cause will no doubt be safe. . . When we see a convention
composed mainly of those who ten years ago were slaves on the plantations of
the South, assembling under the very shadow of the national capital, to deliberate on questions of grave national importance, and conducting them with
such marked ability, as to arrest public attention, we feel sure that the day
is not far distant, when the good sense of our colored friends will lead them
to join us in all honest efforts to make the interests of labor the paramount
interest in our legislation, state and national. Till then, we can afford to
wait. S.P.C.

Samuel P. Cummings in *American Workman* (Boston), December 25, 1869.

8. "AN IMPORTANT STEP IN THE RIGHT DIRECTION "

As was contemplated, one result of the Convention was the organization
of a permanent Bureau of Industry, to have its headquarters in Washington,
with officers and auxiliary associations in all the States and Territories.
The President of the new Bureau is MR. ISAAC MYERS, of Baltimore. Mr. Myers
is at the head of the very successful co-operative Ship Builders Association
of that city. This Association, as our readers will perhaps remember, was
organized by colored mechanics who had been driven out of the Baltimore Ship
Yards on account of their color. Determined not to starve or be outdone, they
organized, and borrowed capital to the amount of $40,000, and to-day they are
out of debt, and are doing fully as much business as any of their white competitors. Nor do they confine their workmen to colored mechanics. Some of
the very white men who a few years ago combined to deprive Mr. Myers and his
associates of employment have since sought and obtained work in their yards.
The name of Mr. Myers at the head of the new Bureau is therefore a guaranty
that it means work, and that good results may be expected from its organization.
Until such time as colored apprentices and mechanics can have access to other
workshops, it will be the aim of the Bureau to open the way for both by co-
operation and organized effort, independent of those now in existence controlled, regulated and exclusively occupied by whites. It will also endeavor to
promote the organization of cooperative Land and Building Associations. It
will need, and we trust will obtain, an adequate supply of money to achieve
a large measure of usefulness. But should its pecuniary cooperation prove to
be limited, the discussion of these industrial problems, already awakened by
the Convention and the organization of the Bureau, will do great good.

This Convention served more fully to confirm the statements we have so
frequently presented in the columns of THE STANDARD, that LAND is an immediate
and pressing need among the freed-people, to the end that their freedom shall
become real instead of nominal, or as at present, at best, but partial. With
great unanimity the Convention seconded the proposition we have urged, that
Congress should provide for a Land Commission to facilitate the selection and
purchase of suitable lands for small homesteads, through Agents qualified for
the trust. Forlorn and helpless as many inevitably are, suddenly emancipated,
with past years of unrequited toil, and left as victims of   monopolists,
they need to be helped to the opportunity to help themselves. Magnanimity
should not be esteemed as the chief of the virtues only when it is shown
towards negro-hating rebels. We urge that the loyal freed-people be not wholly
abandoned to the Ku-Klux and to the grinding and cruel task-masters who, while
they can no longer buy and sell the men and women at the same auction with

their horses, mules and swine, have still the power to render their estate
little better, in the rural districts, than slavery itself. We hope that
early in the present session of Congress due provision will be made whereby
individuals, local associations, and the new National Bureau, may have
government cooperation in securing to the landless freed-people *homesteads*.
The memorial to Congress prepared by Col. Mackay of South Carolina, and an
address before the Convention by Col. R. J. Hinton, replete with important
statistical information concerning the Land question, and an eloquent plea
for the suffering freed-people, we hope in a subsequent issue to present to
our readers.

The freedom of the colored people of this country is still very unlike
that which the whites enjoy. Senator Wright of South Carolina, in coming to
Washington as a delegate to this Convention, though paying first-class fare,
was compelled to come in the second-class car, or be put off the train. It
is but a few weeks since George T. Downing, Esq., was rudely thrust from the
reclining chair car, in which he was entitled to a seat, at Jersey City, by
Camden and Amboy ruffians, solely on account of color. And this same prejudice dominates in the workshops and prohibits in a large measure the landless freed-people from obtaining suitable land for a livelihood, either by
lease or purchase. Labor movements among the white workingmen, manipulated
to their great disadvantage in many cases by political demagogues, will do
little for the colored people. Witness the action of the Bricklayers and
the Printers Union.

We are glad that so auspicious a beginning in the way of organization has
been made by this Convention. The Bureau just organized is an important step
in the right direction. Its advantages are freely offered to all who are inclined to friendly cooperation,--men and women, colored and whites. This is
the true ideal. Political and industrial reconstruction must go hand in hand.
A. M. P.

National Anti-Slavery Standard, December 25, 1869.

9.   FROM MISSOURI

ST. LOUIS, MO., Dec. 7, 1869.

TO GEORGE MYERS, Secretary of the Colored Men's Organization, Baltimore, Md.
SIR.--Since I met you in Washington city last November, I have been so
pressed for a time, that until now have I postponed writing to you, as I then
promised concerning the convention of colored laboring men to meet on the 6th
of this month in Washington city. I learned today that President Trevellick
of the National Labor Union, has left his home and gone to your convention.
It will not be important, therefore, that I should enter into an excluded
explanation of the principles and doctrines embraced in the platform adopted,
or rather reaffirmed, at Philadelphia, last August. Upon some of the questions I gave my views when we met in Washington, and I noted what you complained of, and have given much thought to the subject since. [51]

You and the other colored men that I met with you stated that, although
the colored men now have the same political rights that white men enjoy, yet
there are social rights and privileges denied them; or rather, as society is
now organized, the colored men cannot enter factories and workshops, or be
taken as apprentices to learn the trades, that white men only monopolize to
the entire exclusion, in some instances, of the colored men. That the condition of colored men in the Southern States, although they enjoy the rights
of free citizens, yet are they in a state of quasi slavery, by reason that
they cannot procure land of their own. That the white men of the south will
not sell their agricultural lands to the colored men. That the colored men
must necessarily become tenants, and left to the whim, caprice, or cupidity
of the land owner in regard to the division of the net productions for rent,
leaving the laborer to work on as long as his physical ability will hold out,
without the chance to provide for old age, when he can no longer labor. Now,

under the present unjust medium fixed by Congress for the distribution of the
net productions of labor and capital, and the unjust mode of disposing of the
public lands (the people's lands), the white laboring men have as much cause
to complain as the colored men. Upon these two vital questions the white and
colored laborers stand precisely alike. The question of carrying on factories
and workshops, or taking apprentices to learn trades, are not political questions that legislation can interfere with. These may be called matters of
taste, and being local and conventional different rules may be established
depending on local considerations only. Whilst the other questions although
national, and that can only be effected or changed by national legislation,
yet they must be local in their application as well as national--*per see.*

The National Labor Union party have laid down in their platform certain
principles or dogmas, upon which they will demand such national legislation
as will allow every individual, white or colored, to enjoy the full benefit
of the common inheritance given by God ' to all mankind alike. And as God
requires all men alike to fulfill all the duties required by the law of his
being--"To eat bread in the sweat of his brow"--so He has provided a sufficiency for all whereby man is to obtain his bread by his own labor. In order
that man can carry out that Divine decree, there has been provided a sufficiency of air, water, fuel and land. If these elements had not been provided,
and in sufficiency, then the decree would have been hard--nay, unjust. A
sufficiency of the soil to every citizen is a common gift, and "no one is entitled to a surplus of a common gift which deprives another of a sufficiency."
And a sufficiency of the soil to every citizen is the preventive of social
evil. The Congress of the United States has sold the people's lands and given
the proceeds to corporations. In regard to the public lands, the Philadelphia
platform provides that the thirteen hundred millions of acres that are left,
that have not been alienated, must be hereafter held security in trust by
Congress for the actual settlers, and that every individual being entitled by
inheritance to a sufficiency, a minimum ought to be given, without cost, to
every citizen that chooses to take it. And that by popular legislation a
minimum quantity of land should be held in trust for every citizen that thinks
proper to take it; that this quantity should always be held in trust, that is
to say, the donor should not have power to alienate the soil, only the excess
he adds by his labor could be disposed of, leaving no apology for any one
capable of labor to become a pauper.

But there is another Divine law which we contend has by unwise legislation deprived the laboring men of all colors, of enjoying the fruits of
their own toil. There is a limit imposed by the law of nature to the right
of government to take the earnings or property of a citizen for any purpose
whatever. . . .

The Government, or rather the congress, has committed two great political
blunders since the war commenced. The first was in issuing bonds based on the
credit of the nation and levying a tax on labor to pay the interest. If the
credit of the nation was good security for the bonds, it would have been
equally good for money issued by the Government, as money that has been
issure upon a pledge of the bonds. But the bonds have been issued, and got
into comparatively few hands. The holders of the bonds of course, never
want them paid. The bonds were purchased with greenbacks, and the greenbacks
purchased or obtained by horse traders and other shoddy contractors, we all
know how. But the greatest amount was taken from the soldiers after they
had received them at the rate of $13 per month. Some were purchased with
greenbacks that had been bought with gold, at one gold dollar for two greenback dollars, and some for two dollars and eighty cents in greenbacks. Some
loaned the greenbacks to the government and received bonds bearing gold
interest.

This system of financiering has resulted in saddling a debt upon the
producing classes of over two billions of dollars. Jay Cook says this debt
is a national blessing; and Senator Morgan said the sum of its evils were
not as great as the sum of its benefits to the laboring classes.

. . . For weeks previous to its assembly, we had intimations from authority which we knew to be reliable, that a desperate effort would be made, by prominent political demagogues, to control its action, and secure its influence in behalf of the Republican party; a prediction which subsequent events have proved to be correct, although the *results* cannot have afforded them much consolation. While we should have preferred that the voice of *labor* had been heard a little more distinctly, upon the whole, we are satisfied with the results. A grand inaugural movement has been completed; steps have been taken to consolidate the colored element of the Southern States, which can ultimately, have but one result, viz:--a clear alliance with, and an endorsement of, the principles of the National Labor Union. Of this we have not the slightest doubt. It may take our colored friends, some time to come to this conclusion; but we are perfectly willing to leave it to the inevitable logic of events. The criticisms of our correspondents, we think are somewhat out of place; and, as we believe their publication would not be productive of any beneficial results, we trust they will excuse their non-appearance.

Workingman's Advocate, January 1, 1870.

10. AN APPEAL TO OVERCOME PREJUDICE

. . . We urge the colored laborer to organize his labor, to do it wisely, universally and consistently. We shall seek to illustrate the wisdom of the maxim that labor and capital is one when the laborer is not coerced and when capital is respected, and that therefore all profits should be mutually shared. . . . The pressing need of the hour is education. Seven generations of enforced ignorance and systematic robbery, together with moral degradation to which we have been subjected, make it necessary for we citizens to cast aside all scruples as to the use of public money for the support of non-proscriptive [integrated] schools and to overcome all personal preduces, insuring the benefits of education. . . . so far from being excluded, the "poor white" native of the South, struggling out of moral and pecuniary death into life "real and earnest," the white mechanic and laborer of the North, so long ill taught and advised that his true interest is gained by hatred and abuse of the laborer of African descent, as well as the Chinaman, whom designing persons, partially enslaving, would make in the plantation service of the South the rival and competitor of the former slave class of the country, having with us one and the same interest, are all invited, earnestly urged, to join us in our movement, and thus aid in the protection and conservation of their and our interests.

In the cultivation of such spirit of generosity on our part, and the magnanimous conduct which it prompts, we hope, by argument and appeal addressed to the white mechanics, laborers and trades unions of our country, to our legislators and countrymen at large, to overcome the prejudices now existing against us so far as to secure a fair opportunity for the display and remuneration of our industrial capabilities.

We launch our organization, then, in the fullest confidence, knowing that, if wisely and judiciously managed, it must bring to all concerned, strength and advantage, and especially to the colored American as its earliest fruits that power which comes from competence and wealth, education and the ballot, made strong through a union whose fundamental principles are just, impartial and catholic.

The New Era, January 13, 1870.

III

THE SECOND AND THIRD CONVENTIONS OF THE
COLORED NATIONAL LABOR UNION

THE SECOND AND THIRD CONVENTIONS OF THE
COLORED NATIONAL LABOR UNION

In accordance with the Constitution of the CNLU, a second annual meeting commenced in Washington, D.C., on January 9, 1871. The delegates were requested to inform themselves regarding local employment conditions, educational facilities available to black youths, the extent of cooperative associations founded locally, and the means required to advance the economic condition of black workers (Doc. 1). The real historical significance of the second CNLU convention, however, must be perceived against the background of conflict over racial policy within its white counterpart, the National Labor Union.

The fourth annual convention of the NLU opened in Cincinnati on August 15, 1870. Almost immediately, a bitter dispute erupted between the white and black delegates over the seating of John W. Langston of Ohio, a brother of the more famous John Mercer Langston of Virginia. John Langston was denied a seat on grounds that he was not a workingman, but a politician who had done all he could to prevent the first CNLU from breaking with the Republican Party. The split widened as the convention proceeded. The white assembly adopted a resolution demanding equal pay for men and women, which blacks favored. But the black delegates were annoyed when the convention saw no need for a similar resolution regarding equal pay for black workers. The real conflict, however, arose over the political resolution which declared that the major political parties were dominated by nonproducers who drew their wealth from the exploitation of workingmen. The resolution urged "our colored fellow citizens" to abandon the Republican Party and unite with white workers in a Labor Reform Party. It assured blacks that their true interests would be served by this new political party since blacks were working people.

The black delegates had little confidence that white workers would reward their political support with justice on the economic front, and were more interested in eliminating the barriers against the right to work than in reforming the monetary system as proposed by the Labor Reform Party. This was the last convention of the NLU which blacks bothered to attend. That the split was irrevocable can be seen in the proceedings of the second CNLU convention (Doc. 2-7).

Because of this bitter dispute, and the continued difficulty of organizing black workers in the midst of the "fearful reign of terror" which prevailed throughout the South, delegates at the CNLU convention were in no mood to pacify the white labor movement. Isaac Myers delivered the keynote speech—his last, since Frederick Douglass would be elected the second president of the CNLU—and he took direct aim at the Labor Reform Party as a "grand farcical clap-trap" whose intention to reform the monetary system was "Preposterous." The convention then reaffirmed adherence to the principles of the Republican Party. The committee reports were uniformly militant. For example, the Committee on Capital and Labor, chaired by George T. Downing, reported that freedom for the black worker in the South had turned out to be a cruel hoax. Former masters owned the land, and if blacks agitated for their rights, they were likely to be thrown off the estates. Their only realistic alternative was to move into industrial employment. But here they faced an almost insuperable obstacle in the form of white trade unions which generally refused admission to black workers. It was clear that the main obstacle to cooperation between black and white labor movements was basically economic, while the purely political issues were secondary. That the NLU either would not, or could not, understand the black position is vividly illustrated in Doc. 10.

The third convention of the CNLU was held in Columbia, South Carolina, on October 18, 1871. It was a joint meeting, however, with the Southern States Convention of Colored Men. It is impossible to distinguish between the delegates of the Southern States Convention and the CNLU, but most of the prominent black Reconstruction leaders were present, along with such prominent labor spokesmen as Isaac Myers (Doc. 9).

THE SECOND COLORED NATIONAL LABOR UNION CONVENTION, JAN. 1871

1.   ADDRESS TO THE COLORED WORKINGMEN OF THE UNITED
STATES, TRADES, LABOR, AND INDUSTRIAL UNIONS

In accordance with Article X, Section 1, Constitution of the Colored
National Labor Union, adopted in Convention, December 9, 1869, in the City
of Washington, D. C., the second annual meeting will be held at the Union
League Hall, Washington, D. C., commencing at 12 o'clock M., January 9, 1871.
Your attention is particularly called to Article II, of the Constitution, Section 1: "The National Labor Union shall be composed of such organizations as may now or hereafter exist, having for their object the amelioration and advancement of the condition of those who labor for a living.
Section 2. Each organization shall be entitled to one representative, and
each State Labor Union to three for the State at large, in the National Labor Union, provided that representatives derive their election direct from
the organization they claim to represent."
Your attention is further invited to Article IX, Section 1. "Each local
organization shall pay a tax of ten cents per member; each state or National
organization, ten dollars. The tax of an organization shall be paid upon
the presentation of the credentials of the delegates, and no delegate shall
be allowed to take part in the deliberations of the Union until the tax is
paid." Delegates will be required to furnish certified copies of the number
of members of the associations they represent. Delegates to the meetings of
the Union are admitted without regard to race, color, or sex.
In addition to the regular report of each organization, delegates are
requested to inform themselves upon the following general questions:

First--What are the occupations in which colored men are more generally
employed in your city, county, or state; the rate of wages; the average time
made annually.
Second--The number of schools; their grade, average attendance of
scholars; how many supported by the state; by charitable institutions; also
private schools.
Third--The number of land, building and co-operative associations;
their value in real estate and cash.
Fourth--What means or remedy, in your judgment, can best be applied to
advance the material interest of the workingmen in your locality and in the
United States?

The great importance and necessity of the organization of labor, for
its own benefit and the development of the industries of the country, should
prompt the workingmen of all occupations in the several states to send delegates to this annual meeting of the National Labor Union.
Newspapers throughout the country will please copy.

                                        ISAAC MYERS, President.
                                        LEWIS H. DOUGLASS, Secretary.

The New Era, November 17, 1870.

2.   NATIONAL LABOR UNION

This most important body is to meet January 9th, 1871, in the city of
Washington. The Executive Committee have issued a circular calling the

attention of colored labor organizations to the matter, and inviting them
to a hearty co-operation in the good movement.

The primary object of the Union is, the amelioration of colored workmen
all over the country, especially in the North. In the circular issued delegates are specially requested to bring FACTS to the Convention; such as number of laborers, the number of mechanics, what proportion of them are employed, the wages paid, number of hours demanded for a day's work, &c., &c.
This looks like business. The majority of all our Conventions are afflict-
ed with talkers; men who think they are especially inspired to give council
upon every imaginable subject, from the right of women to vote, to the way
in which the Church ought to be ruled. The Executive Committee seem to have
had an "eye" on these word-mongers, and to have indirectly told them to ply
their business elsewhere. This is as it should be. The era for talk is
past, and the era for work is at hand.

Second only to the work of the Church, is the work of this Association,
and it is a hopeful sign to see its leaders so thoughtful, and exacting.
Let its doings soar high above every political consideration, for it is more
important than either Democratic or Republican rule. If but the heads be
cool and the hands steady to those who have this labor movement in charge,
the desired results cannot but be surely reached.

The Christian Recorder, December 10, 1870.

3. RESOLUTIONS ADOPTED BY THE LABOR CONVENTION

We publish below the most important resolutions, memorials, and reports
adopted at the convention of colored laborers of the nation:

From the proceedings of January 10:

Mr. E. M. Davis, of Philadelphia, after alluding to the necessity of
Government aid to enable the colored people of the South to become useful
citizens, offered a resolution that a committee of five be appointed to petition Congress to appoint a commission to report upon the material condition of the freedmen and the best means of securing their independence as
citizens.

Mr. Harris offered an amendment, which was agreed to, that the commission be selected from known Abolitionists.

Mr. Lewis H. Douglass offered the following:

Resolved, That the president of this convention is hereby instructed to
appoint a committee of five to submit to this assembly a comprehensive plan
of co-operation, which can be made effective in assisting the freedmen of the
South in securing landed property, engaging in such manufactures as they are
by life-long habit familiar with, and to secure the desirable end of becoming
intelligent, useful, and enterprising citizens, and ask the immediate appointment of the above committee.

The resolution was adopted, and the following committee appointed:
Messrs. Nelson, of Texas; Davis, of Pennsylvania; Stokes, of Missouri;
Powell, of New York; and Taylor, of Virginia.

Mr. Downing moved that a committee be appointed to prepare an address to
the African Colonization Society, requesting them to desist from efforts
which tend to unsettle the minds and are hurtful to the prospects of the colored laboring masses. The motion was agreed to, and Messrs. Downing, Loguen,
F. Douglass, Williams, De Baptiste, Nesbit, Jennings, and Harris were appointed.[52]

Mr. Downing, of Rhode Island, from the committee on African colonization, reported as follows:

Whereas two hundred and fifty years of residence in this country is
ample evidence of the colored man's right to consider it his native land; and
whereas, by the organic law of the Republic, colored men are equally with
white men citizens of the United States; and whereas a permanent location is
essential to the peace, happiness, and prosperity of any people; and whereas

the more enlightened part of the colored people have omitted no opportunity
to impress these sentiments upon the public mind; therefore,

Resolved, That it is with the deepest pain and the keenest sense of
wrong that we hear that the American Colonization Society, our ancient enemy, not content with pursuing us forty years before our liberation and enfranchisement, is still upon our track, and is doing all the mischief it can
by teaching our people that this is not our permanent home, and that we must
go to Africa, or elsewhere.

Resolved, That we regard the persistent efforts of that society as im-
pertinent, uncalled for, and deeply hurtful to the interests of our newly-
enfranchised people, and we respectfully entreat the leaders and members of
that society to desist from their efforts to alienate our people from their
native land.

The following are from the proceedings of January 11:

Resolved, That, as the revenue needed for our Government expenses, and
the gradual payment of our national debt, (a sacred debt, growing out of a
great war for the life of the republic, and which gave freedom to all the
people,) call for some $150,000,000 a year from duties on imports, a wise
and just policy requires low duties, or the free import of coffee, tea,
drugs, and other necessary articles not produced by us, and such duties on
articles we both manufacture or produce and import, and the home-product of
which benefit our people, as shall fairly encourage our home-industry, make
wholesome competition possible, leave good wages to the working man, save
him from the pauper pay of foreign workers, give fair prices in a larger
home-market to the farmer, and fit reward to the mechanic and manufacturer;
and that we favor such simplifying and adjustment to tariff and internal
taxes as may be consistent with these vital and important objects.

Whereas varied industry gives employment to labor and skill of all
kinds, develops the resources, increases the internal commerce, gives health
to the foreign trade, and helps the civilization of a nation: therefore,

Resolved, That we desire to see mills, shops, farms, and factories of
every variety built up and prospering all over our country as natural allies
and mutual helps, and that we recognize, as among the evils of chattel slavery, that it confined the South to the production of a few staples, narrowed
the range of industrial occupations, and thus created ignorance and poverty,
not only among the slaves, but the majority of the nominally free people,
irrespective of race; and we hail, as one of the benefits of freedom, the
prospect of varying the industry, and thus helping to elevate and develop
the character and powers of the people in that portion of our country, and
would do all possible in a work so wise and beneficent.

Whereas the American people are compelled annually to pay taxes amounting to over three hundred million of dollars, for the support of the Government, and to meet the interest on a debt incurred to suppress a wicked rebellion; and whereas their ability to bear this enormous annual burden,
without absolute ruin, must depend upon the diversity of labor, the development of our national resources, and the general prosperity of the laboring
classes; and whereas this diversity, development, and prosperity can in no
way be so effectually promoted, and so permanently secured, as by such legislation as shall protect our laboring, mechanical, and manufacturing interests against foreign competition, and, at the same time, create a home
market for our agricultural products: therefore,

Resolved, That we believe in a high protective tariff both a financial
and an industrial necessity in the present condition of the country, and
that it is demanded by every consideration of justice, wisdom, and humanity.

Resolved, That in view of the vast importance of this policy to every
great industrial interest of this nation, and, above all, in view of its
vital importance to the laboring masses, the Republican party be earnestly
advised and requested to engraft the principle of protection to American industry, by a high tariff on such foreign imports as we consume into its
creed, and boldly press its consideration upon the country.

Resolved, That we are irrevocably opposed to the free trade policy of
the Democratic party, which requires that the one hundred and seventy millions of dollars in gold annually received on duties upon foreign imports
shall be hereafter collected by a direct tax upon the American people for

the benefit of British capital and labor, and to the destruction of our own manufacturing industry.

Resolved, That the thanks of the Labor Union be extended to Senator Wilson for his able and timely plea, in the *Atlantic Monthly* of the current month, for the education of the masses, and for his frank recognition of the vital importance of land as a means of that practical education which they require; and that we heartily indorse his recommendation, to men of means, to purchase and dispose of large tracts of land, especially at the South, in the manner proposed by him, with the expression of our conviction that such investments may be made profitable to those who invest as well as to those for whom they are made. [53]

To the Senate and House of Representatives of the United States, in Congress assembled:
On behalf of the National Labor Union, now in session, and representing a large number of American citizens in the different parts of our country, and especially in the South, we would respectfully but earnestly ask your early action in devising and enacting a national system of public school education, somewhat after the plan proposed in the bill of Hon. G. F. Hoar, of Massachusetts, now before the House of Representatives. [54]

Reasons and facts to prove the need and importance of such a plan are abundant in the speeches of Mr. Hoar, and of the Hon. W. F. Prosser, of Tennessee, on the subject, and in the late report of the Commissioner of Education, and we beg leave to call your attention to these and kindred documents.

As workingmen and women, seeing your great development of various industries and the need of skilled labor, we ask that, in any plan proposed, technical education in special industrial arts and avocations be provided for to meet this need to benefit skilled workmen, and to increase the value of our industry, to the signal benefit of our country.

Washington, D. C., January 11, 1871.

To his Excellency U.S. Grant, President of the United States:
On behalf of the National Labor Union, now in session, and representing a large body of American citizens in different parts of our country, and especially in the South, we would respectfully, but earnestly, ask your efforts and influence in favor of a national system of public school education, somewhat after the plan proposed in a bill by Hon. G. F. Hoar, of Massachusetts, now before the House of Representatives. Reasons and facts in support of such a measure are abundant in the speeches of Mr. Hoar, and of Hon. W. F. Prosser, of Tennessee, on the subject, and in the late report of the Commissioner of Education, and we beg leave to ask your attention to these and kindred documents.

As workingmen and women, seeing the great development of various industries and the need of skilled labor in mill-factories, farms, and elsewhere, we would respectfully suggest the importance of making technical education in special industrial arts and avocations a part of the proposed system to meet this need, to benefit skilled workmen, and to raise the standard and value of our industry to the advantage of our country.

Washington, D. C., January 11, 1871.

Resolved, That, for the more perfect organization of the workingmen of the United States, this National Labor Union recommend the holding of State Labor Conventions in the several States of the Union.

Resolved, That said State conventions be requested, when assembled, to form themselves into State Labor Unions, and elect a president, vice president, two secretaries, a treasurer, and an executive board, to consist of one from each county in the State. Said member from each county should be president of the county organization.

Resolved, That said State Labor Unions have full power to issue charters to all labor or industrial organizations in the State, and make such other regulations as may advance their general interest.

Resolved, That said Labor Union, immediately on its formation, inform the president of the National Labor Union, and secure its charter from the National Labor Union.

Resolved, That we recommend, especially in cities, that each branch of skilled labor organize separate associations, and that said city organizations organize State, and that State organize national associations, to be composed exclusively of members of a particular branch of skilled labor.

Resolved, That we recommend the formation of co-operative associations as the best form of organization to protect the rights of labor, and advance their moneyed worth.

Resolved, That we recommend to the State conventions the consideration of the following subjects:

1. The probable number of workmen of each branch.
2. The educational facilities of the State.
3. The probable number of children under 18; how many attending school.
4. The price or wages for all kinds of labor.
5. The prices of real estate in each county in the State.
6. The adoption of a constitution for the State Labor Union.
7. The adoption of constitutions for county and city organizations.
8. Written reports of the actual condition of the people of each county in the State.

Resolved, That this meeting, immediately on the adoption of the resolutions, proceed to appoint an executive committee of one for each State, who shall have full authority to all said conventions.

Resolved, That this National Labor Union endorse the NEW NATIONAL ERA, edited by Frederick Douglass, Esq., in the city of Washington, as the national organ of the National Labor Union of Colored Men of the United States of America.

Resolved, That the presidents of all Labor Unions be authorized agents to obtain subscribers, and circulate said paper in their respective organizations and locality.

The following were adopted January 12:

To the President and Members of the National Labor Union:

GENTLEMEN: Your committee, to whom was referred the resolution making inquiry in regard to the location of public lands in the various States, and the aid that may be given the colored people of the South to locate on those lands, beg leave to report: That, after a careful consideration of this very important subject, and the great amount of suffering endured by the colored people of some of the Southern States for the want of employment and the insufficiency of pay for their labor--in the first place, for the want of capital and political prejudice; in the second place, because of the excess of the supply of labor for the demand--they believe the resolution is of vital interest to the class of persons referred to; that if the information and aid sought can be placed within reach of the colored people of the South, it will materially and politically benefit all classes of citizens. Your committee beg leave to submit the following resolution:

Resolved, That the president of the National Labor Union be requested to correspond with the Secretary of the Interior, and other persons, upon the subject indicated in the resolution, and communicate any information obtained to the executive officer of the National Labor Union of each State.

The Committee on Capital and Labor made the following report:

Among the many agencies at work during the past five years in advancing the best interests of the colored people we may name with pride the system of savings banks. Under a charter guaranteed by Congress, and approved by the patriot-martyr, Abraham Lincoln, these banks have been established at all the principal cities of the South, and the laborer invited to deposit there his savings. In this comparatively brief period more than seventeen millions of dollars of the earnings of our people have been so deposited. Of this large sum about fifteen million have been withdrawn from time to time, the most of it for the purchase of homes of implements of husbandry and of the means of living. These are indeed vast sums of money, but they afford only an earnest of what may yet be done, when all the millions of laborers of the South shall become frugal, economical and saving, each laying by something every day for future need.

The Governor of Massachusetts, in his last annual message, states that the deposits in the savings banks in that State alone is one hundred and

thirty-eight millions two hundred and thirty-two thousand two hundred and
seventy-one dollars and fifty-nine cents ($138,232,271.59.) If the same ra-
tio of savings and deposits prevailed among the laboring people of the South,
the sum in the savings banks would reach the astounding total of four hundred
and thirty-five millions of dollars! And why not? Under the genial sky and
from the fertile soil of the South why should not the proceeds of industry
and thrift be garnered into safe and responsible savings banks by hundreds of
millions? We do not hesitate to recommend the Freedman's savings Banks,
which have already done so much, as worthy the confidence of the people
everywhere.

Resolved by the National Labor Union,
That a committee of three be appointed to memorialize the citizens of the
United States, praying for the passage of a law for the protection of the
ballot-box, and the securement of the purity of the American franchise.

Resolved, That it is the sense of this convention that one of the best
means of promoting the elevation, independence, and enterprise of the colored
citizens of the United States, whose habits for generations have been in connection with tillage of the soil, is that colored farmers of the nation migrate to those portions of the country where they may obtain good land at no
cost.

Resolved, That the Territories of the West and Southwest furnish to the
enterprising emigrant desirable locations for the settlement of individuals
ambitious to acquire independence, education, and power.

Resolved, That this National Labor Union do earnestly indorse the suggestions made by the trustees of the colored schools of the District of Columbia that caste in our public schools should be abolished, and that the
officers of this convention be a committee to memorialize Congress to that
end.

Resolved, That we, the members of the National Labor Union, in convention assembled, do thank our late president, Isaac Myers, Esq., for the very
able manner in which he has conducted the business of the Union for the past
year.

Resolved, That the thanks of this convention are hereby tendered to the
Eight-hour League, of Boston, Massachusetts, for their kind manifestation of
interest in our efforts to improve the condition of our still outraged people.

Resolved, That the grateful thanks of this convention are tendered to
E. P. Rogers, a member of that League, for his able and humane plea to the
religious element in this country in his essay, entitled "Christianity, its
Relations to Capital and Labor."

Resolved, That, while we disavow any intention to environ the efforts
of this organization by unnecessarily introducing politics, yet it is a
duty we owe, as a labor organization, to express our high appreciation of
the Republican party and our devotion to its principles, which have done so
much already for the elevation of labor and the laborer, and which, by its
policy, promises to add so much to the industrial and material interest of
our country.

Resolved, That the thanks of this convention are hereby tendered to the
scholar, gentleman, and one-armed Christian soldier, General O. O. Howard,
for his instructive and encouraging address.

The chairman of the Committee on Cooperation submitted the following
report:
Resolved, That, while upholding the dignity and rights of labor, and
recognizing the fair claims of capital, we would avoid all captious criti-
cism, blind prejudice, or passionate action, and would earnestly urge the
practical wisdom and importance of co-operative plans, whereby intelligent
workingmen can obtain lands and combine labor and capital, sharing the gains
of both.

The following were adopted January 13:
Resolved, That it is a duty we owe our late president, Isaac Myers, to

express our confidence in his entire course as a man and as a consistent
member of the Republican party.

Resolved, That as a convention, representing the intelligence and virtue of four millions and a half of enfranchised colored Americans, and a
voting power embracing a million of loyal electors, we hereby pledge ourselves to an intelligent adherence to the Republican party and its princi-
ples--financial and otherwise--condemning both the Democratic party in its
sentiments of repudiation, and the National Labor Congress, which, in its
"platform," adopted in its meeting held at Cincinnati, Ohio, August 19, 1870,
in which it criticises violently, unfairly, illogically the financial policy
of the present Administration, and declares, in fact, in favor of repudiation of our national obligations.

Resolved, That we condemn [completely] this "platform," and every financial doctrine contained therein, as anti-Republican and false.

Whereas the constitution of the State of Virginia, adopted on the 6th
day of July, 1869, declares that all the citizens of that State "possess
equal civil and political rights and public privileges," and that "all persons entitled to vote and hold office shall be eligible to sit as jurors;"
and whereas a large portion of the citizens of that State are denied the
right to sit as jurors because of their "race, color, and previous condition
of servitude:" therefore,

Resolved, That this convention respectfully petition the Congress of the
United States to take such action as will insure to all the people of Virginia the enjoyment of the equal rights and privileges which the constitution
of that State purports to guarantee to them, without restriction because of
color or race, &c.

Resolved, That a copy of this preamble and resolution, certified by the
president and secretary of this convention, be sent to the Hon. John F.
Lewis, of the Senate, and Hon. Charles H. Porter, of the House of Representatives, with a request that they be presented to the respective Houses of
Congress.

New National Era, January 19, 1871.

4. NATIONAL LABOR UNION

Third Day's Proceedings

WEDNESDAY, January 11, 1871.
The third day's session of the National Labor Union Convention was held
in the Fifteenth street Presbyterian Church, Rev. J. B. Loguen, of New York,
in the chair, and Lewis H. Douglass, secretary.

The Committee on Co-operation Societies submitted their report, which,
on motion, was referred to the General Business Committee.

Mr. Barbadoes, of Massachusetts, presented a series of resolutions of
thanks to Senator Wilson for his able and timely plea in the *Atlantic Monthly* of the current month, and for his frank recognition of the vital importance of land as a means of that practical education which they acquire.

Mr. Myers, of Maryland, offered a resolution asking the convention to
appoint State Labor Unions, and indorsing the NEW NATIONAL ERA as the organ
of the National Labor Union.

The Committee on Capital and Labor presented the following

RESOLUTIONS:

Whereas the American people are compelled annually to pay taxes amounting to over $300,000,000 for the support of the Government and to meet the
interest on a debt incurred to suppress a wicked rebellion; and whereas their
ability to bear this enormous annual burden without absolute ruin must depend
upon the diversity of labor, the development of our national resources, and
the general prosperity of the laboring classes; and whereas this diversity,

development, and prosperity can in no way be so effectually promoted and so permanently secured as by such legislation as shall protect our laboring, mechanical, and manufacturing interests against foreign competition, and at the same time create a home market for our agricultural products: therefore,

Resolved, That we believe a high protective tariff both a financial and an industrial necessity in the present condition of the country, and that it is demanded by every consideration of justice, wisdom, and humanity.

That in view of its vital importance to the laboring masses the Republican party be earnestly advised and requested to engraft the principle of production to American industry by a high tariff on such foreign imports as we produce into its creed, and boldly press its consideration upon the country.

That we are irrevocably opposed to the free trade policy of the Democratic party, which requires that the one hundred and seventy millions of dollars in gold annually received on duties upon foreign imports should be hereafter collected by a direct tax upon the American people, for the benefit of British capital and labor, and to the destruction of our own manufacturing industry.

The chair stated that General Eaton had been invited to address the convention and that he was present.

General Eaton, in response, said he would wish the delegates to make a statement of the educational interest of their part of the country.

Messrs. Myers, Maryland; Taylor, Virginia; Nelson, Texas; Turner and Williams, Alabama; Casten, Georgia; Stokes, Missouri; De Baptiste, Michigan; Bowen, District of Columbia; Downing, Rhode Island, and Barbadoes, Massachusetts, gave interesting details of the school interests in their States.

General Eaton then thanked the delegates for the information they had imparted to him, and addressed the convention on a system of public education, at length, after which Mr. Downing, from the Committee on Capital and Labor, submitted the following

REPORT

The very limited time during the intermission of the convention within which your committee have had to prepare a report on capital and labor, does not permit them to submit such a report as the importance of the subject demands. They would not think of entering into the question, and shall simply confine themselves to one or two practical points.

The committee express the feeling of the colored laborer, when it says he desires, and believes it to be his interest and duty, to cultivate friendly relations with capitalists. Capital is a power to be appealed to. Capitalists should be impressed that there are reciprocal relations between them and the laborer. Let us impress them that they may make their names blessed by using a portion of their means so that those less favored may be benefited.

The efforts of the struggling masses to the present time, the world over, without regard to nationality or race, show that they have not succeeded in results beyond the immediate pressing demands of simple existence. Some have succeeded beyond this.

The above is true, and it is because the masses have not been generally informed; because they have not been educated. Had they been better informed they would have conceived how desirable and profitable co-operative effort would have been in securing the means of administering to their happiness. If this be true, we can hope to be relieved from our present dependent position mainly by education.

This is, however, the work of time; but shall we not be sufficiently enlightened *to-day* to observe and apply the agencies used by others looking to ends similar to those we regard as desirable? The interest of labor calls for some central head to look to its interests. Other interests select certain competent agents to plan, devise, and execute for their interest, compensating such agents as is their due for services rendered. This we must do, or we will not succeed. We have not succeeded as we would had we done so. The interests and success of the laborer depends not simply in creating a bureau of labor, to be located at Washington or somewhere else, but measurably in what is equally as necessary to furnish such bureau with the needful means to carry on its operations.

We come together, talk, resolve, and part; but the essential thing needed, means, is wanted. We admit our poverty, our immediate pressing needs; but we can greatly relieve ourselves by all contributing their mite, which will be a might in benefiting labor.

The colored laborer in America has been the special victim of avarice and cupidity from the time he first set foot on the continent. He has been held in abject slavery, despoiled of all rights; consequently is, as must be the case, extremely poor. He was freed from the chain of an individual master and became more completely a slave to the impoverished circumstances that environed him; he became a subject of the murderous hate now cherished toward him, because of his emancipation and loyalty.

His first two imperative needs--bread and shelter--he had not when he was declared free; the want, without money or land, makes him poor indeed; but without them, and added thereto the lack of a *material* friend makes his situation most deplorable. The colored man is struggling against all this.

It was "necessity" that came to his relief to the extent of freeing him. It also invested him with other rights, justly his as a man without crime--a man to the manor born; but justice or kind offices do not stop here; he expects sympathy and assistance; having been robbed and outraged, he asks for as much as is expected and given to others not thus outraged. It is not expected that the mass will be raised suddenly and completely from their present dependence; but it is desirable for the good of all, the degraded and the elevated, that the most humble of the community should be elevated and made to feel a filial relation to all thereof; universal security and happiness hinges thereon.

For the laborer of the South to properly exercise his convictions as to the best interest of the body-politic he should be placed beyond the restraint consequent upon complete dependence for food and shelter, which dependence exists in the South. It is a common occurrence for the freedman, who is a tenant at will on the lands held pertinaciously by the once man-whipping lord of the South, to be set on the roadside with his family, if he be not murdered, for disregarding as a voter the pleasure of the lord of the soil.

It occurs to your committee how this may, to some extent, be effected. There are certain profitable and honorable pursuits in the South, thoroughly understood by the freedmen, the prosecution of which lead to successful results. Freedmen in the South, industriously inclined, ask the patriotic and humane capitalists of the North not to donate to them any portion of their capital, but to loan the same on sufficient securities, on interest, that they may occupy such an independent position as will enable them as free American citizens to not only freely exercise their judgment as to the best political policy of the nation, but to enable them also to add more extensively to its material prosperity.

Your committee would simply refer to the unkind, estranging policy of the labor organizations of white men, who, while they make loud proclaims as to the injustice (as they allege) to which they are subjected, justify injustice, so far as giving an example to do so may, by excluding from their benches and their workshops worthy craftsmen and apprentices only because of their color, for no just cause. We say to such, so long as you persist therein we cannot fellowship with you in your struggle, and look for failure and mortification on your part; not even the sacred name of Wendell Phillips can save you, however much we revere him and cherish toward him not only profound respect, but confidence and gratitude.[55]

Adjourned to 7:30 P.M.

EVENING SESSION

The convention reassembled at 7:30 P.M., and opened with prayer by Bishop Loguen.

Mr. J. B. Wolf informed the convention that he was from West Virginia and asked to be a self appointed delegate. So ordered.

Delegates Appointed.

The following were appointed as delegates, with power to establish labor unions:

Messrs. John Henry, Maryland; Cassius L. King, Illinois; George L.

Mabson, North Carolina; William I. White, Georgia; J. W. Loguen, New York; Washington Spalding, Kentucky; William L. Leslie, Virginia; William Howard Day, Delaware; J. H. Rainey, South Carolina; Abraham Smith, Tennessee; Richard Nelson, Texas; Robert W. Stokes, Missouri; William Nesbit, Pennsylvania; R. C. Pearce, Florida; Oscar Dunn, Louisiana; Francis Fletcher, Massachusetts; Abraham Ford, West Virginia; Charles Lancaster, Kansas; J. J. Spelman, Mississippi; Elias Ray, New Jersey; A. B. Wolf, Wyoming; Charles Slater, Ohio; A. B. Tinroy, District of Columbia; James Jefferson, Rhode Island; John K. Horner, Indiana; John H. Babtiste, Michigan; Lloyd Wheeler, Arkansas; Charles McLyon, Connecticut, and William Warrick, Iowa.

Affairs in the South

The chair called attention to the impossibility of the people of the country to understand from the public press the real condition of things in the Southern States, and suggested that to-day be set apart for each delegate to speak ten minutes on the state of the freedmen, and invited all the delegates to be present.

Election of Officers

The annual election of officers was then proceeded with, with the following result: Frederick Douglass, president; Bishop Loguen, of New York, first vice president; Lewis H. Douglass, secretary; A. N. Barbadoes, Massachusetts, recording secretary, Anthony Bowen, treasurer.

On motion, the election of nine members of the executive board was deferred until tomorrow.

Messrs. Greene and Downing were appointed a committee to conduct the newly elected president to the chair. The retiring president, Mr. Myers, of Maryland, surrendered the position to Mr. Douglass in a brief and pointed address.

Mr. Douglass, taking the chair, thanked the convention for the honor done him, and hoped that the convention would go in harmony that has been its wont. He advised the delegates when they go home to work up and form local societies, and by so doing send at least five hundred delegates to the convention to be held here next year. He had no strength if the convention had none and if they would make the strength he would try and direct them. He called attention, that during the debate of the convention the strictest decorum was recognized, and thought that if the same harmony was continued it would lead to a grand success.

Mr. Douglass, from the Committee on Labor and Capital, made an additional report, and, on motion, it was adopted.

Mr. Wolf was giving a long history of his working in the old anti-slavery time, when he was called to order by Mr. Downing, who stated that historical statements were not pertinent to the business of the convention.

The Committee on Education, through their chairman, Robert W. Stokes, made a long and comprehensive report, which on motion, was adopted.

Adjourned until 9 A.M. tomorrow.

FOURTH DAY'S PROCEEDINGS

THURSDAY, January 12.

The fourth day's session of the National Labor Union was held at the Fifteenth street Presbyterian Church, Rev. J. B. Loguen, vice president, in the chair.

The session was opened by prayer, by the Rev. A Bowen, of this city.

The chairman called attention to the speech made by Mr. Loguen, in which Mr. Langston had made some uncalled for remarks in reference to Senator Hiram Revels, which remarks, upon making inquiry, he found to be untrue in many respects. He was very sorry that the language had been uttered, and he hoped that in the future deliberations of the convention nothing of the same personal character would be used. Messrs. G. T. Downing and Richard Nelson also made remarks in the same strain.

Mr. L. Douglass moved that a committee of three be appointed to draft a

Memorial to be Presented to Congress,

urging the immediate passage of Senator Sumner's supplementary bill allowing equal rights and privileges on the railroads of the country, and that the same committee be authorized to cover all the gound of prescriptive education.

Mr. De Baptiste offered a resolution tendering the thanks of the convention to their late president, Isaac Myers, of Maryland, which was passed by acclamation.

Mr. Barbadoes offered a similar resolution of thanks to the Eight-hour League, represented by F. P. Rogers, of Boston, Massachuestts.

On motion of Mr. Isaac White, the privilege of the floor was extended to Mr. E. A. Redstone, of California, member and representative of the National Labor Convention of the United States.

Mr. Frederick Douglass introduced General O. O. Howard, who, in response to the invitation, made an extended and interesting address, suggesting to the convention many valuable hints for their future guidance and consideration.

A vote of thanks was tendered to General O. O. Howard, on motion of Mr. Douglass.

On motion of Mr. J. T. Rapier, a committee of three was appointed to ascertain the best manner of

Colonization

of the colored men on the public domain, and Messrs. Rapier, Nelson, and Green were appointed such committee.

Mr. Frederick Douglass introduced Mrs. Colonel Tappan, of Louisiana, who addressed the convention at some length on education and the utilization of the public lands for the benefit of the colored people of the South.

Mr. L. H. Douglass offered the following:

Resolved, That it is the sense of this convention that one of the best means of promoting the elevation, independence, and enterprise of the colored citizens of the United States, whose habits for generations have been connected with the tillage of the soil, is, that colored farmers of the nation migrate to those portions of the country where they may obtain good land at no cost.

Resolved, That Territories of the West and Southwest furnish to the enterprising emigrant desirable location for the settlement of individuals ambitious to acquire independence, education, and power. Passed.

A vote of thanks was tendered to Mrs. Col. Tappan for her entertaining and instructive address.

The convention then took a recess until 7 o'clock.

EVENING SESSION

The convention met at 7:30 o'clock.

Mr. Downing, from the Committee on Capital and Labor, submitted a report on the savings banks, showing that $17,000,000 had been deposited by the colored laborers of the country since the banks have been established. On motion, the report was adopted.

Mr. Downing said that there were now some thirty freedmen's savings banks in the country, with a surplus at the present time of over two and a half millions of dollars, and urged upon the colored people of the nation to husband their resources.

Mr. Frederick Douglass spoke of the importance of having an eye to the future and husbanding their earnings.

Mixed Schools

Mr. Downing offered the following resoultion:

Resolved, That the National Labor Bureau of the colored men of the nation earnestly endorse the suggestion made by the trustees of the colored schools of the District of Columbia, to the effect of abolishing caste in in the arrangements for public instruction in the District, and, that the officers of this convention be a committee to memorialize Congress to adopt the suggestion.

The resolution was adopted without debate.

Mr. Myers, of Maryland, offered the following resolution:

Resolved, That the President of the National Labor Union be requested

to correspond with the Secretary of the Interior and other persons in regard
to the location of public lands, and to communicate the information obtained
to the executive officers of the National Union of each State.

After considerable debate, the resolution was laid upon the table.

On motion, a committee was appointed to nominate officers for the ensuing year. The president appointed Harris, of North Carolina; Taylor, of Virginia, and Stokes, of Missouri, as such committee.

Mr. Stokes offered the following resolution:

Resolved by the National Labor Union, That a committee of three be appointed to memorialize the Congress of the United States praying for the passage of a law for the protection of the ballot-box and the securement of the
purity of the elective franchise.

The president appointed Messrs. G. T. Downing, A. M. Green, and Lewis H.
Douglass the committee.

The Rev. C. W. Dennison was called for, and spoke at considerable
length.

The Committee on Elections reported the following as the Bureau of La-
bor for the ensuing year: Isaac Myers, Maryland; George T. Downing, Rhode
Island; George De Baptiste, Michigan; J. T. Rapier, Alabama; Edwin Belcher,
Georgia; George L. Mabston, North Carolina; R. Nelson, Texas; J. E. Taylor,
Virginia; A. M. Green, District of Columbia.

Mr. Harris, of North Carolina, from the Committee on Finance, submitted
a report, showing the organization to be in debt $187.

Professor Langston, of the Freedmen's Bureau, spoke at length, saying
that his best efforts would be used to keep the negro in the Republican
party. He would use no effort to raise a dollar for the expenses of the Labor Union until he knew whether they were to be entailed upon the Democratic
party.

This last remark created a little stir in the convention.

Mr. Downing said, he for one had some personal pride animating his bosom, and he did not want and would not have, any one beg for him.

A collection and subscription was taken up, and $112 was raised to meet
expenses. The meeting then adjourned until Friday morning.

FIFTH AND LAST DAY'S SESSION

FRIDAY, January 13, 1871.

The fifth day's session of the National Labor Union was held in the
Fifteenth-street Presbyterian Church, the president, Frederick Douglass,
Esq., in the chair.

Mr. Belcher, of Georgia, offered a resolution condemning both the Democratic party and the sentiments of repudiation; also, the National Labor
Congress, which, in its platform adopted in its meeting held at Cincinnati,
Ohio, August 19, 1870, criticises violently, unfairly, illogically, the financial policy of the present Administration, and declares in fact, in favor
of the repudiation of our national obligations, and that they utterly condemn the doctrine contained therein as anti-Republican and false.

This was the cause of a spirited debate, in which some unkind words were
said.

The debate was finally closed by Mr. George T. Downing, who introduced a
resolution indorsing the course of Mr. Isaac Myers, president of the Colored
National Labor Union, in the National Labor Congress, held in Cincinnati,
and expressing entire confidence in his integrity to the principles and policy of the Republican party. The resolution was adopted by acclamation.

Mr. Langston advocated the adoption of the resolutions, eulogizing the
address of Mr. Myers before the convention in Cincinnati, and then delivered
a long address in support of the position taken by him.

Mr. Robert W. Stokes, from the Committee on Homesteads, submitted their
report, which is replete with useful information.

On motion, the report was adopted.

A resolution, indorsing the NEW NATIONAL ERA as the organ of the convention, was adopted.

After brief remarks by several members of the convention, Mr. Douglass
said that he had invested at least $8,000 in the ERA, and did not think it
altogether right for him to saddle the whole expense.

Several members subscribed largely to the stock of the paper.

On motion of Mr. Isaac Myers, of Maryland, it was

Resolved, That the convention hold its next annual session in Columbia, South Carolina. He promised those present that if they went there they would meet with a hearty reception.

The chairman then read a letter which he said he had just received from Hon. D. J. Morrill, in which the writer said he was much gratified at the position taken by the convention on the question of capital and labor; accompanying the letter were several hundred pamphlets, for distribution, on "Protection to American Industry."

On motion, the thanks of the convention were tendered to Mr. Morrill.

After a general discussion the convention adjourned *sine die.*

ANNUAL ADDRESS OF PRESIDENT MYERS

The following is a synopsis of the address delivered by Isaac Myers, president of the Labor Union, at the opening of the convention:

DELEGATES OF THE NATIONAL LABOR UNION: We are meeting in a period of the world's history when all parts of the land seem to be convulsed with revolutions.

Indeed, we may say, that this is the age of revolutions and the revolution of ages.

Religious and political dogmas that have been the devotion and guide of individuals and nations for centuries, and which from their supposed perfectness have been robed in the divine garb of infallibility, have been uprooted by the ideas of an advanced civilization, and their deep-rooted convictions forced to loose their hold on the mind of man by great pools of blood that have dyed the land in mourning.

Had men been governed in their deliberations and conduct by the simple moral law, "Do unto others as you would they should do unto you," we should have had the results without the convulsion.

Not one drop of blood would have been spilled, not one cent of treasure been spent, and not one weeping, wandering widow or orphan would have been seen in all the land, to teach the civilized world that no government or institution can receive an everlasting lease of life only by a strict observance and faithful administration of affairs upon the principles of equity for the common interest of all the people.

No revolution of our day has yet accomplished its mission or purpose. Because of the tenacity with which men hold on to the shattered ideas of an irredeemable past; of the relationship of man to man, and of the duty of those who govern to those who are governed; their Herculean efforts to turn the revolutions backward their challenging of God to battle. We are threatened with another fearful national convulsion that must entail a chronic paralysis of the great national pulse, which is now seemingly convalescent.

Capital and Labor

Not the least, and probably not the most significant revolutionary contest of the times, is the adjustment of the relationship of labor to capital. There is no country in which this question will assume a wider range of discussion, more varied and complex forms and feelings, than in the United States of America, and that, without regard to any fixed laws of political economy. And from the nature of our institutions and privileges of citizenship, there is no country that furnishes so readily the means to solve the problems, and establish some general laws (if they do not already exist) by which labor and capital will be governed in its business intercourse, without endangering the security of the Government or the public peace.

But to suppose a millenium in which labor will get all of its supposed value, and capital will equalize its profit to labor, either by persuasion, reason, or force, is futile, and an utter impossibility. The standard of moral purity, of human nature, that is required to accomplish a revolution so sublime in our present make-up, is too far in the distance for human conception.

There is not a natural antagonism between capital and labor. To admit it to exist, is to admit that there is no Divine economy ruling the world affairs. Their relationship and interest are mutual. One cannot exist or

prosper without the aid and co-operation of the other. If a gulf divides,
and strife is engendered, it is because of a prejudicial investigation of
the cause and effect. The rule is general. Capital is covetous; labor is
prodigal. Capital seeks to gather in and increase its store, while labor
squanders its surplus to gratify superficial tastes. By the management of
their surplus or profits, as stated, capital becomes the stronger, and labor
the weaker power. They grow in opposite directions. Were labor more covetous with its surplus gains, as instanced in the examples of Vanderbilt,
Stewart, and Peter Cooper, of New York; John Hopkins, of Maryland, and a
thousand of other millionaires who commenced life with their brains and
hands, the relationship would be different. Capital would be more equalized.
And until labor learns to be more generally frugal, hold what it gets, and
judiciously invest it, this inequality will forever exist, and no combination that can be formed by the wisdom and cunning of man can control it.

Because of the incapacity and financial weakness of labor and its only
source of revenue--a day's wages--millions of laborers are the absolute
slaves of capital, receiving a pittance of the wealth their labor produces.
And even the honest, industrious, and frugal laborer often receives less
wages than will provide the necessary comforts of life. And very often the
capital employed, by which this labor draws its substance, produces this financial embarrassment of the laborer; for capital is often destitute of
brains. As for instance, in the cotton-growing States, nearly every planter
this year sowed his fields with cotton, expecting, when reaped, without any
ability to control the market, to sell for twenty cents per pound, instead,
it brought but from twelve to fourteen cents. In this margin, between fourteen and twenty cents lie their entire substance, and replenishing of stock
for the next year's working of the farm. It is very easy to see the disadvantage, in this case, to which both labor and capital is put. Thousands of
laborers are robbed of their wages. The land is bare of subsistence, save
wood and cotton, and neither will prevent starvation. This is produced by
the cupidity of capital in the South.

Another instance is the competition between manufacturers on account of
the excess of manufactories for the demand of their products. Not only is
the price of the material reduced to the lowest point between its cost of
production and its marketable value, but the wages of the laborer is reduced
to a point of starvation and desperation, which often results in strikes.
Could there be a corresponding reduction in all the productions or necessaries of life at the same time, then the laborer of a particular branch of industry (in which there is an active competition between capital) may be able
to subsist at the reduction of wages forced upon him; or could the laborer
subsist entirely upon the production of his *own skill,* the same result may
be obtained. But the political economy of the world furnishes us with no
such rule or example. In our immediate observation or history the products
of one branch of industry may decrease in value twenty-five per cent, while
the products of another branch, of more general necessity and consumption,
may at the same time increase twenty-five per cent; and the decline in the
former be the cause of the advance in the latter.

It is but natural that labor should seek (under such circumstances) to
relieve itself from the rapid fluctuations of capital and put itself in a
safe position that it may be able to demand and command a compensation that
will afford it an independent living.

Trades' Unions and Strikes

Trades' unions and other combinations are formed for the purpose of advancing the claims and protecting the interests of the workmen. Unfortunately, by the unwise counsel of brainless leaders, *strikes* are the first
means resorted to as a remedy. Very few instances, if any, can be cited
that strikes have produced any permanent good to the strikers; whilst hundreds of instances can be referred to where they have been disastrous in the
loss of time and money, to all parties, and the bankruptcy and dissolution
of some of the best workingmen organizations in the country. When labor
challenges capital to battle, capital is generally the victor. For strikes
to be at all successful, a combination of all the workmen of a particular
branch of industry must be effected extending over every locality where said
trade is conducted, and be provided with a fund sufficient to pay the rate

of wages demanded during the continuance of the strike. Otherwise it is
folly to attempt the experiment.

The Labor Reform Party

as a means for the elevation of the condition of the workingmen, and to adjust the disputed questions between capital and labor, is a grand farcical
clap-trap, cunningly worked upon the unwary workingmen by intriguing politicians, and is even more disastrous to their cause than the numerous ill-advised strikes.

Its pretentions to a wholesale process to elevate the condition of the
laboring masses to a financial equality with capital, by getting control of
the national and local legislation of the country, is as deceptious and preposterous as the heathen philosophy of producing gold by chemical operation.
Whilst labor has a general interest to be protected by national legislation,
such as a national education law, land grants to actual settlers, and a tariff for protection to American industries, it also has certain special interests, the chief of which is *wages,* in all the varied industries of the
country, which cannot be regulated by any political legislative body that
can be brought into existence.

Rights of Labor to Organize

What is wanting by the laboring men of the country is a fair exchange
for their labor. *Money,* that they can comfortably and independently provide
a living for themselves and families, and have a surplus for an emergency
and old age. To satisfy this demand of labor is to adjust the relationship
between capital and labor and solve the problem.

If labor has any rights that capital is bound to respect, it has a perfect right to be heard through any legitimate organ or organization that does
not trespass upon the legal rights of capital, endanger the principles of our
republican form of government, or the public security.

It has the same right to organization for the protection that the merchant or manufacturer has to form boards of trade and exchanges to promote
their interest. The necessity and practicability of labor organizations for
the material advancement of the workingmen, all reasonable-minded men will
conside. It is but the duty of the laboring men to adopt that form of organization separate and distinct from politics, that will more readily meet
capital in a fair and equitable race.

Co-operative Labor Organizations

seem to be the most effective form of organization to accomplish this result.
The concentration of a certain portion of the weekly earnings for the purpose
of forming capital with which to establish a business in the event capital
will not concede living wages to the laborer. The several co-operative associations in this country are in a flourishing condition; not only are they
paying good wages, but paying a good percentage on the capital invested. In
one instance the dividends upon the capital invested is appropriated to the
purpose of furnishing a homestead for the members of the organization. A
preference is often given these associations by business men because of the
very superior workmanship found in these establishments. Co-operative associations produce these results:

First. They secure the wages demanded by labor, which is the bone of
cooperation.

Second. They are practicable tools for those mechanics and laborers
who are ambitious to become capitalists.

Third. They teach the workingmen the offices, duties, responsibilities,
and make of capital, and how to respect it.

Fourth. They force habits of frugality, temperance, and economy in the
circle of their membership.

Fifth. They impress the members with the importance of an advanced education for their children.

Sixth. They restore order and harmony, and give a fair chance of competition between capital and labor. Next to co-operative associations for
the general advancement of the condition of the workingmen, as well as to
aid them and all other forms of labor organizations, a

Bureau of Industry

should be established in every city in the United States, composed of representives from all industrial and trade organizations, who should meet once a week for the purpose of interchanging opinions, discussing plans of organization, accumulating statistics in relation to workingmen, trades, etc., and passing upon questions of dispute between employer and employee. This Bureau of Industry will be to the laborer what the Bureau of Trade or Chamber of Commerce is to the merchant. Here capital and labor can be brought face to face. The cause for a reduction of wages, or the reasons for an advance, can be dispassionately discussed and amicably adjusted.

In most cases where strikes have existed, and great losses sustained by the contending parties, it is because of the failure or indisposition to submit the dispute questions to a board of arbitration.

Next to co-operation for the elevation of the workingmen is the

Tariff for the Protection of American Industry.

On this national question there should be no division between the laboring men of the United States. It is alike beneficial to all interests that do not receive their support from importing goods of foreign manufacture without any consideration of their effect upon home industry. It is suicidal to the labor interests of this country to support any party or policy looking to a *free trade* in the books of foreign manufacture. Not only must such a policy reduce the wages of American workmen to the standard of European wages, but our industries, vast factories and workshops, that are brought in such unequal competition--their products must be forced out of the markets of the world, thereby reducing the demand, as well as the price of labor.

National Education

This is a question in which the workingmen are more directly interested than any other class of citizens. The rich can be educated at pleasure, without feeling the pressure of pecuniary embarrassment. The poor, who stand more in need of education, as a means for their elevation, must rely mainly upon a free-school system. The opposition to popular education comes chiefly from that class of American citizens who would build up an aristocratic empire, whose footstool would be free trade, ignorance and slavery to the common people. The opposition is not to such a question of taxes or taxation as the objection to educated labor--a class of labor that wants comfortable surroundings, that will not submit to serfdom that is incapable of self-support, independent, inventive, and enterprising.

A system of national education will not only prove a national blessing, but a national necessity at this time. The future peace and security of the Government will be infinitely indebted to a national system of education for the youths of the present generation.

To the common people who make up the working classes it is the manna of Heaven. Appeals and petitions should be sent, as with the raising of a mighty wind, to the halls of Congress until the Congress of the United States gives the country a national school law that will put school-houses and the privileges of a common English education within sight of every poor man's domicile in the land.

"Capital and labor must be both sole and willing to see and consider each other's interests. Make all of either class able to read--able to discriminate correctly between right and wrong--render intelligence and [truth] supreme in deciding their questions of individual interest; lift them up, so that the horizon of each will embrace the interest of all, and the folly and wickedness of an appeal to force or fraud on either hand, will be too apparent to invite the attempt. They would then see how much they have in common, how closely and inseparably they are yoked together. Education, in its large sense; the development of all the powers of man for the best use offers for each the grand instrument for the solution of the difficulties."
. . . .

The unions established by the bureau are generally in a flourishing condition. If their delegates do not arrive to this annual meeting it is because of the great financial embarrassment existing in the Southern States;

but a more effective organization will materially relieve this condition of the laborers.

I need not tell you who are from the Southern States of the

Insecurity of Life in the South,

and its effect upon industry; the fearful reign of terror that in large portions of Kentucky, Tennessee, Georgia, North and South Carolina, Florida, Alabama, Louisiana, Mississippi, and Texas exists at this time. There is little or no value placed upon human life, if it be a negro.

Emigration and Education

seem to be the only means that can raise the condition of the South to the level with other sections of the country. Three millions of foreign emigrants in the Southern States would produce a spirit of independence and enterprise that is absolutely necessary to elevate the condition of labor, both black and white, and to induce and give security to capital. Provision should also be made for the calling of State labor conventions in States at as early a day as is convenient for the people to assemble in their respective counties and send delegates to represent them. Politics should be left entirely out of these conventions, and the business interests of the people considered. We hope to have the co-operation of all classes of the community, because it is to the benefit of all interests to make labor honest, intelligent, economical, and enterprising. There is no desire, upon our part, to have separate organizations based upon color. We believe the condition of the white laborers will be materially advanced by a co-operation with the colored laborers.

New National Era, January 19, 1871.

5. THE NATIONAL LABOR CONVENTION

Any assemblage of [labor], whether large or small, learned or ignorant, if animated by a high moral purpose, is worthy of respectful consideration; and we think the convention above-named possessed this claim to respect in a pre-eminent degree. It was a convention to assist in improving the condition of a class of laborers who, in addition to great social wrongs, are at the same time the least remunerated of all other classes in the country. The recently emancipated slaves are the most destitute of all the laboring classes of the country. They have no past but the past of slavery--the most barren past that it is possible to contemplate. It is a past in which nothing whatever is done for posterity. In its selfish regard for present advantage and gratification, the system treated its victims as a class having no future. The master had in his slave only so much bone and muscle, out of which he could obtain so much work, and he set about getting that amount of work out of him, without any regard to him as a man, a husband, a father, or a member of society. The slave was simply an instrument for the present. Being property himself, he could own no property. He did not own even the miserable shirt on his back, or the peck of corn allowed him per week. In this condition of destitution he lived and died, and was buried at night, without funeral rites, lest a few working minutes should be lost to the master. It was in this destitute condition that emancipation found the whole slave population. The past had robbed him of property, of education, and of everything but his human nature and its absolute wants, and he was compelled to face the present and future in utter poverty. The land on which he had worked belonged not to him who in sweat and blood had earned it, but to him who was clothed in purple and fine linen, and fared sumptuously every day, and whose hands knew no toil. The wretched hut that sheltered him and his little ones belonged not to him, but to the man who formerly owned him and his children.

The Government, in giving the negro his freedom, has given him the freedom to starve, and in giving him the ballot-box has given him a coffin.

It meant well enough to the negro, but the result has been terrible indeed. It attempted to make men free, but withheld the only conditions upon which they can be so. It has attempted to make men independent voters, but left them a prey to conditions which, in many cases, makes such voting impossible. It has attempted to make them loyal to the Government, but has left them where they are compelled to look to their rebel masters for their very existence.

It is in the light of this state of facts that the late labor convention assembled in this city to consider ways and means by which to benefit the colored laboring classes; and it does appear that the convention had good cause for assembling. It may not have succeeded in its object, to any considerable extent, but it, at least, has shown a sense of the necessity of doing something, and doing that something speedily. There was in the convention, at least, the motive and the will to do, however feeble or ill-advised may have been their measures. Something is gained where men feel; something more is gained where they think, and something still greater is accomplished when they resolve to act. All three of these signs of life were given in the late convention; and hence, small as the convention was, and feeble and imperfect as may have been its purposes, we do not regret that it was held. It was a movement in the right direction, and one which may prove the beginning of an important movement for the improvement and advantage of our suffering class.

There was much more ability in the convention than even we expected to find there; and, what is perhaps still more important, there was much more heart in the object to be gained. The colored people of the South have had little practice in the holding of conventions. There was general harmony, and differences of opinion and feeling were exceptional and temporary. Professor JOHN MERCER LANGSTON felt called upon to criticise Mr. ISAAC MYERS, the ex-president of the convention, for his relation to the National Labor Convention in Cincinnati last year, alleging that that convention was, in fact, a mere tender to the Democratic party, and that Mr. MYERS had, by entering and acting with that organization compromised the cause of justice and freedom; but this was a mere shadow on the otherwise undisturbed current of the convention, and even this was generously lifted when Mr. LANGSTON voted for a resolution declaring Mr. MYERS a devoted and consistent Republican, thus showing that his criticisms of Mr. MYERS were the outgrowth of his love of discussion, rather than any thought that Mr. MYERS had greatly sinned in doing what was charged upon him; or, better still, the occasion gave him a chance to send a rattling volley into the camp of his Democratic enemies. At this point the remarks of Mr. HARRIS were admirable. He showed the difference between Mr. LANGSTON and Mr. MYERS to have been simply this: the latter was admitted to the Cincinnati Convention, and the other, for personal reasons, was not. So that, morally, the one had no cause to complaint against the other.

A very bright man came to us, from old Virginia, in the person of Mr. TAYLOR. This man was cut out by nature for important parts--one of the few black men whose mind slavery itself could not extinguish. Old Virginia has been famous for great white men, and it may yet become equally so for great colored men. This Mr. TAYLOR is without education, in the technical sense of the word, but, if a knowledge of men and the possession of the power to wield his knowledge to wise purposes be education, Mr. T. is quite a liberally educated man.

Among the delegates who came here from the North and South, and from whom we are led to expect great results from their efforts in securing the amelioration of the condition of laboring men and women in the South, we find such earnest, energetic, and able men as EDWIN BELCHER, of Georgia; Hon. JAMES HARRIS, North Carolina; RICHARD NELSON, Texas; Mr. PATTERSON, Arkansas; GEORGE L. MABSON, North Carolina; W. V. TURNER, Alabama; JAMES T. RAPIER, Alabama; ROBERT STOKES, Missouri; BISHOP J. W. LOGUEN, New York; ANTHONY BOWEN, District of Columbia; GEORGE T. DOWNING, Rhode Island; JOHN M. LANGSTON, Ohio; GOERGE DEBABTISTE, Michigan.

We publish in another column some of the more important papers passed upon at the convention.

New National Era, January 19, 1871.

6. SOUND POLICY

We are among those who think the National Labor Union Convention of Colored Men, recently held in this city, did several wise things, and that its influence will be fraught with much good in the future. There were many practical, common-sense ideas set afloat, that will spring up and produce good fruit, if honestly acted upon, to the laboring men of this country. But we believe the wisest, most practical, and common-sense measure adopted was the proposition that a high protective tariff is not only a financial but an *industrial* necessity in the present condition of the country, and therefore urging the Republican party to adopt it as a part of their creed. We believe this was a wise, practical, common-sense position for a convention of laboring men to take, because nothing will so surely create a demand for labor and ensure it a just reward as liberal, generous protection to all branches of American industry.

There are now a million laborers engaged in manufactures and mechanical pursuits. The repeal of the tariff which has nursed into existence the establishments that give employment to this mighty army of workingmen, would break down one-half of them at least, and throw half of them out of employment. These half a million of men would therefore, of necessity, be brought into direct and ruinous competition with other laborers. The result would be a great reduction in price of labor, and could not fail to prove more disastrous to them than to the manufacturers themselves. On the other hand, a protective tariff will not only prevent this dire calamity as well to the laboring man as the whole country, but it will gradually add to our manufacturing enterprises, and increase the demand for our laborers till their number is doubled. Every new manufacturing enterprise gives employment to more persons and increases the wages of labor, just in proportion as the demand for it increases. The members of this convention had ability to see this and the courage to recommend the measure best calculated to bring about such a result. They had no nonsense about "a tariff with incidental protection," "a revenue tariff," "revenue reform," and such like clap-trap stuff for gulls. They believed a high protective tariff would call into existence new manufacturing enterprises and create a new demand for labor. They therefore said so, in terms that no one could mistake. For their shrewdness and frankness they deserve the thanks of all friends of American industry.

New National Era, January 26, 1871.

7. THE NATIONAL LABOR CONVENTION

Special to the National Standard

WASHINGTON, D.C., Jan. 11, 1871
The Colored National Labor Convention met here on the 10th inst, and is still in session. Though most of the States are represented, the number of delegates present is considerably less than last year. Several colored men of ability, members of the Southern Legislatures, are among the delegates, also Hon. Wm. B. Turner, representative elect to the XLIst. Congress. Several Committees, entrusted with the business of the Convention, have prepared reports of much value, the substance of which we shall hope to present to our readers hereafter. Addresses have been delivered by the President, Mr. MYERS, of Baltimore; FREDERICK DOUGLASS, Hon. JAMES H. HARRIS, of North Carolina; SUSAN B. ANTHONY, GEORGE T. DOWNING, Esq., EDWARD M. DAVIS, Col. R. J. HINTON, AARON M. POWELL, GILES B. STEBBINS, Rev. A. BOWEN, ROBERT PURVIS, and others. Though not political in its character, the facts presented in the addresses and reports of the condition and needs of the colored workingmen and women of the South are of a most important character, showing conclusively that "Reconstruction" is far from complete, in assuring independence and actual personal freedom and safety to colored citizens. [56]

National Standard, January 14, 1871.

8.   EDITORIAL CORRESPONDENCE

WASHINGTON, D.C., Jan. 14, 1871

The National Labor Convention

The National Labor Convention which has been in session in this city since Monday last adjourned yesterday. The attendance, compared with former years, has been moderate. . . . Reports were made and resolutions adopted to the subjects of Homesteads, Co-operation, Capital and Labor, Education, personal insecurity and political proscription in the Southern States, Temperance, and other topics of vital interest to the colored and white workingmen and women of the country.

Edward M. Davis, of Philadelphia, was in attendance as a delegate, and presented to the Convention an excellent plan, already in successful operation in the vicinity of Philadelphia, for co-operative building associations. It was listened to with much interest and heartily endorsed by the Convention. Mr. Davis also offered a resolution which was adopted, asking the government to appoint a commission to be composed of well-known Anti-Slavery men, to visit the Southern States and to report as to the actual condition and needs of the loyal people, colored and white, of the South. Mr. Davis has recently returned from a Southern tour, and is deeply impressed with the importance of giving to the people of the North such information as the resolution offered by him seeks and would provide for. The condition of many of the colored laborers, especially of the rural districts of the South, is indeed forlorn. They make contracts with rebel land-holders, and work for wages, but in the absence of national protection are intimidated, and defrauded in a most shameful, wholesale manner. The bitter fruits of the "magnanimity" policy towards rebels, the colored and loyal white people of the South are compelled now to reap a harvest of. But the whole country is inevitably to be seriously affected thereby. Under the prevalent reign of terror which the reinstated wealthy rebels have inaugurated through the agency of the Ku-Klux, the South is likely to become again at no distant day substantially a political unit. When this objective point is reached, in alliance with the Northern Sham-Democracy, the excessively "magnanimous" Republican party will be forced to surrender its possession of the national government. The consequences to the colored people in particular, and to the nation at large, of such a political transition it is not difficult to foresee. Fortunate would it have been for all classes if the wise and statesmanlike counsels of Wendell Phillips and Thaddeus Stevens in favor of the confiscation of rebel estates and the policy of small homesteads for the freedpeople and landless poor of the South had been adopted by Congress at the proper time.[57]

It was the concurrent testimony of all the Southern delegates in the Convention that the first and primary need of the colored laborers of the South is personal protection. Landless and dependent as they are, the ballot is to many of them little better than a mockery of freedom. One good result of the Convention will be to disseminate more widely information as to the peculiar perils and trials of the Southern colored workingmen and women. The Caste spirit, too, bears heavily upon Northern colored laboring people--fostered by members of some of the white labor organizations. Afffecte by all the disabilities and the injustice against which white laborers protest, they have also added thereunto the proscriptive influence which in many cases excludes them from workshops simply on account of complexional difference.

Frederick Douglass was chosen President of the National Labor Union for the ensuing year, and it was voted to hold the next Annual Meeting in Columbia, South Carolina, to commence on the second Monday in January, 1872.

National Standard, January 21, 1871.

THE THIRD COLORED NATIONAL LABOR UNION CONVENTION

9. ADDRESS

Reported by the Committee on Addresses, the Hon. ROBERT B. ELLIOTT, *Chairman, to the National Colored Convention held at Columbia, S.C., and by that Body issued to the People of the United States.*

FELLOW CITIZENS: . . .
         In seeking more perfect recognition as members of the great political family to which the interests of humanity have been peculiarly committed, .we desire to recognize our obligations and responsibilities as members of this great family, and to assure the American people that we stand among them imbued with a national spirit--with confidence in and devotion to the principles of representative popular government, and with ideas of policy that embrace every individual and interest of our common country.
         The fruits of the great legal measures that were intended to establish our rights and interests on a common footing with all other citizens of the nation, have, to some extent and in particular locations, been withheld from us by the prejudices and passions left in the hearts of a portion of our fellow citizens as a remnant of former ideas and associations. We need your aid and sympathy to complete the great work begun and carried on in our behalf. We desire to lay before you the facts of our case in a brief but truthful statement. We have not at command the all-important instrument of a local public press, as the medium of communicating with you; the press of the South, with few exceptions, being in the hands of those interested to lower us in your esteem. We have deemed a convention of our representatives as the most efficient means of laying before you the true state of our condition and feeling.
         Since the close of the war a settled policy has controlled the public and private action of the great body of the white people of the South towards us. They have sought to hold us in a condition of modified servitude, so that we should not be able to compete with the industry of the country. They have not been contented to employ the advantages that capital and experience in public and private affairs confer, but have resorted to compulsory means, unsanctioned by the laws of the country, the spirit of American institutions, and the practice of cilivized nations.
         The first great effort to carry into effect this line of policy was perhaps most conspicuously displayed in the adoption of the code of laws commonly known as the "Black Code," passed by the provisional government of South Carolina, in the year 1865, and followed by other States. It is unnecessary to give in detail the features of this system. It established *caste* of the Oriental type. It furnished courts for the trial of questions of *caste*. It provided for legal compulsion as a means of procuring our labor, and fixing the rates of compensation and rules of performance. It provided separate laws--civil and criminal--and separate courts for their enforcement. Finally, it allowed us no voice in the passing of the laws that were to govern us, or hand in disposing of the proceeds of our labor taken from us as taxes for the support of the governments of our respective States. [58]
         The action of the military authorities, followed by that of Congress, and, finally, the amendments to the Constitution of the United States, took from the hands of those seeking to establish a system of slavery scarcely less objectionable than that which had just been overthrown, the means of accomplishing their purpose through the forms of law.
         The next resort was to subsidize and control, through the motives of favor and fear, the political and civil powers conferred by the liberality of the Government. On the one hand, the friendship and patronage of the white citizens were offered as the condition of complete political subserviency, while on the other hand threats of being deprived of homes and employment as the means of subsistence, were made by the landholders and employers of our respective States. These threats were in many instances carried into effect.

It was found, however, that the necessity that existed for our labor left in our hands power sufficient to thwart the efforts for our subjection.

To meet this new difficulty resort was had to secret organizations, with a view to the control of the masses of the colored people by the murder of the prominent representative men of our class, and by the infliction of bodily pain upon a certain number of their followers. As the means proposed involved the commission of the highest crimes known among men, the protection of oaths, secret organizations and disguises were resorted to. We have been hunted like beasts by armed and disguised bands. Many, both men and women, have been killed; vast numbers have received severe corporal punishment; and many more found shelter in the swamps, by day and by night, from this storm of human hatred.

We owe it to ourselves and to our government to acknowledge the well directed efforts that are now being made to bring the perpetrators of these crimes to justice. We are assured that the American people are in earnest to secure to us the fruits of the great measures for our civil and political habilitation, and that the Executive and judicial departments of the Government are thoroughly sincere in their determination to give effect to the Constitution and the will of Congress in our behalf.

We ask of you that you will give to the Government the fullest measure of moral support to enable it to complete that which is so auspiciously begun, and that minor differences of sentiment and policy may be hushed while the nation is gathering up its strength to purge the land of the foulest crimes by the sword of justice. When the nation was threatened with division, political differences yielded to the necessity of maintaining its territorial integrity. Now that it is again threatened from the vertex of passion and crime affiliated, let the same devotion to right and justice induce equal efforts to preserve its moral integrity.

While there remains anything to be accomplished in order to secure for ourselves the full enjoyment of civil and political rights, we shall have class interests calling for the united efforts of persons of color. The moment these ends are secured, the motives for separate action will cease, and, in common with all other citizens, we can take our places wherever the interest of the government, industry or humanity may appoint--recognizing only one standard of duty, interest or policy for all citizens.

We do not ask the government or people of the United States to treat us with peculiar favor, but that, in the policy of the laws, our interest may be grouped with those that receive the consideration of our legislative bodies, and that, in the administration of the laws, no invidious distinctions be made to our prejudice.

We affirm that the colored people of the States represented by us have no desire to strike out a line of policy for their action involving interests not common to the whole people.

While we have, as a body, contributed our labor in the past to enhance the wealth and promote the welfare of the community, we have as a class been deprived of one of the chief benefits to be derived from industry, namely: the acquisition of education and experience, the return that civilization makes for the labor of the individual. Our want in this respect not only extends to general education and experience, such as fits the man to adorn the society of his fellows, but to that special education and experience required to enable us to enter successfully the departments of a diversified industry.

We ask that your Representatives in Congress may be instructed to afford such aid in extending education to the uneducated classes in the States we represent as may be consistent with the financial interests of the nation. Although we urge our unrequited labors in the past as the ground of this appeal, yet we not seek these benefits for ourselves alone, but for the white portion of the laboring class in our States, whose need is as great as ours.

In order to secure the promotion of our industrial interest, you can render us assistance. It is true we have no demands to make of the National Government in this respect; but it is in the power of the people of the United States to aid us materially. In order to advance our knowledge and skill in the industrial arts, it is necessary that we should have the advantages of the means employed in the country at large for these purposes. That in preparing for industrial pursuits and in putting our skill in operation, we should come in contact with educated and experienced workmen and be put in

possession of the results of their skill and knowledge. If the trades and
workshops are shut against us, we cannot reach that point of excellence to
which we desire to attain. We ask your aid and sympathy in placing us on the
same footing in reference to the pursuit of industry as that enjoyed by other
citizens. If after having access to the means of becoming skillful workmen,
we fail to attain that standing, we are content to take rank among the industrial classes of the country according to the degree of our proficiency.
Should we be excluded from these benefits, a state of things will arise, most
prejudicial to the interest of skilled labor, namely: the existence of a
great body of workmen ready to supply the market with poor work, at cheap
rates. While slavery existed, the Northern States were not affected by the
low state of the industrial arts in the Southern States; but labor being now
free to find the best market, it is, beyond question, the interest of the
artificers of the North to raise the standard of proficiency at the South.
It is clearly the interest of the great industries of the North to strengthen
themselves by alliance with those at the South. This result would be practicable to the fullest extent, if those of our color throughout the North could
be placed in a position to bring among us the best knowledge and skill in the
departments of trade to which they belong.

   We would do injustice to ourselves, if, forgetting our own personal indebtedness for the blessings of liberty, and the pursuit of independence and
happiness, to that outgrowth of Christian civilization, the benignant spirit
of our country and century, we should pass unnoticed the condition of those
of our race who are still in the state of slavery. The public sentiment of
this great nation combined with that of Europe, with the good offices of our
Government, is surely sufficient to hasten the abolition of African slavery
throughout the world. We sincerely trust that expression may be given to
such sentiment as will attract the attention and influence the conduct of
those few remaining nations that still maintain slavery as a legal institution.

   It is our privilege, in addressing you, to utter the voice of four millions of citizens of this great country. That voice is addressed to those
whose humane feelings rendered practicable that consummate act that elevated
so vast a body at once to the enjoyment of civil and political manhood. It
is not too much to anticipate that partiality for the work that owes its legal completion to you, will influence you to watch carefully the development
of its practical results; that no perversion from the purposes of your bounty
shall prevent the full fruition of the great principles of justice that actuated you.

   The growth of this nation has shown that its institutions are capable of
blending into an harmonious brotherhood all nationalities and all interests
and industries. In all other instances than that of the accession of our
race to citizenship, the accretion of the elements of its population has been
gradual--giving time to complete the process of assimilation. In our case,
we are well aware that there was much to alarm the apprehensions of those
careful statesmen who hesitated to speculate as to the strength of our institutions much beyond what was demonstrated by the precedents in parallel cases
in Europe and in our own country. The instantaneous embodiment of four millions of citizens who had for years looked upon the government as not only
denying them citizenship, but as preventing them from acquiring that capacity
under any other national existence, was, it must be admitted, a startling political fact.

   But we are happy to point to the proof of the wisdom of those who regarded that course the safest that was indicated by the demands of justice.
We are proud to be able to point to the history of our people since their admission to citizenship as proof that they understand what is due from the
citizen to the government owing him protection. Although they have suffered
much at the hands of those who would deprive them of their rights, they have
appreciated the difficulties and embarrassments that necessarily surrounded
the attempts of the government to vindicate their rights, and have waited
uncomplainingly until relief could be afforded; although many times they could
have found instantaneous relief by imitating their oppressors and taking the
law into their own hands.

   We would call attention to the fact that the conferring of citizenship
on our people, though the occasion, is not the cause of the agitations that

have affected the country. The true cause is the spirit of opposition to
whatever is enlarged and unselfish in our government, and that does not inure
to the exclusive interest of the privileged few which has seized upon the act
of the Government as a means of shutting out of the Southern States liberal
and national ideas.

We affirm, without fear of contradiction, that the colored citizens of
the United States have conducted themselves as good citizens and have displayed aptness to discharge their civil and political duties, as well as an
intuitive fitness for that form of Government which we justly regard as the
highest expression of civic wisdom.

Under these circumstances, and with the proofs of the truth of our
statement abundant on every hand we ask your fullest confidence and sympathy.
We cannot point to the work of our fathers as commingled with that of yours
in the noble structure of Government we all delight to admire and to guard,
but we can claim to have embodied their animating spirit as displayed in our
devotion to the truths that they inculcated and our zeal to render their work
immortal and imperishable.

With this brief presentation of our views and feelings, we beg to subscribe ourselves, in behalf of those we represent, very respectfully, your
humble fellow citizens, and obedient servants,   ROBERT B. ELLIOTT,
                                                   JAS. M. SIMMS,
                                                   RICHARD NELSON,
                                                   J. T. WALLS,
                                                   ISAAC MYERS,
                                                   B. A. BOSEMON,
                                                   F. C. ANTOINE,
                                                   J. F. QUARLES,
                                                   F. G. BARBADOES.

National Standard, November 11, 1871.

10.   THE OTHER SIDE

One of our exchanges contains the following:

Congressman Elliott, of South Carolina, has submitted an address to the
American people asking for "more perfect recognition of the colored people in
the workshops and all industrial pursuits, that they may become proficient in
mechanical sciences and thereby protect skilled artisans from having to compete in the market with workmen of inferior capability."

The first step for the colored race to take to receive a "more perfect
recognition in the workshops and all industrial pursuits," is for them to
throw themselves on their own resources; to discard the advise of those har-
pies, who presuming on their credulity and ignorance, have ridden into place
and power on their shoulders, and who have striven ever since to sow the
seeds of prejudice against the white mechanic. So long as this advice prevails, so long will an antagonism exist.

The National Labor Union has always been opposed to dodging the "negro"
issue by any of our trades or labor organizations believing that ultimately
the colored race, like every other, must stand on their own merits; that if
they shall prove themselves capable of competing with white labor, no legislation can or should keep them down; while on the other hand, if they are
tried and found wanting, no class legislation can maintain them in a false
position.

The National Labor Union is and ever has been opposed, alike from motives of principle and policy, to any unjust discrimination of race or color.
From principle, because it recognised the line of demarcation to be between
the man who, by physical or intellectual labor, contributes to the substantial wealth of the nation, and the man who lives on the product of others'
toil; from policy, because in view of the alarming and increasing power of
capital, it cannot afford to have a house divided against itself; because it
is only by *systematic organization and united effort* it can hope for success.

The action of the National Labor Congress at the Philadelphia session, in admitting colored delegates on terms of perfect equality with the white representatives, spoke volumes in favor of the honesty and earnestness of its members, though strange to say, this circumstance seems to have been over-looked by advocates of the Elliott stamp. The fact that a deep-rooted preju-dice against association with them had existed, and probably then existed in the minds of many, is the highest tribute which can be paid to their good faith, because it conclusively proved that they could and did rise superior to these prejudices, could sacrifice them on the altar of principle for the advancement of the common good.

But it must not be forgotten there are two sides to this question. The National Labor Union is extending the hand of fellowship, did so in the be-lief that it would be accepted in good faith; that the co-operation of the colored race would be secured thereby. It accepted the results as presented; it did not enquire into or discuss the motives which prompted Congress in conferring on them the franchise. It dealt with living issues. It recog-nized that their votes would strengthen or weaken the labor movement; that they would either become allies or enemies, and its subsequent action proved it alive to its interests and duty. It had no idea however, of extending special privileges to any class, of permitting the colored delegates to "run with the hounds and hide with the hare," while it required from the white delegates an implicit allegiance. It did not propose to allow one branch of its members to become the pillars of oppression, the stool pigeons of the very powers, whose aggressions it was organized to resist, and the other to or-ganize to give them battle. It expected from each an equal obligation, an honest, thorough co-operative effort. Unless this has been or can be secured it is needless to talk about a "more perfect recognition of their rights," &c. &c. They must learn to respect the rights of others first.

If they will look at the question for an hour, they must see the futil-ity of arraying themselves against the only class from whom they can expect any material aid; and the worse, than folly of re-arousing the prejudices which happily have been forgotten. The first step to do so, however, is as we have already stated, to think for themselves, to give a wide berth to the scallawags who are leading them to a path fraught with danger and ruin.

Workingman's Advocate, November 11, 1871.

11. SENATOR SUMNER TO THE COLORED MEN

The following letter from Senator Sumner was read at the Convention of Colored Men at Columbia, S.C., on the 23d ult.:

BOSTON, Oct. 12, 1871.

Dear Sir: I am glad that our colored fellow-citizens are to have a Conven-tion of their own. So long as they are excluded from rights, or suffer in any way on account of color, they will naturally meet together, in order to find a proper remedy, and since you kindly invite me to communicate with the Convention I make bold to offer a few brief suggestions.

In the first place, you must at all times insist upon your rights, and here I mean not only those already accorded, but others still denied, all of which are contained in equality before the law. Wherever the law supplies a rule, there you must insist upon equal rights. How much remains to be ob-tained you know too well in the experience of life. Can a respectable col-ored citizen travel on steamboats or railways or public conveyances generally without insult on account of color? Let Lieut. Gov. Dunn of Louisiana des-cribe his journey from New Orleans to Washington. Shut out from proper ac-commodation in the cars, the doors of the Senate Chamber opened to him, and there he found that equality which a railroad conductor had denied. Let our excellent friend, Frederick Douglass, relate his melancholy experience when within sight of the Executive Mansion, he was thrust back from the dinner table where his brother-commissioners were already seated. You know the out-

rage. I might ask the same question with regard to hotels, and even common
schools. A hotel is a legal institution, and so is a common school. As such,
each must be for the equal benefit of all. Now, can there be any exclusion
from her on account of color? It is not enough to provide separate accommodations for colored citizens, even if in all respects as good as those of
other persons; equality is not found in equivalent, but only in equality. In
other words, there must be no discrimination on account of color. The discrimination is an insult, and a hindrance, and a bar, which not only destroys
comfort and prevents equality, but weakens all other rights. The right to
vote will have new security when your equal right in public conveyances, hotels, and common schools is at last established; but here you must insist for
yourselves by speech, by citizens in the enjoyment of equal rights. Of this
there can be no doubt. Among the cardinal objects in education, which must
be insisted on, here again must be equality side by side with the alphabet.
It is in vain to teach equality if you do not practice it. It is in vain to
recite the great words of the Declaration of Independence, if you do not make
them a living reality. What is lesson without example? As all are equal at
the ballot-box, so must all be equal at the common school. Equality in the
common school is the preparation for equality at the ballot-box; therefore,
do I put this among the essentials of education. In asserting your own rights
you will not fail to insist upon justice to all, under which is necessarily
included purity in the Government. Thieves and money-changers, whether Democrats or Republicans, must be driven out of our temple. Tammany Hall and
Republican self-seekers must be overthrown. There should be no place for
either. Thank God! good men are now coming to the rescue. Let them, while
uniting against corruption, insist upon equal rights for all, and also the
suppression of lawless violence wherever it shows itself, whether in the Ku-
Klux-Klan outraging the South, or illicit undertakings outraging the Black
Republic of Hayti. To these inestimable objects add Specie Payments, and you
will have a platform which ought to be accepted by the American people. Will
not our colored fellow-citizens begin this good work? Let them at the same
time save themselves and save the country. These are only hints which I submit to the Convention, hoping that its proceedings will tend especially to
the good of the colored race. Accept my thanks and best wishes and believe
me, faithfully yours,   CHARLES SUMNER.

National Anti-Slavery Standard, November 4, 1871.

12. THE LABOR CONVENTION

      We have received, but have not had room to publish, a two or three col-
umn "brief" presentation of the claims of the colored laborers. It emanated
from a convention recently held at Columbia, South Carolina, the enterprising
Justice Nelson being the Texas delegate. Of all the black men in Texas Justice Nelson was the fittest to represent the working men of color, for he is
the hardest worker among men. His hands are horny with toil. He works like
a blacksmith from sun up to sun down, and knows all about earning the bread
that he eats in the sweat of his brow. Well, Justice Nelson went to South
Carolina representing his over-worked brethren, who generously contributed of
their hard-earned means to send him there. He comes back with a "two column
brief presentation," though we are utterly unable to guess of the way in which
it shall be made to benefit them.
      The doings of the convention were not altogether satisfactory to General
Grant, seeing that he is reported to have footed the bills. With regard to
the annexation of St. Domingo they resolved to approve it as an "abstract
question," but provided that they must not be understood "as casting any reflection on that great and good man, Hon. Charles Sumner." On the whole we
conclude that the convention was harmless, and afforded colored men who don't
labor, a nice little trip and a pleasant time at the expenses of the colored
men who do labor.

Galveston (Texas) News, December 1, 1871.

IV

STATE BLACK LABOR CONVENTIONS

STATE AND LOCAL BLACK LABOR MEETINGS

As the CNLU turned more and more to political action, it was inevitable that the organization would become inextricably linked to the Republican Party. The CNLU itself did not meet again after its joint convention with the Southern States Convention of Colored Men at Columbia, South Carolina, in October 1871.

Although the political events which hastened the demise of Radical Reconstruction in the South also helped to seal the CNLU's downfall, politics alone does not explain the demise of the black organization. It is difficult to see how the Union's failure could have been avoided. Most southern Negroes were isolated and extremely poor, and where that fact did not retard organization, intimidation by hostile employers did. In the North skilled blacks could not find employment because of racial prejudice among both employers and white workers. The only realistic solution lay in effective organization of a unified black and white labor movement, but virulent racial prejudice rendered that course impossible. Black workers had no reliable allies even among their white working-class counterparts who, at their best, completely ignored blacks. White unions usually left discretion to their locals, while some openly excluded Negroes by constitutional mandate. The only course open to the CNLU was to support the Republican Party, which it felt "morally bound" to do. Thus the fate of the black workers was necessarily tied to the fate of the Republicans' southern policies, and when the party yielded its power to the white Redeemers, so did the CNLU.

Even though its life was short, the CNLU influenced the founding of numerous state labor organizations among blacks. Following the first convention in early 1870, Isaac Myers undertook an organizing trip for the union. In Richmond, Virginia, Myers helped launch a convention of workingmen to whom he underscored his belief that "the watchword of the colored men must be Organize" (Doc. 1). Myers spoke to similar audiences in other cities as well. His speeches, reported in the New National Era, the official organ of the CNLU, stimulated black workers to move forward aggressively in organizing local unions. In New York City, for example, black workers were making such headway that a call went out for a New York State Colored Labor Convention. The delegates made considerable progress at the convention, held in Saratoga on August 24, 1870, including the foundation of a State Bureau of Labor (Doc. 2-8).

The most significant spin-off organization established in the South, the Alabama Negro Labor Union, was founded by James Rapier. An officer in the CNLU, Rapier labored vigorously in Alabama to organize black workers in Alabama and represented the moving spirit in the state. After conferring with local black leaders, Rapier agreed to spearhead another state labor convention to consider "the working conditions of colored farmers in Alabama," possible sites where blacks might emigrate, and educational opportunities available for blacks in Alabama (Doc. 9). After a thorough investigation of these topics, about fifty black delegates from across the state gathered in Montgomery on January 2, 1872, to discuss their findings (Doc. 10).

The proceedings of the convention were presented in 1880 before a U.S. Senate Committee then investigating the causes of the Kansas Exodus of 1879, which is considered in Part IX of this volume. Little of the ANLU's history can be reconstructed, but apparently it was still active in November 1873, for the local white press took issue with some of its proceedings (Doc. 11-13).

STATE CONVENTIONS OF BLACK WORKERS

1. MASS-MEETING AT METROPOLITAN HALL
RICHMOND

Proposed Organization for the Benefit of the Mechanical Interest.

Pursuant to announcement published in the "Journal," a large concourse of our citizens, white and colored, assembled at Metropolitan Hall, April 11th.

The floor of the hall and galleries were literally crowded. It was estimated by these knowing the exact capacity of the hall that there were between 1,000 and 1,200 persons present, mostly mechanics, representing the various branches of industry.

The meeting was called to order shortly after eight o'clock, by Mr. Lewis Lindsey, who announced that the first business in order was the selection of officers.

Mr. Henry Cox, member of the Legislature, arose and nominated Mr. John Oliver for president of the meeting.

The nomination was received with enthusiastic applause.

Mr. Oliver came forward and after a graceful bow, said that he esteemed it an honor to have been elected President of the first laborer's meeting ever held in Richmond. He felt honored not only because it was a laborer's meeting, but because he was himself a laborer, being a carpenter. If there was anything he could do, it was to build a house. He believed sincerely that this meeting would meet with fruitful results. It was proposed, as he understood the purport of the call for this reunion to exclude politics. The colored people have had political meetings since the war and nothing good had been achieved. Let us now, said he, learn how to make home comfortable by associating ourselves upon a firmer basis than politics. We should hold meetings for the purpose of exchanging our views and devising the best means practicable for the protection of labor.

Mr. Oliver then read the names of the following Vice Presidents:

Robert Johnson, Charles Thurston, John Adams, Peter Woolfolk, A. R. Brooks, James Turner, Thomas Hewlett, Robert Shelton, Landon Boyd, Wm. Johnson, James Crump, James Carter, Richard Carter, Wm. Isham, Rev. James Holand, Rev. Wm. Troy, William Bartlett, Warner Lindsey, J. A. Taylor, Jos. Cox, H. L. Wigand, J. C. Gaguall, Jas. Morrisey, Wm. Leahey, Peter Stuart, Calvin Griffin and P. O. Brogan.

Secretaries.--Wm. H. Lester, R. L. Hobson, Jas. Bowser and Thos. P. Foley.

The names having been read, Mr. Lindsey said that to do justice to all parts of the country, he would nominate Wm. Bartlett as first Vice President. The nomination was carried unanimously.

It was then moved that the nominations as above read be received. This was also carried.

On motion of Lewis Lindsey, a committee of three, Messrs. J. A. Taylor, David Robertson, and Joseph Cox, was appointed by the chair as a finance committee.

On motion of Mr. Henry Cox, a committee on resolutions, consisting of Messrs. Lewis Lindsey, Robt. L. Hobson, and Wm. H. Lester, was appointed.

The chair requested the officers elected to come forward and take their places on the platform, which was forthwith complied with.

By request of the President, Rev. John Allen then offered a fervent and appropriate appeal to the Throne of Grace for the Divine support and countenance in the efforts then about to be initiated for the benefit of the laboring men.

While a collection was being taken up by the committee on finance, the assembly sang the beautiful hymn, "Blow ye the Trumpet, Blow."

Mr. Lindsey, in behalf of the Committee on Resolutions, then offered the following preamble and resolutions, which were by a unanimous vote, concurred in.

Whereas, By the blessing of Divine Providence, through the agencies of war and the great Republican party of the country, the colored men of Virginia have been released from long and cruel oppression, and invested with full civil and political rights; and whereas, it is the solemn duty of freemen to be grateful at all times to their deliverers, as is exemplified in the devotion of the American people to the illustrious Washington and his compeers; and whereas, all history has proved that the rights of individuals can best be secured and protected by thorough organization, either political or industrial; therefore, be it--

Resolved, That the thanks of the people of Richmond are due to President Grant, his Cabinet, and the Congress of the United States for the prompt legislation tending to complete the work of reconstruction in the South, without which the war and the constitutional amendments would have been absolute failures.

Resolved, That we endorse the National Labor Union of colored men, and appeal to the colored mechanics and laboring men of Richmond to call meetings of their respective branches of industry, for the purpose of immediate organization.

Resolved, That we believe that labor can only secure its rights and the respect due it, by organization, and that all men of whatever color, who oppose the systematized organization of labor, are enemies to the best interests of the working people.

Resolved, That we denounce all agents or agencies who have for their object the inducement of colored men to leave the State; and that we regard such persons as Democratic agencies, whose object is to reduce the Republican votes of this city, and give ascendancy to the Democratic party.

Resolved, That we advise, with a proper application of its importance, the colored men of Richmond against such dangerous demagogues; that their promises are false is evident from the testimony of the large number who have returned penniless from imaginary gold fields.

Resolved, That we advise the colored men of Richmond to be industrious, sober, honest, and true, and peace and plenty will soon enter within our borders and bring joy to the barren fields of this State; when labor and good wages will be found for the whole working people, without regard to race, color, or previous condition.

Resolved, That we endorse the NEW ERA as the national organ of the colored men of the United States, and pledge it our support, and advise our people throughout the State to form clubs and subscribe for it immediately.

After the adoption of the resolutions, on motion of Mr. Cox, Messrs. Edward Fox, James Johnson, and James Massey were appointed sergeants-at-arms.

The chair next introduced to the meeting Mr. Isaac Myers, of Baltimore, President of the National Labor Union of Colored Men, who spoke as follows:

I am happy to meet with you, although I see not more than one or two familiar faces. I am proud to say that I feel myself just as much at home as if I were in my native State. But yesterday we were in chains, deprived of a shadow of the rights of a man. To-day not a cord binds our limbs, and by the authority of the Magna Charta of our liberty--the Constitution of the United States of America--we are authorized to say, each man to his neighbor, we stand equally before the law as American citizens.

What we will be in the future depends entirely upon how we train and apply our minds, in every-day life, to the industrial, moral, religious, and political duties as free men and as citizens, having an equal proportion of the responsibilities of preserving and perpetuating free institutions and a republican form of government.

Each one of these duties which we owe to ourselves, our God, and our country, is a mill through which each man, woman, and child must be ground, and our market value depends upon how fine we come out at the other end. It is said that "the mills of the gods grind slow, but they grind very fine." So it necessarily must be with us as a class, who have been for the last two hundred years deprived of all the rights and privileges of education, and the advantages of accumulating capital. And as it must be slow, let it be extra fine, and when it comes out of the mill, let there be no necessity for its going back again.

Now to get money, man must have employment. And to possess money, if he is a mechanic or laborer, he must have sufficient pay for his labor when employed, as will afford, by temperate and economical living, to buy him a homestead, educate and comfortably clothe and feed his children, and have a few pennies laid by for old age. The value of your labor, then, is what it will cost you to do this, and not what a man or a combination of men would choose to pay you.

We wish to establish and preserve the most friendly relationship between labor and capital, because we believe their interests to be inseparable; because we believe and know in proportion as the laborer is remunerated for his labor, and encouraged in proportion is capital safe and productive. I know an establishment where the mechanics get three dollars and twenty-five cents a day, and so much per centage on all the work turned out. The result is, the shop turns out a third more work, with the same number of hands, than any other establishment of the same kind in the State, and so carefully is the interest of the employer protected, that he seldom visits the establishment.

How can labor be made respectable and productive and protect its rights? We answer, by being organized. By organization men can accomplish almost anything; but, without organization, they can accomplish comparatively nothing. Is there a necessity for the colored mechanics and laborers of the United States organizing? My answer is, there is the greatest necessity; and unless you do organize, in a few short years the trades will pass from your hands— you become the servants of servants, the sweeper of shavings, the scrapers of pitch, and the carriers of mortar.

And why do I make such a broad and positive assertion? It is because I find the white mechanics of the North and South organized for the extermination of colored labor and because I do not find the colored men organized for their protection; and because I know if you do organize you will preserve your labor, command employment, and educate your children in the trades.

Mr. Myers discussed at some length the importance of organization, and as an evidence of what men may do, he referred to the colored Ship Yard Company of Baltimore, and other similar organizations throughout the country. He spoke of the organization of a co-operative association of the carpenters, brick-masons, and plasterers of Richmond, to help the business men to build up the town. He regarded the business men of Richmond who conduct their business with so much prejudice and hate toward Northern men, and combining to prevent the flow of foreign capital useless, and every effort to arrest its progress would be as the little boy who laid under the wheel of Hercules, expecting to stop the car. He thought if the press of Richmond would stop fighting John W. Garrett, and the mine of Northern capital behind him, for building up their railroads and developing the resources of the State, and go in and buy up the stock themselves, encourage railroads all over and through the State, they would be fighting a point that they could carry; if they did not, Northern capital would build railroads all around the city in face of the Legislature, and draw off the trade from this city, as to bankrupt your merchants, and carry your city by greenbacks, as General Grant carried it by bullets.

He pressed upon the colored people the importance of habits of industry, frugality, and temperance. Spoke at length in support of the claim of the NEW ERA, a colored newspaper, edited in Washington, by Sella Martin and Frederick Douglass, and regarded as the national organ of the colored men of the United States.

He particularly enjoined upon his hearers to have confidence in each other and respect for each other, that in proportion as they had confidence in and respect for each other, in proportion would the white people of Richmond respect them.

Mr. Myers here excused himself from the labor question, and asked his hearers their indulgence. He said there were two things he could not understand, and he hoped some one in the city of Richmond would inform his clouded understanding. He could not understand how a colored man could vote the Democartic ticket, or how a Democrat could have the cheek to ask a colored man to vote the Democratic ticket. The Democrats say they have always been, and are now, the friends of the negro. He thought they had a very bad way of showing it. He generally proved his friends by their words. Now, if the Democrats, who say they are our friends, want us to have confidence in the sincerity of their friendship, let them come along with us to the polls on the third Tuesday in May and deposit a Republican ballot, and elect a Republican Mayor; unless they did that they are not our friends, and cannot be so long as they remain in the ranks of the Democratic party.

He said he did hear that Democratic negroes did live in Richmond in peace. He was very glad they were not in Baltimore. He said the legislation is class legislation, and that it was holding in check the prosperity of the State. The State should have a free railroad and a free school law. He claimed that the legislation and acts of the Democratic party looked very much like re-enslaving the negro and he believed that if they got full control of this Government, every negro in the land would be a slave in less than ten years. He advised the Republicans to stand united, and make their leaders stand united; and if they did not, why, throw them all overboard and lead yourselves. The party must forget the past and concentrate and look only to the future for success. Let by-gones be by-gones, and each and every man walk to the polls in May, and cast a solid vote for the Republican nominees.

At the conclusion of Mr. Myers' address speeches were made by Mr. Norton Cox and other members of the Legislature, and by Messrs. Lester and Lindsey, of this city, who strongly urged unity of action in the coming campaign, and severely denounced certain agents who are persuading the colored men to leave the State.

The following resolution was adopted:

Resolved, That our thanks are due the Evening State Journal for its able advocacy of the principles of the Republican party and the equal rights of all men before the law, without regard to race or color, and that we recommend its liberal patronage by our people.

On motion of Mr. Lindsey, a vote of thanks was tendered to such papers as have indorsed the cause of labor.

The New Era, April 28, 1870.

2. CALL FOR A NEW YORK STATE LABOR CONVENTION

In view of the urgan demands now pressing upon the people of all classes for a proper settlement of the conditions of labor in its various departments, and especially as relates to that portion of the people hitherto deprived of a fair apportionment of its benefits both as regards the employment of skilled labor and an opportunity to acquire a knowledge of the Mechanical branches --and in view too of the many avenues necessarily open for such acquirement and employment on the part of those who have controlled the admission of apprentices and workmen in the workshops of the State to the exclusion of the formerly disfranchised class, but now happily enfranchised; and in view too of the great demand for skilled as well as unskilled labor in the future altered and regenerated state of society in our now free State, and free country, the undersigned, impelled by motives of the highest consideration for the welfare and development of our whole country, and the enlarged privileges of every class, do invite a Convention of the colored citizens of our State, as well as others interested in the labor question, to assemble at Saratoga, New York, on Wednesday, the 17th of next August, for the purpose of adopting such views and plans, as shall not only bring out the needs of the people, but tend to enlarge the privileges and dignify the position of general labor.

We invite our brethren to assemble and bring with them statements of all persons engaged as artisans, mechanics, farmers, or any other industrial pursuits of whatever kind, in the several counties, also educational statistics, gathered from official or other sources as well as a list of workshops where workmen are admitted without distinction of color.

NEW YORK

William F. Butler, President of N. Y. L. O.
D. K. McDonough, Vice-President, F. L. I.

G. Lawrence, Jr., Editor of *The Enterprise,*
P. S. Porter, Esq.
N. H. Turpin.
Charles Reason.
Geo. W. Francis.
Stephen Lawrence.
Geo. A. Washington, Publisher of *The Enterprise.*
Peter H. Downing, Brooklyn, N. Y.
Theo. Gould,   "   "
J. N. Freeman,   "   "
J. N. Gloucester,   "   "
David Roselle, Brooklyn, E. D.
Peter Hawkins, Flushing, L. I.
F. Harley, Kingston, N. Y.
Wm. Rich and P. Baltimore, Troy.
Garet Deyo,   Hudson,
Lloyd Tilgham,   "
Anthony Jackson,   "
Wm. Jackson,   "
----Matthews,   "
Wm. Johnson,   "
J. C. Gilbert,   Sarotoga,
O. C. Gilbert,   "
J. W. Loymer,   "
J. P. Thompson, Newburgh.
Jacob Thomas   "
-----Pelham   "
C. E. Verning,   Poughkeepsie
Abram Bolin   "
Isaac Deyo   "
R. Watson   "

Wm. P. Powell. [59]
Jacob Stewart.
J. W. Bowers.
James M. Mars.
E. V. C. Eato.

The National Standard, July 30, 1870.

3. NEW YORK STATE COLORED LABOR CONVENTION

Reports of Committees--Statistics of Colored Labor--Second Day's Proceedings.
     SARATOGA, N. Y., Aug. 25.--The morning session of the State Labor Convention commenced at 10 o'clock. The first paper read was one from New-York, prepared by CHAS. S. REASON, on education, giving statistical facts connected with the schools of New-York City, Brooklyn and Williamsburg, and arguing in favor of education as one of the chief instrumentalities for making remunerative the labors of the working classes.

The Power of Money

     The Committee on Financial Questions presented a report. "The moneyed element of power should be fostered. It cannot take the place of character or education, but is next to them as a mighty power. It assists in carrying out benevolent designs, in building and furnishing institutions of learning, and in developing the mineral resources of the country. Out of the money deposited in the New-York savings banks, it is estimated that $4,000,000 belong to colored persons. Through the freedmen's savings institutions $13,000,000 have been saved by colored persons, while the same people in the South have expended $11,000,000 for business and social improvement. It is impossible for people to stand still; they must either go forward or recede. Though the fields of labor be opened ever so wide, and we enter and gather the fruits, if wanting in the duty of economy and knowledge of applying our gains, we shall not keep pace with the rest of the community. It is a duty to ourselves to labor, economize and think."

Labor Statistics

The Committee on Labor reported. After speaking of the labor problem as being as old as the Pyramids, and yet unsolved, the report regrets the absence of statistics relating to the industrial condition of the colored people. The nearest estimate that can be obtained is, that out of 18,000 colored males in the State in 1850, 2,000 were skilled laborers. Messrs. LEONARD JACKSON, S. J. STOKELY and W. H. DECKER were appointed a Committee on Statistics. On a call for a presentation of facts for the use of the Committee, Mr. GARNET said the Engineers' Protective Association of New-York knew of one hundred engineers, sixty of whom were engaged in saloons and other places in the City because they were unable to obtain employment at their trade, while only forty were working at their trade.

Rev. Mr. SWEARS presented a preamble and resolutions recommending trades and labor organizations.

SINCLAIR TOUSEY, of New-York, opposed the resolutions as leading to strikes and difficulties.

JACOB STEWARD deprecated such a construction of the resolution, and said there was something in labor unions besides strikes, and that something we desire. In answer to some speakers who had advocated humility, care and attention in the performance of work, Rev. Mr. BUTLER said, humility was all very well, and had been practiced for two hundred and fifty years; but the colored people gained more in a short time by taking the musket and shooting rebels than they did by a long practice of humility. He said that out of 3,500 colored voters in New-York City, 104 were shoe-makers, one hundred were engineers, and over eighty were carpenters, with other skilled mechanics, a majority of whom were kept out of the trades' work from class prejudices. One skilled engraver was obliged to work as a waiter, because other engravers refused to work with him. The speaker had been asked to procure colored persons to work in factories by manufacturers, who offered employment if enough colored hands could be obtained to carry on the business. Enough could not be obtained, but a labor bureau would aid such manufacturers.

Afternoon Session.

The resolution offered in the morning regarding the organization of a Labor Bureau was adopted, with an amendment to confine its duty to skilled labor. A resolution recommending the formation of city and county associations under the State Labor Union was adopted. On motion of Mr. GARRETT a committee was appointed to prepare an appeal to the people of the country to give the colored people an equal chance for employment. Messrs. H. H. GARRETT, J. J. SPELLMAN and JAMES STEWART were appointed such committee. Mr. J. J. SPELLMAN, from the Committee on Organization, reported a constitution for the State Labor Union. It makes the principal office in New-York, at No. 185 Bleecker street. At the evening session Rev. Dr. CHEEVER, being discovered in the hall, was called upon and made a short speech congratulatory to the colored people on the advancement made by them, and then digressed to old anti-slavery topics.

New York Times, August 26, 1870.

4.   THE SARATOGA LABOR CONVENTION

The State Labor Convention of colored men met in Saratoga on the 24th ult. The following officers were elected: President, the Rev. William F. Butler, of New York; vice-presidents: The Rev. C. R. Brown, Troy; L. H. Jackson, Albany; the Rev. J. C. Gilbert, Saratoga. Secretaries: E. W. Crosby, Jr., Albany; E. O. C. Eato and S. J. Stokely, New York. Little was done on Wednesday beyond laying out work for different committees to perfect an organization for the benefit of colored laborers.

On Thursday, the 25th, the morning session of the State Labor Convention commenced at 10 o'clock. The first paper read was one from New York, prepared by Prof. Charles Reason, of the committee on education, giving

statistical facts connected with the schools of New York, Brooklyn and Wil-
liamsburgh, and arguing in favor of education as one of the chief instrumen-
talities for making remunerative the labor of the working classes.

The committes on financial questions presented a report: "The moneyed
element of power should be fostered. It cannot take the place of character
or education, but is next to them as a mighty power. It assists moralists to
carry out benevolent designs; in building and furnishing institutions of
learning, and in developing the mineral resources of the country. Out of the
money deposited in the New York savings banks, it is estimated that $4,000,-
000 belong to colored persons. Through the Freedmen's Savings institutions,
$13,000,000 have been saved by colored persons; while the same people in the
South have expended $11,000,000 for business and social improvement. It is
impossible for people to stand still; they must either go forward or backward. Though the fields of labor be opened ever so wide, and we enter and
gather the fruits, if wanting in the duty of economy and knowledge of apply-
ing our gains, we shall not keep pace with the rest of the community. It is
a duty to ourselves to labor, economize and think.

The Committee on Labor reported. After speaking of the labor problem as
being as old as the pyramids and yet unsolved, the report regrets the absence
of statistics relating to the industrial condition of the laborers. The
nearest estimate that can be obtained is that out of eighteen thousand colored males in the State in 1850 two thousand were skilled laborers.

Messrs. Leonard Jackson, S. J. Stokely and W. H. Decker were appointed
a committee on statistics.

Sinclair Tonsey, of New York, opposed the resolutions, as leading to
strikes and difficulties.

Mr. Steward deprecated such a construction of the resolution, and said
there was something in labor unions beside strikers, and that something we
desire.

On a call for a presentation of facts for the use of the committees Mr.
Garnet said the Engineers' Protective Association of New York knew of one
hundred engineers, sixty of whom were engaged in saloons and other places in
the city because they were unable to obtain employment at their trade, while
only forty were working at their trade.

Rev. Mr. Swears presented a preamble and resolution recommending trades
and labor organizations.

In answer to some speaker who had advocated humility, care and attention
in the performance of work, Rev. Mr. Butler, said humility was all very well,
and had been practiced for two hundred and fifty years; but the colored people gained more in a short time by taking the musket and shooting rebels,
than they did by a long practice of humility. He said that out of 3,500 colored votes in New York city, one hundred and four were shoemakers, one hundred were engineers, and over eighty were carpenters, with other skilled mechanics, a majority, of whom were kept out of the trades work from class
prejudices. One skilled engraver was obliged to work as a waiter because
other engravers refused to work with him. The speaker had been asked by manufacturers to procure colored persons to work in factories, and who offered
employment if enough colored hands could be obtained to carry on the business.
Enough could not be obtained, but a labor bureau would aid such manufacturers.

J. J. Spelman presented the report, which provided for a State Labor
Union, with headquarters in New York city, No. 185 Bleecker street, and the
formation of unions throughout the State for the protection of the colored
people in the matter of labor. It was adopted without a dissenting voice. 60

Dr. George B. Cheever 61

being discovered in the body of the hall by the chairman, was requested to
address the Convention. Hesitatingly he complied. He said that the Convention was a remarkable illustration of the progress of the country. It could
not be said that to-day there was but little difference between the colored
and white races. There was a difference, but give the colored race one generation, with the same advantages and privileges as the whites have had, and
would there then be so much difference? No. In that time they would be
fully equal in every particular to any white race. Honesty, courage and
Christianity must guide them, and with these virtues they could not fail.

J. J. Spelman offered the following resolution, which was passed unanimously. His excuse for its introduction was that as the National Labor Convention, just adjourned at Cincinnati, had endeavored to start the nucleus of a third party in the United States, called the "Labor Reform Party," and as it was hardly possible for any body of intelligent men at this juncture to keep out of the political arena, he deemed it in order:--

Resolved, That we, citizens of the State of New York in convention assembled, do hereby pledge our earnest devotion to the republican party and its principles, and that our untiring exertions shall be to aid that party in obtaining a triumphant victory in November next.

Officers of the State Labor Union

The committee appointed to nominate officers of the State Labor Union for the ensuing year presented the following:--

President--Stephen Lawrence, of New York.
First Vice President--Edward W. Crosby, Sr., of Albany.
Second Vice President--Charles L. Reason, of New York.
Secretary--E. V. C. Eato, of New York.
Assistant Secretary--George W. Johnson, of Albany.
Treasurer--J. J. Zuill, of New York.
Executive Committee--H. H. Garnett, O. C. Gilbert, William Rich, J. J. Bowers, D. K. McDonough, M. D.; James C. Matthews, Joseph P. Thomson, D. D.; Rev. William H. Decter, N. H. Turpin.

At the conclusion of this business James C. Matthews, of Albany, and Hamilton Morris, of South Carolina; addressed the Convention. They were eloquent, forcible and pertinent.

With thanks to the Rev. William F. Butler, the presiding officer, and to the people of Saratoga for their manifested kindly sympathy, the Convention adjourned, with the entire audience, white and black, singing the Doxology.

The National Standard, September 3, 1870.

5. CONDITION OF THE NEW YORK COLORED MEN

In the New York Colored Labor Convention, at Saratoga, the Rev. Mr. BUTLER, in answer to some speakers who had advocated humility, care and attention in the performance of work, said that humility was very well, and had been practiced for two hundred and fifty years; but the colored people gained more in a short time by taking muskets and shooting rebels than they did by long practice of humility. He said that out of three thousand five hundred colored voters in New York city, one hundred and four were shoemakers, one hundred were engineers, and over eighty were carpenters, with other skilled mechanics, a majority of whom were kept out of trades work from class prejudices. One skilled engraver was obliged to work as a waiter; because other engravers refused to work with them. The report of the committee on financial questions state that out of the money deposited in New York Savings Banks, it is estimated that $4,000,000 belonged to colored persons. Through the freedmen's savings institutions $13,000,000 have been saved by colored persons, while the same people in the South have expended $11,000,000 for business and social improvement.

New National Era, September 8, 1870.

6. RACIAL PREJUDICE IN NEW YORK

The Saratoga Labor Convention, held recently, was in the interest especially of the colored laborers of New York. A noticeable feature of that Convention was the evidence brought to light of the still powerful feeling of race-hatred with which colored laborers, on account of complexional difference, have yet to contend. While chattel slavery lasted the most forlorn of American laborers were the powerless, unpaid victims of that iniquitous system. The ill effects of the system still survive. In the Saratoga Convention its President, Rev. William F. Butler, of this city, said that "out of three thousand five hundred voters in New York city, one hundred and four were shoemakers, one hundred were engineers, and over eighty were carpenters, with other skilled mechanics, A MAJORITY OF WHOM WERE KEPT OUT OF THE TRADES WORK FROM CLASS PREJUDICES. *One skilled engraver was obliged to work as a waiter because other engravers refused to work with him!*" From the same cause the Rev. Mr. Garnet stated that "of one hundred engineers, known to the Engineers' Protective Association of New York, sixty were engaged in saloons and other places in the city, because they were unable to obtain employment at their trade, while only forty were working at their trade." One of the most pernicious results of slavery, while it was a controlling force in our national politics, religion and social life, was to degrade honest and honorable toil in the popular estimation, and to foster prejudices against the enslaved as a class. We entreat white workingmen for their own sake, as well as for those who are, for no fault of their own, the victims of an unjust race-prejudice, to rise superior to such limitations and make common cause, in the spirit of Christian brotherhood, rather than proscription, with those who are yet more oppressed.

The National Standard, September 17, 1870.

7. NEW YORK COLORED LABOR BUREAU

A large number of colored people assembled last night in Zion Church, Bleecker street, to hear the report of the delegates to the Colored Working Men's Convention, at Saratoga. Rev. Wm. Butler, the pastor of the church, presided, and in a few words introduced the delegation. The report stated that the object of the Convention was to incorporate the colored workingmen's labor organizations with those of the white men, and to establish a labor bureau in this City where skilled colored workmen could obtain places. These two objects had been attained. The white working men showed a most commendable spirit in recognizing the claims of the colored men, and were willing to receive them on terms of equality. Still there was an unfounded prejudice against colored men, and in consequence many who were masters of various mechanical arts were forced to act as waiters in hotels and restaurants. To do away with this state of things the New York Labor Bureau was organized, with Stephen Lawrence as President. From this time, colored who register their names will be provided with employment suited to their capacity and acquirements.

After the report was read, Rev. Henry Highland Garnet made a lengthy and humorous speech, in which he exhorted his hearers to take advantage of the opportunities afforded by the newly established labor bureau, and to cultivate saving habits. He stated that the freedmen of the South had now, four years after their emancipation, $2,000,000 to their credit in bank, and said that the colored men in the North should not be behindhand. After some remarks in a similar strain by Stephen Lawrence, and the enrollment of several persons, the meeting adjourned.--*N.Y. Times.*

The National Standard, September 24, 1870.

8. THE LONG SHORE MEN

There was a meeting of the colored men working along the wharfs, held Thursday evening, at which it was resolved to organize a Longshoremen's Association, to be called the Longshoremen's Association No. 2. The chairman of the meeting stated that every class of workingmen had their organizations, and they found them of great benefit, and why not the black men have theirs. The chairman concluded by recommending the election of delegates from every ward in the city to a convention to be held in Baltimore city on the 24th of February next, and the appointment of a committee to confer with the Longshoremen's Association No. 1 (white). The recommendations of the chair were embraced in resolutions, and adopted.

The Longshoremen No. 1 (White.)

met on the following evening, and shortly after the meeting was organized, the committee of No. 2 made its appearance at the outer door, and was admitted. The chairman of the committee presented the resolutions adopted at their meeting, and was followed by addresses from the members of the committee. A Mr. Pinder said he wanted to see every man at work, white and black, but at not less than 25 cents an hour or $2 per day. This he considered was fair, and they were going to stand up to it. No. 1 passed resolutions similar to those adopted by No. 2, and appointed delegates to the convention of the 24th of next month.

Workingman's Advocate, January 27, 1871.

9.   PROCEEDINGS OF THE ALABAMA LABOR UNION CONVENTION

MONDAY, January 2, 1871.

The Convention of the colored people of Alabama, assembled in the hall of the House of Representatives at 12 m. to-day, representing nearly every county in the State.

Mr. James T. Rapier of Montgomery, Vice President of the National Labor Union, called the Convention to order.

On motion of Mr. Williams of Montgomery, Allen Alexander of Baldwin was elected temporary secretary.

Mr. L. J. Williams moved that a committee of seven be appointed to report upon the credentials of delegates; which motion was agreed to, and the President appointed Messrs. Williams, Thompson of Montgomery, Thompson of Talladega, Greene, Speed, Gaston and Wm. B. Wood, as such committee.

The Convention then took a recess of ten minutes.

After reassembling, the Committee on Credentials reported that ninety-eight delegates were duly accredited to the Convention, representing forty-two counties in various portions of the state; that a majority of the delegates present were farmers and farm laborers, and consequently that interest was more largely represented than any other class of labor.

Mr. Whitfield, of Dallas, introduced a resolution that no member be allowed to speak more than ten minutes upon subjects before the Convention; which was withdrawn.

Mr. Thompson, of Montgomery, moved that a committee of seven members be appointed upon permanent organization; which motion was agreed to, and the following delegates were appointed: Holland Thompson, James K. Green, Ellis Lucas, James Nettles, Henry Duncan, Green Lewis and Henry St. Clair.

On motion of Mr. St. Clair, of Macon, James H. Alston was invited to a seat in the Convention as delegate from Macon.

On motion of Mr. Williams, of Montgomery, Gen. D. E. Coon, of Dallas, addressed the Convention in an able and very appropriate strain, and retired amidst the cheers and applause of the delegates.

The Committee on Permanent Organization submitted the following names for officers of the Convention:

For President--Holland Thompson of Montgomery; Vice President--G. S. W. Lewis of Perry; Secretary--L. J. Williams of Montgomery; Assistant Secretary

--Allen Alexander of Baldwin.

Mr. Williams of Montgomery, offered a substitute for the report, that Mr. Rapier be made President, Holland Thompson Vice President, and Allen Alexander Secretary; which was laid on the table.

The Convention then proceeded to ballot for officers with the following result:

For President--James T. Rapier; Vice President--Washington Stevens; Secretary--Wm. V. Turner; Assistant Secretary--G. S. W. Lewis.

A motion to adopt the rules governing the House of Representatives was then adopted.

Mr. Williams of Montgomery introduced a resolution directing the President to appoint the following committees, which was adopted: On Finance; on Labor; on Homesteads; on Education; on Churches and Societies; on Condition of Colored People; on Printing; on Savings Bank; to Organize State Labor Union.

After the appointment of the committees, the Convention adjourned until 7 o'clock p.m.

At the evening session no business of much importance was brought up, and the Convention adjourned till 9 a.m. Tuesday.

TUESDAY, Jan. 3, 1871.

The Convention was called to order at 11 o'clock this morning by Mr. Rapier, President.

A very able prayer was delivered by the Rev. Mr. Fannin of Talladega.

A resolution tendering the thanks of the colored people to Senators Warner and Spencer, and Representative Buckley in the Congress of the United States, was unanimously adopted.

Mr. Harralson of Dallas, gave notice that he would move a reconsideration of the vote by which the resolution was adopted, so as to strike out the name of Hon. George E. Spencer.

Mr. Cox of Montgomery, chairman of the Committee on Homesteads, presented the following report:

The Committee on Homes and Homesteads, to which was referred the subject of emigration, beg leave to submit the following report:

Your Committee have had the subject under careful consideration, and they have examined and inquired into the prospect of securing homes for our people in this State, and they have come to the conclusion that under existing circumstances it will be impossible for us to procure homes advantageously for the following reasons:

1. The lands in Alabama, fit for cultivation, are held at such prices that the poor man, and especially the colored man will never be able to buy any portion of them.

2. The government lands that are situated in this State are in such large tracts and divisions which will always be unfit for cultivation, and even if the soil was good and remunerative, they lie in a portion of the State in which armed bands of disguised men have created such terrors and committed such depredations upon life, liberty and property, that we cannot remain in such localities in peace; and with these facts staring us steadfastly in the face, we think it would be far better for us to move to a more congenial climate.

Your Committee therefore respectfully suggest the State of Kansas, where the soil is virgin and where homes can be had by simply going to them, and where we will not be murdered and driven from our homes for exercising those inestimable rights of life and liberty which are inherent in every freeman born upon American soil.

Here follows a lengthy description of soil, climate, etc., and the report continues:

As to the point of the advantages to be derived by leaving this State for the above named States:

First, all the improvements we would put upon our place would be our own; our families would pride themselves in making everything agreeable around or about them.

Second, we would be free from paying rent--from $3 to $10 per acre, as is generally paid in Alabama.

Third, we would not be continually on the lookout for another home.

Fourth, we would not be continually harassed by those lawsuits growing out of contracts made, but not complied with.

Fifth, we will not have a man continually riding up and down the rows after us, ready to dock us for every minute we may lose.

In short, we will be able to sit under our own vine and fig tree and none dare to molest or make us afraid. Indeed, we will have a home that we can call home in the true meaning of the word--one which at our death we can will to our children. But when we die now, we are forced to leave our dear little ones to the tender mercies of the charitable world.

These are some of the advantages to be derived by going to this State, whilst I do not know one we can lose.

Here, huddled as we are, so much of the same kind of labor in the market, wages down to starving rates, I do not hesitate to say that I see nothing but misery in store for the masses, and it surely grows out of the fact that we are without land or a house that we can call our own. It is all very well to talk about diversity of labor, what we will do as soon as our mines are opened, as soon as our factories are reared. . . easy enough to imagine the hum of a thousand spindles on our several creeks and rivers. But what hope have we that these things will be consummated in our day? If so, by what reason have we to suppose that it would benefit us? Is it not known that they would employ all white help? Is it reasonable to suppose that capital will flow to this country as long as it can find safer investment, or the same kind in the coal fields of Pennsylvania, or the iron mines of Missouri.

If we owned a considerable portion of land in this State, I would be the last man to say leave, or if I could see that we would be likely to get land, I would say stay. But it is not so; we are today where 1866 left us. Despite our energy the prospects grow less bright, and it can get no better until the laborers get more homes, and wages are better; and, in my judgment, this will not be until a portion of the labor is removed to some place where we can obtain land without money or price. This done, what remains in this country will be better paid.

If the foreigner comes across the briny deep and then travels more than a thousand miles westward, after landing on our shores, it does appear that we ought to have energy enough to go a few hundred miles, in the same latitude, you may say. If the Pilgrim Fathers would leave their shores and seek the inhospitable climate of New England in order that they might enjoy religious privileges, surely we might go a short distance to find a land where we can enjoy political privileges and religious meetings, which we have been denied in this State. If the men from the eastern part of the United States, could form themselves into colonies and cross the Mississippi years ago, (leaving comfortable homes behind them) when the red man met them on the very bank of the river, surely we might not be afraid to go where the country is all civilized; when we know too that we are leaving the Ku Klux, and their midnight hauntings far behind us, going where we can produce abundantly more with the same labor than we can here, and where a man will not be compelled to plant one kind of crop, but can plant whatever pleases him to plant, and will most advance his interest, and above all where peace reigns, where a man can enjoy his political opinions without being murdered; where political and religious meetings can be held without momentary danger of being fired into by Ku-Klux, or men who are opposed to our moral and political advancement.

The report of the committee was unanimously adopted, and a resolution was adopted appointing a committee to proceed to Washington city, to memorialize Congress and also visit Kansas and make a report as to the location for a colony, prices of lands, implements for farming, etc. and the best route of travel, and means of transportation.

The convention then proceeded to elect a Vice President for the State of Alabama of the National Labor Union, and Mr. L. J. Williams was chosen.

The following delegates were chosen to proceed to the city of Washington to attend the National Labor Union, which meets in that city on the 9th inst.: J. T. Rapier, J. K. Greene and L. J. Williams.

The Convention then passed a resolution of thanks to the reporter State Journal for publishing the proceedings, and adjourned until 9 a.m. tomorrow.

Third Day

WEDNESDAY, Jan. 4, 1871.

The Convention was called to order at 10 o'clock, by Mr. Rapier, President.

A prayer was offered by the Rev. Isaac Parker of Elmore.

Mr. Turner of Elmore, chairman of the committee on condition of the colored people, submitted the following report; which was unanimously adopted:

Your Committee on condition of the colored people of Alabama have had the same under careful consideration, and most respectfully beg leave to submit the following report:

After thoroughly canvassing the matter among the delegates from the various counties, and mature deliberation there on, we have come to the conclusion that the present condition of our people, as a mass, is infinitely worse than that of any other class of laborers in any country known to us. To prove this we have the evidence to show that as a people we are practically denied the rights conferred upon us by the laws of the nation, as well as those given us by our Divine Creator, to life, liberty and the pursuit of happiness.

In portions of this State, no colored man is allowed to exercise that highest and dearest privilege of an American citizen--the right to deposit his ballot according to the dictates of his conscience--without endangering his life and jeopardizing the welfare and safety of his family; even the wives of many true and loyal men of our race have been abused and insulted because of the fidelity of their husbands to the general government.

From all over the State there rises a general cry for our oppressed people, of their grievances. The landholders have formed combinations to have their large estates cultivated to their own advantage, at the expense of those who till the soil. The poor colored laborer, on the first day of January, makes a contract, which he thinks will be a sufficient guaranty for his protection from penuary and want at the end of the year, but at the expiration of the year for which he has contracted, after twelve months' hard service, he finds himself as poor or poorer than at the beginning. Educationally, we are making little or no progress, whilst in the cities and some of the larger towns we have some apologies for schools. In the country we are almost entirely deprived of educational advantages of any kind, and in some localities "nigger" schools are not tolerated.

Religiously, we are, if anything, retrograding. The poverty of our people is a serious obstacle in our way of supporting our ministers and keeping up our churches. It is the opinion of your committee that the panacea for the evils enumerated in the foregoing report is emigration. We do not believe it to be consistent with our interests to remain in this or any other State that has been blasted by the curse of slavery. There are millions of acres of the public domain in the broad and free West, where we, in the words of the immortal Lincoln, "a landless, homeless, and houseless people," can find homes, peaceful, free and happy homes for ourselves, our wives and children--homes that after our departure from this world of sorrow, we can bequeath to our children with the satisfaction that it will be theirs for all time to come. We would most respectfully urge this Convention to instruct the delegates to be elected by it to the National Labor Convention, to be held in the city of Washington on the 9th of this month, to consider this subject carefully.

The following resolution was offered by Mr. Forman of Dallas, and adopted:

Resolved, That it is the sense of this Convention that the sum of $1000, expended by the land holders of this State upon each quarter section of 160 acres of tillable land, in comfortable tenements, ditches, fences and in the manufacture or purchase of improved agricultural implements would pay a better per cent. to the landlord, under free labor, than the same amount expended for a slave under the former forced labor system, and would aid much to harmonize and enhance the interests of both capitalists and laborers--whether skilled or common, and would do much to increase the mutual interests, happiness and contentment of all classes.

By these means capital would be largely enhanced, property increased in value, and happiness and good will pervade all classes.

Hon. D. E. Coon was invited to the stand, and delivered the following address:

Mr. President:

I thank you for the compliment you have paid me in calling me to this stand. It is a compliment of no ordinary character, for the reason that your proceedings, if wisely conducted, will prove a great blessing to the entire people of Alabama, white as well as black. If unwisely conducted, you will do great evil to all the people of this nation.

In regard to the objects of this convention, I confess myself almost wholly ignorant and unprepared to express opinion as to the details of its proceedings, but for the call published in the public prints of the State, I have supposed it to be, simply, to elevate the laboring classes of Alabama; if so, then, you have my hearty sympathy.

It has been a long conceived opinion of mine that the more we elevate the laboring men--the more educated, refined and intelligent the laborers of a nation or people--then, the more happy would be that people. And here allow me to intimate that you are to deal with a subject of vast importance. The subject of regulating labor in this country is one of far greater magnitude, not only to yourselves, but to the white man, than many of you have dreamed of.

Your action here will effect, for good or evil, every stratum of society in this State, for the reason that manual labor is the corner stone of all civilized governments and should be handled with wisdom and care.

To illustrate: who raise the cotton of this State? I answer, the laboring man. When I took over this beautiful and fertile State, and calculate the vast amount of wealth produced annually from this one staple, it proves to me that the labor which produces that cotton is of the greatest importance to the people of the State. When in market, it amounts to millions. The millions of dollars obtained for that cotton, to a very large extent, go to make up the sums paid (bread and meat) consumed by both black and white. So you see that the people of this State, black and white, are alike interested in the result of your action in this convention. If you are determined to leave this State, which no one regrets more than myself, you should take at least one year in which to prepare yourselves with the necessary funds to bear your expenses. By no means take such steps here that will disorganize and demoralize the laboring interests of our people, for in so doing the laborer and employer alike would be greatly injured.

Allow me, however, to add that in all laudable measures looking to the education and thereby the elevation of the laboring men of this State, and of the entire Union, you have my heartfelt sympathy and earnest co-operation.

In regard to your emigration, I will state that I do not think you are in a condition to remove from this State at this time. You have very little money to pay your way and no fixed point of destination.

I hope, therefore, that your deliberations will be such as shall prove a blessing alike to the laborer and employer. Deal cautiously with this subject.

I see that your Committee on Permanent Organization is now ready to report, and feeling that your time should be occupied with business rather than long speeches I shall beg to be excused from extended remarks at this time.

Mr. Williams of Montgomery, chairman of the Committee on Permanent Organization of the Labor Union in Alabama, respectfully report the following named officers of the proposed Union:

One president, three vice presidents, five executive committeemen, two secretaries, one corresponding secretary and one treasurer.

The committee also report the following constitution:

This Association shall be known as the Labor Union of Alabama, and it shall be auxiliary to the National Labor Union of the United States.

The object of the Association shall be the furtherance of the welfare and the education of the laboring classes in the State of Alabama.

Its officers shall be one president, three vice presidents, an executive committee of five members, two secretaries, one corresponding secretary, and a treasurer, who shall be elected at each annual meeting of the association, and shall perform the duties usually appertaining to such officers in similar organizations.

Each member of the Association shall pay twenty-five cents annually to the Association.

Warrants upon the Treasurer shall be drawn by the President and countersigned by the Secretary, who shall keep a record of the warrants drawn and the purpose thereof.

Meetings shall be called by the President and Secretary, or by any three members of the Executive Committee and the Secretary, and may be either mass conventions or conventions of delegates, as the call shall state. But no meeting shall be called without three weeks' public notice thereof, published in at least two newspapers of the State.

Mr. Walker of Dallas, introduced a resolution, tendering the thanks of the colored people to Gen. D. E. Coon, for his earnest devotion to their interests; which was withdrawn.

Mr. Greene of Hale, introduced the following resolutions:

Resolved, That it is the sense of this Convention, and we do hereby advise all laboring men in this State who have made contracts for the year 1871, to labor earnestly and faithfully for their employers until the end of the year, and not in any manner violate the obligations of their contract;

Resolved further, That we recommend all laboring men of this State not now under contracts, to engage their services to all planters or other business men who are desirous of securing their services, at reasonable wages; which was adopted.

The Committee to which was referred the subject of wages, made the following report; which was adopted:

Your Committee to whom was referred to subject of labor and wages, beg leave to say that they have not had the time for canvassing so important a subject. They have found that the following prices are generally paid to colored laborers in this State, to wit: mechanics, such as carpenters, blacksmiths, plasterers, painters, etc., from $1 50 to $2 50 per day, farmers from $5 to $12 per month, with board; in many cases they work on shares, the land owner furnishing the land, stock, and meeting all other expenses with the exception of the board of hands, the laborers getting one-third, in other cases they work for one-half and the expenses are equally divided. These are generally the agreements, but we cannot say that they are faithfully complied with on the part of the land owners.

Common laborers are paid from $1 to $1 25 per day, and from $10 to $35 per months. This includes work in cities, towns, etc.

Your committee respectfully submit the above facts without any further remarks, hoping the convention may take some steps that will make the laborer more independent of the combination of the capitalists in this State, as the prices paid are totally insufficient for the support of the colored laborers of this State.

Mr. Green of Hale, introduced the following resolutions; which were reported:

Resolved, That we hail with joy the wise and patriotic measures recently recommended by President Grant and adopted by Congress, looking to the annexation of the territory of San Domingo to that of the United States.

Resolved, That we confidently trust and pray it may prove a blessing to liberty and free labor on the American continent.

The Committee on Churches and Societies beg leave to make the following report:

That the churches and societies are in a very bad condition. Some places in the State are entirely without a place of worship, and are subject to be intefered with by Ku-Klux.

One great cause of their being destitute of places of worship is that they are unable to build. While they have striven hard to obtain means to build their homely temples of worship, they have by bad faith (too often of their employers) failed to receive the reward of their labor. In and about the larger towns they have churches, but in the country and more remote counties they are almost destitute; and in many instances where they have built churches and school houses they have been burnt down by those hostile to the elevation and culture of the colored race. So often have they been disappointed in their earnest endeavors to erect churches and school houses; that they have become discouraged and dismayed, and humbly petition through this Convention to the Federal authorities, to which they have never appealed in vain, for further protection and aid, that the colored race may be enabled to educate their children and worship the God of Israel according to the dictates of consciences, without fear or molestation.

Mr. Williams of Montgomery, made the following report, which was adopted:

The Committee on Education respectfully report:

That ever since an attempt to educate the colored children of Alabama was commenced the work has been steadily pursued in spite of the bitter hostility manifested by the aristocratic classes, the burning of school houses built from the scanty savings of the hard working poor, the persecutions of innocent and defenceless children, and the opposition to every one engaged in their instruction--extending even to the murder of teachers by Ku-Klux assassins. That any progress should have been made under such hell-born opposition may seem wonderful, and yet the progress made by the colored children of Alabama in learning the rudiments of the English language are not inconsiderable.

Thousands have learned to read and write, and all our people are believed to earnestly desire the improvement of the mental condition of their children. . . . The public fund allowable for school purposes is about $500 annually, giving for each child in the schools about one dollar and fifteen cents a year, a sum only sufficient to keep the schools open for two or three months. Many of the Southern States pay less than a dollar a year for each child, and one State less than half a dollar. In New York the public fund allows $6.83, in Massachusetts $16.45, and in the young State of Nevada $19.17 for each child. No comment upon these figures is necessary.

The condition of the Treasury and the hostile public opinion in Alabama, forbid us to anticipate any great improvement upon the present system, if indeed it can be maintained under the attacks constantly made upon it.

The committee have thought it best to recommend this Convention to adopt the following resolution.

Resolved, That the delegates to the "National Labor Union" to be convened in Washington city, on the 9th proximo, be instructed to impress upon that body the importance of urging upon Congress the necessity of enacting a national school system, whereby every child in the Union can at least learn or be taught the rudiments of the English language; experience in this and other States in the South having taught us that without such a system as is here sought for the rising generation (in an educational point of view) will be but very little superior to that of generations gone before.

Mr. Phillips, from the Committee on Savings Bank, made the following report:

Your committee beg leave to submit the following report:

Under an act of Congress, freedmen's savings and trust companies were established in 1865. The principal office is located in Washington, D.C. Branches are established wherever the people show a disposition to support them. Three branches, viz: one at Mobile, one at Montgomery, and one at Huntsville, are now in successful operation in this State. Savings banks are every where recognized as a successful means of educating the people to habits of industry and economy, and in States where the subject has received the most attention, have been encouraged by special legislation. We have examined the system of the bank chartered by Congress and believe it safe to the depositors, and we know of no other system, that can be adopted, preferable to it, and would recommend that our people give it their hearty support, being assured that branches will be established at different parts of the State as fast as it is apparent that they will be sustained.

Mr. Turner introduced a resolution employing the STATE JOURNAL to print 2000 copies of the proceedings of the Convention in pamphlet form.

The Convention went into an election for officers of the State Labor Union, with the following result:

President--Jere Haralson of Dallas.
First Vice President--G. S. W. Lewis of Perry.
Second Vice President--Y. B. Simms of Talladega.
Third Vice President--J. W. Williams of Dallas.

Corresponding Secretary--G. W. Cox of Montgomery.
Recording Secretary--J. B. Simpson of Autauga.
Treasurer--Holland Thompson of Montgomery.
The following delegates were appointed a State Executive Committee:
J. T. Rapier, L. J. Williams, H. H. Craig, L. S. Speed, [illegible].
The Convention then adjourned *sine die.*

Alabama State Journal, January 6, 1871.

10.   TESTIMONY OF JOHN HENRI BURCH
WASHINGTON, D. C., April 9, 1880.

JOHN HENRI BURCH, (colored) recalled.
     BY MR. BLAIR:
     Question. You may go on and state anything further you may have to say
to the committee hearing upon the causes of the exodus.--Answer. So far as
the causes of the exodus are concerned I have one more paper, that I missed
at the time I gave my testimony before, that I desire to call the attention
of the committee to, as the causes of the exodus; and also to sustain the
point that this exodus did not commence a couple of years ago in the South,
but has been in existence and thought of for the last several years.
     Q. You may go on and give us what you have.--A. It is the proceedings
of the labor convention of Alabama. They are marked.
     THE CHAIRMAN. Mark them and give them to the reporter.
     BY MR. BLAIR:
     Q. What is that pamphlet?--A. It is the proceedings of the labor con-
vention of Alabama, relative to whether they would remain in Alabama or not,
and disadvantages under which they labored, so far as their educational privileges and rights were concerned, and their civil and political rights, and
the possibility of their obtaining homesteads in that State. The reports of
the several committees are in it.
     Q. What year was that?--A. Eighteen hundred and seventy-two; also the
report of the agent who was sent to Kansas to look into that country there,
and report back to this convention, which he did, and that report is here.
     Q. His investigation was prior to 1872?--A. It was in 1871. He was
sent in 1871.
     Q. What is his name?--A. Hon. George F. Marlow, chairman of that com-
mittee.
     Q. And you state that the extracts are from his report also?--A. Yes,
sir; his report is very short.
     Q. Well, mark such portions of the proceedings of that convention as you
desire to put in your testimony.--A. Yes, sir; I have done so.
     The marked extracts as indicated by witness follow.

EXTRACT FROM PROCEEDINGS
OF THE
LABOR CONVENTION OF ALABAMA,
Assembled in the city of Montgomery, January 2, 1872.

The following report of Hon. George F. Marlow upon Kansas was read
immediately after the convention was called order, as follows:
     In August, 1871, being delegated by your president for the purpose, I
visited the State of Kansas, and here give the results of my observations,
briefly stated.
     It is a new State, and as such possesses many advantages over the old.
     Is much more productive than most other States.
     What is raised yields more profit than elsewhere, as it is raised at
less expense.
     The weather and roads enable you to do more work here than elsewhere.
     The climate is mild and pleasant.
     Winters short and require little food for stock.

Fine grazing country, stock can be grazed all winter.

The population is enterprising, towns and villages spring up rapidly, and great profits arise from *all* investments.

Climate dry, and land free from swamps.

The money paid to doctors in less healthy regions can here be used to build up a house.

People quiet and orderly, schools and churches to be found in every neighborhood, and ample provision for free schools is made by the State.

Money plenty, and what you raise commands a good price.

Fruit of all kinds easily grown and sold at large profit.

Railroads are being built in every direction.

The country is well watered.

Salt and coal are plentiful.

It is within the reach of every man, no matter how poor, to have a home in Kansas. The best lands are to be had at from $2 to $10 an acre, *on time*. The different railroads own large tracts of land, and offer liberal inducements to emigrants. You can get good land in some places for $1.25 an acre. The country is mostly open prairie, level, with deep, rich soil, producing from forty to one hundred bushels of corn and wheat to the acre. The corn grows about eight or nine feet high, and I never saw better fruit anywhere than there.

The report was adopted.

Hon. Robert H. Knox, of Montgomery, was then invited to address the convention, and spoke as follows:

MR. PRESIDENT AND GENTLEMEN OF THE CONVENTION: While I am deeply sensible of the honor conferred upon me, I shall address you but few words, believing, as I do, that you have met for work rather than to hear long speeches, and that the members of this convention are anxious to finish their labors, return to the people whose representatives they are, who are waiting expectantly for tidings of what may be recommended and accomplished.

You are called together from all portions of the State for the purpose, as I understand, of advancing the interests of labor in Alabama. It is a noble cause, and your duty in connection with it a sacred one--one that will be faithfully discharged only when the subject has been conscientiously considered, and some line of action suggested and adopted which will insure protection and advancement to the labor cause, and extend the privileges and immunities of the laboring man in this State.

The three principal points to be considered by you are, I think--

First. Protection to the laboring masses of Alabama in their exercise of the rights of citizenship, and personal security from ku-klux hate and violence.

Second. Protection to the laborer to securing payment of wages earned.

Third. The protection of labor against the inroads and encroachments of capital.

Work honestly and hard for the consummation of those three great objects; do everything in your power to secure these; and after the subject has been exhausted, if your efforts fail, it is time then to desert Alabama and seek a land--a State--where these rights are accorded.

I have listened with great attention to the report of the commissioner appointed by authority of the State Labor Union to visit Kansas, and while I own that the inducements held out to laboring men in that far-off State are much greater than those enjoyed by this class in our State, yet I would say let us rest here a while longer; let us trust in God, the President, and Congress, to give us what is most needed here--personal security to the laboring masses--the suppression of violence, disorder and ku-kluxism--the protection which the Constitution and laws of the United States guarantee, and to which, as citizens and men we are entitled. Failing in these, it is time then, I repeat, to desert the State and seek homes elsewhere--where there may be fruition of the hope inaugurated when by the hand of Providence the shackles were stricken from the limbs of four millions of men--where may be enjoyed in peace and happiness by your own firesides the earnings of your daily toil--where the bickerings and cavil of party and caste will not be heard, and where the truth asserted by the "Ayrshire Plowboy." [62]

"The honest man, though e'er so poor,
Is king of men for a' that."
may be recognized and maintained by those who surround you.

The true nobility and dignity of labor, are asserted and recognized by
a great part of the intelligent world. It has remained for the spirit of
the nineteenth century to appreciate and confirm the principle that--
Toiling hands alone are builders
Of a nation's wealth and fame.

May God grant this may be the case in our own loved State!

It is a principle of the Mahomedan creed, that I believe is inculcated
in the Koran, that every one should have a trade. This is certainly a doctrine worthy the adoption of all creeds and systems, since individual industry and good character form the sum of a nation's condition and progress.

While our government, and men who have power and opportunity, can and
ought to do much to elevate and ameliorate the condition of the laboring class
as individuals, workingmen can do much more for themselves. Diligent self-
improvement is the road to success and fame and fortune. It is your privilege
to assist these who, already assured of this fact, are toiling up the rugged
path; and it is your duty to incite the indolent to ambition, and the humble
and timid to confidence. What if their station be lowly and their opportunities few? These are the lower rounds of the ladder that have to be ascended
before the great results at the top can be reached. Call the attention of
such to the names of Elihu Burritt, Ben Johnson, the poet Burns, Dr. Livingstone, the missionary traveler; to that of Abraham Lincoln and others, who,
resting from their daily toil, as mechanics or laborers, spent each spare
moment in mental improvement. In private and social life it should be ever
your aim to assist in elevating and ennobling those whose interest you are
now considering in convention. If here calm deliberation and conscientious
counsels prevail, and are remembered and acted upon hereafter, much must be
accomplished, thousands in our State must be benefited, and you will be faithful to the trust confided. [63]

REPORT OF THE COMMITTEE ON LABOR AND WAGES.

MR. PRESIDENT: The Committee appointed by yourself on labor and wages
have had the subject under consideration, and beg leave to submit the following

REPORT

We find here, as almost everywhere, two classes of labor--skilled and unskilled. To the former class belong the mechanics; to the latter, such as
work by the day or month, and all those who work in the fields for a living.

We find the wages of the mechanics differ according to skill, kinds of
trade, and locality; that there are about 4,000 in the State; that the
average wages are about $1.50 per diem, and that work is not plentiful.

The common daily laborers form such a small portion of the labor of the
State that we do not deem it important enough to devote much space to them;
they number probably about 2,000, are confined mostly to the railroads, and
their wages average about $1.25 per diem, without board.

We further find that there are not less than 125,000 laborers engaged in
agricultural pursuits in this State. That this class of laborers have fared
badly requires no report from your committee to prove. But we have taken some
time to investigate their condition, and, so far as in us lie, the causes of
our deplorable state, and find, first, that it is owing to the fact that there
was a very short crop this year, by reason of a very wet spring, followed by a
severe drought in the summer; consequently we failed to make more than two-
thirds of an average crop. Second, on account of high interest we are forced
to pay for the use of sufficient capital to conduct business.

The laborers contract in different ways; a few work for wages, but the
greater portion work on the system known as "shares," the landlord, furnishing the land, stock and implement, draws two-thirds, whilst the laborer
furnishes his provisions, does the work, and draws the remaining one-third of
the crop. But that in order that the case may be understood, we have concluded to count all things outside of our labor as capital, plus the interest
on the same. We must then charge ourselves with all the capital we borrow, as
well as our time, and credit ourselves with whatever the crop brings. If at

the end of the year we find that the crop does not more than pay back the actual cash borrowed, then we have lost our time; if more, then the surplus is just what we have received for our time.

Taking the crop of 1869 as a basis and calculating that this year (as is generally conceded) there was just two-thirds of a crop made, and we have the following result, viz: 1869, the aggregate value of the products on all farms, except cotton, was $38,872,260; two-thirds of this amount $25,914,840. 125,000 laborers, allows each $207.31. Amount of cotton raised, about 5,000,000 bails, at $75.00, $225,000. This divided by 125,000 laborers, $180.00. Total amount for each laborer, $387.31.

To produce this crop the laborer has been compelled to borrow capital as follows, viz:

Land, 25 acres, value.	$300.00	Interest $6 per acre. .	$150.00
One mule	150.00	Interest.	37.50
200 pounds meat.	20.00	Interest.	10.00
13 bushels corn for self	13.00	Interest.	3.25
140 bushels corn for mule. . . .	40.00	Interest.	10.00
Total borrowed	523.00	Total Interest . .	210.75

To this interest you must add the loss of the perishable property, which is the corn, and meat, and percentage of the mules that die, 15 per cent.

Corn	$ 53.00
Meat	20.00
Mule	22.50
Total.	95.50
Sum total of all outlay.	306.20

It will be seen from the above figures that the laborer is compelled to pay, in round numbers, 40 per cent, for all the capital borrowed. We submit this is usury; the capitalist charging just five times that lawful interest.

RECAPITULATION.

Total from all sources	$387.31
Total outlay	306.20
Profits	81.11

Out of this amount ($81.11) the laborer must clothe himself and family, feed the little ones, and furnish medical attendance for the same. Hence his inability to accumulate property. But if the capitalists would strike off half of the interest that they now charge, make it 20 instead of 40 per cent, we could then save $105.37½ and in a few years would be the owner of considerable real estate. There is no earthly reason why capitalists should charge such high interest--upon the whole, the highest charged anywhere in the civilized world. The government to-day is borrowing money at 6 per cent, and finds plenty of it, and we believe it can be safely said that 6 per cent, is the average interest in monetary circles.

Whilst our capitalists are wondering why immigration don't turn this way, we suggest to them that it is altogether unreasonable to suppose that labor will flock to any country where it is confronted with such ruinous interest on money, and the necessaries of life that they may be compelled to borrow.

We suggest further, that labor in one sense is like capital, sees fields where best paid. Not only does this high interest tend to prevent labor from coming to the South, but surely has a tendency to drive off a portion of that already here.

Mr. McKiel then introduced the following resolution, which was adopted.

Whereas the report of the committee on labor and wages shown, and condition of affairs amongst the colored citizens of Alabama, owing in a great part to the fact that we are landless: Therefore,

Be it resolved, That this convention memorialize the Congress of the United States to pass the bill now pending before that honorable body, known as "A bill to incorporate the Freedman's Homestead Company," thinking as we do that such a company would do much good by assisting many poor men to obtain

homes, thereby rendering him a free and independent citizen.
    The bill is as follows:
    A BILL to incorporate the Freedman's Homestead Company

    Be it enacted by the Senate and House of Representatives of the United States of America in Congress assembled, That Charles W. Eldridge and Frederick G. Barbadoes, of Massachusetts; Frederick Douglass and Aaron M. Powell, of New York, E. M. Davis, of Pennsylvania; O. O. Howard, Richard J. Hinton, William D. O'Connor, Daniel R. Eaton, A. F. Boyle, J. W. LeBarnes, and William J. Wilson, of the District of Columbia; John M. Langston, of Ohio; R. W. Stokes, of Missouri; James T. Rapier of Alabama; Abram Smith, of Tennessee; James H. Harris, of North Carolina; Oscar J. Dunn, of Louisiana, and Richard Nelson, of Texas, and their associates and successors, are hereby constituted a body corporate, by the name of the Freedman's Homestead Company, and by that name may sue and be sued in any court of the United States.
    Sec. 2. *And be it further enacted,* That the general business and objects of the corporation hereby established shall be to aid in procuring homesteads in the States commonly known as the Southern States of the Union, and to assist in the settlement thereon of persons formerly held in slavery and their descendants, and to foster industrial pursuits, co-operative enterprises, and the acquirement of useful knowledge among them.
    Sec. 3. *Be it further enacted,* That the corporation shall maintain its principal office in the city of Washington, and District of Columbia, but may establish its branches and agencies elsewhere, and shall have power to acquire, inherit, receive, hold, and convey real and personal property, and to do and perform all acts and things incident to the objects and purposes of the corporation, not inconsistent with the laws of the United States, which any individual or body corporate now has or shall have the right to do.
    Sec. 4. *And be it further enacted,* That the business and affairs of the corporation shall be managed and directed by the board of trustees, who may make, establish, and prescribe all needful rules, regulations, and forms for carrying on the business and government of the corporation, and not less than nine trustees shall be a quorum of the transaction of business at any regular or adjourned meeting of the board. The persons named in the first section of this act shall be the first trustees of the corporation, and the number of trustees may be increased to fifty by the election by the board of additional members; and any trustee omitting to attend the regular meetings of the board for six consecutive months, without reasons satisfactory to the board, may be considered to have vacated the office, and a successor may be elected to fill the vacancy. The board of trustees shall annually, on the first Monday of December, make a report to Congress of the operations of the company for the preceding year; and the books and affairs of the company shall at all times be open to the inspection and examination of such persons as Congress may designate and appoint.
    Sec. 5. *And be it furthered enacted,* That the corporation may receive any gift or bequest of lands or property as a special trust upon such conditions for such purposes, not contrary to the Constitution and laws of the United States, and compatible with the general purposes and objects of the corporation, as may be expressed by the grantor or devisor and accepted by the corporation, which trusts shall be faithfully administered in the interests and for the benefit of those for whom the same may be intended and prescribed.
    Sec. 6. *And be it further enacted,* That if any person, whether under color of State authority or otherwise, shall interfere with, assault, menace, or obstruct any officer or agent of the corporation hereby established while in the proper and legal discharge of his duties, or in the proper and legal prosecution of the business of the corporation, or shall maltreat or by force or menace, and whether under color of State authority or otherwise intimidate, prevent, or obstruct any of the persons designated in the second section of this act from removing to, settling upon, or peaceably occupying the homesteads which may be obtained for them under this act, or of availing themselves of any of the advantages intended to be secured to them by the provisions of this act, or shall in any manner conspire in, counsel, encourage, aid or abet any such interference, assault, menace, maltreatment, or obstruction, such

persons shall be deemed guilty of a crime, and shall, upon conviction thereof, be punished by a fine of not less than five hundred dollars, and by imprisonment not more than five years.

Sec. 7. *And be it further enacted,* That the district courts of the United States, within their respective districts, shall have, exclusively of the courts of the several States, cognizance of all crimes and of each committed against the provisions of this act, and also, concurrently with the circuit courts of the United States, of any cause, civil or criminal, to which said corporation, its officers, agents, or beneficiaries may be a party; and if any suit or prosecution against said corporation, its officers, agents, or beneficiaries, shall be commenced in any State court, the party defendant in such suit or prosecution shall have the right to remove such cause for trial to the proper district or circuit court in the manner prescribed by the "Act relating to habeas corpus, and regulating judicial proceedings in certain cases," approved March three, eighteen hundred and sixty-three and all acts amandatory thereof; and the provisions of the act entitled "An act to protect all persons in the United States in their civil rights, and furnish the cause of their vindication, which, became a law on the ninth day of April, eighteen hundred and sixty-six, shall, so far as the same may be applicable to any proceedings under this act, or to any cause commenced in or removed to any court of the United States under this act, be extended thereto.

REPORT OF THE COMMITTEE ON HOMESTEADS.

Mr. James Green, of Hale County, chairman of committee on homesteads, submitted the following report, which was adopted:

The committee on homesteads beg leave to say that they have endeavored to find out from the several land offices in this State the number of homesteads taken up by the colored people since we adjourned in January last; but in consequence of no record being kept respecting a man's color, it is impossible to tell the exact number of homesteads entered by the colored people. But from the best information at hand, we estimate that no less than two hundred homesteads have been entered in this State under the 'homestead act,' and more than one hundred have been entered in Kansas by colored Alabamians alone, who inform those behind that they now live under their own "vine and fig tree," and none dare to molest or make them afraid--a land in which there are no "Kuklux," and where a man can lie down at night with a reasonable prospect of being spared until next morning.

We think this convention can do nothing better than urge upon the colored people throughout the State to secure homesteads wherever they can be had. If they are not to be found here, then go where they are to be found. Let the colored people exhibit as much earnestness and pluck as the foreigner, who travels thousands of miles from the land of his birth in order to secure a home for his family. We beg to remind this convention that at the rate the government land is now being taken up there will not be any left worth entering on this side of the Rocky Mountains in twenty years; that it will be a sad day for colored men in this country when there will not be sufficient land in the country owned by their own race or in their reach to produce as much bread as is consumed by them in each year. How easy it would be for the land-owners all over the country to unite upon one price for your labor, and close all the corn cribs until you come to terms. There is nowhere else for you to go and find such a country ao this, and if there was, you never would be able to get there.

While we do not advise emigration *en masse*, we do recommend that steps be taken to send out a small number of families as an experiment.

REPORT OF THE COMMITTEE ON EDUCATION.

Mr. John B. Simpson, of Autauga County, chairman of committee on education, submitted the following report and resolutions, which were adopted:

MR. CHAIRMAN: We, the committee to whom was referred the question of the educational condition of the colored people of the State of Alabama, beg leave to report as follows:

We find that the free schools of this State are well patronized by the children of colored people, and thousands are today merrily and prosperously tramping down the school-house paths who four years ago had never seen the inside walls, or even the outside walls, of a free school building. The board of education seem to have done all in its limited power to provide for the education of the colored children of the State.

Normal schools or classes are now provided for, which will tend to supply the schools with competent teachers. Normal schools and normal classes cannot be too highly commended, as our greatest cause of complaint to-day is the want of competent teachers.

Many persons have to be employed as teachers from the fact that as better or more competent person can be procured, who should themselves be students in some private school, and who are totally unfit to teach. The question then, which presents itself is, how is this great evil to be remedied? By holding out such inducements to competent colored men and women of the North, East, and West as will tend to bring them among us as teachers. The too prevalent idea among the domineering and illiberal aristocracy of the State that "anything is good enough for a nigger" is now one of the things of the past, or at least should be.

Now, if the great work of instructing the colored children of the State is to be *effectually* done, it must be done by competent teachers of their own race, who have an abiding interest in them beyond the dollars and cents their quarterly statement may call for.

We hail with pleasure the wise and patriotic move of the board of education looking to a fair division of the funds arising from the sale of agricultural land scrip with the now separate universities for the use of the white and colored races.

We hope the general assembly will not sit idly by and allow this fund to be given alone to *one* race. We think the magnanimous conduct of the colored people toward the University of Alabama in yielding a willing support to the resolution of Mr. Finley, which declared the University of Alabama to be a university for the whites, should impress the general assembly with the fact of our race being in favor of harmony, peace, and good will to all, and should impress said honorable body with the justice and equity of giving a fair part of the agricultural land-scrip fund for the benefit of a colored university. It seems to your committee that this *must* done, or else let the agricultural college be a *mixed* college, and free to all, without respect to race. We think the bill recently passed by the board of education, providing for a university for the benefit of the colored race, a *wise* one, and was dictated by feelings of wisdom, justice, and deep patriotism. We think the present superintendent of public instruction and the members of the board of education deserve great praise for their earnest efforts in favor of educating the children of the laboring masses.

We think the effort now being made to blot out the provisions of our State constitution providing for a free public school system is unwise and mean, and *tends*, as its originators *desire*, sooner or later, to destroy this entire system.

We think that it is a movement that is founded in a destructive prejudice and a deep-rooted hatred for the cause of educating the poor children, both black and white.

We look with deep feelings of sorrow and gloom to the efforts being made in the general assembly to lessen the school revenue. We are pained and somewhat surprised to see the *strength* of the effort that is being made to repeal section 957 of the revised code of Alabama. It is a movement that would more seriously affect the whites than the colored race. It would drive out many of the schools from the "piney woods" and mountain region.

This unwise and reckless movement seemed to have been most strongly supported by many so-called *wise* men, and by many of both political parties, who owe their places almost entirely to the laboring men; some from the mountain region who professed great love for the poor white men, but who had within their bosom a upas-like sword, always ready to be driven to their hearts; and some from the prairie, or cotton region, who got *their* places by or through their *pretended* love of justice and equal rights, and who really despise *all* the poor, and love only themselves, and respect the rich. We think all such should be awakened by the sound of the bugle notes of the trumpets of Wendell

Phillips, Charles Sumner, Henry Wilson, Hoar, and their millions of followers.

There is undoubtedly a strong feeling in the State in opposition to the education of the poor; it has now found its way into our legislative halls, and may God in his infinite mercy have compassion upon such heathen beings and tyrannical wretches as give to it their support.

We think our present school system is gradually gathering into the free public school houses all of the poor children of the State, and soon will they arise, and say, blessed be they (without distinction of political parties) who labored for the interests of the laboring men; and cursed be they who labored only for tyrants, capitalists, and millionaires.

We close our report by referring again to the effort now being made to abolish and obliterate the free school system of the State; and we say, unless the *poor* men of the country, both colored and white, arise to the importance of the times, and hurl from power those unwise aristocrats, unmerciful and unfeeling men, to be found in the ranks of both of our ruling parties, who care nothing whatever for the wants and necessities of the poor and who *think* only with *little* and contemptible bigoted minds, the time is near at hand when the free public school systems will fall, but fall to rise again and flourish over the disgraceful graves of those who now propose and desire its death.

Should the State fail to provide for educating the poor children of the laboring masses, and thus allow the moneyed wolves of the land to go onward in their heartless oppression of the poor, we trust and believe that the national government will come to the rescue of the humble but ever deserving servants. But the State must not fail. "Better that all the colleges, academies, select and high schools in the State *perish*," than have our common school system obliterated from the statute. Let the State "make that which can be done for the *common* people, *better* than that which can be done by the select classes in a community for themselves." We should urge at all times that the State "make such provision for the education of the commonest *common* people, that the richest uncommon people will come suppliantly and ask for *their* children the privilege of participating in the advantages of the common schools."

Extremists can be found in all classes. We propose to be moderate, for God knows we love the country and the country's people; but we boldly say that poor Rosell Cremieux, or Ferre are shining patriots when compared with the blood-sucking capitalists or the moneyed corporations that now seek to trample in the dust all who are called *poor!*

The present school system of the State has done more for the poor man in three years than was ever done for him before in any ten years of the history of our State, the arguments of the enemies of schools and of the poor man to the contrary notwithstanding.

And now, to more thoroughly impress upon the members of this convention the grand and great importance of a continued agitation of the subject, we have deemed it expedient to append to our report the following resolutions, believing that "while there is a silver lining to every cloud," and that "all things come round to him who will but work" and agitate and knowing, too, that governments are strong as they educate wisely; we therefore offer in support of the above the following resolutions;

Resolved, That the delegates to be sent to Washington be instructed to impress upon Congress the importance and urgent necessity of the passage of Representative Hoar's "national school bill," whereby every child in the Union can learn, or at least be taught, the rudiments of the English language; experience in this and other Southern States having taught us that without such a system as is here sought for the rising generation (in an educational point of view) will be but very little superior to generations gone before.

Resolved, That in event the legislature of Alabama refuse to set aside the pro rata share of the "agricultural fund" for the benefit of the colored people, then the executive committee of the State labor union are empowered, and hereby instructed, to memorialize Congress to withhold said "agricultural fund" from the State.

ADDRESS OF MR. RAPIER, SECONDING THE RESOLUTIONS
OF THE COMMITTEE ON EDUCATION

MR. RAPIER said:

Mr. Chairman, in rising to second the resolution of my friend from
Autauga, I wish to say that I do so because I am convinced that it is impossible for the poor children of this State to get a common school education
in any other way.

First. The amount ($1.20 per head for each child) is insufficient to
keep the school-houses open more than two months in the year.

Second. Under this system we have some of the most inferior teachers
on record; in too many cases it appears that there are in the school-houses
more to exhaust the funds than to improve the child; at all events, they
succeed better in the former than in the latter.

Let me compare for a moment the amount per head set aside in several
States for the education of their children. In Alabama we give $1.20 per
head; New York, $6.83; Massachusetts, $16.46; Nevada, $19.17. These figures
show very clearly that Alabama is fearfully behind in providing for the
education of the youth within her borders; and just in proportion as these
States surpass our own in making provisions for the education of their children, so will their citizens in after life excel ours in civilization and
refinement, and outstrip us in the highway of life. Why is it that New
England ideas control the policy of the government today? The answer is
because of the superior education of the people of that section. The superior
education of the New Englanders enabled them to combat the slavery question
successfully; enabled them to settle the question of citizenship in this
country by removing all political obstructions which hitherto confronted a
certain class of American citizens. They also propose a national inquiry
through one of their ablest statesmen (Mr. Hoar), into the vexed question of
the relation of "capital and labor." Where is the man from Delaware to Texas
adequate to such a task? And the reason why they are able to accomplish more
than the citizens of any other section of this country, particularly the
South, is to be found in the fact that they are educated in a way superior
to any other class, and seeing the advantages their own section has derived
from such an admirable system, now propose a like plan for the nation.

There is another thing that militates against our system; that is,
teaching with us is not a profession as in other States but rather a make-
shift. In Alabama the school-teacher, the great civilizer of the day, has not
been properly respected. In North Alabama, where I was raised, he filled but
a very small space in society, consequently, most young men preferred a
clerkship even in a country store to a teacher's desk in a school-house, supposing that the former calling was more honorable than the latter.

We have never had any school system in Alabama worthy of the name; and
when the new order of things overtook us, which necessitated a change from
the old groove, we had not one prepared to take hold of the matter, no one
understood thoroughly the free-school system; therefore a series of blunders
were in store for us, and we were powerless to ward them off. I am satisfied
that we have had more blunders from a want of knowledge of the common-school
system than from all other sources combined.

At first we had the county superintendent appointed by the State superintendent (an elective office), many of whom were never examined by any
competent board, appointed more for political reasons than merit. The system,
then, to a certain extent, was turned into an electioneering machine. At the
Republican convention last year I was told that at least one fifth of the
entire delegation were composed of county superintendents, and I suppose it
will be the same at the next Democratic convention.

Whoever saw such examinations as we have here? Who is it that cannot
get a certificate to teach school in Alabama? Hundreds of teachers (so called)
are to-day drawing pay for putting in their time at the school-houses who
can't work out a simple sum in "interest;" who can't write a half-dozen lines
grammatically; who are wholly ignorant of any of the rules of composition, to
say nothing of etiquette. Can you tell me how we are to succeed with these
dead weights hanging to us?

Why, sir, in every county there should be an examining board, composed
of the best scholars, whose moral character should be beyond question, of
which board the county superintendent should be a member, which board should
meet twice a year for the examination of applicants for certificates to teach
school. The schools should be graded third, second, and first. The pay

should be graduated according to the class. The first step towards procuring
a certificate should be this: The applicant should give the board notice
that he or she intended to make application for a certificate to teach school
(naming the class) inclosing a moral certificate from some minister or magistrate. At the appointed time the meeting should be held. The questions in
the several branches should be submitted in printing, and answers to the same
made in writing, with the name of each applicant subscribed thereto: examination over, which should last several days, the board then should meet, pass
upon the qualification of the applicants, and issue certificates accordingly.
By this opperation many worthless teachers would be cut off, and the calling
would be made to partake more of a profession than it now does, and, as a
consequence, be more respected. This plan is pursued elsewhere.

Now, sir, I do not think that the State will ever be able to carry out
such ideas. Our only hope, then, is in a national system. We want a superintendent of education who shall be a member of the cabinet. All assistant
superintendents should be appointed by the President, upon the recommendation
of the superintendent of education. We want a government school-house, with
letters U.S. marked thereon, in every township in the State. We want a
national series of text-books which will teach the child that to respect the
government is the first duty of a citizen. You may ask, where would the
money come from to sustain such a system? I answer by saying, let the
government, after 1872, turn over the net receipts of the Internal Revenue
Bureau, which will be about $115,000,000. Amount, parceled out amongst the
several Congressional districts, would give to each one about $406,360. At
this rate, Alabama would receive, in round numbers, $2,438,160, a sum
sufficient to keep the schools at least seven months in the year. If to this
be added the "State fund," we will be able to have our school-house doors
open nine months in the year.

U.S. Congress, *Senate Reports,* 46th Cong., 2nd sess., Vol. VIII, Pt. III,
No. 693, 1880.

REFERENCES TO THE 1873 ALABAMA NEGRO LABOR CONVENTION

11.   THE LABOR CONVENTION

The colored folks held a meeting this week to select delegates to attend
a Labor Convention. We understand the question of future wages was discussed,
and that the conclusions reached was, that field hands should demand one
dollar per day.

We want to see labor fairly compensated, and we have no objection to
field hands receiving the wages they ask; provided, they can find employment
at such rates and earn them. But it strikes us that just at this time our
colored friends might be more profitably employed considering where they are
to find employment next year? It is a poor time to strike for higher wages,
when the demand for labor is decreasing, and tens of thousands of laborers
North and South, are being discharged from employment. A man has a right to
fix the price of his services; and another has a right to employ him or not,
as he pleases.--*Livingston Journal.*

The Convention met at the Capital yesterday and its proceedings will be
given to the public, as far as we are able to get them. The remarks of the
Livingston *Journal* are exceedingly pertinent and are worthy of the serious
consideration of the members of the Convention.

Montgomery *Advertiser and Mail, November 11, 1873.*

12. PLAN TO ORGANIZE LABOR COUNCILS

The negro Labor Convention met yesterday pursuant to adjournment.

The Committee on the Condition of the Colored People reported that the Colored people of the State were deprived of the free enjoyment of all their rights as citizens, and recommended the passage of Mr. Sumner's Civil Rights Bill by Congress and a similar bill by the Alabama Legislature.

A resolution inviting Jas. T. Rapier and B. S. Turner to address the Convention was adopted.

The Committee on Local Organizations, in obedience to a resolution of instructions, reported a plan of organization for Labor Councils for each county. The plan provided for the election of an agent for the State at large, and one for each Congressional District, and for the appointment of an agent for each county by the President of the Convention, to organize Councils in each county.

The report of the Committee was adopted. There was considerable excitement in the contest for Agent for the State at Large, the candidates being William V. Turner and Laddie Williams. After a great deal of electioneering and changing of votes during the call of the roll, the Secretary finally announced the result as thirty-four votes for Turner and thirty for Williams.

Montgomery (Ala.) *Advertiser and Mail,* November 14, 1873.

13. WHAT DOES MR. SPENCER MEAN?

The attention of the people has already been called to the following mysterious dispatch sent by Mr. Geo. E. Spencer, claiming to be a United States Senator from Alabama to the Negro Labor Convention which has been in a sort of Bedlam Session at the Capital for several days past. It reads as follows:[64]

I regret my inability to attend and participate in your Convention to-day. My feelings and sympathies are with you and your cause. I am opposed to all monopolies, and particularly to the Land Monopoly that to-day curses the South. GEO. E. SPENCER.

The jargon of the writer of this furious communication must have some intended meaning. Until Mr. SPENCER "rises to explain," we have a right to put upon its language what appears to us to be its obvious construction. It is simply an incendiary document. It denounces the titles and possession of the lands of the State, in the hands of those holding lawful deeds and patents for the same, as an unjustifiable and outrageous monopoly! His sentiments indicate an effort to cast odium on the deeds of possession of the planters and all others holding lands in Alabama, and are designed to encourage the negroes not to labor contentedly for fair wages upon the lands, but to envy their possessors, and even to regard them, in some sense, as a set of Monopolistic Tyrants depriving the negroes of something they themselves should enjoy. He can have no reference, of course, to the large body of Public lands in the State still opened to the settlement of white and black men indiscriminately. His allusion is distinctly to the private lawful possessions of the planters, and he regards their tenures consecrated by the law itself as an odious Land Monopoly. Had such a dispatch been addressed to a Convention of Planters and Landowners in either South, Middle or North Alabama, it would have been arrogant and insulting, but it would, in that case, have been addressed to a body of men having the right to consider the subject. But he well knows the sentiments entertained by the negroes toward the white land owners of the State, and he deliberately attempts to stimulate that hostile sentiment for his own base political purpose. He has already greatly injured the landowners of Alabama, and aided in a large degree to bring the poor, stupid negroes to the door of starvation. The sentiment of distrust and hatred of the great body of the white people of the Commonwealth, such wicked politicians as SPENCER have bred and fixed in their ignorant minds, may be distinctly seen in the spirit of the verbiage employed by WILLIAMS, the Chairman to President GRANT, begging for "rations" during this winter. We give an extract from that Report.

Therefore your committee do urge upon the delegates to this Convention the adoption of the memorial herewith presented. Your committee would respectfully inform the Convention that without the adoption of the memorial, that many of us, in all portions of the State, will be left in a starving condition, which will necessarily compel many of us to emigrate to other States, *which would leave many of our friends in the hands and control of their political enemies, for the reason of their inability to emigrate from county to county, more less from State to State.* Knowing the members of this Convention to be the people's representatives from all parts of the State, knowing the wishes of the people, your committee hope the following memorial will be unanimously adopted by this Convention, and properly signed and forwarded to the executive department at Washington.

Respectfully submitted,

A. E. WILLIAMS, Ch'n.

It will be observed that the Negro Labor Convention, this WILLIAMS, the Chairman of the Committee on Memorial, regard themselves as "the people" of the State, and Mr. SPENCER"S "Land Monopolists," as their "political enemies." It is to a strictly Negro Convention in its officers, organization and delegates, that the so-called Senator sends his Land Monopoly denunciations. No one can reasonably entertain a doubt that any Land owner in Alabama who has lands for sale would sell to an African and be glad to do it for a proper price. No one has ever refused to do so to our knowledge. Mr. SPENCER must also know this. If he means that the land owners should *give* the negro laborers their lands, his appeal should have been made to those who are expected to do such a profitless and disinterested thing. In this sense is it not, when addressed to the Capitol Labor gathering, the baldest kind of demaguism? The negroes at the Capitol all taken together do not *own* two hundred acres of land. They have no land to give away. Mr. SPENCER knows that they can settle under the provisions of the laws of the United States on the Government lands, and that they can purchase lands from private individuals provided they will present the price. He makes no suggestion to the landowners to *give* for either charitable or economical reasons, a portion of their property to the blacks. But he denounces the landowners by plain and designed inference, as Monopolists, to the landless negro laborers! There can be but one construction put upon this impudent and ill-timed despatch. For especial reasons of his own Mr. GEO. E. SPENCER revives the old ridiculous idea of "Forty acres and a mule."

It is for this poor creature--to make him Senator from Alabama in the Congress of the United States--that a number of the Landholders of Alabama helped the negroes last year to bring the present State Administration into power. It was SPENCER who ruled the Nominating Convention and fashioned the ticket, and all to elect himself Senator. It was SPENCER who brought troops into the State during the election. It was SPENCER who brought money into the State and bribed "loyal claimants" and instigated Kuklux prosecutions, and caused citizens of Alabama to be immured in a Northern penitentiary. It was SPENCER that an Insurrection against the rightful Legislature of the State was aided and abetted by LEWIS, the Governor of Alabama, at a cost of several hundred thousand dollars! It was for GEORGE E. SPENCER several "land Monopolists," native Alabamians, or men identified with the State by long residence, voted in a Court House room in this city, in the face of all propriety and in contempt of the laws and dignity of the State, for Senator of the United States from Alabama! They are now well repaid for their criminal folly.

Montgomery (Ala.) *Advertiser and Mail,* November 15, 1873.

V

LOCAL BLACK MILITANCY, 1872–1877

LOCAL BLACK MILITANCY, 1872-1877

The admonitions of the CNLU to organize fell on fertile ground, which was amply demonstrated by the widespread labor militancy of the 1870s. Characteristically, when black workers struck for higher wages and better conditions, their white employers viewed these demands as "a fearful tendency" to be "unreasonable" (Doc. 1).

An interesting diplomatic exchange occurred in 1873 which reveals the economic vice which trapped black stevedores and laborers at Southern ports. Because usually they were confined to unskilled jobs, blacks became desperate when replaced. Thus in 1873, when British subjects temporarily took jobs as stevedores in Mobile, Alabama, Pensacola, Florida, and Washington, D.C., angry black workers drove the foreigners from the docks. These disturbances caused the British consuls to file protests with the Secretary of State, Hamilton Fish (Doc. 2-6).

Labor disturbances involving Negroes, however, generally involved strikes for higher pay and better conditions. Most of these strikes were peaceful, but others were not. In April 1873 about 800 to 1,000 laborers on the Chesapeake and Ohio Railroad in West Virginia stopped work to secure back pay. Some of the strikers sabotaged operations by causing a minor train collision and several landslides which blocked the tracks (Doc. 7). In Jacksonville, Florida, black workers at the saw mills struck for higher wages and demanded a shorter work day. In this case, no serious physical conflicts occurred (Doc. 8-10).

The Louisiana sugar fields experienced some of the most militant black labor disturbances. In January 1874, for example, violence erupted in Terrebonne parish over higher pay. When the governor received a dispatch claiming that the strikers had "broken out into open riot and were murdering white people, burning houses, plantation mills and committing the wildest outrages," he ordered out the militia. When the strike spread to other sugar parishes, the state militia fanned out to quell the disturbances. The trauma such black militia produced among local whites was synthesized in the newspaper headline which proclaimed: "War in Terrebonne" (Doc. 17-26).

During the late summer of 1876, black rice harvesters struck in the South Carolina low country along the Combahee River, demanding a fifty percent increase in their wages. Although many hands appeared willing to work at the current rate, the strikers "visited" each plantation and "persuaded" them to join the strike. The sheriff and a "strong posse" rushed to the area to protect those who desired to work, and the strike was quashed (Doc. 28-30). The Galveston, Texas, strike of July 1877 also exhibited surprisingly little violence. Confined exclusively to blacks, tools were thrown to the ground and about fifty workers marched through the streets stopping work, their numbers swelling as they progressed. The major reason for the stoppage was the inability to rent, buy clothing, food, and medicine for their families (Doc. 32). No sooner had the movement evaporated among the men, however, when the black washerwomen in Galveston struck for better pay, and shut down the Chinese laundry shops which had been undercutting the women's wages (Doc. 33).

Predictably enough, white southerners reacted to these expressions of black militancy with alarm. Many blamed it on Radical Republican rule (Doc. 14), while others thought they saw the beginning of a communist revolution "with its sea of blood and its ocean of fire" (Doc. 16).

The most curious position on blacks and labor unions was expounded in the New National Era. Published in Washington, D.C., by Frederick Douglass and his son Lewis H. Douglass, the newspaper served as the official organ of the CNLU. The paper's editorials, which were written by Lewis, strongly endorsed the Republican Party. Spurred, no doubt by his own negative experiences with white unions, Douglass' basic disposition toward unionism was hostile. In the end, the only solution seemed to be for blacks to become capitalists themselves, or convince the capitalists to obey the Golden Rule, neither of which were very constructive alternatives (Doc. 40-47).

ORGANIZED LOCAL ACTIVISM

1. STRIKES IN ALABAMA

"There is a fearful tendency in this country to the unreasonable, unjust
and unsatisfactory strikes, on the part of laborers, to compel their employers
to accede to their demands for time and wages. The press dispatches for months
for which large sums are paid weekly by those who take them, have consisted
largely of accounts of the parades and movements generally of the strikers.
The newspapers have been filled with fearful accounts of the misdeeds and
violence of those who having seen fit to quit their work, endeavor to force
all other laborers to join with them in enforcing their demands. . . . Large
forces of police have been in constant requisition to preserve the peace, and
to protect property, and the lives of unoffending citizens. In short, the
'strikes' in this country are becoming terribly and wonderfully alarming. ...
     Such measures rarely accomplish the purpose of their inauguration, and
whatever is secured, it is always attended by greater privation, hardships,
and suffering. The cause of all this trouble consists in the nature and
management of the several trades unions with which mechanics of all classes
see fit to restrain themselves. These are generally controlled by young and
thoughtless men, without responsibilities, who can endure the hardships which
they force with terrible results upon their married brethren.

Eufaula (Daily) Times, July 9, 1872.

2. BRITISH VICE CONSULATE

Pensacola, January 8, 1873.

Sir,
     I have the honour to state for your information the following facts:
     The shipment of heavy timber from this port to European markets, during
the winter months gives employment to a large amount of skilled and ordinary
labour in loading the vessels, & a majority of the stevedores & many of the
unskilled men, thus employed, are British subjects residing in Canada, and
who come here during the labour season returning when it is over.
     Their presence and participation in the business of loading vessels have
excited the violent opposition of resident negroes engaged in the same pursuit,
an opposition which after minor demonstrations of hostilities culminated on
the 6th instant in open outrage and violence. The negroes assembled in an
armed mob and by force prevented these British subjects from proceeding to
their labours on board the vessels in the Bay, and throughout the day their
attitude was menacing. At dark, they assembled in large numbers armed with
pistols and clubs and at once proceeded to assail the British subjects referred to, who escaped with their lives only by flight and concealment, the
negroes entering and searching private houses and making deadly threats
against them. The police of the city was powerless and no measure was taken
by its authorities to arrest, or to punish the outrage. On the following
days, the 7th Janry, the British subjects were again by the same mob prevented from going to work. I then called upon the Mayor of the city, to
learn whether or not he would give protection to the lives of these British
subjects who are guiltless of all offence against the laws of the country,
when he informed me that he was powerless to prevent a repetition and continuance of the riot. I then suggested an appeal to the U.S. Naval officer
commanding the navy yard, six miles from the city, and in company with the
Mayor and the Sheriff of the county I called upon Commodore Middleton &

submitted to him a statement of which the indorsed is a copy, the Mayor & Sheriff at the same time representing themselves as powerless to control the riot and asking his assistance. Commodore Middleton promptly sent an officer & twenty marines to the city to cooperate with them & order was restored. As a repetition of these outrages may occur at any moment whereby British interests & lives may be imperilled, I have deemed it proper to report the facts for your consideration.

I am &c (Signed) W. K. Hyer
Vice Consul

J. J. Midland
H.B.M. Consul
Mobile

W. K. Hyer to J. J. Midland, Jan. 8, 1873, Notes from British Legation, Depart of State, Record Group 59, National Archives.

3.   BRITISH VICE CONSULATE
Pensacola, Florida, January 7, 1873

Sir;
    British subjects temporarily living here and employed as stevedores and labourers on the shipping in this Bay are by the force and violence of a riotous mob of negroes not only prevented from pursuing their business, but they have been assailed with deadly weapons and their lives threatened and the rights of peaceable British subjects are invaded.
    Upon application to the Mayor of the city for protection he finds himself unable to afford it with the means at his command & understanding that he has applied to you for a force to aid in restoring order and preserving the peace, I beg leave to submit the foregoing facts for your consideration and to express the hope that his request may be complied with. British subjects pursued by mobs of infuriated negroes armed with pistols and clubs have been pursued through the public streets and as yet no arrest or inquiry has been instituted because of the weakness of the civil authorities to cope with the emergency.

I am etc.
Wm. K. Hyer
1st Vice Consul

Commodore E. Middleton U.S.N.
U.S. Navy Yard
Washington

William K Hyer to Commodore E. Middleton, January 7, 1873,
Notes from British Legation, Department of State,
Record Group 59, National Archives.

4.   DEPARTMENT OF STATE
Washington, January 20, 1873.

Sir,
    I have the honour to enclose for your consideration copies of a letter from Mr. W. K. Hyer, British Vice Consul at Mobile, and of its enclosure. From these you will perceive that an attempt was made on the 6th instant by a riotous mob of coloured men to prevent certain British subjects at Pensacola employed as stevedores and labourers in the shipping of that Port from following their peaceful occupations. The authorities of the town seem to have been unable to suppress the disturbance or to punish the offenders. In the emergency an application was made to the United States Naval Office in command of the Navy Yard, who promptly rendered effective assistance, and I

have much pleasure in expressing my acknowledgments for this timely service
in behalf and for the protection of British subjects.

But you will perceive that fears are entertained that these outrages may
be repeated, and that the interests and lives of British subjects may be
endangered thereby. I venture therefore to hope that it will be in the power
of the Government to send such instructions as will prevent a repetition of
those acts of violence, which I am well convinced, are entirely opposed to
its wishes, as they are to the liberal spirit of the laws and institutions of
the United States.

I have the honor to be, with the highest consideration,

                            Sir,
                            Your obedient servant,
                            Edw. Thornton

Honorable Hamilton Fish

Edwards Thornton to Hamilton Fish, Jan. 20, 1873, Notes from British
Legation, Record Group 59, National Archives.

                    5. DEPARTMENT OF STATE
                        Washington, 24th January, 1873

The Right Honorable
Sir Edwards Thornton KCB
Sir:
I have the honor to acknowledge the receipt of your note of the 20th
instant, and of its accompaniments, relating to an attempt, alleged to have
been made on the 6th instant, by a riotous mob of colored men to prevent
certain British subjects at Pensacola, from pursuing their occupations as
stevedores and laborers in the shipping at that port, and expressing your
thanks for the timely service rendered by the United States Naval office in
command of the Navy Yard at Washington on the occasion referred to.

In reply, I have to state that, with the view to a compliance with your
wishes, a copy of your note together with its enclosures have been sent to
the Attorney General. A copy of your note has also been transmitted to the
Secretary of the Navy, for his information.

I have the honor to be with the highest consideration, Sir,
                            Your obedient servant,
                            Hamilton Fish

Hamilton Fish to Edwards Thornton, Jan. 24, 1873, Notes to Foreign Legations
in the U.S., Record Group 59, National Archives.

                    6. DEPARTMENT OF STATE
                        Washington, February 3, 1873

Sir:
I have the honour to acknowledge the receipt of your note of the 29th
ultimo stating that your Department is informed by a letter of the 27th ultimo
from the Attorney General that he has given instructions to the United States
Attorney for the Northern District of Florida to take the necessary steps to
prevent in the future the attempt alleged to have been made by a riotous mob
of colored men to prevent certain British subjects at Pensacola, Florida, from
pursuing their occupations as Stevedores and Labourers at that port, and I
beg to offer my best thanks for the measures which have been taken, and which

have no doubt will be effectual.
　　I have the honour to be, with the highest consideration,
　　　　　　　　　　　　　　　Sir,
　　　　　　　　　　　　　　　　　　Your obedient Servant,
　　　　　　　　　　　　　　　　　　Edwards Thornton

The Honorable Hamilton Fish

Edwards Thornton to Hamilton Fish, Feb. 3, 1873, Notes from British Legation,
Record Group 59, National Archives.

7.　COLORED TROUBLE AT STRETCHER'S NECK

　　CHARLESTON, W. Va., April 17.--An extensive and important strike among
the laborers upon the new Chesapeake and Ohio Railroad, from White Sulphur
Springs to Kanawha Falls, is in progress.　The strike is for about four
month's back pay, and the number of men engaged in it is estimated at from
800 to 1,000, mostly negroes.
　　The strike began near Stretcher's Neck, on New River, and the negroes
from there marched along the road westwardly, compelling all laborers, of
both colors, with whom they came in contact to stop work.
　　The strikers were augmented in strength as they proceeded, and when they
arrived at Kanawha Falls last night there was a very large force of them.
They have continually shown a very hostile and mutinous feeling towards the
railroad company and its officers.　At the Hawk's Nest, about twelve miles
east of Kanawha Falls, on New River, the negroes took possession of the station, and among other acts of violence broke and turned a switch so that a
train going east a short time afterwards collided with a construction train
upon the switch.　The collision resulted in the wrecking of an engine and
slight injury of several persons on board the train.　At about the same time
a very large rock and two or three stumps were rolled down the steep mountain
next above the Hawk's Nest upon the track, and the probabilities are undoubted
that the strikers were the perpetrators of the acts.
　　The belligerent spirit manifested by the negroes has inspired travellers
and residents of the sections in which they are figuring with fear and anxiety,
and the conduct of the strikers thus far means mischief beyond a question.
　　The amount for which the strike was made is variously estimated, but it
is probably in the neighborhood of $150,000.　Much apprehension is felt by the
people along the line, as the negroes will undoubtedly do a great deal of
sacking and plundering for the means of subsistence, the country in that section being comparatively poor in supplies.　Major A. H. Perry and Colonel
Vancleve, Superintendents of the road, have gone to the New River country to
see what can be done in the matter, but the strikers are bitterly determined
to have their money or hold the road and stop the telegraph and trains.
　　If an adjustment is not effected in the course of forty-eight hours, or
even less, the trains will probably stop running from necessity, as landslides are constantly occurring on the road.
　　　　　　　　　　　　　　　　　　　　　　　　　　E. C. B.

New York World, April 20, 1873.

8.　LABOR AND CAPITAL

　　A number of colored men met in Jacksonville the other day and passed the
following resolutions:
　　Resolved, That the relations now existing between capital and labor in
this vicinity, in common with other portions of the State, are unequally and
unjustly balanced; that the wages paid for daily labor are inadequate to meet

the ordinary requirements of the laborers, and the hours exacted for a day's work too unreasonable and oppressive to allow the laborer that recreation and rest which the laws of his nature demand.

Resolved, That ten hours should constitute a working day, and one dollar and fifty cents should be paid the ordinary, unskilled laborer for a day's work.

Resolved, That we consider the time and rates of pay, above named, just and reasonable for both employer and employee, and that we will do all in our power to establish these relations and exchanges between capital and labor in this county.

The immediate object of the meeting appears to have been in connection with and on behalf of the laborers employed in and about the various saw-mills at Jacksonville. An executive committee of five was appointed, with instructions to visit the owners of the several saw mills, and endeavor to make satisfactory arrangements with the employers in regard to the number of hours and pay of daily laborers, to prepare rules and regulations for the government of the League, and to report at an early day the result of its labors. The mill owners will no doubt receive the committee kindly, but capital will be able to hold its own in this country for many a day yet. And shall we say that it ought to be otherwise?

Tallahassee *Weekly Floridian*, May 27, 1873.

9. STRIKES AND WHAT THEY TEACH

The employees of the saw mills at Jacksonville are on a strike. They demand ten hours as a day's work, and an increase of wages. The employers have refused the demand and are supplying the places of the strikers with new hands. This is more than the strikers bargained for, it being essential to the success of all strikes that the strikers shall not only remain firm themselves, but that no others shall engage to fill their places on the old terms. If, the moment a strike begins, other laborers stop in and fill up the gap, the only effect is a change of workmen, and the end of the movement is worse than the beginning. The strikers simply manoeuvre themselves out of employment. This is well understood by all labor combinations, and hence in order to escape a result so disastrous, it is generally a part of the programme entering into "a strike" to prevent by moral suasion, and, when this fails, by intimidation, by threats, and not unfrequently by violence, the employment of other labor except on the terms demanded. In the present instance, no actual violence has as yet taken place, but the intimidating process has been put in operation and the mill-owners have been compelled to appeal to the authorities about Jacksonville for protection, which of course has been afforded.

No one will deny the absolute right of every class of people to fix the value of their own property, whether it be lands, stocks, labor or anything else, and to sell it at the price demanded or withhold it, as suits their pleasure or convenience. So, on the other hand, the buyer has also a clear right to pay the price demanded or not, as suits his pleasure or interest. Thus far everything is fair and lawful, and no one has a right to complain. But when either party undertakes to coerce the other by means which would constitute a crime if employed under different circumstances, then the combination loses its moral force and its members expose themselves to punishment as law-breakers. We know nothing of the merits of this movement among the mill-workers. They may not be sufficiently remunerated, and the terms they demand may be commensurate with the services rendered, but this has nothing to do with the question of violence. No resort to force to compel acquiescence in the employers is justifiable, any more than it would be in any other combination made up to promote certain interests and the use of force to make it successful.

As a general thing, the utility of strikes is doubtful. They more frequently fail than succeed. There there is the loss of time and the demorali-

zation which always attends a movement of the sort. In the case of common
labor, it is seldom, whether the strike is successful or not, and particularly when the strikers are guilty of acts of violence, that the old hands are
taken back when the trouble is over. It is an easy matter, comparatively,
to supply the places of mill-workers in whom no great amount of skill is
required to make efficient laborers, and this the mill-owners have demonstrated by going on as usual with their work, doubtless to the great disgust
of the disappointed strikers, who were probably told that if they "knocked
off," the "bosses" could not get along and would be forced to yield. This is
not the first time that pretended *friends* of [the] [la]boring man have got him
into trouble and it will not be the last.

"Strikes," says the *Union* with an eye perhaps on the Jacksonville one,
"are not generally caused so much by the suffering injustice, and destitution or helplessness of men who *work* as by the passionate and dangerous
appeals of those who do not *work,* and as demagogues stir up strife and bitter
feelings and animosities, not so much out of regard for the welfare of workingmen, as from a particular regard for men who by politics [illegible] in
some other way desire to live *without work.*"

Tallahassee *Weekly Floridian,* May 27, 1873.

10.   STRIKE AT THE SAW MILLS

The mill owners having refused to allow the reduction of a day's work to
ten hours, in compliance with the demand of the Labor League, the colored
laborers, with preconcerted action, refused to go to work yesterday morning
before 7 o'clock.--The owners of the mills, determined not to yield, told
them that they must continue to work as heretofore, or find other employment.
Both parties stood firm.

Messrs. Alsop & Clark went to work at the usual time, with a few colored
men in their employ. Messrs. Eppinger, Russell & Co., C. A. Fairchild, A.
Wallace and others were occupied as usual the first day of every month, in
cleaning boilers and making general repairs. They fired up last night, and
will go to work this morning with such help as they have been able to secure.
The mill men do not anticipate any serious interference with their business
by the strike.

The Superintendents of the mills claim that the strikers have not heretofore averaged ten hours labor a day, notwithstanding they are required, at
this season of the year, to go to work at 6 A.M., and continue, except for
dinner, until near sunset; that they do not average more than 8 or 8½ hours
in the winter, and from 11 to 12 in the summer. Besides they have a relief
of from one to two hours while changing saws, etc., almost daily.

During the day the strikers endeavored to induce the few men who continued work at Clark's mill to desist, and threatened violence in case they
refused. Mr. Clark sent word to the Mayor requesting the protection of the
police for his employees, which was promptly granted. Up to the time of
going to press no serious disturbance has occurred. A resort to violence is
discountenanced by the leaders of the movement.--

Jacksonville Republican, June 3, 1873.

THE LABORERS'STRIKE.--The strike still continues, and although there is much
excitement among the workmen, as far as we have been able to learn, there is
no disposition to do violence among the majority of them, even to the few
workmen who have refused to join them and still continue working the usual
number of hours.--Yet there are a few who are reckless enough to do violence
to the persons and property of all mill employees who disregard the strike,
as was evidenced by the mob on Monday night throwing brick-bats at a laborer
returning from Wallace's mill. One of the strikers, named Valentine, promptly

interposed and fired a pistol, diverting the mob, while the person assaulted made his escape. We are assured by the Police authorities that there is no reason to fear any serious disturbance.

Jacksonville Republican, June 5, 1873.

The *News* says: "We understand that Gov. Hart counselled the movement of the strikers, but we hope that such a rumor is unfounded, as, in our opinion, it would be lowering the dignity of his exalted position."

THE STRIKE.--The strike of the colored men employed at the eight different saw-mills in this vicinity still continues. The mill owners hold out against the colored men's demand for only ten hours' labor as stubbornly now as on the first day it occurred.

Messrs. Alsop & Clark have succeeded in employing a full crew of white men, mostly from the country, which, if they continue to work, may defeat the object of the strike at this mill.

Penniman's mill is also running every day, being operated by white laborers entirely. Mr. C. A. Fairchild has a small force at work. We are informed that he only intends to run until he can fill an order now on hand. All the other mills remain idle.

At Bradley's mill the hands still hold out, and the mill is not running.

We understand that the mill of J. W. Scott will be shut down for a number of weeks for the purpose of repairs.

Many of the strikers have quit the city and gone to other points in search of employment, which is more commendable than to hang about the streets in idleness.

Tallahassee Weekly Floridian, June 10, 1873.

11. A STRIKE IN THE RAILROAD SHOPS

Precisely at 12 o'clock on yesterday, every hand in the J. P. & M. Railroad shops at this place, including men and boys, white and colored, stopped work simultaneously and demanded their pay, which is now three months in arrears--their wages being due for May, June and July. Superintendent Papy was waited on, and he finally succeeded in lulling the clamors of the men by a promise to pay them off in full in a day or two. The hands, however, all refuse to strike another lick until they *are* paid off, and they cannot be blamed. They have had a hard struggle to live, and could not have got along at all but for the kindness and indulgence of our merchants. "The laborer is worthy of his hire," and it is high time the officers of the Company should make extraordinary exertions and any sacrifice to satisfy the just demands of their faithful mechanics. We believe that Superintendent Papy will "raise the wind" if it is within the scope of human power. The new management succeeds to a mass of debts and embarrassments of every description, the result of the Littlefield mismanagement, and it will be fortunate indeed and deserving of great credit if it is able to afford even temporary relief to the Road.

Tallahassee Weekly Floridian, June 24, 1873.

12. STRIKE IN JACKSONVILLE

The Jacksonville *Republican* of Saturday says that the strike among the mill workers seems to have come to an end. Many of the leaders have gone elsewhere to seek for employment, while others have resumed work at former

rates. Most of the mills are again in operation, others now undergoing repairs, will resume within a few days. No further difficulty in procuring
laborers is anticipated.

Seven or eight of the mill strikers at Jacksonville were tried at the
last term of the Duval County Court upon a charge of riotous conduct in
visiting the house of one Barclay, (an employee of one of the mills), at night,
smashing in the windows, cutting his wife and frightening his children. The
testimony was clear and conclusive against the strikers--nothing rebuttal
being offered by them--and yet the jury, (all colored but one) brought in a
verdict of "not guilty."

Savannah (Georgia) *Morning News,* June 27, 1873.

13.   COLORED COMMUNISM

For some time past it has been known that numbers of the colored people
of Colleton County, South Carolina, have been purchasing large tracts of land,
and dividing them in, or working them on, a co-operative system. The following interesting account of their operations is taken from the *Waterloo News:*

In this country the colored people own, and are successfully conducting,
some of the largest plantations. This is done under a sort of communism.
A number of them, in some cases as many as fifty, form themselves into a
society, elect their officers and adopt by-laws. They have regular meetings,
at which the officers report, and a specified amount is paid into the treasury
by each member. When enough funds accumulate in the treasury, a suitable
plantation is selected and the purchase made; usually the payments are in one,
two or three years, a good portion being paid at the time of purchase. The
land is equally divided by the officers elected for that purpose among the
members of the society, or so much as they wish to cultivate. Each is free
to work as suits him, and each can dispose of his crop as he deems proper.
No new member is admitted except by the consent of the whole society. All
sick are cared for by the society if unable to care for themselves--officers
being elected to look after such cases and report their wants to the society
at its weekly meetings, or at special meetings if the exigency of the case
requires it. All disputes arising among members are brought before the
society, certain of the officers being designated to hear and endeavor to
amicably arrange all dissensions; and it is very seldom, if ever, they fail.
Petty litigation, that is the great bane of the colored people in many sections, is in this way avoided. These societies are principally formed from
people who work for hire--50 cents per day being the sum generally paid; the
plantations are usually bought as soon as sufficient funds are in the treasury
to make the first payment. Upon those that have been in operation three or
four years the land has been paid for, and the members have acquired considerable personal property, and are generally prosperous. A sort of rivalry seems
to spring up between them, which is productive of economy and thrift. These
societies are situated in the low country east of the Savannah and Charleston
railroad. We do not presume to say that only the colored people who have
formed themselves into these societies show thrift and the accumulation of
property, for a number, who six or seven years ago were not worth a dollar,
now carry on successfully large rice and cotton plantations, and are becoming
heavy tax-payers. But in the particular section in which these societies are
formed, more property exists among their members than among those who are
fighting the battle of the life and death on their own account, while from the
formation of these societies they are enabled to purchase more valuable property and secure greater privileges than they could if each laid his money out
in a separate purchase, in which case ten or twenty acres or more of poor land
would be all he would be able to buy, as no planter would consent to cut off
and sell small tracts of his best land and retain himself the poorer portion.
This is undoubtedly one of the reasons of their success, as on nearly all the
plantations in this section a large portion of the land is almost valueless.
By securing the whole plantation they obtain sufficient good land for their

purposes, while he who purchases for himself generally gets such land that it is impossible to make more than a poor subsistence from.

Woodhull & Claflin's Weekly, September 20, 1873.

14. HOW THE RADICAL PARTY IN THE LEGISLATURE ATTEMPTED TO EFFECT A VIRTUAL CONFISCATION OF LANDS

We left this question yesterday at that point where in his furious zeal the State *Journal's* pet LEWIS, let the confiscation "cat out of the bag." The Democratic members who responded so promptly to his incautious statement of the objects sought to be accomplished by the Equalization scheme had, all along, known and *felt* that there was some iniquity covered up in that clause of the bill, but not having been "behind the scenes" they had been compelled to rely upon blind conjecture until this pointed declaration cleared up the mystery. They knew that, in the very nature of things, the Board could not have been intended to do *justice* (1) because its members could not be expected to possess the requisite information, especially with respect to counties they had never seen, and (2) because there was no means provided whereby such information could be obtained. Of these two reasons the first is well nigh self-evident; and of the second it is only necessary to say that the very proposition to establish such a board embodied an indirect charge that the only men competent to prove the real value of lands (the land owners) could not be believed on oath. Each tax-payer swears to the value of his property when he gives it in.--Hence to assert that any one county has failed to return a correct valuation of its real estate must necessarily be to charge that the mass of the tax-payers of such county have sworn to false returns. By whom, then, could any such Board hope to *prove* higher value than the owners of the lands had sworn to? Not by the owners themselves, evidently, because they would hardly consent to impeach their own veracity. Not by the members of the Board, because not one of them would be able to swear truly to the value of one-third of the lands in his *own* county. Not by the assessors, because that would be to put the fees of the assessor in one scale and his oath in the other. It was, therefore, very clear that if the Board acted at all it would be compelled to act upon arbitrary rules--and who could guess the limit to which arbitrary powers might not extend? This reasoning proves that some sort of *injustice* must have been comtemplated by those who proposed and pushed with such relentless vigor this Equalization scheme, because, as we have already shown, *justice* was altogether out of the question. Here we might have been altogether at sea but for the chart so kindly furnished us by the statesman from Perry. That "*injustice*" was to "raise the taxes to such a pitch that GREEN LEWIS, and others of his sort, could buy," at the tax sales, the lands which the large land holders of the State would thereby be "*compelled to sell.*"

But why should the large land holder be *compelled* to sell? Because the negroes, who constitute the mass of the Radical party in the State, acting and speaking through their so-called "Labor Union," had *demanded* it. How do the antimonopolists of the northwest seek to render effective their opposition to high railroad tariffs? By meeting in Conventions and fulminating resolutions against them? No! They rely upon nothing of the sort. They rely upon *legislation!* True, they meet and pass resolutions; but they do so with the deliberate intention of injecting the essence of such resolutions in the laws of the land. Take away the possibility of doing this and we may hear a *protest*--but no resolution. The "anti-monopolists" of Alabama occupy the same ground with respect to the land monopoly that those of the northwest do with respect to the railroad monopoly, so far, at least, as the means of relief sought are concerned. Both look to legislation, because, in the very nature of things, they can look nowhere else. It is also worthy of remark that those of Alabama (disguising their true character under the thin veil of a Labor Union) seized upon the week immediately preceding the assembling of the Legislature to indicate their pleasure by resolutions and to issue their petition any commands to that body. SPENCER, it will be remembered, was in Huntsville at the time the Union assembled. He knew that the members of the Union were not "land monopolists," and had excellent reasons to believe that there was not a land holder amongst them. This being the case what was there about a "Labor union" *per se* to call forth such a dispatch as he sent, about the "curse to the state" of monopolies in land? Doesn't it look a little suspicious, to say the least, that he should be so exactly informed of what that Union proposed to accomplish, if there was no prior understanding--no *conspiracy* between him and the Union? If there was such understanding, is it not fair to presume that SPENCER was not the only white Radical who had been honored with their confidence? THOMAS we know was. If others were thus admitted who shall undertake to say that all the leaders were not? The presumption that there was an organized conspiracy to tax the landholders of Alabama, out of houses and homes is, therefore, created in *advance* of the action of the Radical party in the Legislature, and that presumption deepens into an almost positive assurance when we behold a measure introduced in the Legislature, and championed solely by that party which could not, by any possibility, have resulted in anything *less* than a gross injustice to the tax-paying people of the State and which was, without doubt, entirely *competent,* to effect the precise purposes which the Labor Union must have had in view when the resolutions before referred to were reported and adopted. Conspiracies of this sort are always concocted in secret. It would not do to let the opposition know where the blow is to fall until the axe is sweeping downward upon the neck of the victim. Hence we are almost always compelled to rely upon circumstantial evidence to establish their existence. But in this case we have the positive testimony of one of the conspirators to give force and direction to the circumstantial evidence. He didn't want the clause stricken out.--Why? Because, as he tells us himself, "he wanted the taxes raised to such a pitch that the large landholder would be *compelled* to sell so that he and others like him could buy"--a declaration which, under the circumstances, could not possibly have meant anything else than that the Board of Equalization was the thing to do the work.

Montgomery (Ala.) *Advertiser and Mail,* April 22, 1874.

15.   WHAT DOES IT MEAN?

There was a meeting held at Pike Road Station in this county, composed almost exclusively of negroes, on Saturday last, at which the following resolutions were adopted:

WHEREAS, The crops of the present year have not yielded a sufficient supply to satisfy the demands of the planters and laborers of Mt. Meigs Beat; and

Whereas, The white planters of said beat have held several meetings, for the purpose of devising plans whereby they may better their conditions, without allowing the colored planters and laborers an equal voice, wherein their interests are concerned as well; and

Whereas, We, the laborers, hold that we are in no way responsible for the failure of the crops, and that we have worked as faithful during the present year as we have any year since emancipation, but in consequence of a bad season, wet weather and rain, followed up by the ravages of cotton worms, &c., came the present calamity.--Therefore be it

Resolved, That we consider it nothing but humane and just that the white planters should take our poverty and distresses under advisement, as well as their own, we being the bone and sinew of the beat, and in times past while seasons were favorable rendered them valuable service at their own prices.

Be it further resolved, That we desire to cultivate a friendly relation with the white planters of this beat, but cannot do so, if they insist upon discriminating against us by framing to deprive us of our rightful privilege to have a voice in settling the price of our labor, and the hours in which we shall work.

Be it further resolved, That we believe, and do acknowledge, that a thorough and economical cultivation of the lands of this beat are essential to the peace and prosperity of both white and colored people, and that the most successful way to do that is for each to regard the other's interest as being as sacred as his own.

Be it further resolved, That we are willing to try another crop in the coming year, upon reasonable terms, provided we are allowed to have an equal voice in the settling of those terms and a reliable showing for the procurement of whatever we contract for.

Be it further resolved, That we ask a careful consideration of these resolutions by the white planters of this beat, and a timely response, so that we may know upon what to depend for the coming year.

Montgomery (Ala.) *Advertiser and Mail,* November 4, 1873.

16. THEY KNOW NOT WHAT THEY DO

We feel sure that in the whole course of a long editorial life we never sat down to write an article with a more solemn feeling of responsibility, or with a greater fear of results, than we on which our pen is now engaged. We have watched with much sorrow the gradual, nay rapid spread of Labor Organizations, the beginning of which here we are now seeing. The beginning is here--the little rippling stream, so weak as to be insignificant--the end is like that of Paris. It is the Commune with its sea of blood and its ocean of fire. That movement, which has laid in ashes and bathed in carnage the fairest city of the world, began just where we are now in the organization of labor against capital. An organization of the most fearful import, and of the most terrible conclusion. When the reader looks at the insignificant list of delegates sent to Houston, and sees the absurd labors and professions that they claim, he may laugh at the movement. But we tell him that the movement, of which that Houston gathering will be an insignificant and infinitesimal point, is now almost powerful enough to carry an election to destroy the right of property; and that the day is not very far distant when, unless it is checked, we shall have scenes not unlike those of Paris.[65]

This labor movement is the supplement of the trades' unions. It is the second step, so to speak, in the progress of the principle that labor and capital are antagonistic.

The professed object of this movement is to elevate the laboring classes and improve their condition. They propose to accomplish this result by local combination, united by, delegates, in larger combinations, and so on until a central junta or Commune is reached. Now, to us it is evident that these associations are founded on two wicked, hurtful, and erroneous ideas.

1. That there is, and ought to be, a necessary antagonism between capital and labor.

2. That there is, and ought to be, a class of working men who are to be working men until the ends of their lives, never rising to the dignity of an employer or to the independence of a competency.

There is a third subordinate principle, if we may so call it, to these which assumes that there is not labor enough for all, and that, therefore, no man ought to do all of which he is capable.

We may turn to the platform of labor associations and the constitutions of trades' unions, and we will find, when the mass of verbiage is removed, that these three principles form the skeleton.

In the first place there ought not to be, there is not, any laboring class in this sense. Thrift and industry will raise any laborer in this country at least to any position that he may choose to assume which is within the compass of his intellectual powers. Of this there can be no doubt. We need not recount the evidences of the truth of this position. The freedom of labor, free education, the cheapness of land, and a hundred other considerations, render it easy for the laboring man to rise to a position of greater ease, if not of greater respectability. So that, instead of leaving the course of labor and capital free, each to work out its destiny, as God ordained that they should, demagogues intervene, and seek to band together labor, and wield it as a weapon against the alleged aristocratic influence of wealth. The history of all these organizations is a history of violence, a history of social disturbance, and a history of social degradation.

In England we know what the trades unions have done to the poor and to the rich. We have seen some of the results in this country at the Scranton riots, conducted, as they were by Welsh miners. We have seen an industry paralyzed and men murdered, because, in obedience to their marriage vows they were willing to work for the wives they had taken to their bosoms and the children that God had given them.

The Scranton rioters were a large part of that labor organization, of which the Houston gathering will be an infinitesimal small one. These labor associations, which are one in principle, now number an immense army--an army for larger than most contemplate. The membership of these associations is now as great as was that of the Confederate army at any one time of its existence. But these laborers are law-abiding citizens says one. Certainly they are. We do not charge that there is a man among them all that would resort to violence, but they are the members of a movement which has everywhere led to violence, and which has lately deluged France. They know not what they are doing or whither they are drifting.

This may seem like foolish prognostication, but it is a transcript of history.

Every labor association we have ever known has been composed of two classes, industrious laborers, who supported idling demagogues. Look through the Houston Convention and ascertain if there are any other classes of persons composing it.

The maxim "Let every tub stand on its own bottom" is a good one. If a laborer has intelligence, thrift and industry, he ought not to be curbed in their exercise, or deprived of their profit. That which is should so remain.

Now we shall be told that the Commune was God forsaking, morality denouncing, infidelity loving society, and it was, and this the labor associations of America are not, but they are traveling thitherward. They have begun by a denial of the right of labor, and the advanced members already speak these fearful sentiments. The writer of this heard them, and reported them at a labor convention, twelve years since--sentiments that were identical with those of the Commune--sentiments violating the right of property and the sanctity of the marriage bed. This has in rare instances, cropped out even in America, and it is the mark to which the whole labor movement has tended from its first inception.

These remarks may, perhaps, be the subject of ridicule because of the insignificance of this part of the movement; but it is the small foe of a great giant that is fast growing.

Galveston (Texas) *Tri-Weekly News,* June 7, 1871.

17.   TROUBLE IN TERREBONNE

A Gang of Rioters Interfere with Plantation Work and Prevent Well-
Disposed Negroes from Prosecuting their Contracts.

It appears that the recent action of the planters, with reference to wages, has not been affectionately received by the laborers in Terrebonne. Quite a formidable organization makes its appearance there in consequence of the determination to pay no more than $13 per month, and in many instances violence has already been resorted to. Gentlemen just down from Terrebonne report that during the present week riotous demonstrations have become the order of the day, and that negroes who accepted the new order of things, have been driven from their work and threatened with annihilation in case they accede to the planters' propositions.

The strikers evidently mean mischief as is fully shown by their meetings and the tone prevailing threat. A few nights ago some hundreds of them assembled in the town of Houma, disturbing and alarming the citizens by their conduct. We learn of several instances in which they have driven negroes from the field, cut the gearing of the plows or carts, and turned the mules out, merely because their victims preferred to go to work rather than join their riotous and unlawful league.

These things have been in progress for some days now, and threaten to lead to most unfortunate results unless checked. The planters say they are resolved to resent further interference. They do not wish to force the negroes to work; they freely concede their right to accept or reject the terms offered. But they will not permit the rioters to invade their premises and intimidate laborers who have contracted with them, and are honestly carrying out the agreement.

New Orleans Daily Picayune, January 10, 1874.

18. WAR IN TERREBONNE

The Negroes Murdering, Outraging and Burning.

Further developments of the Terrebonne affair show that late last night a dispatch was received in the city from seven of the most prominent citizens, in Terrebonne parish, addressed to Gov. Kellogg and calling upon him for assistance. It stated that the negro strikers in that parish and district had broken out into open riot and were murdering white people, burning houses, plantation mills and committing the wildest outrages.

Immediately upon the receipt of this information a reporter of the Picayune called upon Gov. Kellogg, who had retired for the night, but immediately arose, and seemed much impressed by the intelligence. He stated that he had also received a similar dispatch, and had ordered a strong force of militia under Captain Snow, fully armed and equipped, to procure a special train and proceed to the spot, and spare no exertion to at once suppress the insurrection. He was unable to state whether the special train had been procured or not, but that in the event of failure, he had ordered the cavalry, with a couple of pieces of artillery, to leave on the 8 o'clock morning train. He had also directed that a dispatch be at once sent to the gentlemen, stating the troops were coming to their assistance, and to use every means to suppress the rioters.

From his words and action, he seemed deeply urgent in the matter, and indeed, stated the peace would be upheld at all hazards and the mobs dispersed.

What the nature of the difficulty was has been already explained, and appears to have been caused by the efforts of the negroes to compel the planters to pay them on their own terms and keep others from working. From threats they proceeded to actions, which appears to have been of the worst kind, the entire parish being overrun by armed bands, and white residents being compelled to flee for their lives.

New Orleans Daily Picayune, January 14, 1874.

19. LABORERS'STRIKE IN LOUISIANA

NEW ORLEANS, La., Jan. 13. The negroes on Barjous, Lafourche, and Tecke are on strike, the landowners having resolved not to pay over $15 per month. They paid $20 last year. A large number of mounted men go from place to place, allowing none to work. The following message was received by Gov. Kellogg:

CHACHAOLUA, La., Jan. 12, 1874.

Dear Sir: Send us assistance immediately. Our section is in a state of terror and alarm. All work is suspended. Armed bodies of mounted men enter

our premises in spite of our remonstrances, and threaten the lives of all at
work. Our peace and safety demand immediate action at your hands.

The message is signed by a number of citizens of that locality. A number of people from that quarter called upon the Governor to-day and urged him
to send immediate relief. The Governor stated that a force would probably
be sent to-morrow.

New York Times, January 14, 1874.

20. LABOR TROUBLES

About a week ago we called attention to the fact that affairs in Terrebonne had reached a threatening stage of development. Armed bands of dis-
affected laborers were roving about the parish, intimidating such negroes as
had accepted the reduced terms of wages, and driving off the mules, oxen,
etc., used in cultivation.

It was thought, at the time, that even more serious results might be
evolved, especially since the planters seemed resolved to submit to no further
interference with their operations; but though there has been no material
change in the situation, we have not as yet heard of any violence beyond that
of arresting on plantations and an occasional raid on the plow-gang. In fact,
the negroes who really wish to work, and who, having the intelligence to
appreciate the situation, are willing to bear their share of the common misfortune rather than aggravate it by violence or disorder, are afraid to give
expression to their actual sentiments. In every instance where they have
made contracts and endeavored to fulfill them, they have been forced to desist from work, their teams driven off, their tools broken, and themselves
warned, on pain of dire injury, to beware of further offense against the
rioters.

This sort of thing has been going on for some time, and we are curious
to see how long that militia which is always ready to be used against the
planters will be withheld from service in their protection.

In Attakapas matters are not so alarming. There is a wide disagreement
between labor and capital as to the rate offered--which, by the way, are more
liberal there than elsewhere, being $15 per month, instead of $13; but no
demonstrations of an unlawful character have taken place. The negroes are
traveling about a great deal--have, in fact, made the fortune of the Bayou
Tecke packet, and they declare as yet an unwillingness to work on reduced
wages. But that is all.

Many have accepted the situation, and entered into the discharge of their
contracts without any interference whatever. There seems to be nothing more
serious at Attakapas than a silent struggle between labor and capital, free
from bitterness and unalloyed by the least ingredient of violence.

The Summing Up is that the planters will have to stand firm no matter
what happens. They have been giving way to extortionists demands for six
years past, and the result is an intimate acquaintance with insolvency. For
that, and for every reason of prudence, consistency, good faith, manhood and
self-respect, it behooves them to abide by the pledges they have made. Better
to let the year's crop go unplanted than add another chapter to the history
of failure, and establish a fresh precedent of weakness and irresolution.

New Orleans *Daily Picayune,* January 14, 1874.

21. WAR IN TERREBONNE

News from the Seat of War. Danger Imminent--A Train Fired Into. The Troops
Go At Last.

It being pretty generally understood Tuesday night, that a company at least of State troops would be this morning sent to Terrebonne parish, a PICAYUNE reporter was down at the train to see them off, but what was his surprise when he found only two officers, Capts. Snow and Joseph, without any assistance, proceeding to the point of destination.

They stated they were going to see what was the real state of affairs, and if soldiers were necessary, to telegraph for them.

Astounded by what seemed to be a direct violation of the orders of Governor Kellogg, the reporter hastened to General Badger's office, where he learned that though no men had as yet been sent, a posse was held ready at a moment's warning. The reasons for this, he stated, were that he believed two officers were enough to settle the whole difficulty, without an appeal to arms.

Thence the reporter proceeded to Gov. Kellogg's where he learned that further advices had been received from citizens in the district which stated that if two officers could be sent up to place themselves at the head of the conservative people, peace could be preserved. The Governor also stated that Gen. Longstreet had complained that the State had no money to send the militia, and that he would have to send a message to the Assembly, asking for an appropriation. This would be forthcoming, and then troops would be sent.

So much for all these statements, but the action is entirely different from that manifested when white people were in arms to protect their rights.

In fact, circumstances warrant a reference to the contrast between the present affair and that which was known as the St. Martinsville War.

Everybody knows how promptly the troops were sent, not only there, but to Livingston and other quarters where the mere recognition of a few carpet-bag interlopers or scalawag frauds was involved. There was no question then of finance or amicable settlement. The troops were promptly forwarded with all the pomp of war and its most effective implements. Half a dozen parishes were overrun, and prisoners brought to New Orleans in scores. It was a question of Radical officers and their emoluments.

Now it is a question of the lives and property of gentlemen who don't happen to admire the Radical administration, and consequently, the greatest caution and deliberation are observed.

The contrast is instructive, and will no doubt be appreciated by the public. It is still further illustrated by subsequent events, which, while we are on the subject, might as well be mentioned.

A cold-blooded murder was perpetrated in the parish of St. Martin, by a man named Veazey. This Veazey is one of the very parish officers, to install, whom the Governor sent his army into Attakapas last spring. Two others were arrested as accessories to the murder; one of them was Judge Theo. Castille, another of the parish officers, in whose behalf the powers did not hesitate for one instant to invoke the arm of violence. These men amongst them butchered a citizen of St. Martin by the name of Guilbeau. There was no concealment; everybody knew it; the local papers contained full accounts of the affair, and did not hesitate to say that Veazey had formally announced his intention of killing Guilbeau, the day previous to the tragedy.

The murderer and his colleagues have been set free. First they imported a judge from another parish. The parish officers of St. Martin being all arrested for murder, they had to call in an outside man. The imported judge first tried Judge Castille, and, having acquitted him, retired. Then Judge Castille, being restored to his office, tried the other two, and acquitted them. They are all free men now. Judge Castille was among the distinguished visitors to New Orleans last Monday evening.

For such men as these, and with no graver object than to secure them in the possession of offices to which their title was at least doubtful, the Governor found no difficulty in sending four or five hundred men with Winchester rifles and Gatling guns into the interior of the State, and filling the rich planting region of Attakapas with all the horrors and excitement of war.

For a Community of Planters and Taxpayers, whose property is being destroyed, and whose lives are threatened by an infuriated, reckless negro mob, there is nothing but the most diplomatic deliberation and pleas of financial necessity.

Look on This Picture and on That!

In one instance it was a question of the positions and salaries of three or four insignificant vagabonds--result, an armed invasion.

In the present instance it is a question of the life and property of an influential element of the population--result, the administration becomes severely economical and sends two men to Terrebonne to see whether anybody really is getting hurt.

It's an instructive contrast, as we said before.

To Return to Our Mattens

We will now take up the Terrebonne affair where it was first brought to Gov. Kellogg's notice in an official manner. On Tuesday afternoon he received the following dispatch:

To Gov. Kellogg:

Send troops at once to quell disturbance and riot.

District Att'y pro tem, Terrebonne. January 13, 1874.

To this he replied as follows:

To Tobias Gibson, District Attorney, etc:

Troops have been sent to preserve the peace.

Wm. P. Kellogg.   January 13, 1874.

As we have already shown, the troops did *not* go. Captains Snow and Joseph were sent to see whether troops were necessary. Meanwhile the rioters are under full headway. On Tuesday evening they fired into the train between Terrebonne Station and Houma, wounding one man. The situation is reported to Governor Kellogg in the following dispatch:

CHACAHOULA, Jan. 14.--Gov. Kellogg, New Orleans: I am unable to carry out the order of court. Excitement great. A collision hourly expected. I call on you officially for aid to quell disturbance and riot. The passenger train has been fired into. Send troops.

PARRICK O'HARE,
Parish Judge of Terrebonne.

I fully indorse the above and trust the assistance may be granted without delay. One man wounded on the cars.

TOBIAS GIBSON,
District Attorney pro. tem.

Corroborative of this we append two Special Dispatches received by the Picayune last evening from prominent citizens of Terrebonne.

CHOCAHOULA, La., Jan. 14.--To N. O. Picayune: Captains Snow and Joseph, of the Metropolitan police have arrived. Negroes still defiant. No murders or outrages as yet, but the condition is very critical. An open collision may be expected at any moment. T.S.C.

CHOCAHOULA, La., Jan. 14. 1 P.M.--To N. O. Picayune: The negroes are still in arms, and they will not be stopped any by United States troops, they say. One negro shot in the thigh this evening, only a flesh wound. The parish is still paraded by armed negroes, in squads of thirty and forty.

W.J.S.

Troops at Last.

At last the troops are sent. The facts were too glaring, the dangers too serious. Captains Snow and Joseph reported yesterday, and the result was instant action by the authorities.

Col. W. F. Loan, A. D. C., and Gen. Longstreet left yesterday evening at six o'clock with a detachment of forty infantry and one piece of artillery, and Col. DeKlyne goes this morning at nine o'clock with a squad of cavalry.

We shall probably have news of importance to-day, for all parties. Captains Snow and Joseph included, agree that force will be necessary to quell the riot.

LATER.

The subjoined dispatches were received by Gen. Badger late this evening.

ELLENDALE PLANTATION, VIA LA FOURQUE, Jan. 14.--Gen. A. S. Badger:

Matters have not been in the least exaggerated. Moral suasion no avail. Send about twenty cavalry to report at Houma. Sheriff Lyons, colored, has a possee of armed men, but can do nothing. Joseph and myself have used all our endeavors to compromise matters, but we consider a few troops absolutely necessary. Please answer at Chachahoula.

W. A. Snow,
Peter Joseph.

HOUMA VIA CHACHAHOULA.--Gen. A. S. Badger: Don't fail to send the
cavalry at the earliest opportunity. Affairs are very precarious. It is
impossible to telegraph particulars. Answer to-night.

                                                          W. A. SNOW

As has already been mentioned, a squadron of cavalry leaves this
morning at nine o'clock on a special train.

New Orleans *Daily Picayune*, January 15, 1874.

22. THE LABOR QUESTION IN LOUISIANA

The wages of field labor in Louisiana have been since the war and down
to the present year higher than elsewhere in the world. The laborer was paid
at the rate of $18 and $20 and sometimes as high as $30 per month, and fur-
nished with cabin, food and a plot of ground for a garden. We venture to
say that no laboring population in the world received better pay for the kind
of work performed. The result was that the men were able to support their
families without calling upon the women to assist them. The women and children
being kept from the field, a tide of negro immigration came flowing from the
less productive portions of Alabama and Georgia. Recently this immigration,
intensified by three successive failures in the cotton and corn lands to the
east of us, has assumed such large proportions as to alarm the land owners
of those States, and to cast upon the richer or more prosperous fields of
Mississippi and Louisiana a plethora of labor. This fact, taken in connection
with the low price of cotton, and the disastrously low price of sugar, following close upon a financial panic which has diminished consumption, contracted
prices in every direction, and thrown thousands of laborers into the streets
without bread, explains the necessity which forced the planters of Louisiana
to offer reduced wages. They could not afford to continue the high prices
which have kept them impoverished, and which, if continued would involved them
in bankruptcy. Deciding to reduce wages from $20 and $18 down to $15 and $13
they are met by insurrection, arson and, we fear, murder. Large sections of
the State are overrun by lawless bands of negroes, who visit plantations,
stop all work, threaten the lives of the peaceful and contented laborers,
and fill the country with terror. This condition of affairs can last but a
few days. The State and municipal authorities, acting in aid of the peaceful
citizens of both races, will promptly and effectually quell the disturbance,
with even less bloodshed and riot than are now witnessed in some of the
Northern cities and States, from the strikes of mechanics and the starvation
of workingmen.

Such a condition of affairs, even for a few days, is a subject of regret;
but the people of Louisiana have the satisfaction of knowing that the recalci-
trant laborers are not, like their Northern brethren, goaded to desperation
by the pangs of hunger. The laborer who can refuse to work for wages which,
even though reduced, are still higher than any paid elsewhere in the South,
or even in the Middle States, is in no danger of starvation. The white men
who have doubtless instigated and the colored men who have participated in
these riots have no claim upon our sympathy.

New Orleans *Daily Picayune*, January 15, 1874.

23. TROUBLE IN THE SUGAR FIELDS

Most of the sugar planters on the Coast have had no difficulty in reducing the wages of their hands to thirteen dollars per month. Last year
it was eighteen dollars. The crop made at this rate of wages has proved
unremunerative; in many cases disastrous. Not a few planters had determined

to abandon the sugar culture if the prices of labor were not reduced. The
negroes on the Coast plantations had the sagacity to discover the danger of
so great a calamity to the State, and especially to themselves, and accepted
the proposed reduction, and everything was going on smoothly on their plantations. Some incendiary demagogues in Terrebonne have, however, taken a
different view of the subject, and have stirred up the agitation and instigated the violence of which a full description appears in our morning's
edition.

New Orleans *Daily Picayune,* January 16, 1874.

24. THE TERREBONNE WAR

Arrival of the Troops.

No Difficulty Apprehended Before Saturday.

By a dispatch to Gov. Kellogg, last evening, from Col. W. J. Loan, it
was ascertained that the troops arrived safely and without difficulty. The
disturbance had been quelled, or rather the mobs, which had paraded the parish with threats of violence, had dispersed to their homes preparatory to a
grand rally and mass meeting on Saturday next, when some trouble may be
apprehended. The troops now on hand consist of a large detachment of infantry, some forty in all, one piece of artillery and a company of cavalry,
all under command of Major Flannagan, Chief of Detectives. They are deemed
sufficient for any emergency, and will probably quell such difficulty as may
arise.

The mass meeting which is announced to take place will be addressed by
the leaders of the strikers, and they may be worked into a fury, though it
is believed more pacific counsels will prevail.

Hamp Keys, the reputed leader of the mob and member of the legislative
committee who sent up as a sort of court of inquiry, had a conversation with
Gen. Badger before he left, and was informed that it would be better were he
to tell the colored people that they must allow all who desired to work at
any wages to do so; otherwise the troops would interfere. Keys replied that
he would see this policy was carried out; and as the committee has doubtless
also arrived, their interference may have something to do with the present
pacific situation.

New Orleans *Daily Picayune,* January 16, 1874.

25. FULL HISTORY OF THE AFFAIR

The Causes of the Riot--Mass Meeting--Threats of the Negroes

Arrival of the State Troops With the Prisoners

The late difficulty which occurred in Terrebonne parish seems to be a
fair example of the manner in which a large number of the negroes in the
State expect to conduct themselves under the prevailing system of Republican
government, and it is hoped the salutary check given them by the State forces
will prove a lesson they will heed in the future.

The first difficulty, it appears, originated on the evening of January
5th, when about two hundred plantation laborers met at the Zion Church, about
a mile and a half below Houma, and organized an association whose objects,
explained by resolutions passed, were:

First--To form sub-associations and rent lands to work by themselves,
they agreeing to waive all laborers' privileges on the crop made to such
persons who would rent them the land and also furnish supplies to make the

crop and subsist themselves.

Second--Binding themselves not to work for any planter for less than $20 per month, rations, etc., the payments to be made monthly in cash.

Third--That they would allow the person furnishing the supplies to appoint an agent on the place to take charge of the interest of whoever should furnish the supplies until the crop should be made and shipped to market, the factor of the furnisher of supplies to have the privilege of selling the crop and deducting the amounts due for the laborers.

To ratify these another meeting was called on the 8th inst., when the most incendiary speeches were made, principally by W. H. Keys and T. P. Shurbem, who advised them if the lands were not given, to seize them by force; also, not to allow any one to work for any wages under those stipulated, which were at the most simply outrageous. After the meeting a mob, headed by a fife and drum, paraded through Houma, threatening the citizens, but doing no harm. On the Tuesday following, a man named Alf. Kennedy and about fifty armed men came down the bayou, and upon arriving at the Southdown plantation of Mr. H. O. Minor, halted, for the purpose of preventing his laborers from working.

Mr. Minor, however, met them and explained that his people were peaceably working, and he would not allow them to interfere. After hesitating awhile they retired, though threatening to shortly return and burn his sugar house. The next day they did return, but were met by the colored Sheriff Lyons, with a posse of white and colored men, and they agreed to disperse upon condition the posse was disbanded. Captains Snow and Joseph, of the State troops, arriving at this opportune moment, however, considerably dampened their ardor; the more, when these gentlemen stated their action would not be tolerated by the State Government. Still persisting in their demands, however, the troops under Col. Flannagan were telegraphed for, and sent as already published; the rioters, before their arrival, firing into the train as it passed Terrebonne, and severely wounding Mr. Gery, who was a passenger in one of the cars. With the troops came Col. DeKlyne, Deputy United States Marshal, who, with the assistance of the cavalry under Capt. Taylor, arrested the ringleaders, as follows: Phillip Gray, Calvin Morris, Robert Jones, James McGinniss, Abe Chestnut, R. Mobly, R. Baron, Alf. Kennedy, Henry White, Ed. Bradford, R. Kennedy, Calvin W. Williams.

After the arrest of these and the arrival of the troops, it was decided that a grand mass meeting should be held. This took place Saturday, when Keys and others made speeches followed by Mr. Minor, when everything was satisfactorily arranged, and the troops yesterday returned to the city. The prisoners were marched to the Parish Prison and locked up, and the soldiers were dismissed to their homes, all apprehension of difficulty--at least for the present--being over.

New Orleans *Daily Picayune*, January 20, 1874.

26. THE TERREBONNE PRISONERS

A number of the participants in the late riots in Terrebonne parish were brought up yesterday before United States Commissioner Weller on the affidavit of Mr. Henry C. Minor, who charged them with unlawful banding together for the purpose of depriving him of his constitutional right to reside and carry on his occupation peaceably in said parish.

Mr. Minor testified that a number of those negroes came to his plantation and endeavored to intimidate his laborers into a cessation of their duties, and Mr. Cage, who was present, identified one of the prisoners, Alfred Kennedy, as being one of the party, armed with a sword.

Assistant District Attorney, Mr. Gurley, suggested that the ringleaders of the party be held under bonds to appear before the United States Circuit Court, and that the residue give bonds for their good behavior during the ensuing six months.

Commissioner Weller held that under the accusation he should require

bonds for re-appearance from all the prisoners, and that the several ringleaders should be held in a higher sum than the others. Accordingly, bonds
were placed in $250 on Alf. Kennedy, Calvin Morris, Perry Jones and Robert
Burrels, and the remainder in $100 each, to appear before the United States
Circuit Court on the third Monday in April next. The bonds were immediately
furnished and the prisoners discharged, the securities being Senator Thomas
A. Cage and Representative W. Ham. Keys.

New Orleans *Daily Picayune,* January 21, 1874.

27. THE LONGSHOREMEN'S PROTECTIVE UNION ASSOCIATION

The annual parade of the Longshoremen's Protective Union Association
took place yesterday morning. The union met at Liberty Hall, Morris Street,
at eight o/clock A.M., and formed the line. On the right were President Green
and other officers, and Mitchell's Band of twelve musicians. Five or six
hundred of the members were in the ranks. The line of march was through
Morris, King, and Broad Streets to East Bay, thence to Market, and along
Meeting, Calhoun and King Streets to the South Carolina Institute building at
the Race Course. The parade was exceedingly creditable, the members being
well dressed and a goodlooking body of men. Banners were displayed, and silver
and gold badges were worn by the Longshoremen. The turnout was composed almost
entirely of colored men. . . .
    The Longshoremen's Protective Union Association has over eight hundred
members and upwards of two thousand dollars in the treasury, besides some
fifteen hundred dollars in the Freedman's Bank. They claim that they are
conservators, rather than disturbers of the public peace, and have only
associated themselves together for mutual benefit and protection.

Charleston News and Courier, January 26, 1875.

28. STRIKE OF RICE HARVESTERS

CHARLESTON, Aug. 22. A serious strike has begun among the laborers on
rice plantations along the Combahee River, the strikers taking advantage of
the harvest season to demand an advance of fifty per cent, in wages. Many of
the hands are willing and anxious to work at the present rate, but the
strikers are visiting each plantation and forcing the working hands, by
whipping and other violence, to join them. The situation is critical, as the
crop must be harvested within a few days or be a total loss. Gov. Chamberlain
has telegraphed the Sheriff of Beaufort to summon a strong posse and protect,
at all hazards, the laborers who wish to work.

New York Times, August 23, 1876.

29. ROBERT SMALL ON THE COMBAHEE STRIKE

Editor, Standard & Commercial:
    BEAUFORT, S. C., Aug. 24th, 1876.
    Having been telegraphed by the Governor and Attorney-General to visit the
disturbed district on the Combahee, I abandoned my trip to Midway, at which
point I was to spend to-day, and with Lt. Gov. Cleaves we left the cars at

Sheldon and upon our arrival at Gardners Corners, we found assembled at Mr.
Fuller's store, between forty and sixty white men mounted and armed with sixteen shooters, Spencer rifles, and double-barreled shotguns, and about one
hundred and fifty colored men with sticks and clubs. Upon inquiry, I found
that about three hundred strikers were collected on the road to Combahee.

I proceeded at once to this point and there found a large body of colored
men and women, I called upon them for the cease of the strike and was informed
by them that they refused to work for checks payable in 1880, and that they
demanded money for their labor, and that if the planters would pay them in
money they would go to work at the usual prices.

I did not find a single colored striker with any kind of deadly weapon
about him, and found that they were peaceably inclined with no other object in
view than to be paid in good money for honest labor; this they are determined
to have or not to work.

The rice planters have been in the habit of using checks instead of money,
which are not good at any but the planters stores for the reason that they are
payable in 1878 and 1880, and that when these checks are used in purchasing
goods at these stores they become checks as change instead of money thus making
it impossible for the laborers to purchase medicines, or employ physicians
or obtain any thing except through the agency of the planter.

So far as violence on the part of the strikers is concerned there were
warrants issued by Trial Justice Fuller, for whipping one of their own number
who had gone to work contrary to the agreement they had made in their own
clubs, not to work for checks. These men upon being requested to give themselves up, walked out of the crowd and came into Beaufort without the Sheriff
or even a guard, and were waiting in town hours before the arrival of the
Sheriff.

The men were first taken to Trial Justice Fuller, but he not being there,
the men arrested came into Beaufort at the request of the Sheriff.

At three o'clock the entire crowd had peaceably dispersed and no sign of
a strike was visible.

It is due to Sheriff Sams to say that he informed the white men that he
did not need their services, and it is due to them to say that they offered
no violence to the strikers, during the time that I was present.

The following is the cause of the strike.

> "50. Due--Fifty Cents, 60.
> To Jonathan Lucas

or Bearer, for labor under special contract. Payable on the first January,
1880. J. B. Bissell

The checks are issued in denominations of 5; 10; 25; and 50 cents.

> Very Respectfully
> ROBERT SMALL

Savannah Tribune, 2 September 1876, p.2.
Courtesy of Joseph Reidy.

30. LABOR MOVEMENT

A serious strike took place recently among the laborers on the rice
plantations in South Carolina. The laborers demanded an advance of 50 per
cent in their wages and the "bosses" of course refused to accede. To make
short work with the strikes Chamberlain, the Republican Governor has ordered
the Sheriff of Beaufort to call out the military and "protect at all hazards
the laborers who wish to work" The interests of black and white laborers
are the same and when they strike they find their friends!, the Republicans,
the Democrats, and the Greenbackers all agreed upon shooting them down.

Labor Standard, September 23, 1876.

31.   STRIKE IN ST. LOUIS

This afternoon great crowds of strikers and some 300 Negro laborers on
the levee visited a large number of manufacturing establishments in the
southern part of the city, compelling all employees to stop work, putting out
all fires in the engine rooms and closing the buildings. . . . The colored
part of the crowd marched up the levee and forced all steamboat companies and
officers of independent steamers to sign pledges to increase the wages of all
classes of steamboat and levee laborers sixty to one hundred per cent.

Scranton (Pa.) Republican, July 26, 1877, dispatch from St. Louis.

32.   THE GALVESTON STRIKE OF 1877

Confined Exclusively to Colored Men, No Drunkenness Among the Strikers An Increase of Wages Demanded and the Impossibility to Live on Present Rates Assigned as the Cause of the Strike.

On Saturday night it was generally rumored that the strike would begin in
earnest on Monday morning, but no one knew who would start it, or what particular branch of industry would be first assailed by the leaders in the movement. During Sunday men would gather in groups late in the evening and talk
in ominous tones of the morrow, but no one seemed to know anything that could
subserve the purposes of a shadow to the coming event, and so everybody would
sigh and say as their groups dissolved, "We will see what we shall see."
Early this morning, at 6:30 o'clock, the movement began by the laborers
on the Girardin building, on Market street, organizing themselves into a sort
of vanguard to the general revolt that was desired by the laboring classes
against the prevailing rates of wages. About fifty men began the movement,
urging all the laborers in the immediate vicinity of the initial point to
cease work and join in the strike. The crowd thus formed marched in a body
down the Strand, at its intersection with Twenty-fourth street, where a block
of brick buildings are in the course of construction. Here some thirteen men
were induced to cease work, and a few of them joined in the procession of the
strikers, who next visited the block of buildings on Avenue A, which are
about being completed, when an additional reinforcement of fourteen men gave
their sanction to the strikers and retired from their duties to join in the
strike.
The Narrow Gauge railroad was the next object that invited the attention
of the force that had now reached in numbers over one hundred men. They first
went to the extended line of this road which runs along avenue A and terminates
a short distance east of Kuhn's wharf. Here the hands engaged in laying track
and ballasting the road were advised by the strikers that they were not being
justly compensated for their labor, and that no measure could repair the wrongs
to which they were subjected except that to which the body before them had
resorted. They urged them to lay down their tools and to "stand by their
rights" until the price of $2 per day was paid them. All the hands employed
at this point immediately assented to the proposition and fifteen more men
entered the list of those who filled out the strength of the column that was
leading the revolutionary movement against a low rate of wages. Mr. Hurley
also advised his men to stop until they would work undisturbed by the influences by which they were surrounded.
From this point the crowd proceeded to Bath avenue, at its intersection
with Market street, where another gang of fourteen men were employed on the
Narrow Gauge Railroad. These men were also induced to cease work and proceeded at once to the round-house of Mr. Hurley's road, and in doing so succeeded in securing four men to give their aid and assistance to the success
of the movement. Mr. Levine's pickery was next visited. This establishment
was closed, three men induced to quite work. The next place that called for
the attention of the strikers was St. Patrick's Church, on Avenue K and

Thirty-fifth street, and which is receiving its finishing touches. Here a few
men were employed, some of whom acceded to the arguments advanced by the
strikers and joined in their crusade against wages that are fixed at a less
rate than $2 per day.

The little planing mill on Winnie st., owned by Stump & Lewis, was next
visited. Here the engine was stopped and five men engaged in attending to
the affairs of the establishment were forced to cease work, which they did.
The engineer was forcibly seized by the men, but when he told them that he was
carrying sixty pounds of steam, and unless he could attend to his engine a
burst was imminent, they let him go after treating him quite rudely.

The Galveston, Houston and Henderson depot, at the western terminus of
Market street, was next visited. Here some few hands employed in scattering
dirt over the yard were admonished that less than $2 per day was an injustice
to the dignity of labor, and to the policy of this argument they yielded,
without resorting to the decision of any higher tribunal for a rule by which
their actions should be governed, but the cessation was a brief one, and with
the departure of the strikers the men resumed their work.

The Galveston Flour Mills were next visited, but it being suggested that
bread was high enough already, no lengthy arguments were employed to occasion
a strike among the employes of this establishment. Having completed the programme of the exercises the crowd left, as they said to report to Mr. McCloskey at the courthouse, who would give them whatever additional instructions
they might require in fixing permanently and successfully the results of what
they had so far accomplished.

Deputy Chief of Police Hutchings, with a detachment of the force, was
following on the heels of the strikers to prevent anything like violence being
done to private property, and to suppress any acts of intrusion that might
occur among the strikers upon premises where their presence was prohibited.
A NEWS reporter inquired of one of the leaders whether any talk of violence had
been indulged in by those engaged in the strike, and was told that not one
word of the kind had been uttered, and furthermore, that no policemen would
be needed to suppress anything of that character, as the men had all agreed
not to molest private property, and to hang any of their number who might be
guilty of such an act.

When asked the cause of the strike the men asserted that they could not
pay house rent, which in no case had been reduced, buy clothing, food and
medicines for themselves and families, at the rates they were receiving for
their labor. There was no drunkenness or riotous conduct among the strikers
up to this point, who evidently endeavored to accomplish the object of their
moevment with as much regard for order as possible. None of the artisans
employed at any of the places visited were interfered with, and none, but
those who live by manual labor were invited by the strikers to desist from
work. At several of the places visited objections were made to the demands of
the strikers by men engaged in work, who felt no desire to lose a day with
only a hope that wages would be increased, and who preferred to work for what
they are receiving rather than idle away valuable time with but a slim prospect of their conditions being permanently improved.

Mayor Stone met the strikers of Mechanic street at its intersection with
Thirtieth street and made them a speech, in which he advised them that they
were in a fair way to become violaters of the public peace, which it was his
duty to protect, and which he would protect at all hazards. He deprecated
the measure to which the laborers had resorted in order to right the wrongs of
which they complained, and in conclusion he advised them to disperse and go
to their homes and think over what they had been doing, and to devise some
more systematic and lawful plan by which they could accomplish the object they
had in view. He advised them further that they could appoint their committees,
who could quietly and orderly confer with the contractors in the city, and
thus, without anything like a tumult, or a single hostile demonstration against
the true interests of the city, they could solve the riddle that they were disposed to master by violent measures. He was listened to respectfully by the
crowd, and after he had concluded the march was again taken up for the court-
house, where it was understood Mr. McCloskey would meet the strikers and give
them whatever additional advice he had prepared for their government.

TAKING IT COOLLY

Capt. M. Quin, superintendent of the Texas Cotton Press, was sitting in the second story of the office building this morning, when he heard an unusual noise in the yard. He put on his hat and started to see what was up. When he looked out of the rear window of the building he saw the yard crowded with colored men. As he descended the stairs he requested those near him to close all the gates of the yard at once. He then wended his way to the yard, and asked the crowd what they wanted there. For some time no answer was given, there being, apparently no leader in the crowd; but at length one of the crowd said, "We want a drink of water." "All right," said Capt. Quin, "there is the cistern--help yourselves." When they had drank all they wanted and no one seemed inclined to tell their business there, Capt. Quin told them as they had all the water they wanted, they had better leave at once. As they looked around and saw that all the gates were closed upon them, they thought it would not be a bad idea to act upon the suggestions, and they did it at once, leaving as they had come, and no harm being done.

The crowd continued to the Court-house, where, as they said, speeches were to be made at 1 o'clock, but when they arrived, finding no speakers, the crowd, which had gathered all the idle colored men they met, numbered about 300. A remark being made that Burnet & Kilpatrick had a lot of hands working in the Tremont Hotel yard, the crowd left to disperse them with more earnestness than had before been noticeable in their conduct.

Arriving at the hotel, not a laborer could be seen, and no bargains being made at $2 per day, they went to Ruff's lumber yard, where several draymen keep horses. There they made no headway, for the draymen were workers on shares, and protesting they would be the losers if stopped, were allowed to go ahead, while the crowd marched to the corner of Thirty-fourth street and Avenue H, where George Lee's dray stables are located. At the gate they met and talked, Mr. Lee endeavoring to convince them if his men wanted $2 he would pay it when he needed them. Finally, wearying of a fruitless argument, he jumped into his buggy and drove off, saying to his draymen, "Come on, if you want to work" all obeying. The crowd followed to the Factors' Press, where they again watered, and started down Avenue F to Hildebrand's mill, where they heard hammering in the boiler, and yelling, "Come out if you are only getting $1.50 per day." Two colored men appeared, but refused to have anything to do with them; one of whom, however, watched his chance and ran up Avenue F, toward the Factors' Press, followed by the crowd. They losing him, seeing Mr. Lee's drays in the yard, they went again to the work of getting the draymen to stop and join them, but the drivers, failing to see the necessity of striking, and disliking to be forced to stop, abused the strikers. They finally yielded to force and drove back into the press, at the door of which the crowd stopped. An occasional yell being heard, "let's go in and take them off." Capt. A. P. Lufkin arriving, advised them to leave there, since the drivers, as they said, had been promised two dollars per day. The crowd remaining, Captain Lufkin drove around into the yard by a rear door, took the reins of a dray in his hands, and drove out through the crowd, followed by Cotton Press employes. Supervisor Burk driving one, Inspector Marrast another, Al. Hawkins another, Albert Arnold another, Mr. Crozier another, and Mr. Timmons another, Capt. Lufkin got through without serious difficulty. Those between him and Al. Hawkins found their drays literally covered with men, their horses' heads held, and the demand, "Get down!" given in a threatening tone. Dray sticks being raised, those on the drays jumped off and gave themselves to the defence of the drays. An indescribable confusion then arose.

Two police officers who arrived grasped men holding the horses, but finding they were too few to cope successfully, drew their clubs and used them in self-defense, or to prevent the rescue of those arrested. For some moments it was difficult to believe they could live long, considering the number of men grabbing and hitting at them, but Al. Hawkins and Mr. Arnold, who had passed through the crowd, came tearing up with Deputy Chief Hutchings, eight officers and a large crowd of citizens. Every one quieted down, and the regular drivers mounted their drays and drove across the street. The confusion was so great, and lasting several minutes, it was difficult for the reporter, though on the top of the wall, immediately above the crowd, to tell who was struck until quiet was restored. Then he found Capt. A. P. Lufkin had received a severe blow on his head, which fortunately was broken by his hat, and he being, as he stated, "the son of an Irish lady," was not easily hurt by a blow on the head. The two officers, though pulled around considerably, received no serious damage.

The most remarkable event was the coolness of officers and citizens, numbers of whom, after drawing pistols, would not use them. Within twenty minutes fully 800 men had reached the press, and the crowd, finding they could not carry their point, withdrew, going down Postoffice to Bath avenue, south on Bath avenue to Avenue F, and on to the Court-house.

The strikers began to rally at the court-house about 3 o'clock P.M. The crowd continued to increase without any exciting demonstrations until 4:30 o'clock, which was the time fixed by the strikers to meet Mr. McCloskey as was stated by one of their number. That gentleman having failed to appear, a considerable feeling was manifested by the meeting against him. It was suggested that Col. Geo. P. Finlay be sent for to address the meeting. He was sent for and came. The meeting was then called to order by Mr. Martin Burns, who said that it was manifest that the leaders who had heretofore figured at the head of the labor movement had gone back on those who had put into practice the principles they had taught them. That he was not accustomed to public speaking, but knew enough to say that the object of the workingmen of Galveston was to secure for themselves a fair and just compensation for every day's labor they might perform. He was in sympathy with the strike now prevailing in the city, and trusted that nothing would be done by any of the laborers of Galveston which they would hereafter regret.

Gilbert Baker then introduced the following resolutions, which were read and adopted without a dissenting voice:

Whereas the reduction of wages paid to the laboring classes, without any corresponding reduction in the cost of living, we believe to be a wrong that should not be tamely and quietly submitted to by those most deeply and vitally interested in securing a fair and just compensation for their labor; and

Whereas the necessity of revolutionizing the rates paid for labor has demonstrated itself in the countless strikes which have occurred in all parts of the country, visiting only those places and affecting only those institutions which have pressed the questions of reduction to that point where further toleration would result in the absolute starvation of the laboring classes, therefore be it

Resolved, 1. That it is not the intention or desire of the workingmen of Galveston to do violence to either the persons or property of its people.

Resolved, 2. That in inaugurating the strike which has taken practical form and existence to-day, we have but yielded to the popular manner of expressing our condemnation of the oppressions to which we have been subjected in the reduction of the prices paid for our labor.

Resolved, 3. That believing the law should be respected, and that all peaceable means should be exhausted by the laboring classes to vindicate their claims for wages sufficient to meet the ordinary wants of life, it is the wish of the working men of Galveston that the co-operation of the civil authorities should be secured in accomplishing the objects of the strike now existing; and in order to effect this end that committee of five be appointed to confer with the officials of the city and county for the purpose of securing not only the advice but the aid of these gentlemen in establishing permanently a fairer schedule in the price for honest labor.

Resolved, 4. That so long as the price of rents that now prevail continue, and the cost of the necessary elements of subsistence remain at the prices they now demand, that we deem $2 per diem for manual labor as a rate sufficiently low; and that we pledge ourselves by all honorable means to secure this rate as the fixed rate for this city, and that we agree to work for no less under any circumstances.

Col. George P. Finlay was then called for, and responded by saying that he was in sympathy with the sufferings of the laboring classes, but that he did not come to indulge in anything that might be calculated to make the workingmen before him laugh or cry. He came to speak candidly his mind touching a question in which every man before him was interested. He then reviewed the conflicts that have for years periodically broken out between labor and capital, and showed how the greatest minds and most eminent economists of the

world have devoted years of patient study to the solution of those causes
that give origin to them, and said that the strikes that are now prevailing
over the country were attributable to known causes that should be remedied,
and that until those causes were removed strikes and other outbreaks would
continue. He then called the attention of his hearers to the dignity of the
law, and said that it was a dignity that stood out above the dignity of labor
or the dignity of anything else. He said that the laws gave to every man
the right to do just as they please so long as they were pleased to do right.
That it was not right to restrain any man from doing as he pleased so long
as he was doing nothing that the laws prohibit. If any man wanted to work
for $1.50 a day let him do it. If you want to raise wages, get together and
organize and do all you can to increase the rate of your pay, but do not go
outside of the law. Stay within legal bounds, and if you can induce enough
of your number to join you in fixing the price of labor at $2 a day, you will
thereby create a corner on that commodity, and thus you will force those who
are bound to have your services to pay you your price. He told the men of
the rumors that were prevailing over the city, and how women and children
were suffering all the terrors of intense fear over the demonstrations of
the day, and which Galveston had witnessed for the first time in its history.
He told them that this demonstration was wrong, and instead of resulting in
good to the working man it was entirely possible and highly probable that all
those who had engaged in it would find themselves coming out of it at the
"little end of the horn." His speech was in favor of respecting the law and
a bold assertion of the fact that strikes never brought any permanent good
to either the country or to those who engage in them. He concluded by coun-
seling the men present to disperse and go to their homes and stop striking,
and he assured the colored men that the white people were taking no part in
the strike, and did not intend to do so, and that the best thing they could
do would be to emulate the example set them by the white laborers of the
city, and return to peaceful avocations.

Mr. Burns, the President, then arose and said that unless something was
done to save honest industry from competition with convict labor that the
time would soon come when every working man would of necessity belong to the
convict class. He assured the colored men that the white laborers of the
city would never go back on the movement.

Mr. Ferrier arose and said that he was a white man, and a laboring man,
and had heard Col. Finlay's speech, which he thought was an effort to throw
cold water on the movement. He assured the colored men that the white men
would never go back on them so long as they were striving to increase the
price of honest industry.

The following is the committee appointed by the President to carry out
the objects of the resolutions: Wm. Ferrier, D. W. Burke, J. McCubbins,
John Wilson, J. L. Washington.

The President suggested that a committee be appointed to go around at
night to the different boarding-houses and induce the men not to work until
the wages were conceded. He thought this a better plan than parading through
the streets.

The following is the committee appointed for this purpose. J. F. Doud,
George Summers, Frank Holt, George Baker and Chas. Eyer.

The meeting adjourned until seven o'clock this morning.

After the adjournment of the meeting, Mr. McCloskey appeared in the
court-room; and after the persons present had expressed their willingness to
hear anything that he might have to say, he ascended the judge's stand and
said that he had had no intimation of the fact that he was expected to meet
the men engaged in prosecuting the strike, except what he had seen in the
evening NEWS, but that he was present to talk to honest men. The Galveston
NEWS, he averred, was an enemy to the true interests of the working classes,
and had its emissaries engaged in watching his movements; that it had made
statements as to the objects of the workingmen that were not true; that it
had announced that meetings would be held when it knew that no such thing was
even in contemplation. [This a representative of the NEWS present denied.]
He then took up the Hurley administration and asserted that the sidewalk improvement bonds issued by Mayor Hurley were a cheat and a swindle upon their
face, and that he had the history of this great fraud from the record; he
knew all the thieves who were interested in it, and was not afraid to name

them. He deplored the burden of taxation which would result to the people
from the recognition given to these bonds by Mayor Stone and his co-operators
in the present city administration. He said that at a great sacrifice to
himself, physically, mentally and financially, he had started a paper which
represented the honest men of the city; that he had given the sale of it to
one of the head boys of the NEWS office, who had failed to settle squarely
with him, and when pinned down to the count of the papers he had received,
and compelled to make a showing for them, he had gone into the NEWS office
and brought the papers forth. He asserted that the NEWS had resorted to
this measure in order to suppress the diffusion of his paper. Most of the
speech was marked by such unmitigated scurrility as to make it unfit to be
literally reported.

Galveston News, July 31, 1877.

33. BLACK WASHERWOMEN STRIKE IN GALVESTON, TEXAS

So-Called Washerwomen, all Colored, Go for Each Other and the Heathen Chinee.

     Monday night colored women, emboldened by the liberties allowed their
fathers, husbands and brothers, during Monday, and being of a jealous nature,
determined to have a public hurrah yesterday of their own, and as the men had
demanded two dollars for a day's labor they would ask $1.50, or $9 per week.
As women are generally considered cleansers of dirty linen, their first move
was against the steam laundry, corner of Avenue A and Tenth street, owned by
Mr. J. N. Harding, who has in his employ several women, as it happened
yesterday all white.
     About 6.30 A.M. colored women began collecting about his house, until
they numbered about twenty-five, seven men being with them. The laundry
women were soon seen coming to work. When met and told that they should not
work for less than $1.50 per day, four cursed back; but, one, a Miss Murphy
went into the house and began working. Seeing this, the women rushed in,
caught her and carried her into the street, and by threats forced her to
leave. As no other laborers were found, a council of war was being held,
when a colored woman passed by and entered the house to collect money for
Monday's labor. The cry was raised that Alice had gone back on them, and
Alice, being generally obnoxious to one or two colored women had spite "agin
Alice anyway." A rush was made for her, but Alice is not slow in her motions,
therefore the first who got in reach went to grass from a well-directed blow,
but they were too many for Alice, who was literally covered with women,
clawing and pulling, until Alice's clothes were torn from her body and they
could get no hold, then the poor woman was let up and driven off.
     This success again emboldened the women to further demonstrations. The
cry was raised, "Let's lock them out for good; here's nails I brought especially." An axe lying in the wood pile was grabbed, and the laundry house
doors and windows secured. Then off they started for the heathen Chinee, who
"washee Mellican man clothes so cheapee allee vile," but before leaving Mr.
Harding was warned that this visit would be repeated at one o'clock and again
to-day. "Now for the Chinee, we'll drive them away. So down Market street
they went, led by a portly colored lady, whose avoirdupois is not less that
250.
     On the way many expressions as to their intentions were heard, such as
"We will starve no longer." "Chinese got no business coming here taking our
work from us." Each California laundry was visited in turn, according to its
location, beginning at Slam Sing's, on Twentieth street, between Market and
Postoffice, and ending at Wau Loong's corner of Bath avenue and Postoffice
street.
     At these laundries all the women talked at once, telling Sam Lee, Slam
Sing, Wau Loong and the rest that "they must close up and leave this city
within fifteen days, or they would be driven away," each Chinaman responding
"Yees, yees," "Alice rightee," "Me go, yees,' and closed their shops. The

women proceeded through Market street to Eighteenth where they scattered
after avowing they would meet again at 4 o'clock on the corner of Market
and Eleventh streets and visit each place where women are hired, and if they
receive less than $1.50 per day or $9 per week they would force them to quit.

Galveston News, August 1, 1877.

34. REPORT OF MEETING OF AMALGAMATED TRADE UNIONS, NEW YORK CITY, JULY 26, 1877
Speech of J. P. McDonnell

It was a grand sight to see in West Virginia, white and colored men
standing together, men of all nationalities in one supreme contest for the
common rights of workingmen (loud cheers). The barriers of ignorance and
prejudice were fast falling before the growing intelligence of the masses.
Hereafter there shall be no north, no south, no east, no west, only one land
of labor and the workingmen must own and possess it (tremendous applause).

Labor Standard, August 4, 1877.

35. MEETING OF BLACK WORKERS IN VIRGINIA

ALEXANDRIA, VA. At a meeting of colored Workingmen in Alexandria county,
Va., a resolution was adopted that the railroad company commencing operations
in our county, near the Aqueduct bridge, promises to be a curse instead of a
blessing, by offering 60 cents only for ten hours hard labor, by the obligation to purchase at their own commissary and at their own rates; and they
further seek to intimidate by representing that laborers from the District
of Columbia be procured upon these terms; and assert their ability to introduce convict labor from the Richmond Penitentiary; that we frown down and
protest against this imposition upon our rights; this unholy advantage of the
already oppressed poor, and that we demand what is just and fair, and respectfully requires laborers of the District of Columbia and the city of
Alexandria to do the same.

Labor Standard, March 17, 1878.

36. COLORED WAITERS' PROTECTIVE UNION

Over 200 of the colored waiters who attend the hotels at the principal
watering places and seaside Summer resorts met last evening in the Bethel
Church, Sullivan street, near Bleecker Street, to protest against the proposed reduction of wages for the ensuing season. The meeting was called to
order by Jesse Potter. Henry Downing was appointed Chairman, and Benjamin
Forde Secretary. The waiters complain that the proprietors of the principal
hotels in Saratoga--the United States, the Grand Union, Clarendon, Congress
Hall, and others--have given notice through the head waiters, who employ the
side waiters, that the wages in future shall be $20 per month, instead of
$25, as heretofore. Out of this sum a man must pay his fare to and from
New York, Washington, or even from Savannah to Saratoga, Sharon Springs or
Newport, and also discharge his wash bills. This the waiters find it impossible to do and continue honest men. They are almost all men of family,
and with the old pay find it very difficult to live. They charge the head

waiters, who get a percentage on the savings, with being the cause of the trouble. They appeal to the proprietors to consider their case and deal fairly by them. A copy of the resolutions will be sent to each of the proprietors of the hotels at the Summer resorts. A committee was appointed to communicate with the colored waiters in the various cities of the States with a view to co-operation.

New York Times, April, 26, 1878.

37. OYSTER SCHUCKERS STRIKE

BALTIMORE, Oct. 23.--The oyster schuckers, white and colored, now on a strike, paraded this afternoon with bands of music, and at night held a mass meeting on Monument Square, where several speeches were made. The strike was against an alleged increase in the size of the oyster measure, by which the schuckers say they are required to open more oysters than heretofore for the same pay. The procession was largely increased by other unemployed workmen sympathizing with the strikers, and numbered several thousand persons. The proceedings were orderly. During the parade a colored striker was shot through the neck and seriously wounded by the accidental discharge of a pistol carried by another striker. It is said that only one packing house in the city is at work at present.

Labor Standard, November 2, 1878.

38. FORMATION OF THE LABORING MAN'S ASSOCIATION OF BURKE COUNTY, GEORGIA

We the laboring men of Burke County, State of Georgia, believe it to our duty for our mutual benefits to organize ourselves into a Laboring man's ciation, the same to be organized and incorporated, into an incorporated company, under and by virtue of the Laws of Georgia made and provided for such organizations, to wit.
That we will organize ourselves, into an incorporated company in and for Burke County, Georgia, To be known by the name and style of the, Laboring Man's association of Burke County. Said company to be governed and controlled by a board of Directors of seven residents, citizens of Burke Co. A President, Secretary & Treasurer. Said Directors elected by the stockholders of said Comp'y, the President, Secretary & Treasurer to be elected by the board of Directors, the capital stock of said co. shall be fifty thousand dollars and may be increased to two hundred; and shall be allowed to commence business. So soon as two thousand dollars in cash is paid, into the Treasurer, the stock shall be ten dollars pr. share, and each stockholder entitled to one vote for each share. Said company shall have the power to establish agencys, in each militia District, of said County of Burke, which Agency shall be allowed to carry on such business, in said District or Districts, as shall be deemed proper by the officers of said Company. Said Company shall be governed by such by-laws, as shall be adopted by said Company and we the undersigned stockholders, doth hereby bind ourselves our heirs and assigns, to be governed by the constitution and by laws adopted by said Company after a legal charter is obtained, in witness whereof we have hereunto affixed our signatures with the number of shares, taken by each of us opposite our signatures: . . .

Official Papers & Writings: Political, 1875-1885, N.d., Bryant Papers, Duke. Courtesy of Joseph Reidy

THE *NEW NATIONAL ERA* AND THE LABOR QUESTION, 1870-1874

39. HORACE H. DAY TO THE EDITOR OF THE *New National Era*

Let us all labor, however humble our lot, for the overthrow of all momopolies, and thus keep on the work, and by the inauguration of such laws as will no longer leave open the door which excites men to avarice.

The ways are already inaugurated in the platform of the Grangers and Labor Reformers for systems of equal justice to all regardless of sex or color. Let us, then, unite and strive to give them the force of law in our nation, that other nations will be compelled to inaugurate and practice the same. [66]

The Labor Reformers are, and have been for many years to this end, and first--most important step now--is for the three sixty-five convertible bonds system in finance, looking to the time when eight hours, or even less, shall be all any toiler need require for a day's work. We the laboring men, not the rich bankers and speculators, pledged our labor and laid down our lives with and for you in the death struggle, in which your friend Sumner sounded the trumpet, and won the orator's plaudit. We now ask the colored race, whose liberty we laid down our lives and pledged our labor to secure, to help us in restoring our liberty, and to break the financial chains, which in this contest were fastened not only upon us, but you as well.

So far as the NEW NATIONAL ERA is concerned, under its present management, we know we shall not ask in vain, but would impress upon you and upon all that until this measure of even justice is the law of the land, there can be no peace or substantial beginning of the work which shall answer Sumner's prayer for "the substitution of arbitration for war."

Horace H. Day

New National Era, April 16, 1874.

40. THE WORKINGMAN'S PARTY

There is, there has been, and there can be, but one real workingman's party in this country. That is the party of equal rights and progress, known as the Republican party. It is the only party which has ever done anything for the workingman, and this it has done in the true spirit of justice, by seeking to secure to every individual the full enjoyment of his natural rights, and an equal voice in moulding the affairs of local, State, and national government. It puts the destiny of the individual in his own hands, by giving all, without distinction of race, color, or previous condition, an equal chance in the race of life. Any party which seeks or pretends to do more or less for the workingman is an injury both to him and to the country at large; for, let it perpetually be borne in mind, that the true interests of the individual and of the nation are identical and never antagonistic, and that what really promotes the one promotes the other. In all cases where their interests seem to clash, either the individual or the Government, if not both, are at fault.

The Republican party, therefore, seeks to improve the condition of the workingman by administering the affairs of the Government in accordance with the principles of equal and exact justice to every individual, class, and race. To this end it has always worked and is steadily working. In the language of the Iowa Republican State Convention, "It has given to the poor man a homestead; it has abolished slavery and established manhood suffrage, crushed treason, given us the Pacific Railroad, settled the right of self-expatriation, and maintained the honor, integrity, and credit of our nation.

It has vindicated the Monroe doctrine by preventing foreign powers from
interfering with the governments on this continent. To perpetuate it in
power is the only safe guaranty for peace and prosperity in the future.

Nearly all these advantages have been secured in the face of persistent
and often violent Democratic opposition. The Democratic party unanimously
opposed the homestead law; it originated and sympathized with the rebellion;
it bitterly resisted emancipation, and even now denounces manhood suffrage;
it has steadily abused the government for its aid in the building of the
Pacific railroad; it advocated the dishonest and pernicious doctrine of repudiation; it fraternized with the invader of Mexico, and now warmly sympa-
thizes with him in his war upon Germany unity. Everywhere, the Democratic
party shows itself to be the enemy of progress and good government, and in
favor of those abominable race and class distinctions which degrade the
workingman to the level of the brute, and must ever continue to so degrade
him as long as they are tolerated.

There is no justice or safety in any organization which seeks to
specially promote the interests of any one class of citizens at the expense
of others. A capitalists' party, a producers and manufacturer's party, or a
workingman's party within the circumscribed meaning of these terms, would be
at once a menace to all other class interests, and would not only provoke the
organization of political parties or factions for the special protection of
each distinctive class, but create such divisions that anarchy and violence
would sooner or later become inevitable. Hence, we must not for a moment
tolerate the idea of arraying the employer against the employee, the capitalist against the business man, the manufacturer and producer against the
laborer, the rich against the poor, the strong against the weak, nor encourage any of the antagonisms, so freely prated about and advocated by the shal-
low if not vicious demagogue. We must seek rather, by just laws and efficient administration, to harmonize all these superficially antagonistic
interests, justice, universal justice, and not special privileges and advantages, is what we should perpetually aim at. Equal justice will wrong no
man, and give no good cause for complaint even to the most selfish.

All who are in favor of a just Government, and of not only doing to
others as they would be done by, but of asking nothing for themvelves that
they are not willing to accord to their neighbors, must elect to go with the
Republican party, which is earnestly laboring to promote the general welfare,
to make the individual free, and to give him equal opportunities everywhere.
This is not the work of a day, but of all time, and demands the earnest attention and co-operation of every lover of justice and humanity. It cannot
be accomplished by throwing power into the hands of a non-progressive, sectional hate breeding and race and class distinction party, like the democratic; nor by getting up political organizations based on special manufacturing capital, trade, or labor interests. Any party, to be successful
and do good, must be organized on principles as universal as those lying at
the foundation of our institutions and based on the natural order of things.
It must not only comprehend every individual and class. Such an organization
is the Republican party, and such are its aims, as is abundantly testified
by its record. It is the working man's and every other man's party, and
deserves the support of all.

New National Era, September 15, 1870.

41. THE TRUE LABOR REFORM

Under the system of slavery Capital owned Labor, and the politicians of
our Southern States affirmed this to be the normal relation of the two forces.
It is a long step from slavery to the wage system--a grand stride, which the
toilers of even Christian Europe were centuries in making. Slavery was the
prevailing system in Rome when their much vaunted civilization was at its
height. It disappeared but yesterday from the United States and Russia, and
is just going in Brazil. It stills lingers like a blighting shadow in a few

dark corners of the globe where the light of the nineteenth century has not yet fully penetrated.

But it is also a long step from the wage system to the complete emancipation of the working people. The relation of laborer to employer is servitude for a consideration--a modified slavery entered voluntarily by the laborer himself, and terminable at his pleasure, subject to forfeiture of pay if terminated before the expiration of a specific contract.

It may be asked, What better system can be adopted to carry on the vast industrial operations of the world? How are the hired laborers to be entirely emancipated from their condition of modified servitude without utterly disorganizing business of every kind? How are they to live without the wages which capitalists pay them, and how are capitalists to dispense with the hired muscle and brain which now render their money valuable to themselves and society? We answer that co-operation--co-operation both in production and distribution--is that better system which is eventually to supplant the present one and join capital and labor in a grand harmonious beneficent union.

Most of the leaders of the workingmen's association make war on capital and denounce it as the chief cause of the poverty of the laboring classes; many of them are more or less adherents of communism. The disproportionate distribution of wealth certainly is one of those evils which puzzle the greatest national economists; but those who merely denounce capital and want to abolish it, are rather fighting a symptom, a consequence, than a cause. We think that real pauperism, wherever it is found, can always be traced back to faulty political institutions; first of all, to monarchism with all the veils and wrongs attending it. A glance on Europe reveals the fact that there is not one country but what is more or less cursed with monarchism, feudalism, serfdom, priest rule, privileged classes, and inequalities of every description. The soil was owned from times almost immemorable by the few, who often exercised an almost unrestrained arbitrary power over the welfare and even the lives of the many. All high offices, all positions of honor being in the hands of the privileged classes, it was only a necessary consequence that the masses of the people, deprived of representation, debarred from owning the soil they were compelled to till for others, shut out from instruction and enlightenment, and consequently without the shadow of a hope to work their way up, should be reduced to abject degradation and poverty. It is true that many of these abuses have disappeared in the course of time, though their remnants are left here and there in the shape of deficient representation, prerogatives of certain classes, and the like. And even where there is perfect equality before the law now-a-days, it cannot undo the consequences of the accumulated wrongs perpetrated through many centuries. The soil, wealth, and political power of a country, to a large extent, remain in the same hands, and with them the means for indirect oppression; and liberty will always be the safest though at best a very slow, remedy.

The aspect is vastly different when we look at our own country, and serves to confirm our opinion about this subject. It is true there is pauperism enough in some of our large cities; but almost invariably it is imported misery, caused by the pernicious influences which continue to work in Europe. The oppressed, the poorest, the most degraded and ignorant from the countries of great and petty despots flee to our hospitable shores; and it is rather a glorious sign of the enormous resources of our country, that so many work their way up in spite of former drawbacks, than to be wondered when others are, like birds, brought up in a cage, who, by long captivity, have lost the use of their wings. Real pauperism among us is indigenous only in those States where liberty and equality have been mere mockeries until lately; where the black man was debarred by law from acquiring knowledge and wealth, and the white man who owned no slaves was the obedient tool and servant of the master of the whip. The American laborer in the Northern States, grown up under free institutions, with the proud consciousness of his equality to any one in the country, is never a helpless pauper. Often by his industry and intelligence he will become a capitalist himself, or, at least, achieve a comfortable and honorable independence. For the others, they have our hearty sympathies, as well as all who have suffered from injustice and oppression; yet we hold that he who devotes his gifts and energy to the cause of liberty and equality generally and everywhere, serves his interests better than all those who attempt to stir up hostility to wealth and encourage outrage and violence.

New National Era, April 20, 1871.

42. THE LABOR QUESTION

Our caption has all the vagueness great issues, yet nebulous and dim,
assume to the conservative mind. Logicians may justly complain of the in-
definiteness, if they see no further than the surface. Whatever there is
embodied in the movement thus rudely designated--and there is much of good
and some of evil in it--must be frankly met and considered. Changes from one
amelioration or modification of conditions to some other, whose form is only
indistinctly perceived, brings with its processes no unmixed benefit. Evil,
or what seems to be such to our finite and limited vision is as necessary a
part of progress as the reverse. It is the law of existence and accompanies
all movement. The labor question--of which in the country the abolition of
slavery, of property in man, was the first grand step--is not free from the
evils of ignorance, passion, ambition, selfishness, and demagogism. It is to
be feared that too many of those who have undertaken to lead in the portentous
discussion it inaugurates, have no higher motive than that of obtaining a
"new deal" for themselves and theirs. Very little of the spirit which seeks
to reach the fundamental conditions of life is found in their mental make-up.
At the best it is but amelioration they seek. The real object must necessarily be to arrive at the principles that affect society in its relations to
production, and especially to comprehend those laws which govern the distribution of labor's results, and which, it must be apparent to the most
superficial thinker, now operate so unequally. The profound truth conveyed
at the apparently paradoxical utterance of Jesus, when he said, "That unto
every one which hath shall be given; and from him that hath not, even that
he hath shall be taken away from him," receives daily and little illustration
in all the operations of our industrial civilization. The new producers now
receive the larger share of what those who labor produce. The result is
natural. Discontent culminates in exactly the same men that intelligence
sustains aspiration. The laborer of to-day cannot by any possibility remain
satisfied with the same surroundings and the same personal results that were
sufficient to his father. The Chinese laborer, who, at home, thinks himself
a rich man, with earnings averaging two dollars per month, will not in this
country long be satisfied with twenty. The Irishman, eating his potatoes and
porridge under his cabin thatched roof at home, must by the very force of
example when he migrates into other surroundings, demand better food and
clothing, and, as a natural consequence, ideas follow and larger mental considerations brood in his vision and stir his brain to unwonted vigor. The
freedman, once content as a slave with his weekly peck of corn meal, piece of
rusty bacon, and one or two tow suits per year, now requires food, lodgings,
and clothing, and, thank God! a higher class of mental conditions and attractions.

Good people, who are appalled with the startling evidences of wide-spread
discontent at conditions which are everywhere visible in this as well as other
countries among the laboring people--or, as they may be for the argument's
sake termed, the wages class--fail to see that their own improved circumstances have not extended in any like equal proportions to those who are
materially considered a grade or two below. The aspiration for the results of
this improved condition is equally as marked among them, though it may not be
as intelligently expressed, are in general, as wisely directed. One fact must
be apparent, that in all older communities, governed by the high-pressure
principle of competition--the idea which is most tersely expressed in the
common saying of "each for himself and the devil take the hindmost"--pauperism
is on the increase, penury has become a fixed institution, and the "poverty of
the masses the rule, not the exception." The question, whether civilization
is designed primarily for Man or for Property, can have but one direct answer,
whatever may be the methods each may think desirable by which to attain that

end. The happiness of man must be the primal condition in which any form of society alone can found a title to existence. The civilization, then, looked at in its material aspect alone, which on the one hand constantly increases its wealth-creating capacities and on the other as steadily leaves out of the direct benefits thereof at least seven-tenths of all who live within its influence, cannot have realized the fundamental condition of its continuance. That society is a failure in which the large majority of its members, without any direct fault of their own, would, if any accidental circumstances deprived them for a month of the opportunity of earning regular wages, be dependent upon private or public charity for daily bread. Yet such is the actual condition of even favored American labor. It is an appreciation of this dependence that gives such formidable impulse to the discontent of labor. It is the general ignorance of equitable remedies which makes that discontent so dangerous. The movement is fundamental. It grows with great rapidity. It will compel a hearing by the very force of numbers if nothing else. It is the duty of those who have been lifted up by this general movement, this attrition of classes, of which the coming struggle of the "proletariat" (to use a word common in European discussions though hardly yet generally applicable to our condition) is the final and natural consequence. We say it is the duty of those first benefited to examine closely and consider fairly the grounds for this prevailing discontent, with a view to finding just remedies, conserving by their operation what is good and destroying what is wrong in present social and economical conditions. No movement which involves vast numbers as this does can be safely denounced or ignored. It must be met, treated fairly, and examined into, or the whole fabric will be wrenched by violent convulsions. There is always justice in the general demand. Ignorance may want prejudice contract, but the guiding impulse is one that seeks to right some wrong.

Inquiry into the condition of labor is the first step. Let the good people know how much truth there is in the reiterated charges that are made, "that the rich grow richer, the poor poorer"; that in all our manufacturing and industrial centres the gulf between classes is steadily widening, and that all the conditions under which the United States have hitherto been the paradise of labor are rapidly changing and steadily deviating; that, in fact, we are taking on the degrading conditions in European society. Somewhat of this is true. Enough, we believe, to warrant full examination into its causes and investigation into the remedies if there be any.

Believing, then, such inquiry to be necessary, we urge upon the attention of the country, of all bodies interested in the questions embraced in the agitation, and of Congress, the important bill presented by the Hon. George F. Hoar, representing the 9th Congressional District of Massachusetts, to the 42d Congress, and which will be included in the bill:

Be it enacted, &c., "That there shall be appointed by the President, by and with the advice and consent of the Senate, a commission of three persons, who shall hold office for the period of two years from the date of their appointments unless their duties shall have been sooner accomplished, who shall investigate the subject of the wages and hours of labor, and of the division of the good profits of labor and capital between the laborer and the capitalist, and the same educational, and sanitary condition of the laboring classes of the United States and how the same are affected by existing laws regulating commerce, finance, and currency.

"Section 2. Said commissioners shall receive a salary of five thousand dollars each, shall be authorized to employ a clerk, and shall report the result of the investigation to the President, to be by him transmitted to Congress."

This measure, with amendments, authorizing the Commission to make in their report such recommendations as they may deem essential a practical legislation, and also allowing their necessary traveling expenses to be paid out of the Treasury, from moneys not otherwise appropriated, should be at an early date "funded into a statute."

We urge this measure upon the consideration of the two important National Colored Conventions about to assemble at Columbia, S.C. The National Labor Union will undoubtedly indorse this proposition. We have no doubt the other body will also do so. The Republican party falls naturally into the consideration of such issues. Having begun the fight, by freeing the slave, it will not weary of well doing. It is not the party of race or color, but of man and his advancement. If there be reasons for criticising its actions in this particular, it will be found that, in the main, the conditions have been misapprehended, and the results have been other than expected. [61]

The inquiry called for by Mr. Hoar's bill will be of especial advantage to colored labor. The country generally does not understand the degrading conditions in which it too largely remains, and therefore fails to see the means which might legitimately be enacted and set a motion to effect the changes so imperatively demanded.

The New National Era, October 12, 1871.

43. "TO LET LIVE."

If ever the time shall come when these organizations of workingmen shall change their character from a contest against all workers not within its charmed circle into a society for elevating labor, for helping the poor and deserving--in short, for raising all men up rather than for putting nine-tenths of them down, and as willing "to let live" as determined "to live", they will find . . . all good men and women, cordinally sympathising and co-operating with them. But till then they can only encounter their op-position.

New National Era, November 9, 1871.

44.   CO-OPERATIVE SOCIETIES

No such radical change can be effected immediately, and any attempt to force its consummation more rapidly than the growth of the working class in intelligence and organizing power warranted, would certainly produce more or less disturbance and distress. The step, however, we have already said, is a long one, and it cannot be taken all at once. The power of united action they are already beginning to learn, and the habit of combining for various other purposes having been established, the working people will perceive in time that the same principle may be more profitably employed than in further-ing such clumsy expedients as strikes and other violent and reprehensible methods of extorting higher wages.

In this country co-operative societies have, with a few notable excep-tions, not succeeded well in attempting to carry on productive industries. Co-operative stores have yielded better results, but, except in New England, very few attempts have been made to establish such institutions. Co-oper-tive banks are practically unknown here, though our analogous building and loan associations which admirably exemplify the principle of co-operation practically applied have flourished for many years, especially in Pennsyl-vania, and have furnished the ladder by which not a few poor men have climbed to competence. The skilled workmen of America are gaining rapidly in know-ledge, self-reliance, and facility for association, and will soon be in a position to start co-operative banks and stores in every manufacturing town, by which they may save and accumulate sufficient capital and gain sufficient administrative experience to embark in co-operative manufacturing and mining enterprises.

Meanwhile, large employers, both individuals and corporations, may take a hint from the information contained in Hon. D. J. Morrell's letter on "Industrial Partnerships," which was published in the Press of November 14. By distributing a certain share of their profits among their workmen, numerous manufacturing firms, both in this country and Europe, have gained a complete immunity from strikes, and aroused greater zeal, faithfulness, and efficiency in the men employed, without diminishing the amount realized from their business exchanges.

New National Era, December 28, 1871.

45. A ONE-SIDED VIEW

Mr. Wendell Phillips' idea seems to be that as soon as a man ceases to work for day wages and begins to hire other men, he is no longer entitled to the fruits of his enterprise, the profits he makes upon the labor of others, and hardly to the protection of the laws. If a man takes a contract to dig a ditch and hires another man to help him, though he labors as hard as his "hired man," he has ceased to be a "workingman," and has become a capitalist and a monopolist. The daily laborer is all right and the employer is all wrong. Anyone who becomes rich by his industry and shrewdness is at once transposed into a tyrant and opposer of the poor. In one of his recent speeches, arraigning the capitalist for the crime of getting rich, he sharply criticises Sir Robert Peel, the great English cotton spinner, because he bought a secret of one of his workingmen, which contributed greatly to his wealth, without giving him a just consideration. The secret was a discovery by the workman of a plan that prevented spinning machines from clogging, a trouble that caused delay and curtailed the daily earnings of operatives. By the discovery of this spinner he was able to earn from two to three times as much as the others. Peel secured his secret for a quart of beer a day and a small sum in cash. By "chalking his bobbins," which was the man's device, Peel accumulated a large fortune; and Mr. Phillips denounces him in good set terms for overreaching or taking advantage of the ignorance of the discoverer, instead of giving him a tenth of his fortune.

Perhaps Peel was wrong; at any rate, we are ready to admit that he was not very generous. But there is another side to the one Mr. Phillips presents, which is presented by an exchange, which comments upon the prejudiced views he expresses, in constantly harping upon the greed of the employer and the wrongs and unselfishness of the employed. It says, correctly, that he quite overlooks the selfishness of the workman who refused to deal generously with his fellows, but kept it to himself and made all he could out of it, while the others were living on smaller wages. Instead of sharing his secret with them, he finally sold it for a pot of beer. The critic thinks that Mr. Phillips has overlooked the "real root of the difficulty in the labor question, which is the mean spirit of one workman toward another. It is this spirit which animates trade unions and the limitation of apprentices, and which has prevented successful co-operation heretofore. Let Mr. Phillips apply to the workman as well as to the capitalist the words: "Thou shalt do unto another as thou wouldst have another do unto thee."

The Golden Rule is a capital rule for the capitalist to measure his duty by, but the workingman needs to carry it around with him, too, and gauge his own conduct by it. If both employer and employed were to realize it as the highest standard of noble living, and live up to its requirements, there would be less complaint on every hand. Work would be better and more faithfully done. Workingmen would be more prosperous and happy. Idle boys, complaining that the apprenticeship system as at present established, instead of keeping them out of the street and the jail, as formerly, thrusts them into them, would have work and opportunities for developing the skill and talent now often employed in picking pockets, forging, breaking into houses, and the various swindles constantly perpetrated. Mr. Phillips needs to revise his speech and tell the whole story.

New National Era, December 14, 1871.

46. LETTERS TO THE PEOPLE--NO. 1

Trades for our Boys:

To the Editor of the New National Era:
    I wish to call your attention to the importance of some movement whereby trades, &c., may be secured to our boys. There are hundreds of boys in this city alone who, after having exhausted every effort to secure employment, from the fact that paper-peddling, boot-blacking, driving, waiting, and choosing, have more than their quota of employees, resort, to petty crimes; thence, through successive stages, to bolder schemes against the peace and security of society, and thus swell the number of criminals and vagrants, and prey upon the community, because an unrighteous public sentiment excludes them from the workshops, and religion, philanthropy, patriotism, have not a word to say in condemnation of the anti-American policy.
    To the son of the German, the Irishman, the Canadian, Scotchman, the far off Pagan Japanese, the doors of your manufactories open wide, the next day after arrival even before one word of the language has been uttered, while against the native-born youth, with the same aspirations as a white American, to appropriate and apply mechanical knowledge, and to improve upon it, by application and invention, the doors are not only closed by individual bosses, but society combines to supplement the injustice by voting exclusion.
    We have in this city, colored mechanics whose work upon inspection equals the very best done by the fairest American or foreigner; these men take colored boys to be taught, but the hand of God is upon them in that He gave them a color which suited Him, so that the large number are so poorly patronized that but a limited number are now instructed.
    The condition of colored youth in this city and District is true of them throughout the country. But the opposition by Americans is not the only cause of this sorry state of things, though mainly so; indifference on the part of leading colored men, and the death-like silence of colored women, contribute to it. A people whose leaders seek to learn the tortuous ways of speculation, and whose women are awed into silence upon vital questions, must for the time take back seats among the people. The white men of this and other countries deal vigorously now with every issue for the good of their youth, and white women are to the front with them in the work as having a common mission; they even unite in our exclusion and mutual congratulations, the result, are neither few nor whispered. Our women must speak out; the boys must have trades. What the crowned heads of Europe, and the poorest of white Americans do for their sons, we cannot afford to neglect.
    I have a boy who must and shall have a trade, (D.V.) and yet where may he learn it, or where exercised it when learned?
    To begin at headquarters, not under Government patronage surely, for there, should a colored lad upon examination distance competitors, let but a persistent Southern rebel, a clamorous foreigner, or a Canadian rebel, seek the position also, and even after given, the well-known out-cry, "reduction of force" is made, which, by interpretation, means change of base, and down comes the headsman's axe upon apprentice, mechanic, clerk, and into his place goes the anti-Government aspirant.
    Where then exercise? The people exclude him. Clannish they worship their kind. As much as may be said about race ostracism by whites, and how much may not be, too much cannot be said against indifference among ourselves. I want our poor tongue-tied, hoppled, and "scart" colored women--"black ladies" as Faith Lichen had the bravery to call them in her Mary-Clemmer-Ames-i-ades--to let the nation know how they stand. White women are getting to be a power in the land, and colored women cannot any longer afford to be neutrals. Never fear the ward-meetings; get the boys started properly in life, and the ward-meetings will come right.
    I want to see the colored preacher canonized, who looking after the great interests of the Master's flock, will, Beecher-like, cry out on Sunday against this sin of keeping our boys from trades, to the fostering of iniquity and the ruin of our souls.

Your millions of "laborers" in the midst of thirty millions of active, energetic people with arts, science, and commerce in their hands, and the love of domination a cardinal point in their creed--four millions that chain to this dank and hoary "labor" carcass--are as certain of subjugation, ultimately, as were the Helots; and this should arouse to action the entire force among the people. I know we have resolutions of conference and of conventions, and have had for a generation; and that each convention is the greatest ever held; but the people know comparatively little about them or their resolutions. We want then, an arousing of the people, and the pulpit must help in the work.

We have no theatres, beer-gardens, opera, nor grand lecture amphitheatres, wherein such questions may be discussed, reshapen, dramatized, made vital issues; the church--the pulpit stands to us in this stead; our preachers, as they should be, are politicians, and do use their churches often as places in which blessed white christians help them to adjust, arrange, and work party laws. No greater party work than this for our boys can they do.

I have not forgotten that we have a few live members of Congress, though I believe no one has as yet got around to trades; and although we must have Civil Rights, I look upon trades exclusion as meanly and wickedly beyond even the reach of that. In parenthesis, another of the many weak places in "your armor," so be it.

I know that we have members of State Legislatures and from whom more may be expected than from even Congress; also, attaches of the learned professions, and aspirants in the field of letters, all of which is enjoyably rose-tinted and gilded as compared with the past, but we, no more than others, can afford to build at the top of the house only. Ill-timed and unseemly as it may appear, the craftsman, the architect, the civil engineer, the manufacturer, the thoroughly equipped citizen, must all come, though silently, surely through the door opened to us by the mechanic. So agitate for the boys!

MARY A. SHADD CARY

New National Era, March 21, 1872.

47. THE FOLLY, TYRANNY, AND WICKEDNESS OF LABOR UNIONS

On more than one occasion we have attempted to convince workingmen of the absolute injury to their interests of the labor unions of the country, and also their oppressions and tyrannical course toward fellow workmen, as well as to their employers. The history of these organizations--generally managed, not by industrious workmen themselves, but by unprincipled demagogues who control them for their own benefit--furnishes abundant proof almost every day of their mischievous influence upon every industrial interest of the country. And we have seen no more sriking illustrations of the ruinous consequences to themselves and the country than in an account given by a correspondent of the New York *Times* of the operations of this organization at Johnstown, Pennsylvania.

At this place the Cambria Iron Works are situated. They are the most extensive and the finest iron works in the whole country, employing on an average seven thousand hands yearly. Mr. Morrell, formerly a member of Congress from Pennsylvania, is the manager of these works, and has ever pursued a most liberal policy towards his employees, after retaining them at a positive loss. That has been especially true since the panic last fall. But that did not satisfy the miserable demagogues who live from the earnings of the unions and control their movements. It has been the rule of the company for twenty years not to employ union men, though twice, in that time, members of Pittsburg unions have got hold of the men and induced them to strike. But in each case the men abandoned the unions and returned to their work at the old rates. Last winter the union men from Pittsburg again visited Johnstown, and again persuaded the men to join as on previous occasions. Trouble has quickly followed, and the works are closed. The men were satisfied with

the hours of work and their wages. They were what they pledged themselves
to abide by when they commenced work with the company. And there was no need
of them belonging to a union to prate about their rights, for there is a
co-operative plan in operation at the works which is more advantage to them
than any arguments the union could confer.

In order to avoid trouble among the men in regard to wages, Mr. Morrell
years ago, offered to agree on a basis and let wages rise or fall from that
basis according to the selling price of rails as quoted in the market reports.
A large number of the employees, after due discussion and deliberation, came
to the conclusion that the proposed arrangement was a very fair one for all
parties and accepted it. Those who preferred to go on in the old way, taking
their chances of good and bad wages, were allowed to do so without the slightest pressure being brought to bear upon them to accept the sliding scale.
Among those who accepted the sliding scale were the miners--the very men who
originated the present trouble. The plan has worked admirably, more especially
to the advantage of the employees; for, during the last few years iron has
been steadily rising in price, the men's wages rising in like proportion.

The consequence is that the thrifty ones have become very prosperous,
are owners of houses, and have money in the banks. But when the panic of
last fall came and iron fell rapidly and heavily, the men were not so well
pleased with the arrangement, though, of course, they had to keep to it. Mr.
Morrell has kept his large works running steadily all through the winter solely
for the benefit of his vast body of work people. Every one knows that orders
for rails on any scale are few and far between, and that the company must have
been working at a loss all the while. Their yards are stacked all over with
immense piles of iron and steel rails, ingots of steel and pig-iron--millions
of dollars worth. And yet to-day there is little or no market for rails. On
the 1st of March last, Mr. Morrell fancied he saw an improvement, which after
all, turned out to be only a momentary spurt, and he, unsolicited by the men,
raised their wages. To his surprise and astonishment, the coal-miners informed him that he had not raised theirs sufficiently, and they demanded five
cents more per ton mined. This he refused, quietly pointing out to the men
their error--an error which they have since acknowledged.

The result was a strike, and Mr. Morrell shut down, and hundreds and
thousands of men found themselves out of employment through the folly of
listening to and being controlled by a set of union demagogues from Pittsburgh.
They were receiving good wages, though they were employed at a great loss to
the company. Numbers of them were really opposed to any strike or trouble,
understanding that they had been kept at work for their own benefit rather
than that of the company. But the union bullied them into it and out of
bread for their families. No human being is benefited but the men who are
paid by the union to do just such work as that at Johnstown.

New National Era, May 7, 1874.

48. FROM ALABAMA

WETUMPKA, ALA., May 16, 1872.

To the Editor of the New National Era:
I notice in your paper of the 7th instant an article headed "The Folly,
Tyranny, and Wickedness of Labor Unions," to which, as State Agent of the
Alabama Labor Union, I beg space in the columns of your excellent "chronicler
of passing events," to submit a line or two in reply.

In the first place I think that the assertion is rather broad when you
speak so disparagingly of *all* Labor Unions without any exception whatever.
I condemn, Mr. Editor, as much as you possibly can, the evil practices of
"demagogues," as in the instance cited by you of the Johnstown, Pennsylvania,
organization; but, to class the *entire* Labor Unions of the country in the
same category, I think unjust, to say the least.

In this State the laboring men are almost entirely colored, and, in consequence of the cruel interdictory laws of ante-bellum times as to education, they are, as a class, in a deplorable state of ignorance. But, ignorant as they are, they have organized themselves, into a Labor Union for their mutual protection against the machination of those that would take advantage of their ignorance.

The institution in this State is intended to do that for the laboring masses that they are not, as individuals, capable of doing for themselves-- that is, they have men in whom they confide to investigate and supervise their contracts, and to see that their interests are not compromised on account of the great lack of the necessary experience on their part. The Labor Union of this State is supplying a want that has long been felt by our people; and in justice to the workings of the institution, so far as Alabama is concerned. I have been prompted to submit the foregoing, with a respectful request that you publish the same.

> Respectfully,
> WM. V. TURNER,
> State Agent Alabama Labor Union

New National Era, May 28, 1874.

49. LABOR UNION

Such labor unions as described by our correspondent in Alabama, W. V. Turner, cannot be objectionable. We welcome any and every organization that will be the means of instructing the colored people of the South. We sincerely hope that the unions of which Mr. Turner speaks, will continue in their good work, and forever steer clear of political, as well other, demagogues. The tendency to entrap every powerful colored organization into political nets, must be checked. Our people must see to it that none but their best men shall be chosen as leaders. Not a few colored men have become proficient in the arts of the demagogue and are capable of doing incalculable mischief. It is gratifying, however, to know that we have progressed, much more rapidly in the direction of earnestness in the work of accomplishing the greatest good for the race.

New National Era, May 28, 1874.

VI

THE KU KLUX KLAN AND BLACK LABOR

THE KU KLUX KLAN AND BLACK LABOR

The distinguished Afro-American scholar W. E. B. Du Bois wrote an aptly descriptive subtitle to his chapter "Back Toward Slavery" in Black Reconstruction: "How civil war in the South began again--indeed has never ceased; and how black Prometheus bound to the Rock of Ages by hate, hurt and humiliation; has his vitals eaten out as they grow, and yet lives and fights (p. 670)." There is little doubt that secret anti-black organizations such as the Ku Klux Klan were symbolized by the Du Bois vulture.

The violence which marred life in the South during the immediate post-Civil War period arose out of the broader struggle for political control between the Democratic and Republican parties. As long as Presidents Abraham Lincoln and Andrew Johnson permitted some southern white elites to participate in politics, southerners believed they could continue to control ex-slaves. But when the advent of Radical Reconstruction made this impossible, these reactionary southerners resorted to violence. Bands of armed men, who considered themselves as guerrilla fighters, made life miserable for agents from Washington in 1866. When it became apparent by 1867 that southern white control would be replaced by Radical Reconstruction, these secret societies multiplied and spread. Scores of them with names such as the White League, the Knights of the White Camelia, the Pale Faces, the Constitutional Union Guards, and the '76 Association--to name a few--spread fear, destruction, and sometimes death, wherever the struggle to control the Negro and to secure home rule called them. It was the Knights of the Ku Klux Klan, however, who became so associated with this movement that contemporaries labelled all such activities "Ku Kluxing."

The extent of the violence against defenseless blacks is still a source of revulsion. Enough contemporaries were concerned enough in 1871 that Congress established a select committee to investigate secret societies in the defeated states. Selected portions of the testimony given before the committee are reproduced in Part VI. The investigators discovered a breakdown in law and order which seemed nearly complete. In the nine South Carolina counties examined by the committee, the Klan had lynched and murdered thirty-five men, whipped 262 men and women, and otherwise shot, maimed, or burned the property of 101 persons. During this same time, Negroes killed four men and beat one other. In Jackson County, Florida, 153 murders were recorded, and accounts proceed in a similarly grim manner. The testimony reveals that over 2,000 people were killed, wounded, or injured in Louisiana within a few weeks' period prior to the elections of 1868. In St. Landry County Louisiana, the Ku Klux Klan killed and wounded over 200 Republicans, most of whom were black.

As a result of the rising public pressure to suppress this wave of violence, President Grant recommended and received the Ku Klux Klan enforcement of April 20, 1871, which declared acts of conspiracy to be tantamount to rebellion and punishable accordingly.

Although there have been many studies of the Ku Klux Klan, little or no attention has been given to its effects upon the labor movement. The documents reproduced in this section offer a small step toward filling this void.

THE KU KLUX KLAN AND BLACK LABOR

1. TESTIMONY TAKEN BY THE JOINT SELECT COMMITTEE
TO INQUIRE INTO THE CONDITION OF AFFAIRS
IN THE LATE INSURRECTIONARY STATES

Spartanburgh, South Carolina
July 6, 1871

CHARLOTTE FOWLER (colored) sworn and examined:
By the Chairman: Where do you live?
A. On Mr. Moore's premises.
Q. Do you know in what township?
A. No, sir; my son does.
Q. Is it in this county?
A. No, sir; I did live in Spartanburgh County with my husband,
before the old man was killed; but now I live with my son.
Q. How long ago is it since your husband was killed?
A. It was the first of May.
Q. What was his name?
A. Wallace Fowler.
Q. Tell how he was killed.
A. The night he was killed--I was taken sick on Wednesday morning, and I laid
on my bed Wednesday and Thursday. I didn't eat a mouthful; I couldn't do it;
so he went out working on his farm. We still had a little grandchild living
with me--my daughter's child. He had two little children living with him on
the farm, but still that little child staid with me. He kept coming backward and forward to the house to see how I got on and what he could do for me.
I never ate nothing until Thursday night. When he came home he cooked something for me to eat, and said: 'Old woman, if you don't eat something you
will die.' Says I: 'I can't eat.' Says he: 'Then I will eat, and feed the
little baby.' That is the grandchild he meant. I says: 'You take that little
child and sleep in the bed; I think I have got the fever, and I don't want you
to get it.' He said, 'No, I don't want to get the fever, for I have got too
much to do.' He got up and pulled off his clothes, and got in bed. He came
and called to the grandchild, Tody--she is Sophia--and he says: 'Tody, when
you are ready to come to bed, come, and grandmother will open your frock,
and you can go to bed.' So he laid there for about a half an hour, and then
I heard the dogs. I was only by myself now, for the children was all abed.
Then I got up and went into my room to my bed. I reckon I did not lay in bed
a half an hour before I heard somebody by the door; it was not one person, but
two--ram! ram! ram! at the door. Immediately I was going to call him to open
the door; but he heard it as quick as lightning, and he said to them:'Gentlemen, do not break the door down! I will open the door'; and just as he said
that they said: 'God damn you, I have got you now.' I was awake and I started
and got out of bed, and fell down on the floor. I was very much scared. The
little child followed its grandfather to the door--you know in the night it
is hard to direct a child. When he said, 'God damn you, I have got you now,'
and he said, 'Don't you run,' and just then I heard the report of a pistol,
and they shot him down; and this little child ran back to me before I could
get out, and says, 'Oh, grandma, they have killed my poor grandpappy.' He
was such an old gentleman that I thought they just shot over him to scare him;
but sure enough, as quick as I got to the door, I raised my right hand and
said, 'Gentlemen, you have killed a poor, innocent man.' My poor old man!
Says he, 'Shut up.' I never saw but two of them, for, by that time, the others
had vanished.
    Q. How did you know there were any others there?
    A. The little boy that was there when they shot his grandpappy ran into
the house; he was there, and when they started I heard the horses' feet going
from the gate. I was then a-hallooing and screaming. After they shot the

old man, they came back in the house--'Chup! Chup! Chup! Make a light.' I said, 'I am not able to make up a light; I have been sick two days." I called to the little girl, "Is there any light there?" She says, "No." But the mantel was there, where I could reach it, where they put the splinters, and I said, "Light that splinter;" and she lit the splinter. He said , "Hand it here;" and she handed it to him; and then he says, "March before me, march before me." That was done in the middle of my room. He says, "Hand me up your arms"--that is, the guns. Says I, "There isn't any here, sir." Says he, "Hand me up that pistol." I says, "There is none here; the old man had none in slavery, and had none in all his freedom, and everybody on the settlement knows it." When he told me about the light he put that pistol up to my face-- so--and says, "If you don't come here I will get you light out of this." He did that when I was a poor woman by myself.

Q. What else?

A. I didn't know that anybody had anything against the old man; everybody liked him but one man, and that was Mr. Thompson. Somewhere along summer before last he had planted some watermelons in his patch; and he kept losing his watermelons, and one day he said he would go and lay, and see who took them; and sure enough he caught two little white boys; one was Mr. Thompson's boy and the other was Mr. Millwood's boy; both were white boys; they had cut up a whole lot of the melons. Jerry Lee lives on the same place with us; that is Mrs. Jones's place; and he comes and says to the old man, "Wally, do you know who took your watermelons?" Wally says, "It is more than I dare to do, to lay a thing on man without I saw with my own eyes." Jerry Lee says, "It is nobody eating your watermelons but Mr. Henley." Then Wally says, "No, I can't put a thing on a man without I saw him do it, and I have got the one that was eating my melons." "Who is it, Wally?" said he. "Well," says Wally, "I have promised not to tell it." Says he, "I have melons too, and if you do not tell who took yours, they will come round and eat all our watermelons." Says Wally, "I cannot tell you who the other boy is, but one boy is Mr. Thompson's son."

Q. Is that the reason you thought that Thompson did not like him?

A. Mr. Thompson is the only one in the whole settlement that has had anything against him. You may search the whole settlement over. Jerry Lee went right on to Mr. Thompson's--that is, to old Mr. John Thompson's house. It was only half an hour; and Jerry Lee didn't tell it as he ought to. You see it was Mr. John Thompson's brother. And Mr. Thompson came immediately as soon as Mr. Lee told his father about the watermelons, and he says, "Halloo." I went to the window. He says, "Where is Wally?" Says I, "He went over to Mr. Jones's; over to the big house." He started on, and met the old man in the road; and he said, "Come along." I listened to them just as they got up to the gate.

Q. What were they talking about?

A. They were not talking a word until they got to Mr. Lee; when Mr. Thompson carried the old man to Mr. Lee. Then Mr. Thompson fetched on so about the watermelons. Says the old man, "Who told you that I said that you took my melons? Did not I know a boy from a man? Tell me who said I took-- your watermelons." Says he, "There is the man." Says Wally to Mr. Lee, "Did I tell you so?" Says Mr. Lee, "I understood you so." And then says Mr. Thompson, "Yes, and God damn you, if you had said I had stolen your watermelons, you would not make tracks out of this yard." That was out of Jerry Lee's yard. I ran to the fence and said "Wally, come out of that yard; and if you don't I will call Mr. Jones. If you had threatened Mr. Thompson, as Mr. Thompson has threatened your life, he would have you in Spartanburgh jail before sundown."

Q. How long was that before the old man was killed?

A. The watermelons were took this summer a year ago, and nobody but him and Mr. Thompson had anything against him.

Q. Do you mean by this that Thompson had anything to do with the killing of the old man?

A. I am going to tell you my opinion about it. I didn't see Mr. Thompson's face, for he had a mask on; but he was built so. He lives close to us, and I saw him every day and Sunday.

Q. Did these men have masks on?

A. Only the one that shot him.

Q. What kind of a mask?

A. It was all around the eyes. It was black; and the other part was white and red; and he had horns on his head. He came in the house after he killed the old man and told me about the light, and I made the little girl make a light; he took the light from her and looked over the old man. Another man came out of the gate, and looked down on the old man and dropped a chip of fire on him, and burnt through his shirt--burnt his breast. They had shot him in the head, and every time he breathed his brains would come out.

Q. Do you mean to say that you believe his being killed was caused by the quarrel about the watermelons?

A. I can tell you my belief. There is a parcel of men who were on the plantation working Mr. Jones's land, and my old man was one of them that tend ed Mr. Jones's land. Mr. Jones had had a whole parcel of poor white folks on the land, and he turned them off, and put all these blacks on the premises that they had from Mr. Jones, and I don't know what it could be, but for that and the watermelons. That was the cause why my old man is dead, and I am left alone. (Weeping.)

Q. Is that all you can tell about it?

A. Yes, sir. That is all that I can tell. I don't want to tell anything more than I know; I don't want to tell a lie on anybody.

By Mr. STEVENSON:

Q. Was the old man dead when the fire was thrown on him?

A. He did not die until Friday between 1 and 2 o'clock; but he couldn't speak a word. He was just bleeding, and his brains and blood came out over his eyes.

Q. Where was he when he was shot?

A. Right by the door. They shot him and never asked a question.

Q. Did you come near him before they left?

A. I never went to the door. I hallooed and screamed where I was standing for some people.

Q. Did you see him by the light where you stood?

A. It was dim moonshine. He lay out there as if he was lying on the bed; his head as white as cotton.

Q. Was he farming or doing anything else?

A. He was the coachman of old Mrs. Shoemaker. His young mistress came up to see about it, and cried about him.

Q. What other business did he do?

A. Nothing but farming. Everytime Mr. Jones wanted anything from this town, he sent him and another old gentleman that lived there. They killed him, and they whipped another nearly to death; and they shot another in the head, but the ball was so much spent that it did not kill him, and the doctor got the ball out.

Q. Was that the same night?

A. Yes, sir. One of them was shot, and the doctor got the ball out; and the other got away. The watermelons and that farming work caused this. That gentleman intended to clean them out off of the plantation. I just tell you the whole truth; I do not want to put a finger on anybody; but they have ruined me. But his name is published to the whole United States. If you ever get a newspaper and read of Wallace Fowler, that is my husband.

Q. That all happened in Spartanburgh County. Do you not know what township it was?

A. I don't know what they call Spartanburgh Township; my son James can tell you.

By the CHAIRMAN:

Q. Was he there?

A. No, sir.

By Mr. STEVENSON:

Q. How old was your husband?

A. I do not know exactly; but he was an old man, with a head as white as that sheet of paper that that gentleman is writing on. But he was a smart man for his age.

Q. Was he seventy?

A. I expect he was over seventy.

By Mr. VAN TRUMP:

Q. You say you are now living on Mr. Moore's farm?

A. With my son, James Fowler.

Q. Where is that?

A. On Tiger Creek.

Q. Is it near where your husband was killed?

A. He was killed three miles from Glen Springs.

Q. In the other direction?

A. Yes, sir; on Mr. Jones's premises.

Q. How long did you and Wallace live there?

A. I could not tell; it was so many years. You see he had belonged to
the Olins; and then Joe Olin sold his land to Mr. Jones. I cannot tell you
how long it has been.

Q. Did you live there before the war?

A. O, yes, sir; many and many a year.

Q. And you never knew what township you lived in?

A. No. I never knew the name after they altered the townships and districts and counties. I don't know.

Q. Do you know what county it was?

A. I know the district.

Q. What was the district?

A. Spartanburgh.

Q. Was your husband as old as seventy-five years?

A. Yes, sir; I reckon he was.

Q. How much older than that?

A. I cannot tell; he was older than I am. You see we poor black folks
had no learning. Old Mrs. Olin had my age and she is dead and gone.

Q. Have you any idea of your age?

A. No, sir.

Q. Are you thirty?

A. I reckon I am more than that; I have children, grown children.

Q. Have you grandchildren?

A. Yes, sir; great-grandchildren.

Q. And you do not know whether you are thirty years of age?

A. No, sir.

Q. How old is your oldest great-grandchild?

A. About six or eight years old. That is the oldest one of all; it is my
daughter's daughter's child.

Q. You say you were sick that night?

A. Yes, sir.

Q. Still you were able to sit up at the door?

A. Yes, sir, after the old man got me supper, because there was nobody
to cook for me but him.

Q. Your husband was working and living in town?

A. Yes, sir; he was living just as spry as he could be.

Q. What was he doing--working in town?

A. No, sir, not in town; he was working at home.

Q. What do you mean by going backward and forward to see him?

A. He came out of the field to see me.

Q. Was he at home every night with you?

A. Yes, sir; and he came in during the day-time.

Q. You sat up about half an hour after Wallace went to bed?

A. Yes, sir; I then heard the dogs bark, and I went and peeped out of the
door to the back of the plantation, and the dogs made a dreadful noise. That
is the time that they were after the other blacks. They went around there at
that time of night.

Q. How do you know that?

A. Because I know the black dog that Mr. Jones had, if anybody is about
the land, would be barking.

Q. Did you hear any shooting? Could you not hear a man as far as a dog?

A. But the boys, when I was talking about the dog, said that was the
very time when they were after them.

Q. That was afterward?

A. Yes, sir; the old man was the last one they came after.

Q. You say that when you were sitting up and heard the dogs barking, was the time when they were after the other black people?

A. Yes, sir.

Q. Did you think so then?

A. I thought so after they killed the old man. That was the time they were after the other ones.

Q. Did you hear a gun or pistol?

A. The boys said they shot at them, but I never heard the gun, as I told the boys the next morning.

Q. Who did this man who shot Wallace tell to march before him?

A. I was the one; he told me to march before him.

Q. Where did he mean to march to?

A. He had shot him at the door, and he came in asked me about guns and pistols, to see if I had any in my house. I told him we did not have any such a thing; that Wally did not have as much powder as he could pick up on a pin's point.

Q. What is old Mr. Thomson's name?[68]

A. John Thomson--the same as his son.

Q. Where does he live?

A. Close by me.

Q. Is he a white man or a colored man?

A. He is white--a young man.

Q. I understood you to state that Thomson complained about his watermelons being stolen?

Q. My husband had lost watermelons.

Q. Did he complain?

A. No, sir; but he laid out to see who was eating his melons, and he came upon those two boys. There were only two.

Q. How many men did you see?

A. I saw only one man with a mask.

Which one shot Wallace?

A. The man with the mask.

Q. From the time they first knocked at the door until they shot was a very short time?

A. Yes, sir; but a very few minutes.

Q. Nothing was said but "God damn you."

A. Nothing; but they grabbed him, and said, "God damn you; I have got you now;" and said, "Don't you run;" and took him out, and then I heard the crack.

Q. Did you know the man who had the mask?

A. No, sir; one came in the gate; he was a long, slim man, and looked down on the old man lying outside of the door. I saw him and the man with the mask.

Q. Did you know the man with the mask?

A. I just know the build of the man, and was just such a built man as Thomson, but I never saw his face.

Q. Was he about the size of Thomson?

A. Yes, sir.

Q. Is Thomson tall or short?

A. He is a short man, and this man was a little short man, but I did not see his face.

Q. Are you not mistaken about fire having been thrown upon the breast of Wallace?

A. I have got the shirt.

Q. Are you sure that cannot be mistaken?

A. I am not mistaken.

Q. Was there not some examination of Wallace by the neighbors afterward?

A. It was no examination; but Dr. Jones came there and saw the blister and burn where they threw the fire on him.

Q. Did any other white persons see him before he was buried?

A. About Saturday two weeks they went and took him up.

Q. Are you sure it was two weeks?

A. I think it was two weeks, but I was not there.

Q. Then you do not know what the persons who took him up know?

A. No, sir; but the burned place was there.

Q. You do not know what the people who took up Wallace's body know?

A. No, sir. I had him dressed and all.

Q. Who was this Mr. Jones?

A. He came from the North.

Q. How long ago?

A. He had been in this country a good many years.

Q. Before the war?

A. Yes, sir; many years.

Q. He had had a good many white persons on his farm, and had turned them off?

A. Yes, sir.

Q. When?

A. New Year's day last.

Q. And Wallace was killed this last May afterward?

A. Yes, sir.

Q. How many white tenants had Mr. Jones on his farm when he turned them off?

A. He had Mr. Millwood, and Mr. Lee, and Mr. Lee again, and Mr. Henley--sir.

Q. Where are all those white tenants?

A. They left the plantation and scattered right down below us, not far from here.

Q. It is your opinion, as given in answer to the question of the chairman, What was the cause of these men killing Wallace? that it was either the difficulty growing out of the watermelons, or the fact that these white men were turned off and black men put on that farm?

A. Yes, sir.

Q. It was one or the other?

A. Yes, sir.

Q. Which is the most probable?

A. I will tell you which I think stronger than the other. These men and Mr. Thomson are all kin.

Q. Were all four of these white men his kin?

A. Yes, sir; to Mr. Thomson. Mrs. Thomson's mother is Mrs. Millwood's aunt, and they are all kin.

Q. Is Mr. Thomson a respectable man in that county?

A. They all said down there that he was a might mischievous man.

Q. Does he tend Dr. Jones's plantation?

A. No, sir; Mr. Foster's plantation.

Q. Where is he now?

A. I don't know. He ran off before I left for some conduct he had done; but his children and wife are there; that is, the old man has run off.

Q. That is since the death of Wallace?

A. The old man was gone before Wallace was killed.

Q. Young John Thomson is there yet?

A. Yes, sir. Young John Thomson and Frank Thomson and Aaron Thomson and Eliphaz Thomson, all his sons, are there with the old lady.

Q. Was this man who was masked a Thomson?

A. I do not know who he was. I tell you the Lord's truth from heaven; I do not know who he was, I am not going to tell more than I know. I do not want to bring trouble on anybody in this world, because I do not want to have anybody hurt for me. My old man is gone, but I do not want to take anything from anybody, or do anything to anybody.

By Mr. STEVENSON:

Q. How long was it before the old man was buried?

A. He died Friday, between 1 and 2 o'clock, and they buried him Saturday, between 1 and 2 o'clock.

Q. Did the coroner's jury come to look at him?

A. No, sir. Mr. Jones wrote for them, too. It was a week after they buried him.

Q. What neighbors came to see him?

A. Not one.

Q. What black neighbors?

A. Only old man Vander Lee's son came with Mr. Jones. Mr. Jones was looking at him, and he came in.

Q. Then Mr. Jones was really the only white man who came to see him?

A. Yes, sir.

By Mr. VAN TRUMP:

Q. Did Lee come in and see him?

A. He came by the gate, and Mr. Jones told him the accident, and he jumped off and came in.

By Mr. STEVENSON:

Q. What are these men called that go about masked in that way?

A. I don't know; they call them Ku-Klux.

Q. How long have they been going about in that neighborhood?

A. I don't know how long; they have been going a long time, but they never pestered the plantation until that night. I have heard of Ku-Klux, but they never pestered Mr. Jones before.

Q. Did your old man belong to any party?

A. Yes, sir.

Q. What party?

A. The radicals.

Q. How long had he belonged to them?

A. Ever since they started the voting.

Q. Was he a pretty strong radical?

A. Yes, sir; a pretty strong radical.

Q. Did he work for that party?

A. Yes, sir.

Q. What did he do?

A. He held up for it, and said he never would turn against the United States for anybody, as the democrats wanted him to.

Q. Did he talk to the other colored people about it?

A. No, sir; he never said nothing much. He was a man that never said much but just what he was going to do. He never traveled anywhere to visit people only when they had a meeting; then he would go there to the radical meetings, but would come back home again.

Q. Did he make speeches at those meetings?

A. No, sir.

Q. Did they make him president of their meetings?

A. I don't know about that.

Q. Did you ever go with him?

A. No, sir.

Q. Did they ever make him president or vice-president, or put him upon the platform?

A. No, sir. Several, I heard, went there and did, but he never undertook such a thing. He would go to hear what the best of them had to say, but he never did anything.

By the CHAIRMAN:

Q. Are the colored people afraid of these people that go masked?

A. Yes, sir; they are as 'fraid as death of them. There is now a whole procession of people that have left their houses and are lying out. You see the old man was so old, and he did no harm to anybody; he didn't believe anybody would trouble him.

By Mr. STEVENSON:

Q. Did he vote at the last election?

A. Yes, sir.

Spartanburgh, South Carolina, *July* 7, 1871

GEORGE W. GARNER sworn and examined.

By the CHAIRMAN:

Q. Do you live in this county?

A. Yes, sir.

Q. What part of it?

A. I live east of this place--about seven miles from here.

Q. In what township?

A. Pacolet Township.

Q. What business do you follow?

A. Farming.

Q. How long have you lived in this county?

A. I have been living in this county since January last a year ago.

Q. Where did you come from?

A. From Union County, in this State.

Q. Are you a native of this State?

A. Yes, sir. I was born and raised in Union County.

Q. Have you suffered any violence at the hands of any person in this county?

A. From persons in this county or some others, I have.

Q. Go on and tell in what manner it was inflicted upon you, and when it was.

A. I had two attacks; the first was on the 4th of March last, on Saturday night; the second was on that night two weeks, which would make it the 18th of March.

Q. Go on and tell what occurred each time.

A. On the 4th of March there came a body of men to my house. They were all around my house before I knew they were there, and were hallooing and beating and thumping the house. I was nearly asleep, and as quick as I awoke I jumped up. They told me to open the door. I told them I would do so. They told me to strike a light before I opened the door. I lighted a lamp and set it on a desk by the side of the house. I opened the door. These men were standing in front of the door with pistols drawn. They were knocking at the other door also. I said, "Gentlemen, somebody is knocking at the other door; let me open it." They let me turn around and open it. There were five men there. While I was opening that door more men came through the other door and into the room where I was. To the best of my mind, there were twelve men in all in my house. My wife thinks there were more, but I did not see them. They asked me to take a walk. I told them I would. I asked them to let me put on my clothes and shoes. They told me to put on my shoes, but not my clothes. They took me out and tied my hands together and hit me a few strokes and sent me back to the house.

Q. What was said?

A. They told me I must be a good citizen to the county. I asked them if I had not been. They said they reckoned as good as any. I told them if I lacked anything, it was from not knowing what a citizen should be. I thought I had done my duty. They said I should quit my damned radical way of doing, and should no longer vote a republican ticket, and if I did they would come back and kill me. . . .

Spartanburgh, South Carolina, July 7, 1871

Alfred Richardson (Colored) sworn and examined:

Q. You say he was killed?

A. Yes, sir; I think they shot seven balls into him.

Q. Was that done by a body of men in disguise?

A. Yes, sir; a body of disguised men.

Q. What was that done for?

A. This black man was keeping a blacksmith shop. He had done work for a man named Kemp. I was not acquainted with Kemp, though I had seen him. Kemp had been having his work done there for about a year or two, and had never paid the black man. The black man complained to the man he was renting the shop from about Kemp's account. He said, "Kemp don't pay me, it looks like he won't pay me. I am getting tired of working for him. Now he has brought a buggy here for me to fix, and I am not going to work for him any more until he pays me." This white man said to him, "I would not work for him any more; put the buggy outside the door and work for somebody else that you can get your money from." Dannons laid the buggy aside, and would not fix it. Kemp came up after awhile and asked why he had not fixed it. Dannons said he did not care about working any more for him until they settled up. Then Kemp took the buggy--the wheels had been taken off--he took the carriage a- part and set it on an anvil, and said, "Don't you move this off until you take off to work on it."

Q. He put the wagon on the anvil so that Dannons could not work on it?

A. Yes, sir; and told him that he should not move it unless he was going to fix it. Dannons then went to the man he was renting the shop from, and asked him what he must do. The man told him, "You take the buggy and set it aside and go on with your work."

Q. Was the man who owned the shop a white man?

A. Yes, sir; Dannons took the buggy off the anvil and set it down. Kemp came along and asked why he had moved that buggy from there without he was going to fix it. Dannons told him he wanted the anvil to go to work and he took the buggy off. Kemp said, "God damn you, I will kill you." He went off and said no more to him. In a night or two about fifteen or twenty men came down there and hallooed to Dannons to come to the door.

Q. Were they in disguise?

A. Yes, sir; they came and told him to come to the door. He told them to hold on until he got his pants on. They told him "Never mind about your pants, come to the door." He came to the door and saw these men all standing in the yard disguised. He turned his back on them and ran into the house. As he turned back they shot him right in the back of the head. I think the first struck him. He fell. They ran in and shot some five or six more shots into him; and then they all went away. That was the last of them that night. . . .

Spartanburgh, South Carolina, July 8, 1871

JACKSON SURRATT (colored) sworn and examined.

By the CHAIRMAN:

Q. Do you live in this county?

A. Yes, sir.

Q. Where?

A. About a mile north of Cowpens Battle Ground, on Mr. Bob Scrugg's land.

Q. What do you do there?

A. Farm.

Q. On rented land or land of your own?

A. I am just working with another man on land.

Q. How long have you lived there?

A. I commenced last Christmas a year ago.

Q. Were you raised in this county?

A. Yes, sir; I was raised below--down below Cowpens Furnace, near sun- rise course from there.

Q. Have you been visited at any time by the Ku-Klux?

A. Yes, sir.

Q. When?

A. About two months ago, on a Sunday night, and the Saturday following.

Q. Go on and tell us all about it. Take the first time and tell us what they said and did.

A. I waked up in my bed, and I heard somebody running against the door. There was two. I hallooed, "Wait, and I will open it." They stopped. When I got up they had bursted a piece off, but it was not open. I opened it wide, and one said, "Have you ever went radical? I told them I had. The other hallooed, "Blindfold him;" and he jerked me out of the door and blindfolded me; and they said "Take a walk with me," and they took me off about fifty yards. I could tell the next day how far it was. They told me to get down on my knees. I got down. He said, "Did you vote radical? I said, "Yes, sir." He said, What made you do it? I said, "Because I was with the white people when I voted that way." They said, "Did you think the white people was right?" I told them I had no other source to cling to. I did not go by myself. I thought it was as right as anybody. He says, "Did the radical party promise to kill all us democrats?" I said, "They never told me that." He said, "If you tell me a lie we will murder you right here." I said, "I

will tell you the truth." They said, "Didn't they say they would kill us?"
"No," says I. Says he, "Are you lying? You are damn good now; but didn't
you get up and vote before breakfast?" I says, "I did, in order to not lose
much time. It was near my home, and I was busy cutting grass, and I didn't
want to lose time." Says he, "You slipped off and went." "No, I didn't,"
says I, "I went along slow." "What made you vote radical?" Says I, "I did'nt
know any better." Says he, "Do you think you will know any better?" I said,
"I will do the best I know how." They said, "Damn you, that is not the best.
You have been talked to, to go democrat, and, damn you, you didn't do it,
and we will show you to-night." Then they said for me to pray for them. I
prayed. They said then, "Just hit him a lick apiece;" and they hit me a
lick apiece, and all the time they had me blindfolded, and they made me run
to the house, and I had just time to look where the house was before I ran.
The house seemed strange to me. I got in. They stood awhile, and I peeped
through the crack. They called my lady out to look at them, and deviled us
a while, and they went off.

Q. Deviled you--what is that?

A. They blackguarded us, and I could not swear to any man of them, for
they were disguised. It looked like paper stuck up beside the head, and it
run up to a sharp point on the top, and they had their coats on and under
their breeches to make them look big--bulging out.

Q. How many were there?

A. They said they all hit a lick apiece, and they gave me fourteen
licks; and after they let me run to the house I heard others off whistling.
I could not tell how many there was in all.

Q. That was on Sunday night?

A. Yes, sir; Sunday night the first time.

Q. Did they come again?

A. Yes, sir; on the next Saturday night they come. They inquired then
for my son. I told them I hadn't any one there at home big enough to do
anything. They said, "We want that one that stays here--your wife's son."
I said he was hired off at Judge Edwards' and didn't come home. The first
time they asked for him. When they came again, I had a clock and it struck
one, and I laid there, and the first thing I heard the yard was full of
horses, and they were rearing and cursing, "Open the door, or we will kill
the last one of you." They started off with me, and they run in the house
and cursed and tore and jerked my daughter out, and jerked my wife and my
wife's son out of bed, and the first thing I knew they were bringing them
all out. There was a man in there cursing and wanted a light. They took
us about seventy yards and made me let down the fence, and made me and my wife
jump two logs together. They made us lie down about three steps apart, and
they began to cut switches. They made us all lie down--my wife and all.
They had us nearly naked. It was getting warm weather. I was in my shirt-
tail. They cut switches, and they hit my wife's son a lick, and asked him
what he was doing. He told them he did not know what he was doing. They
asked one his number, and he said No. 10, and then they hit me ten, and
then they called out eight. The man had cut a switch, and he came to my
head and he looked at me, and then he stepped off the horsemen, and they all
stepped up and looked, and then one hallooed, "Ride up," to the horsemen,
as I was lying there. I said to myself, "I believe if I lie here they will
put me and all my folks through, so that I can't do any good," and I said,
"If my Old Master is for me, he will strike for me to-night and save me, and I
must do my best;" and I rose on all fours and jumped and ran about fifty
yards and stumped my foot, but I raised up and ran on and took right through
the woods, and ran until I run over a log, and I found they were not after me,
and sort of stopped, and though I would take roundings on them, for fear they
would catch me; and I ran back about a quarter of a mile into the swamp, and
that was the last I saw of them.

Q. What did they do with your wife?

A. They said they had not made good hands in the farm. They said that
to my wife and daughter.

Q. Is your wife here, and your daughter?

A. My wife is; my wife's son went off on Friday. He was afraid they
would get after him again. He was a young man, and the person he was living
with dismissed him, and he told me he would go off and try to make something.

It has been last Tuesday a week since I have seen him.

Q. Had you any quarrels in the neighborhood?

A. No, sir; I do not think anybody had anything against me. Everybody spoke well of me. I thought it was all right. All they had against me was voting the radical ticket.

Q. Do you know any of these men who were there the last time?

A. I could not tell for my life who were there.

Q. You say this was about two months ago?

A. Yes, sir:

Q. Have you been living there since then?

A. Yes, sir; part of the time in the woods and at home. I laid about five nights in my house since, on rainy nights when I thought no person could stand it to travel, but at other times I have staid outside in the woods.

Q. Why?

A. For fear these men would come again. I did not know but they were coming, or at what time they would come.

Q. Did you take your family out with you?

A. I had to leave them in the house. My wife had a young baby, and my daughter has not been well enough to go out since they beat her. My wife has the baby.

Q. Had she that young child when she was taken out?

A. Yes, sir.

Q. How old was it then?

A. It is nine months old now, and you can count from that.

Q. It was seven months old?

A. Yes, sir.

Q. Was it taken out that night?

A. No, sir; the child was in its mother's arms, and as she come out she put in the bed and it screamed. I was powerfully uneasy about my baby, and could not keep still for it, and the men still cursed. There were some other little children there, and they crawled to it.

By Mr. STEVENSON:

Q. What sort of whistling did you hear?

A. It sounded like a man whistling out of a key, or something hollow.

Q. Was there more than one such sound?

A. It seemed to me there was one sound like that, but it was in different courses.

Q. In different parts of the woods?

A. Yes, sir; it seemed so to me, but I was scared so I couldn't tell hardly any more than I know they were whistling.

Q. How many men were there the last night?

A. I can't tell, but there was not as many as the first night.

Q. What do you mean by saying if your "old master" was for you he would be with you?

A. I thought Providence was for me, and I put confidence in him to carry me through.

Q. Were you a slave?

A. No, sir; I am not. I was before I was free.

Q. Before the war?

A. Yes, sir.

Q. How old are you?

A. I am going on forty.

Q. Were you raised in that neighborhood?

A. No, sir.

Q. Where were you raised?

A. Some nine or ten miles below.

Q. In the same county?

A. It is divided now. It is in Limestone Township now.

Q. But is it in Spartanburgh county?

A. Yes, sir.

By Mr. VAN TRUMP:

Q. When was it that this conversation about being a radical occurred between you and the members of that Klan?

A. I can't recollect exactly who now, but 'most any of the democrats would get after me about it; almost any of them who saw me would get after me about being in the radical party. They do not believe in it.

Q. You mean democrats that were not there that night?

A. I do not know; I can't tell. They must have been, I reckon. I don't know who they were.

Q. You say that democrats have frequently talked to you about being a radical?

A. They said so.

Q. Who said so?

A. Them Ku-Klux.

Q. What did they say?

A. They said the radicals had said they were going to kill the democrats.

Q. I ask when that took place between you and the Ku-Klux, as you call them?

A. About two months ago.

Q. But at what point of the night did that conversation take place? Where was it?

A. At my home.

Q. Was it when they first got to the door or afterward?

A. It was before they blindfolded me the first time. Before I opened the door they called me; "Damn your old soul, didn't you go radical?" One says "Blindfold him;" and one jerks me right out of the door, and they blindfolded me; and he says, "Take a walk with us;" and I went. He said, "Get down on your knees." I got down. He says, "What made you go radical?" I says, "I did not know any better. I went with the white folks, and am still with the white folks, and don't know any better." He said, "Will you do better?" I said, "I do not know any better." He says, "What made you go radical?" I said, "I didn't know any better;" I was with the white folks--"

Q. Hold on. I did not ask you to go over the whole thing again; I asked you when that occurred.

A. It was the first night.

Q. What made you start to go over the whole thing again?

A. I thought you wanted to know it.

Q. You have been going over that kind of song for some time, have you not?

A. Telling it?

Q. Yes, sir.

A. Yes, sir; I have.

Q. How long have you told it?

A. I do not know.

Q. A good many times?

A. Yes, sir.

Q. To whom?

A. I have told you.

Q. To whom else?

A. To Mr. Tench Blackwell; I told him.

Q. Have a number of people come to you to know about it?

A. Not a great many.

Q. How many?

A. I do not remember of any white persons coming.

Q. None at all?

A. No, sir.

Q. Have you talked with no white persons going through the country?

A. Going through the country they have asked me if the Ku-Klux had whipped me. I said, "Yes, they whipped me."

Q. Did you tell them all about it?

A. I told them they whipped me about the republican party.

Q. Have you talked with anybody within a day or two about it?

A. I don't remember.

Q. Could you recollect if you had?

A. I believe it was about four days that I was talking to some white men about it. One was Mr. Edwards. I went there to see my sons.

Q. Where is that?

A.   Above Cowpens three or four miles.
Q.   How long have you been waiting on this committee?
A.   I came here Wednesday.
Q.   You have been here from that day waiting?
A.   Yes, sir.
Q.   Have you talked with anybody about it since you have been here?
A.   I do not recollect of telling them about this.
Q.   Have none of these people about town here been to see you about this?
A.   Not to examine me.
Q.   You say that?
A.   I do not remember of their having been to me to examine me.
Q.   Have you been down in the yard back here?
A.   Yes, sir.
Q.   Has Rev. Mr. Cummings been to see you?
A.   No, sir. I saw Mr. Poinier.
Q.   What did he say?
A.   He told me to hold on; my time would come to be examined.
Q.   Did he go over there to see you in the yard?
A.   Yes, sir; and another gentleman; I do not remember his name.
Q.   Was it Mr. Fleming:
A.   I don't know Mr. Fleming. I think Mr. Poinier was about all.
Q.   Was it Mr. Camp?
A.   I believe I know him, too.
Q.   Was it Mr. Wallace?
A.   I don't believe I talked with him about it.
Q.   What did Mr. Poinier tell you about it?
A.   He told me he wanted me to give evidence about being whipped.
Q.   Could you not tell that without his telling you?
A.   I could not tell it without being cited by somebody.
Q.   Did he tell you what your evidence was to be?
A.   No, sir.
Q.   Did he not tell you you must tell about that radical matter?
A.   I don't recollect about it.
Q.   Why can you not recollect? It has only been a day or two ago. Did
he not tell you that he wanted you to tell what these men said about radicals?
A.   I do not remember of his telling me that.
Q.   Do you recollect that he did not?
A.   I don't believe Mr. Poinier told me so.
Q.   How long was he with you?
A.   He never staid with me any time.
Q.   Did he come on purpose to see You?
A.   He was just passing through, and I told him I wanted my time to come
off; that my wife was with me.
Q.   Did he stop the other colored people?
A.   Yes, sir.
Q.   Did he talk all around among them?
A.   No, sir; not particularly; only one or another would go to him for
satisfaction.
Q.   Nobody paid you anything for coming here?
A.   No, sir.

                      Spartanburgh, South Carolina, July 8, 1871.

JANE SURRATT (colored) sworn and examined.

By the CHAIRMAN:
Q.   Are you the wife of that man, Jackson Surratt, who has just testified?
A.   Yes, sir.
Q.   We have had from your husband the story of the Ku-Klux coming to your
house and taking you out, and of his running away from them; will you begin
at the point where he left off, and give us what occurred after that?
A.   I will, as well as I can.
Q.   Perhaps you had better begin at the house. Be as brief as you can.
A.   They came to my house and took me out and whipped me. They asked,
did I work; I told them I did; they said I didn't; I said I did, as far as I

was able; I was not able to do hard work; and they just whipped me on.

Q. How many of them came to your house?

A. I was so frightened I don't know; I don't recollect how many, but I think there was six or seven, if I am not mistaken; but I was so frightened that I don't remember.

Q. Did they take out anybody else but you?

A. Yes, sir; my husband and daughter and my son, and whipped them all at the same time. They didn't whip him then; they had whipped him before; he got away; but they whipped the balance of us.

Q. How much did they whip you?

A. I don't know, but I think that they gave me near forty lashes, or quite forty.

Q. On what part of your person?

A. They whipped me from my ankles clear up to about here, above my waist. They made us all lay down.

Q. Were you whipped hard?

A. Yes, sir; they whipped us with things bigger than my thumb.

Q. With what?

A. Switches and sticks, I call them.

Q. Did it hurt you?

A. Yes, sir; Sunday and Monday I couldn't hold my child on my lap to suckle it; I had to lay it on the bed and stand by it. I had no way to rest except on the flat of my belly. I couldn't rest.

Q. What did they do to your son and daughter?

A. They whipped them. They whipped my son miserably bad; they whipped my daughter very bad; she has not been able to do much since; I don't believe she will ever get over it.

Q. Did they say why they whipped you, except that you did not work?

A. That was all. They told her she didn't make a good hand last spring. He was hired out, and they told him he didn't make a good hand; he was at Judge Edwards's.

Q. Who was "he?"

A. My son. They said he didn't make a good hand. They told the man about it. He told the man he was working for about it, and he asked him about it. He had heard that he was whipped for it, and he said, "I never said so." They said my daughter never made a good hand. You see it was my husband and my daughter put in the crop with the man where we staid.

By the CHAIRMAN:

Q. You say there were six or seven at the house. Were there more where you were whipped?

A. One held the horses. I saw the crowd that first came, but I didn't know how many there was, I was so frightened.

Q. Did you know any of the men?

A. To tell the truth, I don't say that I know any one at all; I was so frightened when they came up. They made such a lamentation coming up that it frightened me so that I cannot say who any one was.

By Mr. VAN TRUMP:

Q. Who made the lamentation?

A. They and their horses. I was asleep, and the first thing I knew they burst the door open and took my husband out, and then came back and took me. I had my baby on my arm, and they like to have pulled it out of the bed.

By the CHAIRMAN:

Q. You did not know any of these men?

A. No, sir; I don't know, to say I knew any one.

Q. Have you been sleeping at home since then?

A. Yes, sir; I staid at home. I was afraid about it, but being my little children were there, I couldn't take them about, and I had to bear it. My husband has not slept at home. I have slept the best that I have rested in two months since I have been here in town.

Q. What effect have these whippings of the colored people had upon the colored people in your part of the country? Do they feel safe at home?

A. I can't tell you; I don't know what they mean by it.

Q. Do you know whether the colored people feel safe or not? Have you talked about it with them?

A. No; I don't know whether they do or not; I know I don't.

By Mr. VAN TRUMP:

Q. Have there been any white people to your house since then to talk with you about the abuse these men gave you?

A. There has been nobody only the men we work with; I believe he came in the morning. We were to go out to work and didn't go, and he hallooed to come out there to work, and my husband hallooed, "There is nobody here able to work to-day." We could hear him talking about it with my husband, but I was so bad off that I didn't pay much attention.

Q. Has nobody come to you on purpose to talk with you about it?

A. Not that I know of.

Q. Have you been in town two or three days?

A. Yes, sir; since Wednesday.

Q. Have not white persons in town been talking with you about it?

A. No, sir.

By Mr. STEVENSON:

Q. Did the man for whom your husband worked try to find out who did it?

A. Not as I know of; if he did I never knew it.

By Mr. VAN TRUMP:

Q. Do you believe anybody can find out?

A. He said he was not a friend of killing, but he was a friend of Ku-Klucking.

Q. Who was he?

A. Dennis Scruggs. He called that killing, we were whipped so bad.

Q. Is Dennis Scruggs the man on whose farm you lived?

A. Yes, sir.

Q. When he came down there did he seem satisfied because you were whipped?

A. He didn't say much, only he said that--that he wasn't a friend to killing.

Q. But he was friend to the Ku-Klux?

A. Yes, sir.

Q. Why did he say that he was a friend to "Ku-Kluxing?"

A. I don't know; I supposed it came into his mind then because I was beat so.

Q. Do you know what you are saying now, Jane?

A. Yes, sir; I know.

Q. How far does he live from you?

A. I can't exactly tell you; we just live in sight.

Q. You live now on his farm?

A. Yes, sir.

Q. Have you had any difficulty with him?

A. They are farming together; that is all.

Q. Is it over?

A. No, sir.

Q. Have you had any dispute with him?

A. No, sir.

Q. Has your husband?

A. None; only he has been sort o' angry about getting out o' work, but it was little or nothing.

Q. You say Scruggs was angry about getting out of work?

A. No, sir; about getting out to work.

Q. Was he complaining of your husband?

A. Yes, sir.

Q. Did he work for him?

A. They both worked together; him and my daughter has gone in, and he is to find the horse for them, and he is to get such a part when it is made.

Q. You mean that your husband is?

A. Yes, sir.

Q. He does the work and Scruggs finds the horse?

A. Yes sir; and Mr. Scruggs puts himself in too. My husband finds himself and his daughter, and sometimes I work a little.

Q. Does Scruggs live with you?

A. He is a white man that lives on his land.

Q. There is a daughter in your house; that is your husband's daughter and not yours?

A. No, sir; it is his and mine too; but I say his. I just said his daughter.

Q. Had Scruggs and your husband a dispute?

A. They didn't have nothing worth attention.

Q. Then is your husband's time out on the farm?

A. I don't know. We will not get done now in two weeks, I expect.

Q. Then will the time be out?

A. Yes, sir.

Q. Then he will have to move away?

A. That's what the Ku-Klux told him; he must move from there.

Q. What are the relations between you and Scruggs?

A. He never said.

Q. Has he not told you that you would have to leave when your time was out?

A. No, sir.

Q. You say the time will be out in two weeks?

A. Then we will be done work if it is not wet weather.

Q. Does your husband expect to stay another season?

A. He did talk like moving.

Q. Was that because he had some trouble with Scruggs?

A. No, sir; he said he believed that he would go to the mountains, where he believed that he could get good land.

Q. This land of Scruggs' is not good?

A. A portion of it is tolerable, and some is sorry. He has cleared up his ground this year.

Spartanburgh, South Carolina, July 8, 1871

BARNET RUSSELL sworn and examined.

By the CHAIRMAN:

Q. Do you live in the county?

A. In this county? yes, sir.

Q. In what part of it?

A. I live on Pacolet, about fourteen miles from here.

Q. How long have you lived there?

A. Well, sir, I have lived there, I have been about there--not at the same place, but about the county--for two or three years. I do not know how long.

Q. What business have you been engaged in?

A. I have been farming, sir; and first one thing and another. I have been working for my brother some in the crop. I was married hardly three months ago, and I have been living at my father-in-law's ever since I was married.

Q. Have you been distilling any during that time?

A. No, sir; I have not.

Q. Were you engaged at a distillery at any time?

A. No, sir; I have been plowing ever since cropping time just as hard as I could link it, till yesterday, when they came after me.

Q. Have you a brother there that is engaged in distilling?

A. No, sir; not as I know of.

Q. You do not know of any distilling by you or your brother?

A. If he has done any distilling it is more than I know. I do not say that he has not; if he has it is more than I know.

Q. Have you ever been at any place where there was any distilling done that you know your brother had anything to do with?

A. I have not been at any place where there was stilling going on at the time.

Q. Has there been distilling in the neighborhood?

A. If there has been it is more than I know. I have not been about my brother, near his house, but two or three times since I have been married. I have not been about there, but at home at work ever since crop time, making the crop with my father-in-law, Mr. Edmund Cooley.

Q. Do you know anything of the operations of these persons they call Ku-Klux in that country?

A. No, sir; I do not know any more about a Ku-Kluck no more than a man in the moon about a Ku-Kluck.

Q. Do you know anything about a secret society or organization that is called by any other name up there than the Ku-Klux?

A. No, sir.

Q. Do you know anything of a society called the White Brotherhood?

A. No, sir.

Q. Or of a society called the Invisible Empire?

A. No, sir.

Q. Or the Invisible Circle?

A. No, sir.

Q. Or the Constitutional Union Guards?

A. No, sir; I don't know nothing of no such thing at all. I don't know anything about it.

Q. Have you ever taken an oath of any kind in a secret society or organization of any name?

A. No, sir.

Q. None whatever?

A. No, sir; I have not.

Q. Let me read you an oath, and I will ask you after I have read it what you know about it.

A. Well, sir.

Q. "I do solemnly swear that I will support and defend the Invisible Circle; that I will defend our families, our children, and brethren; that I will assist a brother in distress to the best of my ability; and that I will never reveal the secrets of this order, or anything in regard to it that may come to my knowledge; and if I do, may I meet a traitor's doom, which is death! death! death! So help me, God, and so punish me, my brethren." Have you ever heard an oath of that kind before?

A. I have not, upon my word and honor.

Q. Have you ever taken an oath of that kind?

A. I have not.

Q. Have you ever heard an oath of that kind administered to anybody?

A. I have not. I have not heard no such.

Q. You know nothing about the signs of this order?

A. I know not a thing about it, under the sun; not a thing.

Q. Have there been any persons in that region whipped or taken out by the Ku-Klux?

A. I have heard of it being about the country. I have heard it talked about a good many times, but I never saw a Ku-Klux in my life. I have heard of them whipping about, but never saw them to know anything about them more than you do. If you know anything at all you know more than I do. I know nothing about them. I have heard a great deal of talk about them, but as for knowing anything, I don't know it.

Q. You never saw a raid of the Ku-Klux?

A. No, sir. I have heard of them raiding around several times, but I don't know anything about it.

Q. Are you not under arrest at present for being with a party of these Ku-Klux? . . .

Q. Did you use any of Mr. Cooley's horses that night at all?

A. No, sir.

Q. Were they all in the stable?

A. They were, as far as I know; I never went to the stable to see.

Q. You heard nothing of any disturbance in the neighborhood that night?

A. Not that night.

Q. You heard none going on?

A. No, sir; I didn't know anything about anything going on.

Q. You heard nothing about Isham being whipped at all until you heard it afterward?

A. No, sir.

Q. Remember we are not prosecuting anybody; what is said is not to be given to a jury, or to arrest anybody; but our purpose is generally to see who is guilty. Can you tell us who was the first man that told you about Isham McCrary being whipped?

A. No, sir; I told you I couldn't.

Q. You do not remember?

A. No, sir.

Q. You cannot mind whether it was a white man or a black man?

A. I don't mind whether it was a white man I heard first talk about it, or that it was a black man.

Q. Have you any idea which it was?

A. No, sir; I don't remember. I never tried to recollect anything about it. If I had tried I might have recollected it.

By Mr. STEVENSON:

Q. Have you a gun?

A. No, sir.

Q. A pistol?

A. No, sir.

Q. Have you any kind of arms?

A. No, sir.

Q. I do not mean now, but at home?

A. No, sir; I do not have any use for arms at all, sir. My business is to work and try to make a living. I am married now, and have not a thing under the sun. I am there at my father-in-law's, and have nothing. I am at work there and board there. I have never had nothing, even to a horse or a house. I am a poor boy and have always been so. I have had to raise myself. My father and mother are both dead.

By Mr. VAN TRUMP:

Q. Are you not, Russell, a very light boy for your age, slightly made? Stand up and let us see how big you are?

A. I am a very light man, sir; I am a small man.

Spartanburgh, South Carolina, July 8, 1871

ISHAM MCCRARY (colored) sworn and examined.

By the CHAIRMAN:

Q. Where do you live?

A. Up the other side of Pacolet, not far from McMullen's mill; about a mile from it.

Q. How long have you lived there?

A. I have lived on the same land I am on now, but not in the same house, for three years.

Q. Were you born in that neighborhood?

A. No, sir; I was born and raised in Greenville.

Q. In this State?

A. Yes, sir.

Q. What were you doing?

A. I was living up there--farming.

Q. Have you rented land?

A. Yes, sir; I was on rented land.

Q. Whose land?

A. John McMullen's land.

Q. Did the Ku-Klux come to visit you at any time?

A. Yes, sir; they came on me in March; but I do not know what day it was. I had been working down on the railroad, and just before I got done I went home, about the 15th of March. Pay-day was the 15th; anyway, I went home a little before I got done here. It was Saturday night. They picked the time for me to come home.

Q. Go on and tell how they whipped you.

A. When they came in they broke down one of the doors, and they broke the hinge off the other one, and four came in the doors at once. It was about 2o'clock at night, as nigh as I can tell you; and then they came in and shot twice over my head, and said they were going to kill me; that that was what they came for; and then they gathered me, and I asked them to let me put on my breeches. I did not have my breeches buttoned up; I was out of bed. After they got hold of me, I told them I wanted to get my hat if they were going to take me off; it was handy, and I reached and got it. Then they asked me out. After they shot over my head twice when they asked me out, they told me now to say my prayers, that they were going to kill me. They asked for my arms too. I told them I had no arms. Then they asked me out of the door. I went out. They told me to get down and say my prayers; that they were going to kill me. My wife came out of the door, hallooing to them, and she slipped and fell, and they sort of hallooed. She was about to take her bed; you understand that. Then they commenced whipping me, calling the names by numbers. There were eight of them, as nigh as I could make out, and eight of them whipped me as they called the names. I got to understand the way they called; they called the number that they gave. They gave me twenty-five lashes apiece; four did, and the first whipped me gave me three lashes after they were done whipping me, to make me take the hickories they had whipped me with down to show them to my friends. All of them whipped me around, and they all done give me the same number. Some give me less; four give me twenty-five apiece, and then the others the way they numbered, as nigh as I could understand it. Two give me the same number, twenty-five apiece; four of them gave me twenty-five apiece, and the first one gave me three licks after he was done whipping me to make me take the stubs that he was whipping me with and show them.

Q. Did they say anything to you?

A. Yes, sir; they asked me who I voted for; and said if I told a lie they would shoot me right off. I told them I would not lie; I voted for Mr. Scott. "What did you vote for Scott for?" said he. I told them I did not know how to turn; and if I should tell them another way they would not know but what I was the other way; they would not know whether I turned or not; that I didn't know how to turn. They said, "Scott has turned, and what is the reason you cannot turn?" They said, "How do you like that?" I told them I did not like any such way as that; let a man be what he was; I would not know how to turn any other way; that is what I told them. They dragged me out, as I told you before, and whipped me, after they done whipped me they told me to take the stubs.

Q. Was this before or after they whipped you that this conversation took place?

A. It was before they whipped me that they asked me these questions.

Q. Did they say anything more?

A. They just asked to pray; I don't think there is anything else. I am mighty scattering in telling it.

Q. How many were there of them?

A. There were eight or nine; I cannot say exactly.

Q. How were they dressed?

A. They had just a common--I thought it was cloth, and I reckon it was; anyhow it was white; some white and some black, and bound around with black; and you could see this far around; you could see back of the eyes. The disguise was so that you could see the disguise over the mouth and eyes.

Q. Could you see the face or the eyes?

A. I could see the eyes and part of the face.

Q. How were they dressed below that?

A. Some of them had on--it looked like night-gowns; and this Mr. Russell had his coat turned wrong side out.

Q. What Russell?

A. Barney Russell.

Q. Did you know him?

A. Yes, sir. I knew him by his motion and by his gait, and his beard around here; it just happened so. I was not thinking about anybody; but you see one of my children was made to hold the light and stand right up there, and two or three, I won't say which, but some of them were at the light.

Q. What effect had that holding of the light?

A. That was how I came to see him and know him.

Q. Did you say here he was one of those men?

A. Yes, sir; he was one of the men. When my wife fell down, the next morning she could not walk, and it was pretty nigh two weeks before she could walk; she could not walk across the house. The reason she come out that night was she was afraid they were going to kill me with whipping, and she would bear part of the whipping of me.

By Mr. VAN TRUMP:

Q. Was your wife sick too?

A. No, sir; not then; she was pretty nigh coming to bed. She just got so she could walk about two weeks after she got down.

Q. How did these men come to your house, on foot or on horseback?

A. They came up to the house on foot; but just a piece over the branch --between there and the river I reckon it was about three hundred yards, and may be five hundred yards--they hitched their horses.

Q. Did you see the horses there?

A. I did not see them. I saw the tracks where they came there.

Q. How far is your house from Mr. Cooley's there in the neighborhood?

A. I reckon it is about a mile or a little over; I do not reckon it is more than a mile to go the nighest way, but to go around it is a little over.

Q. Had you any quarrel with anybody to account for this visit to you?

A. No, sir; I never had. I did not know that anybody had anything against me in any way, and that is why I was not afraid of them. I had heard they were coming on me for near about two months before that, but I did not know what for.

Q. Had that made you afraid?

A. It never made me so afraid as not to stay; but I came there on the railroad, and as I would go home they would tell me of it; that the citizens told them they were coming there on such a night, and I laid out some two or three nights, I think, when I went back; I laid out so my wife could rest. I hadn't done nothing, and was not guilty of nothing.

Q. After the whipping did you continue to sleep in your house?

A. Yes, sir; I slept in there until I came off the railroad. I was not quite done at the railroad. I did not have my month out; I was aiming to make a crop anyhow, but they told me when they got done whipping me, that they did not want me to leave that place. I said I did not want to leave neither. I did not expect to leave, because I had done so much work there to get my farm that I hated to leave it. I had about fifteen acres. I have two years on the place; that is the reason I wanted to stay on the place--to get some benefit of it if I could.

Q. Have you told all about this occurrence that you know?

A. No, sir; there is some more men that were there that I knew.

Q. Who were they?

A. Miles Mason; I knew him; I would not have taken notice of him, but when they went to start--I had staid on his land one year, and been working with him backwards and forwards with him, and staid with him off and on--and when he went to start he spoke this word; [whispering] "Tell Isham when he comes to a white man's house to pull off his hat." He whispered that--that when I came to a white man's house for me to always recollect to put it at the door. Then I happened to recollect him, and was surprised at him being there, when him and me always talked so kind; but he was after me several times last summer to plow for him, and I told him I could not do it. That was all I could see that he could have anything against me.

Q. Did you know anybody else?

A. Yes, sir.

Q. Who?

A. William Bush; they call him Billy Bush, but is the same in a common way. Me and him both lived right together; there was not a mile between us; on the same man's land. He married old uncle Bob McMullen's daughter, and we worked the same land together for three years. I knew him, and the way he was fixed, and knew his winter coat that he had over him, and his disguise was not fixed but so I could see his hair right here behind the ears, so that it was kind of turned up; the disguise was turned up behind his ear, so that I could see his hair; and his nose was out--he has got a pretty long nose,

for a slim-faced man, but he has a pretty big body; and I knew him well
enough by that and by his talk; I knew him by his talk if I had not seen
anything.

Q. You have now given Mason, and Russell, and Bush; who else did you
know?

A. I knew another.

Q. Give his name.

A. Mr. Gilbert; Berry Gilbert.

Q. Did you make oath against these men here?

A. I made an oath a while ago against these two; I come to the truth,
I allowed.

Q. Were you sworn before Mr. Poinier about this business?

A. Yes, sir.

Q. How long ago was that?

A. It was Thursday or Wednesday; it was the first day I come; that was
Wednesday.

By Mr. VAN TRUMP:
What day or night in March was this?

A. It was on Saturday night; but to say exactly the night I can't; I
can't read, and I never paid any attention to what day in the month it was.

Q. Cannot you tell the day of the month without being able to read?

A. Yes, sir, when I take notice of it; but I was in so much trouble
I did not know what I could do; it looked like I could not live. I was in a
heap more trouble afterwards than before, just studying.

Q. Do not you know what time it was by having your mind under your command before they came there?

A. No, sir; but as nigh as I can tell, it was about the 1st of March.

Q. For what purpose did you use the 15th of March awhile ago?

A. You see, I had to come down back to the railroad and stay until the
15th; I did not have my month out, and I told them I had to go back to the
railroad, because I did not have my money for it to begin my crop.

Q. What has that got to do with fixing the time when these men called
to see you that night?

A. They asked me if I was going back to the railroad.

Q. Who asked you?

A. These Ku-Klux. I told them yes, I was going back, and I had to work
until the 15th of March to get my money.

Q. How came it that you did not tell before that those Ku-Klux asked
you whether you were going to work at the railroad again?

A. I did speak about the railroad.

Q. You did not speak about the Ku-Klux asking you about it?

A. They asked me about that.

Q. Why did not you tell that they said that to you awhile ago?

A. It slipped my mind.

Q. When they asked you whether you were going back to the railroad,
what did you tell them?

A. I told them I owed Mr. McMullen some; and I wanted to raise the money
to pay him.

Q. What has that to do with the 15th of March?

A. I had something like two or three days to stay to get my month out,
and then I had to work a little longer to stay until the 15th of March--I
think it was only three days.

Q. How many days had you to work, after the Ku-Klux came, before the
15th of March when you got your pay?

A. I think it was four days.

Q. That would make the Ku-Klux visit about the 10th or 11th of March?

A. Yes, sir; I reckon so.

Q. Is that the day instead of the 1st of March?

A. I tell you it was some time in March. Coming to study about it, I
reckoned it was about the 1st of March.

Q. I know you stated it was some time in March, and afterwards said it
was the 1st of March; are you now satisfied it was at least so far as the
10th or 11th?

A. I think it was about the 1st of March; it was the 1st or 11th of

March, as nigh as I can tell.

    Q. Do you say you think it was the 1st or 11th of March?

    A. It might have been about the 1st of March, but I cannot exactly tell how many days.

    Q. You do say you had to work about four days after the Ku-Klux came before the 15th, when you were to have your pay?

    A. Yes, sir; I think they came Saturday, and I worked that many days, and three days over, I think.

    Q. Did you work until the 18th?

    A. No, sir; until the 15th. It was on Saturday, in March.

    Q. Did not you say your time expired on the 15th?

    A. Yes, sir.

    Q. Why did you work three days over?

    A. I did not get the money, because the money had not come, and I worked three days and then I went home.

    Q. Is not your mind so much confused about the expiration of the time on the railroad that you cannot fix the time by that at all? How can you fix it by that fact?

    A. By its being so many days between that time and the 15th. I think it was about the 1st of March. That is the way I think it.

    Q. Why do you think it was the 1st of March?

    A. The way I went and came. I think it must have been the 1st of March, because I worked down here on the railroad so many days, and it was wet weather all the time, and I might have missed some days, and it was Saturday night in March. I know it was no piece in March, for March had not begun hardly.

    Q. You say your time was up in March, on the 15th?

    A. Yes, sir.

    Q. You say you worked four days after they visited you?

    A. Yes, sir. I worked my time out, and some days I did not work on account of the rain.

    Q. What effect does that have?

    A. I am telling how many days I worked before I went home.

    Q. How does that explain the time the Ku-Klux came?

    A. That is the way I tried to get the exact time. It was about the 1st of March. I said on the 1st of March, because I knew it was not long in March.

    Q. You know it was on a Saturday night?

    A. Yes, sir; I know that.

    Q. And you know it was the 1st of March?

    A. I believe it was the 1st of March.

    Q. How many men came to your house?

    A. Eight or nine. I said there was eight men, but I never counted them.

    Q. Had you heard they were going to visit you before that?

    A. Yes, sir.

    Q. How did you hear that?

    A. From this Free Tobe McMullen; he is called Free Tobe; he had been free all his life-time. Every time he would meet me when I came up he would tell me what the Ku-Klux said they were going to do to me.

    Q. What did he tell you that they were going to do?

    A. He said they were going to raise me before many days.

    Q. Was he a black man?

    A. Yes, sir.

    Q. Did he say he belonged to them?

    A. No, sir; he did not say he belonged to them, but he said what night they were coming.

    Q. Coming to you?

    A. No, sir; he didn't say; he said they were going out such a night.

    Q. How did he know?

    A. I do not know.

    Q. Did you ask him?

    A. I asked him who said so; he said a man told him, but it won't do to talk.

    Q. How often did he warn you that the Ku-Klux were going to be after you?

A. He warned me twice.

Q. Did he seem to be in earnest about it?

A. Yes, sir; he said that they said they were coming to raise me. I asked him what they were going to raise me for. He said he did not know; he said he could not tell what it was, but they were going to do it, so they said. I asked him who said so. He did not say he heard them talking about it, but he said "some men that live not far from you is going to do it."

Q. But he said it would not do to talk about it?

A. He said it is close times now, and it will not do to talk about it.

Q. He said he knew they were going to call on you?

A. Yes, sir; he said he heard they were coming, but he did not say he knew it.

Q. He did not tell you who told him?

A. No, sir; he said that it would not do to talk.

Q. Are there other colored men in the neighborhood?

A. Yes, sir; there is another one.

Q. More than one?

A. There is one right close to the cabin.

Q. Are they within a mile or two of where you live?

A. Not on that side of the river.

Q. On any side of the river?

A. Yes, sir; there are several.

Q. You say four of these men gave you twenty-five lashes apiece?

A. Yes, sir.

Q. Did you count them?

A. You see the first man whipped me, and called the numbers, and then I counted; one counted them, and then another counted them.

Q. Do you mean that one of the Ku-Klux counted them?

A. Yes, sir.

Q. Did he count them out loud?

A. Yes, sir; he said, "That is twenty-five, stop."

Q. And then he called another?

A. Yes, sir.

Q. And so four gave you twenty-five apiece?

A. Yes, sir.

Q. Making how many altogether? That made one hundred lashes?

A. Yes, sir.

Q. Did two others give you twenty-five cuts apiece?

A. No, sir, just four; and then the others they gave me--they whipped me so that, with the others, it made a hundred and fifty.

Q. Right there, after describing their whipping you, you started off without a question being asked after you had replied that there were eight or nine of them, which was the last question asked, and you said this man Russell had his coat turned wrong-side out. Nobody asked you about Mr. Russell?

A. No, sir.

Q. But you stated right out that Russell had his coat wrong-side out, and you said you knew him by his coat and his beard?

A. Yes, sir.

Q. Had he a black beard?

A. No, sir; a dark beard.

Q. A long beard?

A. No, sir.

Q. A heavy beard?

A. No, sir.

Q. A dark beard?

A. Sort of dark and fine, as if he never had shaved hardly; he is just like one that has never been shaved hardly. I could see his beard was almost, you might say--well, it was his beard, as nigh as I could see.

Q. What was there in the coat being turned wrong-side out, that you could tell it?

A. The lining of his coat, and the make of his coat, and his size.

Q. Had you ever seen that coat wrong-side out before?

A. Yes, sir.

Q. Where?

A. I did not see it all turned wrong-side out, but I have seen the
lining along here; because I was about him so often.

Q. What kind of lining was it?

A. It was store-cloth; black and white. I cannot tell exactly the
stripe.

Q. You do not remember the stripe?

A. Yes, sir, I recollect it, but I cannot explain it.

Q. What color was it?

A. It was a black stripe and then red.

Q. You have seen a good many coats like that, have you not?

A. Yes, sir; but nobody right close around here had any just like it.
I knew him by his features.

Q. What was peculiar about this coat?

A. Nothing more than the lining.

Q. You have seen many other coats lined that way?

A. I have seen lots of coats lined that way since.

Q. You never saw one before like his?

A. I never noticed it before.

Q. You never noticed a coat just like that before that night?

A. Not with that lining. You see, I had seen that lining before, and
that made me think of it.

Q. Where had you seen it? On him?

A. I had seen it on him.

Q. Was that the first coat with that kind of lining you had ever seen?

A. I reckon I had seen others like it.

Q. But you say all you have seen like it were since you saw that coat?

A. He got it out of the store, and I have not seen many like it, because
I had not been out much, and had not seen anything like it there.

Q. Do you say it is remarkable that a white young man, twenty-one years
of age, should get a coat out of a store?

A. It was not got out of a store, it was a store lining. It was home-
made jeans.

Q. Is it anything remarkable that a young fellow should buy a piece of
goods like that out of a store?

A. No, sir; I do not suppose so.

Q. You say it was a jeans coat?

A. Yes, sir.

Q. Are you sure of that?

A. Yes, sir.

Q. What color?

A. Dark; not black, not right black.

Q. Is that the only jeans coat in this country?

A. 0, no, sir.

Q. It was not because it was jeans coat that you thought it was Russell?

A. No, sir. It was because I saw enough of his face.

Q. How much of his face?

A. I could see some around here and here, [the eyes,] and his beard.

Q. Was the top of his head covered?

A. Yes, sir.

Q. Was the mask over his eyes and mouth?

A. I could see a little under the back part of the jaw.

Q. Did not you in describing his hair a while ago say his hair was
turned up behind?

A. That was another gentleman.

Q. How were the masks fastened on?

A. It looked like it was tied on.

Q. Was it tied under the chin?

A. It was tied some way or another under the chin, and there were holes
for his nose and everything.

Q. Did his nose come outside of the mask?

A. It was so everybody could see it.

Q. You saw there was a hole for his eyes and another for his nose?

A. Yes, sir.

Q. How was that?

A. It was cut to come across in this way.

Q. Was there a slit for his nose to come out?

A. It was cut so that he could have air through it. It was not tied.
It came out over his mouth, and by his holding the light I came to notice.

Q. At what particular time was it that you noticed this particular
head so as to know it was Russell's head and face?

A. I was not thinking about it then to know who it was, but I just
happened to know it right then, and I says that's Russell.

Q. You said so?

A. Yes, sir.

Q. Who to?

A. Just as soon as they quit whipping me I said that was Russell.

Q. Who did you say so to?

A. To my wife and children.

Q. You did not say anything to the Ku-Klux about it?

A. No, sir; it was after they left.

Q. At what point in the proceedings did you discover that this man was
Russell?

A. It was when they were talking to me; asking me questions.

Q. Russell did not ask you any questions?

A. No, sir; Russell did not talk to me.

Q. How far from you was Russell standing?

A. He came out when they called the number.

Q. Was Russell one of the four that whipped you?

A. There was more than four that whipped me.

Q. How many more?

A. As near as I can tell it was eight, and there was one that never
came up. That is, I do not think so. I think there was nine of them. I
know eight whipped me.

Q. Did you keep the count so accurately as to know that eight men
whipped you?

A. You see when they gave me this hundred lashes--

Q. This, then, made four?

A. Yes, sir.

Q. How many did the other four give you?

A. They whipped me in a manner that caused me to take notice of their
counting.

Q. They were counting the number of licks, were they not?

A. Yes, sir.

Q. They were not counting the number of men?

A. No, sir.

Q. How came you to notice that eight out of the nine whipped you?

A. Because it was just one hundred and fifty; the way I counted it.

Q. How many did the other four give you apiece?

A. I cannot say exactly; but two of them whipped me to make twenty-five.

Q. How did you ascertain that?

A. By the way they counted. You see one whipped me on until it got
about half. You see there is a difference in the two whippings; one gave me
a little more than the others, a lick more anyhow, it made twenty-five for
the two. Then the other two gave me about the same. The way they called it
over, I just averaged it myself. I said that is about fifty for the whole
four.

Q. To which of the two divisions of four men each did Russell belong?

A. The last one.

Q. He gave you twelve or thirteen strokes?

A. Yes, sir; somewhere there.

Q. He was not among those who gave you twenty-five apiece?

A. No, sir.

Q. Did you look up to see him; how did you know him; in what position
were you?

A. I was just standing up, and they were facing me; and they would just
go behind me; and every time they called the number they would go around.

Q. Were you blindfolded?

A. No, sir; I was not blindfolded.

Q. They all stood right before you, and as some man called out the
particular man to whip you he stepped behind?

A. Yes, sir; the one that was whipping. They stood far enough so that
I could see all around both sides, and there was a narrow place in my yard,
and some of them held their guns pointed towards me if I would run.

Q. How long after they commenced did they bring the light?

A. They brought the light before they whipped me.

Q. Do you say the light was brought before the whipping began?

A. Yes, sir, that was fetched up just as soon as they got in the house.

Q. How long before the whipping commenced was the light brought?

A. There were one or two got the light from one of my children.

Q. They had the light in the house, had they not?

A. Yes, sir.

Q. Did they take the light when they led you off?

A. Yes, sir; they made one of my children stand and hold the light.
It was not further from the door than that door is from me, [three or four
yards.]

Q. Was it a dark night?

A. Yes, sir, not very. It was dark, for they had a light. I am sort
of bothered in talking, but I want to be straight, if I can.

Q. Do you know that you are swearing here positively that one of those
men that night was Barnet Russell?

A. Yes, sir.

Q. You swear to that positively?

A. Yes, sir, positively; he was one of them.

Q. Are you just as positive in regard to Mason?

A. Yes, sir.

Q. Are you just as sure in regard to Billy Bush?

A. Yes, sir.

Q. No mistake about it.

A. No, sir, no mistake about it. I do not feel it betwixt me and my
heart. I know if I swear a wrong thing it will be against me in the coming
day. What I swear here I want to swear right.

Q. Then it is between you and your soul, rather than your heart.

A. It is between me and God. God is the manager of it.

Q. You have no hesitation in saying that three of these men were Russell,
Mason, and Billy Bush.

A. There were four of them I knew.

Q. And Berry Gilbert; are you positive in regard to him also?

A. Yes, sir.

Q. Were you sure of it that night?

A. Yes, sir. I was sure of it that night.

Q. Particularly sure of this young man Russell?

A. Yes, sir.

Q. Did you wake up in your senses next morning?   ·

A. I never went to sleep. I could not sleep for the whipping.

Q. Where did you go the next day?

A. I went over to the mill.

Q. Champion's mill?

A. No, sir. Bob McMullen's mill.

Q. Is he a white man?

A. Yes, sir.

Q. Did you tell him about this transaction?

A. No, sir; I never told him, but I told a black man that was there;
I never saw him.

Q. When did you tell a white man about it?

A. I never told a white man about it at all; that is about knowing these
men.

Q. But about the whipping?

A. I told any white man that asked me.

Q. Did a good many ask you?

A. They did not ask me that day, but in days or weeks afterward.

Q. Was there not more than one white man in this county who knew it a
few days afterward?

A. On Monday I came down to the railroad, and no white men had asked me.

Q. When did it become known through the country that you had been
whipped by the Ku-Klux?

A.   I do not know how soon it was known, but I never told nobody; no white man, that I recollect; not before Monday.

Q.   But when was it known by white men and black men that you had been whipped by these marauders; was it not within a few days afterward?

A.   O, yes, sir.

Q.   Everybody knew it?

A.   I do not know whether everybody knew it, but I did not keep it a secret at all; if anybody asked me I told it, but I did not tell anybody that did not ask me.

Q.   When did you tell anybody that you knew Russell that night?

A.   I told my wife so the next morning.

Q.   Who else?

A.   That is all I did tell.

Q.   Why did you not tell others?

A.   Because I heard that if any one told anybody on the Ku-Klux, that they knew any of them, they would kill them right off; and I would not tell anybody.

Q.   When did you tell anybody?

A.   I never told anybody in that settlement.

Q.   What other settlement?

A.   I did not tell it anywhere then that I knew them; hardly anybody knew it; I do not know as anybody knew it, until I explained here the other day.

Q.   When?

A.   Wednesday.

Q.   How came you to tell it then, if you were afraid to tell it before that?

A.   Because I was afraid of its getting out; if I said it was such men I would be killed.

Q.   Were you brought up a few days ago; you say you told somebody a few days ago?

A.   I told that I was whipped.

Q.   You said you told the next Monday that you were whipped.

A.   Yes, sir; I told anybody that asked me, that I was whipped.

Q.   But I am asking about your telling as to your knowing any of these particular men; you say you were afraid to tell that you knew any one, fearing that they would kill you.

A.   I say I would not tell anybody that I knew them, for fear they would betray me.

Q.   Did I understand you correctly as saying that you told somebody a few days ago?

A.   I said, "until a few days;" not who it was. I did not tell that.

Q.   Who did you tell?

A.   Mr. Poinier.

Q.   How did you happen to meet him?

A.   He called me up to give it in.

Q.   In where?

A.   To give in what was done to me.

Q.   To give it in where?

A.   Down here. Down in the room.

Q.   Whose room?

A.   In the post office.

Q.   How did he know anything about it?

A.   Somebody put it in here.

Q.   Put what in?

A.   Put my name there, that I had been whipped.

Q.   You know that everybody knew you had been whipped about the 1st of March.

A.   Yes, sir; but I did not report it to any body about my being whipped.

Q.   You did the next Monday morning; and everybody knew you had been whipped.

A.   I never reported anybody to put it down for me but Ben Jackson. He is the one that put it down. He got here before I did, and did it.

Q.   Did what?

A.   Told men here that I was whipped.

Q. That was nothing new; did he tell who whipped you?

A. No, sir.

Q. How do you know?

A. Because he did not know, I reckon.

Q. Up to that time nobody except your wife knew who had whipped you?

A. I never told anybody I knew who did it except my wife.

Q. How did Jackson know?

A. He only knew to say I was whipped.

Q. When did you tell anybody who whipped you?

A. I never told it until here, beside my family.

Q. You say a few days ago you told somebody who had whipped you?

A. But not before.

Q. But then you did. Whom did you tell a few days ago the names of these four or five men that you recognized?

A. I did not tell anybody.

Q. Is this the first time you have told anybody in the world, except your wife, the names of these four or five men?

A. I never told no white folks, so that they would get them. I have told some that I thought were my friends about it; but they will keep it.

Q. Told them what?

A. Told them I knew who whipped me.

Q. I thought you said a while ago that you never had told a human being except your wife who these men were?

A. I was speaking about white men; I wanted to keep it secret from white men.

Q. I was speaking about white men and black men. You have said repeatedly that you never told it to any man until within a few days.

A. It has not been long since I did tell them.

Q. Who were these friends that you told that you thought would keep it?

A. Uncle Harry Lipscomb. I told him about it.

Q. When did you tell him; directly after it occurred?

A. No, sir.

Q. How long afterward?

A. It was two months, or a month, or more--over a month.

Q. You think it was about a month after it occurred before you told Lipscomb? Was that the first time that you saw Lipscomb after the Ku-Klux had visited you?

A. Yes, sir; the first time I ever got acquainted with him.

Q. How did you know he was such a good friend?

A. He said he had been whipped, too.

Q. You then told him about a month after you were whipped who four or five of the men were who whipped you?

A. He told me he was whipped; but I never would tell until I told him.

Q. Who else did you tell beside Lipscomb?

A. There is nobody I know of I told. To tell the truth, I told him, finally, who whipped me. I think he was all the man I told.

Q. When did you first get the thought in your head that you would prosecute those men for being here that night?

A. I was not thinking about prosecuting them.

Q. When did it first enter your mind to prosecute these four or five men for being in that band of Ku-Klux that night who whipped you?

A. I did not think about prosecuting them at all.

Q. Who did?

A. I did not think it was right.

Q. It would have been very right for you to have prosecuted them the first moment you had the chance.

A. This here was the only chance I got here.

Q. That never entered your mind; whose mind did it first enter into?

A. I have thought it was right that they should be, but I did not see any ground that it could be done, and I thought it would go away like a heap of other things have gone, and nothing would be said about it.

Q. When did you first hear that they would be prosecuted?

A. I heard it talked about a little, but I can't say exactly when.

Q. How long ago?

A. I cannot tell exactly how long since I heard it.

Q.   When were you first sent for to come to town to swear to it?
A.   Tuesday.
Q.   Who came for you?
A.   The Yankees came. The Yankees came to our house.
Q.   Who are the Yankees?
A.   We call them Yankees.
Q.   Who are they?
A.   These men out here. They came up to the still-house there, and sent
Uncle Harry Lipscomb to tell me to come to Spartanburgh.
Q.   Who are the Yankees?
A.   I mean them men out here in camp.
Q.   Do you mean the soldiers?
A.   Yes, sir; we always call them that way.
Q.   Do you know who sent the soldiers?
A.   No, sir; I thought some men had sent them.
Q.   Tell me why it was, that although this outrage was committed upon you
about the 1st of March, and you knew the names of four or five of those who
did it, and had told several persons, still the prosecution has been postponed
until this particular time, when this congressional committee is to visit
Spartanburgh; can you explain why this thing has been allowed to lie since
the 1st of March?
A.   I thought it had to lie, because my life would be taken if I had
told.
Q.   I am not asking why you did nothing; but do you know why this thing
was postponed until now?
A.   No, sir, I don't know; unless it was because the men that are doing
the business now did not get into the light of it until this time.
Q.   Whom did you go to see when you came to town--when these Yankees left
word that you must come to town?
A.   I came to see whoever was holding the committee.
Q.   What committee?
A.   This here.
Q.   The committee at this table?
A.   I thought it would be likely a court.
Q.   Then you seem to have understood that the word the Yankees left with
Lipscomb was for you to come before this committee and swear here?
A.   Yes, sir.
Q.   But you have not sworn somewhere else, before you came here?
A.   They called me in there; but I didn't know but what that was the
place.
Q.   You say "there." [Pointing out of the window.] Where do you mean?
A.   I mean the post office down there.
Q.   Where is Mr. Poinier's office?
A.   I don't know where it is.
Q.   I want to distinguish between the time when you came here to swear
against these young men, and the time you came here to swear before us as a
committee. When did you come to make oath in order to have these young men
arrested?
A.   It was Wednesday.
Q.   Are you sure it was Wednesday?
A.   Yes, sir.
Q.   Who told you to come then for that purpose?
A.   Uncle Harry Lipscomb told me it was necessary to come. They had sent
him; and they said they were going to take me right on then.
Q.   Did you understand that Lipscomb, having received word from the
Yankees, left word for you to come to swear before Mr. Poinier, and before us
also?
A.   I do not know who it was. Tuesday they came.
Q.   You have been here since?
A.   Yes, sir.

By Mr. STEVENSON:
Q.   What did Uncle Harry Lipbscomb tell you?
A.   He just told me we all had got to come down to town that had been
abused by the Ku-Klux, to explain ourselves.

By Mr. Van Trump:

Q. Was anything said about how much money you would get for it?

A. No, sir; I never heard about that.

Q. Was there something said to you about two dollars a day and mileage?

A. I do not know as Uncle Harry said a word about it to me. Before we got down here I heard that they got two dollars a day here; and I heard a dollar and a half; and I heard two dollars and a half.

Q. Was it talked pretty generally among the colored people out there that all colored people who came here and swore would get two dollars a day and mileage?

A. No, sir.

Q. You have come here and have not been back since; did you swear before anybody else before you swore here, since you have been here?

A. I did not hold up my hand to swear; he wanted to know who I knew, and asked could I swear; I told him this, I could swear.

Q. What was done then?

A. I said that these were the men.

Q. Who asked you that question?

A. Mr. Poinier.

Q. He asked you whether you could come before us and swear that those were the men?

A. Yes, sir.

Q. And you said "yes?"

A. I told him I could.

Q. How many men did he name that you could swear to?

A. Four.

Q. I still cannot get at what I want, which, I suppose, is a fact. How often have you sworn in town here? Were you not sworn before somebody else before you were sworn here to-day?

A. On this here?

Q. Yes; about this Ku-Klux visit to you; have you not sworn that these four or five persons were among the men that abused you on that night?

A. No, sir; not as I can recollect.

Q. Then how were these men arrested?

A. I just said what I told you. I did not have the Bible, but I told them I could swear to them.

Q. Did they write down anything you said?

A. Yes, sir.

Q. Did you sign it?

A. No, sir.

Q. Did you make a mark to it?

A. No, sir.

Q. But they had paper and were writing?

A. Yes, sir.

Q. And wrote it down?

A. I think Mr. Poinier wrote it down.

Q. Was he writing on paper partly printed and partly white?

A. I do not know whether he was or not, exactly. I never noticed.

Q. Did he read to you what he wrote?

A. No, sir; he never read it out after I stated it.

Q. Did he ask you whether you were willing to swear to what was written down, and what you were telling him?

A. Yes, sir.

Q. And you told him you could?

A. Yes, sir.

Q. But you did not swear?

A. That is all I did, to say swear; I said I could do it.

Q. Did they make you hold up your hand and swear?

A. I do not remember now of holding up my hand.

Q. Did not they make you hold up your hand and put the question, "whether you would swear by Almighty God that what you were saying was true?

A. I do not think they did.

Q. You did not kiss the book?

A. No, sir.

Q. You did make a statement which Mr. Poinier set down in writing?

A. I think it was him.

Q. What did he say he was going to do with it?

A. He did not say what.

Q. Did not they talk to you about sending for these young men?

A. He did not say when he was going to send.

Q. Did he say he was going to send?

A. He said they were going to have them taken up. He did not say when he was going to send.

Q. How came you to know Miles Mason?

A. I knew him right well.

Q. How?

A. I knew him; you see I catched his voice so good; and I looked at him when he started off.

Q. Had he a strange voice that you could tell it?

A. It is not so strange, but I have heard him talk so much that I caught it when he said, "tell him to pull off his hat."

Q. Then he was just whispering to you?

A. He was right close to me.

Q. The way in which you tried to represent it to Senator Scott a while ago, was that he whispered, "If you come to a white man's house to take off your hat." You repeated it, whispering the words yourself. Was that the way?

A. No, sir.

Q. What did you whisper it for?

A. I couldn't think. He just told me to come to a white man's house; or told him, "Tell him, when he comes to a white man's house, to take off his hat."

Q. Did you not make a motion to show how Mason told you these words; put your head up as if to another, and whisper?

A. No, sir. It was to the other man, that did the talking, that he did that.

Q. To what other man?

A. That one who was talking. That was the one Mason talked to.

Q. Who said to you, "Take off your hat when you come into a white man's house?"

A. No, sir; he did not say it to me; he said it to a man; I didn't know that man.

Q. He whispered to him?

A. Yes, sir; I just catched his voice.

Q. How could you tell his voice in a whisper?

A. I was so I could hear it to catch it.

Q. Did he do it in about the way in which you did when you were answering Senator Scott?

A. He did to the white man.

Q. Did he do it as you did it a while ago?

A. That is the way; he motioned to the other man.

Q. You say you knew his voice when he spoke the words?

A. Yes, sir.

Q. Now, the way in which he said these words was in a whisper, was it not?

A. He talked low; I called whispering--that is, talking low.

Q. Did he do it just as you attempted to do it a while ago in describing it?

A. He just turned his head close to him.

Q. Did he do it in the way in which you attempted to show it a while ago?

A. The way I was trying to do; just talking low.

Q. Was that the way he did?

A. Yes, sir.

Q. In that kind of a whisper you recognized the voice of Miles Mason?

A. Yes, sir.

Q. How did you know Billy Bush?

A. I knew him by the way I saw part of his hair and his face, and I knew his talk and his movement--that is, in his motions.

Q. You are satisfied you knew him?

A. I knew him just the same as my brother.

Q. You saw his hair behind his ears where his disguise was turned up?

A. It was at the side his hair was out.

Q. What sort of hair had he?

A. Pretty nigh black hair.

Q. You think it was Billy Bush because it was black hair?

A. It was by the shape of his face.

Q. Had not he a mask and disguise on?

A. Yes, sir.

Q. What sort of one?

A. A white one.

Q. All over his face?

A. No, sir.

Q. How much of his face?

A. Part of it showed along his eyes and all the holes.

Q. Was it tied under his chin?

A. Yes, sir.

Q. And over his forehead?

A. I don't remember of its being tied.

Q. Did you see any part of his face except through the holes for the eyes and mouth?

A. No, sir; only back here I saw his hair.

Q. Is that all of his face that you saw?

A. I saw his face betwixt the holes and his mouth.

Q. What particular expression was on the face where the holes were that you could tell him? Had he a wart just at that hole?

A. No, sir; he hadn't a wart.

Q. What made you think it was Billy Bush?

A. I could see enough by the light to satisfy me it was him. I was satisfied it was Billy Bush.

Q. How did you know Berry Gilbert?

A. He sort of grinned, and let his mouth open pretty nigh across him. He is a tall slim fellow. He tried to alter his voice, but he could not do it enough but what anybody could tell it, and by that I knew him; but I was not thinking about noticing to know these men.

Q. You have no doubt that these five men were there.

A. Yes, sir; I have no doubt about it. I would be willing to be put to death on it, knowing it was them men.

Q. Why did not you complain against them directly after the 1st of March?

A. I was afraid to do it.

Q. Why are you not afraid now? Do you think these men have got any better? Are they not as much ruffians as then?

A. I knew I couldn't get any protection then.

Q. Who will protect you now?

A. It looks like here was the place; they told me to come here.

Q. Who promised to protect you if you would swear to this?

A. I allowed that these men would protect me.

Q. Who promised to protect you?

A. The Government.

Q. The Government cannot promise; some person may promise for it. Who did it? Who made the promise that if you would come and swear--

A. I took my oath to hold by the United States.

Q. When did you take an oath to support the United States?

A. To support it and the radical principles in any difficulty or anything; to be just and true to it; and this is what I was trying to do; and I thought that there was a chance for it now, for me to explain myself with these gentlemen.

Q. You have come here to-day to swear, and charge these men with this crime, because you had sworn, some long time ago, that you would support the radical cause. Is that it?

A. Yes, sir. I was aiming to stand up to them, and I thought if the other radical men could not stand up to me I could not stand myself. If I did not come to them that they would not protect me.

Q. Is it because you took this oath to protect radical men and measures that you come here to-day to swear that these are the men?

A. No, sir; it was because I thought may be there was a chance for me to get what was justice, what was right.

Q. You did not think of that before?

A. Yes, sir; but I did not know of any way to get into it or have anything done.

Q. Did not you know you could have these men arrested on the 1st of
March if you came in and swore to it?

A. No, sir.

Q. Why not?

A. I did not know it.

Q. How do you know it now?

A. I thought it was better now because they had their backers, and there
was such confusion in the country that I thought I had better keep still.

Spartanburgh, South Carolina, *July* 10, 1871

TENCH BLACKWELL sworn and examined.

By the Chairman:

Q. Where do you live?

A. I live near Cowpens' battle ground, in this county.

Q. What is your business?

A. My occupation is farming.

Q. How long have you lived there?

A. I have lived there or near there for fifteen or sixteen years.

Q. Are you a native of this State?

A. I am a native of North Carolina. I was born right on the line.

Q. Were you a manager of elections at the last general election?

A. Yes, sir.

Q. Go on and state if there were armed men appeared at the time of your
holding that election; and if so, what they said?

A. There was an armed party appeared there. I was very busy. There were
two or three election-boxes thrown together--at least there were one or two
others where they did not hold the election. I was very busy, and there are
some things that I don't recollect. There was an armed party came up to the
box. . . .

A. No, sir; they said that they wanted to whip me because I voted the
radical ticket.

Q. What did they whip your wife and children for?

A. Just because they could, I reckon.

Q. Did they whip your child because you voted the radical ticket?

A. Yes, sir; my little girl, nine years old. They told me that after
I got back.

Q. Did they whip her much?

A. Three lashes. They give my son four, and my wife a few licks.

Q. Your wife told you that?

A. Yes, sir.

Q. What did she say it was for?

A. They said, "Get up and let us whip you." They whipped them in the
yard. One came into the yard after they were through and said, "I didn't
whip none yet;" and he hit them all a lick apiece again.

Q. How many were there with you?

A. Three.

Q. How many were at the house?

A. Six. There were three carried me off.

Q. Did they say why it required six to stay at the house to whip the
children, and only three for you?

A. No, sir; I don't know what they said. Three run me off, and six
staid behind.

Q. You say there were nine, and they gave you twelve licks apiece?

A. That was their law.

Q. Why do you say it was their law?

A. They said it was their law.

Q. Did they threaten you afterward?

A. They told me if I did not leave in ten days they would come back and
kill me.

Q. You did not leave?

A. Yes, sir; I moved away.
Q. Where?
A. Two miles and a half.
Q. They could still reach you quite as easily, could they not?
A. It looks like they could; but they told me to leave that place, and
I did.
Q. Did you know any of these men?
A. No, sir; none of them.
Q. Were they completely disguised?
A. I did not know them no more than I do you or your name.
Q. Do you know whether they were white or black?
A. No, sir; because they run me in an old field. After they did what
they wanted to at the house, then they all came out and whipped me.
Q. Who did you tell about this?
A. When, before now?
Q. Yes.
A. I never told any one, only that the Ku-Klux came.
Q. You have told people, then, before this time that the Ku-Klux had
visited you?
A. Yes, sir.
Q. How soon did you do that?
A. I told that next morning.
Q. To whom?
A. I forget who, but I told them the Ku-Klux had been on me. I had been
laying out for about three months, and it looked like it was no use to lay
out; they caught me anyhow.
Q. How laying out?
A. To keep them from whipping me.
Q. Sleeping out of your house?
A. Yes, sir.
Q. What made you do that?
A. They were so strong in there that I was afraid of them. They whipped
all around there.
Q. Have you slept out of your house since?
A. No, sir.
Q. You are not so afraid of them now as before?
A. I am afraid of them yet; but they never pestered me since.
Q. Did you tell anybody that they whipped you and your wife and children;
you say you told that the Ku-Klux had visited you?
A. Yes, sir.
Q. Did you tell them that they had whipped you?
A. Yes, sir; that they had whipped us all. Some asked how many; I told
how many there was in the family.
Q. And you did not know any of them?
A. Not one of them.

Spartanburgh, South Carolina, *July* 10, 1871

HARRIET HERNANDES (colored) sworn and examined.

By the Chairman:
Q. How old are you?
A. Going on thirty-four years.
Q. Where do you live?
A. Down toward Cowpens' Furnace, about nineteen miles from here.
Q. Are you married or single?
A. Married.
Q. Did the Ku-Klux come to your house at any time?
A. Yes, sir; twice.
Q. Go on and tell us about the first time; when was it?
A. The first time was after last Christmas. When they came I was in bed.
They hallooed, "Hallo!" I got up and opened the door; they came in; they
asked who lived there; I told them Charley Hernandes. "Where is he" they said.
Says I, "I don't know, without he is at the Cowpens; he was beating ore there."

Says he, "Have you any pistol here?" Says I, "No, sir." Says he, "Have you
any gun?" Says I, "No, sir." He took on, and, says he, "Your husband is in
here somewhere, and damn him, if I see him I will kill him." I says, "Lord
o' mercy, don't shoot in there; I will hold a light under there, and you can
look." I held a light, and they looked. They told me to go to bed; I went
to bed. Two months after that they came again.

Q. How many men were there at that first visit?
A. Eight.
Q. How were they dressed?
A. All kinds of form; but the first ones that came would not look me in
the face, but just turned their backs to me, for they knew I would know them.
Q. Had they disguises?
A. Yes; horns and things over their faces; but still, that did not hinder
me from knowing them if these things were off.
Q. Did you know any of them?
A. I did not know any of the first ones, to say truthful, but the last
ones I did know.
Q. Had the first ones arms--guns or pistols?
A. Yes, sir; they had their guns and pistols. They came with a long
gun, and told me they were going to shoot my damned brains out if I did not
tell where my husband was.
Q. What time of night was it?
A. Away between midnight and day.
Q. How long had your husband lived there?
A. We have been living there three years now.
Q. Is he a mechanic or laboring man?
A. He is a laboring man.
Q. He was working at the furnace?
A. Yes, sir.
Q. Go on to the second time; you say it was two months afterward?
A. Yes; just exactly two months; two months last Saturday night when
they were at our house.

By Mr. Van Trump:
Q. Two months from now?
A. Two months from Saturday night last. They came in; I was lying in
bed. Says he,"Come out here, sir; come out here, sir!" They took me out of
bed; they would not let me get out, but they took me up in their arms and
toted me out--me and my daughter Lucy. He struck me on the forehead with a
pistol, and here is the scar above my eye now. Says he, "Damn you, fall!" I
fell. Says he, "Damn you, get up!" I got up. Says he, "Damn you, get over
this fence!" and he kicked me over when I went to get over; and then he went
on to a brush pile, and they laid us right down there, both together. They
laid us down twenty yards apart, I reckon. They had dragged and beat us along.
They struck me right on the top of my head, and I thought they had killed me;
and I said, "Lord o' mercy, don't, don't kill my child!" He gave me a lick on
the head, and it liked to have killed me; I saw stars. He threw my arm over
my head so I could not do anything with it for three weeks, and there are
great knots on my wrist now.

By the CHAIRMAN:
Q. What did they say this was for?
A. They said, "You can tell your husband that when we see him we are
going to kill him." They tried to talk outlandish.
Q. Did they say why they wanted to kill him?
A. They said, "He voted the radical ticket, didn't he?" I said "Yes,"
that very way.
Q. At what time did they say that to you?
A. That was this last time.
Q. Had your husband any guns or pistols about his house?
A. He did not have any there at all. If he had, I reckon they would
have got them.
Q. How old is your daughter?
A. She is fifteen.
Q. Is that the one they whipped?

A. Yes, sir.
Q. Is this all you know about it?
A. I know the people that came.
Q. Who are they?
A. One was Tom Davis, and there was Bruce Martin and his two sons.
There are only four I knew. There were only six that came that last night.
Q. When did your husband get back home?
A. He went back yesterday.
Q. When did he get back home after this whipping? He was not at home,
was he?
A. He was lying out; he couldn't stay at home, bless your soul!
Q. Did you tell him about this?
A. O, yes.
Q. What caused him to lie out?
A. They kept threatening him. They said if they saw him anywhere about
they would shoot him down at first sight.
Q. Had he been here as a witness?
A. No, sir. They never saw him, but they told us what to tell him.
Q. When you said, in reply to my question, that he went home yesterday;
had he come up here as a witness?
A. No, sir; he came here with me.
Q. Had he been afraid for any length of time?
A. He has been afraid ever since last October. He has been lying out.
He has not laid in the house ten nights since October.
Q. Is that the situation of the colored people down there to any extent?
A. That is the way they all have to do--men and women both.
Q. What are they afraid of?
A. Of being killed or whipped to death.
Q. What has made them afraid?
A. Because men that voted radical tickets they took the spite out on the
women when they could get at them.
Q. How many colored people have been whipped in that neighborhood?
A. It is all of them, mighty near. I could not name them all.
Q. Name those you remember.
A. Ben Phillips and his wife and daughter; Sam Foster; and Moses Eaves,
they killed him--I could not begin to tell--Ann Bonner and her daughter,
Manza Surratt and his wife and whole family, even the least child in the family,
they took it out of bed and whipped it. They told them if they did that they
would remember it.

By Mr. Van Trump:
Q. How do you know that?
A. They told the black people that was whipped.
Q. You know it by the people who were whipped telling you of it?
A. Yes, sir.

By the CHAIRMAN:
Q. You have seen those people that were whipped?
A. Yes, sir; and I have seen the marks on them, too.

By Mr. STEVENSON:
Q. How do colored people feel in your neighbothood?
A. They have no satisfaction to live like humans, no how. It appears to
me like all summer I have been working and it is impossible for to enjoy it.
Q. What do they do?
A. They just shoot down as they come to them, or knock them down.
Q. What do the colored people do for their safety?
A. They lie out all night.
Q. Is that generally the case?
A. Yes, sir; some families down there say they don't think they can get
tamed to the house in five years.
Q. Does this fear extend to women and children and whole families?
A. Yes, sir; they just whipped all. I do not know how bad they did
serve some of them. They did them scandalous; that is the truth--they did them
scandalous.

By Mr. VAN TRUMP:

Q. You may say they just shoot down and whip all through there?
A. Yes, sir.
Q. Tell us how many they have shot down in your neighborhood.
A. I cannot exactly tell you; I have heard so much.
Q. Heard of so many being killed?
A. Yes, sir.
Q. How many?
A. Some five or six, that I know of.
Q. Up there around Cowpens?
A. Yes, sir; and the other side of that, down the river.
Q. How far off?
A. Not more than ten miles down.
Q. Can you name any one that was shot down?
A. Charity Phillips was shot down and whipped bad. As for any more I cannot tell to be certain; it was done only as I heard it. I will not tell no lie about it.
Q. You say all the colored people up there are sleeping out?
A. In general. They are mighty near the last family sleeps out.
Q. That is the case with almost all of them?
A. Yes, sir.
Q. What do you mean by the last of the families?
A. All.
Q. All in that neighborhood?
A. Yes, sir.
Q. How wide a stretch of country around about do you speak of?
A. It is mighty near six miles.
Q. How many colored people live in that space?
A. I cannot tell you, to tell the truth, how many live there.
Q. Do you know how many colored votes are in that township?
A. There are five or six on Cowpens Hill, right around me.
Q. But in the whole Cowpens country?
A. Lord o' mercy, I can't tell.
Q. Have any colored people moved away from there?
A. Yes, sir; about two months ago Moses Eaves and his family, and Sam Foster and his family moved away.
Q. Where to?
A. To Tennessee. They said if they did not leave they would kill them.
Q. How many do you say there were when these men first came?
A. Eight came in the house.
Q. What they seemed to be after and asking for were pistols and guns?
A. Yes, sir.
Q. They said nothing else?
A. Yes, sir; they asked for my husband. I told them, "At the furnace, I reckon."
Q. They seemed to be after him, too?
A. Yes, sir; as well as guns; and he says "You tell him when we get him here that I will kill him for certain." They talked outlandish. They would not turn their faces to let me see them. One said,"You look like you were scared." I says, "I am scared;" and one rubbed his pistol in my face.
Q. Were those that came the second time the same as those that came the first time?
A. No, sir.
Q. How do you know?
A. I knew they were not.
Q. How do you know?
A. Because those that came the last time lived right at us in about a mile and a half, or worked right in that neighborhood; and ever since we have been there nigh them they can't face me, can't look at me.
Q. But how do you know that these six were not part of those who came the first time?
A. People say the others came from below, and these came from right above us.
Q. How did the people know they came from below?

A. They had been after them so much, and these here wanted me to work for them a good while, and I could not work for them then.

Q. You say the first one would not let you look at their faces?

A. No, sir.

Q. So you could not tell who they were?

A. No, sir.

Q. Then they might have been the same as the second ones?

A. No, sir; I do not think so.

Q. Is that only because the people said they were from below?

A. No, sir; I could not say they were the first one at all; not any of them.

Q. What is your belief?

A. They were not the same men at all.

Q. You say one of the last six was Tom Davis?

A. Yes, sir.

Q. Was he disguised?

A. Yes, sir.

Q. What had he on?

A. His horns and a long blue coat. He was the one that told them to lay us down, and then just jumped right on the top of my head.

Q. Could you see his face?

A. Not all of it. I had just seen him the day before.

Q. Had you never seen him before?

A. Yes, sir; I knew him all the time.

Q. Why should seeing him the day before make you know him better than seeing him generally.

A. I see him passing about generally.

Q. Could you see him that evening?

A. Yes, sir.

Q. How could you see his face under the disguise?

A. I knew it was him; I could hear him catch himself in talking.

Q. Did not you say he talked outlandish?

A. Yes, sir; but they would catch themselves in talking.

Q. Did they all talk?

A. Yes, sir.

Q. Every one?

A. No, sir; one held the horses.

Q. Only five acted?

A. Yes, sir; only five whipped us.

Q. Had they six horses?

A. Yes, sir; they took my little gal and one of the horses tails struck her, for she was nigh the horses.

Q. Were the horses disguised?

A. No, sir.

Q. It was a pretty bold fellow that came that way?

A. Yes, sir; that was one of Martin's sons.

Q. Which one?

A. I don't know; both were along.

Q. What are their names?

A. Romeo and Tine.

Q. Which one was it?

A. I think it was Romeo.

Q. Why?

A. He was so brickety.

Q. What do you mean by that?

A. Fidgety--somebody that wants to get into business and don't know how.

Q. That you call brickety?

A. Yes, sir.

Q. He got into business that night?

A. Yes, sir; and I did not like it much.

Q. Why was he brickety?

A. Because he jumped on top of me and beat me.

Q. That is the reason you knew it was Romeo?

A. Yes, sir; and I have seen them so often since, and I know their talk.

Q. Were they not all brickety?

A. I think they were all brickety.

Q. What other reason have you to think that was Romeo that took your child to the horse?

A. Because I knew it was not any person else.

Q. Then if you are correct it must have been him.

A. I knew it was not any person else; and the truth is the prettiest thing any person can come up here with.

Q. I am glad you are attached to the truth; but what was the reason why you thought it was Romeo?

A. Because that family wanted me to work for them and I could not work for them; I was working for another man.

Q. How long was that time when they wanted you to work before this whipping?

A. Not more than a month.

Q. Before the last visit?

A. Yes, sir.

Q. What took place that you could not work?

A. My husband rented some land and I had to come home.

Q. Did they get mad?

A. Yes, sir.

Q. What did they say?

A. They said they were going to have me Ku-Kluxed.

Q. What did they say?

A. They told me right there, bless me.

Q. Bless you?

A. I say bless you.

Q. I say bless you; they told you they were going to have the Ku-Klux on him?

A. Yes, sir.

Q. Who was present?

A. Only old Missus Williams, and she said,"Harriet, you'll be Ku-Kluxed for that."

Q. Who is she?

A. She is a white woman. It was her son I was to work for. He wanted me to work for him.

Q. What is his name?

A. Augustus Williams.

Q. I thought it was the Martins you had the trouble with?

A. They were the ones that whipped me. I thought it was Mr. Williams that held the horses.

Q. You said the Martins wanted you to work for them and you could not?

A. Yes, sir, all the family; they were all kin.

Q. And when you could not work for them they said they would have you Ku-Kluxed?

A. Yes, sir.

Q. Who said that, Bruce Martin?

A. Yes, sir.

Q. Was Mrs. Williams there?

A. Yes, sir.

Q. She heard them say that?

A. Yes, sir.

Q. They were bold enough to say before you and Mrs. Williams that you would be Ku-Kluxed?

A. Yes,sir, that I would be Ku-Kluxed.

Q. That is the reason you think old Martin and his two sons were there?

A. Yes, sir, and I knew they were there.

Q. Is that the only reason why you think they were there?

A. Yes, sir.

Q. You considered that it was them for the reason that they had said they would Ku-Klux you because you could not work for them.

A. That is why I know it was, for--

Q. That is why you think it was them that did it?

A. Yes, sir.

Q. Not because you saw them that night and knew that they were the Martins?

A. No, sir; I saw them that night and knew that they were the Martins.

Q. But you knew them because they had threatened you? If they had not threatened you you would not have known they were there?

A. Yes, sir; I would have known they were there to-night.

Q. But you would not have known it was these particular people if they had not threatened you?

A. No, sir; the man came and bruised me in my arm, taking me out of bed, and I saw his face then.

Q. Did not he have a disguise tied over his face?

A. No, sir, he could not have it over; it was too short; and there were two horns, and in their devilment at my house they broke off one of their horns, and I kept it about three weeks, until one day I got mad with it and throwed it in the fire.

Q. Why did not you keep it and bring it here.

A. Everybody said they would not do anything with this.

Q. You think the Martins did this for the reason that they were so mad because you would not work for them, that they Ku-Kluxed you?

A. Yes, sir; they got so mad that they could not stand it.

Q. Are they white people?

A. Yes, sir.

Q. How did you know Tine Martin?

A. By his size and his ways, and all.

Q. What sort of ways has he?

A. Fidgety ways, brickety ways.

Q. Unlike everybody else?

A. Not unlike everybody else, but like all the Ku-Klux.

Q. They must be a brickety family, if both the boys are brickety?

A. They are all brickety.

Q. What did they do, that you knew them?

A. Their father was there and they all tried to be brickety. One took hold of one arm of my little child and the other took the other arm, and I said, "Lord, don't kill my child;" and he knocked me down with the pistol and said, "Damn you, fall! Damn you, get up!" and I went to get up and he said "Damn you, get over the fence;" and when I tried to get over he kicked me over, and I knew the horses.

Q. What horses?

A. One big black and four big sorrels and a mule. There were two of the Martins, and I reckon they had borrowed a mule of Gus Williams.

Q. Did you talk to him about it?

A. No, sir; if I told them I believed it was them they would have come the next night and killed me.

Q. Did you know the mule?

A. I knew it; it was Gus Williams' mule. He must have been holding the horses. He must have known that I would have known him if I had touched him almost.

Q. Did not the Martins know that you would recognize the horses?

A. I don't know.

Q. You knew Bruce Martin?

A. Yes, sir; he is a high, tall man.

Q. Is he the only tall man in that country?

A. No; he is a high man and a mean man, too.

Q. You and the Martins cannot get along?

A. We can't get along, and couldn't if I wanted to.

Q. Have you had any quarrels?

A. No, sir; I give them no chance.

Q. Did they get mad?

A. Yes, sir; he got mad. They got mad enough to Ku-Klux me.

Q. This was two months ago?

A. Yes, sir.

Q. Is there any justice of the peace up there? Have you any squires?

A. I know there was a squire named Blackwell.

Q. You could have come here and made complaint?

A. But I was afraid.

Q. Afraid of what?

A. Afraid of the Ku-Klux.

Q. What Ku-Klux?

A. Of the Martins.

Q. Why are you not afraid of them now?

A. I am; I am afraid to go back home.

Q. Are you going home?

A. I don't know whether I shall go back or not.

Q. You do not look very frightened.

A. I am. I have got the trembles, sir.

Q. You will not go back home?

A. Not unless I see that I can have peace.

Q. Have you your children with you?

A. No, sir; one.

Q. Where is the other?

A. With my sister.

Q. Where?

A. At home.

Q. You were not afraid to leave that girl at home?

A. Yes, sir; I was afraid, too; but all could not be at home at once.

Q. Does not the whole neighborhood know that you are down here as a witness?

A. No, sir; I do not know that they do. It was night when I came home and people told us to come here, to be here at Friday dinner time.

Q. The people then knew you were to come here?

A. The people told us to come.

Q. What people?

A. The people were from town. I do not know what you call them.

Q. What do you call them?

A. We call them Yankees.

Q. Were they soldiers?

A. Yes, sir.

Q. How many?

A. Twenty-six.

Q. Did the whole neighborhood know that twenty-six soldiers were there?

A. Yes, sir; but I was off at work when they came, and my little gal; but they got my husband to tell me.

Q. You have come down here to be a witness, and twenty-six soldiers told you to come?

A. Yes, sir.

Q. In full military array in the neighborhood, so that all the people must have known it?

A. I do not know whether they knew it or not.

Q. The Martins must have known it?

A. I do not know.

Q. You were not afraid to leave your little daughter?

A. Yes, sir, I was; but I had to come; and there was the cow; there had to be somebody there.

Q. Which was the dearest to you, your cow or your daughter?

A. The daughter was, but Charley wouldn't fetch us both.

Q. Who is Charley?

A. My husband. . . .

Testimony Taken By The Joint Select Committee To Inquire Into The Condition of Affairs in the Late Insurrectionary States, South Carolina, Vol. I (Washington, D.C.:Government Printing Office, 1872), pp. 386-91.

2. TESTIMONY TAKEN BY THE JOINT SELECT COMMITTEE
TO INQUIRE INTO THE CONDITION OF AFFAIRS
IN THE LATE INSURRECTIONARY STATES

Columbia, South Carolina
July 20, 1871

JACK JOHNSON (colored) sworn and examined.

By the CHAIRMAN:
Q. Do you live in this county now?
A. Yes, sir.
Q. What county did you come from?
A. From the lower edge of Laurens County.
Q. How long had you lived in Laurens?
A. I had lived there since I was born.
Q. How old are you?
A. Forty-five on the 25th of next August.
Q. What did you do there?
A. I was farming pretty much all the time until emancipation, and then I still farmed on, but cut rock and built chimneys.
Q. You were a stone-mason, then?
A. Yes, sir.
Q. Were you called on there by the Ku-Klux at any time?
A. Yes, sir; I was called on by one man on the way from the riot at Laurens from the fuss.
Q. By one man?
A. Yes, sir, just one man. He said he had been out three nights, and his horse hadn't eat a bite. I heard him tell that gentleman after he got done beating on me.
Q. What did he do to you?
A. He came up to the gin-house and jumped off of his horse and said to me, "Didn't I tell you I would give you as much for your cotton in the seed as anybody?" I told him yes, and I told him Mr. Johnson told me to get my cotton ginned up and pay him what I owed him for bacon and corn, like a gentleman. He says to me, "What ticket did you vote?" I told him I voted the republican ticket. "God Damn you," says he, "have you got a tie-rope here?" Says I, "Mr. Reizer, I don't think I have done anything to call for that." He says, "No, God damn you, you haven't done anything; you go against our party; you go against us who have been a fried to you all your days. I suppose you hallooed the other day, Hurrah for Governor Scott. Didn't you vote for Governor Scott?" I told him I did, and I thought I was right in doing so. He says, "Why did you think so?" I told him I thought that was the right way, and it was right for me to go that way. He says, "Suppose you want to be burned right here?" I says, "No, I am not prepared to die," and I stooped down to pick up some cotton on the ground, and he struck me on the head and knocked me down on the face.
Q. What with?
A. With a club about a yard long, and I turned and got hold by his coat and tried to struggle up, and he jerked out his pistol and said, "God damn you, if that is what you're after, I'll kill you right now." I told him I didn't want him to kill me. He beat me on the head. I don't know what passed, but he beat on me to his satisfaction, and I went to raise again, and he says, "God damn you, I've a great mind to shoot you through and through." I says, "Mr. Reizer, you are beating me for nothing. O Lord, I hope you'll not kill me." He says, "Do you think the Lord has any feeling for you or anybody else that voted the ticket you have?" I told him yes, I thought he ought to have. When I said that he struck me right across the top of my forehead, and I caught his hand, and he says, "God damn you, I left eight of your republican party biting up dirt at Laurens, and you'll be biting dirt before morning;" and he said then, "I don't say I'll kill you, but, God damn you, there's men from Tennessee to kill you;" and he turned around and said to Mr. Miller, "I ought to kill this God-damned nigger right here." Those gentlemen were standing there and not one of the white gentlemen standing around said a word noway. He went on then toward the house to have his horse fed. I struggled along to the fence and got on the fence and got over and went through to my wife's house, and she said they had been there hunting me. I told her to please give me a little piece of bread and meat and I would try to get away from there. She cut off me off some bread and a bit of bacon, and I put it in my pocket and made off to Newbury Court-House. When I came on the road by Squire Hunter's they were camped on the road, about thirty men. They had their horse-feed lying in the corners of the fence, and taken down

fence rails to put up pens to put their horses in. I went through the field and on down to the Lutheran church, and there was another company that I knew nothing at all about. I thought I had better keep the woods all the time to Newberry Court-House, and I did keep the woods and held all the way. I had to part the brush with my hand to get this arm through, for I had but one arm then to use. I had to keep this arm here for nine weeks, and never will use it again. I can't turn the drill in the rock with that arm. One finger he broke so that it hung down.

Q. Who was that Mr. Reizer?

A. George Reizer, the son of old Billy Reizer.

Q. How far did he live from you?

A. About three miles.

Q. What is he?

A. A farmer and a store-keeper. He has a large store.

Q. Who were these other men that you spoke of?

A. Mr. Frank Miller and Elam Ritchie and Henry Johnson.

Q. Did they come with him?

A. No, sir, they were tending about the gin-house; Mr. Johnson was with me.

Q. What were their politics?

A. Henry Johnson told me he was sorry. I asked him wasn't that awful that I was beat that way for nothing. He said, then, "I am sorry, but my advice would be for you to get away from about here." I asked his advice. He said, "Get away for fear they will kill you; and I made my escape.

Q. Were they the men you worked for?

A. Mr. Johnson was working with me that day, because I had a good mule and he had two young mules that I raised to haul these loads. He had me to help him haul his cotton and he helped me. We were swapping work.

Q. Had you been to the election the day before?

A. Yes, sir.

Q. Where?

A. At Clinton.

Q. Had these men been to the election, too, that were there with you?

A. No, sir, only one.

Q. Who?

A. Young Adams, a colored man.

Q. Were they of the same party with you? Were they republicans or democrats?

A. There were no republicans there but black men; the other two were democrats, but they were powerful opposed to what Reizer did to me.

Q. Did you ask them for protection?

A. No, sir, because I knew it was no use.

Q. Why?

A. Because I knew it was no use for nobody to ask protection from men as vigorous as they were, because they were all principally against us voting, and Mr. Johnson had told me before to vote a reform ticket if I wanted to save myself; and I knew it was no use.

Q. Was Reizer drunk or sober?

A. I never saw him drunk in my life.

Q. You say he is a farmer and store-keeper in that neighborhood?

A. Yes, sir, he has a farm going on right there. He went the next day after he beat me and rode up to my house and asked for me. My wife told him she didn't know where I was, I was gone to my father. I didn't tell her I was going to Newbury, for I knew she would go crazy entirely if I did. He asked what he should do to get his money out of that farm. She told him to do what he could. He said, "By God, he knew what he would do." He turned around and galloped off and came back and took away my fodder and things. It took four loads to haul my fodder. And he took off my cotton.

Q. What became of your crop?

A. He took it all off. I owed $70 and he took off my mule. He took my cow up there to sell her, and Mr. Boyd wouldn't let her be sold. He said he claimed the cow in my behalf; he hated to see all my property go for nothing. There was my hogs. I think they brought $8. I had two hogs in the pen to have weighed two hundred by Christmas. That mule I had refused $175 for. All the men in the settlement knew that mule. I loved the mule. It was as

large a mule as I have seen since I have been here in Columbia. He took my
fodder and he sold my corn. He sold it for twenty bushels, more or less. I
had measured my corn when I put it up, and I had eighty bushels, and he sold
it for twenty bushels, more or less.

Q. Did you owe anybody else but him in that neighborhood?

A. Yes, sir, I owed some other men. I owed the lady I rented the land
from. I bought the land off for a hundred dollars a year. She said she
would rather I should have it than anybody else, for I would work it. Mr.
Dave Boyd and Billy Young came and told my wife she had better go off to some
other place, because Mr. Reizer was going to take my truck away, and she had
better hunt a home some other place.

Q. Where is your wife?

A. She has come here.

Q. Have you any children?

A. No, sir; I have one boy driving a carriage now, down below, for the
hotel.

Q. How much was your crop worth that you left there?

A. Well, the man taking the census around was at my house just about
four days before the election came off, and he came into the cotton-field
where my wife was picking cotton and asked for my property, and I told him,
and he said my property at the house was worth $600 besides my crop--that is,
my hogs and cows. I had one cow and calf and another heifer and two yearlings.
I wouldn't have taken one hundred dollars for my cow, because when we drove
her up she would give two gallons of milk every night and morning, and we
needed no begging with her.

Q. Have you been back since?

A. No, sir.

Q. Do you feel afraid to go back?

A. Yes, sir.

Q. Why?

A. I know one thing. Mr. George Reizer don't care for money no more
than you for a chaw of tobacco, and if he didn't kill me, he would have it
done; because he had been at me so long before the election to vote the conservative ticket, and I would not tell him what I would do. I told him I
couldn't promise nobody I would vote such a ticket for I would have gone
against my principles and against my own feelings. He came to there a day or
two before the election and asked me what I would take for my cotton in the
seed. I told him I didn't want to sell my cotton in that way. He said I
might go to any white man in the settlement and ask him what the cotton was
worth in the seed, and leave it to him which would be best for me to do. I
left home immediately, and went over to Jared Johnson, one of the strongest
democrats in the settlement, but one of the best men who wouldn't tell anybody anything wrong about it. He is a magistrate. I asked him what was best
for me to do. I told him Mr. Reizer was powerful mad at my house yesterday;
I wouldn't promise him not to vote the republican ticket. He says, "You go
home and let everybody see you are gathering your crop and paying your debts,
and when you get your cotton ginned, pay Mr. Reizer half and Mrs. Dillon half
until you get them both paid." I rented my land from her. He says, "I got
some meat of George Reizer on a lien, and he wrote me an insulting letter,
and I let him know I am not a nigger."

Q. How is it there in regard to the other colored people? Do they feel
at liberty to vote as they please, or has this system of intimidation been
carried on to any extent?

A. Well, they are down up there now, for all the republican men that
have been the leaders, speaking and going about through there, has left there
--has come out and left them. My wife come from there about four weeks ago.
She is just as well brought up as a white child. Her old master and mistress
had no children, only her to take care of, and she was respected; and she
said they refused to speak to her there, and told her she had better go away
from there to Columbia, for that was a bad place for negroes, it was a harbor
for negroes; nobody there seemed to have no use for us--no old friends.

Q. What do you know about the liberty of the colored people there to
speak or do as they please? How was it at the election?

A. All voted that could vote, only they were persuaded to vote the other
way.

Q. Was there any violence of this kind before the election of last
October?

A. Yes, sir; there were lots of threats. You could hear rumors of
threats all through the settlement. There was Mr. Tom Ware. The day of the
election I walked up, and I had a chill on me that day. I put in my vote,
and some of them says, "There's Old Jack voting for Scott!" Says I, "Suber"
--he is school commissioner at Laurens now, a colored man--"Did you notice
how they voted; there are some going in I don't think is right. Dr. Tom Ware
spoke up, and says, "Now, the last God damned one of you are voting yourselves
into your graves."

By Mr. VAN TRUMP:

Q. What did you mean, saying it was not going all right?

A. What I meant was this: When I went to go out of the gate to go to
vote, I had no ticket, and I asked a gentleman for a ticket. I had just got
there. I catched him by his coat, and pulled him around, and asked for a
ticket. He handed me a ticket, and I says, "What are you; are you a republican?" He says, "I am as full-pledged a republican as you ever saw." I took
the ticket and went back in the yard; they told me I couldn't go in then;
enough time had gone. Only ten voted at a time. I showed the ticket to a
white man in the yard there, and he says, "That's a democratic ticket, you'll
not vote it." I says, "No, not for this world." This man, Al. Daggan,
pulled me. He is a colored man, and he says, "I'll give you a right ticket."
And then I went in and voted.

By the CHAIRMAN:

Q. Can you read.

A. No, sir.

Q. Had you taken any part in politics--been a candidate for office?

A. No, sir.

Q. Did you do anything else than vote?

A. No sir, only to vote; only this, I took a great propriety in counsel-
ing the people which way to vote--the colored people. I had been riding about
a good deal. I was the only colored man that had a mule anywheres nigh my
house, and I would go 'way off to speeches, and come back and tell the news
how the speeches were; that was all I did, and for that they were very down
on me.

By Mr. Stevenson:

Q. Did you say the scar was still on your head?

A. Yes, sir, here is the scar of his lick. [Indicating.] He struck me
here, and struck me again, and this finger he broke entirely, so that I can't
turn a drill in my hand.

Q. Was that done with a club?

A. Yes, sir.

Q. Had he a pistol?

A. Yes, sir. When he was beating me his cartridges began to fall out of
his pocket, and he gathered them up, and said, "Those are sort of things for
you, God damn you."

Q. How many white men were there?

A. Three grown white men, and one young man nearly grown.

Q. Did they do anything to protect you?

A. No, sir, they just stood and looked on.

By Mr. VAN TRUMP:

Q. How old a man is this George Reizer?

A. I should suppose he is twenty-eight or twenty-nine years old.

Q. Who was the other man with him when he came up?

A. There was no other man; he came up by himself.

Q. Who was the other man begged for a horse feed?

A. He begged for it.

Q. Of you?

A. No, sir, of this other white young man. That was at Mr. Miller's
house, where this was done. It was at Mr. Miller's gin-house.

Q. Where did Reizer come from? Did he come to see you particularly?

A. He left the crowd at Mr. Joe Hunter's. They had all come down there together.

Q. How far was that from Miller's?

A. Three miles.

Q. How do you know he left a crowd there?

A. My wife and all the rest said so. He came by my house first, and asked for me, and they told him I was gone to the gin-house with a lot of cotton.

Q. How far is that?

A. Three miles, about. They were all shooting up at Mr. Hunter's.

Q. How far is Hunter's house from your house?

A. About half a mile.

Q. Was your wife there?

A. No, sir, she was at Mr. Sanderson's.

Q. How far is that?

A. It was only about a quarter of a mile, and she could see all around the door and around the store where they were.

Q. What time did he leave Hunter's?

A. I don't know. I know about the time he came to where I was.

Q. What time was it?

A. I think the sun was about two hours high.

Q. Was there anybody with Reizer when he came up?

A. No, sir.

Q. No crowd in sight?

A. No, sir; not that I saw. But after I left for home and got my meat and bread, coming back to the road, there were fifty-three men going right down to where Mr. Reizer beat me.

Q. Was that the first crowd you met?

A. Yes, sir.

Q. How came you to say there were thirty?

A. There were fifty-three that night. There was more than me saw them. This man Johnson, that was at the gin-house with me, met them in the night. They said they heard Dr. Pink Johnson hail as they passed his house, and asked them where they were going, and they said they were going over to the other road.

Q. Were they Ku-Klux?

A. Yes, sir.

Q. Were they disguised?

A. They were just on the way from the raid at Laurens.

Q. Had they disguises on?

A. No, sir.

Q. How do you know they were Ku-Klux?

A. They were acting very much like it.

Q. Do you know that what you are telling here you are swearing to?

A. Yes, sir.

Q. And yet you call them Ku-Klux?

A. Well, what is the difference between the Ku-Klux? A man that will kill a man I always call him a Ku-Klux.

Q. There were fifty-three of them?

A. Yes, sir.

Q. Would they all kill a man?

A. I don't know what else but that business they were there for. Why should they be out? If I were to start out in that sort of a crowd, knowing so many men had been killed above and below here, take up my gun and gone to join them, I would say I would kill a man just like they did.

Q. You think all those fifty-three men were Ku-Klux not disguised?

A. They had guns and ammunition.

Q. Had they been up to this riot?

A. There was where the Ku-Kluxing had been done.

Q. Was the Laurens riot by Ku-Klux?

A. That is what they say. I don't know what Ku-Klux is.

Q. Who says it?

A. Everybody. They don't call them anything else. These men that are killing men about, they are Ku-Klux.

Q. You don't know much about the Laurens fight; how it was begun or what it was?

A. No, sir; I was not at it, but I knew many of the men who were killed.

Q. That is your opinion of the Laurens raid, that all who were engaged against the colored people were Ku-Klux?

A. I can't think anything else, because if they had not been, I would not have thought they would have killed Mr. Henry Johnson and Frank Miller, and the people were right smartly opposed to them and never left their homes for them. Mr. Hunter and Mr. Bond, and Calvin Adams and Tom Hutton would all leave their homes to go to that riot, but Johnson and Frank Miller never left their homes. They said they wouldn't take part in anything of the kind.

Q. How far is that from Laurens?

A. Eighteen miles below Laurens.

Q. You do not think Frank Miller and Johnson were Ku-Klux?

A. No, sir.

Q. How do you account for the fact of four men standing there, seeing this one man come up furious as a mad bull and attack you, without taking your part?

They are like all other men. They knew that if they took any part in that they would be called taking a negro's part. That is the way they do up there. When a white man goes in and speaks in behalf of the negro, they put him in above all the negroes.

Q. You think all the white men are for killing all the negroes?

A. Some were for peace, and some were not.

Q. There is no peace between the white men and the negroes?

A. I should not call it so; because I tried for four years to be as humble as I could, and to get along with them in some way, and I couldn't do it.

Q. All the white men opposed to the negroes you think are Ku-Klux?

A. I don't know that I can say that they are.

Q. You say the assessor, when he came around a day or two before the election, said your property about the house was worth $600?

A. Yes, sir; besides my corn and cotton.

Q. And your cow?

A. No, sir. I talked a little too fast; I had gathered my corn and counted it.

Q. But he did not count your cotton?

A. No, sir.

Q. He counted the cow?

A. Yes, sir; both times. I had a cow and a heifer.

Q. Did he count your mule?

A. Yes, sir.

Q. Then he estimated the amount of your property at $600, including all your property, except your cotton crop?

A. Yes, sir.

Q. What was your cotton crop worth?

A. My cotton crop, from what I can understand--Mr. Reizer sold three bales and I had about a hundred pounds lacking to make two bales when--

Q. Was that worth about $100?

A. I can't say what.

Q. What was cotton worth?

A. Cotton was worth nineteen and quarter, I think.

Q. What would it come to--about four hundred pounds in a bale?

A. Yes, sir.

Q. Would not that be about $120 or $130?

A. Then he hired hands and picked out another bale.

Q. Then you had three bales?

A. Yes, sir. Then he sold about twelve hundred pounds in the field to John May, a colored man.

Q. All this property is gone?

A. Yes, sir; I have never received it.

Q. The $600 worth, and the cotton and everything else; cows, mules, and everything else?

A. Yes, sir.

Q. Who had it sold--Reizer?

A. Yes, sir.

Q. On execution?

A. I don't know how he did it; he just went there and gathered it. I owed him some for bacon.

Q. How much?

A. I give him the lien. I bought my mule and got me some little feed to go on to feed my mule along until I could get somebody to help me out, and rented me the land and went to work. I went to the store and asked Mr. Reizer to let me have bacon and corn. He asked, how much. I told him about $70 worth of bacon and corn together. He asked me if I would give him a lien on my crop. I told him I would give a lien on everything I made, outside of the rent.

Q. Then you owed him $70?

A. Yes, sir; he wrote it down that he was to let me have $70 worth in bacon and corn.

Q. You owed him $70.

A. Yes, sir.

Q. Your contract was to pay Mrs. Dillon $100 rent?

A. Yes, sir.

Q. Then you owed $170.

A. Yes, sir.

Q. Who else?

A. Well, I owed some little debts up there, but I don't know that it concerned him.

Q. It concerns me just now. How much did you owe besides that $170?

A. I can't tell you without I saw my account. I owed Mr. Bob Callomy $30.

Q. That makes $200.

A. Yes, sir.

Q. Who else did you owe?

A. I don't know anybody else.

Q. You said you owed little debt?

A. Yes, I couldn't tell who they were now until I could see. They were little things. I don't know that anybody had any charges against me.

Q. Part of the cotton had to be attended to, and Reizer attended to that and made twelve hundred pounds of it?

A. Yes, sir.

Q. Have you not heard what disposition he made of that property?

A. He wrote me out a few papers and sent me.

Q. Here?

A. Yes, sir. My wife went up there and sent to him for a settlement, and he sent her $2, and sent her the papers, and said that was all he owed me; and I think he claimed that I owed him something over a hundred dollars.

Q. How much over?

A. I don't know that, but she said she thought, from the way he did, that he claimed over a hundred dollars. But when I went to him the last time for bacon--I was out of bacon--and told him I wanted some--

Q. Never mind that.

A. He told me I was up with my lien.

Q. You gave him a lien for $70.

A. Yes, sir.

Q. Then you owed $200?

A. Yes, sir.

Q. You owed $230, if Reizer was honest in saying that you owed him thirty more. He claimed that, did he not?

A. I don't know; I can't go to see him. Mr. Moore has got it.

Q. What papers did he send you?

A. Mr. Moore has it. I sued him just day before yesterday.

Q. Where?

A. Here in Columbia.

Q. How did you sue him here? He lives in Laurens?

A. I have given it to the lawyer. The lawyer said if I would pay his way there, he would attend to it. I told him I couldn't go up there.

Q. How was this property disposed of?

A. It is gone; he sold it.

Q. Did he get a judgment against you?

A. I don't know what he did, for I cannot tell.

Q. Then you do not know anything about it?

A. I know he sold it, and I got nothing.

Q. Did Mrs. Dillon get her pay?

A. I don't know.

Q. Did Mr. Callomy get his pay?

A. I don't know.

Q. You do not know anything about it?

A. No, sir; I left my property. All I hear from my wife is that it is all gone; that he took it away.

Q. And you are going to sue him for it?

A. Yes, sir, and assault and battery.

Q. If what you stated here is true, both about taking your property and about assaulting you, you ought to sue him?

A. Yes, sir; and I think, according to the law the white man told me, he ought to be prosecuted for taking my property without anything.

Q. When he rode up was he on horseback?

A. He jumped off his horse at the fence.

Q. What did he first say?

A. He said, "What the hell are you doing here?" I said, "I am hauling cotton." He said, "Didn't I tell you I would give as much for your cotton as anybody else?" I said, "Yes; but you told me to leave it to two men, and Mr. Johnson told me what to do."

Q. What were you going to do?

A. I was going to have it ginned. I was going to let Mr. Bond gin it and sell it for me, and pay Mrs. Dillon some and Mr. Reizer some.

Q. Did he appear to be mad because you would not let him have your crop of cotton?

A. He wanted to buy it in the seed.

Q. Then he asked you right away what ticket you voted?

A. Yes, sir. Then he said, "God damn you, you have done everything against the party you could."

Q. Did he whip you for voting that ticket, or for the cotton?

A. I just put it that way. I don't know whether it is right or wrong. I believe he brought that excuse of the cotton to pick a quarrel to beat me.

Q. Is Reizer understood to be so bad a man as all this?

A. He never had much of a good name with the colored men.

Q. Has he had other difficulties with other people?

A. He had difficulties way in back times; I don't know about lately, but he has no feeling for black men.

Q. What other black man has he beaten for voting the republican ticket?

A. I don't know that he has knocked any about.

Q. You say you believe he made this cotton an excuse to beat you, because you were a republican?

A. Yes, sir; I believe it, and shall always believe it. I don't know as he had any right to do it.

Q. He had no right to whip you for either cause, but you say he made the cotton a pretext to get up a quarrel and beat you for voting the republican ticket?

A. Yes, sir.

Q. Are there any other black men republicans?

A. Yes, sir; but he had no chance at them. He had a chance at me because he made a crop with me.

Q. Have you heard of his beating any other negro men?

A. No, sir; only he shot one man. He didn't kill him, but he shot him to pieces nearly. That is since that. I didn't blame him so much for that, for if he hadn't caught up with who it was he would have always sworn it was me. A man went and bored into his store-house, and he shot him up pretty bad. A black man was trying to get into his store.

Q. That is, a black man was trying to get into his store and shot him?

A. Yes, sir.

Q. That is all you have heard of his feeling against the black people?

A. I don't know about that; he has a bad feeling toward me.

Q. You say you do not blame him for shooting that black man?

A. No, sir. I should have done so in his place. I should have tried to find out who he was if balls could find out.

Q. You had no difficulty except about this cotton?
A. No, sir. He would halloo, "How are you getting on?" and "Hurry!"
Q. Has not Mr. Reizer been kind to negroes there, to help them?
A. Very kind for their money. Nobody ever had much dealing with him except that way. That is the way with the black people there; they work all the year as hard as they can, but when Christmas comes the whole bandanna of them got nothing.
Q. What is the "bandanna?"
A. I say the whole bandanna of the colored people have no money when Christmas comes.
Q. Whose fault is that?
A. It is because many of them can't read or write.
Q. Do you think those white people cheat them out of what they should get?
A. Yes, sir; pretty much. Some of the black people wastes what they make.
Q. Do the republican white people hate them?
A. They don't have any white republican people in that county. In Laurens County there are a few, but I don't think there is a republican white man in our neighborhood.
Q. Does the negro population carry that county at the election?
A. They have been doing it so far.
Q. All the time?
A. Yes, sir.
Q. There is a much larger number of black people than whites?
A. I reckon there is.

By the CHAIRMAN:
Q. Did you say he told you he had been up where they killed people?
A. He told me, "God damn you, I've left eight of your republican party biting dirt up here at Laurens, and you'll be biting dirt before day. I don't say I'll kill you, but, by God, there's men from Tennessee will kill you. . . ."

Testimony Taken By The Joint Select Committee To Inquire Into The Condition of Affairs In The Late Insurrectionary States, South Carolina, Vol. II (Washington, D.C.:Government Printing Office, 1872), pp. 1165-73.

3. TESTIMONY TAKEN BY THE JOINT SELECT COMMITTEE
TO INQUIRE INTO THE CONDITION OF AFFAIRS
IN THE LATE INSURRECTIONARY STATES

Yorkville, South Carolina,
July 27, 1871.

ANDREW CATHCART (colored) sworn and examined.

By the CHAIRMAN:
Q. How old are you?
A. I am about seventy-seven years old, the first day of last March.
Q. Where do you live?
A. Down forenenst Squire Joe Miller's, on a plantation that I bought in slavery times. I bought myself about twenty years ago, and then worked and bought myself a little plantation.
Q. How long is it since you bought that plantation?
A. About twelve years.
Q. How long since you bought your freedom?
A. I reckon it has been twenty-one or twenty-two years; I cannot tell exactly.
Q. Do you recollect what you paid for it?
A. Yes, sir; I do.
Q. How much?

A. I paid $190 for a tract for--

Q. But for your freedom, how much did you pay?

A. I paid $330 for my freedom.

Q. How many acres do you own down there?

A. Ninety; I bought another place, a place that Willburn Ward owned, adjoining and together it makes ninety-eight acres.

Q. How much did you say you paid for it?

A. I paid $190 for the first, and $350 for the last part--the Ward place.

Q. Have you got it all paid for?

A. Yes, sir; all.

Q. Go on and tell us what you know of the operations of the Ku-Klux in your neighborhood--what they did to you.

A. When they first came in to me, they said, "Ku-Klux, Ku-Klux, Ku-Klux," and catched hold of me, and says one, "Have you any arms?" I said I had a rifle up there. They said, "Take it down and break it all to pieces." I got it and went to my hearth and broke it all to pieces there on the rocks of my fire-place, and then bent the muzzle, and they struck me a few licks while I was at it. The men talked to me; I think it was one Henry Reeves spoke to me; and I looked at him, and every time I would go to look at him, he would slap me in the face; but still I would look at him when I got a chance, because I had not heard his voice in twelve months, and yet I thought of him then. He was a man that had lived with me, and I knew his voice when I heard it, and so I would look at him from head to foot. I knew the man's temper; I have seen him in good humor and in ill humor. He is a fractious sort of a man. The next thing they said was, "Where is your money?" I told them I had no money. Says he, "Open the chest, or I will break it open, and open it damned quick." My wife handed him the keys and they opened the chest. They did not do anything but just throw it open. "Come," says he, "damn him, take him out and hang him, kill him, shoot him, take him out and shoot him." As they marched me out of the door one stood inside of the door and turned back as they marched me out. I took him to be one Jimmy Jones, that I had worked with for five years. His father is an old man. I farmed for him, and made him corn and cotton, and took care of it until he died. He came back and sat down and commenced plundering the chest. The old woman sat right by him; her knees were right against it, and his gown fell off he was so busy plundering, and then she look and saw his pantaloons, and knew the pantaloons; she knew the coat and the pockets of his coat; she knew them well; she saw his chin; it had a little beard coming out. Then after he had plundered and taken out several things, such as would be useful to him, they marched me out, and he went on with Henry Reeves. Says he, "Where were your children when they were run away?" You see five years before that they belonged to an Irishman. He was a curious sort of a man, and sold them to a man named Davies, and we did not know where he took them to. I told him I did not know where he took the children to. He talked in the Irish way. He is a passionate man; that is Reeves I am talking about now. Says he "Damn you, tell me where they are or I will kill you." I told him I did not know where they were, and I could not tell. He took the butt of an Army gun and struck me on the head, and dropped me to my knees. I scrambled a while and got up. Says he then, "I will kill you if you do not tell me." I told him I could not tell where they were. He just took and struck me a solid lick here on the head, and I thought it would burst my head open. It was a hard lick, and I fell with my breast on a stump. I spit blood after that for two months from that blow. As I was going on to tell you, I scrambled and raised up, and he said he would be damed if he did not kill me if I did not tell him, and they presented their guns at me. I turned around and said, "O Lord, have mercy upon me! Lord have mercy on my soul!" I said, "You can kill me if you see cause." I expected that was to be my last word. Then they started. But I must tell one word here. As I came out of the door they knocked me right here in the hip and they carried me out, and I have not been able to plow since, I am so lame. I do not believe I will ever be over it. When I go to the field to hoe for half an hour I have to sit down to rest. They told me to go in the house and to run and jump the bars. I scarcely could drag myself. I went in as well as I could. When I got in the house they told me to shut that door and not say anything. Then they marched me down to the house where my daughter and another woman taught school. They had authority to teach from Mr. Lathan and Mr. Johnson agreeable to the law. They went down there and tore the school-house all to pieces; they worked on it half to quarter of an hour, and not only treated it rough but broke it all to pieces. Tore the tenons out and broke it all up. One hallooed, "Burn it up;" but another one hallooed, "No burning," but they raised a fire; they had a pile of boards and they put stuff under and then put the fire there, but after they went off I crawled under there and put the fire out, and saved it.

Q. Had that building been used as a school?

A. Yes, sir; for two years.

Q. For white or colored children?

A. For colored children. It was on the place I bought of Ward. It was a frame house, worth forty or fifty dollars, that they tore up for me. They shot one ball in the end of the house by the window, and shot another through the door, and it went just above the bed. They seemed to shoot for somebody in the bed. My daughter was living there in the house. It is one hundred and fifty yards from the house I staid in. She ran out and got away; but they got all of her things out of the chest and threw them on the floor and tramped over them, and took two or three pieces of clothing, some silver thimbles, and several other things that I do not remember now. They took a jug of vinegar and bursted it among them. They destroyed a heap of things.

Q. Is that all of it?

A. I think that is all. Then they went off.

Q. How many were there of them?

A. I could not tell you now, because everytime I would go to look at them they would slap me in the face and over the eyes; but I saw there were fifteen or twenty of them; there might have been a little over fifteen and a little under twenty, or there might be twenty; I know there was a large company.

Q. Did you see the kind of disguises they wore?

A. Yes, sir; they had on some sort of caps--one thing and another--and sort of horns one had. But they would not let me look at them, but slapped me whenever I looked; and I could just look at them from the body down.

Q. Did you recognize any others than the two you have mentioned?

A. I can mention this Ben Presley; Ben Presley is my nigh neighbor; I knew him by his walk and by his looks and by his motion; and when he first began to talk he said that I was a ruler--"You think you will rule; but, God damn you, you shall not rule." I told him I always kept myself as humble since my freedom as before, and I did not want to rule anything. He says, "You have got a bald-faced horse that you ride up and down the road." I told him I did not ever ride him. He said, "Well, your son does." I told him, "He didn't ride often." He talked in his plain, natural voice then, and I knew him. He is a man I am used to; he seemed to get mad when he talked.

Q. Who is Ben Pressley?

A. He is Richard Pressley's son; he is not here now.

Q. Is Richard Pressley a farmer?

A. Yes, sir.

Q. Does he own the land he occupies?

A. Yes, sir; a large place; Ben manages it for him; he has been almost dead for a year.

Q. How old is Ben?

A. I reckon he is near thirty.

Q. Is he a drinking man?

A. Yes, sir; he drinks pretty smart at times. The same night they came on Charlie Bryant's, I think it was the 11th of March; I got June Moore to write it down; I could not write myself; here is the paper [producing scrap written as follows: "Thay Night the Ku Klux Come to my house Was March 11th 1871. ANDREW CATHCART."] Charlie Bryant heard them throw the house down, Mr. Currance heard it, and they heard it at old man Wallace's; they could hear them two miles off shooting and knocking and hallooing.

Q. What did they do with Charlie Bryant?

A. He was out, not at his place, but they abused his wife pretty bad; they liked to have killed her. They knocked her down, I think, with a pistol. They knocked her down and beat her, so her child said, after she was down.

She did not know much about it, for she was as bloody as a hog that had been stuck.

By Mr. VAN TRUMP:

Q. Was that the same night on which they had been to your house?

A. Yes, sir. Charlie said when they started part of them came right up to his house again, and another part came up the York road.

By the CHAIRMAN:

Q. Have you ever reported this case here in town before to anybody?

A. Yes, sir; I think June reported it. I never reported it myself, but I think June Moore made mention of it up here.

Q. Is that all you know about it?

A. Yes, sir, that is all.

Q. Have you taken any part in the public affairs of that township except in getting up this school-house?

A. No, sir.

Q. Did you get up this school-house on your own land?

A. This had been a kitchen built on the land, and then the big house was there, and I let them teach in the kitchen. I just let it be for a school-house. That house was worth as much as forty or fifty dollars.

By Mr. STEVENSON:

Q. Had you been a republican leader?

A. I had never been leader of nothing, but I voted the republican ticket.

Q. You did not undertake to lead?

A. No, sir, I led nothing.

Q. You are seventy-seven years old?

A. Yes, sir.

Q. What makes you think that is your age?

A. I have it on a book at home--the Old Testament. I had my brother's son's age, and he was nearly a year younger than me, and from that we counted it up, and it makes me seventy-seven last March.

Q. You counted up by your brother's son's age?

A. Yes, sir; I was about seven months older than him.

By Mr. VAN TRUMP:

Q. Had you a brother so much older than you that he had a son nearly as old as you were?

A. Yes, sir. And counting his age off, and giving me seven months more, makes me seventy-seven.

By Mr. STEVENSON:

Q. You spoke of an Army gun; what did you mean by that?

A. I mean by an Army gun, one of those rifles such as the blacks had mustering with--the colored militia. They had bayonets on the guns that night that they beat me.

Q. They had one of those guns?

A. Yes, sir, more than one. I saw two or three, maybe.

By Mr. VAN TRUMP:

Q. When did you get your gun?

A. It was an old rifle I had got long before; I allowed to sell it, but I did not; I made no use of it.

Q. What part of the county do you live in?

A. In York, on the lower edge of the county, fornenst Squire Joe Miller's; north of here on the Charlotte road; seven miles from here.

Q. If you have named the right men here, Andrew, I hope you may catch them and punish them as they deserve.

A. I pray God I have spoken the truth as I understand it.

Q. It is my duty to see whether you are mistaken or not. Who is Henry Reeves?

A. He is Henry Reeves; he lives down here not far from Nely Miller's.

Q. What is his business?

A. Only a farmer. If he came on me I think he came out of spite, because my children that ran away used to belong to his sister.

Q. What do you mean by their running away?

A. They left with that Irishman?

Q. Was it since freedom?

A. No, sir; it was five years before freedom. They were slaves to them,
and it was thought by many that he sold them, but it was not known whether he
sold them or what it was. One Davis took them away.

Q. What interest had Reeves in them?

A. That's it. They were his sister's negroes, and he had ambition
against me, thinking I harbored them.

Q. Do you think that Reeves has a hatred--

A. He has a spite against me. Whatever man it was he spoke in such
ambition and spoke in a great rage.

Q. Is that the reason you think it was Reeves?

A. No, sir; after he spoke I knew his voice, and I looked at him and
he would put his face right up in mine and slap me.

Q. You did not have much chance to see?

A. Yes, sir. After he did that I would keep looking. I looked at his
body and shoulders, and I knew the make of the whole man, and knew his voice
and everything.

Q. Did you know him by his dress?

A. No, sir; I did not know him by his dress, but I knew the shape and
make of the man.

Q. Is not that a very dangerous way to prove a man guilty, because he
is made like somebody else?

A. Yes, sir; but did you never see a man you were so used to that you
could tell him by looking at the build of the man and the voice. Now look
at a blind man how he can call a man by his voice. Here is Mr. Cook and Mr.
Campbell; anybody that they know they can call by their names. And this man
was like one of my home folks to me. He had not talked to me for a year, but
when he spoke I looked up like it was one of my home folks.

Q. But do you not know that a blind man has the faculty of hearing much
more sharply and accurately than we who see?

A. Yes, sir, but I know him; he is a hasty-tempered man.

Q. Are there not many such in the South?

A. Yes, sir, a great many; but he had a hasty stammering sort of a way
that I knew.

Q. Do you say that Henry Reeves stammers?

A. He sort of stammers and whines like, as it were, and is crabbed when
he quarrels.

Q. Is it a stutter?

A. No, sir; a sort of whining, grumbling.

Q. Will not almost any man grumble when he is mad?

A. Yes, sir.

Q. Does Reeves have a particular grumble?

A. Not when he is not mad, but I had seen him mad so often that I knew
him at once.

Q. Let me ask you now--as an old man of seventy-seven years, who cannot
expect to live very long--

A. No, sir, of course not.

Q. Let me ask you, if Henry Reeves's life depended on the fact would you
swear that he was there?

A. I would swear that it was a man made just like him, and talking like
him, and acting like him in passion and temper; a man that had vengeance in him
whenever he talked of those children. If you were coming to me in that shape
you would not come raging in that way unless you were interested. You would
not want to knock my brains out about a thing you were not interested in.

Q. Did this man Reeves talk about the children that night?

A. Yes, sir; he knocked me down, and said he would be damned if he would
not kill me if I did not tell where the children were. I could not tell.

Q. But your children had gone away before freedom?

A. Yes, sir; five years.

Q. Then of what value would they be to him?

A. No value, but it seemed an old grudge five years old. He held a spite at me because they were his sister's children.

Q. How near did you live to Henry Reeves?

A. About four miles.

Q. From the time your children ran away before freedom until the present time you have seen Reeves as a neighbor; have you seen him several times?

A. Yes, sir.

Q. Has he had any difficulty with you about the children?

A. No, sir; never. I saw him over at Mr. Gillespie's, and I had seen him pass on the road.

Q. Was he kind toward you?

A. No, sir; he never appeared to have much to say.

Q. Did he ever talk to you about the children?

A. No, sir.

Q. Never named them?

A. I never heard a complaint about it, but when he spoke in that angry way I knew his voice.

Q. If this man among the Ku-Klux was not Henry Reeves, but some other man, and he wanted to keep you from knowing who he was, and had to talk to you about something, would he not be likely to talk about something which he thought you would put on Reeves or some other man that he might assume to be or talk about or for?

A. No, sir; I do not think there is a man in my section would do it, or could.

Q. Who is Jimmy Jones?

A. He has just got to be a man. I worked for his uncle for about five years when he was a boy and unable to work for one or two years; then he came up and worked with me.

Q. What is his business?

A. Farming. As I went to come out of the door when they marched me out, he stood in the door and turned and came right back and commanded the chest to be unlocked, and called for my money--my cotton money. I told them I had sold it, but I had not yet got the money. I said I had no money. He went and began to scramble for it; he went right to the chest; he had often seen me put it there. He sometimes worked with me, working a little farm. He went at it just as orderly as if he knew all about it.

Q. But how did you know it was Jones?

A. He had on a pair of pantaloons, when I met him at the door and looked at him, that I knew, and I am particularly confident that I knew his walk; as I went out I looked at him.

Q. What kind of a walk has James Jones--the real Jones?

A. A sort of a teetering walk, a sort of swing that made me look at him.

Q. Is James Jones the only man you ever saw who had a swinging walk?

A. No, sir; but if it is a person you have been working with a long time and have noticed particular you can tell the walk. There may be a walk like his, but to the best of my knowledge that was him.

Q. Would you swear it was him?

A. I will tell you more. My wife looked at him, and his gown that he had on fell off while he was there. He had been to our house several times before that, and she had looked at his clothes. He is like one of our home folks, and she knew them. There was the same pantaloons and the same coat pockets, all agreed just for him, and he stammered a sort of talk like this. [The witness assuming an unnatural bass tone.] He tried to talk a sort of Irish, outlandish like that--to keep us from understanding him or that it was him, until they got mad, and then they talked naturally.

Q. Did Jimmy Jones get mad too?

A. No, sir, but he talked with a different voice from natural.

Q. Did that help you to discover him, by his voice?

A. Yes, sir.

Q. Is it easier to discover a man by a counterfeit voice than by his natural tone?

A. Sometimes he would talk pretty naturally in his own voice again, and we knew his foolish ways; he is a mighty brickety fellow.

Q. What business does he follow?

A. He is the one that took my money.

Q. What business does he follow as a profession?

A. Farming.

Q. Does he own a farm?

A. Yes, sir; cotton and corn.

Q. Does Reeves own a farm?

A. Yes, sir.

Q. Does Presley?

A. Yes, sir.

Q. I thought you said Presley was the son of a man who owned a farm.

A. Yes, sir; the land belongs to his father but he manages it.

Q. You are satisfied that these three men were there that night and Ku-Kluxed you?

A. I believe it with the bottom of my heart.

Q. They asked for your money?

A. Yes, sir; they asked for my cotton money.

Q. Did they get the money?

A. Yes, sir; $31.40.

Q. Then they were robbers as well as Ku-Klux?

A. Yes, sir; I told it to the neighbors all about, and everybody said "Who was it?" but I knew that such a company could not have gone and made the fuss and noise they did and nobody know it.

Q. Did you tell anybody that you found or discovered Reeves, or Jones, or Presley?

A. No, sir; I never told that to anybody.

Q. Who did you first tell it to?

A. Here is the first place I ever made the discovery to anybody, when I told it here today.

Q. Then this is the first time you have told who these men were?

A. Yes, sir; the first time I have told it plainly. I gave little scattering hints, but I never made it plain.

Q. Who did you give scattering hints to?

A. Dr. Barron was talking to me, and I told him I knew the men, and he told me it was a very difficult thing without I was confident. I would not positively say. One of them had a scar under here, [under the chin,] where he had had a boil, and my daughters both saw the scar and knew it, and I saw it. He was about the size of that young man, [a young man of slight build, and less than ordinary height.] He looked maybe a little bigger; he was a common-sized man. I will not say who he was, but that scar was in the company, and if any one knows the company that was along that night, if there was any such one in that company they might know it was him. It might point out the man.

By Mr. STEVENSON:

Q. Why did you not tell these names before today?

A. Because they would have killed me. I began to talk a little about it, and I heard something. They laid a trap. There was a paper that they would be on me again. I went to Mr. Jerome Miller's and Dr. Miller's and laid there several nights. I expected to be shot. Dr. Miller told me and Jerome did, that I need not be afraid; that they would guarantee that I would not be disturbed any more; that they had attended to it. I took them as friends. They told me I need not be afraid; they had attended to it. Mark you, I am a negro and cannot read or write, but I know some few things.

Q. You think that Reeves had a grudge against you because of the loss of the slaves?

A. Yes, sir; I say that now. I never told it before.

Q. Is he the only man in that neighborhood who has a grudge because of the loss of negroes?

A. I do not believe there was a man in the country cared about it except him. I would not have thought it of him unless he had been in such a passion--a temper raised to such a height.

Q. Are not all the old slave-holders more or less mad about the loss of their slaves?

A. O, yes, sir; but that was nothing to my children running away.

By the CHAIRMAN:

Q. How many children had you?

A. Three were run away.
Q. Were they slaves at the time you bought your freedom?
A. Yes, sir; and several years afterward.
Q. Do you know where they are now?
A. Yes, sir; they are living with me now. Two of my daughters looked
at those Ku-Klux the other night, and they said they would be qualified as
to these men. One of my daughters had the measles and was in bed; the other
was in bed, too; but when they came they looked at the Ku-Klux and knew them,
and said they could swear to them.

NOTE BY MR. VAN TRUMP. --In the event that the general committee, at
their meeting in September, shall decide on taking further testimony, I
hereby give notice that I shall take additional testimony in relation to the
evidence of one William K. Owens, a witness examined at Yorkville, South
Carolina, not having time now to take the same.

                                            P. VAN TRUMP.

*Testimony Taken By The Joint Select Committee To Inquire Into The Condition
of Affairs In The Late Insurrectionary States,* South Carolina, Vol. III
(Washington, D.C.: Government Printing Office, 1872), pp. 1590-97.

VII

BLACK SOCIALISM AND GREENBACKISM

BLACK SOCIALISM AND GREENBACKISM

   During the 1870s, the black worker was caught in the vortex of contracting alternatives. The federal government began, and finally completed, its
withdrawal from the commitmemt to full equality for freedmen. As the federal
government retreated from Radical racial policies, white southerners regained
home rule and succeeded in all but eliminating blacks from political power.
Moreover, at that very moment when black workers were most in need of white
union support, those same unions became even more vigorous in excluding blacks
from the ranks of the organized.
   Against this general background, it is not surprising to find some blacks
concluding that a major change in the American political and economic system
was in order. One of the black leaders was Peter H. Clark of Cincinnati.
Clark's grandfather, William Clark, was the "Clark" of the Lewis and Clark
Expedition sent by Thomas Jefferson in 1804 to explore the continent and find
a route to the Pacific. In 1849 Peter Clark became a teacher in the city's
colored public schools, and after a brief flirtation with African colonization, decided to stay in Cincinnati. He launched his own newspaper in 1855,
the Herald of Freedom, and in 1866 became principal of Gaines High School
(colored). Although an ardent Republican prior to and during the Civil War,
in the immediate post-war years Clark steadily moved to the left. In a
speech delivered on March 26, 1877, Clark became the first Afro-American to
identify himself publically with socialism, announcing his support for the
Workingmen's Party of the United States, the first Marxist political party in
this country (Doc. 2). Peter Clark's basic ideas are presented in Documents
1-5.
   The Greenback Party emerged from a series of agrarian conventions in
1875, and pledged itself to a repeal of the resumption of specie payment
act as a means for improving the farmers' economic position. In other developments, the brutal force used to break the great strikes of 1877 taught many
mechanics that some form of political action outside the traditional party
structure was necessary. Consequently, workers' parties sprang up across the
country. Out of mutual necessity, they soon began to merge with the Greenback Party in states such as Pennsylvania, Ohio, and New York. The election
returns of 1877 accelerated the formulation of a national unity platform for
the farmers and the mechanics, which finally took place in Toledo, Ohio, in
February 1878. Both groups agreed in principle that the economic woes of
laboring men resulted from the machinations of speculators and monopolists,
and they agreed upon the need to reduce the hours in a work day, and both demanded an expansion in the money supply. Yet, the alliance between Labor and
the Greenbackers essentially was unstable. The Greenbackers believed that
financial reform would cure all of society's ills. On the other hand, workers
wanted much more, demanding that the government operate the railroads and other
public facilities upon which the unemployed would be put to work, ownership of
land and prohibition of large accumulations of wealth in the hands of a few,
and other goals such as the shorter work day, direct elections, and a graduated
income tax. Inevitably the two groups split and by 1879 the joint Greenback-
Labor movement was all but dead.
   Still, here was a platform with which black workers could readily identify,
even if the greenback panacea aroused little interest among them. The extent
to which southern blacks supported the movement is open to further study, but
as historian Herbert G. Gutman has suggested (see note 71), many southern
blacks undoubtedly shifted their hopes to the Greenback-Labor movement as a
reaction to the Republican retreat from Radical Reconstruction. A majority of
the Greenback clubs in Mississippi and Texas, for example, were probably composed of blacks. At least some of the Nationals in Arkansas and Alabama also
found support among black radicals. The letters reproduced as Documents 6-35
reveal that probably more blacks than whites were attracted to the movement in
Alabama. Nationals at Helena, Jefferson Mines, and Warrior Station, located
in the coal fields near Birmingham, exemplified a progressive inclination for
working-class solidarity among black and white coal miners who belonged to
the movement.

PETER H. CLARK AND SOCIALISM

1. CLARK ADDRESSES THE WORKINGMEN'S PARTY OF THE UNITED STATES[69]

Address to Working Men

Mr. Peter H. Clark lectured before the Workingmen's Society, in one of
the committee rooms of Arbeiter Hall, yesterday afternoon, his subject being
"Wages, Slavery, and the Remedy." The room was packed during the speaking
by a crowd of very respectable and intelligent looking workingmen, who
listened attentively, and occasionally applauded the speaker's remarks. Mr.
Clark addressed himself to the present relations of capital and labor, and
showed how the inordinate concentration of the former operated against the
interests of the latter, bringing about the evils of unemployed capital on
the one hand, and unemployed labor on the other. The speaker's remedy for
these would be gradual, and he would bring about a reformation of the laws
of society and of the Government. He would show that the selfish gaining and
holding of large fortunes was contrary to the welfare of society and to the
interests of capital itself. Furthermore, as the Government placed signals
on the coast as a warning against the wrecking of ships and loss of commerce,
he would have devised some means to restrain reckless speculation, large
business failures and commercial panics.[70]

On the other hand, he would have the law recognize the rights as well as
the duties of labor, by offering facilities of information through which there
might be a better distribution throughout the branches of industry. For labor
he advised thorough, intelligent, honest and faithful organization, the collection and study of statistics, &c., in order that each man might judge for
himself the best and most profitable occupation to engage in; and he further
counseled the affording to children of the best educational advantages that
they might, when they in turn assumed the responsibilities of life, the better
look after their interests.

In short, he would have capital give up some of its assumed selfish
rights and give labor its share, still bearing in view the principle that all
should not be bound down to a common level, but the genius and skill, and
perseverance and industry should have full scope and enjoy its full reward.

Mr. Clark was followed by several other speakers. Another lecture will
be delivered at the same place next Sunday afternoon by some person who will
be selected during the week.

Cincinnati Commercial, December 11, 1876.

2. THE WORKINGMEN'S PARTY
MASS MEETING IN ROBINSON'S OPERA HOUSE LAST NIGHT

The call for a mass meeting of the Workingmen's party filled the lower
part and gallery of Robinson's Opera--house with an attentive and well-behaved
assembly. . . .

Tuesday Evening, March 27, 1877

Peter H. Clark was the next speaker, who stated first, that lest he
should be misunderstood and regarded as inconsistent, he had to say that long
before there was a Republican Party he was a socialist. He did not know that
what he had to say would have a bearing directly upon the questions immediately
at issue with the workingman's party, but he certainly sympathized with the
Socialist Democracy. He reviewed the history of the country to show that the
men who produced its wealth were slaves, white and black, and never received
the benefits of their labor. He denied that labor and capital were the fast

friends that some would have us believe, and showed that the conflict between them drenched the streets of Paris with blood, accounted for the barrings out and strikes in England, the evictions of the small tenants in Ireland, and the denial to the freemen of the South of the right to purchase the land they till. He also instanced the fact that men are now living in prison under sentence of death for crimes committed in the contest between labor and capital.

He depicted the hopeless drudgery of the poor seamstresses of the city. He classed society under three heads: Millionaires, wage slaves, and paupers. Some time ago there were few of the first class, but now they jostle each other in the streets, while the men--who toiled and moiled to make the city what it is, have passed away in poverty and obscurity.

He did not agree with the words of Christ, "The poor ye have always with you." It was necessarily so. He thought society could be organized, so that at least the number of the poor could be reduced to a minimum. He deplored the words of Governor Young that "produce is high and labor is low."

He hoped that the cry for relief would reach the ears of our legislators, and they would do something to lift the burden from the shoulders of labor. He made no threats, but the French Revolution taught a lesson that cannot be forgotten. The cause did not lie with the people.

Capital must not rule, but be ruled and regulated. Capital must be taught that man, and not money, is supreme, and that legislation must be had for man. The mass of men North and South as voters were pretty much alike-- they were both obliged to vote for the interest that secured them bread.

He had no plan to present: perhaps they would obtain their desires for a better condition one by one. He alluded to the railroad monopolies, and instanced how the poor operatives were kept out of their wages while the money went to pay dividends and keep up the credit of the corporations in Wall Street.

Government is good; it is not an evil; and he believed that aside from securing life and liberty, it owed to society the duty of organizing labor.

He related from his own personal experience the incident of suffering in this city for months for want of employment to earn bread for his wife and babe, and how, not finding it, he felt like throwing himself in the river, and thus end all his misery. It was then he understood the *genus* tramp, and learned to sympathize with men out of employment and unable to obtain it. He felt that it was the duty of Government to so organize society that honest labor should not feel such oppression as to drive it to desperation.

Mr. Clark's remarks were heartily applauded. . . .

Cincinnati Commercial, March 27, 1877.

3. SOCIALISM: THE REMEDY FOR THE EVILS OF SOCIETY

Speech delivered by Peter H. Clark, Cincinnati, July 22, 1877.

GENTLEMEN: If I had the choosing of a motto for this meeting, I should select the words of the patriotic and humane Abraham Lincoln, "With malice toward none, with charity for all, with firmness in the right God gives us to see the right." These words so full of that charity which we should exercise toward each other, are especially suited to this day and time, when wrongs long condemned have at last been resisted and men are bleeding and dying in the busy centers of our population, and all over the land other men, with heated passions, are assembling to denounce the needless slaughter of of innocent men who, driven by want, have appealed to force for that justice which was otherwise refused to them. . . .

I sympathize in this struggle with the strikers, and I feel sure that in this I have the cooperation of nine-tenths of my fellow citizens. The poor man's lot is at best a hard one. His hand-to-hand struggle with the wolf of poverty leaves him no leisure for any of the amenities of life, his utmost rewards are a scanty supply of food, scanty clothing, scanty shelter, and if perchance he escapes a pauper's grave [he] is fortunate. Such a man deserves

the aid and sympathy of all good people, especially when, in the struggle
for life, he is pitted against a powerful organization such as the Baltimore
and Ohio Railroad or Pennsylvania Central. The Baltimore and Ohio Railroad
was taken possession of by the government during the war, and was rebuilt in
a manner, from end to end. Such a firm roadway, such tunnels and bridges,
are rarely seen as are possessed by that road, and at the end the road was
turned over to its owners in a better condition than it had ever been, so
that much of the outlay which other roads are compelled to make was saved to
this. They were paid for the use of the road many millions of dollars and
the managers have lately declared a dividend of ten percent, and if their
stock was watered, as I have no doubt it is, this ten percent is equivalent
to fifteen or twenty percent upon the capital actually invested in it. Yet
this road, so built, so subsidized, so prosperous, if we may judge from its
dividend, declares itself compelled to put the wages of its employees down
to starvation rates. Either they were not honestly able to declare that
dividend or they are able to pay living wages to the men whom they employ.
The blood of those men murdered at Baltimore cries from the ground against
these men who by their greed have forced their men to the desperate measure
of a strike, and then invoked the strong arm of the government to slaughter
them in their misery.

The too-ready consent of the state and national governments to lend
themselves to the demand of these wealthy corporations cannot be too severly
condemned. Has it come to this, that the President of a private corporation
can, by the click of a telegraphic instrument, bring state and national
troops into the field to shoot down American citizens guilty of no act of
violence? For you observe that neither at Grafton, Baltimore or Pittsburgh
was there violence offered to persons or property until the troops were
deployed upon the scene. At Grafton it is noticeable that women, wives and
mothers, were the chief forces employed by the strikers to keep others from
taking their places.

The sight of the soldiery fired the hot blood of the wronged men, and
they met force with force. Whether they are put down or not, we are thank-
ful that the American citizen, as represented by these men, was not slave
enough to surrender without resistance the right to appeal for a redress of
grievances. When that day comes that a mere display of force is sufficient
to awe a throng of Americans into submission, the people will have sunk too
low to be entrusted with self-government.

Those men will be avenged--nobly avenged. Capital has been challenged
to the contest; and in the arena of debate, to which in a few days the
question will be remanded, the American people will sit as judges, and just
as surely as we stand here, their decision will be against monopolists and
in favor of the workingmen. In twenty years from today there will not be a
railroad in the land belonging to a private corporation; all will be owned
by the government and worked in the interests of the people. Machinery and
land, will, in time, take the same course, and cooperation instead of competition will be the law of society. The miserable condition into which
society has fallen has but one remedy, and that is to be found in Socialism.

Observe how all civilized communities pass from a condition of what is
called prosperity to one of depression and distress. Observe how continually
these fluctuations occur; how the intervals between them grow shorter; how
each one is more violent than the last, the distress produced more widespread.
Observe, too, that after each the number of capitalists decrease, while those
who remain grow more wealthy and more powerful, while those who have failed
join the great army of workers who hang forever on the ragged edge of pauperism.

The so-called periods of prosperity are more properly periods of unrestrained speculation. Money accumulates in the hands of the capitalists,
[through (?)] some governmental device as a tariff or the issue of greenbacks.
This abundance tempts men to embark in business enterprises which seem to
promise rich returns. For a time all goes well, shops are crowded with busy
men, and all [are] ready to say, "Behold how prosperous we are!" But there
comes a check to all this. The manufacturers begin to talk about a glutted
market. There has been overproduction. There comes the period of sharp
competition. Prices are reduced, goods are sold at cost--below cost--then
comes the crash, bosses fail, shops are closed, men are idle, and the

miserable workmen stand forth, underbidding each other in the labor market.
If the competition be too sharp, they resort to strikes as in the present
instance. Then comes violence, lawlessness, bloodshed and death.

People who talk of the anarchy of socialism surely cannot have considered these facts. If they had, they would have discovered not a little
of anarchy on their side of the question.

It is folly to say that a condition of poverty is a favorable one, and
to point to men who have risen to affluence from that condition. For one
man who is strong through the hindrances of poverty, there are ten thousand
who fail. If you take ten thousand men and weigh them with lead and cast
them into the midst of Lake Erie, a few may swim out but the majority will
be drowned.

This condition of poverty is not a favorable one either for the individual or for the nation. Especially is it an unfavorable condition for a
nation whose government lies in the hands of all its citizens. A monarchy
or an aristocracy can afford to have the mass of its citizens steeped in
poverty and ignorance. Not so in a republic. Here every man should be the
owner of wealth enough to render him independent of the threats or bribes of
the demagogue. He should be the owner of wealth enough to give leisure for
that study which will qualify him to study and understand the deep questions
of public policy which are continually demanding solution. The more men
there are who have this independence, this leisure, the safer we are as a
nation; reduce the number, and the fewer there are, the more dangerous the
situation. So alarming has been the spread of ignorance and poverty in the
past generation, that whole cities in our land--whole states, indeed--are at
the mercy of an ignorant rabble who have no political principle except to
vote for the men who pay the most on election days and who promise to make
the biggest dividend of public stealing. This is sadly true, nor is the
Negro, scarcely ten years from slavery, the chief sinner in this respect.

That this evil of poverty is partially curable, at least, I am justified
in thinking, because I find each of the great political parties offering
remedies for the hard times and the consequent poverty. Many wise men,
learned in political economy, assure us that their doctrines, faithfully
followed, will result in a greater production of wealth and a more equal
division of the same. But as I have said before, there is but one efficacious remedy proposed, and that is found in Socialism.

The present industrial organization of society has been faithfully tried
and has proven a failure. We get rid of the king, we get rid of the aristocracy, but the capitalist comes in their place, and in the industrial organization and guidance of society his little finger is heavier than their loins.
Whatever Socialism may bring about, it can present nothing more anarchical
than is found in Grafton, Baltimore and Pittsburgh today. . . .

To increase the volume of the currency, which is the remedy proposed by
some, means simply that money shall be made so abundant that the capitalist,
in despair of any legitimate returns in the way of interest, shall embark in
any and all enterprises which promise returns for the idle cash in his coffers.
It means a stimulation of production in a community already suffering from
excess of production; it means speculation, competition, finally a reduction
of values, bankruptcy, ruin. The American people have traveled that path so
frequently in the past fifty years that it requires no prophetic powers to
map out the certain course which will be pursued. Already our capitalists
rush to invest their money at four and a half percent in markets which a
short time since gave readily two percent a month. Increase your volume--let
it be either greenbacks or silver--and we enter on the career I have described with a certainty that the gulf at the end is deeper and more hopeless
than the one in which we now wallow.

Trades-unions, Grangers, Sovereigns of Industry, cooperative stores and
factories are alike futile. They are simply a combination of laborers who seek
to assume toward their more unfortunate fellows who are not members the
attitude that the capitalist assumes toward them. They incorporate into their
constitutions all the evil principles which afflict society. Competition,
overproduction mark their stores and factories as much as do those of individual enterprises, and when the periodic crash comes, they succumb as readily
as any.

All these plans merely poultice the ulcer in the body politic which needs

Constitutional treatment. The momentary improvement they produce is always succeeded by a corresponding depression. The old fable of Sisyphus is realized, and the heavy stone rolled to the top of the mountain with infinite labor rolls back again.

The government must control capital with a strong hand. It is merely the accumulated results of industry, and there would be no justice should a few score bees in the hive take possession of the store of honey and dole it out to the workers in return for services which added to their superabundant store. Yet such is the custom of society.

Future accumulations of capital should be held sacredly for the benefit of the whole community. Past accumulations may be permitted to remain in private hands until, from their very uselessness, they will become a burden which their owners will gladly surrender.

Machinery too, which ought to be a blessing but is proving to be a curse to the people should be taken in hand by the government and its advantages distributed to all. Captain Cutter wrote in his song of steam:

> Soon I intend ye may go and play,
> While I manage this world myself.

Had he written, ye may go and starve, it would have been nearer the truth. Machinery controlled in the interests of labor would afford that leisure for thought, for self-culture, for giving and receiving refining influences, which are so essential to the full development of character. "The ministry of wealth" would not be confined to a few, but would be a benefit to all.

Every railroad in the land should be owned or controlled by the government. The title of private owners should be extinguished, and the ownership vested in the people. All a road will need to meet will be a running expense and enough to replace waste. The people can then enjoy the benefit of travel, and where one man travels now, a thousand will travel then. There will be no strikes, for the men who operate the road will be the recipient of its profits.

Finally, we want governmental organization of labor so that ruinous competition and ruinous overproduction shall equally be avoided, and these commercial panics which sweep over and engulf the world will be forever prevented.

It will be objected that this is making our government a machine for doing for the citizen everything which can be more conveniently done by combined than by individual effort. Society has already made strides in the direction of Socialism. Every drop of water we draw from hydrants, the gas that illumines our streets at night, the paved streets upon which we walk, our parks, our schools, our libraries, are all outgrowths of the Socialistic principle. In that direction lies safety.

Choose ye this day which course ye shall pursue.

Let us, finally, not forget that we are American citizens, that the right of free speech and of a free press is enjoyed by us. We are exercising today the right to assemble and complain of our grievances. The courts of the land are open to us, and we hold in our hands the all-compelling ballot.

There is no need for violent counsels or violent deeds. If we are patient and wise, the future is ours.

Cincinnati Commercial, July 23, 1877.

4. AN EDITORIAL REPLY

Mr. Peter H. Clark can not understand why it is that the military are always against the strikers. It ought not to be a great mystery to a man of his analytic powers. A notifies B that after a given date he can not pay him but eighty cents a day, and B knocks off work because A will not pay a dollar. B, not satisfied to quit A's employment, takes possession of his

property, and undertakes to dictate to A what he shall or shall not do. A
appeals to the civil authorities to protect his property. If the Sheriff
and his *posse* find they can not do it, an appeal is made to the Governor of
the State, and if the emergency is such as to warrant it, he calls out the
militia. And that is where the military comes in. It is probable nine-
tenths of the militia who are thus called upon to sustain the laws, and
assist the State in (what it is bound to do) protecting the property of its
citizens, sympathize with B. But B has put himself in a false position.
He had done an unlawful thing. He has taken possession of property not his
own. He has put himself outside the law, defied the civil authority, and
has made himself penally liable. It seems to us if Mr. Clark would give
his mind to the subject for a few hours he would be able to discover why it
is that the military are in such crises as the present on the side of law
and order.

Cincinnati Commercial, July 24, 1877.

5.   A PLEA FOR THE STRIKERS

To the Editor of the Commercial:
    I have no idea of when or where I confessed to the state of ignorance
attributed to me in the Commercial of this date. Certainly I have never had
any difficulty in understanding why the military are always against the
strikers. In the words of the writer of "Ecclesiastes," "I beheld the tears
of such as were oppressed and they had no comforter: and on the side of
their oppressors there was power: but they had no comforter." With this
fact imprinted on my memory by many years' sympathy with and service in
unpopular causes, I do not marvel when I see the oppression of the poor, and
violent perverting of judgment and justice."
    Perhaps your informant was endeavoring to report a contrast which I
perceive between the course of the General Government. Now, when military
aid is demanded to protect property against labor, and then, when military
was demanded to protect the laborers against the aggressions of the powerful.
That a vast deal of cabinet meeting and consultation with Attorney Generals
and other magnates was needed, before the requisitions of the Governors of
Maryland, Virginia and Pennsylvania are answered is wonderful, if not admirable.
    I am, sir, in every fiber and nerve a law-abiding citizen. When the
will of a majority of my fellow citizens is enacted into a law, I implicitly
obey the law, as long as my right of free speech and of free press is reserved to me. I deprecate violent words and violent deeds as much as any
one can. I am, sir, emphatically a law-and-order man.
    But all the violent deeds and violent words are not on the part of the
strikers and their friends. The law-and-order party are responsible for
their full share of this violence. A score of times during these disturbed
days I have been told of mysterious armings of men, who were to "wipe out"
the strikers and their sympathizers. Thumbs have been drawn significantly
across the throats, and law-and-order men have pulled at imaginary ropes to
give me an inkling of the throat-cuttings and hangings in reserve. Now this
was harmless enough expended on me, but there are fiery spirits in the strike
who might accept the challenge. Is it not best that all parties observe the
caution to be prudent in word and deed. The press of the country is nearly
or quite unanimous in its inculcation of respect for law and property, but
this same press is actually more responsible for a lack of respect to law
and property than all the influence combined.
    The man who at the Sunday meeting exclaimed, "To hell wid the Govern-
ment," had learned from the press of the country that every man concerned in
public affairs was a scoundrel or a fool. I am a reader of newspapers of all
shades of politics, and the abuse so uniformly and copiously heaped upon men
in public affairs justifies the opinion that there is not a single wise or
honest man in public life in America. As for railroad corporations, we need

only to call Mr. Thos. Scott, who I think, enjoys the distinction of being the most universally abused man in America, for while your ordinary political sheet will defend the reputation of the public man who represents its ideas, all unite in the abuse of railroad corporations. Tirades about their "mismanagement," their "greed," their "ill-gotten gains," can be found daily in the newspapers of the land. Now, when the able editor calls his political opponent a villain, or expatiates on the scoundrelism of railroad managers, he may mean it in a Pickwickian sense. He may be ready to drink the champagne of the one or accept the pass of the other. But the people take him to mean what he says, and the consequence is a widespread belief in the wickedness and incompetency of public men, and a belief that railroad men are public plunderers. The man there who cried "To hell with the Government," and the misguided men who attempted to burn the Ohio and Mississippi bridge last night, are the product of newspapers, not of communistic teachings.

If more care had been taken in the past to state only facts and to criticise in a fair spirit, the necessity for this volume of good advice which they are now giving might have been avoided.

I do not doubt for a moment that the railroads are losing money. There are too many of them, and sharp competition has caused them to reduce their rates below a remunerative price. The facts of the case could and should have been communicated to the men, who are not fools nor soulless. But when they see high railroad officials receiving the salaries of princes, when they hear of dividends on stock and interest on bonds, they cannot understand why there is no money for the man whose labors earn these vast sums. They naturally regard themselves as wronged, for the sentiment, "Thou shalt not muzzle the ox that treadeth out the corn," finds a sanction in human nature, as well as in Scripture. When they complain, they are told that they are at liberty to quit and take their services elsewhere. This is equivalent to telling them that they are at liberty to go and starve. Let them look where they will and they find the close-ranked array of employes shutting them out of hope of bread should they let go their present positions. Hence they make the effort to obtain an increase of wages and to retain their places at the same time. Understanding their motive, and the dire necessity by which they are driven, I pity, but I can not condemn them. Mr. John H. B. Latrobe once said in this city, "Before the end of this century there will be twenty hands stretched for a single loaf of bread." The century is not yet closed, and what I deemed a mere rhetorical flourish seems almost an accomplished fact.

Then too, the door of justice seemed shut in their faces.

They have no representation on the Board of Directors. Every State has laws punishing conspiracy, punishing riot and unlawful assemblages, but no State has laws providing for the examination and redress of the grievances of which these men complain. The whole force of the State and National Governments may be invoked by the railroad managers, but the laborer has nothing.

In this respect we are worse than monarchial England, where the laws provide for juries of arbitration, to whom disputes between laborers and their employers may be referred.

The right to resist wrong resides in every man, and no laws can take this right from him. There may be questions of expediency, which he must settle, but the right remains. Hedged in and despairing, the railroad men have exercised this right, with consequences which we all deplore.

These strikers are our fellow-citizens, for the justness of those motives and moderation of whose conduct, I refer to the columns of your own paper, where proof may be found that the strikers themselves, are neither destructives nor men of blood.

The exercise of a small degree of patience at Pittsburgh would have prevented the horrible scene of arson and death which that doomed city presents.

The "wiping out" policy is not the true one. Much bitter invective is heaped upon the Workingmen's party because of this outbreak. I venture to say that there is not a section of that party in any one of the centers of disturbance. Had there been there would have been less tendency to disturbance. When workingmen understand that there are peaceful influences at work to relieve them of the thraldom of wages slavery, they will be more patient.

There was never a slave insurrection in the United States after Wm. Lloyd

Garrison began to agitate for the abolition of slavery, though there were
many before.

The railroad managers would do well to plant a section of the Workingmen's party at every station. They would guard their property more effectually than the whole United States army can do it.

Hoping for the speedy prevalence of that peace which arises from the
practice of justice, I remain,

Respectfully yours,

PETER H. CLARK

July 24, 1877.

Cincinnati Commercial, July 26, 1877.

THE GREENBACK-LABOR PARTY

THE "ALABAMA LETTERS" TO THE EDITORS [71]
OF THE NATIONAL LABOR TRIBUNE

6.

Jefferson Mines, June 25, 1878.

Allow us a small space in your paper to give account of the meeting
here by the members of our National Greenback-Labor club. The white people
of this place have solicited the colored men to join their clubs here, which
we have done largely. The officers of this club are: George McDonald,
President; James Moran, Secretary. The club meets on Thursday evening. At
our last meeting James Dye gave a most delightful lecture on the questions
uppermost among the people. He was loudly applauded. W. J. Thomas, a new
colored member, was then called on for a few remarks, but he was rather
diffident about coming forward and it is but just to say he made a most
brilliant effort. He warmed up the crowd in a most lively manner, and gave
both of the old parties "what Paddy gave the drum." His speech brought eight
new colored recruits forward, who joined the club. All classes of people who
heard Mr. Thomas accord him the highest need of praise for his masterly effort. He is an up-and-down Greenback-Labor man, and the colored people here-
abouts have settled upon him for a leader in the coming campaign, and he is
not afraid to speak what he thinks.

Our club is growing rapidly here. We have chosen Messrs. McDonald and
Moran delegates to the County Convention. We hope to have W. J. Thomas as
a delegate to the next convention. Messrs. Moran and Thomas report prospects
good for a club among the farmers east of Jefferson. They are working for
it too. We believe these two men were sent here for a special purpose, and
that purpose to be to show the working people the legitimate way out of their
slavery to the money power.

Faithfully for humanity,

WARREN KELLEY

National Labor Tribune, June 29, 1878.

7.

W. J. Thomas, the colored Alabama orator, is doing noble service for the
National Greenback-Labor party in that state. He is forming clubs rapidly,
and both the white and colored men join the clubs with avidity. Push on the
good work; strengthen and hold up his hands, men of Alabama, and you will be
rewarded in the end by this, the party of humanity.

National Labor Tribune, August 3, 1878.

8.

Our regular Jefferson Mines, Alabama, correspondent, Warren Kelley,
writes:
"Our meeting held here Monday night, July 22, was a good one. We elected
W. J. Thomas to organize clubs through this country. After he had been out
sixteen days, we concluded to call him in to see how he had improved, and to
find how many clubs he organized, and how many members in each club. There
was one member from every club ordered to meet with us to bear witness to
Mr. Thomas' testimonials. Four clubs sent their secretaries, and six others
a report, stating that they had been organized, and the names of their officers
and the members all corresponded with Mr. Thomas' statement exactly. Mr.
James Martin was called upon to address the council in regard to Mr. Thomas'
improvement, and he gave a most eloquent lecture. He said to the council
that so far as he was concerned he was perfectly satisfied with what W. J.
Thomas had done, and that he did not believe any other man in the State of
Alabama could do as well among the colored voters of Jefferson county as
Thomas had. He has done extremely well, and we should keep him at this
business. He is doing more for the cause than any other man in the State of
Alabama, and with but little assistance--about $4. Mr. Martin encouraged the
council all he could to assist Mr. Thomas and keep him stumping this county.
He stated that all that W. J. Thomas asks for is the money to send to the
editor of the NATIONAL LABOR TRIBUNE at Pittsburgh, Pa. to pay for papers he
had got, and to get 100 copies more to hand around as he traveled. Mr. Kelley
was appointed to receive and answer all correspondence. He was also directed
to furnish the NATIONAL LABOR TRIBUNE with official notices of our doings in
Alabama. The notices will all be read by W. H. Galloway or M. Johnson to the
club before being published.

National Labor Tribune, August 3, 1878.

9.

Jefferson Mines, July 29, 1878.

After the speech of Mr. Thomas, the leading member of the white club,
Mr. Walker, addressed the council, saying to the Warrior club that they would
have to spur and lay whip to the horse, or Jefferson would soon ride out of
sight. He also stated that Jefferson club had the best order and held the
most regular meetings of any club in this State, white or black. He never
thought such work would ever be carried on by colored people. Mr. Thomas is
the leading spirit of the Jefferson club, and the Jefferson men here said
that if he were to leave their club would soon go to pieces. Mr. Thomas is
the right man for the business, because he speaks what he thinks in any crowd.
The council then adjourned, having an understanding that the regular
meeting time for Warrior club should be on Wednesday night of every week, and
the regular meetings of Jefferson will be held on Friday night of every week,

and we will visit each other every meeting time. Meetings held at any other
time shall be for special business.

On the 4th of July W. J. Thomas bid the boys good-bye for a few days,
and on Saturday, July 12, he returned, and instructed the Secretaries to call
a meeting the same night. Mr. Thomas brought in his reports, with good witness to prove everything to be true. All the reports from the different
clubs that he had organized were read by the secretaries. The crowd was over-
whelmed with joy when they found that Mr. Thomas had organized seven clubs,
making twelve in this county. Mr. Thomas was attacked by the Democrats, who
tried to keep him from putting up notices for public speaking, or making any
speeches in favor of the Greenback party. They told him that he was heaping
up war upon himself and millions of others, and threatened to take him down.
But Mr. Thomas slipped his hand in his vest pocket and brought out his authority, asking them to read for themselves. They soon handed the paper back.
They said to a white man the next day, who was a Greenbacker, "Our country has
gone to the dogs." "Why?" said the Greenbacker. "Because I saw a negro nail-
ing up a sign on the Eureka Co. storehouse door. It was to notify all colored
voters or whites that there would be public speaking at Oxmore on the 10th of
July; that W. J. Thomas would address the people in regard to the National
Greenback-Labor Party. The notice stated that the platform would be read by
him." "What platform?" said the Greenbacker. "Why, the platform of that infernal Greenback party," says the Democrat. "Now, to think that a negro has
that much authority in a good Democratic State, is enough to make a white man
commit suicide. John, you know three years ago if a negro dared to say anything about politics, or public speaking, or sitting on a jury, or sticking up
a notice, he would be driven out of the country, or shot, or hung in the woods.
He was not allowed even a trial. Now white people are backing them in doing
such things. I am told by responsible white men that this fellow Thomas has a
carpet-bag full of newspapers that are printed in New York, Terre Haute, Pittsburgh, Chicago and Toledo. I suppose, from what I can learn from some sensible
negroes, who don't pay any attention to the negro Moses, but have been to his
speaking once or twice, that W. J. Thomas has advised all the colored people
to subscribe for these papers, and not pay any attention to the papers that are
printed here in the South. He says the papers here are printed by our masters,
and they keep all the good news away from us, and give us their old papers to
read, and keep us fooled all the time. The nigger advises them to let these
papers alone and take these good ones. He has got some with him to show what
good papers they are. Now, he has one among them that he calls *Labor Nashel
Cribbune*. This paper is wrote in Pittsburd, Pinsalvany, so the niggers tell
us. I don't know how true it is, but Ned will tell a white man anything he
knows. Ned says he will get holt on one of them next time he goes to nigger
meeting, and give it to his master, Jim. If he does, I will get it and see
what it is. The nigger tells them in his speaking to subscribe for this
Cribbune; he says it is the best paper in the bunch. But I tell you, John,
if we let this nigger alone he will ruin our whole State. It is a dam shame.
They tell me he has organized four or five clubs in Jones Valley, and more
coming. Some white men that heard nigger Thomas say he is the best speaker
in Jefferson county, white or black. He is too saucy; he don't care what he
says to white nor black in his speeches. John Smith says that he heard the
niggers in Jones Valley the other night crying out, 'Three cheers for W. J.
Thomas!' So this is what is doing with our party. Greenback clubs organized
by niggers! In two years our editors will have to go to the plow-handle, and
these Pittsburgh, New York, Chicago and Terre Haute editors will have all of
the negro subscribers and half of our white subscribers. Well, good-bye,
John; I will let you know when Ned gets that paper and let you see it. We
can scare the niggers in Jones Valley, and run the carpet-baggers and elect
Billy Walker. Come over, John."

Now John was a full-blooded Greenbacker, and let the cat out of the wallet.
He came to our meeting last night and told us the whole secret, and advised us
to have Thomas on the line. He asked us to have these facts published, so
that Greenback men would be on the watch. There should be money made up for
Mr. Thomas and keep him on the road. He will have to watch his own color, for
the other party will hire them to betray him.

If W. J. Thomas is let alone he will turn the State of Alabama upside down
in the course of twelve months. The Greenback men will win if he keeps on.

Mr. John Brown rode forty-two miles to meet us and tell us how to manage it.
He is a stranger to Thomas and says from what he can learn Mr. Thomas is
doing all he can for the National party, mostly at his own expense.

W. K. [Warren Kelley]

National Labor Tribune, August 10, 1878.

10.

Jefferson Mines, July 29, 1878.

Please permit a small space in your paper to state the condition of the
National party among the colored people in this county. As I stated before,
W. J. Thomas is considered the leader of the Nationals in Alabama among the
colored people, having his headquarters at Jefferson Mines. We elected him
chairman of the committee, giving him authority to organize clubs over this
county. Several white men met with us and advised us to organize in haste.
It was moved and seconded that the Warrior and Jefferson clubs should unite
and make a collection in order to get money to support one man while travelling through the country to organize. So we named W. J. Thomas as a delegate
to meet the Warrior club at their regular meeting, on Wednesday, July 13,
1878. After the house was called to order the Warrior club proceeded to
business.

It was moved and carried that they should hear the report of the Jefferson club. W. J. Thomas had caused the Jefferson club to hold meetings three
nights in succession, and had everything posted up to a gnat's heel. Mr.
Thomas requested that the minutes of the Jefferson club be read before any
further proceedings be had. This was done by the secretary of the Warrior
club, which were approved. This gave satisfaction, and a collection was made
by the Warrior club to help support the organizer. They were very poor, but
showed a willing mind and assisted all they could. A motion was made to select
from Warrior white club some good man to run against Mr. Thomas, but they refused. They said that they all knew Thomas, and they would rather have him
than any man in Jefferson county. The Warrior club then turned all the money
over to the Jefferson treasurer. The Warrior men robbed their own treasury to
help Mr. Thomas, and said that they were willing to help in this cause at any
time. Then the power was given W. J. to organize and rule over all the
colored clubs in Jefferson county.

W. J. Thomas was then called to address the council. This he did, and
it was asserted by all who heard him, that such good words had never been
heard from the lips of a poor coal miner before.

W. K. [Warren Kelley],

National Labor Tribune, August 17, 1878.

11.

Jefferson Mines, July 30, 1878.

We had a central committee meeting to hear the report of our general
organizer, W. J. Thomas, who was present, and reported that he had organized
four new clubs. A collection was raised in our central club for him, which
resulted in placing him once more upon the road. He has done wonders in this
section of the State. The people clamor for meetings. One was held here, and
Mr. Thomas made a stirring appeal and address to the assembled people. The
ladies turned out in force and gave countenance to our young orator. One of
the friends suggested that the young ladies "go behind the door" until he got

started, but they wouldn't do it, and sat still. Mr. Thomas came forward, and after a few preliminary remarks, said: "Where there is little known there is little required." He took the Bible and made some quotations. He spoke of Moses, of Joseph and others. He spoke of Christ, and his love for the people, and indeed the meeting looked, for the moment, more like a missionary meeting than a political one. He made a remarkable speech, surprising even those who had heard him before. He read the Toledo platform all through. He also read articles from the LABOR TRIBUNE, which were received with unmistakable evidences of approbation. He also read from "Pomeroy's Catechism" with great effect. After taking extracts from other documents, he called upon any one who had aught against the documents read to them to come forward and defend his position. No one appearing, he advised them all to come and join in the good work. "Called for mourners," the boys said. This meeting added ten names to the roll of the Irondale club, thirteen to the Newton club, and eighteen to the Jonesboro club--a pretty good night's work. The other speakers were called upon, but said there was no room left for them to say anything as Mr. Thomas had fully covered the ground. Thomas then asked pardon for his having kept the audience waiting so long, but they shouted "Go on! go on! We'll stay here a week longer to hear you talk the greenback gospel." Deacon Hockens, of the Baptist church, sang a hymn, and Parson Jones called on them to pray, which he led, after which they were dismissed.

Persons who were present at this meeting tell me that it was more like a camp-meeting than a political gathering. W. J. Thomas will be long remembered here for his effective work, and all accord the young man great praise for his speech and gentlemanly demeanor toward the people. This was the master meeting of the Greenback-Labor Party in this county. Mr. Thomas is going to work in a few days, but we will raise another collection, and send him on the road again soon. The clubs in this State should all contribute toward his support, and to keep him going, for he is competent to show the people the true way to prosperity and happiness. . . .

W. K. [Warren Kelley]

National Labor Tribune, August 17, 1878.

12.

The following letter was received from Colored Club No. 3, . . . Haygoods Cross Roads, Ala., July 9, 1878:

WARREN KELLEY--Dear Sir: I learn from Mr. C. C. Anderson that you are in correspondence with the editors of the LABOR TRIBUNE. If so, I wish you would manage to subscribe for a copy for me. I can read a little, but don't understand how to subscribe for papers. I have not got the money, but as you have to pay five cents a pound for flour, I will let you have the same quality of flour at two and a half cents, to get that paper for six months. A colored man from your place brought some here and handed them around, and told us to subscribe for them. He seemed to be in a hurry. He made a speech here, and it beat anything we ever heard. He organized a Greenback club here, but the most of our boys were afraid to join it. Some say the Democrats have hired him to do this; others say it is to get up war; so that he had better make his tracks scarce here, as the white folks will upset him in a minute. If you know anything about him, let us know. He seems to be a good friend to colored and poor people. He is a small, spare made black man, and signed his name Willie Johnson Thomas. I hope he is the right kind of a man, but we have been fooled so much, that we can't trust him yet. But I like this paper called the TRIBUNE. Please answer soon, and oblige yours respectfully,

Henry Hospun.

Another letter dated Oxmoor, Ala., July 10, says:

MR. WONE COOLEY--Sir: Do you know W. J. Thomas, a colored man? Our neighbors were roused up here last night by a carpet-bagger, who had about a hundred newspapers, handing them around, and storming and crying out something

about greenbacks, public lands, banks, bonds, convicts, Chinese and poverty
and starvation. He got eight or ten to join him, but I had no use for his
Democratic foolery. He said he came from Jefferson Mines, and showed that
he had authority to organize clubs of gold or greenback or silver bank bonds,
or something. He said if we did not believe him to write and ask you. He
left this morning before breakfast. Do you know anything about him, or not?
He said his name was W. J. Thomas. These white folks say they will Thomas
him if he comes here any more.

B. JONES

Faithfully,

W. K. [Warren Kelley]

National Labor Tribune, August 17, 1878.

13.

Helena, December 28, 1878.

This place is on the North and South Alabama Railroad. The principal
works in this vicinity and along this road, is the Central steel works,
located at Helena, and operated by Cobb & Fell. The mill has stopped for the
winter, throwing 75 men out of employment. Now comes the Eureka coal and
iron company, which employs about 82 freedmen at mining and coke making.
There are about 95 convicts in mining who are shipped here from the State
Penitentiary. You seem to be something to be an American citizen after all.
If you don't like convict labor or farming you can go to the State warden of
the prison and put on a suit of striped clothes and be appointed a coal miner,
provided the judge and grand jury are favorable. Next comes the Cahaba mines,
which have been idle for twelve months. Then comes the North Cahaba mines,
owned by Davis & Carr, who employ about ten men. Next we have the Oxmoor
furnace, located at Oxmoor, and operated by the Eureka company, which employs
about two hundred men. At Birmingham, at the junction of the North and South
Alabama and Chattanooga railroads, are located the new mines of Debort, Laboring, Sloss, Aldridge & Co. This is a new mine, and is calculated for the
manufacturing of coke. The ovens are already in course of erection. The number of ovens will be about ninety. The Coalburg mine, two miles north of New
Castle, owned by Sharp, who employs about 35 men, comes next. Then we have
the New Castle mine, owned by John T. Milner. This is another model of our
free institutions, as the mining is done by convicts. This fellow told the
few freemen who worked for him that if he found out that any of his men voted
the Greenback-Labor ticket they could find work some place else. But the men,
I am proud to announce, stood manfully to our cause, Milner is a Republican
bulldozer. Then comes the Jefferson mines, owned by Aldridge & Morris, who
employ about 65 men. There is a strong element of Greenbackers here. I paid
this place a visit last summer, and found some good workers here, among them
Mike and Jim Moran and Tom Murray from Dunbar, Pa. They are working like
beavers for the cause of humanity and freedom. . . .

"Dawson"

National Labor Tribune, January 4, 1879.

14.

Jefferson Mines, January 20, 1879.

I would ask space in your columns to state the condition of things here.
The Greenbackers are still betting on a majority in 1880. They seem to be

increasing very much south of Jefferson. They elected a Greenback man in the
city of Birmingham a few weeks ago, and it stings the old parties like yellow
jackets in a bushy head. Work here has been tolerabie [sic] scarce for two
months on account of the pump being out of order. They got it in order again
about December 20th. The prospects now look bright for steady work all winter.

George W. Griffin, a mule driver, was on the downward cage, at noon of
December 23rd, 1878, when it stuck. By his moving about on the cage it
started, and fell a distance of nearly 40 feet. His cries attracted the
attention of one of the miners, who lifted him out of further danger. He
was laid up some time, but is now at work. The men quit work until the cage
was made safe, but after being idle awhile, again went in. Three days after
this accident a man named Posey had his foot crushed by a fall of coal.

One Monday morning about nine o'clock a cry was raised in the mines for
a strike. "What is the matter now?" said some. "We are cheated in our
weight," was the answer. The men who first struck did not wait to have any
understanding before going to the top, and before all had been notified the ones
who went up were coming back. Nearly all of the men, both white and colored,
were opposed to the strike. Several men went up and examined the scales,
when the pit boss gave an order that all who were not in that evening to
square up and bring out their tools. Some eight or ten quit, and the rest
went back to work. It is said by some of the men that the miners who first
got up the strike were in debt to the company, and wanted to leave. We
don't know how true it is, but we know that the thing was brought up foolishly,
and the men working now have been here a long time, the largest portion of
them at least, and have been well treated by the superintendent and company,
and would not like to go into a strike unless they were satisfied beyond a
reasonable doubt that there was something wrong about the weight. As once
members of the Miners' National Association we say: First, do all in your
power to keep down a stike; then, if that won't do, strike with an understanding and a resolution. The thing broke up in a row. The clerk struck
one of the miners, and the superintendent and clerk then went to his house
to take some blankets for debt, and was [sic] bluffed out by the miner drawing a pistol. We don't know how the thing exactly stands. I will just state
however, the next morning the miner and the clerk were shooting at one
another, and the last we saw of it was the miner running and the clerk following, shooting at him with a pistol. The superintendent followed with a
shot gun, but no one was shot. The man with the shot gun tumbled and fell
before shooting, and it is said that this saved the life of the miner. We
learned further that the end of it would be a big law suit.

W.J.T. [Thomas]

National Labor Tribune, February 8, 1879.

15.

Jefferson Mines, N.N., N.D.

Things are going on very smoothly here. Work is regular, and prospects
seem very bright for the future. The shooting scrape between the superintendent, operators and Little George, the miner, is in the courts. They
have had one trial of the cause [sic], but it has not been decided yet. We
heard that Little George was in jail before the trial, but we have not
learned whether he was released or not. The Warrior mines are going on very
well at present. We received some extra copies of the TRIBUNE, and have
handed them around. We have several promises of clubs, but money is so
scarce outside of the mines that we can't rely on any promises unless we see
the cash, and feel it, too.

National Labor Tribune, March 1, 1879.

16.

Warrior, March 28, 1879.

On the first of March J. T. Pierce reduced the price of mining coal
from $1 per ton to 75 cents, which we, his miners, refuse to submit to.
We are offered 75 cents for mining a ton of 2240 pounds of coal, which
Pierce sells in [the] market for 2000 pounds to a ton, not saying anything
about the irregularity of the overweight. The following is an exact account
of J. T. Pierce's store prices compared with the stores in the town of
Warrior, distance from Pierce's mines about one and one-half miles; but the
miners are not allowed to deal in Warrior unless after night, when they will
not be seen carrying contraband goods to their homes. A more damnable system of tyranny as practiced by this firm I have never seen, and I doubt
whether there is a cursed pluck-me in the United States that can compare with
the aforesaid Pierce. These are his figures:

	PRICES		PRICES
	At J. T. Pierce's Store		*At the Warrior Stores*
Flour per barrel.	$ 9.00	Flour per barrel.	$6.00
Meat per 100 pounds	13.00	Meat per 100 pounds	7.00
Corn meal per sack	2.75	Corn meal per sack.	1.75
Sugar 6 lbs. for.	1.00	Sugar 9 to 10 lbs. for.	1.00
Coffee 3½ lbs. for.	1.00	Coffee 4 to 6 lbs. for.	1.00
Tea per pound	1.00	Tea per pound	.50
Cheese per pound.	.20	Cheese per pound.	.12½

. . . Here is a sample of Mr. Pierce's Christian charity toward his fellow
man: There is a man here by the name of G. B. Elliott, who sent to New York
and had a lot of tea shipped here to sell as cheap as he could to his fellow
miners, and he commenced to sell tea at 65 cents per pound. It got to Mr.
Pierce's ear, and he at once sent his partner to Mr. Elliott's house to
ascertain if the report was true, when Mrs. Elliott informed him that such
was the case. At the same time Pierce was selling tea in the pluck-me store
(I mean the robber's den) for one dollar and fifty cents. He immediately
ordered Mr. Elliott to emigrate from his mines, or to put it a little plainer,
to take out his tools, which I believe was perfect right, for a man that
would undertake to sell a miner anything lower than a pluck-me store belonging
to a coal operator ought not to be allowed to run at large, because he is
calculated to ruin the public reputation of the noble pluck-men system.

"Dawson"

National Labor Tribune, April 5, 1879.

17.

Jefferson Mines, March 28, 1879.

Perhaps your many readers are somewhat surprised at not hearing anything
from this place for so long a time. As matters are stirred up so here I am
much surprised myself. . . .
First, the Warrior mines went on strike, as Pierce, the Alabama Co. and
their neighbors all reduced wages from $1 to 75¢ per tone for digging coal.
Two weeks later the superintendent called the miners together, in order to
reduce the price of digging at Jefferson mines from $1 to 87½¢ per ton. After
about a month's work at the old price, the miners proposed a strike after
working out the old price notice. Men have flocked in here from every direction, not knowing the condition of things until they got here. They overcrowded the mines, and the company stocked coal. The conclusion was then
reached, what good would a strike do against a large pile of lump coal in the

summer season when work is dull? This is all on account of men not being
notified as to how things were here.

"A Close Looker"

National Labor Tribune, April 5, 1879.

18.

Helena, April 16, 1879.

. . . The Montgomery workingmen have a full ticket in the field for the
coming city election, and there is nothing under heaven to hinder them from
succeeding if they but stand firm in the faith. The people of Alabama are
tired of ring rule. The Democratic papers call the workingmen the riff-raff
and fag ends of society. Workingmen, how does this go down? So long as we
remain in the traces we are the brawn and sinew of the land; that's when the
oily, office-seeking politican comes around to take a view, so to speak, of
his cattle that do the voting. Here is a sample of Democratic legislation in
Alabama: there was a ventilation bill presented the House of Representatives
for protection of the miners of Alabama, and one of the men elected to the
Legislature recommended the appointment of one of the penitentiary inspectors
for mining inspector, a man that never was inside of a coal mine unless when
he came there to see how the convicts were treated. I have heard that one
of the bosses of the Eureka Co., at Helena, asked another one what was the
meaning of two outlets, and the other fellow said it was a way for the men
to come out of the mines in case of danger, or to keep from getting in the
way of the cars. The other said the next thing the miners would want would
be a law to have a barroom in the mines.
The farmers here are very eager to organize for their better protection.
There will be a move made in a few days to organize them into a combination
for mutual protection. They are willing to wipe out convict labor by legislation. Workingmen of Alabama, rally your forces! Now is the time for action!
In peace prepare for war. The writer is at your service day or night, without
fear or compensation. . . . Miners, ironworkers, farmers, and every son of
toil, must come to a general understanding. We are falling one by one, and
amalgamation is the only thing that will bring us out of our present state of
servitude to tyranny. Now is the time to use calm judgment. The colored
man of the South can be no longer made use of by the political henchmen of
Republicans or Democrats, but we who are compelled to work side by side with
him must drop our prejudice and bigotry. This is the lever that's keeping
labor in bondage to capital. . . .

"Dawson"

National Labor Tribune, April 26, 1879.

19.

Warrior Station, May 13, 1879.

I write to let you and the boys along the line know that we of the Pierce
& Haney coal mines are still allowed the privilege of breathing, and as yet
have not been called upon by the operator to get an order for the same, but
how long we will be permitted to enjoy this privilege is more than I can tell,
as measures used by the taskmasters, let them be ever so bad, to crush our
manhood, have become so severe and occur so often that it seems as though we
will become hardened, and ere long lose the respect our wives have or once
had for us. Some of my brother workmen will say, Why don't you better your

condition and stand firm like men for that which rightly belongs to you? My
answer must be that we have been most shamelessly betrayed by men whom we
placed trust in. On the first of April last the operators dropped the price
of digging 25 cents on the ton, and the men all came out from both mines in
one solid body. Little did I think that we would be blacklegged; but such
was the case, for inside of three weeks sixteen blacklegs showed their colors.
I ask my brother workmen what we are going to do with those worthless things
who call themselves men? My advice to those who stood firm during the strike
was and is to give them all the rope they want and they will soon hang themselves. Perhaps the solid men who read your paper would not believe that we
have a man among us who did accept a suit of clothes (and a very superior
suit by the way) to act the rascal, and *did* use his influence in getting the
men to accept from the operator overtures which he knew at the time would
prove injurious to himself, his fellow workmen, and finally bring his family
to want. I am glad to say that this place of operation will not last much
longer, from the fact that coal cannot be dug here as cheap as other places
on this road, therefore those blacklegs will be brought to a speedy account
when they want to shift their base of operation. This is the only way to
treat those who prove false to the trust that others repose in them--herald
their names to places where they wish to go. I will here conclude by saying
that we have men here who will uphold the cause of labor.

"Reno"

National Labor Tribune, May 24, 1879.

20.

Jefferson Mines, May 24, 1879.

     I drop you a few lines to let the many readers of the TRIBUNE (the most
valuable labor paper in the Union . . .) know that we have not forgotten
them yet. Neither are we dead, d--k nor d--d. You all may know that we have
not had much work here since the last of March. We had 16 or 17 idle days
in April. The boys called it "a squeeze." They all got through it but three
of lads, who were denied at the store,and they "hit the railroad a week"
at 80 cents a day. The other boys made sport of them at first, but before
the work started old Pete knocked some of their stomachs about considerably,
but they got through, and went to work a day now and then. I suppose work
is as good here as anywhere down here, at this season. Warrior is working
about the same, or a little better. It might be well to state that we tried
the neighborhood to get up three clubs of subscribers to the TRIBUNE during
the "squeeze," and the only objection the farmers had to the paper was, as
they said, "We can never see anything in it for labor except for miners, mill
workers and puddlers. If those fellows would tell us all about corn, cotton,
wheat, potatoes, rice, eggs and so on, we would take it in a minute." So I
will start it for them. The fruit was all cut and dried by Mr. Jack Frost
the nights of the 3d, 4th, and 6th of April. Wheat is very promising on
Turkey Creek, five miles east of Jefferson. The gardens are young, but look
flourishing. Cotton and corn looks well. Hail and rain fell here on the
14th and 15th, accompanied with much wind. . . .
     The Jonesboro Greenback club is the boss of the county. Irondale is
next, and they held regular meetings every week. They are both composed of
colored men.
     Our brother Greenbacker, Michael Moran, at Helena, Alabama, is still
fighting for the cause.
     Warren Kelley, one of our best men, is out on a piece of land, two miles
from the mines. He bought a sore-footed mule from Mr. Pierce, of Warrior,
for $15, on credit, and the boys though they had the laugh on hom, but the
mule shed his hoofs, and is sound and well, and the boys now "laugh on the
other side of their mouths," says Peter Walker.

Kelley carried a girl 7½ miles last Sunday. She is a farmer's daughter, and went to the milliner shop this morning with a lot of fine goods. Her mother is gathering up flour and saving eggs, and her sister is scouring up the rooms. Kelley is loading two cars more every day. Is this a good sign?

W. J. Thomas

National Labor Tribune, May 31, 1879.

21.

Jefferson Mines, May 24 [1879].

Work continues dull in this section of the country. We get about three days in the week. The farms and gardens are looking fine. The young corn and cotton look nice and green. Turkey Creek wheat is looking bully. Eggs and butter are cheap.

"I am a Greenbacker," says Ad. Jackson, "But how is this thing fixed? I hear that six men are going to run for President, Brick Pomeroy, Peter Cooper, Gen. Butler, Gen. Grant, Tilden and Hayes, and the white Greenbackers here want Tilden elected. If so, I's not Greenback mor nothin' else." And Kelley said in reply, "Take the LABOR TRIBUNE and ask the editor or some of its readers, through the TRIBUNE, and you will get full satisfaction about who is on our side between now and next November one year. We, as laboring men and workers in the cause, should not be so quick to give over because we hear others say they want so and so. It is their business to want and our business to keep them out of their want. If I can see straight this is what is the matter now: When money was plenty and wages good, some big monopoly with tender hands and stud-horse clothes and Boston shoes on said, I want less money in circulation, wages reduced, more cotton and less corn, big public works and pluck-me stores, more convict labor and less wages for free labor. Then we would say, 'I am a Republican, or I am a Democrat; but if this be true I ain't nuthin'.'"

I would say to you and all others of the same mind, if you are a Greenbacker stand firm; be a man all over; have a strong constitution and a good resolution. . . . Because hypocrite Greenbacker says, I want Tilden elected, don't give up and say 'I ain't nuthin'. If we do we will soon be nothing, and what we once were—rich man's slave. . . .

Corn is worth 60 cents in cash—90 on time and a mortgage. In Birmingham the other day a man said to a merchant, "What is your corn worth?" "Ninety cents," he answered. "But for cash, I mean." "Got some to sell for cash," he answered. He wanted a mortgage.

The reason Mother Brown's funeral was postponed from the first Sunday in April to the second Sunday in July was because Rev. J.J.S. Hall was conducted to jail for kissing a colored woman with a rock. A witness against him went and found the rock at 10 o'clock in the night without a light, and brought it before the justice of the peace next morning. Two weeks later the same witness carried the rock to the Circuit Court and it was decided on court that no man could throw the rock. Now how did the witness feel? His name is Willis Harris. The kissing of the woman cost the parson $5, but it was a small rock, and she had just called him a bad name.

W. J. K. [Kelley]

National Labor Tribune, June 7, 1879.

22.

Warrior, June 30 [1879].

A short time ago I arrived in this little mining town, located 137 miles
south of Montgomery, on the South and North Alabama railroad, and am sorry
to have to say that work here, in the way of mining coal, is not brisk. The
men do not get more than half time, but seem to be able to support their
families even on this. The miners have experienced poverty to such a degree,
and for such a length of time, that they and their families do not shudder
at it, but look it squarely in the face, like little men. I have ofttimes
thought how proud the operators must feel to know they have employees who
possess the nerve to serve them regardless of the comforts of their families
or the education of their children. Nothing I admire in men more than a
steady nerve, but I must admit that this pleases me a little too well. When
I speak about the education of children, it causes me to dwell on the ignorance of the mining population of this town. Some of the men argue with me
that it takes thirty hundred weight to one ton of coal, and tell me they are
satisfied to give this, for if they do not the operator will come out behind
the return at the end of the month! Some of the men have figured to show me
that they are correct about this 3000 business. Ignorance seems to have as
great a hold on the toiling masses here as elsewhere. Some of the miners
contend that a scale drawing five tons can be fingered with by putting a block
of wood or gum underneath: that a car of coal that should weigh 1700 will
not draw much more than 1200. I contend that such cannot be done. Do you
suppose that the standard scales of our country (Fairbank's) can be made to
tell lies? Never! The men here are too superstitious, and if they are not
careful they will all have to be supported by the country, as they are so
extravagant, and cannot maintain their families at the rate they are now
going. . . .

"Reno"

National Labor Tribune, July 5, 1879.

23.

Jefferson Mines, July 6 [1879].

Work continues dull here, but we are promised better work for the future.
Some men get about all they want to do, as they have what we call a snatch
game—grab all the empty cars from the side track at noon and at night. If
there is work to-day and none to-morrow, these chaps will go in to-night and
load the empty cars left from to-day, and make a day, and rest with the other
men on the idle day. This is not taken off of them the next day. They work
—these greedy grabbers—nearly double as much as the other men, as their
booms show at the end of the month. A few of the men met to pass resolutions
against such acts, and decided among themselves that they would stop it
shortly. In two days after one of the leading men against the act was seen
going up the entry pushing an empty car at the rate of ten miles an hour.
About an hour later, two loaded cars were found standing in his room! He will
so stop his part of it, as at that rate overwork is liable to make him stop a
hole in a "wooden overcoat." Now, as the leading man against the act is guilty
of such tricks as these, there should be some plan devised to end it. . . .
Again I will say if any of your readers come this way looking for work,
you had better bring an extra piece of pie or bread and butter along with you
for the trainers and drivers. Good grub will send out more coal for you in
a day than two picks and a helper. Don't fail to bring it if you come. If
you have any to spare, you might bring me some, and I will stay outside and
eat it, and not give it to the 5 drivers.
George W. Griffin, our worst rumseller, is gone. He stabbed Sidney

Rogers, leaving three or four bad cuts in his left side, and two on his arm. Sidney Rogers is a colored man, and staunch Greenbacker, and one we all love, and the rumseller had better not show himself here any more.

"A Close Looker"

National Labor Tribune, July 12, 1879.

24.

Helena, July 25 [1879].

As it has been some time since you had any news from this place, I will endeavor to jot down a few lines to give the friends of our manly paper an understanding of the condition of our people in this section of the sunny south (not the solid south by a long way, for we are pulling off the mask of the political hulks, and by eighteen hundred and eighty they will find us tramping on their corns with a vengeance.)

Labor in the mines is very dull at present, except for convicts, and they get all they can do, and about as much as two common men can do. Well, this is a Democratic State, and [the] Democracy is the champion of labor, and so is the devil. I see a plank in the Pennsylvania platform of the late Democratic convention (I believe it is the eighth) which says in so many words that Democracy is the friend of labor. Said plank is a flaming lie, and the actions of the Democratic party throughout the land proves it to be so. Alabama, Tennessee, Georgia, Ohio, New York and New Jersey are all governed by Democratic governors, and said States have the infernal audacity to bring their convict labor in competition with free labor. Ask the miners of Ohio what Democracy has done for them, and their answer will be: "Well, a Democratic governor gave us a Chinese lantern for a mine inspector." Ask the cigar maker of West Virginia what the Democratic governor and House of Representatives has done for them, and their answer will be: "It has deprived us of the honest means of a decent support for our families by sending thieves and felons of the State's prison to work in competition at twenty-five cents per day." Alabama has about 300 convicts working in the coal mines who are used far worse than mules or oxen. Tennessee has about 600 working in and about the mines. Georgia has several hundred, and the Democratic politicians have begun to shoot and kill each other in order to get the spoils of their thieving legislation. The notorious robbers belonging to that party first enact a law to degrade free labor and deprive it of work, and the next step is to pass what is called the tramp law. By this law they grab up some good Democratic workingman whose father has been a Democrat all his life time, and if the devil should take him he is going to stick to the old party, so he wakes up some fine morning with a shackle on his leg, to find out that a Democratic governor has sold him to a coal mine robber for the enormous sum of $6 per month--the money, of course, to go into the state treasury. . . .

The mines here have changed hands from Eureka Company to the Pratt Coal Company. No. 1 mines are working steady, with 70 convicts. The coal is used for coking purposes. The company are sinking two new slopes. The Williams mines will be worked by 240 convicts, and the Conglomerate by what is called free labor. L. W. Johns has been made general superintendent of the Pratt Company, and Peter Thomas mine boss. Davis & Carr's mines are working steadily, employing about six men. Coketon mine, five miles from Birmingham, employs 50 miners. It is a new mine, and George McDonald is mine boss. New Castle mines are working with 106 convicts and about 25 free men; the principal part of the work done there is iron ore mining. The Jefferson mines are working with a full force. . . .

"Dawson"

National Labor Tribune, August 2, 1879.

25.

Helena, August 5 [1879].

It seems to me that the miners along the line of the North and South
Alabama railroad are the most cowardly set of men it has been our lot to
witness in this free land of ours. We have been making some powerful efforts
to organize the laboring class of people in this State for some time back, and
among the various branches of trades. We find the miners are the worst, notwithstanding the various schemes and devices practiced by their employers
to deprive them of their just rights. Some time ago we were invited to the
town of Warrior, and on arriving there we were convinced that the men had a
good share of manhood in their breasts, but their actions since our visit
among them proves to the contrary. If those men knew what sacrifices we
made in order to bring them among our grand whole temple of man's industrial
rights they would not treat us as if we were some mongrel hyena. The men
along this road will have to shoulder a little more manhood if they intend
to ever raise their children up to the standard of a Christian race of people.
There are some as good men at Warrior as walks the land to-day, but the men
at the helm will have to show a little more determination to be men, or else
we will all sink together. Now is the critical time to stand. . . .
        The cause of labor is advancing in our State. The colored race can be
no more hitched up to the infernal car of Juggernaut. The colored men of
Alabama have one of the truest men in the labor movement amongst them--W. J.
Thomas; he is a miner at Jefferson Mines; his heart is in the right place.
Would to God every miner in the State had the same courage that he embraces
in his manly bosom. I hope to see the men there prepare to put Mr. Thomas
in the field in 1880. This will be a year when bigots and fanatics will have
to fall to the rear and let men of brave hearts come to the front. It will
be a question of whether we will be ruled by a plutocracy or aristocracy of
money-bags who care not for the industrial power so long as their rapacious
maw is satisfied. Then, fellow workmen, let me, in the name of a just and
merciful God, beg of you to cast aside your religious and national prejudices;
let labor have no religion or nationality. Remember God made all of us, and
will require a strict account of each of us at the last day.
                        "Dawson"

National Labor Tribune, August 16, 1879.

26.

Jefferson Mines, August [1879].

It seems as though Mr. Dawson, at Helena, has lost confidence in the
miners along this line of road, or at least he calls the most of them "cowards."
There is a volume in that word! In the first place, he means the miners no
harm, but their good. He has labored long and faithfully, and it is no
wonder the man is disheartened. But he should consider, as the good old man
did when he was called on to lead in prayer. He began in this way: "O Lord!
O Lord, ah! we are in a might bad fix, ah; and we all have fell in the ditch
together, ah." And so it is with the people in this part of the country. In
the first place, the colored people are all slaves, and the white laboring
men are all in bondage. The man that has a moral influence is so blinded with
prejudice that he leads his hundreds to the ditch, and all fall in. Sure
enough this is the aim and object of the few that aspire to rule, and have all
this country under their control. Had it not been for the great and noble
principles slowly unfolding to our minds, we, no doubt, to-day would have been
so engulfed that we would never have dared to make the start. I hope to see
the day when it unfolds itself as a canopy which will shade the trees of liberty, when all sons of toil may be clothed with its principles, and come out

from under the yoke of bondage.

The people in this part of the country are very superstitious. The most of them believe that there is a secret organization pointing directly or indirectly to their persons and property. This is not so. If they will only take the TRIBUNE, and read it, and study its principles, they will find out their mistake. If I am not deceived, it is for the protection of all honest *industry*. But it is pointed directly and indirectly against all extortioners, thieves and swindlers in our government. It will take time and patience, in this part of the country. The people see that the Greenback-Labor party is the party to hold to, and I hope that by 1880 we can say, as Kanawha country, West Virginia, has said, "Get thee hence, Satan." In conclusion, I will say, take the advice of your friend Dawson, and say, "we will stand shoulder to shoulder."

D. J.

National Labor Tribune, August 30, 1879.

27.

Jefferson Mines, August 27 [1879].

. . . Work is plentiful in the mines, as the men have all they can do, and the prospects look bright for the future. Some of the Greenbackers hereabout still stand for the right, and some of the "Democratic Greenbackers," who voted what we call a mixed ticket last August, still urge the colored people to stand to the Greenback ticket, while they themselves are astraddle of the fence, and deeply in love with the Democratic party. I will say one thing plainly, the colored people in this county, one with another, have been bull-dozed and fooled as long as they intend to be. We organized into the Greenback party last year, and intend to stand as long as there is a paper printed in that name. We mean business, and nothing more, but there is a "fly in the mug" somewhere, and when it comes out we will see it. Now, if the white men here and elsewhere want us to stand by them in the way of standing up for wages, and voting the Greenback ticket, and on many other things that they ask us to join them in, they must come out on the square, and stand up like men, and do more themselves, as well as tell us and do nothing themselves. There are some good, sound Greenbackers here among the whites, but they are not so plentiful as strangers might think. . . . There is no use in advertising a great mess [sic] in favor of men being Greenbackers, and they dead out the other way. Now if the men will come out solid on the platform, and let us hear from them often, and not raise a dust about election times, and then lie down and sleep until the time comes again, there will be better hopes kindled. . . .

Mr. M. Moran is a solid Greenbacker and a gentleman, and treats every poor man alike when he can, but know there are some men in society that cannot bear good treatment. They want colored men to come in on the edges until it comes to tax-paying and voting for their party, then the Negro is called "colored gents," and must come into their party, and feast off the best. Mr. Moran is a good hearted, manly gentleman, and should be in the field in 1880. Greenbackers that will not follow him are no friends to labor, and ought to be slaves, as there is no chance for anything else the way men are doing. May God bless this man and make Helena bloom.

"A Close Looker"

National Labor Tribune, September 13, 1879.

28.

Birmingham, September 15 [1879].

As the miners all over the country are doing something to advance and protect their interests, I think it is short time that we, the miners of Alabama, should endeavor to do something towards getting at a little more uniform system of mining. In looking for work at mining, in that section of [the] country I find that miners are divided to a considerable extent among themselves. For instance, the miners at Pierce's mines are mining at 75 cents per ton and the Alabama mine the same price. The vein is a 3 foot vein of coal, and at Neighbor & Worthington's the miners are working a 2 to 2-1/2 ft vein for the same price. Then there is the Jefferson shaft miners working at 87-1/2 cents per ton, in from 20 inches to a 2 foot vein. But here comes the softest snap of all, the New Castle men mining coal at about 35 cents a car. Then comes the Pratt mines, at Coketon, where there are from 3 to 4 feet of coal mined for 40 cents per ton. But here are the grandest set of tools in the whole region; the Helena miners are working at from 35 to 25 cents per ton in a 3-1/2 foot vein, and pay $3.50 per keg for powder. This coal was formerly paid for at 40 cents per ton, but some of the men down there refuse to move in regard to the question of a just price for coal mining. The fact of the matter is, we have here a class of men who would consider themselves union men of the first water if they were in the northern or western coal fields.

The miners in Alabama have no organization to protect their interests or advocate their cause, and they are in a different position from any mining locality in the United States, viz: All capitalists employing labor in this part of the country have two sorts of labor, and some of them three sorts of labor. First, the poor white man, who is dependent on capital for his daily bread; second, the colored man, who is in the same fix; and third, the convict, who has no alternative but to go where his taskmasters choose to lead him in chains. . . . Can any man that casts an eye around him help seeing at a glance that capital has no religion or nationality in its ranks? You never find these causes at work among any other class except it be the poor, unfortunate laborer who keeps the thousands of idle paupers and swindlers rolling in luxury by their stubbornness in not protecting or advancing their own interests. In bringing this matter before the laboring men of this place, I hope I have not hurt the feelings of any man who earns his living according to just methods.

"Olympic"

National Labor Tribune, September 27, 1879.

29.

Helena, October 4, 1879.

. . . In the TRIBUNE of September 27th I showed how divided the miners on the North and South railroad of Alabama are as regards a uniform price for mining coal. One would suppose that all emigrated from China or some other heathen country, to see the way they conduct themselves. There is no system whatever among the miners of this region, and I would suggest that a general convention to be called for November 1st, 1879, to come to some conclusion as regards a system to work by, the same as other trades have all over the country, and not be, as we are at present, blacksheeping each other out of work.

The Greenback-Labor men of Alabama are at work already preparing for that conflict in 1880, viz., the overthrow of the money power. In the northern part of the State, Hon. W. M. Lowe, member of Congress, is speaking day and night; another man is also busily engaged, Paul Jones. They are making the valleys ring with the shouts of the honest farmers rallying to the Green-back standard. In Jefferson County we are confident of sweeping the rotten dynasty of Bourbonism out of existence. The Bourbons have threatened the shot-gun argument up in North Alabama. That shows how they are the people's party. Their hardware, bond-mongering press yell that the Greenback party is made up of Republicans! Where are all the Democrats that left the rotten old hulk in Maine in '66? The Greenback-Labor men of Mississippi are swarm-ing like bees in a hive. Bourbonism threatens a shot-gun diet there. The other day the Greenback-Labor men were going to hold a convention, but the Spartan band were not made up of rum-shop material and they marched to the hall three hundred strong, and nominated their officers, and dispersed like men who know what freedom means. I tell you the animal is very near dead down South. Will the working classes of the North, West and East see to it that they cast their ballots for home and liberty in 1880, and not for the money-grabbing machine that is run for the benefit of the sharks of wall street?

Jefferson county, Alabama, has sixteen Greenback-Labor clubs, and several more have in view an organization during the coming fall. Well, we are all right down here. There are men here who go to work at two and three o'clock in the morning, and then after spending fifteen or sixteen hours in their cakes, come out and swear by their maker that they are the best miners on the works--just and honest men! Pass those animals by with contempt and scorn. Shun them as you would a viper.

                                                    "Olympic"

National Labor Tribune, October 18, 1879.

                                    30.

                                            Montgomery, October 20 [1879].

    . . . Birmingham, Ala., is the center of the iron and coal region, and is the livest [sic] town I have seen in the South. There are three foundries, three machine shops, and the S. and N.A.R.R. shops are located there, and a large iron furnace is building. If the place is not killed by rings and monopolies, it will make a good town. Politically, Alabama is in a bad fix. All things are run by Bourbons, and they are in all the rings. There is no organization amongst labor, no Brotherhood of Engineers, no union of the miners.

    I am told that the charter of the S. & N.A.R.R. requires that the Presi-dent of the company shall reside in the State of Alabama. Col. Stass draws a salary of the aforesaid office, and it said he is a very nice man. and gives liberally to the churches. He is also a fine politician and runs the Oxmoor furnaces. The Governor of the State is interested in the coal mines, and in the labor of the penitentiary convicts. He would make an excellent charter member for a new Standard Oil Co. He has a 'grab all,' or a train with groceries and merchandise running over his division of the road to sell to employees only, many of whom get only 80 cents per day. The railroad is generally two and a half month's behind, and when the pay car arrives there is not much money to pay. This bonanza is said to be worth a cool $40,000 per year. I am told that the "grab" will not offer to sell here, as they are afraid they will have to pay license. If I was a merchant on that road I would examine and see if there was no law to make them pay license. On the Memphis and Charleston and the S. & N.A.R.R. many Negro firemen and brakemen are employed. Many engineers and conductors prefer Negroes as they can make them wait on them, black their shoes, etc., and I have heard it intimated that some Negroes give as much as $15 per month to them to retain their jobs.
    . . .

                                            "New Deal"

National Labor Tribune, November 8, 1879.

31.

Helena, November 17 [1879].

Fellow miners and workingmen, the time has come for us to act together.
Our fellow toilers are moving in one grand mass all over this noble land of
ours, (it ought to be ours, only for our cowardice). Therefore, I ask you,
men of Alabama, to be up and doing your duty. The time is coming when labor
will assert its rights all over the land, and I hope all over the earth,
for "earth is the Lord's and the fullness thereof," but it seems our paternal
government don't think so, as they have given a very large slice of to the
mine and railroad robbers. Well, there are two ways to rectify wrongs in
this country, and if we fail in the legitimate way, we will have the best
side of the question in the second way, as muscle will be the ruling factor
when the day comes. Therefore, let all who love liberty and justice band
together in one noble industrial army. Self-preservation is the first law
of nature, and eternal vigilance is the price of liberty. While the sluggard
of labor slept the national bankers and the railroad kings were in the halls
of legislation riveting the chains of slavery on the toiling masses. They
can send their agents with a few silver or gold dollars over from London,
and buy more legislation in one hour in Congress, than the forty-eight millions of so-called freemen can in ten years.

Messrs. Editors, you never hear those fellows fighting about their
"nationality" or their "religion" when they meet. No! they have no nationality or religion. The click of the dollar is the only God Shylock kneels to
adore. It is left to the ever-worked half-starved, under-paid serf of
American freedom to drink rotgut whisky and squabble about such matters,
and the more he uses of the tangle-foot the easier he is to manage! It only
takes one short day or night for him to invest his little capital, and then
there is no need of a clerk or agent to take care of his book account. He
returns to his den the next Monday morning to serve his master for a small
pittance, and when earned he even begrudges it to his wife and children! . . .
We prefer to leave our few dollars at the bar-room, and when meeting night
comes around our seat in the lodge is vacant. John Tippler has no time to
attend to the labor question. When one o'clock in the morning comes, he
must be getting ready to go into the mine, or shop, or factory, or on the
railroad. He gets up out of his bed at 12 or 2 o'clock at night, and leaves
the land of dreams and goes forth to spend 15 or 16 hours in a coal mine, and
he comes perhaps at eight or nine o'clock at night. What does he resemble?
Well, there he is, look at him yourself; I won't tire you, as it costs
nothing to see him after he is out of the works, but you will not dare to go
down in the mine to see him for fear you might tell him some dangerous idea
about how mankind in general ought to live--not as they are at the present
trying to rob and swindle each other, however. Let us have a little light
on the question of organization. . . . Let all the miners in the United
States band together under the standard ****, and all the organizations we
want is there.

Michael F. Moran

National Labor Tribune, November 22, 1879.

32.

Jefferson Mines, December 9 [1879].

. . . We are still working at 87-1/2 cents for 2240 pounds, and it is
a drag sure enough. We all want the other 12-1/2 cents to make it $1.,
though none of us come out plainly and ask for it, though we still live in
hope that the company will comply with the request that we made on the 1st
of November, and which I saw stated in the TRIBUNE of November 22d. Since
then several of the men have left here and got work at other places, and

seem well pleased with the change, though the most of us still here have
families, and don't want any strike. We are willing to uphold free capital
as long as possible, but I think the time has come that something must be
done, or we will be living as Henry Ward Beecher says we should live, though
I don't think that there will be much love left with our wives, if we bring
them and the little ones to bread and water. I think that times will take
a change in this part of the country soon, for we are moving slowly but
steadily in the right direction. The Greenback element, which the aristocracy thought to be dead, our good old farming citizens have been watching.
They have been weighing the principles of the party until they are satisfied
they are sound, and if they only knew the principles of the organization,
there would be a brotherhood in this country strong enough to carry the day
at any and every election in spite of the influence of aristocrats, supplemented by the codfish aristocracy of the country.

A letter was recently sent by the miners of Pierce's mines to the men
working in the other pits, and signed "So called Blacklegs," in which they
proposed that a meeting be held and the question affecting them be discussed.
The Jefferson shaft miners declined to meet them as a body, but [said] that
if they desired they could meet their accusers face to face. We also offered
to discuss the future of labor in this district with them, which they also
declined. I am in favor, if they can prove themselves clear of the charges
against them, to lift the ban from them and make them free men once more.
They certainly can prove themselves clear of the charges made against them
if untrue, and owe it to themselves to do so. The columns of the NATIONAL
LABOR TRIBUNE will certainly be open to them to do so, if they will do it.
Will they do it?

Henry Ovenlid

National Labor Tribune, December 20, 1879.

33. A BLACK MINISTER EXPLAINS HIS SHIFT FROM THE REPUBLICAN

TO THE GREENBACK-LABOR PARTY

A few days ago, while passing the streets in Terre Haute, I saw a black
dog, and a gentleman passing by, snapping his fingers at the dog, said, "That
is a little Republican." (Laughter) His remark was in keeping with the
sentiment of the Republican party, that every man whose face is tanned must
necessarily vote and affiliate with that party. . . . I am glad I have lived
to see the day when we can make our own selection, and when the colored people
of the United States are making their own selection. . . . I read in the
Book of Truth that God sometimes chooses weaklings to confound the mighty.
. . . The laboring men of the country understand their business as well, and
I think probably a little better, than our former leaders. . . . While many
men have gone south to guide the color there, after the elections our people
have been left to the mercy of the south; and I am informed by a gentleman
supposed to know, they are willing to come into the National party at any
moment, and with the assistance of the laboring masses, the colored men of
the north and south will preserve this country as the land of the free and
the home of the brave. . . .

Speech of Reverend H. Anderson before Indiana State National Greenback Con
vention, quoted in the *National Labor Tribune,* July 6, 1878.

34.   THE PEOPLE'S LEAGUE

The New Organization of Colored Voters

When the so-called States Equal Rights League was in session in Pittsburgh it will be remembered that a number of delegates of Nationalistic and Democratic proclivities were ejected from the meeting because they declined to indorse a resolution pledging their support to the Republican party. The resolutions emanated from Mackey's man, W. D. Forten, a colored politician of Philadelphia, whose family is well provided for in the way of official position, and who for that asked the colored men of Western Pennsylvania to support his party. For two days past these ejected delegates have been in session, and here is the result of Friday's session:

THE SO-CALLED EQUAL RIGHTS' LEAGUE

In the absence of the Chairman, J. Grandison, R. A. Hall was called to the chair. The minutes of the last meeting were read and adopted. The report of the Committee on Grievances, Messrs. A. Hawkins, P. A. Noler and J. G. Hawkins, was read and adopted, as follows:

Pittsburgh, Aug. 29, 1878.

To the citizens of Allegheny county and State of Pennsylvania: Fellow Citizens, Members and
Gentlemen:

We deem it essential that we should bring to your notice the action of the so-called Equal Right's League that met in Avery Hall, Allegheny City, on the 20th of August, in denouncing all the western delegates, not by the constitution or parliamentary law, but from their malicious tyranny. There was a Committee on Credentials appointed but no Committee on Contesting Delegations. When the Committee on Credentials was announced to make its report, it was as follows:

"Mr. President--These are the names of the men the Board decides shall be the delegates to this convention."

And, we, your delegates, not hearing our several names called, rose to ascertain the cause. We were told that our credentials were thrown in the scrap and waste basket. We then wanted to know why we got no other redress. The reply was that we were not members until we signed a pledge to support the whole Republican ticket and candidates, which we would not do. We therefore submit this resolution for your considerations:

Resolved, That we organize ourselves into a league, to be known as the People's League.

The resolution was unanimously adopted.

Mr. Paul J. Carson reported that he had interviewed a large number of the colored citizens of Western Pennsylvania in relation to the unjust action of the State Equal Rights' League, and learned their sentiments concerning the contemplated organization of the People's League, many believing that such an enterprise would be a great assistance in advancing the best interests of the colored people in Pennsylvania and their race in general. Mr. Aveler, in a brief address, related the unjust action of the League.

PLATFORM ADOPTED

After a consultation, Prof. Wm. Howard Day presented the following platform, which was also unanimously adopted:

Opposed to the later methods and tyrannical action of the Pennsylvania State Equal Rights League, which has, by a few men, been made merely the appendage to the Republican party, and which has demanded a political test which sought to pledge us, willing or unwilling, to the support of the Republican candidates in the campaign of 1878; knowing the pledge to be unconstitutional and impolitic, and believing that the Pennsylvania State Equal Rights League, with its present methods and control, to be barren of usefulness; and also believing that the colored citizens should unite for their own intellectual, industrial, mechanical and social improvement, with permission to hold such political views as they choose, and to vote as they may deem best, we form a new State organization "of the people, by the people, and for the people," working out our political salvation through existing or new political parties, as may seem wise to each of us.

OFFICERS ELECTED

The chair appointed a committee of three on nominations, Messrs. Aveler, Harkers and Carson, who reported the following, who were unanimously elected as officers of the People's Equal Rights League:

President--C. M. Brown, Harrisburg.

Vice Presidents--D. B. Bowser, Philadelphia; R. A. Hall, Pittsburgh; J. B. Popel, Harrisburg; P. J. Carson, Pittsburgh; A. Bettencourt, Philadelphia; W. L. Ramsey, Wilkesbarre.

Corresponding Secretaries--R. W. Bell, Pittsburgh; Chas. O'Donnell, Pittsburgh; S. P. Hood, Philadelphia.

Recording Secretaries--John H. Jones, Pittsburgh; S. P. Irvin, Philadelphia; I. C. Harris, Pittsburgh.

Treasurer--Francis A. Hall, Pittsburgh.

Chaplains--Rev. J. P. Hamer, Carlisle; Rev. Jesse Cowles, Pittsburgh; Rev. Geo. M. Bonner, Harrisburg.

COUNCIL OF ADMINISTRATION

Chairman--Wm. Howard Day, Harrisburg; Alfred Hawkins, Pittsburgh; Thos. L. White, Chambersburg; Peter R. Tucker, Philadelphia; Wm. H. Still, Reading; B. F. Towns, Wilkesbarre; J. W. Henry, Franklin; Jos. Lebar, Lancaster; S. T. Linsey, Pittsburgh; D. M. Robinson, Harrisburg, Pedro A. Aveler, East Liberty; James Armstrong, Marietta; Philip Peterson, Allegheny City; C. W. Harley, Harrisburgh; M. Cupit, York; R. Knox, Huntingdon, John L. Griffith, Lewistown; S. J. Jordan, Carlisle; Jno. Turfley, Pittsburgh; Wm. H. Rex, Wilkesbarre; M. S. Pugh, Pittsburgh; Geo. Barnes, Shippensburg; J. C. Brown, Pittsburgh; M. J. Terry, Reading.

ANOTHER MEETING

The committee further reported that a mass convention of the colored people of Pennsylvania who are opposed to the action of the Pennsylvania State Equal Rights League, and in favor of the formation of a People's League, be called to assemble in the city of Pittsburgh, on Tuesday morning October 18th, 1878, at 10 o'clock.

The meeting was well attended and very enthusiastic, and after routine business, adjourned to reassemble again on Tuesday, September 10th and to hold a ratification meeting in the evening.

National Labor Tribune, September 7, 1878.

35. ARKANSAS GREENBACKERS

From a private letter to Mr. Isaac Cline, from his brother in Little Rock, Ark., we take the following extract:

Yesterday morning I was ordered to go out of town about one mile to Jacoby's Grove, and write up a barbecue. I got into a carriage and reached the grove before the speaking began. Now, a Southern barbecue and political meeting differs widely from the same thing anywhere else. I found here one large ox, three sheep and a calf on the spit, all being cooked by colored men, to be served up free of cost to all who wished to eat. As I wandered through the grove I saw dozens and dozens of revolvers hanging in belts on the Southern bloods, all prepared and ready for use. The barbecue was given by the Greenback club, and the candidates on the Democratic ticket were invited to discuss the questions at issue. Quite a number accepted, and twenty-minutes were allowed each speaker, and in all my life I never saw men so badly beaten as the Democrats were. You must understand this county, and in fact the State, has three negroes to one white person, and those negroes to a man are solid Greenbackers, and some few of them are the best speakers I ever listened to in all my life. They carry their lives right in their hands--brave, cool and determined to have all their rights. One to three shooting affairs have occurred every week since I have been in the State.

National Labor Tribune, August 10, 1878.

VIII

BLACK AND WHITE LABOR RELATIONS, 1870–1878

BLACK AND WHITE LABOR RELATIONS, 1870-1878

The complex cross-currents of race relations within the American labor movement crystallized during the 1870s. Within the span of a few short years, the Republican Party retreated from Radical Reconstruction, the economy slumped with the Panic of 1873, and industrial production was severely disrupted by massive strikes, especially the nation's first general strike in 1877. In this convulsive atmosphere of turmoil, it was natural that conflicting attitudes regarding the role of black workers in the labor movement would dramatically come to the forefront. The reform press in particular, such as the National Anti-Slavery Standard and the Workingman's Advocate, official organ of the National Labor Union, steadfastly argued for the inclusion of blacks in working-class organizations. The Advocate reminded white workers that "enlightened self-interest" alone required that blacks be organized, for those workers who did not belong to the movement certainly would be used to break it (Doc. 1-6, 28).

The facts seldom conformed with the ideal, however. For example, the Bricklayers' National Union met in convention in January 1871. On the subject of the admission of Negroes, local chapter representatives vowed that they "would never admit a nigger into their fellowship" (Doc. 7). Even though the Workingman's Advocate opposed the Bricklayers' stand on admission (Doc. 8), the paper exerted no influence in such matters. Actually, only the Marxist International Workingmen's Association (First International) actively practiced racial equality in its admissions (Doc. 11, 14, 16). In Galveston, Texas, for example, the Workingmen met to consider a proposal requesting that blacks join the organization. Even though the local racist faction opposed the move and split with the union over the issue, the Workingmen leaders insisted on adherence to the principle of inclusion (Doc. 19-21, 34-39).

Although the Internationals, the Colored National Labor Union, and the reform press, all supported labor solidarity (Doc. 18), most unions continued to bar Negroes. Even worse, they threatened the continued existence of blacks in the skilled crafts by restricting black youths from the crucial apprenticeships required for learning most trades (Doc. 17). Less prestigious employment was barred to blacks as well, for as one observer noted, "the foundry, the factory, the workshops of every kind, are closed against us, whether they are public or private" (Doc. 24). The bedrock racial conservatism among America's white workers seemed impervious to the egalitarian idealism of the more progressive labor reformers (Doc. 27).

As the labor reformers predicted, if black workers were excluded from the movement, they would be used to undermine its success. Thus, when white coal miners in the Hocking Valley of Southern Ohio struck for better wages in 1874, 300 or 400 strikebreakers were imported to work the mines. Since whites themselves restricted blacks from joining unions there seemed little reason for blacks to respect union picket lines when those same whites went out on strike (Doc. 29-32).

RACE RELATIONS BETWEEN BLACK AND WHITE WORKERS

1. A QUESTION OF COLOR

In a report of the committee of the Labor Reform party, given in the
second number of the new Labor paper, the N. Y. *Workman,* we find this statement of Mr. Browning the editor of that periodical:

"Mr. Browning's district being called, he stated that although his district was chartered, he would bring his associates at the next session, and
go through the required formalities in presence of the committee. He had
postponed this for the reason that a colored gentleman of influence among his
brethren in the district might be added to the list, and he desired information
on that point."

Mr. D. S. Griffin moved that the admission of the colored gentleman be
disposed of, and Mr. Browning complete his charter. Mr. Taylor seconded the
motion, and hoped that the question of color would be postponed until the
organization of the General Committee. Mr. Walsh said he belonged to a race
of people who had been disfranchised for a long time, and he recognized no
nationalities or colors; to him they were equally eligible, but he deemed it
unwise to introduce the question of color at present. This was all that was
said at the meeting upon the subject. In our opinion it was a meritorious
action in Mr. Browning to endeavor to obtain an answer to the question. In
the present state of the Labor Movement it is important to the public to know
whether our workingmen in power are likely to prove more select than the
present Senators and Ambassadors of the United States, and more aristocratic
than the titled dignitaries of any court in Europe.

H.

National Anti-Slavery Standard, April 9, 1870.

2. "A FELLOWSHIP THAT SHALL KNOW NO CASTE "

GEORGE E. McNEIL, of Boston, in forwarding a club of subscribers for the
new series of THE STANDARD, writes:

"Now that the black man has come out of the bondage of chattel slavery,
as his white brother, centuries ago came out of villenage, it is well that
you, who have so earnestly and faithfully worked for his enfranchisement,
should unite him to us his fellow workers in unity of purpose and harmony of
action. For through our joint agitation of the "great question of labor"--
an agitation made possible by the old STANDARD and its old standard bearer--
shall come a fellowship that shall know no caste. Then labor, emancipated
from the thraldom of wage service, shall make *Land monopoly* and *Ballot monopoly* disappear before the rising sun of cooperation, made practicable through
the enlarged culture, increased product, and equitable distribution, that comes
by less hours of toil. Gladly shall I hail the day when THE STANDARD, crowned
with the laurels of achieved victory, shall wave above the hosts of labor,
marching forward toward an enemy more firmly entrenched than any that have yet
retreated before its hero legions."

National Anti-Slavery Standard, April 9, 1870.

3.   "LOYALTY" AND "THE NIGGER "

We are sick of having to daily encounter the blanket sheets full of meaningless twaddle, which greet our vision upon taking up our exchanges for perusal. The entire trashy mass, if reduced in the crucible of common sense to its legitimate proportions, would be found to be nothing more nor less than the words that we have selected to caption this chapter. We are full to satiety, of the vicious stuff. That which emanates from radical quill-driver's empty pates, containing less knowledge of good Saxon, than of filthy billingsgate, and less ordinary common sense than either, is a rascally swindle, a contemptible cheat, designed as a cover for the most outrageous of official malversation, a screen behind which a privileged few may toy with the rights of a sacrificed people. What we find in Democratic vehicles of mental garbage, for it is a scandalous libel upon the language to call them newspapers, is little or no better. Sometimes in terms of sufficient filthiness, to befoul the mouth of a Manchester fishwoman, or a Massachusetts congressman, never in intelligible parlance, we find them continually catering to vicious prejudice, the only outgrowth of which is unfit for decent entertainment. A negro, for he is not a "nigger," is as good as a white man in his proper place, and his proper place is as high up the social ladder as he can get, without trespassing upon the rights of others.

We have no scruples in ventilating this belief, though it may be, and no doubt is out of accord with views entertained by some who read the ADVOCATE. The manacles recently taken from the black man, he who is blindly fighting to keep the former as deep in the mire of ignorance, as ever he was in the palmiest days of slavery, is laboring with all his main to assume, and he deserves no better reward for this infamy. The proper sphere of the black man is by the side of his white citizen brethren, in a duel to the death with the odious money tyranny, which entertains for each an equal love.

Tammany Hall and Beaumont, or Union Leagues and Claflin, are no more the friends of the white, than of the black workingman. The perpetuation of their soulless regime, depends upon their ability to enforce a continuance of this blind battle of prejudices, purposely generated by the political excesses of each. Loyalty, which should be a sacred word to every Republican citizen, has become nauseating in the ears of common sense. Not that we would have any disloyal; we would have a loyalty of the greatest comprehensiveness conceivable. We would have a man loyal, first to his God, then to his family, and then to his country. If a man be loyal in the legitimate sense of the word, to the two former, he must be so to the latter. But loyalty does not mean simply an ever-present readiness to resist those who would take up arms against a wicked regime, into which it may have fallen. It means the duty of the citizen to be, a careful, honest and logical inquirer into the causes of the alleged grievances for which some would rebel, and if it be found that these so-called grievances are really such, then the part of loyalty is to apply the political remedies, always accessible, and always efficacious. A loyal people is a people of peace. A disloyal people, one which goes to war with unholy prejudices. Let us have no more of this wicked as well as silly cant about loyalty. Let our ears be no longer daily saluted with the disloyal outcries of unholy prejudices against "the nigger," whose greatest crime is the accident of his birth, which made him black. Let us rather turn to political pursuits, more befitting the loyalty, due God and our families, and the early future will bring with it a millenium, such as even in the imagination of the most sanguine has never been pictured. A millenium of honesty and fair dealing, in and out of politics, of rewarded labor, and of comfortable homes for tired toil. "How like you the picture?" Is it not worth the trying for? [72]

Workingman's Advocate, April 9, 1870.

4. APPEAL TO COLORED LABOR UNIONS

The action of the National Labor Congress at Philadelphia, in admitting colored delegates from Maryland, Pennsylvania, and Virginia, on terms of perfect equality with the white representatives, must convince the most skeptical that we are sincere in our declarations, while from present indications, nearly every Southern State will be represented at the Annual Convention to be held in Cincinnati in August next, and in that body you are cordially invited to be represented.

Friends, it is now for you to act. The issue has been made up. Our programme--lands for the landless; the substitution of a national currency, receivable for all debts, public and private, bearing a just rate of interest, in place of the present swindling National Banking system, by which labor is robbed, the shortening of the hours of labor, the establishment of co-operative enterprises, by which the services of the middleman can be dispensed with; the enforcement of the law prohibiting the importation of Coolie labor, and the abolition of class legislation, is one which we believe, must, and will command your judgment. It is more than probable at the next election, a ticket representing the interests of the working classes, will be placed in the field, when we trust, it will receive from our colored citizens a hearty and undivided support.

A. C. CAMERON,
FRED RETZ,
WM. YOUNG.

Workingman's Advocate, April 30, 1870.

5. THE FIFTEENTH AMENDMENT

A few days ago, under the signature of U. S. Grant and Hamilton Fish, there appeared a document scarcely second in importance--and the influence it is destined to bear on our national character--to the Declaration of Independence--an official promulgation of the ratification of the Fifteenth Amendment, by which the privileges of American citizenship were conferred upon the colored race in every State of the Union. The fiat has gone forth, and right or wrong, the American people have set the seal of approbation to the work of their legislators. Henceforth, the colored voters will exercise as much influence in sections where their numbers preponderate, as those of fairer skins have done in our Northern States, and in many localities where the partisan vote is nearly balanced, there is no doubt, their united efforts will, for the time being at least, virtually constitute them the *law-making power*.

Under these circumstances, we have no patience with that class of labor reformers, who, instead of accepting the situation, and turning it to the best account, continue to deplore the degeneracy of the times, and drive into the ranks of the enemy the very men whose assistance is essential to secure success. If they will but take a lesson from either the Republican or Democratic faction, they will find that a fierce struggle is now being waged alike in the Southern and Northern States, to secure a controlling influence in their ranks; and is it, we ask, either politic or right that the party of all parties most deeply interested in securing their influence, should stand listless and indifferent at this important juncture?

Granting all that our dissatisfied friends claim--that a lust for party power was the controlling motive in the enfranchisement; and that the bitterest enemies of the white laborer, was the most loud-mouth advocates in their behalf, how does this admission change the result? Will it deprive the colored citizen of his vote? Will it change the complexion of affairs, or undo an act which has been sealed by the American people? Will it make them any less a power for good or for evil? All such speculation is useless. Is it the part of wisdom to fight *dead* issues, when *living* ones meet us at

every point? We believe not, and we trust the leaders of the movement will
realize the fact, before it is too late.

We may perhaps, be alone in our opinion, but we firmly and honestly
believe that the success of the labor movement for years to come, depends on
the co-operation and support of the colored race, and further, that it will
be only through the grossest culpability and mismanagement that they can be
driven into the ranks of their oppressors. *Their interests are our interests;
our interests are theirs;* and they have studied the antecedents of either the
Republican or Democratic parties to little purpose, who believe that the
leaders of either will have more respect for the welfare of the black, than
they have for the white mechanic. It stands to reason, however, that an
attempt will be made to prove an antagonism of interest, hoping thereby to
secure a new lease of power, while the victims of both shades will be ground
to powder between the upper and nether millstones.

We certainly have no desire to see our leaders act the demagogue, and
there is no need that they should. The action of the Philadelphia Convention
in the admission of the colored delegates, speaks louder than words, and if
followed up consistently, will do more to convince our Southern friends of
the sincerity of our motives and intentions, than the speeches of a dozen
blatherskites of either party. What we do want to see, is some steps taken to
counteract the poison being instilled, insidiously, it is true, but nevertheless, persistently, into their minds by the veriest class of demagogues, who
ever *misrepresented* a constituency. An appeal from President Trevellick,
containing a review of the situation, their future prospects, and the aims of
the National Labor Union, would, we believe, be fraught with the happiest
results. From it, there is everything to gain and nothing to loose. As
there are several journals in the Southern States who are devoting more or
less attention to the labor problem, there would be no difficulty in securing
its general circulation. Certain it is, some such effort must be made, and
we know of no one so well qualified to put it forth, as the President of the
National Labor Union.

Workingman's Advocate, May 7, 1870.

6.   "DAMNED NIGGERISM"

The principles of the ADVOCATE are in advance of the age. The masses
are not prepared to receive them, and will not.

THE ADVOCATE has advanced ideas on the negro and the Caucasian, and the
relation of both to labor, which are far in advance of other journals and
parties, but which were objectionable to our Baltimore workpeople, and gained
for it the reputation of an "abolition organ." The effect of such a reputation was just what the oppressors of labor desired, and the workingman cannot
play at a better game to suit the employing, than to be indifferent as to the
success of so valuable a labor organ. What will be the course of those men
who have denounced THE ADVOCATE as an abolition paper, simply because it
contended for the right of the black man to be protected in his labor, and
that the white man should take steps to organize him into labor associations,
now that the Democratic party of this state has elevated him to the high
position of a citizen, by conferring upon him the right of suffrage, and providing for his registration the coming fall. Will it not be amusing to see
men who denounced THE ADVOCATE for its "damned niggerism" playing toady to
that self same niggerism in the next election campaign. Verily the world
moves, and strange things move with it. But now that the negro is a voter,
that the great Democratic party of this state is willing and eager to take
him into its fold--that the Republican party has made him "brother" of high
degree, and now that the abolition question is a dead cock in the pit, cannot
something be done to advance the circulation of THE ADVOCATE.

Workingman's Advocate, May 21, 1870.

7. CONVENTION OF THE BRICKLAYERS NATIONAL UNION,
JANUARY 9, 1871

AFTERNOON SESSION

The National Union was called to order by the president, Mr. M. Moore,
and the roll was called. A majority of the delegates answered to their names
and the usual routine of business was pursued, until the reports of committees
were called for. None being ready to report, the union went into a session
for the "general good of the order."

The subject of the admission of negroes to the rights and privileges of
the union was introduced, and provoked a lively discussion, in which many
members engaged.

Among others, Mr. A. Martin, of No. 2, Kentucky, gave a history of
affairs in his vicinity. He said that in Lexington, Cynthiana, and Paris,
the negroes were standing up for regular prices, and he was in favor of organizing colored unions.

Josiah Bradley, of No. 1, Kentucky, followed, and said that his union
would never admit a nigger into their fellowship. As an instance showing the
feeling of bricklayers toward colored men, he told a story in regard to the
erection of the Galt house in Louisville. A large number of men were engaged
on the job, and one negro was put to work, but, as soon as he put in an appearance, all hands quit, and would not go to work until the negro was discharged.

Thos. Newton, of No. 6, New York, obtained the floor and made a long
speech against receiving negroes into the union, either local or national.
"Although, I am willing to admit that we have got to consider this subject
of colored bricklayers, yet still I am not willing to have them on an equality
with me, and I know the Union I represent will endorse my position. The
idea has been broached that we organize them into unions by themselves, but
that will not do gentlemen; they are a sensitive race, as sensitive as we
are, and will not accept any such proposition. Either they will demand an
equality on this floor, a right to hold office, and all the privileges of
the order, or they will have nothing to do with us. I, for one, am not ready
to grant them these privileges, and consider that the time has not yet arrived when negroes are better than white men.

T. C. Tinker, No. 1, Wisconsin, said, "although he represented a state
so far north as Mason and Dixon's line, yet, still once in a while we see
the color of the negro's face; indeed one of our unions has a member who
has some negro blood in his veins, and yet can handle a trowel as well as any
other bricklayer I ever saw, and is the corresponding secretary of the union.
I want to ask for information whether if we give him a travelling card, it
would be regarded by other local unions? For my part, I believe in elevating
the negro, not for his sake, but for our own, as if he goes forth and cannot
get into a local union, he will go to work for any one, and at any price."

Josiah Bradley, No. 1, Kentucky, in reply, remarked, "that he would
never recognize the travelling card borne by a negro, and if the national
union saw fit to be displeased thereat, union No. 1 of Kentucky, would
withdraw."

T. C. Tinker replied that he was no ultra-republican, but that he could
not refrain from asking, "Is it not an accomplished fact that the negro has
become a voter by the law of the land? Are we not butting our head against
a fact?

W. S. King, of No. 1, Maryland, arose very much excited, and had the
constitution of his local union in his hand, from which he read a clause
which inflicted a penalty of fifty dollars on any member who worked with a
negro. That put aside all chance for discussion on his part, and he would
only say, "the fifteenth amendment made a nigger a white man, and in Baltimore
we had to allow him to vote because we could not get around it, but we don't
allow him in our union. I wouldn't let a nigger into our union, and if he
came in I would get out. We will not recognize a nigger bricklayer in Baltimore.

Dr. Lewis [illegible], District of Columbia, mada a statement in regard
to the condition of bricklayers of a sable hue in his vicinity; "We are
flooded with negroes, who flock to the national capital and come under the

protection of the government, to the injury of white men, although their work was inferior in quality and quantity.

John Van Kuren, No. 14, New York, said he had traveled all over the south, and worked in several states, but his experience was that a white man had to stand over negroes in order to get a day's work out of them.

A large number of speeches were made, but "troubled waters" were stilled by Mr. Bradley, who offered the following resolution, which was adopted.

Resolved, By the national union, in convention assembled, that the question of admitting the negro bricklayers into the jurisdiction of the national union bereferred to the local unions for their final action, and the delegates for 1872 be empowered to act.

Workingman's Advocate, January 28, 1871.

8. EDITORIAL AGAINST THE BRICKLAYERS' STAND ON THE RACE QUESTION

We regret that the "negro" question was not disposed of in a manner which would forever remove it from future deliberations as a "bone of contention." Shirking will do no good. *The issue can't be dodged*—it must be met sooner or later—and the sooner the better. The reactionary element may delay, but it cannot prevent the ultimate recognition of his claims. It is just such action that gives demagogues an opportunity to poison the minds of the colored race and penny a shine partisans their stock in trade. As matters stand at present, it is the privilege of the Baltimore union to refuse admission to a colored Bricklayer, who brings a card from a Philadelphia or Milwaukee union—a state of affairs which must eventually be settled by the action of the national body. It may take a year or two to bring every local union in the traces, though we have no fear of the result. Discussion, will follow, however, and discussion is what is wanted and all that is wanted to bring about the correct solution.

Workingman's Advocate, January 28, 1871.

9.   LABORERS STRIKE SETTLED

The laborers' strike at Washington ended Saturday. There was a conference with the contractors, some of whom agreed to pay $2 at once, and the others will pay that sum on the new contract. The different districts are to form a labor union.

Workingman's Advocate, July 17, 1871.

10.   RESOLUTIONS OF THE NATIONAL LABOR UNION CONVENTION, 1871

Mr. Johnson offered the following resolutions, which were, on his motion, referred to the committee on organization:

WHEREAS, We deem it essential to the highest interests of the Workingmen of the country that there should be both a National Trades Assembly or Industrial Congress, to be composed exclusively of delegates from protective and co-operative labor associations, to meet annually or oftener, to discuss and decide upon purely industrial questions, and a National Labor Union to give expression to the political ills of our country's workmen, and to propose and force upon the government, by the power of the ballot, the method of their removal, a national organization, with auxilaries in every State, to give character and support to the Labor Reform party, and prevent its getting into the hands of political tricksters; and[73]

WHEREAS, The necessity of keeping them separate and distinct is mainly due to the presence in the constitution of nearly every trades union or purely industrial association, of a clause or clauses wisely prohibiting any interference by their members, as Trades Unionists, with matters of an exclusively political character; therefore,

RESOLVED, That we hereby openly proclaim and declare this National Labor Union to have for its paramount if not its only object, the advocacy and support, politically as well as morally of the eminently equitable principles that are now, or may hereafter, become a part of our platform; and

RESOLVED, That we call upon the workingmen of every color, nationality or creed, and in every section, to organize Labor unions, take out charters from this body (until there are a sufficient number of local organizations in any State to form in accordance with our constitution a State organization) to pledge themselves to support our principles with word and pen and at the ballot box, and redeem their pledges as becomes honest men engaged in an ennobling cause; and

RESOLVED, That we urge upon the Presidents of the several National and International Trades and Co-operative Associations the propriety of calling at an early day a National Trades Assembly, to be composed as herein--before advised, exclusively of delegates from purely industrial organizations, and

RESOLVED, That this National Labor Union promise its undivided support to any recommendations of such assembly or congress that do not conflict with our published principles or are not subversive of the common rights of all; and

RESOLVED, That a committee of three be appointed to modify the constitution of this body in accordance with the declaration herein contained.

Workingman's Advocate, August 19, 1871.

11. THE EIGHT-HOUR DEMONSTRATION IN NEW YORK

The Largest Display Ever Made By the Workingmen in America

The workingmen of New York may well feel pround of their demonstration last Wednesday.   There were not less than 25,000 men in the procession, and had it not been for the rain in the forenoon, which made the walking very disagreeable, as well as the threatening of more rain in the afternoon, it is fair to presume that from ten to fifteen thousand more men would have been in line. All along the route after cheer rent the air from these who stood on the sidewalks and housetops, and from the windows the daughters of toil saluted them by the waving of handkerchiefs and the clapping of hands. Never was there a more well behaved, peaceable and orderly procession in the metropolis, and looking at the men as they filed by, one could not help but notice the earnest, determined look in their faces. The centers of attraction appeared to be section 2 of the Internationals, carrying the red flag, and the colored men, both of whom were enthusiastically cheered by the citizens at every point. The Internationals numbered about two hundred men. They carried a large banner with the old watchwords inscribed--"Liberty, Equality, Fraternity."[74]

Workingman's Advocate, September 23, 1871.

12.   NEGRO HATE TRIUMPHANT

New Rochelle, 10th mo. 27th, 1871.
To the Editor of the National Standard:

The opening and grading of a new road in the quiet little, unpretending
town of Scarsdale, that cannot even boast of a grogshop within its limits,
was made the occasion of the following disgraceful scene:
   The farmers adjoining volunterred their services to open and grade the
road, taking with them their hired laborers, composed of colored men and Irish,
about equal in numbers. The dinner was got up on the picnic plan, each
farmer furnishing his share of provisions. The table was set in an adjacent
barn, at which some of the farmer's wives presided. The cooking was done near
at hand. All things being ready, and the dinner smoking on the table, the
employees and the Irish laborers were invited, and all seated at the same
board, while the colored laborers were left to toil on until the rest had
finished, and then they had the privilege of partaking of the remnant of a
cold dinner.
   What makes this flagrant breach of common courtesy and good breeding
appear so very ridiculous, is the fact that all the managers (with one exception) vote the Republican ticket. Such conduct as the foregoing was the
legitimate cause of the July riots, and assuredly will, if continued, produce
a repetition of them. It is virtually putting the Irishman's feet on the
colored man's neck. O! how I have longed for the pen of a Lydia Maria Child,
or the tongue of a Wendell Phillips, that I might be enabled to do justice
to the subject that I have attempted to discuss, and the despised and down-
trodden class that I have alluded to.
   It is indeed a sad condition in the social structure of civilized society
to have in our midst a class of human beings, differing from us only in
color, that the public sentiment of the community in which we live actually
forbids us to treat respectfully.

                                                  JOSEPH CARPENTER

National Standard, October 23, 1871.

13. MORE CONVICT LABOR WANTED

   General Nathan B. Forrest arrived here yesterday, from Memphis. We
understand that he comes with a view to contracting for the labor of convicts
to be worked upon his Selma and Memphis Road. President Wicks, of the Memphis
and Charleston Railroad, is also here for the same purpose. It is believed
that no action will be taken in regard to the matter by the Penitentiary
Commissioners until some determination is reached by the Legislature as to
the manner in which convicts shall be hereafter employed.[75]

Nashville *Republican Banner,* October 29, 1871.

14. PROCESSION IN NASHVILLE

   A correspondent, writing from Nashville, Tennessee, under date of October
29th, says:
   Yesterday we had a splendid turn-out of workingmen. There were nearly
two-thousand in the procession, and of that number but five were white men.
We marched through the principal streets, had several banners, and two bands
of music. William Cobb, a white man, was our chief Marshall. On tomorrow
night there will be a meeting in the city, and on Thursday night there will

be two meetings in the 13th district, one for our white and one for our colored citizens: the whites to reorganize Nashville Labor Union, No. 1, the other for the purpose of organizing a new union. Strange as it may seem, our colored citizens are more active in the cause than the whites, and exhibit far more independence of capital and party influence.

There is a considerable feeling here upon the subject of employing convicts as common laborers, and we are taking all advantage of the agitation we can. We are leaving no stone unturned to get our workingmen to act together in the premises.

Workingman's Advocate, November 4, 1871.

15. WOMEN OF COLOR

The Philadelphia Morning Post, in reply to one of its recent excellent editorials urging, in view of the coming winter, charity to the needy without regard to color, race or creed, has received a communication from "*A Colored Woman,*" which feelingly speaks of the yet prevailing caste spirit in our midst, depriving deserving, respectable colored people in all our large cities from obtaining employment. Upon this head she touchingly speaks:

"When respectable women of color answer an advertisement for a dressmaker, either in families or with a dressmaker, they are invariably refused, or offered a place to cook or scrub, or to do housework; and when application is made at manufactories immediately after having seen an advertisement for operators or finishers, they meet with the same reply, sometimes modified by bidding you "call again," "just suited," "will want more hands in the course of a few weeks," etc. There are many respectable workmen of color competent to fill any of the above named positions, and who eke out a scanty livelihood sewing at home, who would gladly take permanent situations, to sew, operate or finish; and some have advertised to that effect, making their color known, and received no answers."

National Standard, November 11, 1871.

16. MEMORIAL PARADE IN NEW YORK

Parade in Honor of the Martyrs of the Commune--The Red Flag in Fifth Avenue--Quiet and Orderly Procession of the Internationals--The Streets Filled With Spectators.

The parade of the Internationals in honor of General Rossel yesterday afternoon, was just what its projectors intended it to be--a quiet, orderly procession, wholly of the nature of a funeral and not all of a political demonstration. As far as the procession itself is concerned, it needed the assistance of the police as little as the officers could have desired. Everywhere it met with the respect which everybody seemed to feel due to a body of men earnestly and sincerely doing honor to a martyr to a great idea. . . . It was an exhibition of the universal feeling of condemnation for the policy which put Rossel to death. It was a proof of how widespread are the ideas it endeavored to set forth. It showed that the Internationals, with all their fire and rashness, possess a sincere earnestness of purpose and quiet determination--qualities with which they have not been generally accredited. It combined all shades of opinion, and had representatives of every nationality whose people claim to be struggling against oppression and despotism. There were men from Poland, from Cuba, from Germany, France, and England. There were women from everywhere, too, and the International idea could not have been better embodied--there could not have been a more characteristic representation of the best phase of the Commune. . . .

The Military were drawn up on the north side of Eighth street, and were composed of one company of Skidmore Light Guards (colored) under Captain Brown. They presented a fine sight, too. Scarcely one of them under six feet, with their burnished muskets and tasteful trappings, blue uniforms, light blue facings, and regulation chapeaux, they furnished a far from unimposing advance guard. On Seventh street was a delegation from the Cuban League of New York, about 180 strong. . . . Quite a number were not of the Caucasian race however, but nevertheless placed in the ranks without the least distinction as to race or color, the Cuban mulatto and black being found in many files side by side with his fellow-countrymen of the fairer race, all in perfect concordance no doubt with the Internationals' demand for "liberty, equality, and fraternity," particularly the two last. . . .

New York *World,* December 18, 1871.

17.   THE APPRENTICE QUESTION

Editor of the National Republican:

SIR: I notice in your journal of Monday, a communication from "Book-binder," in which reference is made to my action on the apprentice question, with an effort to justify the determination of the Bookbinders Society that there shall be no increase of apprentices in the bookbindery of the Government Printing Office. I should not feel called upon to make any response to that effort if I did not know that "Bookbinder" reflects the feeling, sentiment, and purposes of a somewhat formidable organization, which has evidently placed itself in the way of the young men of the country who may desire to be educated in the art of binding books, and is interfering materially with the business interests of the country by imposing unjust and oppressive restrictions upon this branch of industry.

The issue between the bookbinders and myself is a plain one. They attempt to restrict the education of young men in their trade to such numbers, here and elsewhere, as may suit their peculiar views and purposes, and thus hold, as far as possible a monopoly of the art they possess. It is to this that I object, and on this point I take issue with the society in its interference with this branch of the Government service.

I have no quarrel with the bookbinders as such. In his sphere, unless his character is reproachable, the journeyman bookbinder is entitled to full respect and consideration; but when he steps outside his legitimate sphere and attempts to interfere with the rights and interests of others he forfeits that respect and exposes himself to prejudice. Having devoted a portion of his life in acquiring a knowledge of his business, at his majority his trade is for capital. He has a right to invest his skill and abilities in business on his own account or to lease them to others who are prosecuting the trade. If the latter course is pursued; in engagement for a fixed salary or rate of compensation to serve another, rests in that employer, for the term of the engagement, or unreserved rental and use of the knowledge, skill, and industry of the journeyman during the proper hours of labor. This service entitles him to a full and just compensation therefore. The terms and purposes of the relation end at this point, and good faith on both sides entitles both parties to mutual respect.

This issue, however, originates at a point beyond that named above. The employers and the young men of the country are aggrieved for the reason that the journeymen combine resolve, and determine that the service of no more apprentices shall be engaged than their organization shall dictate. It is with this the fault is found, for the journeymen transcended the bounds of their legitimate power and rights when they array themselves against the young men who seek to make themselves useful in that department of trade. In taking such position they interfere with the prerogatives of the employer, and, what is more, they assail the rights and interests of business, and call upon themselves a feeling of prejudice, if not of open hostility, which they should avoid.

Reference having been made by "Bookbinder" to the negotiations heretofore held on the subject of apprentices between myself, and the bookbinders' and printers' associations in this city, I will state that when I entered upon my duties as Congressional printer I was surprised to find organizations outside of Congress passing laws for the government of this office in regard to who or what number of persons the Congressional printer should and should not employ. Having respect for the men thus combined, though regarding them as stepping entirely outside the pale of their jurisdiction, I did consult with them and induce on their part a more liberal line of action, though they clung to the idea that they could and should dictate the number of apprentices to be employed. Finding myself embarrassed and annoyed by the restriction imposed, I some months since suggested to the bookbinders' and printers' societies that they remove it altogether, and leave that question to the judgment of the officer at the head of this bureau of the Government, where it belongs. The printers' union have had the question under advisement without taking definite action, while the bookbinders' society has informed me, through its president and secretary, that they decline to accede to the proposition.

In this I did all I could, consistently with my sense of duty to the Government and its people, to bring the question to a proper and amicable settlement, and having failed in that, I have no alternative but to yield the partial government of the national printing office to these societies, or take the stand I did in the letter which has led to this discussion.

Regarding the position taken by these societies on the apprentice question as unjust, oppressive, and untenable, I shall not hereafter recognize any power over the management and policy of the Government printing office, except that which is to be found in the laws of Congress, under which it has been organized.

In defence of his position and that of his associates, "Bookbinder" says "As to the abstract right of our side of the question of restriction, we would simply say that, although the employer is the part who selects the boy and the work that he is to do, the journeymen are the parties to instruct him, and we do think that we have as good a right to place a limit upon the number we instruct, as the employer has to compel us to instruct any."

This is poor logic, and goes farther to betray the hostility of journeymen to the education of young men than to establish any right on their part to impose restrictions. The above quotation from the communication of "Bookbinder" reveals very clearly that the purpose of imposing this restriction is to circumscribe the numbers engaged in their calling, and thus force the services of that class of mechanics upon the business interests of the country at greater expense.

To avoid this, and secure trades to hundreds of lads in this country who should be saved from lives of idleness and shame, I, for one, so long as I remain at the head of the Government printing office, propose to do all in my power to secure an increase of mechanics in this line, and thus advance the interests of mankind.

Respectfully, &c.,   A. M. CLAPP

New National Era, January 18, 1872.

18. INTERROGATORY

Reader, were you ever a colored boy? Have you ever gone to school with your heart thumping tramp, tramp the boys are marching, and been obliged to walk round a crowd of white boys, because they chose to put themselves right into your path, and had it leap into your throat by a--"cuff that nigger" yelled into your ears, and after doing all that one pair of fists could do against half a dozen other pairs, were you unmercifully beaten (two or three policemen passing meanwhile) while some old woman with a bundle of tracts and a marvelously large bonnet came along and rescued you? Did you trudge on at her side, your boyish heart swelling with gratitude and revenge, the former greatly in the ascendant, and have her ask you what you did to those boys to make them mad? and you replied "nothing!" and did she walk you a square or two out of your way, and compel you to listen to the story of the boy who could not tell a lie; while visions of doing without recess, sitting with the girls, or wearing the dunce cap, singly and unitedly, flitted before your blurred organs of sight, until you wished in your tortured mind that that virtuous youth had never been born, or that a kind hand had strangled him at his birth? To be sure you might have run away and left the old lady to ponder upon the ingratitude of the human race in general, and the negro portion of it in particular, but wouldn't do that, no you would have borne anything, even to the loss of that bright little pin-cushion which you bought at the Anti-Slavery Fair to give Jennie Brown; and which took the larger portion of your little hoard, earned, by holding horses, shoveling snow, and the like, and which you smile through your tears to know is safely pinned up in the breast-pocket of that waistcoat mother bade you "wear to school and never mind." O, If she only knew!

Released at length, have you made your appearance just in time to "hold out your hand, sir," for the reception of six or eight stinging blows from a heavy rattan in the hands of a white teacher, whose one article of faith was "spare the rod and spoil the child?"

Have you ever studied Smith's Geography with a carefully cut card held over that very worst type of the negro, presented in painful contrast to the most perfect of the Caucasian on the opposite page? Have the words "superior to all others," referring to the latter, ever stuck in your throat while flashes of heat shot out all over your body, and defiant pride made you "go down," while some other boy, no more ambitious but less sensitive, "went up?"

Have you ever tasted the sweet revenge of sticking pins into the eyes of that soul driver in the picture of a cotton field at the head of the lesson on Georgia? No! then you don't know what a jolly experience belong to nine-tenths of the free-born colored men in this land of liberty; then you can't see the necessity for all this commotion among them about the Supplement to the Civil Rights Bill. You who do not know what it is to have been kicked in byways, hooted on highways, dragged off railways, driven to the decks of steamboats, hurled from the communion table in your Father's House, till in your agony and humiliation, your wretchedness and despair, you cursed God and--lived. [76]

FAITH LICHEN.

New National Era, January 25, 1872.

19.   INTERNATIONAL WORKINGMEN'S MEETING, I [77]

A workingmen's meeting, for the purpose of forming an International Union, was held last night at the Hall of the Mechanics' Fire Engine Company. Present, about twenty-five persons. Mr. Berry, the Chairman of the Painters' Union, stated that the object of the meeting was for formation of a Workingmen's Association.

Mr. McMakin, of the Painters' Union, being called on, addressed the workingmen--asserting that the rights of workingmen were ignored, and that the slavery they endured was worse than that which was endured by the negroes, or worse than that suffered by brutes. He contended that there never was a time when workingmen were shaking governments and aristocrats as now. Bismarck dare not touch them. France was prostrate at their feet, and that England was trembling. Here in the United States there is no need of fighting. By the ballot, he said, they could equalize the "wealth gathered at our expense," and that monopolies could be sent broadcast over the land.

The speaker then drew a picture of workingmen's wants. When we lift, said he, our voice to tell of our wrongs, we are called infidels, socialists, everything that stinks in the nostrils of these would-be Christians. If this is Christianity then let us retrograde back to the time when a man was man everywhere.

Mr. O'Brien of the Carpenter's Union was then called for. He said that the Carpenter's Union was a failure, but he heard that it was embodied in the International. He thought there should be a combination society including all trades, and it should be made a branch of the International.

The Chairman stated that he could not understand the International and its objects. He then explained the workings of the amalgamated engineers which seemed to be an ordinary trades union.

Mr. McMakin spoke in praise of the International Workingmen's Association, and read the entire constitution and plan of operation, and claimed that it was only the amalgamation of the different Trade Unions. "Although," said he, "this movement has been characterized by many a bloody day, it was but a lake beside the ocean of blood spilled by the aristocrats." Thereupon it was unanimously resolved to turn the meeting into an International Section, which was done, by Mr. McMakin taking the chair, in doing which, he again eulogized the Society, and contended that the crimes of barbarism were not equal to those of civilization. The International does not aim to distribute property, but it does claim that the men who produce wealth shall possess it.

The meeting then proceeded with the details of organization, Mr. Gallagher being made Secretary. Mr. Burgoyne was made the Treasurer.

Galveston Daily News, February 20, 1872.

20.   INTERNATIONAL WORKINGMEN'S MEETING, II

Citizen James E. Gallagher, Secretary, called the meeting to order. He explained that an imposition appeared to prevail that no one was allowed to join the society or. . .the meeting unless they were actual laborers--men who had some trade. He stated that this was an erroneous idea; as any one who desired to join could do so, but no one who did not sympathize with the principles of the organization should think of associating themselves with them; that they proposed to make war not, strictly speaking, upon *capital,* but upon that combination of capital that had proved so oppressive to the workingman. He claimed that they were aggressive only to the extent of putting down *monopolies,* and that they would gladly welcome anybody into the organization who would openly and sincerely join hands with them in their efforts to strangle this hydra-headed monster. Citizen Gallagher showed a conciliatory spirit, and if his policy prevails the organization can, by no means, be regarded so dangerous to the well-being of society.

After the explanatory remarks of citizen Gallagher citizen J. H. Kennedy was, upon motion, chosen chairman.

The reports of the committees of the various trades were then heard, all of which were more or less favorable to the organization.

A motion was then made to appoint a committee to wait upon the colored working men to ascertain if they would co-operate with the society. Upon this motion Mr. Bernard Lochery arose and spoke in substance as follows:

Gentlemen, I came here to-night to join, if agreeable, your society. I have co-operated with every society wherever I have lived that had for its object the amelioration of the condition of the working man. But if I understand by the resolution that the colored man is to be taken into full fellowship in this society, socially and politically, I must decline to become a member.

Mr. McMakin thereupon arose and spoke at some length, with much genuine eloquence, in explanation of the objects and principles of the society, favoring, however, the motion to invite the co-operation of the colored men, and indulging in some personalities against his opponents.

Mr. Lochrey, as the representative of the opponents of the motion to ask the co-operation of the colored men, indulged in some equally personal remarks, and with his party quitted the hall.

The motion was put and carried, and a committee appointed to wait upon the colored people to invite their co-operation in the society.

Some other matters of minor importance were passed and the society adjourned.

It is perhaps not our province to speculate upon this matter, but we fear that the negro question will prove a subject of discord in the society.

Galveston Daily News, March 3, 1872.

21.   THE INTERNATIONALS - JOHN MCMAKIN'S ADDRESS

The attendance at Trube's Hall last night, to hear the speech of that remarkable young Irish orator, John McMackin,was unexpectedly large. He is, by trade, we believe, a painter, and is in full sympathy with the movement, of which he has become such a popular champion in Galveston.

Suffice it to say that Mr. McMackin is as much a natural born orator as was the gifted young Emmett, and in his crude, unpolished way, excels any one in natural eloquence we have heard in the city.

After the speech of Mr. McMakin, the Secretary, Mr. Gallagher, read the platform of principles of the Association, which we hope at an early day to find space to print in full.

After the platform of principles had been read, a number of persons subscribed their names as members of the association, and the meeting adjourned.

Galveston Daily News, March 21, 1872.

22.   TO THE INTERNATIONAL SOCIETY

CITIZENS--Since our last meeting I have received from the Corresponding Secretary some copies of a circular containing a new programme collated from the decisions of the several general Congresses.

Section 5 of this programme reads: "Complete political and *social* equality to all, without regard to nationality, sex or condition."

Section 8 reads: "No interference with, or preference for, religious opinions. No religious differences or creeds to be recognized."

Now, as those two sections are not in unison with the ideas put forward in the platform of the Association, so adopted by this section, I don't propose to be bound by them. No human effort can make all socially equal, as I believe; and as to women's rights, personally I have no sympathy what- ever with that movement.

This question of social equality has been debated again and again at our meetings, and it is clear to me that no such meaning could be drawn from the programme under which this section was organized. However, as I do not wish to control the opinions of others in any way, I should be happy to meet any of the members wishing to discuss these matters, at my room, No. 226 Tremont street, this afternoon.

Gentlemen, with respect,
            I am your obedient servant,
                        J. E. GALLAGHER,
                                    Secretary.

Galveston Daily News, April 14, 1872.

23.   THE COLORED NATIONAL LABOR UNION AND THE LABOR REFORM PARTY

In reply to the several communications addressed to us in relation to
giving support to the Labor Reform party, we take the occasion to say that
it is well understood by you that the Colored National Labor Union is not a
political organization. The object for which it is organized, is to develop
the intellectual and improve the material condition of its members. No
political test is applied as a qualification to membership, yet we feel
morally bound to give our support to that party whose principles and legislation conform to the interest of American labor.

The Labor Reform party has no connections whatever with our organization. It is not a national organization, nor indeed, can it be. If, by the
organization of our Government, or the customs of society, there were
established a permanent laboring class, then there would be a reasonable
pretext; but no such condition of society exists. . . .

Never before in the history of the country have the working people
received so large a remuneration for their labor, and been so prosperous and
happy, for which we are especially indebted to the legislation of a Republican Congress in its policy of protection to American industry. By this policy
there has been a steady and unprecedented development of the resources of the
country, an increased demand for all kinds of labor, native and foreign, and
better wages than is paid in any other part of the inhabited globe.

Nothing could be more disastrous, especially to the workingmen of the
United States, than the financial and tariff dogma of the Democratic party.
Whilst professing great friendship for the laboring classes, its legislation,
when in power, has invariably been in the interest of a privileged few,
against the development of home productions, but in aid of foreign manufacturers and workshops.

Under the policy of the National Administration of the Government, three-
fourths of the workshops in the United States must be closed and their millions
of honest, skillful workmen seek less remunerative employment or be forced
back to the overcrowded workshops of Europe. The prices of all labor, which
would be thus placed in an unequal competition with foreign labor, would be
reduced fifty percent, while there could be no visible reduction in the
prices of the necessaries of life, house, rents, etc. Therefore your duty is
plain. Cast our fortunes with the party whose record and aim is to make
labor abundant and remunerative, education universal and cheap, and to secure
equal and exact justice and equal rights to all the citizens of the United
States without distinction of race or color. That party is the Union Republican party. . . .

New National Era, April 11, 1872.

24.   CLOSED AGAINST US

The foundry, the factory, the workshops of every kind, are closed against
us, whether they are public or private. Our whole female population form no
part of the many thousands of workwomen that crowd our thoroughfares at the
close of every day's labor. We propose to aid in the creation of a public
sentiment, by commencing at the fountain head, that will modify, and that
early, if it does not remove, this terrible grinding ostracism. I have no
anxiety about danger to the Republican party from these criticisms. I would
have fear rather for its principles if these criticsms dare not be made. I
am sure that nothing but an abandonment of its principles will ever change
the settled convictions of the intelligent voters (of whatever color) of
State and Nation; that the vigorous, patriotic, progressive Republican party
is the proper custodian of the people's liberties and the nation's honor; and
this being true, I shall hew to the line of political and civil righteousness,

no matter how the chips fly in my face.

Isaiah Weir.

The Christian Recorder, May 1, 1873.

25.   REPORT OF COMMENCEMENT EXERCISES AT PHILADELPHIA INSTITUTE OF COLORED YOUTH

An oration, subject: "Trade Unions," was next given by W. Alexander Merrill. The orator spoke distinctly, and pronounced well. He compared the condition of the employer and employed to-day with their state during the Middle Ages. He maintained that combinations are not in themselves unlawful if not made for an unlawful purpose. The violence of strikes is not attributable to trades unions, since in countries where these do not exist, strikes are more violent in their character than where they do exist. This being the case he argued that "they should receive the sanction of every philanthropic heart."

New National Era, June 12, 1873.

26.   DELEGATES TO FOUNDING CONVENTION OF THE INDUSTRIAL CONGRESS

C.C. Collinberry, Labor Union, Peoria, Illinois.
John Schley, Trades Assembly, Indianapolis.
Solluna Keefe, cooper, Philadelphia.
John Magly, Machinists' and Blacksmiths' Union, Cincinnati.
Warwick J. Reed, (colored) Tobacco Union, Richmond, Va.
P. Van Allen, Machinists' and Blacksmiths' Union, Meadville.
J. R. Bradborn, Coopers' Union, Madison, Indiana.
John O. Edwards, Henry Clay Forge, Kentucky.
Wm. S. Erwold, Machinists' and Blacksmiths' Union, Reading, Pa.
M. Humphrey, Iron City Forge, Pittsburgh.
Thomas Carr, Trades Assembly, Quincy, Illinois.
Wm. Bailey, (colored) Coopers' Union, Richmond, Va.
E. D. Barthe, Labor Reform Union, Plymouth, Pa.
Thomas Mears, Coopers' Union, Martin's Ferry.
Robert Reed, Miners' and Laborers' Benevolent Association, Mahoning Valley.
Robert O. Sullivan, Coopers' Union, Ohio.
James Greener, Trades Assembly, Water Valley, Mississippi.
John P. Davis, Cataract Forge, Newburgh, Ohio.
Edward Sniggs, Machinists' and Blacksmiths' Union, Buffalo.
T. C. Skinner, Machinists' and Blacksmiths' Union, Newburgh.
Joseph Magley, Machinists' and Blacksmiths' Union, Cincinnati.
N. F. Dubois, Typographical Union, Cleveland.
C. Muth, Iron Molders' Union, Evansville.
John Stuart, Coopers' Union, Cleveland.
H. G. M. S. Smith, Machinists' and Blacksmiths' Union, Cleveland.
W. T. Blatterman, Machinists' and Blacksmiths' Union, St. Louis.
Jeremiah Lillie, Iron and Steel Heaters' Union, Chicago.
John Siney, Miners' and Laborers' Association, Pottsville, Pennsylvania.
T. A. Armstrong, Workingmen's Protective League, Pittsburgh.
P. McManus, Machinists' and Blacksmith's Union, Milwaukee.
L. S. Stanton, Cigar Makers' Union, Cleveland.
George Jones, Iron Rollers' Union, Chicago.
T. A. Myer, Machinists' and Blacksmiths' Union, Hamilton.
Charles Cox, Machinists' and Blacksmiths' Union, Cleveland.

T. P. Jones, National Iron and Steel Heaters Lodge, Chicago.
David Ellis, Iron Molders' Union, Dunkirk.
James O. Hallern, Miners' and Laborers' Benevolent Association, Plymouth, Pa.
George O. McDonnell, Trades Assembly, Cleveland.
George Flack, Machinists' and Blacksmiths' Union, Hanover, Pennsylvania.
Harvey Salisbury, Machinists' and Blacksmiths' Union, Norwalk.
J. W. Wheeler, Memphis, Tennessee.

Workingman's Advocate, July 9, 1873.

27. A MECHANIC'S IDEAS

MONTGOMERY, November 13, 1873.
    Editors Advertiser:--With permission, I would like to say a few words
concerning the doings of the Radical party, and also my firm conviction as
to what is in store, in the future, for the working class (that is the laborers and mechanics) of this section of the country. I will simply say to both
white and black people that this is our country and in it, not only we, but
our future generations to come after us, will have to abide, and it is with
us whether we have a good Government, or not, or be taxed to death or live
comfortably. We have tried the present Radical Government of this country,
and we see the result. Thousands of our craftsmen are out of employment,
their families are in a starving condition, with a cold and dreary winter
before them while the Radical politicians, with their cliques and rings, sit
around their comfortable fires and discuss the propriety of starving them out
or making them work for barely enough to sustain life, and burdening the
country with a debt we cannot pay and perchance, if they should resist, force
a war upon Spain and have them butchered like dogs, and Grant declared an
Emperor. The way to break up this state of affairs is to put down Radicalism
everywhere in the neighborhoods, towns, cities, counties and States and let
us begin right here at home. My fellow mechanics and laborers, the above is
what I firmly believe, and unless we put our shoulders to the wheel and roll
the old conservative party into power we are lost beyond redemption.
                                                                        MECHANIC

Montgomery (Ala.) *Advertiser and Mail,* November 14, 1873.

28. COLORED LABOR

    The condition of the negro as a slave, and the moral and economical
effects of slavery, has been discussed by the press, from the public rostrum,
and, the halls of congress for sessions, with energy and zeal; what shall or
ought to be his status as a freeman is at present a matter or no less national anxiety. But aside from this, his interest as a workingman, and especially the part he is to take in advancing the cause of labor have as yet received from those most deeply interested but little consideration. It is in
this last respect exclusively that the question has a vital interest for the
friends of labor reform; an interest of such importance that, delicate as the
question may be, and not withstanding the impossibility of expressing an
opinion in reference to it, which would meet with the universal approval of
workingmen in general, the principle involved and its growing importance
demand that the truth should be fearlessly expressed no matter at what cost.
    The primary object to be accomplished before we can hope for any great
results is the thorough organization of all the departments of labor. This
work, though its beginning is of comparatively recent date, has progressed
with amazing rapidity. Leagues, labor unions, granges, and trades associations exist in all our large towns and cities, and in thousands of villages

and county districts. There are central organizations in many of the States,
and a National Industrial Congress, the result of whose deliberations on the
future welfare of the county can scarcely be overestimated. In this connection we cannot overlook the important position now assigned to the colored
race in this contest. Unpalatable as the truth may be to many, it is needless to disguise the fact that they are destined to occupy a different
position in the future to what they have in the past; that they must necessarily become, aye, have become in their new relationship an element of
strength or an element of weakness, and it is for the workingmen of America
to decide whether that position shall be that of an enemy or that of an ally.

The systematic organization and consolidation of labor must hereafter
be the watchword of the true reformer. To accomplish this the co-operation
of the African race in America must be secured. If those most deeply interested fail to perform their duties, others will avail themselves of it to
their injury. What is wanted, then, is for every union to inculcate the
grand, ennobling idea that the interests of labor are one; that there should
be no distinction of race or nationality; no classification of Jew or Gentile,
Christian or Infidel; that there is but one dividing line--that which
separates mankind into two great classes, the class that labors and the class
that live by others' labor. This, in our opinion, is the true course for
workingmen to pursue. The interests of all on one side of the line is the
same, and should they be so far misled by prejudice or passion as to refuse
to aid the spread of union principles among any of their fellow toilers,
they must prove untrue to themselves and the great cause which they profess
to have at heart.

But aside from all this the workingmen of the United States have a
special interest in seeking their co-operation. This race is being rapidly
educated, and has already been admitted to all the privileges and franchises
of citizenship. That it will neither die out nor be exterminated, is now
recognized as a settled fact. They are here to live amongst us, and the
question to be decided is, shall they make them their friends or shall capital be allowed to turn them as an engine against them? They number four
million strong, and a greater proportion of them labor with their hands than
can be counted from among the same number of any other people on earth.
Their moral influences and their strength at the ballot box would be of incalculable value to the cause of labor. Can they afford to reject their proposed co-operation and make them enemies? By committing such an act of folly
they would inflict greater injury upon the cause of Labor Reform than the
combined efforts of labor could accomplish. Their cherished idea of an
antagonism between capital and labor would be realized, and as Austrian
despotism makes use of the hostility between the different races, which com-
pose the empire, to maintain her existence and balance, so capitalists,
North and South, would foment discord between the white and colored race, and
hurl the one against the other, as interest or occasion may require, to maintain their ascendency, and continue the reign of oppression. Lamentable
spectacle! Labor waring against labor, and capital smiling and reaping the
fruits of the mad contest.

Taking this view of the question we are of the opinion that the interests
of labor demand that all workingmen should be included within its ranks, without regard to race or nationality; and that the interests of the workingmen
of America especially requires that the formation of trades unions and other
labor organizations should be encouraged among the colored race; that they be
instructed in the true principles of Labor Reform, and that they be invited
to co-operate with their white co-laborers in the general labor undertaking.
The time when such co-operation should take effect has already arrived, and
we believe a recognition of this fact by our representative organizations
will redound to the best and most lasting interests of all concerned.

Workingman's Advocate, February 7, 1874.

29. NEGROES WORKING THE COAL MINES--
     FLATTERING INDUCEMENTS HELD OUT
     BY THE STRIKERS--A FORMIDABLE
     BAND OF RIOTERS DISPERSED

Special Dispatch to the New York Times

NELSONVILLE, Ohio, June 12.--Both the old and new miners were astir early this
morning to take a look at the situation of affairs and lay their plans for the
remainder of the day. Both parties--unionists and non-unionists--had their
lines strongly picketed with armed men throughout the night. The silence of
the night was occasionally broken by sharp firing along the picket lines. No
one after dark was permitted to enter or leave the lines of either party,
except the corps of newspaper correspondents, and even these were frequently
brought to a standstill, by the word of command from unionists in ambush,
accompanied by the sharp "click" of their rifles and revolvers--not the most
pleasant sound at the dead of night. They permitted us, however, to pass un-
molested to the telegraph office.
     Early this forenoon the strikers congregated on the outskirts of Long-
streth's mine, and tried to induce the negroes to come over to them, where
they would be received with open arms and kindly treated. Flattering inducements were held out to cause them to lay down their arms and desert. A large
number of women, supposed to be relatives of the strikers, were out in force,
and occupied the line of the railroad. They carried baskets, containing
bottles of whisky, which was freely offered to the negroes. This plan worked
like a charm, and in a short time no less than twenty-five or thirty negroes
deserted to the enemy amid loud cheers. This only lasted for a short time,
however, for they returned to their former quarters again. A report soon
reached camp that 800 miners had arrived from Straitsville, and were forming
to make an attack on Longstreth's mines. The Private Secretary of the
Governor and the Sheriff of the county immediately intercepted them, and for-
bade them to make any demonstration of any kind, or go near the mine, and
informed them that if they persisted in doing so troops would be telegraphed
for immediately. This menace had the desired effect, and they dispersed.
     At 10 o'clock this morning about sixty-five of the negroes were put to
work in the mines, and by tomorrow a similar force will commence operations.
It is surmised that when the Sheriff and the Governor's Private Secretary
feel satisfied that sufficient order has been restored to enable them to
leave town the rioters will resume their aggressive tone. There is a good
deal of regret expressed because Gov. Allen does not consider this matter of
sufficient importance to call out the militia to restore peace and order,
and protect the property of the operators. The miners this afternoon were
scattered around the village in knots of a dozen or two, discussing whether
they should exterminate the blacks or not. A strong force will be out to-
night to do guard duty, and to prevent a midnight attack.

New York Times, June 13, 1874.

30. NEGRO COMPETITION

     Shortly after the close of the war of the rebellion, a prominent
Southern General in speaking of the freedom of the negroes, said: "You
Northern people don't know what you have done. You will yet see these blacks
you have freed go North and come into competition with free white labor."
     In Illinois, Indiana and Ohio there have been strikes of Miners within
the past **three** years and in such strikes negroes have been imported to take
the place of the white men. Only recently have three or four hundred negroes
been imported to the Hocking Valley to supplant the white labor now refused
employment for adherence to the principles of Trades' Unionism.
     Let us consider this Hocking Valley outrage. The Miners in this Valley

saw fit last fall and winter to establish amongst themselves branches of the Miners' National Association. This action was partly due to the utterly inadequate compensation which the chicanery and artifice of the proprietors forced upon them. They have been obliged to work generally at 2-1/2 cents per bushel when Miners in other localities were earning four cents per bushel and even then they were compelled to remain idle most of each winter consuming the savings of the preceding summer. Their earnings ran from thirty to forty-five dollars per month, in busy seasons, while Miners elsewhere were earning from seventy to one hundred dollars per month. [78]

Under the management it was impossible for these men to have a dollar left them at the end of a year's work, besides this, they were compelled for fear of dismissal to deal at company stores and pay enormous profits. Under these exactions coal mining in the Hocking Valley became like white slavery. To obtain grip upon the men the proprietors associated with them a so-called Benevolent Association, a number of men devoid of principle, who, for the sake of their employers favor, acted as spies and informers on the rest, and repressed all efforts at organization to break up the unfair system which existed. The "pets" made good wages and had the best "places."

When the National Association was organized, the Hocking Valley flew to it for protection, and the proprietors' so-called "Benevolent Association," which never spent a dollar in benevolence, fell to the ground. They saw their power over the Miners to maintain a low rate of wages was at an end. To regain their power they resolved to precipitate a strike.

Under cover of the panic, they declared a reduction in the price of mining to 62-1/2 cents per ton, which is less than two cents per bushel, and demanded the unconditional breaking up and surrender of the Union. [79]

The gauntlet of war thus thrown down was picked up by the long oppressed boss-ridden Miners. Fifteen hundred of them stood up as one man and declared they would accept starvation rather than surrender their manhood and independence.

There was no other alternative. If they worked, it was but a mere pittance their labor brought them. For six months, almost, have they stood together in their resistance to the surrender of their Unions. Their employers, vexed at their determination and angered at their obstinate adherence to their Unions, resolved to seek a pretext to calling in military force, and under cover of this, compel the men to accept their terms. Toughs and cut-throats were secretly employed to go among the Miners creating quarrels. On the occasion of a demonstration the employers employed about forty men and armed each with two or three flasks of cheap whiskey and picketed them so as to interrupt the Miners as they congregated for the demonstration, with orders to distribute the whiskey freely. The purpose came to the ears of the Union leaders and they placed an outer line of pickets with the instructions to warn all comers to not touch the gratuitous whiskey, or take it home to their chagrined masters, and the demonstration took place without a militia of the peace.

The governor was next appealed to. A [illegible] of threatened riot were poured into his ear, and assistance to save from fire that threatened property of the proprietors was prayed for. Finally troops were dispatched to the scene of threatened riot, only to find all quiet. The agents of the associated press were on the ground, and did their duty manfully by keeping the public mind on tiptoe of excitement on the threatened outbreak. The newspapers did their duty manfully by keeping the flaming headline, in black letters, "The Coal Miners' Riot" standing, when no riot was thought of.

All these artifices failed, and the troops were compelled to return home without glory.

But the proprietors were not thus to be beaten. A riot they must have. They at once dispatched agents to Louisville, Richmond, Memphis and Little Rock, and gathered together five hundred negroes from those cities, vagrants who lived about the city wharves and eked out a precarious existence by picking up stray jobs only as starvation stung them to it.

This crowd, composed mostly of ignorant, dissolute villains from the dregs of those cities were hurried from their miserable, filthy dens, into the beautiful Hocking Valley Ohio, where a few hundred honest, hardworking Miners have for years past been struggling to build themselves and their children little homes, where they can enjoy in an humble way, some of the comforts of life.

This Valley is their home; some of them have homes paid for out of the labor of their strong arms in the bowels of the earth; others have lots and houses on them partly paid for; others are trying to save enough out of their hard earnings to buy themselves homes. They have helped to build the churches and school-houses, which they took upon with pride, and where their children receive instructions. These men are citizens. Many of them have carried the banners of Grant and Sherman over the battle-fields of the slave-holders' rebellion. Their labor aids wealth in the nation. They are the support of its institutions, they obey the laws of society, its taxation.

National Labor Tribune, June 27, 1874.

31. COAL MINERS' STRIKE

COLUMBUS, Ohio, July 8.--A force of sixty-five colored men and twenty white guards left for Straitsville Mines to-day. The train was met at Straitsville by a turbulent crowd of about 150 striking miners with their wives and children. Private Secretary Putnam made a speech to the crowd, requesting them to obey the laws and disperse, as they were on private property. The crowd refused to disperse until assured that a box of arms on the train were not there by State authority and should not be unloaded. The crowd then slowly dispersed into no good humor, but contented themselves with telling the colored men they had been deceived and begging them not to go to work. Mothers held up their children in their arms, pointing out the negroes to them as those who came to rob them of bread. A special force has been sworn in by the authorities at Straitsville to preserve order. Dispatches received here to-night state that this afternoon some of the strikers got drunk and were firing pistols in the vicinity of the colored men's quarters.

New York Times, July 9, 1874.

32. FROM KENTUCKY

Earlington, Oct. 27, 1874.

To the Editor of the WORKINGMAN'S ADVOCATE.
      I have seen a letter in the columns of your valuable paper of Oct. 17, from this place, in which the writer of said letter says that there is a great change in the minds of the men in this place. True enough for my friend, "Determined Struggler." There has been a change in their minds, but allow me to inform you and the readers of the ADVOCATE that it is a change for the worse that has come over them.
      The strike here is a thing of the past. It ended in a most inglorious manner for all engaged in it. It came to an end on the 14th of the present month.
      It was the poorest excuse for a strike that ever I saw in all my travels. Never have I seen men so completely cowed down as the men are in this place at present. They have degraded themselves in the most abject manner possible for men to degrade themselves. Never were men on a strike better encouraged than they were by all disinterested parties.
      There was only a few families here that were really in need during the first few days of the strike, and as soon as their circumstances became known their wants were supplied immediately. But allow me to state these were not the men who went to work first; but it was the men that stood the least in need of anything, the men that caused the strike to end in such a disgraceful manner; and the very men that were mostly in favor of a strike were the first to cave in, as is generally the case in most strikes.

But allow me to inform your readers that some of these very men are now reaping the reward that they richly deserve. The St. Bernard Co. brought a lot of niggers here to work in the white men's places; so when the strike was over those men whose places were taken up by the negroes had their choice either to break rooms away for nothing or leave the place, as a good many did. But others, of less independence, are turning rooms away for nothing. Others, who had entries, had to vacate their places to make way for some of the bosses' pets, so I leave the readers of the ADVOCATE to judge for themselves what trash of men there is in this part of the country. Men who are always ready to do anything the tyrannical bosses bids them to do, are not worthy of the respect or sympathy of any honest working man; and I would advise my fellow workmen to keep away from this place and give it a wide berth, for the St. Bernard Coal Co. have no use for white men any more. They are employing almost every nigger that comes along this way. They have turned several families out of their houses to let those wooly-headed gents have room, and it makes these worthies feel big to think that they are superceding the white man.

There were a few white men who went in to blackleg here with the niggers. Their names are John Grey, James Grey, George Grey, father and two sons, Joe Edgar, Henry Phillips, W. Shrelkil and Tandy James and Will James, two brothers. They were working for the company before the strike at two dollars per day, so I am informed; but when the strike came on they quit to go in and blackleg. They will fill a good man's place, and keep him out of a job. I am sorry that my friend, "Determined Struggler," should be deceived so much in the men of this place as to cause him to speak of them in such glowing terms, and to misrepresent them to the readers of the ADVOCATE and the country at large.

There are a good many men, no doubt, who would like to know who are the bosses under the St. B. Co. They are three brothers: Ben Robinson, Tom Robinson, and George Robinson. They are the tools of the tyrannical St. B. Co., and they are at subjects for anything that is mean in men. They stop at nothing, if it is to the advantage of the company. Let it be ever so mean or low they are always ready to go ahead with it, which some of the men in this place know to their sorrow. They not only rule the mines, but they rule the whole town, but I hope the day is not far distant when the citizens of this vicinity will look better to their interests and deprive them of the power which they presently pursue.

Hoping that you will insert this in your valuable paper, I remain,

Very respectfully,

H. J. E.

Workingman's Advocate, November 7, 1874.

33. "TURNED OUT UPON THE CHARITY OF THE WORLD"

. . . They have no capital, and I may say, they just merely live, I have asked many why they did not remain in the country and till the land. Some say, "We come to the city in order that our children may enjoy the advantages of the schools;" others, "because we have no church," and still another large number remarked, "that they cannot receive pay for their labor." Several said to me recently, that "we worked all of last year, and at its close were in debt to the planters." They work on shares but find that it will not pay. Many of these men have large families. Still they wander about, from town to town, city to city, year after year, looking for work, leaving their wives and children at home in distress, and unaccustomed to city life, fall into all kinds of vice. I think that there is not a single parallel in history where a whole race, comprising so large a number as this does, has always been turned out upon the charity of the world, without homes, money or friends. All the land is in the hands of those who held them in bondage two hundred and forty years and more. There is no State in the South suffering so much as Virginia is for the want of some regular system of

labor. Thousands of acres of land all over the State are growing up in
bushes and weeds, and in many parts of the State you can purchase land from
one dollar to five dollars per acre, and thereon, timber of all kinds can
be obtained and readily shipped away, as the lower part of the State is in
direct communication with the cities of the North by means of water. The
only hope they have for the South is Northern emigration. What the colored
people and poor whites of this State want, is some means of getting land.
If the situation of the rich men of the North could be turned in this direction, a great change would surely be visible in the condition of the
laboring classes of the South. I hope that your plea may not want for sympathy among good people, and that it may be accompanied with success, as
I believe it is the really true method of elevating those who have been
kept down by slavery and the poor generally. Not a single day should be
lost in the prosecution of this work. Humanity is groaning under a great
burden, which should be lightened by willing hearts and hands.

Yours respectfully,

J. W. Dunjee

New National Era, September 18, 1874.

34. OUR COLORED BROTHERS IN THE SOUTH

Editor, Labor Standard.

The condition of our colored fellow workmen in the Southern States is
very deplorable. They have been taken from one kind of serfdom into another.
But yet they are not willing slaves. There is a wonderful amount of intelligence amongst them and it only needs the introduction of the labor
movement to rouse them from their prostrate state. Having recently been in
different parts of this State--Beaufort, Morehead and other places--I have
had an opportunity of conversing with our colored brothers and I assure you
that I found them deep in their hatred of oppresion and ready to embrace
any means by which they can emancipate themselves. Many of them are in a
more wretched condition than they were in during the worst days of chattel
slavery. The latest attempt being made to humbug them is the colonization
scheme of Liberia. The planters and capitalists generally favor this scheme
in the hope that they will be able to get rid of a rebellious element (for
the colored men are really less slavish than the whites) and also in order
that they may substitute them by white and submissive slaves from the North.
The colored population should beware of this vile trick and the white working people should be no party to it. The interests of white and black
workmen are alike and they must stand by each other.

I am glad to say that copies of the LABOR STANDARD have been distributed
in Beaufort and other Southern towns and you may look out for a large support
from these places. I hope steps will be taken to bring our colored fellow
workmen into the proposed Labor Union.

Yours fraternally,

A White Slave.

Raleigh, N.C., Nov. 7th.

Labor Standard, November 25, 1877.

35. CAPITALISTIC PRESS

The Chicago *Times* remarks: "It is the opinion of southern papers, almost without exception, that the negroes in the south are dying at the rate
of four to one as compared with the whites. The causes are uncleanliness,

lack of proper food, clothing, shelter, and cooking, sensual excesses of all kinds, drunkenness, neglect of the sick, the preference of 'conjurors' to physicians, and absence of proper precautions against contagious diseases." Do not the same reflections apply with equal truthfulness to the *white* negroes or wage-slaves of the North? Can our fellow-workmen of the North fail to see in the above mirror an exact reflection of their own condition? Starvation wages and long hours of labor produce the same effect upon all wage workers whether white or black, either men or women. Then we all have a common interest in organizing against the robbing capitalists who steal our labor and work us to death.

Labor Standard, December 16, 1877.

36. CONVICT LABOR IN GEORGIA

Georgia has no State prison. Over 1000 convicts have hired out at whatever they bring, the present price being $11 a year, the party hiring out being bound to clothe, feed and guard them. The greater part are employed on farms, railroads and mines. In this manner the slave owners of the south are beginning to get back their old slaves. North and south the voice of labor should be raised against contract convict labor and the causes which give birth to a criminal class.

Labor Standard, April 14, 1878.

37. ADOLPH DOUAI'S SUGGESTION TO THE INTERNATIONAL LABOR UNION[80]

The Negro population of the South deserves our kindest and most careful attention. They are almost the only laboring people there. Few of them are anything but wage slaves. Without their gathering into our fold, one half of this country must remain adverse or indifferent to our movement. Beginning with their enlightenment in our purposes in such places as Baltimore, Washington, Louisville, St. Louis, and wherever our Labor Unions are spreading, we might achieve what otherwise cannot be done. We might loosen the hold of their white employers on them.

Labor Standard, May 5, 1878.

38. "IGNORANT, DOCILE AND PEACEABLE"

Virginia--It is boasted that the colored people of this State are "ignorant, docile and peaceable" and that, they will join no labor or communistic organization. The papers say that they do not grumble at the hard times, and that they are a good set of people. It is claimed that the only available material for the labor movement are the white mechanics and laborers employed in the foundries and on railroads, whose wages have been so often reduced and who are generally paid in scrip. Even these, says the N. Y. *Herald* are too conservative to--well we may as well add what the *Herald* means--to organize for the protection of their health, their labor and the happiness of their homes. The press of the bosses is wrong. The white and colored workingmen are conservatives, but their conservatism is of the *right kind*. They want to conserve their health and labor, and to

prevent any further depredations of legal highwaymen, known as capitalists
and bosses.

Labor Standard, May 26, 1878.

39. LABOR IN THE SOUTH

                                                Philadelphia, June 16th, 1878.
Editor, Labor Standard.
    Allow me to make a brief description of the situation of the Southern
States, that is, Carolina, Georgia, Florida and Louisiana.
    In social relations the population of these States, so far as I know,
divided in three classes.
    1st. Whites who had possession before the war--patricians;
    2nd. Whites who had no possession before the war--crackers, plebians;
    3rd. Negroes who do all the labor and are considered only when needed
          --outcasts.
    Politically these States have two classes--Democrats comprising Nos.
1 and 2; Republicans No. 8.
    During election times the negroes are flattered and deceived by both
parties. These men should be rescued from the vile parties which trade in
their flesh and blood. White workingmen in the Southern States should do
their utmost to create splits in the political parties, and to bring our
colored brothers into the labor ranks. I have done this in Florida and hope
on my return to be able to continue the good work. Let others do likewise.
                                        Yours fraternally,
                                                P. E. Collie,

Member of the C.C.I.L.U. of America.

Labor Standard, June 23, 1878.

40. HOUSE COMMITTEE TESTIMONY

    JEREMIAH E. THOMAS, a colored man, next appeared before the committee,
and was questioned as follows:
    By the CHAIRMAN:
    Question. Where do you live?--Answer. 252 West Twenty-sixth street.
    Q. Are you a delegate?--A. No, sir.
    Q. What is your business?--A. Waiter and porter.
    Q. Have you been studying the causes of the present distress?--A. Since
I have been out of employment I have had occasion to study it.
    Q. What is the difficulty in your branch of business?--A. The diffi-
culty in my branch of business has been for the last three or four years that
the cities have been promising good wages, and a great many of my people have
come to the city, and now we have got down, and we have not got money to get
out; and I want you to relieve the poor colored people and help them to do
something; and it is this, give the men in the city of New York, or any other
city, who are out of employment, money, and let them go South or West, and
provide for them for eight or twelve months. If you do that, I guarantee you
will do a very great many of my race, our people, and myself, good; and I
will go any day that any man give me the opportunity to do so. That is what
I ask, and no more.
    Q. You want the government to give more money to all people who are out
of employment to go somewhere else?--A. No, sir.
    Q. Suppose government could not find any place where they could get

employment?--A. But, sir, there are.
    Q.   Do they want waiters down South?--A. Yes, sir. I am not particular
about waiters' work. I would rather have anything else that I could get.
    Q.   Was there a demand when you went away?--A. Well, they were paying
$4 or $5 a month, while here they were paying $15 or $16; but now they have
no work. I thought I could have a farm, and live with a full stomach, and
be as free as anybody else, but I can't do it now.

House Miscellaneous Document, No. 29, "Investigation By a Select Committee
of the House of Representatives Relative to the Causes of the General
Depression in Labor & Business, Etc.," 45th Congress, 3rd Session, Washington,
D.C., 1879, p. 145.

THE LABOR LEAGUE [81]

    41.   ADDRESS OF CENTRAL COUNCIL OF THE LABOR LEAGUE OF THE UNITED
          STATES TO HIS EXCELLENCY RUTHERFORD B. HAYES, PRESIDENT OF
                          THE UNITED STATES

    John Pope Hodnett, President of the Labor League, delivered the follow-
ing Address at the Executive Mansion in the presence of the President, surrounded by white and colored delegations, and by the officers of the Executive Mansion.

    MR. PRESIDENT: In a country like ours men are likely to forget the
main object for which governments are created, and after a long continuance
of power in their hands to abuse and distort the power given them from its
proper channels, and generally become oppressors instead of benefactors of
the people from whom all power springs,--for the people are the law making
power of this Country, and all power springs from them.
    This delegation of the Labor League is a representative body of white
and colored working men, of all races and creeds, who call to pay their respects to the President of their Country. They want no offices, they have no
axes to grind,--they are here for other and for nobler purposes. They come
to strengthen your hands in the good work of reformation, and to ask you to
aid them in developing the great natural resources of our infant republic.
At present the industrial elements of our republic are unemployed, and the
once busy hum of mechanical and laboring industry which was so long heard in
our flourishing cities is now hushed, and the avalanche of American pauperism
created by the enforced idleness of millions of American working men takes
the place of industry, frugality, wealth, and personal independence!
    A nation like ours, constituted and built up by labor, upon which all
the elements of success revolved, and upon which the business and the capital
of the country depends, cannot sustain itself without the employment of the
masses, who are in reality its only wealth, to develop its unlimited resources. We are not like any one of the European countries where the soil
has been utilized until the very marrow has been withdrawn therefrom. On the
contrary, our virgin soil has not yet been wedded to universal husbandry, and
generations yet unborn will flourish on its generous bosom ere decay sets in
such as that which works King ridden Europe. Too much stress cannot be
laid upon the present misery, the present want, the present starvation--a
new word in American homes--of American working men, and the man, or the
President who solves the problem of labor by opening up national improvements
to employ the unemployed of his country will go down to history as the next
benefactor of labor to Abraham Lincoln who emancipated four millions of
laborers in the south, and called a new nation into existence. For the first
time, Mr. President, in the history of the republic the working men recognize

the fact that neither color nor creed protects them from the heavy hands of
injustice; that the public corruptionists, the organized monopolists, the
public officials who betray all alike, white and black, native and naturalized; and feeling and knowing these things we have clasped hands for mutual
protection and proclaim to you that we have been plundered and pauperised by
profligate corporations and corrupt public servants. We look to you for the
restoration of public honor and public virtue. By vice and corruption labor
becomes degraded and pauperised. By public virtue and public honor alone
can the nation flourish and labor prosper. When we consider how much a
President of the United States can do for his fellow men we are not saying
too much in calling you in the language of the Indian "Our Great Father,"
for if ever there was a man who has had a chance to be a "Great Father" to
his people beyond all controversial historical events you are that man, and
you can only become a "Great Father," a great benefactor to your countrymen,
by aiding the laboring classes of the United States out of their present
enforced idleness and involuntary pauperism. Labor is the source of all
wealth, of all power, and of all greatness. Labor commences at the birth of
man, and ends only when the earth closes over his coffin. Before this country was settled by the white man the Indian held it, and for want of labor
what a barren wilderness the Pilgrim fathers found it! Look at it today--
what a contrast it presents! And let me ask, what made it the present
paradise it is? I answer, "Labor!" And now the creator of this republic is
to be destroyed by the despotic hand of monopolizing the capital! But, Mr.
President, if the creator is to be destroyed then the creator's work, the
republic itself, must also fall! Napoleon the First created the empire of
France; it was his own conception; it was his own idea. The despotism of
Europe vanished before his genius as the wilderness does before the sublimer
genius of Labor! When Napoleon fell, France--*his* France--also fell! So it
will be with this country. As labor was its creator so it is its strength
and freedom, and when labor falls the republic must fall with it, for it
created the republic, and under its fostering care it has flourished for one
hundred years, and by its prosperity and protection can the republic also
prosper, and the arts and sciences abound.

The greatest rulers of nations were those who, regardless of consequences
protected the industries and subserved the rights of the people, which are
only the rights of labor. What does the soft, silk-fisted banker do for
this country? Point to me a canal he has built; point to me the steam boat,
or the machine he has created or invented.

On the contrary he produces nothing, invents nothing, and, if left to
himself without the aid of labor would actually starve. Labor therefore is
the creator of all capital, and all capital that does not subserve itself to
labor is a curse to the country, and becomes a means in the hands of designing men to enslave the people who created it.

We read in history that Queen Mary had her regular hours of labor, and
had one of her maids of honor read history to her while she labored with her
needle; and our own Washington and his lady are examples of industry and
painstaking labor for all American households to copy from. Judson says,
"labor also induces men to be better citizens. Idleness leads to vice and
crime. Indolence is no part of ethics or theology, nor is it recommended by
pagan or Christian philosophy, by experience or common sense. Man was made
for action."

"Noble, sublime, and god-like action. Let him see well to it that he
does not thwart the design of his creator, and plunge headlong into an abyss
of misery and woe."

Jefferson says, "sometimes it is said that man cannot be trusted with
the government of himself. Can he then be trusted with the government of
others, or have we found angels in the form of Kings to govern him? Let
history answer this question." And he also says in closing his inaugural
address (and I think it would be well for all presidents to study this pro-
foundest of all American statesmen, who is the only man in America erudition
who stands side by side with the great Commoner, Edmund Burke) still one
more thing, fellow citizens, a wise and frugal government, which will restrain men from injuring one another, shall leave them otherwise free to
regulate their own pursuits of industry and improvement, *and shall not take
from the mouth of Labor the bread it has earned!*"

The men by whom you are now surrounded represent in themselves and their associates those who have been robbed by the contractors of the Board of Public Works of this District, and laborers are today starving in our Capital while this District owes them over $15,000 for labor performed! Thus unpaid labor to which all the avenues and streets are indebted for their present appearance and cleanliness, and without whose sweat and toil they would have remained in the same rude state that major L'Enfant left them in the days of Washington.

There are now 20,000 men in this District out of employment, in a state of utter destitution, half clad, half fed, and forced, in many cases, into unwilling mendicancy for want of work to sustain life. We ask you in the name of God! in the name of American Centennial Independence! to embody in your message to Congress a recommendation for the payment in full of all the demands of the laborers of this District on the government, an adequate appropriation to carry on the improvements, and enable the 20,000 men who are now idle to follow honest avocations by the sweat of their brows, and make this City the first Capital of the world to show to the Kingly despotism of Europe that a free people can also excel in magnificence, and that the Capital of their country can be mentioned by travelers as the most picturesque and the most elegant city of the civilized world, as it was intended by Washington its founder it should be. This District presents an anomaly. It is the seat of government of the United States. It is the source from whence the laws emanate, and yet its citizens have no political rights! No suffrage! The people here are the mere serfs of a few masters placed over them without their consent, and in fact, here at Washington we live under a little despotism formerly unknown to American institutions. There are today no Kingly governments that would dare deprive the people of the capital cities of the natural right of suffrage, still we are deprived of that right in the 19th Century--one hundred years after we won our independence! This, Mr. President, is something you should call the attention of Congress to, and not allow the District to remain without its legal liberty any longer! This District of ten miles square is the only black spot upon the sun of American liberty. And it is a disgrace to the American republic to have two hundred thousand slaves at its Capital City, and all its other cities free as the wind. Do this and all mankind will celebrate your advent to the Presidency, and the people of Washington, and of the whole Country shall call your name holy for all time to come.

I, also in behalf of the whole mass of American white and colored Workingmen, ask you to embody in your message to Congress a request, asking them to pass such measures as shall inaugurate a system of public improvements throughout the whole country, such a system as will benefit the country as well as adequately employ and compensate the now unwillingly-idle millions of American mechanics and laborers, and also for the imposition of such a tariff on foreign imported articles as will protect our infant manufacturing industry against the unremunerated pauper labor of Europe.

I am requested by the Central Council of the Labor League to convey to you their thanks and congratulations upon your prompt withdrawal of the military from the legislative precincts of the conquered states. Instead of blows, insults and curses let us extend the hand of American brotherhood to the erring children of the South who have wandered away from the teachings of their fathers, and who can only be brought back to their first love by the wooings of affection, and the teachings of "meek eyed peace" so ably demonstrated in your recent master stroke of policy. Verily may it be said, *Washington founded, Jefferson educated, Jackson defended, Lincon emancipated, Grant conquered, but Hayes united and saved the whole Union!*

Your idea of an independent Cabinet, rising above party, which at most is only the representation of one section of the country, carries out practically the idea of Washington who said in his farewell address:

"The alternate domination of one faction over another, sharpened by the spirit of revenge natural to party dissention, which in different ages and countries has perpetrated the most horrid enormities, is itself a frightful despotism. But this leads at length to a more formal despotism. The disorders and miseries which result gradually incline the minds of men to seek security and repose in the absolute power of an individual, and sooner or later, the chief of some prevailing faction, more able or more fortunate than

competitors, turns this despotism to the purposes of his own elevation on
the ruins of public liberty." Therefore, Mr. President, we extend to you
the honest hand of labor and bid you God speed on your mission of peace.
Workingmen in this country want no war, for should war come they, and they
alone, would be the sufferers; they, and they alone, would do the fighting;
they, and they alone, would be the slave on both sides. What workingmen
want is *work*. What the American people want is an honest administration,
and a president like Jackson who will protect their interests against the
encroachment and power of capital. God has now given you the power to be
that man if you will it yourself, for "where there's a will there's a way."
In you today are concentrated the hopes of the whole millions of American
workingmen, and I may add the hopes of mankind, for this country is the
harbor of the oppressed, and a beacon to struggling nations for freedom
throughout the globe. The president who saves the country from the grave
dug for it by encroaching monopolists will go down to history by the side
of Washington, Jefferson, Jackson, and Lincoln, and the man who has the
chance and does not avail himself of it may only be remembered for what he
could but would not do. May God serve your hand for the right! May God
strengthen you against the enemies of the American people! May God, who
has placed the helm of the ship of State in your hands, guard you from the
rocks and invisible dangers ahead, and hedge you about with honest, god-
fearing men! May you perpetuate in living example the model President of
Washington's republic, and all mankind gazing upon our unrivalled greatness
in the arts and sciences, and modern freedom shall chant the inspiring words
of Berkeley:

> "Westward the course of Empire takes its way:
>   The four first acts already past,
> A fifth shall close the drama with the day:
>   Times' noblest offspring is the last."

Washington, March 26th, 1877.

Rutherford B. Hayes Papers,
Rutherford B. Hayes Library,
Fremont, Ohio.

IX

THE BLACK EXODUS

THE BLACK EXODUS

By the late 1870s, those blacks who had become convinced that the future held nothing for them in the South began to emigrate to the West, most of them to Kansas. Once there, many settled on the frontier to endure hardships for which even they were totally unprepared (Doc. 17, 25).

The movement itself sprang from unpretentious origins, but must be sought in the conditions of southern life. An 1874 contract for black agricultural laborers in Alabama (Doc. 2), indicates how much power to control the black work force rested in the hands of whites. The earliest organization established to promote emigration was founded in Tennessee in 1869 when 400 blacks decided to leave the state (Doc. 1). In 1873, Benjamin "Pap" Singleton, a fugitive slave from Tennessee who had escaped to Canada, returned to lead 300 Negroes to Kansas to start "Singleton's Colony." Already seventy when the exodus began, Singleton spent the remainder of his life organizing colonies and relief for Kansas settlers (see note 82). Apprehension that disfranchisement was eminent, weariness over the "interminable agitation," and inadequate compensation, even the possibility "of ever receiving any reasonable remuneration" for faithful labor (Doc. 3, 20, 39), all accelerated the emigration of other southern blacks to Kansas. The causes of the exodus gained national attention by the late 1870s. Even the eastern newspapers, such as the New York Times, carried numerous articles about the gruesome details of oppression and suffering (Doc. 10-15).

Others saw the promised land in Africa, rather than in Kansas. In South Carolina the Liberian Joint Stock Steam Ship Company, founded in 1876, claimed to have enrolled 150,000 exiles for Liberia (Doc. 6). Richard H. Cain, a black congressman from the same state, wrote in 1877 that thousands were ready to leave for Africa (Doc. 7). This general groundswell of discontent erupted in 1879 and 1880 when thousands packed their meager belongings and vacated the plantations. Some, such as the 100 poor blacks from Arkansas who arrived in New York bound for Liberia, felt that they "would rather starve in Africa" than continue to be persecuted in the South (Doc. 30-34). But most seemed bent on going to Kansas. How this spontaneous movement developed, and how the grass-roots leadership functioned, is vividly illustrated in Document 36, the testimony of Henry Adams (see note 85), a Louisiana laborer who organized the local emigration movement to Kansas, before a select Senate investigative committee. Men like Henry Adams were the unsung "heroes" of the movement, which, like poet Langston Hughes' figurative raisin in the sun, swelled and burst forth.

Reaction to the exodus was mixed. Many white southerners believed that the blacks were being led astray by subversives and attempted to stop the migration by nefarious means, such as the "Common Road Law" (Doc. 19). Others proposed that white immigrants could be an even better source of labor than Negroes (Doc. 5). Politicians of the race, such as W. P. B. Pinchback, a mulatto ex-governor of Louisiana, deplored the conditions under which blacks lived, but remained unconvinced that emigration would be "productive of more good than harm" (Doc. 10). The New York Times' basic editorial policy was openly sympathetic to the exodusters, charging that there was little wonder that blacks chose "another and a better country" considering the systematic oppression which prevailed (Doc. 23). Other white northerners shared the Chicago Tribune's ambivalence, believing that the only solution to the problem was for blacks to leave the South, even though fear was widespread that these poor freedmen would come north to compete with white workers. This, the Tribune lamented, would "only be changing the location of the race conflict." These people agreed with the position expressed by President U. S. Grant that Santo Domingo should be annexed as a United States Territory and then utilized as a colony for Afro-Americans (Doc. 21).

Vol. II concludes with the Kansas Exodus, a short-lived movement which, for all its drama, revealed the problems of black workers rather than solved them. Vol. III primarily will examine the attempt by the Knights of Labor to create a solidified labor movement by black inclusion rather than exclusion.

THE EXODUS OF BLACK LABOR FROM THE SOUTH

1. THE NEGRO EMIGRATION MOVEMENT

A colony of some 400 negroes, in Maury County, Tenn., has been forming an organization to emigrate. The similar movement set on foot at Macon, Ga., would indicate that the subject of emigration from their old homes in the South is growing popular with the negroes, who are growing weary of the interminable agitation of their rights in the South. A large number of them apprehend that they will be disfranchised in a short time, and their fears are increased by the tone of several of the Memphis papers and some of the country press. If the exodus once gains headway no human persuasion can stop it. The last negro will leave the South. Whether Tennessee can afford to lose the bone and muscle of nearly 300,000 laborers, is a very serious question.--*Nashville Press*.

National Anti-Slavery Standard, September 11, 1869.

2. CONTRACT FOR AGRICULTURAL LABORERS, ALABAMA, 1874

1. He will be required to be ready for work by sunrise in mornings, then repair to same and render good and faithful service until noon, when he will be allowed for dinner one hour, during winter and spring and one hour and a half during the summer months. Then to perform faithful labor until sundown. Then feed stock or perform any other necessary duty demanded of him by his employer or agent.
2. All time lost to be deducted from the wages of the laborer, to be assessed by his employer.
3. Bad or unfaithful labor, careless breakage or loss of tools, willful destruction of property or abuse of stock will be charged for, and deducted out of the wages of the laborer.
4. The laborer binds himself to be obedient to his employer or agent. To obey all orders willingly and cheerfully of either employer or agent, and to render good and faithful service at all times.
5. It shall be the duty of the laborer to attend faithfully to the stock of his employer on the Sabbath.
6. The employer binds himself to furnish three pounds and a half of sound Bacon and twelve pounds of good meal per week, and quarters free of rent.
7. It is understood that the laborer is to receive one half of his wages per month, at the expiration of each month, and the remainder at the expiration of the contract in case he shall leave before expiration of his term of service without consent of his employer, he thereby forfeits all claim upon the employer for the unpaid part of his wages. It is, however, understood that the employer has the right to discharge the laborer at any time by a liquidation of all dues.

Henry E. Cobb, "The Negro as a Free Laborer in Alabama, 1865-1875," *Midwest Journal*, 6(Fall 1954):43-4.

3.   RESOLUTION ADOPTED BY NEGRO CONVENTION –
MONTGOMERY, ALABAMA, DECEMBER 1, 1874

An experience of nine years convinces us that it is to the interest
of our people . . . to leave this state for some other state or territory
more favorable to their material, social and intellectual advancement.

We have labored faithfully since our emancipation for the landed class
of Alabama, without receiving adequate compensation, or without the possibility of ever receiving any reasonable remuneration. . . . And consequently,
instead of advancing our material interests . . . our condition is becoming
worse . . . and many of our people are on the verge of starvation. And inasmuch as there is no prospect of our opportunities being any better . . .
we recommend the formation of an association to be called the "Emigration
Association of Alabama."

Henry E. Cobb, "The Negro as a Free Laborer in Alabama, 1865–1875,"
Midwest Journal, 6(Fall 1954):48.

4.   DELUDED NEGROES

THEIR EXPECTATION OF FREE TRANSPORTATION TO KANSAS, AND FORTY ACRES AND HALF
A YEAR'S RATIONS WHEN THERE

Rev. Edwin Horn, formerly Pastor of a colored church in Edgehold, but
now of Giles County, was in the city yesterday. He said he had been criti-
cized by some five hundred colored people in Giles County to investigate
whether the idea entertained that free transportation was given between
Nashville and cities in Kansas and Missouri was a reality. They had gotten
to believe that free transportation was furnished and there is no getting it
out of their heads. It almost amounted to a superstitious belief, so much
had the story been told, and there was no controverting it, and especially by
those who had no written documents upon which to base an argument against it.
It was a singular fact that the idea was traceable to no particular person.
No single person appeared to advocate such emigration as was proposed by the
blacks in Giles and Maury Counties, Tenn. and Limestone County, Ala. No one
had any knowledge as to the route they would take for the West, or even the
amount of money required to be expended on the way. They hardly knew where
they were going, nor when they would stop. They were led on by the one vague
idea of receiving forty acres of land and six months rations at the end of
some insubstantial rainbow.

Many had stopped their plows in the field, packed up their little all,
buried it under the hammer, and sold it at whatever it would bring--a beggary
sum. Many led on by these illusions, broke their contracts, sold their cabins
and wandered out with all the rest of the flock who had the Western fever.
They were spending what little they possessed, and many would soon reach a
point near unto starvation. Mr. Horn confessed having said to many of them
to have it they thought they would later advance their fortunes, and many
had confessed the opinion that the greater the number when it departed for
another country, the greater the opportunity afforded for those remaining to
better their fortunes, because of a more active demand for their labor. The
best of labor was leaving the country, as only those who had, by their industry, accumulated at least a small amount of money, could think of removing
to so distant a country as Kansas.

He intended going back to Giles with a view to discouraging the emigration, as it could result in no good to the emigrant who was far better off
at home than he would be among strangers.

Desiring to have some positive evidence of the [illegible] of the free transportation, forty acre illusion, he had applied to Mr. J. N. Brooks transportation agent, for information upon the subject and he asked him to write a letter which he might read to his people. The letter mentioned this:

"There is no free transportation from Nashville to the West. The only free transportation given or that is offered is by the Atlantic and Pacific Railroad, of St. Louis, Kansas City and Northern from St. Louis and that is to the effect that they promote to sell certain lands adjoining their line of railroad in seven years' time, with the understanding that one-tenth of the purchase money is paid down to the real estate agents in St. Louis, and when this is done they will give the purchaser free transportation to the lands. This is the only kind of free transportation known by me. If there is a large number of persons that wish to go, the railroad company will make a reduction from regular rates, and give them the lowest possible rate from any point on the line of the Decatur division to St. Louis or Kansas City."

Twenty-five deluded blacks came here yesterday, with the intention of going to Kansas. Out of the number only ten were enabled to pass on their way, nearly all of their limited means being required to pay their passage to St. Louis. The remaining fifteen, like others who have come to Nashville in the past few days, were out of money, with no place to lay their heads, and dependent entirely upon the charity of the cold world for subsistence. These indigent would-be emigrants spend their last dollar to reach Nashville and reaching Nashville are forced to remain, wishing they had never left home.

Nashville (Tennessee) *Banner*, March 5, 1875.

5. THE LABOR QUESTION IN THE SOUTH

The time is rapidly approaching when the Southern people must give special attention to the immigration and labor question. That the colored labor of these States is declining, both in numbers and in quality, no intelligent Southern man can deny. That 700,000 square miles, or seven-eighths of Southern territory, lies idle and uncultivated is certain. That the raw materials of wealth exist in these States in sufficient quantities to enrich the nation, is equally clear.

The planters are divided on the labor question; some of the most successful favoring white labor on the share system, while others prefer the colored man, though the negro has obstinately voted to destroy the State and the planter ever since he became a voter; and the white laborer has faithfully voted to save the State.

The question is settled that white men can cultivate land, and work in the open air, and have good health, in all parts of Louisiana and all along the Gulf coast. White laborers are as healthy and as long lived as colored laborers throughout this coast country.

Why do planters approach white labor with such caution and even timidity? Why try experiments with the worst specimens of white laborers, and then condemn all field hands who do not wear a black skin? There are numerous instances of the complete success of white labor on sugar plantations in every sugar parish in this State. We can find hundreds of instances where the white share hand has made money on sugar plantations, and the planter has made money, and both parties were satisfied. A good working farmer can hardly ever fail to make money out of these lands. Many white share hands on sugar plantations have made money enough in a few years to buy farms, and have nice homes of their own.

There are thousands of poor men now working poor lands in Alabama and Georgia who would be glad to work these plantations. But they know nothing about them. Why does not the sugar planter send for these white men as he has been sending for colored men in the last twelve years? Thousands have gone to Texas from those States since the war with just money enough to carry them there, and not a dollar to start with in their new homes. The sugar

planter could give such immigrants houses to live in, and a chance to make
money the first year. The advantages which the planter can offer to the poor
immigrant are better than can be offered anywhere else. And as fast as these
new laborers make money enough to purchase farms and leave, plenty of others,
ambitious to do the same thing, would be found to take their places.

Now is the time to commence considering and discussing this subject. A
strong movement should be made in this direction next fall and winter. The
first immigrants from these States could be secured in season to help make
up the sugar crop. Let the sugar plantations be the gates through which
immigrants pass into Southern Louisiana to possess and work small farms of
their own. Then, as the negro passes away, his place will be promptly supplied by a more skillful and ambitious labor. The planters will then become
the promoters of white immigration and the friends of the small farmer, instead of importers of colored voters to sink the State, and the planter,
and all other classes and callings.

New Orleans *Daily Picayune,* April 5, 1877.

6.   "150,000 EXILES ENROLLED FOR LIBERIA "

> *Rooms of The Liberia*
> *Joint Stock Steamship Company*
> *Charleston, S.C.*
> *November 6th, 1877*

To the President of the Republic of Liberia:
Dear Sir,--This will inform you that the colored people of America and especially of the Southern States desire to return to their fatherland.

We wish to come bringing our wives and little ones with what wealth and
education, arts, and refinement we have been able to acquire in the land of
our exile and in the house of bondage. We come pleading in the name of our
common Father that our beloved brethren and sisters of the Republic which you
have the high and distinguished honor of presiding over, will grant unto us
a home with you and yours in the land of our Fathers. We would have addressed
you before on this subject, but we have waited to see what would come of the
sudden up-heaval of this movement. We are now in position to say, if you
will grant us a home in your Republic where we can live and aid in building
up a nationality of Africans, we will come, and in coming we will be prepared to take care of ourselves and not be burdensome to the Government.
By our present plan of operations, we will be able to furnish food, medicine
and clothing to last us for from six months to a year.

We desire to ask you the question, can we come? Will you be able to
furnish us with a receptacle, where we could spend the first few weeks of our
arrival, or will it be necessary for us to build our own? Would it be convenient for us to settle on the St. Paul's river? We hope to hear your decision at your earliest convenience.

Yours, for and in behalf of 150,000 exiles enrolled for Liberia.

> *Benj. F. Porter*
> Pres. Liberia J.S.S.S. Co.

African Repository 53 (1977):75.

7.   RICHARD H. CAIN TO HON. WM. COPPINGER

January 25, 1877

Dear Sir, The deep and growing interest taken by the Colored people,

in the south in the subject of Emigration, prompts me to write you, requesting information as to whether the society will send a vessel this spring to
Liberia, and if so about what month, and what are the arrangements for the
passage. There are thousands who are willing and ready to leave, South
Carolina, Georgia, Florida and, North Carolina, but are not able to pay their
way; Many are willing to do so. Will you be kind enough to send me any
information on the subject. What vessel the society has now employed? Could
not some shipowner be induced to put a couple of vessels on a line regularly
from this country to Africa? Putting the passage at a low rate; if so there
are fifty thousand people who would lease and pay their own passage and a
brisk trade, could be established between the two countries. And would pay
the owner well. The Colored people of the south, are tired of the constant
struggle for life and Liberty with such results as the *Missippi Plan* [sic]
and prefer going where no such obstacles are in their way of enjoying their
Liberty.

An early reply will greatly oblige yours Respectfully,

Richard H. Cain.

American Colonization Society Records, Container 227, Series I, Library of
Congress.

8. THE LABOR QUESTION SOUTH

The recent discussion regarding the relative prosperity of cotton
factories North and South have developed the fact that during the twelve
years since the war, under a system of free labor, there were produced in
this country 2,772,371 bales of cotton more than during the twelve years
before the war under the old system of slave labor. The planters are more
independent than they ever were then, their crops are seldom mortgaged as
they were formerly, and instead of being dependent upon the farmers of the
West for their supplies, they grow a great part of their corn and bacon at
home. That the emancipation of the slaves has been the first great cause
of this result there can be no doubt. The free colored man, having more
self-respect, a greater feeling of responsibility, more knowledge, and from
the necessities of the case being more industrious and faithful, is much
more valuable as a laborer than was the negro slave. Unfortunately, there
is a very large class of persons in the South who are not willing to acknowledge these facts, or who are so blinded by prejudice that they cannot
regard them as do practical business men in other parts of the country. There
are, indeed, in several of the cotton States, notably in South Carolina,
Alabama, and Louisiana, a number of so-called leaders who freely express the
belief that the negro, to be made useful must be ,kept in a state little
better than bondage, in short, as nearly in a condition of slavery as is
possible under the law.

To bring about this result, the Rifle Clubs of South Carolina and a
number of the most prominent Democrats in Alabama and Louisiana are engaged
in a determined effort to reorganize the old Labor League, and secure such
legislative enactments as will place the unfortunate black laborer absolutely
under their control. The demands made by the promoters of the movement are
not exactly calculated to find favor in the eyes of the men who call themselves citizens of a free country. They ask, in the first place, that agricultural labor of all kinds shall be performed under contracts to be drawn
by individual employers, or drawn by them and approved by the Labor Leagues.
The share system, by which the negro receives bacon meal and implements, and
in return gives the white landowner one-half or two-thirds of the entire
crop raised by himself and family, is to be continued, but under the laws
which it is hoped may be passed every violation by a colored man of such a
contract would be considered a misdemeanor, to be punished by imprisonment,
forfeiture of crops, or, as is proposed in Edgefield and other White League
strongholds, by the lash. Further than this, it is proposed that all colored

men found out of employment or trespassing upon the lands of the whites
shall be regarded as vagrants, and punished accordingly. Should such laws
go into effect, and their advocacy by the powerful Labor Leagues of South
Carolina and the secret organization known as the State Grange of Louisiana
leaves no doubt that there is grave danger of this being the case, the
Southern black men would be almost as completely at the mercy of their white
masters as they were twenty years ago. Even under Republican Governments,
where the State, county, and Judicial officers were all pledged to do full
justice to every class of citizens, the negro laborers who worked on the
share system with the landowners were frequently defrauded out of all their
earnings. The white men were quickwitted and greedy of gain; the negroes
ignorant and easily satisfied; and so at the end of the season, when the
crops were harvested and the accounts made up, they were only too often obliged to repeat that verse familiar to all the laborers of the Black Belt:

> "Nought's a nought, figure's a figure
> All for de white man--
> None for de nigger."

    Still the negroes did not complain; their wants were easily supplied,
and if they had enough to eat and a cabin to shelter them, they went on with
their work without a murmur. That they should rest quietly under such laws
as those proposed, however, is not to be expected. Indeed, we have no doubt
that in this new movement of the Labor Leagues is to be found the secret
spring which impels so many of the freedmen to listen to the glowing and, as
the result has proved, the delusive, promises of the Liberian emigration
swindlers. They certainly have every reason to be alarmed at the prospect
before them, for even should the law-makers, who are being appealed to, have
the good sense to refuse the demands of the land-owners, the Labor Leagues
threaten, as a last resort, to openly take the law into their own hands, as
they have already substantially done in secret, and agree among themselves
not to rent land or give work to any laborer without the consent of his
former master, or to buy corn, cotton, or produce of any kind from any employee
without the consent of the proprietor of the land upon which it has been
raised. In the same way, that is by an agreement among themselves, it will
be a very easy matter for the Labor Leagues to determine what rates of wages
they will pay their laborers. It will thus be said that under the new re-
conciliation plan, which has so effectually broken down the color line, the
outlook for the black man is not exactly the rosy one that gentlemen of the
Stanley Matthews school of politics would have the country believe.

New York Times, January 14, 1878.

9.   THE LAND THAT GIVES BIRTH TO FREEDOM

Words By Mrs. Hester Hickman.   Arranged By A. D. DeFrantz
                       Nashville, Tennessee, 1877.

1. We have held a meeting to ourselves, to see if we can't
    Plan some way to live. (Repeat).
       Chorus:--Marching along, yes we are marching along,
                To Kansas City we are bound. (Repeat).
2. We have Mr. Singleton for our President, he will go on before us,
       and lead us through. (Repeat)
       Chorus   8?
3. Surely this must be the Lord that has gone before him, and opened
       the way. (Repeat)
       Chorus--
4. For Tennessee is a hard slavery State, and we find no Friends in
       this country. (Repeat)
       Chorus--

5. Truly it is hard, but we all have to part, and flee into a
    Strange land unknown. (Repeat)
         Chorus--
6. We want peaceful homes and quiet firesides; no one to
    Disturb us or turn us out. (Repeat)
         Chorus--

10. W.P.B. PINCHBACK DESCRIBES THE EXODUS [83]

Ex-Gov. Pinchback, writing from Delta, Madison Parish, La. on March 11,
thus describes the exodus: "Before leaving New Orleans I heard of the Kansas
fever among the colored people of this section, but did not attach much importance to it. I was, therefore, surprised on nearing the Delta ferry-
landing, to find the banks of the river covered with colored people and their
little stores of worldly goods. The crowd awaiting transportation at this
point was estimated at 300, but I learn it was swollen to 500 yesterday, when
the people took their departure on the St. Louis packet Grand Tower for Kansas. A noticeable feature about their departure was the fact that not one of
that vast number was permitted to board the steamer until fare was paid to
St. Louis. This fact explodes the erroneous idea that these people are
having their expenses paid by some outside agency, and that the movement is
not a spontaneous one on their part. Numerous reasons are alleged for this
remarkable exodus, but so far as I have been able to learn, the real cause is
an apprehension of undefined danger in the near future. They religiously
believe that the Constitutional Convention bodes them no good; that it has
been called for the express purpose of abridging their rights and liberties,
and they are fleeing from the wrath to come. They are absolutely panic
stricken. Every road leading to the river is filled with wagons loaded with
plunder, and families who seem to think anywhere is better than here. On my
way yesterday to Milliken's Bend, I saw a large crowd camped on the landing
at Duckport. A still larger crowd awaited transportation at Milliken's Bend.
There is no doubt in my mind that this movement has assumed formidable shape,
and, unless some means are devised to arrest it, this portion of the State
will soon be entirely depopulated of its laboring classes.
    "The entire congregations of two of the leading Baptist churches of this
parish have already gone, and the estimate of the number that has left since
the movement began is placed by the white planters as high as 1,500. While
I deeply deplore the condition of things up here, I am not certain but what
it will be productive of more good than harm in the end, in that it has
taught the white people of Louisiana that there is a point beyond which even
negro endurance cannot last."
    Gov. Pinchback says meetings have been held in Madison Parish at which
Gen. Morey, William Murray, himself and others have attended and addressed
the blacks, and he expressed the belief that their efforts will lead to a
mutual understanding between the planters and the laborers.

New York Times, March 24, 1879.

11. AN APPEAL FOR AID

ST. LOUIS, MO., April 2. A number of prominent colored gentlemen who
have been most active in relieving while here and assisting to their destination colored emigrants from the South, issued this afternoon the following appeal for aid:
    To all Generous and Charitable People Throughout the Country:
    For three weeks there have been almost daily landed at our wharf scores,

sometimes hundreds, of colored refugees from the South, fleeing from a
second slavery. Their accounts of oppression and inhuman treatment by
White Leaguers and planters are terrible. Their struggle to make their way
to the free West should receive the attention of liberty-loving men and
women everywhere. And we appeal to all such for means to assist them in
finding new homes. The colored people of this city have not encouraged
them to come; the transportation companies have offered them no inducements
to emigrate; but, according to their own testimony, they have started for
Kansas because they heard they would be free there, and because it was impossible for them to live longer at their old homes. These refugees at the
best have but slender means. A large proportion of them are destitute when
they reach here, having spent all their money for their passage to this
point, and are thus dependent upon others for means to reach their destination. The colored people of this city are doing all in their power to help
them. So far, they have fed and sheltered them while here and have forwarded several hundred to Kansas, but still they come, and we are now compelled
to appeal to generous and benevolent persons everywhere to aid us in our work.
We need both money and clothing. In the name of God and humanity we ask aid
for the refugees. Any contributions sent to the following named persons will
be most thankfully received and acknowledged: Rev. Moses Dickson, No. 1,211
Morgan street; Rev. John Turner, No. 1,512 Morgan street, Rev. S. P. Anderson,
Eighth Street Baptist Church; Rev. William R. Lawton, No. 1,015 Christie
avenue; J. Milton Turner, ex-United States Minister to Liberia, No. 2,513
North Tenth street.

New York Times, April 3, 1879.

12. LEAVING MISERY BEHIND

THE BLACK HEGIRA FROM THE SOUTH

NEARLY THREE THOUSAND NEGROES ALREADY SENT FROM ST. LOUIS TO KANSAS--THE
DESTITUTE CARED FOR BY COLORED CHURCHES--A POSITIVE REFUSAL TO RETURN BE-
CAUSE OF POLITICAL OPPRESSION.

ST. LOUIS, April 4.--The sensation of the day in this part of the
country is the exodus of blacks from the South. The Southern colored people
are making for the river, and nothing but the most determined efforts of the
persons interested in staying their flights from intimidation will prevent
the depopulation of large sections in Mississippi and Louisiana. The tide
of emigration is toward Kansas. Altogether, 2,760 emigrants have passed
through this city on the way to the Mecca of their dreams, and 250 others are
now here, unable to obtain transportation. The notable departures from this
city to Kansas have been those of the steamers Joe Kinney on March 22, and
E. H. Durfoe on March 30, each with 300 persons on board. The fare from
Vicksburg and other Southern points to St. Louis is $4 by steam-boat, and $7
by rail; luggage on the former at 25 cents per hundred pounds, and on the
latter at double the price. The charge from here to Wyandotte, Kan., is
$2.50 by river, baggage free, and to Kansas City by rail is $2.50; baggage at
the regular rate.
The hegira was begun at Vicksburg on the 6th of March, when 280 refugees
boarded the steamer Belle of Memphis, bound for St. Louis. Their expectations
were the same as those of their followers. They believed Kansas to be a land
of "milk and honey," where they could rise to affluence in a very short time.
They were confident they would be furnished with free transportation from
here to Kansas, and on their arrival there be given 20 acres of land, a team
of mules and farm-wagon, household goods, and a large quantity of food by
the Government. All of these things were to be paid for, they thought, at
such times as they had money to spare. They knew nothing whatever of the
nature of Kansas or its people. Of the 2,760 emigrants who have gone to
Kansas, not more than 400 paid their own way. The other 2,360 were helped
along by colored citizens of St. Louis. Three African congregations have

given most of the assistance. When the first boat-load arrived, the doors
of these churches were thrown open to shelter the indigent refugees, and
never since have they been closed when there was an emigrant at the thresh-
hold. The members of these churches are not in very good circumstances, but
they have cheerfully given their labor and their earnings to their unfortunate brethren. A committee of 25 prominent colored men has charge of the
emigrants, who are lodged and fed and clothed. This committee has expended
about $2,000, and has collected by subscription $1,683, with which it has
paid for the passage of helpless refugees to Kansas.

REFUSING AID TO THE EMIGRANTS

So far, the white people here have shown no sympathy for the emigrants,
and have offered little assistance. The Mullanphy Emigrant Relief Fund
Association has given $150, and that is about all the assistance the colored
people have received from the whites. Other contributions of worthless
articles of clothing have been handed to the committee, but their value is so
trivial that it is useless to speak of them. There is a significance in
this--the city is thoroughly Democratic, and its citizens have the old Bour-
bon instincts. In regard to this the TIMES correspondent has had an interview with the Rev. John Turner, a colored minister, whose first exclamation
was: "Shame! Shame! I say, on the inhabitants of St. Louis, that they
should thus allow suffering to continue in their very midst. So far, the
whites have shown no inclination to help us through; they have been reminded
of the urgent necessity for action time and again. If they don't do something soon for the refugees, they will have cause for regret; for unless
these immigrants are shipped off they will become a heavy burden to the city
and remain so for a long time. And while they are waiting for boats they
must not starve. Each minute spent impassively witnesses the growing heavi-
ness of the burden. Every boat that arrives brings more emigrants, and meanwhile they have to be fed and clothed and sheltered by poor colored people;
I say poor, and knowingly, for of the 40,000 colored citizens of St. Louis
there are not 40 who can be considered well-to-do. We have received no
encouragement in our charitable and humane work from white ministers; they
have evinced no desire to help us, though they should, if they are Christians,
forget their prejudices to our race, and bind closer the tie that exists between all Christians, whether white or black. Verily, I believe there is
a strong color line in this city."

Mayor Overstolz, on being asked whether he had assisted emigrants to
Kansas, replied: "No, I see by a dispatch that the citizens of Topeka
entertain the opinion that the St. Louis municipal authorities have provided
free transportation, for the purpose of ridding the city of the burden which
was sure to ensue if they remained here. There has been nothing in the action
of the authorities here to justify such a conclusion. The city has not paid
a dollar for transporting the negroes."

"Have the authorities done anything for the prevention of the exodus?"

"Yes, when it became apparent that the exodus threatened us, I informed
the authorities of cities along the river below that the emigrants were deluded; that they were being misled, and that it was not to their interest to
come North unless they were provided with means. We considered the advis-
ability of stopping them at quarantine and taking some action to induce them
to return South, the Anchor Steam-boat Line having offered to take them back
gratis."

"Is the offer of the line still open for acceptance?"

"Most certainly. We concluded that if we provided for them at quarantine there would be no inducement for them to move, and we would have to care
for them all Summer, an expense which the city could not afford."

"Then the city is doing nothing for the refugees?"

"Nothing except watching over their health. Most of them have been
examined to see whether they did not have yellow fever, and have been vac-
cinated. As those in the city are now quartered, their presence is dangerous,
and if disease should break out among them it would work sad havoc. A few
days ago it was reported that 21 of these unfortunates were crowded into a
squalid, ill-ventilated, and small room in one of our down-town alleys. I
think the Ingalls bill to encourage emigration to Kansas is in a large measure answerable for the exodus."

"Have you been informed of the action of any municipal authorities?"
"Yes; Kansas City has taken vigorous stops to prevent an influx of refugees. She has informed us that she would not permit any transportation
company to land any large number of emigrants within her limits unless they
were provided with means to meet their wants. St. Louis could take no such
action as that, nor is it desired."
"Have you warned the negroes that St. Louis is not able to support them?"
"Yes; I have sent copies of this to Southern towns." The Mayor here
handed me a placard, on which was printed:

TO COLORED PEOPLE COMING NORTH!
A WARNING FROM THE MAYOR OF ST. LOUIS.
The following notice has been issued from the Mayor's office of the
City of St. Louis:
MAYOR'S OFFICE, ST. LOUIS, March 15, 1879.
To Whom it may Concern:
A large number of colored people having recently arrived in this city
from different points in the South on their way West, and entirely destitute
of means to make the journey, and as I am informed that many more may be
soon expected, it is my duty to warn the colored people against coming to
this city without money to support themselves and to pay their fare West.
The City of St. Louis is wholly unable to support them, or to furnish them
means of reaching their destination. There are no opportunities of obtaining
employment here at present; much suffering and death . . . must certainly be
endured by colored people coming to this city without money or friends. As
I see and understand this fact, and have no power or means to prevent its
consequences, I urgently warn all colored people against coming North under
such circumstances. Do not leave your homes on false premises. Do not start
on the long journey westward unless you have money enough to pay your way.
                    HENRY OVERSTOLZ,
                    Mayor of St. Louis.

CAUSES OF THE EXODUS
The exodus itself is a terrible condemnation of the bull-dozing policy
now pursued by the white people of Mississippi and Louisiana. According to
the refugees, who have made affidavits to the facts, they are robbed of their
political rights; they are not permitted to hold political meetings of any
kind, and their lives are in danger if they attempt to vote the Republican
ticket--all this in the two bulwark States of the Democracy. A well-organized
system of terrorism prevails there. The whites cannot and will not tolerate
a smart negro; they look upon one as a fire-brand, who is a constant menace
to Democratic supremacy. There is no doubt that the Southern whites are
determined to keep the colored people in a condition of poverty and ignorance
quite as degrading as slavery was. They are aware of the fact that the crops
on which the South is dependent can be raised only by negro labor, and they
dread lest those colored men whose minds are cultivated should unlink their
chains of tyranny and demand for their race a just return for their labor.
Ever since the war closed and the agricultural interests of the cotton States
began to resume their former importance, the negroes have done the work, while
the whites drank whisky, gambled and improved their skill as marksmen by
shooting, off-hand, at a servant who did not please them. The laborers have
served their old masters faithfully under this system for 14 years, and now
they find themselves no better off than when they began, and what is worse,
they see no hope, under the present mode of government, for the future. White
men from the North have tried to introduce improved methods of agriculture,
but they have been invariably driven back. "Pinching poverty is a great
educator," and some of its lessons have been learned by the colored people,
amid desolation, scenes of sorrow, of rapine, and of murder. They have concluded that so long as the reign of the bulldozers continues in the South they
cannot hope for any amelioration of their condition in the future.
What then shall they do? When a man is convinced of the uselessness of
attempting to improve his condition at home he usually thinks of changing his
abode. So with the negroes. In the hour of their adversity they cast their
eyes toward the West, and lo! among them suddenly appeared agitators, who told
fairy stories of the wealth in Kansas that awaited their coming. The first

blacks to think of emigrating lived near Vicksburg, Miss. They sent six
men to Kansas as did the Israelites to the promised land. These six men
returned with plethoric pockets, and an opinion of Kansas that had its
foundation on the greenbacks which had been kindly presented to them. Under
the inspiration of rose-colored accounts of the blessings offered by Kansas
the exodus began.

One familiar with the bad treatment accorded to the negroes in Louisiana and Mississippi, and unfamiliar with the reasons for that treatment,
would naturally suppose that Southern planters would be glad to get rid of
them. Such is not the case. Violent opposition was made to their departure
at many places, and in some cases the whites went so far as to seize upon
their portable property to prevent their leaving. In a few instances, however, the whites assisted them to go, but those who assisted were what they
termed "agitators"--in other words, sensible men, more enlightened and with
a better idea of justice than their neighbors. One of these was the Hon.
Curtis Pollard, who was State Senator from the upper district of Louisiana
during reconstruction. He hauled some goods to the boat one day for a neighbor, and had no intention of leaving his home in Delta. When the approaching
departure of the boat was announced by the ringing of her bell, a stern voice
behind him cried, "Curtis Pollard, you ---, if you come off that boat we'll
plug you," and Curtis Pollard, glancing up, saw the barrels of 40 or more
guns glistening in the sun, and concluded to stay where he was. So he left
his home without a dollar in his pocket, left his wife and children, his
horses and mules and land, and came North to starve--for that is what he did
for several days. He was rescued from death by the Rev. John Turner and
others of the Relief Committee, and is now in Kansas.

What the negroes were charged for the necessaries of life in the South
can be seen from the following items, taken from a bill rendered by a store-
keeper to Louis Woods, a colored emigrant: One bushel of corn-meal, $2--
wholesale price in St. Louis markets $2.10 per barrel; four pounds bacon
sides, $1--wholesale price in St. Louis 5 cents per pound; one plug of to-
bacco 50 cents; one gallon molasses $1.50--St. Louis price 30 cents per
gallon; one bushel corn $1.50--worth here about 35 cents; one steel plow $12;
one pint whisky 75 cents. The total bill from March 1 to Nov. 28 footed up
$137. 64, and when three bales of cotton had been sold, and the proceeds
turned over to the storekeeper, the darkey was still $4.62 in debt.

A LOUISIANA LEASE

The following is a literal copy of a plantation lease, the lessee being
Louis Woods, of whom the items of the bill given above were procured:

This agreement, made and entered into this 31st day of January, 1877,
between D. O'Brien, party of the first part, and Louis Woods, party of the
second part, witnesseth: That the said party of the first part, for and in
consideration of $100, to be paid to the said D. O'Brien, as hereinafter
expressed, hereby leases to said Louis Woods, for the year 1877, a certain
tract of land, the boundaries of which are well understood by the parties
hereto, and the area of which the said parties hereby agree to be 10 acres,
being a portion of the O'Brien plantation, in Madison Parish, La.

The said Louis Woods is to cultivate said land in a proper manner, under
the general superintendence of the said D. O'Brien, or his agent or manager,
and is to surrender to said lessor peaceable possession of said leased
premises at the expiration of this lease, without notice to quit. All ditches,
turn-rows, bridges, fences, &c., on said land shall be kept in proper condition by said Louis Woods, or at his expense. All cotton-seed on said land
shall be held for the exclusive use of said plantation, and no goods of any
kind shall be kept for sale on said land, unless by consent of said lessor.

If said lessor shall furnish to said lessee money or necessary supplies,
or stock or material, or either or all of them during this lease, to enable
him to make a crop, the amount of said advances not to exceed $75, the said
lessee agrees to pay for the supplies and advances so furnished out of the
first cotton picked and saved on said land from the crop of any year, and to
deliver said cotton of the first picking to said lessor, where he may designate, to be by him brought or shipped at his option, the proceeds to be
applied to payment of said supply bill, which is to be fully paid on or before
the 1st day of October, 1877.

After payment of said supply bill, the said lessee is to pay to said lessor, where he may designate, the rent cotton hereinafter stipulated, said rent to be fully paid on or before the 1st day of October, 1877. All cotton raised on said land is to be ginned where he may designate,--dollars per bale for ginning same. To secure payment of said rent and supply bill, the said lessee grants unto said lessor a special privilege and right of pledge on all of the products raised on said land, and on all his stock, farming implements, and personal property, and hereby waives in favor of said lessor the benefit of any and all homestead laws and exemption laws now in force or which may be in force in Louisiana, and agrees that all his property shall be seized and sold, to pay land rent and supply bill in default of payment thereof as herein agreed.
Any violation of this contract shall render the lease void.

D. O'BRIEN.
LOUIS WOODS.

Witnesses: S. KAHN, JOHN WALKER

THE SUFFERINGS OF THE BLACKS--A PROTEST

What the refugees have suffered can be imagined when the following, which is the text of a memorial now being extensively circulated for signatures, is read:

The undersigned, your memorialists, respectfully represent that, within the last two weeks, there have come by steam-boat up the Mississippi River, from chiefly the States of Louisiana and Mississippi, and landed at St. Louis, Mo., a great number of colored citizens of the United States--not less than 2,000--and composed of men and women, old and young, and with them their children. This multitude is eager to proceed to Kansas, and, without exception, so far as we have learned, refuse all overtures or inducements to return South, even if the passage back is paid for them. The condition of the great majority is absolute poverty; they are clothed in thin and ragged garments for the most part, and while here have been supported to some extent by public, but mostly by private charity. The older ones are the former slaves of the South; all now entitled to life and liberty. The weather, from the first advent of these people in this Northern city, has been unusually cold, attended with ice and snow, so that their sufferings have been greatly increased, and if in their hearts there was a single kind remembrance of their sunny Southern homes, they would naturally give it expression now. We have taken occasion to examine into the causes they themselves assign for their extraordinary and unexpected transit, and beg leave to submit herewith the written statements of a number of individuals of the refugees, which were taken without any effort to have one thing said more than another, and to express the sense of the witness in his own language as nearly as possible."

Then follow the stories of suffering and terror. The story is about the same in each instance--great privation and want from excessive rent extracted for land, connected with the murder of colored neighbors, and threats of personal violence to themselves. Election days and Christmas, according to this concurrent testimony, seem to have been appropriated for the sole purpose of killing "peart niggers," while robbery and personal violence in one form or another appear to have been going on every day in the year. In the small number of affidavits taken a large number of murders are mentioned, caused by the Republicans proclivities of the victims.

Dave Marshall states that when they went to the polls to vote they were made to go away by white men who said they would shoot if the negroes put a ballot in the box. Clarence Wren says; "If we voted the Republican ticket, the Democrats would get up in a mob and kill us off; at the last Presidential election, after the voting was done at Ravia, doors were broken open and ballots taken, and the colored men in charge driven off." James Brown states: "The agent of the place I rented said: 'Jim, we are going to carry this thing our own way; you--niggers have had things your own way long enough, and we white folks are going to have it our own way or kill all you ---- ----Republican niggers.'" These are only a few of the outrages sworn to by the refugees. The memorial continues:

"We submit that the great migration from the South is in itself a fact that overbears all contradiction and proves conclusively that causes must exist at the South to account for it. Here they are, in multitudes: not men

alone, but women and children, old, middle-aged, and young, with common consent leaving their old homes in a natural climate and facing storms and the
unknown dangers in Northern Kansas. Why? Among them all there is little
said of hope in the future. It is all fear in the past. They are not drawn
by the attractions of Kansas, they are driven by the terrors of Mississippi
and Louisiana. Whatever becomes of them, they are unanimous in their un-
alterable determination not to return. There are others coming. Those who
have come and gone to Kansas must suffer, even unto death we fear--at all
events, more than any body of people entitled to liberty and law, the possession of property, the right to vote, and the pursuit of happiness, should
be compelled to suffer under a free Government--from terror inspired by
robbery, threats, assaults, and murders. The occasion is we think, a fit
one for us to protest against a state of affairs thus exhibited in those
parts of the Union from which these negroes come, which is not only most
barbarous toward the negro, but is destructive to the constitutional rights
of all citizens of our common country.

"It is intolerable to believe that with the increased representation of
the Southern States in Congress, those shall not be allowed freely to cast
their ballots upon whose right to vote that representation has been enlarged.
We believe no Government can prosper that will allow such a state of injustice to the body of its people to exist, any more than society can endure
were robbery and murder to go unchallenged. We protest against the direful
necessities impelling this exodus, and against the violation of common right
natural and constitutional, proved of most frequent occurrence in the places
named and we ask such action in behalf of our representatives and our Government as shall investigate the full extent of the causes leading to this unnatural state of affairs and protect the people from its continuance--not
only protect liberty and life, but enforce law and order.

The memorial has received the signatures of nearly every resident
Republican, and of many Democrats.

AN APPEAL FOR AID

The following appeal to the white ministers of this city is the latest
action on the part of the colored Relief and Finance Committee.

St. Louis, April 4, 1879.

*To the Pastors of all Christian Churches, Catholic and Protestant, of St.
Louis:*

An emergency compels our Committee on Finance to instruct me to address
you, and ask the aid of all Christian people whose teachers you are. You
are well advised through the press of this city that there are hundreds of
colored refugees from the South in this city, on their way to a distant home,
where they hope to enjoy for themselves that freedom which is the inalienable
right of men and God-given. The great Apostle to the Gentiles, whose teaching you profess to follow, declared that God created all nations of one blood,
and that greater than faith or hope is charity. These people are of our race
and look to us to make an appeal to you in their behalf. I ask you, therefore,
in the name of our common fatherhood and Christianity, to request your congregations on Sunday next to contribute of their means to the relief and aid
of these poor sufferers, and our prayers shall follow you all your lives long.

J. MILTON TURNER
Secretary Financial Committee.

The above will be published in the daily newspapers to-morrow, and will
probably cause some action by the churches.

New York Times, April 7, 1879.

13.   WHY THE BLACKS ARE EMIGRATING

INTEREST IN THE MOVEMENT IN NORTH CAROLINA--THE WELFARE OF COMING GENERATIONS
THE RULING MOTIVE--POLITICAL ASPECT OF THE HEGIRA

NEWBERN, N.C., April 3.

The interest in the exodus of colored people from the South is very greatly increased to one who has been familiar with the status of affairs here from actual observation during the past few years, by the fact that it is only one of the many indications that the universal feeling of the colored race is one of unrest and insecurity. That this movement is either local or sporadic is simply absurd. The feeling is as deep and universal as the sentiment which led Israel to flee from Egypt, and of much the same character. It is the result of a profound conviction, which has been growing in the minds of the most thoughtful, thrifty, and capable of the race, that they can never achieve a fair position, command respect, or secure their rights in a land where they have been bondmen. It is a feeling which is fast becoming, if it has not already assumed the proportions of a race movement. The Liberian movement was its first exponent, and very few, even of those who had the opportunity, appreciated the significance of that movement. The Southern white man is inconvertibly fixed in the belief that the negro is incapable of any such thing as an independent, self-assertive movement of any kind or in any matters. He looks upon every migrative or aspiring tendency as the result of some outside, and, usually, some malignant influence. They thought, almost without exception, that the Liberian movement was a sharp or rather unscrupluous "Yankee trick" to filch money from the gullible negro, and regarded the wide-spread enthusiasm in its favor as more manufactured excitement. In truth, it was considered with the utmost seriousness by the very best of the race as offering a possible outlet for the deepseated feeling of unrest which pervades their people. It was a consequence and not a cause. Hundreds of those who have acquired a modest competence are so fully convinced of the imperative necessity of such a movement that they regret their investment in land. Many more, who have been saving for the purpose of securing homesteads, have, during the past two years, refused to buy, under the conviction that they will see an opportunity to take part in a general exodus to some region where their children will reap the benefits of freedom without suffering from the drawbacks of previous bondage. The writer brought from the Centennial one of the volumes issued by the State of Kansas, in regard to its opportunities and advantages. His servant, an intelligent colored man, examined it with great care, asked many questions, and finally borrowed it. Since that time, he tells me, several copies have been procured by colored men of his acquaintance, and it is beyond question that this detailed statement of Kansas free homes, which was scattered broadcast through the country, had much to do with directing attention toward that State. It was not the cause, however, but only an opportunity for the development of the feeling which has been growing for years.

The causes are, perhaps, as intangible as those of any other great race movement in history. It partakes not a little of that blind, uneasy restlessness which has so often impelled half-barbarous peoples to face every conceivable hardship and danger for an indefinite some thing which they hoped to acquire by migration. In this instance it is greatly to the credit of the people that the good they desire and expect to attain is, in almost every instance, the freedom, advancement, and ultimate elevation and happiness of their children. To every inquiry, made by one whom they feel that they can trust, the response is: "I do not want my children to grow up here to lead the life which is before me." Mere personal fear has little, if anything, to do with the movement. The conviction that the law does not protect them, and cannot protect them under the social organism which at present surrounds them, either in their rights of person or of property, while considered a grievous burden, seems yet to impress them as ominous of a future of hopeless woe for their descendants. This is, in my opinion, the great impelling cause of the present exodus. That it will become all but universal is a fact which must be apparent to any one who has studied their characteristics. By very many the fact that the yellow fever last Summer, for the first time, gathered its victims "without regard to race, color, or previous condition," is

regarded as a signal manifestation of Divine displeasure, of a like character with the plagues which troubled Israel and led to the flight toward a
promised land more remote and inaccessible than any point upon the continent could now be considered. This action upon the fervid religious natures
of these people, has been a powerful means of convincing them of the necessity of such a course. Should that scourge resume its ravages this Summer,
no power could prevent a universal hegira.

It is useless to discuss its effects, or to talk of climatic fitness.
The masters in the old days used this argument to deter the runaway. That
very fact now tends to discredit the wisdom of the *savants,* with those whom
it is desirable to affect. Besides that it has already been exploded by the
robust health of the thousands of colored people in the North, and has been
put to rest in the tomb of departed scientific truths along with the profound
crudity, "Cotton is King." Politically, it may bring a retribution so sudden
and overwhelming that the arrogance of the dominant party may well stand
appalled before it. A tithe of the suppressed Republican majority of South
Carolina would make Indiana anything but doubtful. The idea that Kansas is
regarded as a peculiar sort of promised land is true only of a few. The
land of promise which they seek is one where their children may have the
protection of the law, the advantages of free schools, and a fair chance for
the future.

New York Times, April 7, 1879.

14.   URGING THE NEGROES TO MOVE

THE WORK DONE BY A BOSTON EMIGRATION ASSOCIATION IN THE SOUTH--A SCHEME FOR
GIVING THE BLACKS HOMES IN NORTHERN TEXAS

BOSTON, April 6.--The *Advertiser* will publish to-morrow some information
regarding the work of Northern associations in the South among the negroes
to induce them to emigrate from the South to the freer and more promising
Western States and Territories, the result of which is, to some extent, seen
in the present exodus. This movement, it is said, began soon after the
Presidential struggle. The popularity of the Liberian movement among the
South Carolina blacks led the "exodus magnates" to open correspondence with
Western land and railway agencies, and just as they were about ready to talk
up the advantages of the chosen Western paradise, the railway land nego-
tiators themselves rushed in their glowing prospectuses and precipitated a
stampede. The long oppressed and dissatisfied colored people, rushing into
the current, landed at St. Louis, the official rendevous; took breath and
began to realize their improvident haste; but, having started, pushed on,
trusting that the haven of political freedom, social rights, and security in
real estate acquisitions would be found. Letters have been received in Boston, within a week, from leading Southern colored men, stating that the tide
will swell until there will be a sufficient decrease in the population in
the Southern States, to reduce the representation in Congress, in the next
apportionment, by at least 15.

The locality in which these new settlers were to have been collected
was Texas, in that unoccupied northerly part lying between New Mexico and the
Indian Territory. Here, starting with about 200,000 men, one-third of them
with families, it was anticipated that in time the Territory might be set
off by itself as a State, to be called Lincoln. In the furtherance of this
scheme there was formed, some months ago, in this city, the National Farmer's
Association. This association engaged from the Dallas and Wichita Railroad,
a Texas corporation, 65 alternate sections of land, which was to be paid for
at the rate of $1.50 an acre. The association issued lots of 200 shares of
stock, each share at $100. These are sold to the colored people, and are
accepted by the railroad corporation as cash in their purchase lands. When
each lot of stock is issued $19,000 is paid to the railroad, the $1,000 retained (200 shares at $100 making $20,000) being used in the work of

canvassing among the negroes, and of removing them. This land comes to the
railway company as a subsidy from the State of Texas. The sections between
the railway lands belong to the State, and these are to be pre-empted at
$1.50 an acre, the State being paid in tenths, yearly, and without interest.
It is understood that there are now about 2,800 families ready to start, who
have stood out against the tempting offers of competing Western agents. It
is supposed that these people will start about April 19--Emancipation Day.
The association, however, does not dictate to the colored men their choice of
section, but recommends Texas, arguing that the soil produces what they best
know how to cultivate, and the climate is better adapted to their needs.

It is understood that the association has issued and sold stock covering
20 sections in Texas, in all 12,800 acres. More than four times as much
State land will be pre-empted under the same patronage. This organization
has been in existence about five months, and is one of several in the North,
their formation being preceded by the circulation of political documents
among the negroes during the past two years. Probably the most influential
of these documents have emanated from Boston. The Boston tracts were four
by six inch 25-page pamphlets, printed in good, clear type, and very handy
to carry about in a blouse pocket. These were known as the first principle,
or "Principia Club papers," and the latest, No. 9, issued in August last,
is entitled "A Plan to Transfer the Freedmen of the South to the Government
Lands of the West." This details the plan for the formation of the National
Farmers' Association, and presents reports of abuses of negroes in the south
occurring since the issue of No. 8 in the previous Spring.

New York Times, April 7, 1879.

15. THE SOUTHERN FUGITIVES

MASS-MEETING OF COLORED CITIZENS

THE GREAT EXODUS TO KANSAS--WHY THE NEGROES LEAVE THE SOUTH--AID TO BE GIVEN
TO THE REFUGEES.

A mass-meeting of colored citizens was held last night at Zion African
Methodist Episcopal Church, Bleecker street, to consider the question of the
present great exodus of the emancipated slave population from the Southern
States to Kansas and other Western States or Territories, and to devise means
for affording temporary assistance to this great mass of poverty and terro-
stricken fugitives until they can begin to provide for themselves. About a
dozen colored men occupied seats on the platform, among them being the Rev.
H. M. Wilson, George T. Downing, W. A. Dixon, the Rev. Mr. Spellman, William
C. H. Curtiss, the Rev. W. H. Dickinson, and the Rev. W. A. Hodges. The
meeting was opened with prayer by the Rev. H. M. Wilson, and the Secretary
announced the circumstances under which the call had been issued. The Rev.
Abraham Anderson was chosen Chairman, and a list of Vice-Chairman and Secretaries was read. The Chairman said the objects of this gathering invited and
merited the most serious attention of those assembled. The Secretary next
read a letter from the Rev. Henry Highland Garnett who is on a lecturing tour.
He regretted his inability to be present, but urged that the object of the
meeting be ardently pressed. He would aid it in every way in his power--with
his voice, his influence, and his money. He would dig, sift, grovel, carry
a hod, if necessary, to aid in this work of building up homes for his poor
black refugee brethren in Kansas. [Applause.] The Secretary also read from
a newspaper a graphic account of the freedmen's hegira, in order to explain
more clearly to the audience its origin, scope, and progress.

George T. Downing was then introduced, and in the course of an earnest
speech said: "When the President's Southern policy was announced, we realized
that we were offered up; we had no alternative but to submit. We knew that
it had to take its course. The preverseness of the South had well-nigh worn
out the North. The resolute South, having failed in a contest at arms,
adopted the policy to badger the North, which, being tired and anxious for

peace and prosperity, exhibited a disposition to yield. From the first,
we are fully persuaded that the President's policy would not elicit the
response which its general yielding to the South, its appeal to its honor,
should have called for. We were confident that the President's yielding to
the South would not be accepted in good faith; that the yielding and submission on the part of those in the North who hoped by so doing to win re-
conciliation and peace would eventually mortify those who yielded. No. The
South is not ready to accept as a principle and rule of action equality before
the law for all men. It cherishes the education, the ends, the peculiar
civilization, with intensified hate that has moved it in seeking dominion in
the land. The amount of evidence already before the country proving the
existence of wide spread outrage, intimidation, and brutal murder, to the
end of subjugating the black vote of the South and of controlling it to further the ends of that section, is sufficient for all who are willing to accept
reasonable evidence. The south has a deliberate purpose. It designs to increase and strengthen the power, and to dominate in the land. To that end it
will stop at nothing. Outrage and murder will be common, agencies in intimidating those in her midst who favor equality before the law of all men.
The present exodus of the robbed and outraged colored people of the South
who are fleeing West in the hope of being freed from persecution, who look for
protection and an existence in that far-off part with hope to profit there
by labor--is not only an important event but it is most touching. It, and
the heroic movement a short time ago on the part of a large number of colored men in the South to go forth and brave the dangers of the broad and, to
them, unknown Atlantic, and land on the pestilential shore of heathen be-
nighted Africa, even daring there to fight grim death's embrace, should
appeal to the better nature of any human being possessed of sympathies keener
than those belonging to brutes. The scenes now witnessed in Louisiana, in
Mississippi, at St. Louis, and enroute to Kansas, along with the general
suffering condition of our people in the South, have especially moved us to
this expression. We are poor, we have but scanty means, but we will give
therefrom, and we appeal to the rich, to those who are able to assist our
native brethren struggling to be free. Fear of personal harm, a failure to
realize from labor, faithlessness as to contract, the desire to educate their
children and to "be somebody," induce these poor people to endure all the
hardships of a trip to Kansas. The name of John Brown, who was willing to
lay down his life for their freedom, is associated in their minds with free-
dom-loving Kansas, and to Kansas they are marching on. They are fleeing
precipitately, because of an awful fear that has seized upon them. They are
made to feel an increasing insecurity as to their lives and little possessions in the South. They observe that they work from year to year to produce
that of which they are robbed. They feel that the Federal arm, on which they
have relied for protection, is withheld; that they cannot rest in the South
under its broad aegis, though the Constitution designs to protect them. Life,
liberty, and the pursuit of happiness to them in the South is a mockery.
They have fears as to 1880. They are considering the possibility of being
found in the South with the Presidential chair, once filled by Lincoln and
Grant, their protectors, occupied by a party who fought the constitutional
amendments which secured their freedom, affirmed their citizenship, and gave
them the ballot. It is not necessary that there should be a resort to force
in defense of the principles of the Government lately formulated into law.
But it should be understood that there is a law, that the South, like all
other sections, are subjects of the same, and that the North will be a unit
in defending it. Let the South at once understand that a public sentiment to
this effect exists in the North, and that it is not to be trifled with;
then, and only then, will the South begin to realize its situation and think
of adopting the Declaration of Independence and the declaratory amendments
to the Constitution that are in conformity therewith as laws for its guidance. We would remark as to State rights and to those who would make so
much ado in regard to them, that they remember the axiom that "those who seek
justice must themselves act justly." Let the North, from any fancied pecuniary interest or from indifference as to outrages perpetrated upon their
fellows, permit the South to obtain control of the Government, and it will
rue the day. For not only will their principles be outraged, but also their
pockets.

The Rev. Mr. Dickerson, in an address full of pathetic eloquence, urged the adoption of Mr. Downing's address, and hoped that from that night there might be no sleeping, no slumbering, until all over this broad land right shall have triumphed over might.

The address was then adopted.

Mr. Downing offered the following resolutions as embodying the sense of the meeting:

Resolved, That it is most evident that the dominant element of the South is opposed to a fundamental principle of the Government, namely, equality before the law for all men and that that element will oppose with murder and outrage this doctrine of the Government and the people.

Resolved, That all concessions to this subversive policy do not only tend to the offering up of the colored people, but to a violation of the spirit and letter of the Government and will, instead of producing conciliation and peace, result in continued agitation throughout the land.

Resolved, That owing to the existence in the South of the old slave-holding sentiment, and, of fostered prejudices, because of the innumerable advantages that have been taken by employers in making and carrying out contracts for labor; because of violations of agreements, because the possession of lands and to become educated have been discouraged; because of systematic plans to intimidate and create a feeling of insecurity; because of brutal outrage, even unto death, has been a policy; because the ballot could not be fully used, the colored man's condition in the South has become desperate and hopeless, involving fears of a still more frightful future.

Resolved, That we urgently press upon the oppressed, our brethren now seeking new homes in the West, not to remain in cities and towns, but to settle permanently on lands which they must make every sacrifice to possess; to till the same, educate their children, be most frugal, and thus improve their material condition and develop that higher manhood that we know them to possess.

Resolved, That while the fleeing in great numbers of the colored people of the South may have been started without the consideration more experienced persons may have given the subject, nevertheless, we see in it a hopeful side; it will open the eyes of the colored people to the fact that there are other parts of their country than those in which they are oppressed; it will teach their oppressors a lesson, make them realize their dependence, and perhaps induce them to become wise.

Resolved, That we ask the people of the States and Territories to which our persecuted brethren are fleeing to consider the cause of their flight, and for them to consider it is a laboring class that is coming within their borders, and that it may be utilized in benefitting their States and Territories.

Resolved, That no one can fail to see that these wanderers from their homes to distant parts, persons who have been fleeced and outraged, need not only sympathize in the form of dollars, and that it is a case in which the generous, those loving liberty and their fellow-men, are called upon to aid and that therefore we do call upon all such to contribute as liberally as their means admit.

Resolved, That the Rev. William F. Dickerson, James W. Mars, Lewis Williams, the Rev. H. H. Garnett, John M. Thomas, J. Tullie, and George T. Downing, to be Corresponding Secretary, be an advisory committee to act in all cases as they may deem advisable in furthering the interests of those fleeing from the South and seeking homes in the West; that they receive, disburse, and account through the press for such moneys and other donations may be given to aid these wanderers seeking a new home.

Resolved, That the press be respectfully requested to receive donations in aid of this movement.

Resolved, That one of the most striking instances of brutal outrages at our very doors was the outraging of the Rev. Willis A. Hodges, in Virginia, within a few hours ride of Washington, by destroying his property, by imperiling his life by imprisonment, and finally banishing him judicially from the State, because he told his people to stand for their rights.

Messrs. Downing, Hodges, Sewell, and Thomas, the latter gentlemen being a delegate for the colored people of Flushing, also addressed the meeting. Mr. Hodges described some of the wrongs he had witnessed or been subjected to in Virginia, and exhibited a circular written and published by him in 1877, and circulated among the colored people, urging them to leave the State as soon as possible, and go to the Western Territories and settle there. . . .

New York Times, April 11, 1879.

16. THE WESTERN EXODUS

It is right. Let it go on till the miserable bulldozers of the South shall learn to appreciate their absolute helplessness without the brawn of the Negro. This is the exodus we endorse, if exodus there must be; and it is impossible to read the *Tribune* accounts elsewhere given, and not conclude that some such thing is a real necessity. The exodus of our Charleston folks had Africa for its objective point. The Windom exodus had *one spot* somewhere in the great West where the whole colored class would eventually be brought to settle for its objective point. To both these we were set in our opposition as we would be set in opposition to seeing the poor and inexperienced of any class huddled together. The present exodus, however, unlike the two mentioned above, has every point of the great North and West as its objective points, scattering the hundreds and thousands, and we trust even millions all through these enlightened and on the whole Christian sections of our country. We say again, it is right. Let it go on. Great suffering will doubtless ensue. But it is the kind of suffering that is sustained with the prospect of future good. The region from which they come is warm, that to which they go is cold. This feature alone will increase the suffering of the change. But, there is naught to do but grit the teeth and push ahead. A cheerful fact is, there are already thousands of our people scattered in all these regions. In the larger cities of Northern Missouri, Kansas and Nebraska we have large and flourishing congregations well attended and ably ministered. These can and will bestir themselves for these fleeing exiles.

People's Advocate (Washington, D.C.), April 19, 1879. [84]

17. THE SOUTHERN REFUGEES

AN APPEAL FOR AID BY THE NEW YORK COMMITTEE

The committee of colored citizens having in charge the movement for aiding the colored emigrants to Kansas make the following appeal to the public:

The startling migratory movement now in progress among the colored laborers and people of the Southern States, creates a demand upon the humane impulses of all thoughtful and kindly disposed persons, regardless of sect, race, color, nationality, or party. We put aside, in the face of the great needs that the movement creates, all personal questions of cause, motive, and policy. Benevolence belongs to no party, and charity is not limited by "color, race or previous conditions which, to them at least, seem degrading. There must be much, wheresoever the fault lies, in surrounding circumstances that can induce a home-loving people to abandon everything, and seek new connections and new homes for themselves--and, above all, for their children-- in surroundings where the environment will, in their opinion, tend to elevation and not degradation. The motive is one honorable to our people, and must appeal to the considerate in all classes. The Southern colored emigrant is willing and able to work. He needs aid in this new effort. Give him such assistance as will tend to make him self-supporting. The whole land will ultimately be enriched by a movement which seeks to make a free yeomanry out of a class of dependent wage-laborers. Give him books, farming utensils, seed, clothing, and such other aid as will be needful for him to have in starting life anew. Anyone who shall send their address to the Young Men's Union Christian Association, No. 122 West Twenty-sixth street, will be waited on to secure whatever may be given. Be careful not to give to un-authorized parties. The New York *Herald*, Times, *Tribune, Evening Post* and *Mail* will receive subscriptions.

G. T. Downing, the Rev. H. H. Garnett, J. W. Mars, the Rev. W. F. Dick-erson, P. T. Downing, the Rev. A. Anderson, J. E. Crosby, S. W. Smith, the Rev. W. T. Dixon, Louis Williams, the Rev. J. J. Zuille, the Rev. Henry Wilson, John M. Thomas, S. W. Clay, the Rev. A. C. Garrison, John Lucas, Charles Thomas, E. V. C. Eatt, William H. Freeman, G. M. Rice, W. M. Stewart, David Bush, P. M. Gallezo, N. B. Ashley.

GEORGE W. MYERS, Chairman

CHARLES H. MINNIE, Secretary.

New York Times, April, 21, 1879.

18.   FREEDOM IN KANSAS

WELCOME EXTENDED TO THE FLEEING NEGROES--THE NEED OF OUTSIDE AID.

It is quite evident that the time has come when more efficient measures will be necessary to meet the exodus of colored refugees to this State. How large the movement will become no one can tell. It has already burdened the Wyandotte people beyond all their ability to successfully cope with it. These people congregate at Wyandotte because that is the first place where they strike the State of Kansas. It is not just or proper that Wyandotte should be left to cope alone with this burden. Indeed, she cannot do it. The thing has come upon us all so suddenly that we are taken by surprise. But there are some things that the impulse of the moment is sufficient to properly decide.

These people are refugees fleeing from what had become to them an in-tolerable condition of affairs. Talk with them, and in their simple, homely way they all tell one and the same story. They were oppressed. Many of them were in fear of their lives. They had heard of Kansas as the home of liberty. They have a pretty correct notion of the Homestead laws. They want to get on to Government land. They have no definite idea of how they are to get there or how they are to sustain themselves after they get there; but they have fled from evils that were sufficient to make them sacrifice everything to get away and to brave everything to get here.

Under these circumstances there is but one thing for the people of Kansas to do. These people must be received and kindly cared for. Unpleasant as the responsibility may be, it is upon us, and must be met in the same spirit that has always animated our people with reference to the great ques-tions of freedom. There is something infinitely honorable to the State of Kansas that its name has become the synonym of freedom all over this land, so that the oppressed turn their eyes toward us as they used to toward the north star. We have a great State of almost a million of people. We need labor to develop all of our industries, and by wise measures we can find homes for these refugees, and in a short time they will add largely to the production of the State. Nor will we have to bear the burden of their settle-ment alone. The great, rich, free-handed North has only to know the facts and the necessities of the case to respond as she has done in every hour of past distress. The same spirit which sustained the Sanitary Commission during the war, and which sent millions of dollars South last Summer to re-lieve the wants of the sick and dying from yellow fever, will meet this em-ergency as well. But what is needed now is a State organization that can speak with authority; that will command confidence at home and abroad, and that will devise means for meeting the emergency. Topeka is the proper place, and a convention should at once be called. The Government of the State is the

proper man to issue such a call. We hope he will move in the matter at
once.

New York Times, April 29, 1879.

19. COLORED LABOR IN THE SOUTH

The prevalent idea is that the group of questions connected with the
Colored Exodus is found in full force only in the Southwest, and particularly in those of the Southwestern States which have acquired an odious distinction by their treatment of the colored vote. In Louisiana and Mississippi
the desire to escape from the harsh administration of unjust laws, and the
yet harsher conduct of lawless whites has seemed to be natural, perhaps
inevitable. The Liberian movement in South Carolina has been similarly regarded as the result of a condition of things not likely to exist save where
cruel oppression has manifested itself as a means of producing certain
political results. States not made infamous by partisan methods have been
supposed to be exempt from the operation of causes which, if not confined
within narrow limits or checked by the early efforts of remedial agencies,
obviously tend to disorganize staple industries of the South, and to increase the bitterness felt at the North with regard to the general course of
Southern affairs.

We now print a statement that imparts another aspect to the subject.
The facts recited on apparently trustworthy authority from North Carolina
raise the presumption that, apart from familiar political considerations,
the treatment of the freedmen by Democratic authorities, and by planters,
farmers, and other employers of labor, is neither just nor humane. Certainly
the condition of the small colored farmers, and of the colored laborers, as
described by intelligent representatives of the race, differs from the old
bondage in little beyond the name. The aim of the makers and administrators
of law, and of the great body of white land-owners, appears to be to reconcile
the nearest possible approach to slavery with the nominal continuance of
freedom. It must be confessed that the North Carolinians are very near the
consummation of this purpose. Two of the laws referred to in the statement
exemplify a certain class of the hardships that are complained of. One is
known as the "Common Road law," and is so ingeniously contrived that the
white Supervisors of a county may fasten upon black citizens the bulk of the
labor on its roads. The other, "the Landlord and Tenant act," is several
degrees more iniquitous than laws of a kindred character which in other days
attracted attention to the crimes of English rule in Ireland. Under the
first of these acts the industrious black men who have tried to acquire farms,
or who have rented farms which require all the time and labor they can command, are at the mercy of Democratic officers. Under the second act, the
tenants are exposed to the worst phases of Old World landlordism: they may
toil, but they have no assurance of reward; they may starve, but the landlord will have all; eviction may follow robbery, and they have no redress.
Add to these evils the abuses of the credit system, and the absolute power
of the creditor-trader over the farmer who needs current supplies, and it
is not difficult to understand the loss of heart and hope which impels a deserving class of a grade above the laborer to plan removal to localities
where these situations of discouragement do not exist.

Such being the position in North Carolina of the colored owners and
tenants of small farms, the state of the farm laborers may be imagined. The
object of the white farmers seems to have been to discover the point at
which the laborer may be kept face to face with starvation, with a constant
reminder of the fate that awaits him if he tries to better his position. They
have succeeded. The food allowances are wretched, and the miserable pittance
paid in the form of wages is still further cut down by a system which robs
the laborer of nearly half of the sum he nominally receives. The farmer
grinds and cheats him, and in both operations is helped by the neighboring
storekeeper. The negro is helpless as against the employer and the trader.

If he complains he is turned adrift, and as the employers make common cause
he cannot obtain other work. Then the terrors of a vagrancy act come into
play. Under its provisions a negro out of work may be arrested and consigned to the "the vagrant gang." Even his poor semblance of freedom is
thus lost, it may be indefinitely. The prospect of this treatment keeps
laborers who have families in abject subjection to their masters. "The
oldest negro in North Carolina," we are told, "fails to remember a time when
the slavery was more complete or the hardships greater."

All this, it will be seen, is wholly irrespective of politics. That
the negroes are to a large extent practically disfranchised, we may infer
from the general condition of poverty and helplessness to which they have
been reduced. Men who are kept all the time at starvation point, and who
dare not murmur or move lest they be thrust into the vagrant gang, may be
controlled, politically, without the intervention of the Mississippi plan.
If they vote, their ballots are not counted. And to this assured ascendency
of the Democratic Party the possibility of treatment so cruel and unjust may
be traced. But for Democratic laws, administered by Democrats, the outrages
described would be impossible. From this point of view, the North Carolina
case is political. The immediate occasion of the desire to migrate is however, mainly industrial. The great body of the negroes, whether working
land as nominally its owners, or working on land as the laborers of the old
slave owing class, have abundant reasons for the discontent that prevailed
among them. They would be fit only for bondage if they could submit contentedly to the hopeless wretchedness which is now their portion. The misfortune is, that they are unable to move. Such poverty as they endure pre-
cludes migration. A fortunate few may escape; the many must remain to suffer.

In other Southern States the natural forces at work to continue the
Exodus are identical in their general nature with those reported from North
Carolina. Enough has appeared in the more independent of the New Orleans
journals to prove the presence in Louisiana of solid causes of discontent;
and the unfulfilled promises of the Vicksburg convention are negative testimony to the strength and reasonableness of the feeling that pervades the
colored farm laborers and tenants of Arkansas and Mississippi. We have
uniformly deprecated attempts to use the Exodus for partisan effect, and we
have doubted the wisdom and humanity of encouraging indiscriminate migration
to parts of the West where the market for hired labor is necessarily limited.
Evidently, however, the condition of colored labor at the South gives rise
to problems that will not always remain unsolved. The South cannot with
impunity rob and oppress the race on whose toil it is dependent for prosperity.

New York Times, September 23, 1879.

20. REPORT OF THE COMMITTEE ON ADDRESS TO THE NATIONAL
CONFERENCE OF COLORED MEN OF THE UNITED STATES, MAY, 1879

Fifteen years have elapsed since our emancipation, and though we have
made material advancement as citizens, yet we are forced to admit that obstacles have been constantly thrown in our way to obstruct and retard our
progress. Our toil is still unrequited, hardly less under freedom than
slavery, whereby we are sadly oppressed by poverty and ignorance, and consequently prevented from enjoying the blessings of liberty, while we are
left to the shame and contempt of all mankind. This unfortunate state of
affairs is because of the intolerant spirit exhibited on the part of the men
who control the State governments of the South today. Free speech in many
localities is not tolerated. The lawful exercise of the rights of citizenship is denied when majorities must be overcome. Proscription meets us on
every hand; in the school-room, in the church that sings praises to that God
who made of one blood all the nations of the earth; in places of public
amusement, in the jury-box and in the local affairs of government we are
practically denied the rights and privileges of freemen.

We cannot expect to rise to the dignity of true manhood under the system of labor and pay as practically carried out in some portions of the South to-day. Wages are low at best, but when paid in scrip having no purchasing power beyond the prescribed limits of the land owner, it must appear obviously plain that our condition must ever remain the same; but with a fair adjustment between capital and labor, we, as a race, by our own industry, would soon be placed beyond want, and in a self-sustaining condition.

Our people in the North, while free from many outrages practiced on our brethren in the South, are not wholly exempt from unjust discriminations. Caste prejudices have sufficient sway to exclude them from the workshop, trades, and other avenues of remunerative business and advancement.

We realize that education is the potent lever by which we are to be elevated to the plane of useful citizenship. We have the disposition and natural ability to acquire and utilize knowledge when equal facilities are accorded, but we are denied the necessary advantages, owing to the defective common-school system and non-enforcement of laws in most of the Southern States. We therefore favor and recommend a national educational system embracing advantages for all, the same to be sustained by the proceeds derived from the sale of public lands.

Wholly unbiased by party considerations, we contemplate the lamentable political condition of our people, especially in the South, with grave and serious apprehensions for the future. Having been given the ballot for the protection of our rights, we find, through systematic intimidation, outrage, violence and murder, our votes have been suppressed, and the power thus given us has been made a weapon against us.

The migration of the colored people now going on from several of the Southern States, has assumed such proportions as to demand the calm and deliberate consideration of every thoughtful citizen of the country. It is the result of no idle curiosity, or disposition to evade labor. It proceeds upon the assumption that there is a combination of well-planned and systematic purposes to still further abridge their rights and privileges, and reduce them to a state of actual serfdom. It is declared in Holy Writ "that the ox that treadeth out the corn shall not be muzzled."

If their labor is valuable, it should be respected. If it is demonstrated that it cannot command respect in the South there is but one alternative, and that is to emigrate. But as the South possesses many advantages for them, they would prefer to remain there if they could peaceably enjoy the rights and privileges to which they are legally entitled and receive fair and equitable remuneration for their labor. The disposition to leave the communities in which they feel insecure, is an evidence of a healthy growth in manly independence, and should receive the commendation and support of all philanthropists. We, therefore, heartily indorse the National Emigration Aid Society recently organized at Washington, D.C., and bespeak for it a successful issue in its laudable undertaking.

We view with gratification the recent efforts of the planters of Mississippi and Louisiana, at the Vicksburg Convention, to effect an adjustment of the labor troubles existing in that section of the country. Believing that through such movements it is possible to establish friendly relations, adjust all differences between the races, and secure a final and satisfactory settlement of the grave causes underlying the unsettled and inharmonious condition of affairs now obtaining among them at the South, we would respectfully recommend to both classes the adoption of similar action in the future for the settlement of all disturbing public questions which may arise between them.

Having said so much with regard to the disabilities under which we labor on account of influences over which we have no control, we are not unmindful of the all-important fact that we are to a great extent the architects of our own fortunes, and must rely mainly on our own exertions for success. We therefore, recommend to the youth of our race the observance of strict morality, temperate habits and the practice of economy, the acquisition of land, the acquiring of an agricultural education, of advancing to mercantile positions and forcing their way into the various productive channels of literature, art, science and mechanism. The sooner a knowledge of our ability to achieve success in these directions is acquired, the sooner we will overcome the apparently insurmountable obstacles to our elevation.

In the struggle for independence our blood mingled with that of the
white man in defense of a common cause. When our flag was insulted on the
high seas and naturalized citizens outraged, we sprang promptly to our
country's call in the war which followed. We did not stop to consider the
fact that, although Americans, we were not citizens; that, although soldiers
we were not freemen. In the war of the rebellion, after emancipation, we
responded by thousands in the country's defense; and on the high seas, in
tented camp and rifle parapets, the prejudice of race and caste were forgotten in the heat of conflict, and the cause of secession disappeared be-
neath the bodies of white and black alike. In the light of these facts we
demand, in the name of the citizenship conferred by the organic law of the
land, in the name of humanity and Christian brotherhood, the same treatment
accorded the other nationalities of our common country--nothing more, nothing
less. If the government has the right to make us citizens, surely it has
the power to enforce the laws made for our protection. We have reached a
crisis in the history of the race. With us it is a question of citizenship
upheld by the moral sentiment of the country and protected by its physical
power, or of citizenship in name invaded, outraged and winked at whenever
party necessities and exigencies require the stifling of the will of a
majority in the interest of party ascendency--more than that, it is a question of life and existence itself. We have submitted patiently to the
wrongs and injustice which have been heaped upon us, trusting that in the
fullness of time a generous and humane public sentiment would bring to our
relief the enforcement of all laws passed for our protection. If the nation
desires to maintain the proud position it has attained, it must say and
prove to the world that every man in our midst is free and equal, and that
the same means will be used to protect its colored citizens in the right of
citizenship as have been used to avenge the insults and outrages against
the country's flag; and for the accomplishment of these ends, we invoke the
prayers and sympathies of all liberty-loving citizens.

*Proceedings of the National Conference of Colored Men of the United States.
Held in the State Capitol at Nashville, Tennessee, May 6, 7, 8, and 9,
1879. (Washington, D.C., 1879), pp. 94-98.*

21. NEGRO COLONIZATION

The following paragraph is an extract from a private letter written by
a gentleman who served in the Union army during the War, and who afterwards
settled in the South, where he now lives and where he held a prominent office
under the last Administration. The writer is a Republican in politics, a
man of good judgment, and long enough a resident of the South to be entitled
to respect for any opinion he may express upon the race conflict going on
in several States. With special reference to the emigration of the blacks,
he says:
"The 'exodus' is the only solution of the Southern question. The persons
who once owned the negro as a slave will never live in peace with him as a
political equal. The Anglo-Saxon will never submit to be governed by any
so-called inferior race; hence the irrepressible conflict will go on in the
South till the exodus removes at least a part of the negro race, which is
weakest mentally though strongest in number in some of the States. But I
don't like the idea of an exodus to the North. That will only be changing
the location of the race conflict. Gen. Grant's idea was the true one, and
ought to have been carried out. Annex San Domingo, a territory capable of
supporting ten millions of people in comparative luxury, and give it to the
negro. Let national vessels ply between the principal Southern ports and
that island, giving free transportation to the emigrant, and you will see an
'exodus' worthy of the name. In that event the South would fill up with a
labor like that in the North, which would not submit tamely either to the

lash of the bulldozer nor to the deprivation of its political rights."

It is a notable fact that many of the Northern men who have lived in the Cotton States since the War, and who have no sympathy whatever with the material discrimination and political oppression practiced upon the blacks, are still of the opinion that it will not be possible to harmonize the relations between the two races. If this judgment be correct, then it is true that an "exodus" is "the only solution of the Southern question." The same view of the situation has been taken by many Northern men of ability not residing in the South, and it has been the inciting cause of various projects for emigration and colonization of the blacks, among which may be enumerated the following: A scheme to agree upon some one or two negro States, with encouragement for the settlement of the blacks and the removal of the whites; the purchase of San Domingo, which was urged by Gen. Grant largely upon the ground that the new island in our possession would furnish a congenial home for the oppressed blacks of the South; Senator Windom's scheme for black emigration to Dakota, Montana, and other lands open for settlement in the Territories of the cold Northwest, and especially along the line of the Northern Pacific Railroad. The recent flight of black laborers from Louisiana and Mississippi was not the result of any organized effort, but a spontaneous movement among themselves to escape oppression and injustice, stimulated, of course, by the usual promises held out by railroad circulars; and hence it attests the eagerness of the negroes, as a class, to quit a section of the country where they have labored for fourteen years without improving their condition. The palpable manifestation of this disposition on their part, which the Southern whites cannot reasonably ignore, may be the turning point in the conflict of races in the South. It may warn the land-owners of the South that they cannot longer maintain this conflict without incurring the risk of losing the labor which supports them, and the apprehension of such loss may teach the Southern "Anglo-Saxon" that he can better afford to give the negro his position and social rights and a fair share of his earnings than to lose black labor altogether. If this warning be heeded, and the white population of the South adapt itself to the situation, then the prediction that the two races cannot live together in peace will prove to be wrong; otherwise, there is little doubt that more comprehensive schemes will be organized to release the blacks from their *quasi* condition of bondage at the South, and furnish them with homes where material prosperity and political equality will depend upon their own industry, frugality, and ambition of purpose. In the latter event, the revival of Gen. Grant's San Domingo project will probably be received with more popular favor than was accorded it when it was first proposed. It would seem now that Gen. Grant was gifted with more prescience than his opponents, and it is safe to say that, if the Republican party had the same political control now that it enjoyed at the time when Grant was urging the purchase of San Domingo, renewed negotiations would result in the acquisition of that island with special reference to the colonization of the blacks. It may be that recent Democratic blunders may restore to the Republicans in Congress in sympathy with Northern civilization and political methods, and in that case the anxiety of the blacks to escape from the hardships of their present existence may find a response and practical aid in the Americanizing of San Domingo for their benefit. Even if the ex-Confederation shall prevail in the Administration of the next four years, strict honesty would require that they should further some such project for the colonization of the negroes, for most of them pretend that their country would be better off without the blacks. Renewed emigration from the Cotton States in the winter and spring, after the gathering of the present crop, may be confidently expected. That will serve to convince the Southern whites that the movement is not transient and unimportant, but actually threatens a loss of the black labor. It will then be for the "running class" to determine whether they desire to keep the blacks, or to let them go their way. If the former, then they must treat the negro as an equal before the law, and, if the latter, they should further any proper scheme for facilitating black emigration and for colonizing the negroes in such a way as to provide a final settlement of the race problem.

Chicago Tribune, July 3, 1879.

22. THE NEGRO'S NEW BONDAGE

--

CRUEL LAWS OF THE DEMOCRATIC SOUTH

NORTH CAROLINA COLORED PEOPLE ANXIOUS TO GO WEST--THEIR PRESENT CONDITION
WORSE THAN SLAVERY--HOW THE WHITES SWINDLE AND OPPRESS THEM--A PETITION FOR
AID.

WASHINGTON, Sept. 22.--Two very intelligent-looking colored men have recently
arrived here from North Carolina. They come as agents of a very extensive
society of colored people in the Second Congressional District of that State,
and bring with them a petition which is signed by 163 respectable colored
people, well known in the community in which they live, 150 of whom are
heads of families, each averaging from five to ten in number. The petition
is addressed to the National Emigration Aid Society, and reads as follows:
     "We, the undersigned colored people of the Second Congressional District
of North Carolina, having labored hard for several years under disadvantages
over which we had no control, to elevate ourselves to a higher plane of
Christian civilization; and whereas, our progress has been so retarded as to
nearly nullify all our efforts, after dispassionate and calm consideration,
our deliberate conviction is that emigration is the only way in which we can
elevate ourselves to a higher plane of true citizenship. As our means are
insufficient to emigrate without the aid of friends, we therefore petition
your honorable body, through our worthy agents, Samuel L. Perry and Peter C.
Williams, for aid to emigrate to some of the Western States or Territories.
And we furthermore agree to be bound by any contract which they may enter
into in their efforts to secure aid for our transportation and settlement."
     The two agents referred to are both young men--neither of them over
30 years of age--and were selected, no doubt, on account of their intelligence
and conservative manner of speech. Neither of them has ever held any political office of any kind, one being a school-teacher and the other a Methodist
Minister. They are fully empowered to make any arrangements on behalf of
those they represent, and they hope for success, and will probably succeed,
from the fact that they expect to prove the justness of their people's purpose to emigrate, not so much by tales of a bloody-shirt character as by a
calm and business-like narration of the conditions under which the colored
people in North Carolina are compelled to work and exist. They both called
the offices of THE TIMES in this city a day or two ago and made a very clear
and intelligent statement of the circumstances which are now impelling the
exodus movement. The source of all their troubles is the State laws adopted
by Democratic Legislatures. These laws virtually make the negro as much of
a slave now as he was before the war; and as the negro seldom, if ever, gets
his voice counted, though he may be allowed to put it into the ballot-box,
there is no hope of ever changing their present condition. With them all
hope has fled, and even the most prosperous of them despair of better times.
According to the statements of the two agents, their greatest hardships are
in consequence of the two laws known as the "Common Road law" and The Landlord and Tenant act. The former requires every man in the counties, between
the ages of 18 and 45, to work on the road not less than 10 days each year,
and as many more days as the County Supervisors may require. There are few
exemptions to this law, and as the colored people are usually the ones called
upon to perform this road labor without compensation, it frequently works
great hardship to families that exist only by the labor of day to day. The
Landlord and Tenant act requires that farm rent shall be paid before any
part of the crops are sold or consumed. In other words, the colored man who
rents a small farm is not permitted to gather any part of his crop, either
for sale or for home consumption, until he has gathered and delivered one-
third of it to his landlord. It therefore sometimes happens that the colored
farmer's family want even the common necessaries of life while he is gathering
the one-third of his crop for the landlord, and he must gather it himself,
alone, as he is not permitted to sell any part of it to procure money to hire
help. Another great hardship of the colored farmers is the result of the
mortgage system. A man is forced to get advances, sometimes of money, but

generally of bacon, flour, meal, and other produce, and gives mortgages on
his crops. The prices charged for the produce advanced, are invariably
high, while the prices afterward allowed for the crops are correspondingly
low. The consequence is that the mortgages take nearly the whole crop, and
the remainder goes for rent. It sometimes happens, however, that after the
mortgage is satisfied, there is nothing left to pay the rent with, and the
inexorable landlord seldom shows mercy, but drives the poor family from the
farm.

The hardships of the colored farm laborers employed by white farmers
are no less rigorous. Farm laborers are paid $6 a month and "found", which
means that they are given shelter and just enough to eat to keep them from
starving. The average food allowance for each laborer per week is four pounds
of pork or bacon and one peck of corn-meal. They can cook these two articles
as they please, but they never get a varied bill of fare. A laborer who has
a family is allowed to keep them on the farm, but unless they do work they
are not fed by the "boss." Indeed, the general rule is that laborers must
feed their own families and they have only $6 a month to do it with. Out
of this amount must also come the money paid for clothes and a little tobacco.
The laborers on public works of the State were formerly allowed $18 a month.
That amount was reduced, however, to $12, and it is now proposed to give them
only $8 a month. The colored people judge from this that the wages of farm
laborers will also be reduced next year, as laborers on public works always
get about double that paid to farm lands.

Even this small sum of $6 a month, however, is not paid in cash. The
white "boss" almost invariably pays his hands in scrip, and the country
merchants or cross-road shop-keepers take this scrip in payment for goods at
a discount of about 25 per cent. The "boss" subsequently redeems the scrip
at a reduction of about 10 per cent, on its face value, so that both "boss"
and merchant profit by the business. The cheated negroes have no option in
these transactions, and even if they had the cash to buy with, they would be
compelled to pay at least 25 per cent more for the necessaries of life than
Northern laborers pay in Northern communities.

Under these circumstances, the negroes are utterly helpless. If any one
of them murmurs or complains, or is suspected in any way of being disposed to
create dissatisfaction among his co-laborers, he is at once discharged. In
this way the negroes are cowed. The "boss" is always on the watch, and his
constant threats to discharge somebody keeps the negroes under the most perfect discipline. The fear of discharge alone, however, is not the secret of
the meek submission of the negroes. The white legislators have, by a complex
system of Democratic legislation, succeeded in successfully co-operating with
the tyrannical "bosses." Under what is known as the Vagrancy act, any person
without occupation may be arrested and put to work in the vagrant gang of
laborers. A negro who is discharged by one "boss" seldom gets hired by another, and he is doomed to the vagrant gang, for he cannot obtain employment,
however willing he might be to work.

All these things keep the negroes in abject servility to their old masters.
Indeed, the two agents above referred to declare positively that the oldest
negro in North Carolina fails to remember a time when their slavery was more
complete or their hardships greater. They say that very few, if in fact any,
of the negroes own farms. Some of them, a few years ago, purchased small
tracts of land on time and paid for them in monthly installments. Of late,
however, the installment plan has proved a farce. One man, after paying up
$5,000 on his farm, was unable to pay the last installment, and his land was
sold and he got nothing. It was bid in for the amount of the last installment
due.

In reference to public schools, the colored people have nothing to boast
of. No new schools of any size have been built since the Republicans had
control of the State Government, and as it is now the public schools for the
colored children are only kept open three or four months in the year. Colored
school-teachers'formerly received $60 a month, but now they get only $10 and
$15. Everything possible is done to discourage and limit education, and the
colored people understand this fact only too well. The two agents said these
things were not all, but that they could talk for hours, telling of their
disadvantages in the South. Their people expected to suffer for a while in the
West, or at whatever point they should move to, but there they could hope for

better times. As it is, they suffer in the South, and have no hope of a
change. On the contrary, things grow worse each year, and there is not a
hamlet or a farm-house of colored people in the South in which dissatisfaction, not to say despair, does not reign at all seasons of the year. The
163 signers of the petition referred to above are not destitute. They have
farm implements, &c., and they are anxious to go to any eligible place. They
hope for a little aid expecting transportation, but will emigrate, they say,
if they have to journey on foot.

NASHVILLE, Tenn., Sept. 22.--Cheap excursion rates having been extended
to St. Louis, Kansas City, and Topeka, Kan., 100 colored people left here
to-night for Kansas, and more will follow to-morrow.

New York Times, September 23, 1879.

23. SOUTHERN LABOR TROUBLES

It seems to be considered in some parts of the South that the departure
of many colored laborers has been facilitated by the means of a conspiracy.
A Georgia paper for example, commenting on the efforts of a well-known
colored man to help those who were bound to Kansas, says that the colored
people of the region are "as invincible to the arguments of the accomplices
of the base Radical section, whose aim it is to use them in filling their own
coffers with the proceeds of their labor, as the earth upon which they stand."
It is taken for granted that the negroes would not think of going to Kansas
or elsewhere unless some base person--an accomplice in a conspiracy--were at
hand to make the wicked suggestion that they might be better off somewhere
in the North. In North Carolina, as we have lately seen, a more vigorous
remedy than mere argument is applied to prevent the so-called exodus. The
negroes who have been sent out to prepare the way before the intending emigrants are notified from home that it would be unsafe for them to return, so
violent are the threats made against them by their former masters and present
employers. By an ingenious system of financial contracts, supplemented by
State laws designed for the strengthening of the bonds of the colored race,
it is possible for the employers to so impoverish and hamper the blacks that
it seems as if they may as well give up all hope of escaping from the house
of bondage.
It does not appear to have occurred to any of the astute political
managers of the South that there is too much protesting that the negroes do
not desire to go away, and would not go if it were not for the "arguments
of the accomplices of the base Radical section," which is supposed to desire
the unpaid labor of these people. The elaborate preparations made to obtain
the colored people are inconsistent with the theory that nothing but a conspiracy will be effectual in alluring them away from their comfortable and
happy homes in the South. They are to be cajoled by the base accomplices
who seek to entrap them into Northern fields of labor, and they are to be
kept at home in the South by all sorts of legal and illegal contrivances.
The negro is happy in the South, but he is open to the arguments of the base
accomplices, whoever they may be. In passing, it should be noticed that the
term "Radical" is used in the South to express the bitterest feeling of hatred
and contempt. To say of the part of the United States to which some of the
colored people have gone that it is a "base Radical section" is to confer
upon it the most scathing of epithets. But if the condition of the negro in
the South is so blessed and serene as has been described, why are the arguments of Northern emissaries so potent that it is necessary to use force and
legal entanglements to detain him? In most free countries laborers change
their place of abode, passing from State to State, without hindrance, whenever
it suits their whim or convenience, and without exciting remark.
The uneasiness, to use a mild term of the colored people of the South is
only one of many indications of the fatuous policy which has been attempted
by the Southern leaders ever since they have resumed political power. This

policy is an attempt to keep the reins of government in the hands of a few.
Before the war the South was governed by an oligarchy, and this seems to be
the natural tendency of things in that section of the country to this day.
Southern newspapers are filled with complaints of hard times and depressed
business; and yet, the chief occupation of the people is politics. As in
the old times, the leading white men of each section do nothing but grumble
and curse the hard fate which keeps them poor, their poverty being, somehow,
due to the Government, or to the neglect of some financial power dwelling in
another section of the country. If the white people of the South were not
so intent on political control, they would be in a far happier condition and
frame of mind. The persistent effort to maintain an artificial state of
society, in which one class shall constitute a servile substratum, monopolizes
all the energies of the Southern people. It is a conspicuous fact that the
negroes do prefer not to leave their homes in the South. It is notorious
that nothing but adversity or oppression would drive them forth. One would
suppose that the policy of the white men of the South would have been to
secure the confidence and affection of their late slaves when freedom became
a fixed fact, and thus to forestall all attempts to alienate them. If the
freedmen had been assisted, in good faith, to make for themselves comfortable
homes among the people who had been once their owners, or had even been left
to their own devices, does anybody suppose that they would now be looking
eagerly to emigration as a way of escape from something dreaded? It is asserted, and with some show of reason, that the negro votes as he is told.
If this is true, and nobody knows it better than the Southern man, why have
no steps been taken to allure the colored people into the Democratic fold?
If the negro is so simple and ignorant that the base emissaries of the Kansas
farmers have some success in their seductive plans, how does it happen that
nobody in the South has ever tried kindness and fair treatment as a means of
detaining these confiding people? It would really seem as if the allurements
of fair wages and good homes on the one side were only met with threats of
forcible detention on the other. These flies are to be tempted with vinegar.

Of course, the obvious answer to this inquiry is that the men who are
in a position to conciliate and quiet the disturbed negroes are afraid of the
ruling public sentiment. It is not the custom in the South to concede that
the negro has any political rights. If he has these, the sceptre must depart
from the hands of the old oligarchy. To treat the ex-slaves as intelligent
human beings, endowed with reasoning faculties and entitled to absolute freedom of action within the law, would be a subversion of all notions of social
and political order. To preserve the normal balance of things, it is necessary that the negro should "be kept in his own place," and where that place
is, the experience of the many unfortunate martyrs to a thirst for knowledge
and an awakened ambition has testified. It has been necessary to keep the
negro in his place by forcible means. Is it any wonder, then, that he seeks
another and a better country? Thus the folly of the men who desire to maintain a false and artificial state of society reacts upon themselves. No
matter how far successful they may be now in detaining the uneasy colored
people, no matter how the men who fret at this feeble exodus try to check it,
there will be migration from the South just so long as the laborer, white or
black, is oppressed. While labor is considered servile, and the condition of
the laborer made irksome, there will be discontent and flight. More than
this, there can be no white migration Southward so long as the land is filled
with violence and tyranny, however disguised these may be. Until the Southern
people learn that the laborer is free to go and come as he pleases, seeking
his own happiness and comfort in his own lawful way, there can be no substantial prosperity among them.

New York Times, October 6, 1879.

24.   AN ENGLISHMAN'S PERCEPTIONS OF BLACKS IN KANSAS CITY

In Kansas City . . . the negroes are more numerous than I have yet seen.
On the Kansas side they form quite a large proportion of the population.
They are certainly subject to no indignity or ill-usage. They ride quite
freely in the trains and railways alongside of the whites, as I myself experienced, and there seems to be no prejudice whatever against personal contact with them. I did not hear them at all abused or slanged. Coming along
in the train-car a cart was found standing on the line, and detained us some
time. When the owner at last appeared, he was a black man. A white waggoner
in London would certainly have been most unmercifully slanged by a bus driver,
and would have deserved it, but our driver said nothing that I could hear.
He may have moved his lips or said something low, *but it was the negro* I
heard defiantly call out "What do you say?" . . . The blacks are civil and
attentive as waiters in the hotel and railway cars, but sometimes ill-man-
nered. . . .

Here the negroes seem to have quite taken to work at trades; I saw them
doing building work, both alone and assisting white men and also painting
and other tradesman's work. On the Kansas side I found a negro blacksmith,
with an establishment of his own; he was an old man, and very "negro," and
I could extract a very little from him. He grumbled just like a white man--
he made a living; did pretty well; "But things are dear. But there you are
expected to work cheaper." He came from Tennessee, after emancipation; had
not been back there, and did not want to go. Most of the schools here are
separate and not mixed. "Perhaps that suits best. Some black boys go, and
some don't."

Sir George Campbell, *White and Black--The Outcome of a Visit to the United
States* (New York, 1879), pp. 225-26.

25.   COLORED IMMIGRANTS IN KANSAS

PRESENT CONDITION OF THE REFUGEES FROM THE SOUTH

TOPEKA, Kans., Dec. 31. A staff correspondent of the Chicago *Inter-
Ocean,* who has been making an investigation of the exodus in Kansas during
four weeks' travel through the State, writes a letter from here, giving his
conclusions. He estimates the number of refugees in the State at 15,000.
Of these, he thinks that probably one-fifth were able to buy a little land
and are making a good progress in farming. Most of the remainder have found,
through the Freedman's Relief Association, places as laborers, and are giving
good satisfaction. In no county did he find them burdens upon corporated
charities; but the demand for these laborers has been stretched to its fullest
capacity, as the accumulation of refugees at the barracks now nearly 700--for
whom no places can be found, clearly indicates. Judging from what he has
learned from refugees themselves, and from the increasing number--now from
25 to 50 arriving every day, he predicts that the movement to Kansas will soon
assume such proportions again as to astonish the country, and unless the tide
can be turned, or the charity of the North more readily bestowed, that suffering which the Relief Committee, although laboring faithfully with the means
at their command, has not been entirely able to relieve during the recent cold
weather will soon be turned to general destitution and great suffering among
the pauper refugees.

New York Times, January 1, 1880.

26. BLACKS IN THE WEST

Cincinnati, January 2.

The charge that Hoosier emissaries are laboring in North Carolina to induce the blacks to go to Indiana is denied by the people who have arrived. The Rev. Mr. Williams answers the question why they came to Indiana without hesitation or reserve. "After laboring and economizing for 14 years, he says, "my people find themselves as poor, and ignorant, and despised as they were at the close of the war--a condition differing from absolute slavery only in this, that they are now at liberty to emigrate without being hunted down by bloodhounds." The policy of emigrating, therefore, has long been the principal topic of discussion at the fireside, in the prayer-meeting, and at public gatherings. As a result of it, small emigration societies have been organized in many of the counties, collections taken, and plans matured, that at the proper time an exodus might begin. During the past Summer, aroused by the Mississippi emigration, these arrangements were vigorously pushed, and by September enough money had been collected by the Lagrange Society to defray the expenses of a single delegate, who should go as far west as Indiana or Illinois to find suitable places to locate, until such times as they might be able to go upon Government lands. Mr. Williams was chosen such representative, and being a minister of the African Methodist Episcopal Church, he stopped at points having similar churches, to whose Pastors he confided his mission. From these he took letters of introduction to others further on, and in this way reached Indianapolis. There he found a large colored population, who entered readily into the plans of their Southern brethren. They organized local relief committees, turned colored churches into hotels, and canvassed the city for means to feed and help all who should come. Thus Indianapolis became a sort of centre where all might congregate and thence be distributed wherever laborers were needed. Capt. Langsdale, editor of the Greencastle *Banner,* volunteered to aid in finding homes for all who should come. But beyond receiving and answering letters, Mr. Langsdale finds that his services are not needed. The Rev. John H. Clay, Pastor of the colored church, has stood at the wheel and guided the affair. Colored people take entire control of the matter. The assistance of white men beyond giving money to feed the immigrants on their arrival, has neither been sought nor needed, and to charge the movement upon Republicans is quite as absurd as to argue that Democratic opposition to their coming is keeping them away.

That there is a demand for the labor of these people is made evident by the number of applications that come from all parts of Indiana, and from the adjoining States of Ohio and Illinois. Mr. Langsdale receives a handful of these letters every day. The Rev. Messrs. Clay, and Williams, at Greencastle, have their pockets full. Mr. Trevan, of Indianapolis, is equally burdened with applications, as is every one else whose name is mentioned in connection with the movement. Farmers want them. The plan of having two or three hired men, with their families, settling on a farm, in little homes of their own, is a new one in Indiana. In Winter or Summer their labor can be depended upon. If sickness enters the farmer's home, colored nurses are at hand. The women, too, can milk and wash and make gardens, if necessary, they can go into the field or take care of the stock. Their children can run errands and do the lighter work. Thus a farmer becomes independent of all outsiders. Said one farmer the other day, "I would take them even if ordinary farm laborers were plenty, which they are not . . . The coming of these colored families, therefore, is a necessity, and is solving the labor question for the rural districts."

New York Times, January 3, 1880.

27. THE APPEAL FROM KANSAS

To the Editor of the New York Times:

In your issue of Friday last, Jan. 30, you state on the authority of
Gov. St. John, of Topeka, Kans., that 16,000 colored refugees have located
in that State since last April. In view of that fact, it seems to me that
we old Abolitionists ought to feel that our work is not yet finished; we
have for years been endeavoring to teach colored men that their true position
is that of free American citizens; we have fought and paid dearly to prove
the sincerity of our efforts in their behalf, and now, when the fruits of
these lessons begin to crop out, when our scholars begin to realize the truth
of our teachings, and attempt to exercise the rights we have conferred upon
them, their former masters, true to the instincts generated by the accursed
institution of slavery, opposed their exercise of practical liberty, by in-
stituting a system of kukluxing, bulldozing, and tissue ballot swindling.
The effect of this systematic opposition has been to convince our colored
brethren of the Southern States that their position to-day is no better than
that of the Israelites under Egyptian bondage, and, like their prototypes
of old, they have determined to emigrate. We are, more than others, responsible for this state of things; we taught them freedom, and urged them to
exercise their rights as freemen; they have taken our counsel and made the
attempt. What then, is our duty in the matter? Shall we fold our arms and
say, "We have opened the way to you, now work out your own salvation? I say
no. The spirit that prompted a man to be an Abolitionist 30 years ago will
prompt him now to make still another effort to finish so noble a work. These
poor people appeal to us to aid them until they can raise their first crop.
Gov. St. John seconds their appeal and offers to become your almoner. Let me
urge my friends to accept this services in that capacity, and do as I do.
Enclose a dollar bill every month to his address.
                                        GEORGE S. McWATTERS.

New York, Friday, Feb. 6, 1880.

New York Times, February 7, 1880.

28. THE COLORED REFUGEES

A MOVEMENT AMONG NEW YORKERS TO AID THEM IN THEIR EFFORTS TO SETTLE IN KANSAS

New York, Feb. 13, 1880.

Touched by the account of the sufferings of the colored refugees in
Kansas, the undersigned appeal for help for them. There are already 15,000
to 20,000 of them in the State. They continue to come day by day, arriving
ragged and bare-foot and without money. Many are sick from exposure to the
severe climate, and a number have been frozen to death. They are willing
to work, but at this season of the year unable to get employment, as most of
them are only accustomed to labor on a farm. A considerable part of those
who came in the Summer have contrived to pick up a living, and now offer to
help those who have followed in their distress. Gov. St. John says he "has
seen *no tramps* among them."
We are gathering up money and supplies for the Irish, which is right.
Ought we not to remember our starving fellow-citizens in our own country?
The Freedman's Relief Association of Topeka, Kan., with which Gov. St.
John is connected, calls urgently for aid, especially for money to buy fuel
and food, and to pay railroad fares, as the association forwards the refugees
as fast as possible to all places where the people are willing to care for
them till Spring comes, when they can set them at work. Contributions should
be sent promptly to

New York Times, February 17, 1880.

29. THE TIDE OF COLORED EMIGRATION

WASHINGTON, Feb. 26. There arrived at Washington to-day 150 colored
emigrants from North Carolina. They came from Warren and Lenoir Counties,
and are destined for Indianapolis. They proceeded on their journey to-night
by the way of the Baltimore and Ohio Railroad. About two-thirds of the
party are women and children. They report that others will follow them as
soon as they can command the means necessary to pay for transportation, and
that the negroes will leave North Carolina in large numbers in the Spring
months.

New York Times, February 27, 1880.

30. THE EXODUS TO LIBERIA

DRIVEN FROM ARKANSAS BY WHITE PERSECUTION

ONE HUNDRED MEN, WOMEN, AND CHILDREN WHO WOULD RATHER STARVE IN AFRICA THAN
LIVE SOUTH--THE STORY OF THEIR SUFFERINGS--ANOTHER PARTY ON THE WAY.

One hundred colored men, women, and children, dusty, travel-worn and
scantily-clad, dismounted from the 10:28 train at the Pennsylvania depot, in
Jersey City, yesterday morning, on their way to Liberia. The party, who are
all from Phillips County, Ark., started from Helena just a week ago, and have
spent the interim on the crowded decks of Mississippi and Ohio River steamboats and in the dingy and closely-packed emigrant cars of the "Pan Handle"
Route. The journey from Philadelphia was made in two emigrant cabooses, with
an extra freight car for their luggage. The party is under the guidance of
Richard Newton, an intelligent, hardworking black man, who, despairing of
decent treatment for himself and his brethren at the hands of the ex-rebel
whites of Arkansas, has determined to seek a new home for them in Liberia. The
present party are but the *avant couriers* of a colonization army, said to
number 10,000 in the State of Arkansas alone, who are organized into companies
of 100 each, with the object of emigrating to the North or to Liberia--any-
where, in fact, to get out of the clutches of their unreconstructed task-
masters. The stories that these unfortunate people tell of the cheating,
swindling, and grinding oppression to which they have been subjected for years
past, are most pitiable. That their statements are true is abundantly proved
by the concurrent testimoney of both blacks and whites, as well as by the
frequent though reluctant, admissions of Southern newspapers.
    In crossing the Desbrosses Street Ferry, the party were objects of mingled
curiosity and pity to all who saw them. Huddled together like   in a
corner of the men's cabin, they said little, and seemed desirous of avoiding
observation as much as possible. There were old black men, with snowy wool,

roughened cheeks, and hard, cracked hands, little molasses-colored picka-
ninnies with frightened faces, clutching hold of their mothers' skirt, goodlooking young mulatto and quadroon girls, old women with sunken cheeks and
bowed heads, anxious fathers toil-worn and husky-voiced, clad in rough home-
spun and keeping an anxious look-out for their charges. They numbered 24
men, 33 women, and 43 children, all told. Half a dozen battered packing-
cases and a score of dry-goods boxes contained all their worldly goods--
bedding, furniture, and provisions. Every man who had owned a mule or a
plow or anything salable had disposed of it, generally at a hard bargain, to
get the wherewithal to come North. Many of the women and children had not
a change of clothing. On landing, Newton formed his ragged regiment into
something like military order, and marched them up Sixth avenue to Thirty-
third street. Here they were quartered for a short time in the house No.
130, on the north side of the street, but as the proprietor asked a larger
price for his lodgings than they could afford to pay, they were taken to the
rooms of the Young Men's Colored Christian Association, No. 124 West Twenty-
sixth street. During the evening John J. Freeman, editor of the colored
paper, the *Progressive American,* T. T. B. Reed, J. W. E. Grey, and other
well-known colored people, called at the house and offered their services to
Newton in providing employment for his people until the sailing of a ship
for Liberia, which will not occur for fully six weeks. Some of the emigrants
have sums of money, $50 and $100 apiece, in gold and silver, but the majority
of them are said to be destitute. They ate a frugal supper last night on a
table of boards spread in the centre of the room, and then lay down to sleep
on the floor. The room, which is only 30 feet long by 13 wide, was crowded
almost to suffocation with men, women, and children, and the ceaseless crying
of half a dozen babies added to the discomfort. When their destitute condition became known, one or two small tradesmen of the neighborhood sent in
donations of provisions and groceries, and a baker at the corner of Seventh
avenue and Thirty-third street contributed two barrels of bread. The great
fear of the negroes is that they will not have money enough to pay the passage to Liberia. Newton says that after the white bull-dozers at Helena had
exhausted every other means of keeping them there they sent the Sheriff down
to the landing and forced them to pay from $2.50 to $8 apiece for taxes.
Many of them had already paid these taxes before, and had receipts showing
that they had done so, but the Sheriff was inexorable, and said they must pay
or stay. Newton consulted Republican and Democratic lawyers, who told him
that the exaction was a monstrous one, and was clearly illegal, but advised
them to pay if they could possibly raise the money, as a lawsuit would only
make their plight worse. They clubbed together and satisfied the Sheriff's
demands, those who had money paying for those who had not. Women were taxed
$2 and $2.50 a head, and every person having a piece of baggage with his or
name on it had to pay something to the Democratic Sheriff, "Bart" Turner,
before he was allowed to go. In some cases the original poll-tax of $1.50 a
head--which had already been paid--was raised to $2.50.

Richard Newton, Rufus Patton, Ephraim Holmes, and other heads of families
described the suffering and swindling which they have endured at the hands of
ex-rebel land-owners and storekeepers as being worse than any possible amount
of suffering they could undergo at the North or in Liberia. Their crops were
always mortgaged beforehand to the storekeepers, and, struggle as they would,
they could not get out of debt. Some of the landlords made them give up one-
half the cotton they raised for rent; others took one bale out of three. Out
of the two-thirds that were left they had to pay the cost of planting, har-
vesting, and the storekeeper's bills, which were always swollen in proportion
to their crop. No matter how hard they worked, or how big the crop, the store-
keeper's bill for advances of provisions and clothing swamped it. Bills were
"raised" from $150 to $200 and $250 at a stroke of the pen, and if the un-
fortunate negro protested he was terrified into paying by threats and abuse.
Ephraim Holmes said he had seen a colored man knocked down and beaten in Dr.
Jack's store, in Helena, because he refused to take $2 worth of purchases and
$1.50 in change for a ten-dollar bill. Others were raided by night-riders,
and had their barns burned and their crops destroyed out of pure deviltry.
One old woman had her hay-rick fired and her house burned over her head
because she sheltered some "Radical niggers" about election time. Girls and

married women were violated by drunken white ruffians and if their husbands
or fathers sought redress they were "raided" by the "night-riders." Women
who defended themselves against attempts at violation, were first outraged
and then nailed by their ears to trees. The local authorities, who were all
Democrats and ex-rebels, were not only powerless to prevent this state of
things, but often winked at it. None of papers dared to take up the black
man's case, and in the greater number of instances the outrages were either
hushed up or palliated by lying stories set afloat. At election time in
1878 the country was overrun with armed military companies and night-riders;
and the negroes were told to vote the Democratic ticket under threats of
continued outrage if they did otherwise.

At Cincinnati, Richard Newton left with the Recorder of the city a
blurred and misspelled document, which, divested of its inaccuracies, is as
follows:

"We were to start from Helena on the 17th of March, but by the help of
the Lord we got away on the 18th of March. We say that God was with us, for
the people at Helena did all they could to induce us to remain. We were
citizens of Phillips County, Ark., and we had paid our taxes, but when they
saw we were determined on leaving they attached all we had on the wharf-boat
for taxes. We, being brothers, went to the Court-house and paid what was
demanded; but we do say that many of us paid them twice. We furthermore say
that we have been treated like dogs. I would not treat a dog as colored men
are treated in Arkansas. We humbly beg the people at large to help us out
of the South. I believe God will reward you if you do so. I cannot tell
all of the sufferings of the colored people of the South. But pray to God
to help us to get out of the South."

Another party of 300 are expected here by Tuesday.

New York Times, March 27, 1880.

31. WRONGS OF THE COLORED RACE

ONE OF THE ARKANSAS REFUGEES TELLS OF THE PERSECUTION OF HIS PEOPLE IN THE
SOUTH.

The Rev. Simon Davis, minister, and one of the Arkansas colored refugees,
occupied last evening the pulpit of the Rev. Dr. H. H. Garnet, at the Shiloh
Presbyterian Church, and spoke about the persecution to which his race has
been subjected in the South for some years past. The colored people, he said,
were so oppressed in the South that sometimes they almost doubted whether they
were human beings. They had tried every means in their power to earn an honest
living and to lead a religious life, but at every step they were met with
opposition and outrage. If a colored man purchased and cultivated a farm he
would be called upon by a white man who demanded rent. If the owner claimed
that it was his property, the white man would then bring a lawsuit, and by
some legal means prove ownership and make the real owner a tenant. If a
negro settled on Government land it was taken away as soon as he had improved
it. Those who worked for white proprietors were hardly paid one-half of
wages at which they had been engaged, and many were not paid anything at all,
and were deeply in debt. Hundreds were thus brought to the verge of starvation, and if to preserve life they confiscated food they were sent to the
Penitentiary. At election time bands of masked white men rode about the
country at night and broke into the houses of the colored men who they
thought were opposed to them. For a trifling political offense the colored
political offender was flogged; if the whites had a special spite against a
colored person they took him out and killed him. The speaker was told by
several Southerners, on several occasions, that the blacks were their property, and that the whites were going to live off them so long as they staid
there; that they had been preparing for this state of affairs for several

years, and had the State in just such a condition as they wanted, and if the
blacks were not satisfied they could leave, and their places would be filled
with another class. The blacks were charged with having helped the North to
crush the South; "and now," some whites said, "your Northern friends have
gone and left you in our hands, and we are going to do just what suits us,
and stuff ballot-boxes as we please." What the Southern colored people want,
continued the preacher, so to gain an honest living by hard work, and to live
in peace with all. When the Liberian question was first agitated in his district, Mr. Davis strongly opposed it, but he has since become convinced that
God was in favor of this movement, and, referring to the text read in the
lesson, "Ethiopia shall soon stretch out her hands unto God," he declared
that God's had was directing this movement to Liberia to carry out His own
wonderful plan.

New York Times, April 5, 1880.

32. THE ARKANSAS REFUGEES, I

     The General Relief Committee for the Arkansas refugees met in the rooms
of the Young Men's Union Christian Association yesterday afternoon, Vice-
President Philip A. Walton in the chair. The committee appointed at a previous meeting to investigate and report on the condition of the refugees
presented a long report, through its Chairman, T. T. B. Reed. The report
said the refugees were very independent and refused to go to work by the
month, although employment on farms had been offered to some of them. A few
of them have money and are able to take care of themselves, and the committee
found that, while appealing for aid, the refugees had turned over to the
Liberian Colonization Society $78 in money. In view of these facts, the re-
port recommended that the General Committee solicit no further aid from the
public in money, food, or clothing; that it "refuse, deny and prohibit" to
the moneyed element of the refugees board, lodging, or clothing; that the
Superintendent be ordered to turn over to the refugees all the provisions now
in his care, cooked and uncooked, and that the refugees be instructed to do
their own cooking and care for themselves hereafter, being allowed the use
of their present quarters in West Thirty-seventh street only until May 1.
The reading of the report caused a long discussion, much of which was wholly
irrelevant. The Rev. W. F. Dickerson and the Rev. J. S. Atwell opposed its
adoption, and the former said that if the committee abandoned the refugees,
there were other black men in New York who would stand by their brothers.
After three hours of angry debate, Mr. Atwell offered a resolution referring
the report back to the committee "for such modifications as will present a
more business like aspect on the part of the General Committee, and less reflections on the unfortunate refugees," and this was finally adopted.

New York Times, April 20, 1880.

33. THE ARKANSAS REFUGEES, II

To the Editor of the New York Times:

     The report of T. T. B. Reed to the General Relief Committee for the
Arkansas Refugees, noticed in your issue of Tuesday morning,   an entirely
erroneous impression regarding these people. The committee was organized that
they might not be obliged to use the small pittance which has been gathered
by years of hard work and self-denial. The people from Arkansas have stated
frankly from the first that they had such money. This all who have witnessed
the honest, straightforward bearing of the men feel they deserve to keep and
that it a duty to provide for them so long as they are (unavoidably) detained
here.

Being turned out of their homes in Arkansas, when the purpose of leaving was known, they reached here some weeks before time for sailing. Notwithstanding that a persistent effort has been made since their coming to intimidate them, and shake their resolution to go to Africa, they cannot be moved, and for this are reported "very independent." As it is hoped that money for the passage to Africa can be raised by the 1st of May, they, of course, "refuse to go to work by the month," feeling that it would be dishonest to enter upon any engagement which it will be out of their power to keep. The few who had money paid to the Treasurer of the American Colonization Society $478 toward passage; (this, if equally divided, would give the party scarcely $8 apiece.) The Treasurer was so impressed with the sincerity of the men, and the evident desire to help themselves, that he only accepted this money lest a sufficient sum might not be raised, and, therefore, unasked, gave to them a written pledge that, if possible, the money should be returned. The report of T. T. B. Reed does not in any sense express the views of the colored men of New York, and it is their purpose to aid these people so long as they may be compelled to wait here. While I believe that our land has ample space for all its citizens, yet, at the same time, if any choose to seek homes in other countries, they have a perfect right to go where they will.

                                        HENRY HIGHLAND GARNET.
                   Shiloh Presbyterian Church, West Twenty-sixth street.

New York Times, April 22, 1880.

34. THE ARKANSAS REFUGEES, III

To the Editor of the New York Times:

A report having gone forth to the world through the medium of the Press that the Arkansas refugees were rich and were dishonest, we, the undersigned, were appointed as a special committee from the General Committee having them in charge to disabuse the public minds concerning them. We would say that they are among the most unfortunate of all persons who have ever come in our midst. They are poor and the majority of them have no means of subsistence. They are not lazy; they are willing to work, and many of them are at work daily. The General Committee have unanimously voted to continue their benefactions as long as the necessity for the same exists. We submit that the published statements concerning their internal affairs were most unfortunate, and quite at variance with the truth in the case. We are directed to state that the "refugees" are still in need, and the charitable public is very earnestly requested to continue its donations as long as the sufferers are in our midst and are in an unavoidable condition of need. We have not abandoned our brethren and do not propose so to do. Money, food, and clothing are still needed. Donations may still be sent to the Rev. H. H. Garnet, No. 165 West Twenty-sixth street; the Rev. J. H. Cook, No. 1460 Second avenue; Mr. Peter S. Porter, No. 252 West Twenty-sixth street; the Rev. W. F. Dickerson, No. 218 Sullivan street. Respectfully submitted,

                                        WILLIAM F. DICKERSON,
                                        T. T. B. REED,
                                        J. W. STEVENS.

New York Times, April 26, 1880.

35.   THE EXODUS QUESTION

Mr. Editor:--I see that the Committee on Exodus reported that the cause in North Carolina was Northern politicians and negro leaders in their employ, &c. We do not tolerate any such deceitful report. The cause of our people leaving this part of the State was, first, for a living. The average wages in North Carolina for men is from eight to ten dollars per month, and they have to take half of that up in trade. The man will tell you that he has no money and will give you an order to some white man's store, and in three hours after you leave he comes along and pays for what you purchase. He has his family to take care of and educate his children off this eight or ten dollars, and is compelled to take half of it in trade. And you need not leave one man and go to another, for it is understood from the oceans to the mountains this is done to keep us from ever being able to buy lands, and thus they hope to be able to keep us on theirs to work for them and their children, and should you ever become able to make them an offer they will charge you from $10 to $12 per acre for land that would not produce five bushels of corn to the acre. The women get from three to four, five and six dollars per month and find their own rooms. Should they accidentally break an old plate while in their service, they charge them from 50 to 75 cents for it. This they take out of her four or five dollars.

As for colored juries, there is not one in Orange county, nor never has been; but ah! there is no use in trying to write--it would take an angel's pen to do it.

I had a minister's certificate given to me by the Superintendent of the Railroad. When I go to buy a ticket he marks on that ticket second-class-- as much as to say all negroes are second-class. A white minister purchased one at the same time and they marked it first-class; and if I go into the first-class car they make me pay extra. This was done last week. But half can't be told.

Hillsboro, N.C.

The Christian Recorder, July 8, 1880.

36.   TESTIMONY OF HENRY ADAMS BEFORE THE SELECT COMMITTEE OF THE UNITED [85] STATES SENATE TO INVESTIGATE THE CAUSES OF THE REMOVAL OF THE NEGROES FROM THE SOUTHERN STATES TO THE NORTHERN STATES:

Q. What is your business, Mr. Adams?

A. I am a laborer. I was raised on a farm and have been at hard work all my life.

Q. Now tell us, Mr. Adams, what, if anything you know about the exodus of the colored people from the Southern to the Northern and Western States; and be good enough to tell us in the first place what you know about the organization of any committee or society among the colored people themselves for the purpose of bettering their condition, and why it was organized. Just give us a history of that as you understand it.

A. Well, 1870, I believe it was, or about that year, after I had left the Army--I went into the Army in 1866 and came out the last of 1869--and went right back home again where I went from, Shreveport; I enlisted there, and went back there. I enlisted in the Regular Army, and then I went back after I came out of the Army. After we had come out a parcel of we men that was in the Army and other men thought that the way our people had been treated during the time we was in service--we heard so much talk of how they had been treated and opposed so much and there was no help for it--that caused me to go into the Army at first, the way our people was opposed. There was so much going on that I went off and left it; when I came back it was still going on, part of it, not quite so bad as at first. So a parcel of us got together and said that we would organize ourselves into a committee and look into affairs and see the true condition of our race, to see whether it was possible we could stay under a people who had held us under bondage or not. Then we did so and organized a committee.

Q. What did you call your committee?

A. We just called it a committee, that is all we called it, and it remained so; it increased to a large extent, and remained so. Some of the members of the committee was ordered by the committee to go into every State in the South where we had been slaves there, and post one another from time to time about the true condition of our race, and nothing but the truth.

Q. You mean some members of your committee?

A. That committee; yes, sir.

Q. They traveled over the other States?

A. Yes, sir; and we worked some of us, worked our way from place to place and went from State to State and worked--some of them did--amongst our people in the fields, everywhere, to see what sort of living our people lived; whether we could remain in the South amongst the people who had held us as slaves or not. We continued that on till 1874. . . .

Q. Was the object of that committee at that time to remove your people from the South, or what was it?

A. O, no, sir; not then; we just wanted to see whether there was any State in the South where we could get a living and enjoy our rights.

Q. The object, then, was to find out the best places in the South where you could live?

A. Yes, sir; where we could live and get along well there and to investigate our affairs--not to go nowhere till we saw whether we could stand it.

Q. How were the expenses of these men paid?

A. Every one paid his own expenses, except the one we sent to Louisiana and Mississippi. We took money out of our pockets and sent him, and said to him you must now go to work. You can't find out anything till you get amongst them. You can talk as much as you please, but you have got to go right into the field and work with them and sleep with them to know all about them.

Q. Have you any idea how many of your people went out in that way?

A. At one time there was five hundred of us.

Q. Do you mean five hundred belonging to your committee?

A. Yes, sir.

Q. I want to know how many traveled in that way to get at the condition of your people in the Southern States?

A. I think about one hundred or one hundred and fifty went from one place or another.

Q. And they went from one place to another, working their way and paying their expenses and reporting to the common center at Shreveport, do you mean?

A. Yes, sir.

Q. What was the character of the information that they gave you?

A. Well, the character of the information they brought to us was very bad, sir.

Q. In what respect?

A. They said that in other parts of the country where they traveled through, and what they saw they were comparing with what we saw and what we had seen in the part where we lived; we knowed what that was; and they cited several things that they saw in their travels; it was very bad.

Q. Do you remember any of these reports that you got from members of your committee?

A. Yes, sir; they said in several parts where they was that the land rent was still higher there in that part of the country than it was where we first organized it, and the people was still being whipped, some of them, by the old owners, the men that had owned them as slaves, and some of them was being cheated out of their crops just the same as they was there.

Q. Was anything said about their personal and political rights in these reports, as to how they were treated about these?

A. Yes; some of them stated that in some parts of the country where they voted they would be shot. Some of them stated that if they voted the Democratic ticket they would not be injured. . . .

Q. State what was the general character of these reports?

Q. I have not yet got down to your organization of 1874--whether what
you have given was the general character; were there some safer places found
that seemed a little better?

A. Some of the places, of course, were a little better than others.
Some men that owned some of the plantations would treat the people pretty
well in some parts. We found that they would try to pay what they had
promised from time to time; some they didn't pay near what they had promised;
and in some places the families--some families--would make from five to a
hundred bales of cotton to the family; then at the end of the year they would
pay the owner of the land out of that amount at the end of the year, maybe
one hundred dollars. Cotton was selling then at twenty-five cents a pound,
and at the end of the year when they came to settle up with the owner of the
land, they would not get a dollar sometimes, and sometimes they would get
thirty dollars, and sometimes a hundred dollars out of a hundred bales of
cotton.

Q. What were the best localities that you heard from, if you remember,
where they were treated the best?

A. In Virginia was what they stated was the State that treated them the
best in the South; Virginia and Missouri and Kentucky, and Tennessee.

Q. There the treatment was better was it?

A. Yes, sir; it was better there.

Q. Had you any reports from North Carolina? Some few from North Carolina.

Q. Do you remember anything about them; or is your knowledge of that
State only general?

A. Well, they reported that some parts of North Carolina was very bad
and other parts was very good. . . .

Q. I am speaking now of the period from 1870 to 1874, and you have
given us the general character of the reports that you got from the South;
what did you do in 1874?

A. Well, along in August sometime in 1874, after the white league
spring up, they organized and said this is a white man's government and the
colored men should not hold any offices; they were no good but to work in
the fields and take what they would give them and vote the Democratic ticket.
That's what they would make public speeches and say to go and we would hear
them. We then organized an organization called the colonization council.

Q. The result of this investigation during these four years by your
committee was the organization of this colonization council. Is that the
way you wish me to understand it?

A. It caused it to be organized.

Q. It caused it to be organized. Now, what was the purpose of this
colonization council?

A. Well, it was to better our condition.

Q. In what way did you propose to do it?

A. We first organized and adopted a plan to appeal to the President of
the United States and to Congress to help us out of our distress, or protect
us in our rights and privileges.

Q. Your council appealed first to the President and to Congress for
protection and relief from this distressed condition in which you found yourselves, and to protect you in the enjoyment of your rights and privileges?

A. Yes, sir.

Q. Well, what other plan had you?

A. And if that failed our idea was then to ask them to set apart a
territory in the United States for us, somewhere where we could go and live
with our families.

A. You preferred to go off somewhere by yourselves?

A. Yes.

Q. Well, what then?

A. If that failed, our other object was to ask for an appropriation of
money to ship us all to liberia, in Africa; somewhere where we could live in
peace and quiet.

Q. Well, and what after that?

A. When that failed then our idea was to appeal to other governments
outside of the United States to help us to get away from the United States
and go there and live under their flag.

Q. Have you given us all the objects of this colonization council?

A. That is just what we was organized for, to better our condition one way or another. . . .

Q. Now, let us understand more distinctly, before we go any further, the kind of people who composed that association. The committee, as I understand you, was composed entirely of laboring people?

A. Yes, sir.

Q. Did it include any politicians of either color, white or black?

A. No politicianers didn't belong to it, because we didn't allow them to know nothing about it, because we was afraid that if we allowed the colored politicianer to belong to it he would tell it to the Republican politicianers, and from that the men that was doing this to us would get hold of it, too, and then get after us.

Q. So you did not trust any politicians, white or black?

A. No; we didn't trust any of them.

Q. That was the condition of things during the time the committee were at work in 1870 to 1874?

A. Yes, that was the condition.

Q. Now, when you organized the council what kind of people were taken into it?

A. Nobody but laboring men. . . .

Q. At the time you were doing that, was there anything political in your organization?

A. Nothing in the world.

Q. You were simply looking out for a better place in which you could get work and enjoy your freedom?

A. Yes, sir; that was all.

Q. When did the idea first enter your council to emigrate to the northern and northwestern States; if you remember, what were the first movements in that direction?

A. Well, in that petition we appealed there, if nothing could be done to stop the turmoil and strife and give us our rights in the South, we appealed then, at that time, for a territory to be set apart for us to which we could go and take our families and live in peace and quiet.

Q. The design of your organization, then, as you understood it, was not so much to go north to live among the white people in the Northern and Western States as it was to have a territory somewhere that you could occupy in peace and quiet for yourselves?

A. That is what we wanted, provided we could not get our rights in the South, where we was. We had much rather staid there if we could have had our rights.

Q. You would have preferred to remain in the South?

A. Yes, sir.

Q. And your organization was not in favor of your moving, providing you could get your rights and be protected in the enjoyment of them as any other men?

A. No, sir; we had rather staid there than go anywhere, else, though the organization was very careful about that, and we said so from the first; and then, if that could not be done under any circumstances, then we wanted to go to a territory by ourselves.

Q. Well, about what time did this idea of a territory first occur to you; did it occur at all during the organization of your committee, or after the council was organized?

A. After the committee had made their investigations.

Q. Well, what did you do after that?

A. We organized the council after that.

Q. About what time did you lose all hope and confidence that your condition could be tolerated in the Southern States?

A. Well, we never lost all hopes in the world till 1877.

Q. Not until 1877?

A. No, sir. In 1877 we lost all hopes.

Q. Why did you lose all hope in that year?

A. Well, we found ourselves in such condition that we looked around and we seed that there was no way on earth, it seemed, that we could better our condition there, and we discussed that thoroughly in our organization along in May. We said that the whole South--every State in the South--had got into the hands of the very men that held us slaves--from one thing to another-- and we thought that the men that held us slaves was holding the reins of government over our heads in every respect almost, even the constable up to the governor. We felt we had almost as well be slaves under these men. In regard to the whole matter that was discussed, it came up in every council. Then we said there was no hope for us and we had better go.

Q. You say, then, that in 1877 you lost all hope of being able to re- main in the South, and you began to think of moving somewhere else?

A. Yes, we said we was going if we had to run away and go into the woods.

Q. Well, what was the complaint after you failed to get the territory?

A. Then, in 1877 we appealed to President Hayes and to Congress, to both Houses. I am certain we sent papers there; if they didn't get them that is not our fault; we sent them.

Q. What did that petition ask for?

A. We asked for protection, to have our rights guaranteed to us, and at least if that could not be done, we asked that money should be provided to send us to Liberia.

Q. That was 1877, was it?

A. Yes, sir; that was in 1877.

Q. Still, up to that time you did not think at all of going into the Northern States; at least you had taken no steps toward going into those States, had you?

A. No, sir.

Q. When did that idea first occur to your people?

A. In 1877, too, we declared that if we could not get a territory we would go anywhere on God's earth, we didn't care where.

Q. Even to the Northern States?

A. Yes, anywhere to leave them Southern States. We declared that in our council in 1877. We said we would go anywhere to get away.

Q. Well, when did the exodus to the Northern States from your locality, or from your country you are acquainted with best, begin?

A. Well, it didn't begin to any extent until just about a year ago.

Q. It didn't begin to any extent until 1879, you mean?

A. No, sir; not till the spring of 1879.

Q. But you had prior to that time been organized and ready to go some- where, as I understand you?

A. Yes, sir; we had several organizations. There were many organizations; I can't tell you how many immigration associations, and so forth, all spring- ing out of our colonization council. We had a large meeting, some five thou- sand people present, and made public speeches in 1877 on immigration.

Q. What was the character of those speeches as to what you intended to do?

A. We intended to go away, to leave the South, if Congress would not give us any relief; we were going away, for we knowed we could not get our rights.

Q. Where were these meetings held?

A. Some were held at Shreveport, in Caddo Parish, some were held in Madison, and some were held in Bossier Parish.

Q. Was there any opposition to these meetings in which you talked about going away?

A. No, sir. There didn't nobody say anything to us against our having our meetings, but I will tell you we had a terrible struggle with our own selves, our own people there; these ministers of these churches would not allow us to have meeting of that kind, no way.

Q. They didn't want you to go?

A. No; they didn't want us to go.

Q. Why?

A. They wanted us to stay there to support them; I don't know what else. Mighty few ministers would allow us to have their churches; some few would in some of the parishes. There was one church, Zion, in Shreveport, that allowed us to talk there.

Q. Were the ministers opposed to it?

A. Yes, sir; they was opposed to it. . . .

Q. Your meetings were composed, then, of men in favor of going away?

A. Yes, and of the laboring class.

Q. Others didn't participate with you?

A. No, sir.

Q. Why didn't the politicians want you to go?

A. They were against it from the beginning.

Q. Why?

A. They thought if we went somewhere else they would not get our votes. That is what we thought.

Q. Why were the ministers opposed to it?

A. Well, because they would not get our support; that is what we thought of them.

Q. They thought it might break up their churches?

A. Yes; that is what they thought; at least we supposed the ministers thought that.

Q. About how many did this committee consist of before you organized your council? Give us the number as near as you can tell.

A. As many as five hundred in all.

Q. The committee, do you mean.

A. Yes; the committee has been that large.

Q. What was the largest number reached by your colonization council, in your best judgment?

A. Well, it is not exactly five hundred men belonging to the council, that we have in our council, but they all agreed to go with and enroll their names with us from time to time, so that they have now got at this time 98,000 names enrolled.

Q. Women and men?

A. Yes, sir; women and men, and none under twelve years old. . . .

Q. How many of your people have gone from that part of the country to the North, if you know?

A. I don't know exactly how many have gone.

Q. Of course you cannot tell us exactly, but as near as you know; give some idea of the number, if you can.

A. My reports from several members of the committee, in parts I have not been in and seen for myself--I take their words and put their words down as mine, because they are not allowed to lie on the subject. And so from what I have learned from them from time to time I think it is about five thousand and something.

Q. Do you mean from that section of country down there?

A. Yes, sir.

Q. From Louisiana?

A. Yes, sir. . . .

Q. Now, Mr. Adams, you know, probably, more about the causes of the exodus from that country than any other man, from your connection with it; tell us in a few words what you believe to be the causes of these people going away.

A. Well, the cause is, in my judgment, and from what information I have received, and what I have seen with my own eyes--it is because the largest majority of the people, of the white people, that held us as slaves treats our people so bad in many respects that it is impossible for them to standit. Now, in a great many parts of that country there our people most as well be slaves as to be free; because in the first place, I will state this: that in some times, in times of politics, if they have any idea that the Republicans will carry a parish or ward, or something of that kind, why, they would do anything on God's earth. There ain't nothing too mean for them to do to prevent it; nothing I can make mention of is too mean for them to do. If I am working on his place, and he has been laughing and talking with me, and I do everything he tells me to, yet in times of election he will crush me down, and even kill me, or do anything to me to carry his point. If he can't carry his point without killing me, he will kill me; but if he can carry his point without killing me, he will do that. . . .

Senate Report No. 693, Part 2, 46th Cong., 2nd Session, 1880, pp. 101-05, 108-11.

37. NICODEMUS

Nicodemus was a slave of African birth,
And was bought for a bag of gold.
He was reckoned a part of the salt of the earth,
But he died years ago, very old.

Good times coming, good times coming,
Long, long time on the way;
Run and tell Elijah to hurry up Pomp
To meet us under the cottonwood tree,
In the Great Solomon Valley,
At the first break of day.

Walter L. Fleming,   "Pap Singleton, the Moses of the Exodus," *American Journal of Sociology,* pp. 67-69.

38. "THE ADVANCE GUARD OF THE EXODUS"

One morning in April, 1879, a Missouri steamboat arrived at Wyandotte, Kansas, and discharged a load of colored men, women and children, with divers barrels, boxes, and buddles of household effects. It was a novel, picturesque pathetic sight. They were of all ages and sizes. . . . their garments were incredibly patched and tattered, stretched, and uncertain; . . . and there was not probably a dollar in money in the pockets of the entire party. The wind was eager, and they stood upon the wharf shivering. . . . They looked like persons coming out of a dream. And, indeed, such they were . . . for this was the advance guard of the Exodus.
Soon other and similar parties came by the same route, and still others, until, within a fortnight, a thousand or more of them were gathered there at the gateway of Kansas--all poor, some sick, and none with a plan of future action. . . .
The closing autumn found at least 15,000 of these colored immigrants in Kansas. Such of them as had arrived early in the spring had been enabled to do something toward getting a start, and the thriftier and more capable ones had made homestead-entries and contrived, with timely aid, to build cabins; in some cases, small crops of corn and garden vegetables were raised. . . .
. . .Numerous cabins of stone and sod were constructed while the cold season lasted; . . . in many cases, the women went to the towns and took in washing, or worked as house-servants . . . while the men were doing the building. Those who could find employment on the farms about their "claims," worked willingly and for small wages, and in this way supported their families, and procured now and then a calf, a pig, or a little poultry; other obtained places on the railroads, in the coal-mines, and on the public works at Topeka. Such as got work at any price, did not ask assistance; those who were compelled to apply for aid did it slowly, as a rule, and rarely came a second time. Not a single colored tramp was seen in Kansas all winter; and only one colored person was convicted of any crime. . . .

Scribners' Monthly 8 (June, 1880): 211-15.

39. LABOR IN THE FAR SOUTH

HOW COLORED WORKMEN ARE DEFRAUDED

It has from time to time been fully proved in these columns that the colored men of the South were not regarded as equals before the law; that they were not permitted freely to exercise the rights of suffrage conferred upon them by the national Constitution, and that the Democratic State and local Governments gave them next to no opportunity of educating their children. But these are not the only wrongs of which the freedmen have to complain. From a number of facts which I obtained during a recent visit to the Gulf States--facts which will not be successfully disputed--it is evident that in every material relation the negroes are cheated and taken advantage of by the whites. From year's end to year's end they have been made to work for the profit of the land-owners, and each year they have found themselves growing poorer and poorer. Of course, there are isolated exceptions to this general rule. Here and there may be found a black man who, by dint of hard work and close economy, coupled with circumstances of a peculiarly fortuitious character, has gathered together enough money to buy a small farm, and who has a few thousand dollars in good securities. But such cases are very rare, so rare, in fact, that when one of them is discovered the Southern newspapers have much more to say about it than they would about half a dozen murders. In the great majority of cases the negroes are living actually from hand to mouth. They and their families are kept alive very much as they were in the days of slavery. That they are in any of their material relations more independent than they were during those days there is very little evidence. Since the results of the war made them free all sorts of means have been resorted to by the whites, who had and have all the money, to keep them from bettering their financial condition, and thereby placing themselves in a position to make more favorable terms with their former owners. One of the earliest of these devices was known as "the share system." Under its provisions the white capitalists supplied the land, provisions, seeds, and implements, the negroes, with their wives and children, gave their labor, and it was understood that at the end of the year the profits of the crops which were obtained should be divided between all those engaged in raising them. When the time for a division came, however, it was almost invariably found that all the money which had been made was by one means or another placed in the pockets of the land-owners, while the black laborers were declared to be in debt for extra supplies, to provide for which they were coolly required to give a lien on the share of the next year's crop which was supposed to be theirs. For a time this pretty little scheme worked admirably and to the very great advantage of the capitalists. But by degrees the negroes began to see that they were being systematically cheated out of their hard earnings, that, indeed, for all practical purposes, they might just as well be slaves as freemen. Knowing this, they ceased to take any interest in their work under "the share system" which never brought any "share" to them. They neglected the fields, and after a time convinced the land-owners that some new and less transparent means of defrauding them would have to be devised. To a very great extent the latter have succeeded.

In the far South, but particularly in Mississippi, the "share system" has now given place to what is known as the "lease system" and the "hire system." Under both of them the whites continue to get very much the best of the bargains which are made with the colored men. For instance, under the so-called hire plan the land-owner usually contracts to pay an able-bodied and experienced farm-hand, who is aided by a wife and perhaps by children, $16 a month, or a total of $192 a year. It is also understood that the negro is to be supplied with a "furnish," which consists of certain stipulated quantities of meal, pork, sugar and coffee, and which is to be given at certain stated periods in the year. This "furnish" costs the capitalist $85. One mule and the farming implements necessary for the use of the negro, the ownership of which rests with the land proprietor, costs him about $200. The wear and tear of mule and implements, at a very liberal estimate, is $50 a year. These are the usual expenses which have to be borne by the land-owner under the "hire plan." It will be seen that they foot up a total of $327 a year; but, to be on the safe side, and to include a liberal sum on account of interest on the capital invested by the owner, let be assumed that the total expense to him is $400 a year. On the other hand, what are his profits from the negro, the mule, the implements, and the land upon which he is supposed to expend this sum? It is always expected that the negro and mule will cultivate during the year 12 acres of ground. It is usual in Mississippi to plant nine acres of this in cotton and three in corn. In a reasonably good year nine acres of the rich bottom lands of the Mississippi, to which the figures given are applied, yield 12 bales weighing 500 pounds each. At 10 cents a pound, the total derived from the sale of this product would be $600. From the corn land 60 bushels are usually expected from the acre. From three acres the yield at this rate would, of course, be 180 bushels, which, if sold at the average price of 70 cents a bushel, would bring $126. From these figures it will readily be seen that the total yield in money from the 12 acres would be $726. If the $400 which was allowed for expenses be deducted from this sum, it will be found that the land-owner has realized from his 12 acres the handsome profit of $326. And the majority of them are not content with these returns. By every conceivable trick, by extortionate charges for extra provisions which they may or may not have supplied to the negroes, they continue to evade payment of a large portion of the wages which it was agreed should be given to the laborer and the blacks in ninety-nine cases out of a hundred at the end of the year find themselves precisely where they commenced--that is to say, penniless and entirely dependent upon the white land-owner for the food which keeps them from starvation and the miserable cabin which gives them but scant protection from the elements.

Still bad as it is, many of the negroes with whom I talked on the subject said that they preferred the hire to the lease system. On the surface there is no good reason why this should be so. The inquiring stranger is always told that the negroes can lease land at $8 an acre, or $96 a year, for 12 acres, which in many cases is true. It is also stated to those who make such inquiry that a negro can feed and clothe himself for $100 a year, get a mule for $110, farming tools for $50, a wagon for $75, and that all other expenses for himself and a small family could be covered for $100, or a total of $536 a year. On this basis his crop should yield him $190 clear profit the first year, and subsequently, when he need make no expenditures for mule or implements, such profit should be largely increased. But, unfortunately for the negro, the figures given are only superficial ones. Close inquiry reveals the fact that there is one set of prices for a black man in the far South and another set for the whites. It being always assumed that the negro buys on credit, he is obliged on an average to pay $160 for the mule which costs the white man $110, $110 for the wagon, $75 for the farming implements, and for meal, bacon, sugar, coffee, calico, and everything else in the same proportion. The plantation storekeepers who charge him these prices are, in nearly every instance, in partnership with the land-owners, and divide with them the profits. In addition to everything else, the negro debtor is charged by these all-powerful oppressors interest on all his purchases at the average rate of 18 per cent. To secure payment of their advances made on these outrageous terms the storekeepers in every case exact from the negroes a deed in trust on the mule and all implements furnished, and also on all growing crops which may be raised by their use. So, at the end of the year the unfortunate Mississippi "freedman" who has been bold enough to venture upon farming under the lease system is lucky if he escapes from his creditors with the clothes on his back. And for these wrongs there is next to no redress before the Democratic courts. In the great majority of the counties in Mississippi it is impossible to find record of a case in which a negro has successfully sued a white man. Their only escape from oppression seems to be in leaving their old homes and emigrating to other States. This, they have already done to a greater extent than is generally supposed. In all parts of Louisiana and Mississippi there is a growing complaint of a scarcity of labor. To such an extent is this true that the planters in the Teche country have been making earnest effort to get Chinese from Cuba to move their sugar crops, and at this moment the steamboat men at New Orleans, Vicksburg, and Memphis are not able to get men sufficient to handle their cargoes, and this is the case despite the fact that they are offering prices to this class of laborers which three years ago would have been looked upon as little short of fabulous. The land-owners and capitalists of the South should be warned in time. When it is too late they may be only too forcibly reminded of the fact that they killed the goose which for generations has laid their golden eggs.   H. C.

New York Times, November 26, 1880.

40. INTERVIEW WITH SOJOURNER TRUTH [86]

"You are now on your way to Kansas?"

"Yes, I am going out there to see the colored people; but I must stop and hold meetings to pay my way from Battle Creek and back again. I have prayed so long that my people would go to Kansas, and that God would make straight the way before them. Yes, indeed! I think it is a good move for them. I believe as much in that move as I do in the moving of the children of Egypt going out to Canaan, just as much. It will also be a benefit to the South, to the ungodly people there. The blacks can never be much in the South. They cannot get up. As long as the whites have the reins in their hands, how can the colored people get up there? I tell you they can't do it, for there is nothing to let them up. But if they come here to the North, and get the Northern spirit in them, they will prosper, and returning down there, some of them will teach these poor whites. They will go down there, and these colored people will bring them out of Egyptian darkness into marvelous light. The white people cannot do it, but these will; before forty years, they will teach the slave holders the truth that they never had and never knew of. God works in a mysterious way. In Battle Creek a tramp came along, and looking upon him, a colored man recognized his old master, and gave him assistance to help him on; gave him his breakfast and supper. I tried my best, right after the war, to have colored people go to Kansas and settle on homes. I traveled there myself for this purpose, hoping to get the government to give a home to those colored people who were in Washington, living there at government expense, paying people great sums to feed them, when the money might carry them out to Kansas lands and fix it so they could support themselves. I was there in Arlington after the war, and for three years I hoped to get the people away. General Howard and General Butler approved of my general ·recommendation, and I see that my going to Kansas, though for the time being a failure, has been approved by the Lord, who is finally taking my people there in such numbers. The movement means the regeneration, temporally and spiritually, of the American colored race, and I always knew the· Lord would find some way. I said his holy purpose must be fulfilled, and now he has put into their hearts to go out there, and not to stay South and be abused and heathenized any longer. There will be, chile, a great glory come out of that. I don't expect I will live to see it; but before this generation has passed away, there will be a grand change. This colored people is going to be a people. Do you think God has had them robbed and scourged all the days of their life for nothing?"

The old lady's voice had ·risen to a still higher note, and the closing sentences were pronounced with solemn gestures, including a slight swaying to and fro of the body and shaking of the head.

Interview in Chicago *Inter-Ocean,* taken from *Narrative of Sojourner Truth* (Battle Creek, Michigan, 1884), pp. 18-20.

1   For a biographical background on Isaac Myers, see the introduction and Doc. 7 in Part XI, Vol. I.

2   Henry McNeal Turner (1843-1915) was born in Columbia, South Carolina, of free Negro parents, and in 1855 moved to Macon, where he joined the African Methodist Episcopal Church and became a preacher. "His eloquence," a church paper noted later, "attracted the attention of the white citizens, who considered him to be 'too smart a nigger' to remain in the South, and he was obliged to leave." Turner went to Baltimore and finally to Washington as pastor of Israel Bethel Church. Here he rapidly became a leader of the Negro community and an outstanding and militant fighter for racial justice in the capital. In 1863 he was appointed by President Lincoln as chaplain to the first United States Negro troops. After the war Turner moved to Georgia, where he continued preaching and played a prominent part in Reconstruction politics.
    Before he was declared ineligible for membership in the Georgia House, Turner had introduced two bills of a progressive nature, neither of which was passed. One called for an eight-hour day for laborers and the other sought to prevent common carriers "from distinguishing between white and colored persons in the quality of accommodations furnished."
    In 1880 Turner was ordained Bishop in the African Methodist Episcopal Church.
    During the years between Reconstruction and World War I, Turner became the chief advocate of emigration of black Americans to Africa. He became convinced that there was no future for the Negro in the United States, dominated as it was by white racism, and his conviction was fully fixed in 1883, when the Supreme Court nullified the Civil Rights Act of 1875, in a decision which declared that the federal government could not prevent racial discrimination by private parties. During the 1890s Turner organized several attempts to transport blacks to Africa and through his newspaper the *Voice of Missions*, urged Afro-American emigration. He died in Windsor, Canada in 1915.
    Jefferson Franklin Long (1836-1900) was born a slave near Knoxville, Georgia. As a youth he moved to Macon, where he learned the tailor's trade, and eventually opened his own shop. After the Civil War, Long entered an equally successful political career. In 1871 he became a member of the United States House of Representatives, the only black congressman from the state of Georgia. In March 1871, when his term expired, he returned to Macon and declined to run for political office again.

3   The Freedmen's Savings and Trust Company was chartered by the federal government in 1865 specifically to provide banking services for freedmen. Two-thirds of the deposits were to be invested in United States securities. Between April 1865 and 1872 thirty-four branches were established, nearly all of them in southern cities and deposits totaled about $3,000,000. Throughout its existence poor investment policy and faulty business practices plagued the institution. In an attempt to save the bank, Frederick Douglass became its president, but it was too little too late. Political influence secured loans for a few privileged financiers, such as Jay Cooke who borrowed large sums at excessively low interest rates, while still other speculators saddled the bank with bad loans. Douglass' efforts failed and the bank was closed in June 1874. Thousands of black depositors lost their hard-earned savings.

4   Joseph E. Bryant was a leading figure in the Republican Party of Georgia. He edited a Radical newspaper, the *Loyal Georgian*, published in Augusta.

5   The Union League of America was organized in the North to rally support for the Union effort during the Civil War. After the war it became
a (sort of) benevolent association operating in the South to protect
Republican Party gains, and recruited members primarily among the freedmen. Negro members were taught their political rights, and in return,
blacks looked to the local League for advice when they knew it would not
be forthcoming from other quarters. Consequently, the Union League became important in the South during Reconstruction as a mechanism for
delivering black votes to the Republican Party.

6   For a discussion of this practice among planters of "dealing in supplies for their hands" and its abuses, see pp. 24, 26, 349.

7   "John Chinaman" was a common expression, sometimes of derision, referring to the Chinese labor which entered the United States through
California during the post-Civil War industrial expansion. Usually contracted for pitifully low wages in order to receive passage to America,
they depressed the price of labor and thus stirred considerable resent-
ment among Euro-American workers.

8   The Fifteenth Amendment was passed in 1870 as part of the Radical
program for Reconstruction. It states that the right of citizens to vote
shall not be denied or abridged "on account of race, color, or previous
condition of servitude." Although the intention was to ensure Negroes
the right to vote, it remained a dead letter until nearly a century later
when the mechanisms utilized to subvert the amendment were outlawed
during the civil rights movement of the twentieth century.

9   The city referred to was New York City where the National Anti-Slavery
Standard was published.

10   For biographical background on Lewis H. Douglass, see the introduction
to Part IX, Vol. I.

11   For biographical background on George T. Downing, see note 48, Vol. I.

12   For background on the Chesapeake Marine Railway and Dry Dock Company,
organized by Isaac Myers in Baltimore, Maryland, see Part XI, Doc. 7, 11-
13, Vol. I.

13   Prior to the Civil War blacks in Baltimore had no building for public
meetings, except churches. Consequently, in 1863, several local black
leaders purchased a large three-story building on Lexington Street for
that purpose. They named it the Douglass Institute after Frederick
Douglass, "the grand old man from Maryland." In addition to public entertainment, the hall also provided a meeting place for fraternal orders.
Douglass Institute served in this capacity for twenty years until it was
converted to a fire-engine house.

14   Robert Browne Elliott (1842-1884) was born free in Boston, of West
Indian descent. Although there is some debate over the authenticity of
his own account, he claimed to have been educated first in Jamaica and then
in England, where he graduated from Eton with honors in 1859. While in
England he also studied law, and was admitted to the bar and practiced in
Columbia, South Carolina. After serving as a member of the South Carolina
House of Representatives from July 6, 1868, to October 23, 1870, and as

assistant adjutant general of South Carolina, 1869-71, he was elected as
a Republican to the Forty-second Congress from the Third District of South
Carolina. He was reelected, but resigned on November 1, 1874, and returned to the South Carolina House of Representatives, where he became
speaker. Elliott spoke French, German, Spanish and Latin, and had the
largest private library in the state of South Carolina. He was considered one of the greatest black orators up to that time in American
history.

15   The Hon. Franklin J. Moses, Jr. (1838-1906) was born in South Carolina.
His father was a prominent Carolinian, serving in the state Senate from
1842 to 1862, as circuit judge, and then as chief justice of the state
from 1868 until his death in 1877. As a youth Franklin went into politics, but enlisted in the Confederate Army when the Civil War broke out,
and rose to the rank of colonel. In 1866 Moses was admitted to the bar
and began editing the *Sumter News* between 1866 and 1867. Moses'
editorials became so radical, however, that he was dismissed from the
editor's post. In 1868 he was elected as a delegate to the constitutional
convention, and served in the new state government as Speaker of the
House of Representatives. In 1872 he was elected governor by a landslide
and served for two years. When he finished his term as governor, the
scandal and corruption which characterized his administration left him a
ruined man. His wife, family, and friends deserted him, and he moved to
Massachusetts where he was plagued by poverty, drug addiction and served
several prison terms for theft.

16   Jonathan J. Wright (1840-1885) was the first Negro admitted to the
Pennsylvania bar. In 1865 he went to Beaufort, South Carolina, to organize schools for freedmen under the auspices of the American Missionary
Association. From 1866 to 1868, Wright served with the Freedmen's Bureau
as a legal consultant, then left the Bureau for politics. He was elected
as a delegate to the 1868 constitutional convention, and then became state
senator from Beaufort, South Carolina. In 1870, Wright was elected
associate justice of the state supreme court where he served until 1877
when he resigned from the post.

17   Francis L. Cardozo (1836-1903) was a freeborn son of a Jewish economist
in Charleston, South Carolina, by a woman of mixed blood. After his
elementary schooling, he became a journeyman carpenter. His savings,
gained through summer employment and a $1,000 scholarship, enabled him to
go to the University of Glasgow and then for two years to a theological
school in London. At the outbreak of the Civil War, he was a Presbyterian
minister in New Haven. When the conflict ended, he went as a principal
to Avery Institute in Charleston and entered politics. Cardozo served as
a delegate to the 1868 constitutional convention and subsequently was
elected South Carolina Secretary of State. In 1872 the people elected
him state treasurer and he was reelected in 1877. In 1878, Cardozo received an appointment in the Treasury Department in Washington, D.C., and
between 1884 and 1896, he served as principal of Colored High School in
the capitol city.

18   Alonzo J. Ransier (1834-1882) was born free in Charleston, South
Carolina, where he worked as a shipping clerk. After the Civil War he
became active in politics, and in 1866 attended the state's first Republican Convention. In 1868 Ransier served as chairman of the Republican
State Executive Committee. He accepted the nomination for lieutenant
governor and in 1870 was elected to that post. In 1873 Ransier was elected
to a seat in the United States House of Representatives, which he occupied
for two terms. When the state was regained by the White Democrats in
1876, Ransier's fate was sealed, and when he died in 1882, he was a day-
laborer for the city government.

19   Robert Carlos De Large (1842-1874) was born a slave in Aiken, South
Carolina, where he became a successful farmer. Entering politics in
1868, he served as a delegate at the constitutional convention, and later
won election to a two-year term in the state assembly. When his term
was up in 1870, De Large became Land Commissioner and then was nominated
and elected to a seat in the U.S. House of Representatives under suspicious conditions. The election was challenged and the seat declared
vacant. When he returned to South Carolina, he was appointed a magistrate
in Charleston, but died soon afterward.
        Thomas J. Mackey was a white Republican who played a secondary role in
the Republican government of South Carolina after the Civil War. A vice
president of the Liberty League, he was elected as a delegate to the
state constitutional convention in 1868. He also was a delegate to several Republican conventions and became a county judge, probably for his
active campaigning for the corrupt administration of Franklin Moses.
Even though Mackey held no major political office, he ranked high in the
Charleston *News Courier's* "guilt by association" list (November 25, 1874).
That Mackey's Radical Republicanism was a matter of convenience rather than
principle was evidenced in 1876 when he dumped the Republican candidate
Daniel Chamberlain to support the Redeemer candidate Wade Hampton after
it became apparent that Republican rule was over.

20   For biographical background on the Hon. William Whipper, see Vol. I,
note 29.

21   Joseph Hayne Rainey (1832-1887) was the first Negro to serve in the
House of Representatives. Born in Georgetown, South Carolina, he received
a limited education and followed the trade of barber. In 1862 he was
drafted to work on the Confederate fortifications in Charleston harbor, but
he eventually escaped to the West Indies and did not return to South
Carolina until the end of the Civil War. In 1868 Rainey became a delegate
to the state constitutional convention, and a year later he was elected
to the state senate. He resigned in 1870 and was elected to the Forty-
first Congress from the First District of South Carolina.

22   "H. H." refers to Henry Highland Garnet. For biographical background
on Garnet, see Vol. I, note 54.

23   A. A. Bradley was a black state senator in the Georgia legislature.

24   Alexander H. Troup was the treasurer of the National Typographical Union,
and represented the Boston Workingmen's Assembly at the founding of the
National Labor Union.

25.   *Magna Carta,* the Great Charter of the liberties of England, was granted
by King John to the barons at Runnymede on June 15, 1215. The main provision granted that no freeman could be imprisoned, banished, or put to
death except in accordance with the established law.
        "Christopher Attick" apparently refers to Crispus Attucks, a black
sailor of Boston who was shot in the so-called Boston Massacre. A runaway
slave, the forty-seven year old Attucks was in a tavern with several of
his associates when a disturbance in the streets brought them out to join in
the harassing of a column of British troops. Attucks was supposed to have
shouted, "The way to get rid of these soldiers is to attack the main
guard." Several of Captain Preston's company fired upon their tormentors,
and Attucks fell first followed by two others who died with him. An
additional two men died later from wounds.

Saint Crispin was the legendary saint of shoemakers, dating back to early Medieval European mythology. He was honored each year in a festival on October 25, generally conducted by the shoemakers' guilds. Under the strains of high unemployment in the American shoe industry during the post-Civil War years, Saint Crispin was recalled into service.

Newell Daniels and six other tradesmen met in Milwaukee, Wisconsin, on March 1, 1867, and formed a union called the Knights of St. Crispin. The K.S.C. focused their attention primarily on gaining control over the labor supply by control over the apprenticeship programs. Although most of the K.S.C. members opposed the introduction of machinery into the industry, the K.S.C. acquiesced to the inevitable if skilled shoemakers operated the machines. The union grew quickly, but the loss of the 1872 strike at Lynn, Massachusetts, presaged its downfall, and within a few years the union was dead. A new K.S.C. appeared in 1875, but it had an insignificant impact and disappeared in 1878.

26   The "efforts to oust Mr. Douglass from the Government printing office" is a reference to the exclusion of Frederick Douglass' son Lewis H. Douglass from the Columbia Typographical Union. See Vol. I, Part IX.

27   Richard F. Trevellick (1830-1895) was born on St. Mary's in the Scilly Islands off the southwestern tip of England. He became a ship's carpenter and traveled to the Far East. Even as a youth he was known as an outspoken labor reformer, especially favoring the eight-hour day. He arrived in New Orleans in 1857, where he became the local union president for the ship carpenters' and caulkers' union, and successfully fought for the nine-hour day. When the Civil War came, he moved to Detroit and became the first president of the Detroit Trades Assembly. In 1865 Trevellick became president of the International Union of Ship Carpenters and Caulkers, and in 1869, 1871, and 1872, respectively, served as president of the National Labor Union.

A tireless labor organizer and reformer, Trevellick fought for the eight-hour day, led the fight against the blacklist, and advocated complete exclusion of Chinese contract labor. After the Panic of 1873, Trevellick fell under the influence of the Greenback movement, and thereafter advocated inflation as a means of relieving depressions. Helping to establish the Greenback Party in 1876, he served as temporary chairman of the 1878 convention in Toledo which formed the National Greenback-Labor Party and chaired the 1880 convention. Trevellick was one of the most influential leaders of the early labor movement.

28   For biographical background on John M. Langston, see Vol. I, note 61.

29   James T. Rapier was born in Florence, Alabama in 1839 of a white and black mother. His father acknowledged him as a "natural son" and sent him to Montreal College in Canada and the University of Glasgow in Scotland. Returning to Alabama after the Civil War, Rapier was successively a delegate to the Reconstruction constitutional convention, newspaper editor, labor organizer and secretary of the Alabama Equal Rights League. In 1872 he was elected to Congress from the second Congressional District of Alabama. He served one term, during which he fought repeatedly for civil rights. Rapier died in 1883.

30   "Patriots of Cuba" is a reference to the liberation fighters in Cuba. In 1868, young Cubans met secretly and drafted *el grito de yara* calling for the island's independence from Spanish rule. The declaration marked the beginning of the Ten Years' War (1868-1878) between Spanish troops and the poorly armed guerillas. No less than 200,000 lives and about $700 million in property were lost in the struggle. While this war seemed futile, it did fix the determination of the Cuban people to be

free, and produced heroes who became the idols of future generations.
Perhaps the most significant of these heroes was Antonio Maceo, a
mulatto.

31   Oliver Otis Howard (1830-1909) was born at Leeds, Maine, and attended
Bowdoin College from which he graduated in 1850. He attended West Point
and graduated in 1854. After brief service in Florida, and a teaching
post at West Point, he became a colonel of the 3rd Maine Regiment when
the Civil War broke out in 1861 and rose to the rank of brigadier-
general in the regular army. During the war he participated in numerous
battles, and commanded the right wing of Sherman's army as it cut a
wide and destructive swath through the South on its way to the Atlantic
coast.
    On May 12, 1865, President Andrew Johnson appointed Howard Commission-
er of the newly established Bureau of Refugees, Freedmen, and Abandoned
Lands. Charges of corruption troubled Howard and the Bureau, and in
1870 a congressional committee investigated the Bureau and exonerated
him. Howard championed the rights of the freedmen and put up a vigorous
fight against racial prejudice. He was otherwise active in organizing
a Congregational church in Washington, D.C., and demanded the admission
of blacks. He was instrumental in founding Howard University, becoming
its president between 1869 and 1874 when he resigned. Howard also
served as president of the Freedmen's Bank for a time. In 1874 he was
given command of the Department of Columbia, and during the late 1870s
campaigned against several of the northwestern Indian tribes. In 1886
Howard became commander of the Division of the East until his retirement
in 1894.
    Howard retired to live in Burlington, Vermont, where he died. In
his last years he wrote a number of books on a variety of topics and
constantly contributed articles to magazines.

32   *The New Era* became the *New National Era* in the summer of 1871. It
was published by Frederick Douglass and his son Lewis H. Douglass in
Washington, D.C., during the decade of the 1870s.

33   Jermain W. Loguen (1814-1872) was born a slave in Maury County,
Tennessee. Escaping to Canada, he moved on to Oneida, New York, where
he studied and became an African Methodist Episcopal Zion minister.
Loguen served as pastor, successfully, in Ithaca, Troy, and Syracuse,
New York. A tireless advocate of human rights, and an ardent opponent
of slavery, in 1859 Loguen published his autobiography, and in 1868 he
was elected an A.M.E.Z. bishop.

34   Henry Wilson (1812-1875) was born at Farmingham, New Hampshire, and
given the name Jeremiah Jones Colbath. So poor were his parents that
the boy was indentured at age ten. Neighbors instructed the youth until
he was thoroughly well-read in the classics. At twenty-one he was released from bonded labor, and immediately changed his name.
    Once on his own, Wilson learned the shoemaker's trade, hoping to save
enough money to study law. Meanwhile, he read voraciously and learned
the art of public speaking and debating. On a trip to Virginia, Wilson
witnessed the heated debates over slavery in the nation's capitol, saw
slaves being sold in pens, and vowed to spend his life in the cause of
emancipation. Back in Natick, Massachusetts, Wilson established a
moderately successful shoe factory. But his interest lay in politics
rather than business, and Wilson immersed himself in Whig politics and
anti-slavery. In 1848 he helped establish the Free Soil Party when the
Whigs made no stand on the Wilmot Proviso. From 1848 to 1851 Wilson
edited the *Boston Republican,* and helped Charles Sumner (see note 39)
win election to the U.S. Senate. In 1851 and 1852 Wilson served as
president of the state Senate. After a brief flirtation with the Know-

Nothings, he led a walk-out of anti-slavery men which effectively dis-
membered that party.

In January 1855 Wilson was elected to fill a vacant U.S. Senate seat,
and in his first speech aligned himself with the Anti-slavery men, a
position he adhered to without wavering. When the Civil War broke out,
he returned to Massachusetts and organized about 2,300 men in a little
over one month. He constantly urged emancipation as a war measure, and
reported a bill which would establish the Freedmen's Bureau. He opposed
Johnson's Reconstruction and joined the Radicals in demanding harsher
penalties of the ex-Confederates. In 1872 he was nominated for the
Republican vice-presidential slot. An effective presiding officer,
Wilson was, however, in poor health, and in November 1875 he suffered a
paralytic stroke which caused his death. Wilson was one of the true
"crusaders" of anti-slavery, and blacks recognized and respected him
accordingly.

35   Jay Cooke (1821-1905), financier, was born in Sandusky, Ohio, to a
father who practiced law and served in the U.S. Congress. After serving
as a clerk for several years, Jay Cooke went into banking and, for the
rest of his life he resided in Philadelphia. In 1861 he formed a
partnership of his own, Jay Cooke & Company, one of the best-known firms
in the nation.

Cooke enjoyed intimate relationships with key government officials
such as Salmon Chase of Ohio, who became Secretary of the Treasury in
1861, and used his connections to good advantage. During the Civil War,
Cooke successfully sold $2,000,000 in short-term bonds to Philadelphia
bankers in order to help finance the war. A few days later, he sold
another $50,000,000 to New York bankers. To capitalize on these govern-
ment connections,Cooke & Company established an office in Washington,D.C.
After 1864 he helped to promote the purchase of $500,000,000 in govern-
ment bonds to over one million citizens. In 1865 Cooke once again became
the government's "fiscal agent" and helped promote the sale of over
$600,000,000 in government securities.

When the war ended, Cooke & Company expanded into the general banking
business with branches in all the key financial markets, such as New York
and London. Cooke became involved in numerous industrial schemes which
required large amounts of capital, such as the Central Pacific Railroad.
Cooke & Company speculations were too expansive, however, and when the
company shut its doors in 1873, a general depression ensued.

36   The "finest landscape painter" in America is a reference to one of
two black painters, both of whom might qualify for that distinction.
Edward M. Bannister (1828-1901) was born in New Brunswick, Canada, and
without formal instruction became one of the great landscape painters
in America. In 1876 he was one of the two black artists to exhibit at
the Centennial Exposition in Philadelphia. Bannister also founded the
Providence Art Club in Rhode Island, where he made his home.

Robert Duncanson (1821-1872) was a native of Cincinnati, Ohio. In
1840 the local Freedmen's Aid Society sent him to study art in Glasgow,
Scotland, for three years. Although he painted several well-known
portraits, his forte was landscapes and he received international recognition for his work.

The "finest sculptress in America" is an obvious reference to Edmonia
Lewis (1845-1890), the first black woman to be recognized as a sculptor.
Born in Greenhigh, Ohio, to a Chippewa Indian mother and Negro father,
she was educated at Oberlin College with the financial assistance of
several abolitionists who recognized her talents. After graduation she
moved to Boston and studied with Edmund Brackett.. She resided in Rome
from 1867 to 1884 but sent much of her work to the United States to be
exhibited. Her most famous work, "The Death of Cleopatra," was exhibited
at the Philadelphia Centennial Exposition of 1876. The only other Negro
artist to have his work on exhibit at the Exposition of 1876 was Edward
M. Bannister.

"The noble Andrew of Mass." probably refers to Andrew C. Cameron (1834–1890), printer, and an active member of the Typographical Union. Cameron also edited the *Workingman's Advocate* of Chicago from 1864 to 1880, and was known as the greatest labor editor of his time. For six years he served as chairman of the Platform Committee of the National Labor Union, and was its delegate to the International Workingmen's Association convention in 1869 at Basle (now Basel), Switzerland.

37   William D. Kelley (1814–1890) was a native of Philadelphia, where his father was a leading jeweler. Kelley himself became a jeweler's apprentice, and moved to Boston when his term of indenture expired in 1834. Kelley studied on his own and in 1838 returned to Philadelphia to read law. Admitted to the bar in 1841, by 1847 Kelley was appointed judge of the court of common pleas.

Kelley abhorred slavery and became one of the founders of the Republican Party. In 1860 he was elected to Congress, and thereafter reelected to fourteen terms. He supported a vigorous prosecution of the Civil War and backed all measures for the abolition of slavery. During Reconstruction he became a leading Radical in the House. Kelley also became a leading advocate of protection for American industries through a high tariff, especially for iron and steel (for which he received the nickname "Pig Iron").

38   Josephine Sophie White Griffing (1814–1872), social reformer, was born at Hebron, Connecticut, a farmer's daughter. She married Charles Griffing, a Hebron mechanic, in 1842 and the couple moved to Ohio. Both became intensely involved in the abolitionist movement, organizing and lecturing against slavery in the West, and maintaining a station on the Underground Railroad.

Josephine Griffing also became involved in the feminist movement in 1848. She constantly worked for these twin movements and made her messages more palatable by blending them with a musical program. When the Civil War erupted, she volunteered to work with the freedmen, and in 1863 journeyed to Washington to petition for aid in their education, acquistion of land, and emergency relief. Helping to establish the Freedmen's Bureau, she became a commissioner of the Bureau.

Following the war Mrs. Griffing assisted in founding the Universal Franchise Association in Washington, D.C., to lobby for woman's suffrage, and also served as corresponding secretary for the National Woman's Suffrage Association.

39   Senator Charles Sumner (1811–1874) was the most notable of anti-slavery senators to serve in that body. Born in Boston, Massachusetts, Sumner attended Boston Latin School, Harvard College, and Harvard Law School (1831–1833), where he became a close associate of the famous jurist Joseph Story. He found the work in a law office weary, but finally entered upon his true calling when, in 1845, he was selected as the orator for Boston's Independence Day celebration. The magic of his oratory captivated the massive audience and brought Sumner into close association with leading lecturers and reformers of his day. Henceforth, Sumner became a leading spokesman for the peace movement and the abolitionist movement.

Sumner entered the U.S. Senate in December 1851, where he thrilled the northern reformers and angered the southern conservatives. He played a large role in the formation of the Republican Party and took a lofty position on most issues which were agitated during the stormy decades of the 1850s and 1860s. For one outspoken speech, Sumner was severely beaten with a cane by Representative Preston S. Brooks of South Carolina, and sustained injuries from which he never fully recovered.

At the October 1861 Republican convention, Sumner was the first significant politician to urge emancipation of the slaves. As early as

February 1862, Sumner had begun the struggle to secure equal civil rights
for all Americans, and articulated his belief that the southern states
abdicated their constitutional rights when they seceded. In cooperation
with Thaddeus Stevens (see note 57), Sumner led in the implementation of
Radical Reconstruction in the post-war South. Sumner also came into
direct conflict with President Grant over the acquisition of Santo
Domingo, which resulted in the senator's demotion from his powerful position as chairman of the committee on Foreign relations. It was the
beginning of Sumner's rapid downward slide from the pinnacles of power.
He was considered an anti-slavery man, and for years spoke out on the
issue. After the war his emotionalism on the point of equality rendered
him little service in that fight. The Civil Rights Bill of 1875, which
guaranteed open access to public accommodations, was, however, largely
a result of his labors.

40   The "Vicksburg general at the White House" refers to General Ulysses
S. Grant who became President of the United States from 1868 to 1876.

41   "John Brown's Body" was the popular title of the "Battle Hymn of the
Republic," which immortalized the radical anti-slavery John Brown who
led an attack on the arsenal at Harpers' Ferry, Virginia, in October
1859 as a protest against slavery.

42   In 1619 a Dutch vessel anchored off Jamestown, Virginia, and traded
"20 negars" for water and provisions. These twenty Africans are tradi-
tionally accepted as the first African slaves in the American colonies.

43   For biographical background on Denmark Vesey, leader of the abortive
plot to lead a slave insurrection in 1822 in Charleston, S. C., see
Vol. I, note 2.
        For biographical background on Nat Turner, the leader of America's
bloodiest insurrection, which occurred in 1831 in Southampton County,
Va., see Vol. I, note 2.
        Regarding the identity of "a colored lady by the name of Deveaux,"
Henry Allen Bullock says the following: "The foundations for a freedmen's school system was strong. With the strong and obvious motivations
had come white and Negro teachers whose past deeds in the field of Negro
education left no question of their sincerity. . . . there were those
who through sheer courage and moral commitment had managed to maintain
schools for Negroes throughout the crisis [Civil War]. One such educator, found in Savannah, Georgia, when the Union Army moved in, was a
Negro woman whom tradition knows only as 'Miss Deaveaux.' She had been
teaching a private school in the same building since 1838. Although
quite advanced in years, she was still teaching with great earnestness
and zeal. Her stories of how she had carried out her work in secret,
eluding for more than a quarter of a century 'the lynx-eyed vigilance of
the slave-holders,' adequately reflected the tenacity of the leadership
that kept the Negro's hidden passage open until revolutionary changes
could bring it from underground."
Henry Allen Bullock, *A History of Negro Education in the South, From
1619 to the Present* (New York, 1967), p. 25.

44   For an explanation of the Emancipation Proclamation, issued by
President Abraham Lincoln which took effect January 1, 1863, see
Vol. I, note 14.

45   For background on the American Colonization Society, see Vol. I,
note 45.

46   For an explanation of the "eight-hour law," see Vol. I, notes 58 and 69.

47   The term "land monopoly" is a reference to the practice among southern white property owners in the Reconstruction South of refusing to sell land to Negroes.

48   During the ante-bellum period, the major evangelical denominations in the United States were fractured over the issue of slavery, and tended to split into northern and southern wings. Even though the Congretationalists had no southern churches at all before the war, they were plagued by the issue as well, with pro and anti-slavery forces within the church jockeying for power within the denomination. The American Missionary Association was founded in 1846 when the abolitionists failed to gain control over the Congregational missionary societies. Although the AMA was nominally nonsectarian, it nevertheless remained primarily a Congregationalist organization. During the war the AMA founded the first schools for freedmen in the South, and thereafter education of blacks became its primary concern. The AMA was responsible for the founding of many black secondary and collegiate institutions in the South, including Fisk, Straight and Clark universities, and Tougaloo, Claflin, and Morgan Colleges.

49   For an explanation of the National Bureau of Labor founded by the Colored National Labor Union, see p. 69, Article III of the CNLU constitution.

50   Samuel P. Cummins was highly active in the labor movement of Massachusetts during the 1860s as a leader in the Knights of St. Crispin (see note 25). He also played a prominent role in the National Labor Union.

51   George Myers was the brother of Isaac Myers, founder and first president of the Colored National Labor Union.

52   African Colonization Society is used in the original document, but it is clear from the text of the resolution, and the subsequent reference to the American Colonization Society, that the latter is the organization to which the protest referred. For a background discussion of the ACS, see Vol. I, note 45.

53   Henry Wilson, "New Departure of the Republican Party," *The Atlantic Monthly* 27 (January 1871): 104-120. In this article Senator Wilson called upon the Republican Party to reaffirm its commitment to the advancement of equal rights for all Americans regardless of race.

54   George F. Hoar (1826-1904) was born in Concord, Massachusetts, and educated at Harvard College and Harvard Law School. In 1849 he entered the practice of law in Worcester and launched a political career by assisting in the foundation of the Free Soil Party in Massachusetts, and later the Republican Party. In 1852 he was elected to the state House of Representatives, and later served in the state Senate. In 1869 Hoar was elected to Congress where he served until 1877 when he was elected to the Senate. Hoar was noted for his tolerant views of others, and held in utter contempt those he believed to be bigots.

55   Wendell Phillips (1811-1884), a leading orator and social reformer, was born in Boston to affluent parents. Phillips received his education at Boston Latin, Harvard College, and Harvard Law School. He established a practice in Boston during the mid-1830s and immediately became active in the abolitionist movement. In December 1837, at the age of twenty-six, Phillips delivered an impromptu diatribe against slavery, the eloquence of which brought him to the public's attention.

Relieved of the necessity of earning a living by personal wealth, Phillips began a career as a lyceum lecturer, speaking mostly on the topic of slavery, and he contributed regularly to the abolitionist press. After the Civil War, Phillips continued to advocate other moral issues, such as prohibition, penal reform, women's rights, and the labor movement.

56   Susan B. Anthony (1820-1906), was born into a wealthy Quaker family in Adams, Massachusetts, and grew up in a family tradition when encouraged strong and independent women. A precocious child, Susan learned to read and write at age three. Well educated for her day, Anthony became a teacher and eventually the head of the Female Department of Conajoharie Academy in New York from 1846 to 1849. She never felt compelled to become a homemaker, preferring to remain single and give herself over to reform.

She returned to Massachusetts in 1850 and there entered into association with the many famous reformers who rallied at the homestead, becoming particularly close to Lucretia Mott and Elizabeth Cady Stanton. In the early 1850s, she assisted in organizing the Woman's State Temperance Society of New York, and began her fight for equal rights for women. She also took a radical abolitionist stand on the slavery issue. Her life was one of constant lecturing and convention organizing. When the National Woman Suffrage Association was organized in 1869, she became chairperson of the executive committee. When the Association was reorganized in 1890, Miss Anthony served as vice-president, and from 1892 to 1900 served as president. She retired at age eighty.

57   Thaddeus Stevens (1792-1868) was born in Danville, Vermont. His father deserted the family, but the mother sacrificed to see that Thaddeus received all the special care the sickly child required. From his youth Stevens acquired an intense distaste for the aristocratic. After graduation from Dartmouth in 1814, he took a position as instructor at an academy in York, Pennsylvania, where he also continued to read law. In 1816 he moved to Gettysburg to practice. After a few years of earning a meager income, Stevens became both rich and famous as a successful attorney. In 1826 he entered the iron business with a partner, formed Stevens & Paxton in 1828, and constructed several furnaces in the area of York.

Stevens emerged into political prominence in 1831 at the anti-Masonic Convention in Baltimore, and two years later was elected to the Pennsylvania House where he served until 1841, becoming well-known for his advocacy of free public education and other reforms. In 1848 Stevens, now living in Lancaster, was elected to Congress on the Whig ticket. In the House Stevens became known for his uncompromising stand on anti-slavery, a position he had long held. A prominent participant in the formation of the Republican Party, Stevens warned the South to secede at its own peril. When the South did secede and the war came, Stevens had become chairman of the House ways and means committee, which gave him considerable power over revenue bills. On the prosecution of the war, Stevens took a vigorously aggressive stance, and that same vigor carried over into Reconstruction following the cessation of hostilities.

Stevens opposed Lincoln's and then Johnson's mild approach to Reconstruction, believing that the South had left the Union and enjoyed no constitutional rights whatsoever, and along with Charles Sumner in the Senate, did battle with both presidents. In December 1865, he became chairman of the House committee on Reconstruction, which accepted his view that the South was a conquered province. Through this committee much of the Radical Reconstruction program was implemented.

Stevens also played a prominent role in the impeachment of President Johnson. By then, however, his health had failed and he died not long after the president's acquittal.

58   When the Civil War ended in 1865, white southerners were willing to concede to adopt the Thirteenth Amendment, putting an end to slavery. But as they gradually reassumed power in 1865 and 1866, they adopted laws which revealed the conviction that black freedmen must be controlled in order to prevent bloodshed, and to insure the continuation of their role as the South's labor force. These laws, called Black Codes, bore a strong resemblance to the antebellum Slave Codes. While they varied from state to state, most attempted to limit property ownership among blacks, outlined vagrancy laws, and among other restrictions, laid down rules governing black labor. Blacks and whites who had prosecuted the war in order to abolish slavery saw little evidence of freedom in these codes, and provided them with further justification for Radical Reconstruction.

59   For biographical background on William P. Powell, see Vol. I, note 19.

60   James J. Spelman (1841-1905?) was born and educated in Norwich, Connecticut. After moving to New York in 1855, he entered a career as a newspaper reporter, editor, and publisher, establishing the sprightly *Anglo-African*. When the Civil War came, Spelman actively recruited for the black regiments, becoming a major in a battalion known as the "Show Cadets," named after the hero of Fort Wagner. In 1868 he went to Mississippi to do educational work with the Freedmen's Bureau, and in 1869 was appointed alderman of Canton, Mississippi. That year Spelman won election to the state legislature where he remained for six years. Spelman served in numerous important public positions in Mississippi as well.

61   George B. Cheever (1807-1890), clergyman and reformer, was born in Hallowell, Maine, and received an education at Bowdoin College and at Andover Seminary (1830). After preaching at various posts, he settled in New York where he served as a Presbyterian pastor from 1838 until 1867. In 1845 Cheever was editor of the *New York Evangelist*. After 1867, he became involved in publishing, the profession of his father.

An uncompromising reformer, Cheever favored temperance and was fined and jailed for libel against a distiller because of a newspaper story Cheever printed. He advocated capital punishment on biblical grounds, opposed rituals of the Episcopal and Catholic Churches, and favored Sunday "blue laws." Moreover, Cheever was a stern abolitionist and fearlessly supported equal civil rights and educational opportunities for blacks. His large library, in fact, was bequeathed to Howard University. Cheever was a gifted writer on all topics, publishing many books, pamphlets, and articles.

62   The "Ayrshire Plowboy" refers to the poet Robert Burns, of Ayrshire, Scotland, who spent many years as a farmer. See note 63.

63   Elihu Burritt (1810-1870), a self-educated forgeman of New Britain, Connecticut, learned to read nearly fifty languages. The "learned blacksmith" also published the pacifist *Christian Citizen*, and wrote voluminously. He was a leading figure in the American peace movement, organizing the League of Universal Brotherhood (1846), and was the leading spirit of the second Universal Peace Congress held at Brussels in 1848.

Benjamin Jonson (1572-1637) was born and educated in Westminster, England. For a time he worked with his stepfather as a bricklayer. By 1597 he was an actor and playwright, and after killing a fellow actor in a duel, was imprisoned for a number of years. He wrote a great variety of plays, some of which were produced by William Shakespeare's company. From 1605 onward, Jonson wrote plays for the court, and when he died, he was buried in Westminster Abbey.

Robert Burns (1759-1796) was born at Alloway in Ayrshire, the son of a cottar who set him to work as a farm laborer while still a youth. From 1784 to 1788 he farmed 118 acres in partnership with his brother, and during this time wrote some of his best work. In 1786 he published a volume of poems which made him famous. A second edition earned Burns enough money to provide an income, which he supplemented by writing songs and poems until his death.

Dr. David Livingstone (1813-1873) educated himself while working at a cotton factory near Glasgow, Scotland. In 1840 he embarked for the Cape of Good Hope on the first of his many explorations of the African interior. His travel journals provided the first detailed information on the African interior and its peoples available in English. He died while trying to discover the sources of the Nile River, and was buried in Westminster Abbey.

64   George E. Spencer (1836-1893) was born in Champion, New York, and educated in classical studies at Montreal College, Canada. After graduation he moved to Iowa and became secretary of the State senate in 1856. He studied law and was admitted to the Iowa bar in 1857. During the Civil War he joined the Union Army at the rank of captain. When Spencer resigned in 1865 he had been promoted to brigadier general for bravery on the field of battle. Following the secession of hostilities, Spencer settled in Decatur, Alabama, resumed his legal practice, and became active in the state Republican Party. When Alabama was readmitted to the Union, Spencer was elected to the U.S. Senate where he served until 1879, at which time he retired to his ranch in Nevada. The Montgomery (Alabama) *Advertiser and Mail* was a conservative white Democratic newspaper, and the comment contains an obvious note of sarcasm.

65   "Commune" was the term applied to the period in the history of the Paris from March 18 to May 28, 1871, when the commune (an administrative division) of the city attempted to establish its own authority against the National Assembly at Versailles. The instigators of this movement hoped to replace the centralized system of government with a federation of communes. This struggle had nothing to do with the Marxist revolutionaries, even though contemporary anti-Marxists in American confused the two movements.

66   "Labor Reformers" refers to the Labor Reform Party, which was launched in 1872 by the National Labor Union to pressure government to be more sensitive to the needs of tradesmen and mechanics. "Grangers" refers to members of the Patrons of Husbandry which began to organize the agricultural sector of the nation's work force into local "Granges" in 1867. While the Labor Reform Party was a miserable failure, the Grangers succeeded admirably. One year after the Panic of 1873 the Grangers boasted a total membership of 1,500,000, mostly in the mid-West. They became a potent political force in the states where they were strongest, and won legislation which abridged the financial power the railroad companies exerted over the isolated farmers. In a series of important court cases tried between 1876 and 1886, known as the "Granger cases," the Grangers won significant victories which controlled the railroads and paved the way for the Interstate Commerce Act.

67   The "two important National Colored Conventions" referred to, assembled

in Columbia, S. C., as a joint session of the Colored Men's Convention and the third Colored National Labor Union Convention.

68   Both spellings--Thompson and Thomson--appear in the text. The correct spelling is unknown.

69   American sections of the International Workingmen's Association were organized by Socialist groups in this country. In October 1867, the Communist Club of New York, founded by F. A. Sorge, Conrad Carl, and Siegfried Meyer in 1857, became a section of the International in America. By 1872 there were about thirty sections and five thousand members of the First International in the United States. Sections were formed in Chicago, San Francisco, Washington, D.C., New Orleans, Newark, Springfield, and New York City. The minority of the membership in America were "plain wage workers," observed Sorge.

The socialist movement in the United States remained split between the Marxists, who favored organization of the working classes into a movement controlled by themselves (unions), and the followers of the German, Ferdinand Lassalle, who advocated political action to affect reform. Unity within the Socialist movement was formally established in July 1876, when delegates from nineteen American sections of the International met in Philadelphia and dissolved the International Workingmen's Association. A few days later, a meeting of socialist organizations was held to form the Workingmen's Party of the United States. The platform of the new party adopted the trade union policies of the International, but conceded to the Lassallean's request that a national organization be established. Participation in politics was to be delayed until the party was strong enough to exercise a perceptible influence. Until then, the party would focus its energies upon economic issues and organizing workers into unions. The party did not advocate that it embodied the labor movement, but rather saw itself as an advance guard of the inevitable struggle between capital and labor.

70   For a biographical account of Peter H. Clark, see Herbert Gutman, "Peter H. Clark: Pioneer Negro Socialist, 1877," *Journal of Negro Education* 34 (Fall 1965): 413-18.

71   These letters have also been published by Herbert G. Gutman, "Black Coal Miners and the Greenback-Labor Party in Redeemer, Alabama: 1878-1879," *Labor History* 10 (Summer 1969): 506-35.

72   Tammany Hall was the headquarters for the Tammany Society in New York City. Tammany societies were organized as patriotic associations during the American Revolution. The New York society, chartered in 1789, was the only one to endure. During the 1830s it became influential in the Democratic party, and by 1850 was the most important political organization in the city. By the 1870s, under the leadership of William Tweed, Tammany controlled state politics and refined the definition of the "boss" system of political power.

73   The National Labor Union represented the first successful federation of trade unions in the post-Civil War period. The Industrial Congress, precursor to the NLU, met between 1845 and 1856, but collapsed when it proved unable to retain the allegiance of affiliate trade unions. Most probably it was this short-lived organization which prompted the use of the term "Industrial Congress" mentioned in this resolution.

74   For a discussion of the International in America, see note 69.

75   General Nathan B. Forrest (1821-1877) was born in what is now Marshall
County, Tennessee. His father died when Nathan was only sixteen and left
him with the responsibility for maintaining a large family. Dealing in
horses, cattle, slaves, and real estate, Forrest eventually accumulated
enough capital to buy the plantations which made him wealthy. In 1861 he
enlisted in the Confederate army, raised and equipped a battalion himself,
and was appointed lieutenant colonel. Following several heroic acts, he
was promoted to colonel, fought at Shiloh, and became brigadier-general in
1862. His bold cavalry raids made him famous, and he was promoted to
major-general. The one major blotch on his military record was the Fort
Pillow Massacre. Although he did not order the murders, he was in command
when a unit of over 200 Negro Union soldiers were captured, slaughtered
in cold blood, and buried in a mass grave after they had surrendered.

76   The Supplement to the Civil Rights bill is a reference to the bill
sponsored by Senator Charles Sumner (see note 39) which sought to ensure
equal access to public accommodations. Eventually it emerged as the
Civil Rights Act of 1875.

77   For a discussion of the International Workingmen's Association, see
note 69.

78   The Miners' National Association was the first union of miners organized in the United States. Its constitution provided for an all-
inclusive union that would embrace all miners without distinction. When
the miners met in a national convention in Ohio on October 14, 1873, to
form the Miners' National Association, John Siney, head of the organization, stressed the necessity of unity of black and white. Responding
to this appeal, the convention called upon all miners to join including
"our colored brethren." *Workingmen's Advocate,* October 25, 1873.

79   "Under cover of the panic" refers to using the current economic
depression, or Panic of 1873, as an excuse for reducing the wages paid
to workmen.

80   Adolph Douai was born in Germany in 1819 and played an active role in
the German Revolution of 1848. He emigrated to Texas in 1852 and established the *San Antonio Zeitung,* an anti-slavery paper. Moving to Boston,
he established a three-graded school which included the first kinder-
garten in America. He also became the editor of the *Die Arbeiter Union*
until 1870, and in 1878 became co-editor of the Socialist newspaper,
New Yorker Volkszeitung, a position he held until 1888. He played an
important role in the early Marxist organizations in the United States.

81   The Labor League appears to have been a temporary body of representatives from the various trade unions organized to voice the concerns of
labor to President Rutherford B. Hayes.

82   Benjamin ("Pap") Singleton (1809-1892) insisted on the title "Moses
of the Colored Exodus," and testified before a congressional committee
investigating the Kansas Exodus that he was the "cause of it all." This
assertion, along with his age and kindly disposition, led his followers
to dub Singleton, "Pap." Born a slave in Tennessee and sold a dozen
times into the deep South, Singleton finally ran away to Canada before
settling in Detroit where he resided until 1865. Returning to Tennessee
after the war, Singleton believed it was his "mission" was to colonize
blacks in separate territories where they could develop their own
"national experience." He believed that blacks must have a separate

nation in order to survive. With that in mind, Singleton labored
tirelessly to promote emigration to the western territories. When it
became apparent that Kansas would not be the Negro "Canaan" as hoped,
Singleton suggested emigration to Canada, Liberia, and then Cyprus.
Pap Singleton died in Topeka, Kansas, at the age of eighty-three.

83   Pinckney B. S. Pinchback was born May 10, 1851, near Macon, Georgia,
of a slave mother, Eliza Stewart, and a white Mississippi planter father,
William Pinchback. His father subsequently manumitted the mother of his
children and moved his family to the North. Pinchback was educated,
first at home, and then at school in Cincinnati. After the death of
his father, he was forced to make his own living, and followed steam-
boating on the Ohio, Missouri, Red and Mississippi rivers, becoming a
steward, the highest position a man of his race could then attain in
this line of employment. In 1862, he recruited a company of black
soldiers (Corps d'Afrique) in response to a call of Maj.-Gen. Benjamin
F. Butler that free colored men take up arms in defense of the Union.
Pinchback became the captain of the company; but practically white in
appearance, he refused to pass as a white man and was forced by indig-
nant whites to resign the captaincy. He was active in Louisiana as
lieutenant governor, and when Governor H. C. Warmoth was impeached,
Pinchback became acting governor of the state for a month. Following
Reconstruction, he held the posts of Internal Revenue agent, and Survey-
or of Customs for the Port of Orleans. He was admitted to the bars of
federal and state courts in Louisiana and practiced law until his death
in Washington, D.C., in 1921.

84   The *People's Advocate* was a black newspaper published in Washington,
D.C., during the post-Civil War era.

85   Henry Adams (1843- ?) was born a slave in Georgia. Even though he
did not achieve national fame, Adams was an important and articulate
leader of ordinary freedmen. In 1850 he was moved to Louisiana, Texas,
and back to Louisiana again as the Civil War ended. After the war Adams
became a peddler until September 1866 when he enlisted in the U.S. Army.
He was promoted to the rank of quartermaster sergeant, but left the army
in 1869. While in the army, Adams learned to read and write, and gained
the worldly experience which served him well at the grass-roots level
of leadership he was to attain.
        During the early 1870s, Adams worked as a rail splitter and plantation
manager and was moderately successful. By 1870 Adams and several other
black ex-soldiers of Caddo Parish organized a secret committee to gather
intelligence, with as many as 500 people participating. He also became
involved in grass-roots Republican politics, and continued his faith-
healing practice among the ill, having become an expert "herbs doctor."
In 1874 he was president of the Shreveport Republican Club and when the
White League organized to pressure blacks into submission, Adams lost
his job.
        In 1876, Adams and other black leaders met and formed a committee which
suggested that migration out of the South might be an answer to the oppression they experienced. By 1877 Adams made his first speeches ad-
vocating migration. The Colonization Council found that emigration to
Liberia was economically unfeasible, and thereafter the Council concentrated on the West. Moving to New Orleans in 1878, however, Adams lost
contact with the Council, but continued to seek assistance for emigration
to Liberia. While he maintained hope for African emigration, black
people caught the "Kansas fever" and public concern and black interest
was diverted westward to Kansas rather than eastward to Liberia. Henry
Adams slipped away into historical obscurity, and after 1884 was heard
no more.

86   Sojourner Truth gained a national reputation as an anti-slavery and
woman's rights lecturer before the Civil War. Born into slavery in
New York, probably in 1797, and given the name Isabella Baumfree, she
eventually ran away from the last of her several masters when he refused
to acknowledge New York's emancipation act of 1827. Isabella settled in
New York City where she was drawn into a religious cult led by a fanatic
named Mathias. Growing disillusioned by 1843, she resolved to perform
the Lord's work independently of the cult, and adopted the name "Sojourner Truth" because God told her that the name revealed her spiritual
mission. Becoming deeply involved in the struggle for equal rights
for blacks and women, she lectured on either topic wherever someone
would listen, and soon became the leading black woman on the lecture
circuit. After the Civil War, she continued her struggle for equal
rights until she died on November 26, 1883, in Battle Creek, Michigan.